D1571178

JOSEPH CHAMBERLAIN
AND THE TARIFF REFORM
CAMPAIGN

"Hear! for thy children speak from
the uttermost parts of the sea."

Kipling's Song of the English

J. Chamberlain
March 11th 1905.

JOSEPH CHAMBERLAIN

AND THE TARIFF REFORM

CAMPAIGN

THE LIFE OF JOSEPH CHAMBERLAIN
VOLUME SIX · 1903–1968

JULIAN AMERY

MACMILLAN
LONDON · MELBOURNE · TORONTO
ST MARTIN'S PRESS
NEW YORK

First published 1969 by
MACMILLAN AND CO LTD
Little Essex Street London WC 2
and also at Bombay Calcutta and Madras
Macmillan South Africa (Publishers) Pty Ltd Johannesburg
The Macmillan Company of Australia Pty Ltd Melbourne
The Macmillan Company of Canada Ltd Toronto
St Martin's Press Inc New York
Gill and Macmillan Ltd Dublin

Library of Congress catalog card no. 33–286

Printed in Great Britain by
R. & R. CLARK LTD
Edinburgh

TO MY SON,
LEO

CONTENTS

LIST OF ILLUSTRATIONS

ACKNOWLEDGEMENTS

The author and publishers thank the following, who have kindly given permission for the illustrations to be reproduced:

Pages 536, 568, 569, 665, 696, 697, 793, 825, 889 originally appeared in the *Westminster Gazette,* and are now reproduced by permission of Associated Newspapers; 888: Birmingham Reference Library; 664 (upper): Birmingham University Library; 537 (top right): Constable and Co.; 537 (top left), 664 (lower right): Mansell Collection; 824: *Punch*; 537 (lower left and right), 664 (lower left), 792, 920 (both), 921 (both): Radio Times Hulton Picture Library.

BOOK XXIV

TARIFF REFORM:
THE FIRST CAMPAIGN
(1903–1904)

THE GLASGOW PROGRAMME

(*October* 1903)

The Public Meeting Then and Now — The Pattern of the Campaign — 'Getting Up' the Speeches — Glasgow : The Case for Preference — Greenock : the Case for Retaliation — Liberal Reactions — Asquith at Cinderford — The Newcastle and Tynemouth Speeches — First Doubts about Balfour — Liverpool : the Bid for Trade Union Support — The Stanleys and the Fiscal Question.

I

W E have followed in some detail Chamberlain's efforts to reform the Fiscal policy of the country from within the Government. We have seen him persuade the Cabinet to give the Colonies a drawback on the Corn Duty. We have seen the Cabinet go back on that decision during his absence in South Africa. We have seen him bring forward the issue of Tariff Reform in public in his speech of 15 May 1903 and in subsequent speeches. We have also seen his failure as yet to capture either the Cabinet or the Unionist Parties in Parliament for his new policy. No course remained open to him, therefore, but to appeal to the constituencies and try to win public opinion to his side during the parliamentary recess. This he had determined to do from the time of the truce reached in the Cabinet in the previous June.

The knowledge that Chamberlain was to enter upon a speaking campaign in the autumn had been indeed the immediate cause of the Cabinet crisis of September. So long as Ministers were silent, a decision on Fiscal policy could be postponed. But once Chamberlain spoke out his colleagues must either submit or contradict. A public wrangle between Ministers was unthinkable. The choice had lain, therefore, between reaching agreement or breaking up the Government. Balfour had sought in vain for a compromise formula. At one time he had seemed near to success. His efforts, however, had failed, basically because any formula deviating from the orthodox canons of Free Trade would, in practice, have enabled

Chamberlain to preach his full doctrine in the country. Hence the resignations of Ritchie, George Hamilton and Balfour of Burleigh. Hence Chamberlain's resignation designed to enable Balfour to keep Devonshire. Hence Devonshire's own resignation once he was made to feel that by staying in the Government he was only helping to keep Unionist Free Traders loyal to a Retaliationist Prime Minister himself in league with Chamberlain.

Chamberlain's First Tariff Reform Campaign — as it has come to be known — was a direct appeal over the heads of Ministers, and of Parliament to public opinion and the Constituency associations. To understand the form it took, we must briefly recall the conditions of the time.

The franchise was already very wide, but there was no single medium through which the electorate could be reached. There was, indeed, an old-established national Press which reported statements and speeches of leading politicians practically verbatim. It was of decisive importance; for it was carefully studied — much more than today — by the leaders of opinion and by all educated people in the provinces.

In the days of a more restricted franchise, indeed, it had enabled our statesmen to reach the whole electorate without stirring beyond the House of Commons or their constituencies. But now its reports were no longer enough. It was not read by the average shopkeeper or working-class voter any more than *The Times*, the *Manchester Guardian* or the *Daily Telegraph* are today. Nor had there yet arisen the great popular dailies which were to play such a part in the political life of the next generation. The *Daily Mail*, indeed, had been transformed by Harmsworth; but it is doubtful if its circulation had yet reached the million. In the absence of a national medium for reaching the electorate, there was no choice but to go to the people; to speak to thousands and tens of thousands from the platform; and, by making big local news for the provincial Press, to reach some thousands more.

This period between the granting of a wide franchise and the rise of the popular media of information — the great dailies, the radio, the cinema and the television — was the golden age of the Political Meeting. Each meeting was an event. Its sponsors were at pains, by the banquet which preceded it and the torchlight procession which often followed it, to raise the temperature and underline its importance. The visiting statesman was looked on as a cross between a film star, a football hero and a religious preacher.

Thousands came to study his 'form' as well as to consider his arguments, and tens of thousands discussed his opinions, his personality and his idiosyncrasies for days afterwards in club and pub. The statesman himself had to play a double part. He must appeal to the emotions of a still backward and largely illiterate mass audience. But he must do so in the knowledge that every word he said would be on the breakfast tables of the whole British Middle Class next day.

Chamberlain's campaign was conceived on a quite unprecedented scale. For a statesman to speak once or twice on a provincial platform during a recess had become more or less accepted in the previous ten years. But to 'stump' the country was still regarded as a very questionable proceeding. Even Gladstone's great Midlothian campaign had been confined to the triangle Glasgow–Perth–Edinburgh : the general area of the Midlothian constituency. Besides it had only lasted a fortnight and had been confined to general attacks on the Government such as might have figured in an election campaign.

Chamberlain's purpose resembled more his own campaign in South Africa for 'reconciliation' or William Jennings Bryan's crusade against the Gold Standard. Over a period of three months, he proposed to deliver a dozen major speeches, all on Tariff Reform, in the principal industrial and commercial cities of the Kingdom : Glasgow, the industrial heart of Scotland, and neighbouring Greenock once the stronghold of our sugar refining ; Newcastle-on-Tyne, centre of the industrial north, and Tynemouth with its great shipyards ; Liverpool, the second city of the Empire ; Birmingham, his own city and the capital of the Midlands ; Cardiff, the industrial capital of Wales and Newport with its iron and steel ; Leeds, the metropolis of Yorkshire's varied trades ; and finally the Guildhall in the City, at the very hub of Britain's commercial Empire.

Many other towns claimed his presence, but of the industrial centres there were two major omissions. He would not speak in Sheffield ; for it was there that Balfour had defined the official Unionist policy. Nor would he go to Manchester. That was Balfour's constituency. At this time, indeed, he would not even let Vince, his agent, accept an invitation to speak to the Liberal Unionist Committee in Manchester. 'Manchester', he said, 'is Mr. Balfour's town ; if you are known there at all you are known as my man. I should be supposed to have sent you ; and I will not be suspected of trying to interfere with Mr. Balfour.' [1]

The agricultural centres were deliberately omitted from the

[1] Vince to Locker Lampson, 22 April 1920.

programme. Not that Chamberlain failed to realise the importance of the agricultural vote. On the contrary his correspondence with Chaplin, Pearson and others in these months shows his close concern with the problem. He believed that the farmers would vote for him anyway, but feared that if he spoke to agricultural audiences he would have to stress too much the Protectionist side of his policy ; and this might frighten off both the Colonial exporter of foodstuffs and the consumer in the towns. The following letters give some picture of his mind.

CHAMBERLAIN TO PEARSON

10 *October* 1903.—*Private.*—I am a little doubtful whether I ought to go into the Country. I have to convince the towns, and arrange my arguments accordingly. I have also to avoid any misapprehension on the part of the Colonies. If I went through the Agricultural districts dropping little speeches here and there I might get into some pitfall or other and say something which my opponents would declare with more or less of reason was inconsistent with my principal speeches, but there is plenty of time to think over this, and circumstances may change meanwhile.

CHAMBERLAIN TO ONSLOW

11 *November* 1903.—I am quite prepared to deal later on with agricultural audiences, but I think it best to carry the towns with me first. Townspeople are, of course, quicker to see points, and at the same time their influence ultimately permeates to the villages ; especially to those in their neighbourhood. If I had taken the agricultural audiences at the same time, it would have been difficult to avoid inconsistent inferences, even if the arguments themselves were consistent.

My own idea is that the farmers will be with me everywhere. I may not be giving them much, but I am giving them something, and possibly they may hope in their hearts that they will ultimately get more. In any case, they were all in favour of the 1/- tax. They must therefore approve of a tax of double the amount, plus a tax on meat and dairy produce. The labourers are the real difficulty. To them I shall have to go over the ground already traversed, in order to impress upon them that the cost of their living will not be increased. But it is a little difficult to show any direct benefit, although, if the country prospers and there is more employment they will sooner or later derive advantage. G........ has tried tariff reform in a number of villages in Lincolnshire and is greatly encouraged by his success. . . . I shall finish my present campaign just before the opening of Parliament, and if I live to carry through another, next autumn I will include some of the centres of agricultural industry.

There were besides limits to his strength ; to say nothing of the difficulty of maintaining public interest on a single theme over so long a period. No statesman of the front rank had ever attempted such a campaign before. Nor has any since.

II

Economic and social conditions seemed favourable to the campaign. 1903 had been a year of unbroken gloom on the stock exchange. Consols had fallen to their lowest point since 1866. There had been few new issues. Shipping was depressed. Railways were depressed. Cotton had been hit by the increase in raw cotton prices. Coalminers' wages had been cut. Unemployment was increasing, and a conference was being prepared to consider its problems. *The Times* was instituting an enquiry into the growth of 'pauperism'. When the final trade figures for the year were published, the situation would seem less gloomy. At the time it could hardly have looked darker.

Chamberlain's preparation for the campaign had been thorough, at least by the standards of research of the time. His brains trust of economists and journalists had been at work since the end of May. He himself had spent long hours reading books and memoranda on the subject; and his papers contain lengthy abstracts of what he had read, written on foolscap in his usual careful way. He had also made use of his official position to obtain all the statistical information available to the departments. He was, in particular, in close touch with Ryder and the chief officials of the Customs Board.

CHAMBERLAIN TO CHAPLIN

27 *October* 1903.—All my calculations as to budgets are based (please keep this entirely confidential) on estimates which I obtained from the Customs before I left the Government. I do not want to produce them, at present at any rate, as of course every additional figure only gives new opportunities of contradiction, but I believe they are absolutely correct and could be justified before a Committee. They are accompanied by long memoranda explaining them, and when I get a little more time I will see if I can have a summary made for your private information.

The course of the campaign would reveal a number of inaccuracies in his calculations. But apart from one or two glaring errors of fact — schoolboy howlers almost — these were mostly due to the extreme poverty of economic information available.

Besides this intellectual preparation, we must also remember the activities of the Tariff Reform League and the Birmingham Tariff Committee. These had been at work for some months. They had formed centres up and down the country and their leaflets, articles and speeches had already prepared the ground.

The general economic circumstances, the careful preparation of the campaign and its unprecedented form would have been enough to command a wide and attentive audience. The Cabinet crisis, besides, had created an atmosphere of drama. Chamberlain's campaign now had a clear and definite purpose. He had resigned so as to be free to convert public opinion. Failure would mean the doom of his policy and probably the end of his public career. Success, on the other hand, would lead to his rejoining the Government to make Tariff Reform and Imperial Preference the official policy of Unionism. He had staked all on a single campaign. As he said to Monkbretton shortly before the opening meeting at Glasgow, 'I shall triumph or fail altogether'.[1]

Chamberlain's decision to throw up office and take his political life in his hand made him the man of the moment. The clearness of his purpose was underlined by the Delphic mistiness of Balfour's speech at Sheffield. The leader of the Unionist Government had decided not to lead. All eyes were now turned to Chamberlain.

Powell Williams caught the mood of the Unionist party in the following letter:

POWELL WILLIAMS TO CHAMBERLAIN

3 *October* 1903.—I send you a line to wish you an immense success at Glasgow — such as will quite satisfy you. I do not doubt that you will have it.

. . . The speech of the Prime Minister has disappointed everyone in the street. He lacks the qualities of a great leader of people. Letting 'I dare not' wait upon 'I would' never won a political struggle, and never will win one. '*Not practical politics*' is — not practical politics when a great policy, as a whole, is in men's thoughts.

His failure, however, is not a misfortune for you, but quite the reverse. Had he been freer and more generous towards the complete fiscal scheme many folk would have said 'Well, let that suffice for the present'. But now people are more than ever looking for the entire policy, and looking to *you* to make it clear to them. The lead has come round to you again, and the unexpected absence of a lead from Balfour has left the game with you only in a way that may, perhaps, otherwise not have been so complete.

III

Opinion in Glasgow was divided on the Fiscal Question. The Chamber of Commerce had passed a resolution favourable to Chamberlain's proposals. On the other hand, Cameron Corbett,

[1] Monkbretton in conversation with Garvin: from a note in the Garvin papers.

one of the city's leading Unionist M.P.'s, was a strong Free Trader and had organised an extensive distribution of Free Trade pamphlets written by James and Goschen. The *Glasgow Herald*, too, was lukewarm.

Chamberlain had decided, from the first, that his visit to Glasgow should not be confined to a speech. He wanted a strong resolution committing the meeting and more particularly the members of the Platform. The local Unionists rather jibbed at this.

CHAMBERLAIN TO MAXWELL

25 *August* 1903.—I am very much obliged to you for your letter and shall at all times be disposed to pay great attention to your advice. At the same time I must say at once that, according to my present views, it would be a sign of weakness, if not of cowardice, to address a meeting at Glasgow without some Resolution more definite than that proposed, and it is in my opinion made much more urgent by the leading article in the Glasgow 'Herald' in which the local organisations are publicly advised to hold aloof from my meeting if anything more than a non-committal Resolution is proposed.

My whole object would, I think, be destroyed under such circumstances. Like every other statesman I can do nothing without popular support. If public opinion is against me the sooner I know it the better. If it is with me, it will be better that other people should know it also.

The Resolution actually suggested is a very mild one. It only commits the meeting to an expression of opinion that the time has come for reconsideration of our fiscal system, and therefore only carries the matter very little further than inquiry.

You will remember that Mr. Balfour will speak as Prime Minister at Sheffield a week before me. He will certainly advocate such reconsideration, and the Resolution will therefore be one of approval of the policy of the Government as a whole, while it will not commit anyone in matters of detail.

Parker Smith has written to me on the subject taking the same line, and I believe that Bonar Law agrees with him although I have not heard from him at present.

I do not see that under such circumstances any member of the Unionist Party need be kept from the platform. They need not vote for the Resolution if they do not approve of it. But even if they stayed away I should think their absence would be fully compensated if such a Resolution were adopted by a popular meeting.

You will have noticed that the opposite Party invariably propose strong resolutions condemning the new policy root and branch. They will certainly triumph if we dare not or do not give our meetings the opportunity of expressing some opinion.

Please understand that this is not a final decision, but I think it right to tell you how the matter appears to me.

The first meeting makes the question of great importance, because, if I yield now the weak members of our Party will press the same conclusion at all the other meetings that I attend and the net result after all my work will be that I shall apparently have accomplished nothing. My instinct tells me that the bolder course is the wiser one.

CHAMBERLAIN TO COCHRANE

27 *August* 1903.—In my opinion the leader in the Glasgow 'Herald' makes it absolutely necessary that there should be a rather definite Resolution. I cannot allow myself to be frightened by half-hearted friends like the 'Herald' or active opponents.

Chamberlain's view prevailed. But after the resignations new difficulties arose. The Conservative Association which was to be co-sponsor of the meeting with the Liberal Unionists began to get cold feet.

PARKER SMITH TO CHAMBERLAIN

20 *September* 1903.—Some of the members of the National Union of Conservatives feel difficulty under the changed position in having your meeting under their auspices.

They refused to have anything to do with a Hicks Beach meeting on the ground he was outside the Government and feel difficulty in treating you differently.

I urged on the man who talked to me that the case was different as you supported Government as far as they went while Hicks Beach was against them ; also that they should not go back from action already taken, and in any case that they should privately consult Balfour first.

The Executive met yesterday, were divided in opinion, and are I believe consulting Balfour. They meet again tomorrow and the Joint Committee on Wednesday.

Of course they are not the least hostile to the meeting, and desire that it should take place under L.U. auspices and there is not the least doubt of an overwhelmingly crowded meeting.

I am anxious to keep the meeting a joint one if possible, but under the changed circumstances I don't attach the same importance to that as I did previously. If you attach importance to the matter will you let me know.

CHAMBERLAIN TO PARKER SMITH

21 *September* 1903.—. . . As regards Glasgow, — Personally I do not care a 'damn' whether the Conservatives join or not, but I beg you to impress upon them in the strongest way that they could not render a worse service to Balfour or to the Party than by retiring at this stage. I have left the Government while wholly agreeing with it in principle and in policy, and I am going to give it all the support I can.

If now the Conservatives of Glasgow, or anywhere else, separate themselves from me or from the Liberal Unionists, they will give rise to the opinion that in spite of my correspondence with the Premier we are really at loggerheads. I am quite sure that my people, by which I mean not necessarily Liberal Unionists, but my supporters in the country, will not take any slight to me lying down, and the result of such cowardice as some of the Conservatives seem to contemplate will be a certain destruction of the Government and a breach which it will take years to heal. I have made *my* sacrifice, and the least they can do is to show some appreciation of it. I am not prepared to be put in the same category with Hicks Beach whose support of the Government would in any case have been very lukewarm and of no value; and, although I do not value the support of such men for itself, I feel that they will make a fatal mistake if they establish a distinction between myself and my followers and other loyal supporters of the Government.

This letter of Chamberlain's shows us the mood in which he entered on his campaign. The time for compromise and diplomacy was over.

IV

Chamberlain left Birmingham for Glasgow on the morning of 6 October. His wife's parents who were sailing to New York next day accompanied them as far as Crewe.

MRS. CHAMBERLAIN TO HER MOTHER

7 *October* 1903.—After we parted from you at Crewe we continued our journey through torrents of rain, which seemed only to increase the farther North we got. At every station there was a little knot of people, which became a regular crowd the nearer we got to Glasgow. Cheers and 'Good old Joe,' and 'He's a jolly good fellow,' followed the pauses.

At Glasgow there was a big gathering on the platform, and Mr. Parker Smith was on hand, together with the principal political people of the place and a good many from the surrounding district. As we emerged into the street, in spite of the steady downpour, for several hundred yards beyond the station there were crowds on either side, five and six deep, to whom the sight of closed carriages could have hardly compensated for the wetting which they had got. However, this did not seem to damp their ardour, for we found the same thing outside the Hotel and at the entrance to St. Andrew's Hall.

As soon as we arrived I scurried upstairs and made a lightning change, and was actually ready before Joe. Sir Matthew and Lady Arthur entertained us at a dinner, which turned out to be a miniature banquet — three or four long tables beside the head one at which we sat. The local magnates and many of the Peers who had come to attend the meeting were present. Just after we sat down Joe came to me to ask if I had got any lozenges as he felt extremely hoarse, and was much disturbed in his mind as to what the consequences might be. Happily, fortune had favoured me, for just before we left Highbury I rushed upstairs and got a box of tabloids. These saved the situation, for without them I think his voice must have broken down. As it was it held extremely well. He made a short speech at the dinner in reply to the toast of his health, and at eight o'clock we were at the meeting.

As I came in I was recognised and they gave me a most kindly greeting. The scene was really very striking, for the Hall is an exceptionally large one and there were certainly six thousand people packed into it. The unbroken sea of heads reached far up the galleries as well as on the floor and composed, as it was, almost entirely of men, it made a great effect. Scotch audiences are always intelligent, though they have the reputation of being very quiet. *This* could hardly have been called that, for it gave itself up to sympathetic enthusiasm. I have rarely, if ever, seen a meeting which was more quick to see the points, or more ready to applaud them.

The Glasgow speech is the most important in the series. Nothing is more difficult than to propose a policy without going into detail, except perhaps to go into detail on a platform. Yet this is precisely what Chamberlain did. In an hour and fifty minutes he set out the basic assumptions of the Tariff Reform movement and then explained, in detail, what he would do, what his Fiscal budget would be, if he had the power. It is not just a policy speech or manifesto. It is a programme. As such we must consider it in some detail.

Chamberlain began by observing that he was speaking in the city 'in which Free Trade took its birth . . . in which Adam Smith taught so long'. He then proceeded to cite Adam Smith in his support.

When I read his books I see how even then he was aware of the importance of home markets as compared with foreign; how he supported the Navigation Laws; how he was the author of a sentence which we ought never to forget, that 'Defence is greater than opulence.'. . . he had a broader mind, a more Imperial conception of the duties of the citizens of a great Empire, than some . . . who claim to be his successors.

He went on to define his personal position. 'I am no longer a party leader . . . but I am still a loyal servant of 'the party.' As to Mr. Balfour':

I agree with the principles that he has stated. I approve of the policy to which he proposes to give effect . . . in no conceivable circumstances will I allow myself to be put in any sort of competition, direct or indirect, with my friend and leader, whom I mean to follow. What is my position? I have invited a discussion upon a question which comes peculiarly within my province, owing to the office which I have so recently held. I have invited discussion upon it. I have not pretended that a matter of this importance is to be settled off-hand. I have been well aware that the country has to be educated, as I myself have had to be educated before I saw, or could see, all the bearings of this great matter ; and therefore I take up the position of a pioneer. I go in front of the army, and if the army is attacked, I go back to it.

Meanwhile, putting aside all these personal and party questions, I ask my countrymen, without regard to any political opinions which they may have hitherto held, to consider the greatest of all great questions that can be put before the country, to consider it impartially if possible, and to come to a decision ; and it is possible — I am always an optimist — it is possible that the nation may be prepared to go a little further than the official programme . . . one of my objects in coming here is to find an answer to this question. Is the country prepared to go a little further ?

His objects were the prosperity of the United Kingdom and the Unity of the Empire. Seemingly these objects were already achieved and he had, therefore, to answer the question, 'Why cannot you let well alone ?'

Well, I have been in Venice — the beautiful city of the Adriatic — which had at one time a commercial supremacy quite as great in proportion as anything we have ever enjoyed. Its glories have departed ; but what I was going to say was that when I was there last I saw the great tower of the Campanile rising above the city which it had overshadowed for centuries, and looking as though it was as permanent as the city itself. And yet the other day, in a few minutes, the whole structure fell to the ground. Nothing was left of it but a mass of ruin and rubbish. I do not say to you, gentlemen, that I anticipate any catastrophe so great or so sudden for British trade ; but I do say to you that I see signs of decay ; that I see cracks and crevices in the walls of the great structure ; that I know that the foundations upon which it has been raised are not broad enough or deep enough to sustain it. Now, do I do wrong, if I know this — if I even think I know it — do I do wrong to warn you ?

He now unfolded his analysis of the threat to the British economy. In the first place our export trade was stagnating :

The year 1900 was the record year of British trade. The exports were the largest we had ever known. The year 1902 — last year — was nearly as good, and yet, if you will compare your trade in 1872, thirty years ago, with the trade of 1902 — the export trade — you will find that there has been a moderate increase of £22,000,000.[1] That, I think, is something like 7½ per cent. Meanwhile, the population has increased 30 per cent. . . . In the same time the increase in the United States of America was £110,000,000, and the increase in Germany was £56,000,000. . . . Meanwhile the protected countries which you have been told, and which I myself at one time believed, were going rapidly to wreck and ruin, have progressed in a much greater proportion than ours. That is not all. . . .

[1] The figures given in the then recent Board of Trade Blue Book are as follows : total exports of British produce — 1872, £256,000,000 ; 1902, £278,000,000.

When Mr. Cobden preached his doctrine, he believed . . . that while foreign countries would supply us with our food-stuffs and raw materials, we should . . . send them in exchange our manufactures. But that is exactly what we have not done. On the contrary, in the period to which I have referred, we are sending less and less of our manufactures to them, and they are sending more and more of their manufactures to us.

He next explained the change in the structure and character of Britain's trade. 'I have had a table constructed and upon that table I would be willing to base the whole of my contention.'

Table showing rise and fall of U.K. exports of manufactures between the years 1872 and 1902

To U.S., Germany and Protected European countries	− £42,500,000
To 'neutral' or low tariff countries, *e.g.* Egypt, China, S. America	+ £35,000,000
To British Colonies	+ £40,000,000

Our loss of trade with the Protectionist countries was thus almost exactly balanced by the increase in our trade with the Colonies. From this Chamberlain drew the conclusion :

. . . that our Imperial trade is absolutely essential to our prosperity at the present time. If that trade declines, or if it does not increase in proportion to our population and to the loss of trade with foreign countries, then we sink at once into a fifth-rate nation. Our fate will be the fate of the empires and kingdoms of the past. We shall have reached our highest point, and indeed I am not certain that there are not some of my opponents who regard that with absolute complacency. I do not. As I have said, I have the misfortune to be an optimist. I do not believe in the setting of the British star, but then, I do not believe in the folly of the British people. I trust them. I trust the working classes of this country, and I have confidence that they who are our masters, electorally speaking, will have the intelligence to see that they must wake up. They must modify their policy to suit new conditions. They must meet those conditions with altogether a new policy.

He now ventured on what would prove dangerous ground. Why had we lost our trade with the United States and the countries of Europe ? Because those countries had become Protectionist, and Protection had enabled them to industrialise. If we had offered them Reciprocal Preferences twenty years ago we would have kept much of our trade with them. The Colonies were also Protectionist.

They were industrialising, and unless we made concessions to the Colonies now, we should lose the Colonial trade as well:

If we had gone to America ten or twenty years ago and had said, 'If you will leave the tin-plate trade as it is, put no duty on tin-plate . . . we in return will give you some advantage on some articles which you produce,' we might have kept the tin-plate trade. It would not have been worth America's while to put a duty on an article for which it had no particular or special aptitude or capacity. . . . We did not take that course. We were not prepared for it as a people. We allowed matters to drift. Are we going to let them drift now ? Are we going to lose the Colonial trade ? This is the parting of the ways. You have to remember that if you do not take this opportunity it will not recur. If you do not take it I predict, and I predict with certainty, that Canada will fall to the level of the United States. . . . The Colonies are prepared to meet us. In return for a very moderate preference they will give us a substantial advantage.

In the first place, I believe they will reserve to us the trade which we already enjoy. They will arrange for tariffs in the future in order not to start industries in competition with those which are already in existence in the Mother Country.[1]

They will not — and I would not urge them for a moment to do so — they will not injure those of their industries which have already been created. They will maintain them, they will not allow them to be destroyed or injured even by our competition, but outside that there is still a great margin, a margin which has given us this enormous increase of trade to which I have referred. That margin I believe we can permanently retain, and I ask you to think, if that is of so much importance to us now, when we have only eleven millions of white fellow-citizens in these distant Colonies, what will it be when, in the course of a period which is a mere moment of time in the history of states, that population is forty millions or more ?

Preference would bring increasing trade with the years; but already the immediate advantages of adopting a preferential system would be substantial. His calculations showed that £26,000,000 of goods imported by the Colonies from foreign countries would be imported from Britain under a preferential system.

What does that mean ? The Board of Trade assumes that of manufactured goods one-half the value is expended in labour — I think it is a great deal more, but take the Board of Trade figures — £13,000,000 a year of new employment. What does that mean to the United Kingdom ? It means the employment of 166,000 men at 30s. a week. It means the subsistence, if you include their families, of 830,000 persons ; and now, if

---

[1] The passage shown in italics suggested that Chamberlain wanted to keep the Colonies as food and raw material producers. He saw the slip as soon as his critics. In the official version of the speech issued next day, the first sentence was modified as follows, 'They will give us in the first place, I believe they will reserve to us *much at any rate* of the trade which we already enjoy'. The second sentence was omitted altogether.

you will only add to that our present export to the British possessions of £96,000,000, you will find that that gives, on the same calculation, £48,000,000 for wages, or employment at 30s. a week to 615,000 work-people, and it finds subsistence for 3,075,000 persons. In other words, your Colonial trade as it stands at present with the prospective advantage of a preference against the foreigner means employment and fair wages for three-quarters of a million of workmen, and subsistence for nearly four millions of our population.

This was the end of the economic argument. Now came the Imperial appeal :

I have appealed to your interests, I have come here as a man of business, I have appealed to the employers and the employed alike in this great city. I have endeavoured to point out to them that their trade, their wages, all depend on the maintenance of this Colonial trade, of which some of my opponents speak with such contempt, and, above all, with such egregious ignorance.

But now I abandon that line of argument for the moment, and appeal to something higher, which I believe is in your hearts as it is in mine. I appeal to you as fellow-citizens of the greatest Empire that the world has ever known ; I appeal to you to recognise that the privileges of Empire bring with them great responsibilities. I want to ask you to think what this Empire means, what it is to you and your descendants. . . . Is such a dominion, are such traditions, is such a glorious inheritance, is such a splendid sentiment — are they worth preserving ? They have cost us much. They have cost us much in blood and treasure ; and in past times, as in recent, many of our best and noblest have given their lives, or risked their lives, for this great ideal. But it has also done much for us. It has ennobled our national life, it has discouraged that petty parochial-ism which is the defect of all small communities. I say to you that all that is best in our present life, best in this Britain of ours, all of which we have the right to be most proud, is due to the fact that we are not only sons of Britain, but we are sons of Empire. . . . But . . . remember that each generation in turn has to do its part, and you are called to do your share in this great work. Others have founded the Empire ; it is yours to build firmly and permanently the great edifice of which others have laid the foundation. And I believe we have got to change somewhat our rather insular habits . . . I have been in communication with many of the men, statesmen, orators, writers, distinguished in our Colonies. I have had intimate conversation with them. I have tried to understand them and I think I do understand them, and I say that none of them desire separa-tion. There are none of them who are not loyal to this idea of Empire which they say they wish us to accept more fully in the future, but I have found none who do not believe that our present Colonial relations cannot be permanent. We must either draw closer together or we shall drift apart.

He now led up to his practical proposals.

Can we invent a tie which must be a practical one, which will prevent separation. . . . I say that it is only by commercial union, reciprocal

Preference, that you can lay the foundations of the confederation of the Empire to which we all look forward as a brilliant possibility. Now I have told you what you are to gain by Preference. You will gain the retention and the increase of your customers. You will gain work for the enormous number of those who are now unemployed; you will pave the way for a firmer and more enduring union of the Empire. What will it cost you? What do the Colonies ask? They ask a Preference on their particular products. You cannot give them, at least it would be futile to offer them, a Preference on manufactured goods, because at the present time the exported manufacture of the Colonies is entirely insignificant. You cannot, in my opinion, give them a Preference on raw material. It has been said that I should propose such a tax; but I repeat now, in the most explicit terms, that I do not propose a tax on raw materials, which are a necessity of our manufacturing trade. What remains? Food.

He went on to explain that, though he proposed to tax food, he believed that could be done without adding a farthing to the cost of living.

I have been asked for a plan. I have hesitated, because as you will readily see, no final plan can be proposed until a Government is authorised by the people to enter into negotiations upon these principles. . . . At the same time I recognise that you have a right to call upon me for the broad outlines of my plan, and those I will give you if you will bear with me.

Now came the plan:

1. 2s. a quarter on foreign corn, with no duty on corn imported from the Empire. A corresponding duty on imported flour. This he hoped would restore the milling industry thus helping to check the drift from the countryside to the towns, and providing cheap feeding stuffs for pig-keepers. There would be no duty on maize, partly because it was 'a food of some of the very poorest of the population', partly because it was an animal feeding stuff.

2. A 5 per cent duty on foreign meat and dairy products; bacon to be excluded from the duty, again as a food of the poorest section of the population.

3. A Preference on Colonial wines and, perhaps, fruits.

4. These new taxes were to be balanced by the following reduction in existing revenue duties:

(i) The Tea Duty to be reduced by 75 per cent.

(ii) The Sugar Duty to be reduced by 50 per cent.

(iii) Corresponding reductions on cocoa and coffee.

Assuming that the consumer paid the whole of the new duties, Chamberlain's scheme, according to Board of Trade estimates of working class consumption, would increase the agricultural labourer's bread, meat and dairy bill by 16½ farthings a week and reduce his tea and sugar bill by 17 farthings. The increase in the artisan's weekly budget would be 19½ farthings balanced by a reduction of 19½ farthings. On the most unfavourable calculation, therefore, the artisan's cost of living would be unaffected, while the agricultural labourer would actually be half a farthing better off!

Chamberlain, however, did not believe that the consumer would pay the full extent of the duty. He had been advised by 'one of the highest of the official experts whom the Government consult' that 'the incidence of a tax depends upon the proportion between the free production and the taxed production'. This meant that if, as in the case of meat, two-ninths of the total consumption was imported from abroad, the consumer would bear two-ninths of the tax. On this calculation, Chamberlain reckoned that his proposals would make the agricultural labourer better off each week by 2 pence and the artisan by 2½ pence.

One further point remained. The proposed cuts in the tea, sugar, cocoa and coffee duties would deprive the revenue of £2,800,000 a year. 'How is it to be made up? I propose to find it, and to find more, in the other branch of this policy of fiscal reform, in that part of it which is sometimes called "reciprocity".' He went on to propose a 10 per cent duty on foreign manufactures. This would yield between £9,000,000 and £15,000,000 a year, thus leaving the Chancellor a substantial margin. He could use it 'for the further reduction both of taxes on food and also of some other taxes which press most hardly on different sections of the community'. Or he might remit some of the duties on foreign manufactures, 'if we could get corresponding advantages from the country whose products were thus taxed'.

He had spoken with great deliberation and, inevitably, most of the speech had been businesslike, matter-of-fact. But he had held his audience throughout. He came now to the peroration, 'and the strength and force and passion with which he made it was like that of a great actor — dramatic in the highest sense of the word and full of a feeling which caused his voice to break'.[1]

It remains to ask, what will the Colonies say? . . . They have not waited for an offer. Already Canada has given you a Preference of 33⅓ per cent., South Africa has given you a Preference of 25 per cent., New Zealand has offered a Preference of 10 per cent. The premier of Australia has promised to bring before Parliament a similar proposal. They have done all this in confidence, in faith which I am certain will not be dis-

[1] Mrs. Chamberlain to her mother, 7 October 1903.

appointed — in faith that you will not be ungrateful, that you will not be unmindful of the influences which have weighed with them, that you will share their loyalty and devotion to an Empire which is theirs as well as ours, and which they also have done something to maintain.

It is because I sympathise with their object, it is because I appreciate the wisdom, aye, the generosity of their offer, it is because I see that things are moving and that an opportunity now in your hands, once lost, will never recur ; it is because I believe that this policy will consolidate the Empire — the Empire which I believe to be the security for peace and for the maintenance of our great British traditions — it is for all these things, and, believe me, for no personal ambition that I have given up the office which I was so proud to hold, and that now, when I might, I think, fairly claim a period of rest, I have taken up new burdens, and come before you as a missionary of Empire, to urge upon you again, as I did in the old times when I protested against the disruption of the United Kingdom, once again to warn you, to urge you, to implore you to do nothing that will tend towards the disintegration of the Empire, and not to refuse to sacrifice a futile superstition, an inept prejudice, and thereby to lose the results of centuries of noble effort and patriotic endeavour.

Mrs. Chamberlain came away sure that he had really done all that one could have wished to give a clear outline to his policy. 'As I passed through the crowds everyone was talking and one heard such expressions as "that's convincing", "I don't see that there is any answer to that", and "there must be many convictions settled tonight".'[1]

The impact of the speech on Unionists up and down the country was almost as strong as on the immediate audience. Staunch old Chaplin who had travelled to Glasgow to show his support wrote as follows on the following evening.

CHAPLIN TO CHAMBERLAIN

7 *October* 1903.—I have heard so much that is encouraging since I got back to London that I think you will like to know it.

. . . I went into the Carlton Club on my way from the station first — not very full but there had been a fair sprinkling during the afternoon. They crowded round me to ask about Glasgow and I asked in reply what they thought there — Ah ! we are all for him here to a man ! ! was the answer.

Next a well-known City member told me, taking me on one side, that your speech had had a remarkable effect in the City — This was confirmed at dinner when I met 3 City men, Alfred Rothschild among them. I asked in an innocent way what they thought of the Glasgow Speech in the City and they all burst out at once. Only one opinion ! ! ! ! ! Some well-known and prominent Free Traders and others who had always been

[1] Mrs. Chamberlain to her mother, 7 October 1903.

opposed — come round entirely, general satisfaction, followed by a
boom — Consols going up 1 or ¾ — the precise details in City matters I
never can remember and it doesn't matter.   Alfred R, whom I asked
afterwards privately, more than confirmed all this.   He has been in the
City today, and entirely agreed that there is no doubt as to the impression
you have made in those circles, and after all, the City is very important.

I shall go down into those parts tomorrow or Friday myself, and see
what can be done in the way of Funds for our friends in Victoria St.
I told them I would take round the hat as soon as I got back ; and from
the 1st man I've tried I've got £1,000 today — nothing like striking while
the iron is hot.

Altogether I am delighted, and chiefly because I rejoice to see your
pluck and patience and resolution already rewarded.   Devonshire's resignation, they told me, I should add, was already forgotten in the general
excitement about your speech today.

Away in Dublin, Balfour's protégé George Wyndham was moved
to something like enthusiasm.

WYNDHAM TO CHAMBERLAIN

Private.—7 *October* 1903.—I must break my resolution not to add to your
correspondence only to say that I have never felt such exultation in the
joy of battle since the anti-Home Rule meeting at Her Majesty's theatre
which swept me into politics in 1886.

The speech, of course, had its defects.   1872, the year after the
Franco-Prussian war, had been in many ways a freakishly unfavourable year from the point of view of trade.   To choose it as the starting
point for his statistical comparisons did not greatly strengthen
Chamberlain's case but laid him open to the charge of special
pleading.

More serious had been the implication that an object of his preferential policy was to keep the Colonies from pressing on with their
own industrial development.   He never repeated this mistake but,
as we shall see, he never quite lived it down.   To the end, a suspicion
remained, particularly in Canada, that British Imperialists wanted
Preference to keep Canada a primary producing country.

Finally we cannot help noting that in speaking of the way in which
the Chancellor of the Exchequer might dispose of the proceeds of the
duty on manufactures, he made no reference to Old Age Pensions.
It is easy to understand why he had played down this side of his
original proposal when his first aim had been to win over the party
in the House of Commons.   But now his appeal was to the constituencies, and here was the golden chance to put a great social reform
in the forefront of his programme.

But these defects were small compared with the positive quality of the speech. Anyone who has taken part in political life knows that there is a longing in the rank and file of active constituency workers for 'a concrete, definite, black and white' statement of policy. They want something easy to remember and factual; not a declaration of principles but a statement of what you mean to do. Such programmes have usually been the prerogative of movements of the left. The People's Charter, the manifesto of the Anti-Corn Law League, and the Radical Unauthorised Programme, are obvious instances. The Unionist parties, in social and economic affairs, had pursued a broadly defensive strategy coupled with occasional opportunist sorties. They had principles but they had no programme. It was the strength of Chamberlain's speech that it gave Unionism for the first time, a positive social and economic programme. The Glasgow programme would be the basis of Unionist domestic policy for years to come.

'Chamberlain was very tired after it [the Glasgow meeting] but that did not affect him the next night at Greenock.' [1]

The Glasgow speech had stressed the importance of Colonial trade, argued the case for Preference and given the outline of a Tariff Reform budget. The Greenock speech put the case for Retaliation.

I begin with a confession of faith. I was brought up in the pure doctrine of Free Trade. . . . I accepted it as a settled fact; and nobody could have surprised me more than if, twenty, or still more, thirty years ago, he had told me that I should now be criticising the doctrine which I then accepted. But thirty years is a long time. Has nothing changed in thirty years? Everything has changed. Politics have changed, science has changed, and trade has changed. . . . In the last thirty years the whole conditions have changed; and it seems to me to be not the policy of a Liberal or the policy of a Radical, as I understood such a policy twenty or thirty years ago, but the policy of a rabid and reactionary Tory to say that when all the conditions have changed you should not change your policy too.

He went on to discuss the rise of Protectionism in other countries. What was its purpose? How far had it succeeded?

We are a great people, but, after all, I have never been able to believe that all the wisdom in the world was absolutely domiciled in this country. I have a great opinion of our American cousins. . . . I have some considerable respect for the German people. . . . I have a great regard for our neighbours the French. . . . I do not believe that all these people are fools. . . .

[1] Mrs. Chamberlain to her mother, 11 October 1903.

What is the policy of these . . . nations ? It has been, not a hap-hazard policy, but a policy deliberately adopted and deliberately pursued. It is a policy to use tariffs to increase home trade, and, if you like, to exclude foreign trade. All these nations to which I have referred, and every other civilised nation on the face of the earth, have adopted a tariff with the object of keeping the home market to the home population and not from any want of friendship to us. I do not believe they have been in the slightest degree actuated by ill-feeling to Great Britain ; but because they thought it was necessary for their own security and prosperity, they have done everything in their power to shut out British goods. . . .

That was a deliberate policy ; there is no doubt about that. Has it succeeded ? It has, whether it was right or wrong. What these people intended to do they have done ; and if you look back for any term of years you will find that the exports of British manufactures have fallen off to these countries, while their exports to us have risen. There may be some-thing wrong in my constitution, but I never like being hit without striking back again. But there are some people who like to be trampled upon. I admire them, but I will not follow their example. I am an advocate of peace, no man more so. I wish to live quietly, comfortably, and in harmony with my fellow-creatures, but I am not in favour of peace at any price. I am a Free Trader. I want to have exchange with all the nations of the world, but if they will not exchange with me, then I am not a Free Trader at any price.

Now came a series of direct appeals to the Working Class. He began by arguing that it was illogical to protect Labour with social legislation and Trades Unions if you gave no protection to the results of Labour.

. . . what can be more illogical than to raise the cost of production in this country in order to promote the welfare of the working classes, and then to allow the products of other countries — which are not surrounded by any similar legislation, which are free from all similar cost and expendi-ture, freely to enter our country in competition with our goods, which are hampered in the struggle ? . . . If these foreign goods come in cheaper, one of two things must follow : either you will have to give up the condi-tions you have gained, either you will have to abolish and repeal the Fair Wages Clause and the Factory Acts and the Compensation to Workmen Acts, either you will have to take lower wages, or you will lose your work. You cannot keep your work at this higher standard of living and wages if at the same time you allow foreigners at a lower standard and lower rate of pay to send their goods freely in competition with yours.

He then rounded on the Free Trade argument that it was in the National interest to buy in the cheapest market.

Yes, but think how that affects different classes in the community. Take the capitalist — the man living upon his income. His interest is to buy in the cheapest market, because he does not produce. The cheaper he can get every article he consumes, the better for him. He need not buy a single article in this country; he need not make a single article. He can invest his money in foreign countries and live upon the interest; and then, in the returns of the prosperity of the country, it will be said that the country is growing richer because he is growing richer. But what about the working men? What about the class that depends upon having work in order to earn wages or subsistence at all? They cannot do without work; and yet the work will go if the article is not produced in this country. This is the state of things against which I am protesting.

From the general he turned to the particular. Greenock had been the centre of the sugar refining industry.

Greenock was one of the great centres of the sugar trade. You had many refineries; it was a profitable trade; it not only employed a great number of work people itself, but it also gave employment in subsidiary industries to a great number of your countrymen.

Then came foreign competition, aided by bounties, and your trade declines so seriously that only the very best, the very richest, the most enterprising, the most inventive, can possibly retain their hold upon it. If there had been no bounties, and no unfair competition of this kind, what would have happened? In the last twenty or thirty years the consumption of sugar throughout the world has increased enormously. The consumption in this country has increased enormously; and you would have had your share. I do not hesitate to say that, if normal conditions and equal fairness had prevailed, at this moment in Greenock, quite independently of the other industries you may have found to occupy you, there would have been in sugar alone ten times as many men employed as there were in the most palmy days of the trade. But normal conditions have not obtained. You have been the sufferers; and a great number of your refineries have disappeared altogether. The capital invested in them has been lost, and the workmen who worked in them — what has become of them?

Free imports have destroyed this industry, at all events for the time, and it is not easy to recover an industry when it has once been lost. They have destroyed sugar-refining for a time as one of the great staple industries of the country, which it ought always to have remained. They have destroyed agriculture. . . . Agriculture, as the greatest of all trades and industries of this country, has been practically destroyed. Sugar has gone; silk has gone; iron is threatened; wool is threatened; cotton will go! How long are you going to stand it? At the present moment these industries, and the working men who depend upon them, are like sheep in a field. One by one they allow themselves to be led out to slaughter, and there is no combination, no apparent prevision of what is in store for the rest of them. Do you think, if you belong at the present to a prosperous industry, that your industry will be allowed to continue? Do you think that the same causes which have destroyed some of our industries, and which are in the course of destroying others, will not be equally applicable to you when your turn comes? . . .

What is the remedy? What is it that the Prime Minister proposed at Sheffield? He said — I am not quoting his exact words — Let us get rid of the chains which we ourselves have forged, and which have fettered our action. Let us claim some protection like every other civilised nation.

Then in a sounding passage he attacked the fears of the Treasury and Board of Trade that by imposing import duties we should invite foreign retaliation against our exports.

Then we are told that if we do this the foreigners will be angry with us ! Has it come to that with Great Britain ? It is a craven argument ; it is worthy of the Little Englander ; it is not possible for any man who believes in his own country. The argument is absurd. Who is to suffer ? Are we so poor that we are at the mercy of every foreign State — that we cannot hold our own — that we are to fear their resentment if we imitate their own policy ? Are we to receive their orders 'with bated breath and whispering humbleness' ? No, if that were true, I should say that the star of England has already set ; it would not be worth anyone's while to care to speculate on her possible future. But it is not true. There is not a word of truth in it. We have nothing to fear from the foreigners. I do not believe in a war of tariffs, but if there were to be a war of tariffs, I know we should not come out second best. Why, at the present time ours is the greatest market in the whole world. We are the best customers of all those countries. There are many suitors for our markets. We may reject the addresses of some, but there is no fear that we shall not have other offers. It is absolutely absurd to suppose that all these countries, keenly competitive among themselves, would agree among themselves to fight with us when they might benefit at the expense of their neighbours. Why, at the present time, we take from Germany about twice as much as she takes from us. We take from France about three times as much, and from the United States of America we take about six times as much as they take from us. After all that, do we stand to lose if there is to be a war of tariffs ?

As yet the main concern of the speech had been with the need for protection against foreign competition. He now looked outward and developed what in our time has been called the concept of 'the common market'. The main cause for the prosperity of the United States was that they had a market of 70,000,000 consumers. But Britain with her Colonies could, if she took the necessary steps to organise it, have a 'home market' of 350,000,000 consumers, including a White population of over 50,000,000. Would we take the necessary steps ?

. . . all history is the history of States once powerful and then decaying. Is Britain to be numbered among the decaying States ? Is all the glory of the past to be forgotten ? Are we to prove ourselves unregenerate sons of the forefathers who left us so glorious an inheritance ? Are the efforts of all our sons to be frittered away ? Are all their sacrifices to be vain ? Or are we to take up a new youth as members of a great Empire, which will continue for generation after generation, the strength, the power, and the glory of the British race ?

That is the issue that I present to you. . . . I have in times past more than once taken my political life in my hand in order to teach that which I believe to be true. No man as a statesman is worth his salt who is not prepared to do likewise. I care nothing about the personal result. I beg you not to consider it for a moment ; but I appeal to you to consider that in this matter the interests of your country, the interests of your children, the interests of the Empire are all at stake, and I ask you to consider impartially the arguments that I have put before you. I pray you may give the right decision.

After the Glasgow meeting, Mrs. Chamberlain had noted that Chamberlain's arguments for Imperial Preference had evoked a much greater response than his references to Protection. At Greenock it was the other way about. The reference to the decline of the sugar-refining industry and the warning against the dangers of foreign competition were received with tumultuous enthusiasm. They established an immediate link between the speaker and his audience. Chamberlain was powerfully influenced by the experience. He realised then to the full how much easier it was to rouse the working man against the danger of foreign competition with his own industry than to lead him on to the hope of new markets in the Colonies. Hitherto, Imperial Preference had been the main element of the programme. We shall now see the Protectionist part coming more and more to the fore.

We may let Mrs. Chamberlain take up the tale :

MRS. CHAMBERLAIN TO HER MOTHER

11 *October* 1903.—We went back to Glasgow, still in the pouring rain, and I marvelled at the crowds gathered outside the Hall and the station, who were cheerful under the downpour.

We left the Parker Smith's on Thursday morning, and arrived at Crawford Priory in time for lunch. There we found a gathering of M.P.s, actual and prospective : Sir Charles Tennant, who is a Liberal who has deserted his son-in-law, Mr. Asquith, on this question ; Mr. Garvin, alias 'Calchas', and 'Tariff Reformer' and author of the article you read in the National Review ; the owner of 'The Scotsman', Mr. Richard Cavendish and his wife, etc., etc. After we left the dining-room the gentle-men had a regular parliament, which lasted till five o'clock, to Lady Gertrude's despair. Then it was re-assembled round the tea-table and was continued through dinner. That ended our stay, for at ten o'clock we took the night train for London. Just after we left Edinburgh the train was stopped for Mr. Brodrick and Mr. Alfred Lyttelton, and so we had another pow-wow for about an hour, all talking as hard as we could. Poor Mr. Brodrick ! He was rather pathetic, for he feels that he has made a failure, but with the task before him too much was expected of him, and I could not but sympathise with this. Mr. Lyttelton was very nice and I was glad to be able to meet him so soon, and give him my congratulations.

R

The opening phase of the campaign was over. Chamberlain was well satisfied with the result. 'If I live,' he wrote a few days later, 'I am going to win on the issue I have raised, and probably earlier than I had ventured to anticipate. Scotland was very kind to me.' [1]

v

Chamberlain's two speeches in Scotland called forth seven replies from the Liberal leaders in almost as many days. The first to the attack was Asquith speaking at Cinderford, with Dilke as Chairman, the day after the Greenock speech.[2]

The most patient reader will not expect us to analyse the many powerful speeches which swelled the Fiscal controversy that autumn ; nor even all of Chamberlain's. We have, however, considered in some detail the Glasgow and Greenock speeches which contain all the main points of the first Tariff Reform campaign. It is necessary, therefore, if the reader is to have even a general idea of the great debate to give some analysis of at least one representative Free Trade speech. Harcourt thought Asquith too reasoned for the platform and rated Campbell-Bannerman's replies to Chamberlain higher. Most contemporary opinion, however, gave the palm to Asquith ; and it was by his relentless pursuit of Chamberlain through the country that Asquith really established his reputation. We shall, therefore, give some little consideration to his speech at Cinderford.

Asquith began by giving his interpretation of the relationship between Chamberlain and Balfour.

Mr. Balfour declared, in the first instance, that he personally had an open mind. . . . An open mind needs to be informed. Accordingly a so-called inquiry was set on foot under that pretext during what remained of the Parliamentary Session. . . early in August the Prime Minister composed and circulated amongst his colleagues an academic treatise on fiscal retaliation. It was, if I may say so with respect, a most elegant and learned disquisition ; but for all it had to do with the proposals of Mr. Chamberlain it might just as well have been written and published in Mars. . . . Another month passed, and at the end of that we were given to understand, first by correspondence which took place between Mr. Balfour and Mr. Chamberlain, and then by the speech of the former at Sheffield, that under some undefined influence the open mind of the Prime Minister had closed. His fluid opinions had crystallised into convictions, and in principle he had become a convert to Mr. Chamberlain's fiscal proposals.

It seems that there is a wide gulf between a convert in principle and a

[1] Chamberlain to Lady Jeune, 11 October 1903.　　　[2] 8 October 1903.

fellow-worker in the mission field. 'I do not think,' said Mr. Balfour at Sheffield, 'that public opinion in this country is ripe for the taxation of food.' It is not as though he, the leader, as he reminded us, of a great party, were giving a lead to that party upon a critical occasion ; it is not as though he professes to agree with public opinion. On the contrary, he does not disguise his view that public opinion upon this topic is the slave and the dupe of ingrained political prejudice and perverted historical analogies ; but, bad as he thinks it, and wrong as he thinks it, he is not going to engage his party to combat and to convert it. No ; for himself and his colleagues he has abandoned the open mind, but the open field he leaves to Mr. Chamberlain. He is asked to give a lead, and what is the lead that he gives ? In effect what he says to his followers is this :— For the moment we will all combine to talk generalities about retaliation or freedom of negotiation, which may mean anything or which may mean nothing, so that the unity of our party will be secured ; but none the less our lamented colleague, Mr. Chamberlain — who, as all the world can see, has parted from me and I from him in a glow of mutual appreciation and regret — our lamented colleague will continue to conduct, ostensibly from outside, his propaganda for the taxation of bread and of meat. In the meantime, I, the Prime Minister, having shed my Free Trade colleagues, will contemplate his operations from afar with undisguised, though for the moment inactive, sympathy, waiting with my sickle ready for the ripening of the harvest.

Dealing first with the policy of Retaliation, Asquith began by claiming that our policy of free imports was essential to the strength of our export trade. The proof of this, in his eyes, was that although the Protectionist countries were growing increasingly self-supporting — as, he argued, they were bound to do — Britain was still exporting more to the main Protectionist countries than they were to each other.

He then raised the question : 'What are you going to retaliate upon ?' According to his statistics, eleven-twelfths of our imports from Russia and five-sixths of our imports from the United States consisted of food and raw materials. Was there really any need for a policy of retaliation against foreign manufactures ?

The moment you begin to translate these vague platform phrases into practice you find that they cannot be carried out as a policy without doing to you here in Great Britain as great and probably more harm than to the persons against whom that policy is used.

From Balfour's policy of Retaliation, Asquith now turned to Chamberlain's policy of Preference.

Let us pass from Sheffield to Glasgow. I must say that from one point of view it is rather a relief to do so. It is something like passing from the atmosphere of the footlights after the curtain has been rung down upon a rather sorry farce to the bustle and animation and reality of life in the open air. Mr. Chamberlain may be right or he may be wrong. For my part I think he is profoundly wrong. At any rate, he knows what he thinks, he says what he means, and he does not 'let I dare not wait upon I would.' . . . Mr. Chamberlain says he has two objects in view. The first is to maintain and increase the prosperity of the United Kingdom, and the second is to cement the unity of the Empire. We all agree as to these two objects, to which I will venture to add, not by way of qualification, but simply by way of supplement, that the one end must not be sought, and cannot be attained, at the expense of the other. In the long run, depend upon it, you will not promote the unity of the Empire by anything that arrests or impairs the material strength of the United Kingdom. Mr. Chamberlain says, and says truly, that the Colonies ought not to be treated as an appendage to Great Britain. I agree, and neither ought Great Britain to be treated as an appendage to the Colonies. . . . Any one who strikes a blow at the root of the prosperity of the United Kingdom is doing the worst service which can be done to the Empire to which we are proud to belong.

He went on to question the truth of Chamberlain's warning that our economy was decaying and that our trade had been virtually stagnant over the last thirty years :

Let me ask my fellow-countrymen to see what has been our condition during this era of stagnant trade. During that period the amount assessed to the income-tax has doubled ; the interest upon our foreign investments has more than doubled ; the deposits in our savings banks have multiplied two and three fold ; the bankers' cheques cleared, taking the annual average, have risen in amount from 530 millions to over 800 millions sterling ; and last, but not least, the wages of the working classes have risen, measured not merely in terms of money, though there has been a considerable rise in our money wages, but much more measured in their real terms, in the terms of that which money can buy. As the Board of Trade has told us, 100s. buys as much as 140s. twenty years ago. Talk about Germany and the wages of a protectionist country ! I hope you will compare, from the material the Blue-books place at your disposal, the wages, the standard of living, and the hours of labour of the German workmen and your own.

The truth was, he continued, that Chamberlain altogether over-looked the importance of our home trade. The export trade did 'not employ more than one-fifth or one-sixth of the whole labour of the country'.

Moreover, in calculating the value of our exports, Chamberlain had altogether left out of account the value of our earnings from shipping, investment and other services. He closed this passage with a sharp attack on the accuracy of Chamberlain's statistics and more particularly on his choice of the year 1872 as a standard for his comparisons. This he declared was 'an absolutely unpardonable error — unpardonable in a man who has acquainted himself with the ABC of the subject'.

Asquith now came to Chamberlain's contention that unless the Preferential policy was adopted the Empire would break up :

> I come to the other assumption, which is, that unless we are prepared to establish a preferential tariff we must look for a break up of the Empire. That is a pure assumption that we are asked to accept and act upon without a shadow of proof or a scintilla of evidence. For my part, I believe it to be — I use very plain language about it — I believe it to be a calumny on the Colonies and a slur upon the Empire . . . anxious as we are to do all that is prudent and practicable to develop our trade with the Colonies, we Free Traders do not believe, at least I do not believe, it is in any way desirable that we should have what is called a self-contained Empire between which and the rest of the world there are none of those commercial relations which are so fruitful of peace and amity and good will . . . let me point out that the Colonies have absolutely no grievance of any kind against us. We give them free admission through our open door into the largest and best market in the whole world. On the other hand, they have at home complete fiscal autonomy.

The existing Canadian Preference was not of much value to us, as the Canadian tariff was so high. Nor should we gain much if the Canadian tariff was raised still further against the foreigner. Then came a more telling thrust :

> . . . the Colonies are to be asked to agree not to start new industries in competition with ourselves . . . these great and growing countries are actually to be asked to stereotype their industrial condition, to arrest their industrial development in order that the Mother-country may keep and increase the hold she has on their markets. And that is the proposition seriously made in the name and the interests of Imperial unity. I should like to know what Sir Wilfrid Laurier would say. He said the other day that he would sooner face the disruption of the Empire than that Canada should part with her fiscal independence. To my mind, it is impossible to imagine a proposal seriously meant which would more certainly tend to engender friction, to foment quarrel, and in the long run to kindle disloyalty.

The duties Chamberlain had proposed were admittedly small. But if the Empire was really in danger of breaking up would small duties avert the catastrophe

> . . . it is ridiculous to suppose that a duty of 2s. on corn is going to turn the whole wheat supply of the world into the, at present, undeveloped fields of Canada. I warn you of this. This would only be the first step, and it is a step which would operate so slowly and so partially that the demand would become irresistible. Your 5 per cent. would become 7 per cent. and your 10 per cent. 20 per cent. before you had time to turn round. Do not let any one be misled by this talk of what duty you are to put upon

corn and wheat. Protection is an inclined plane. Once you put your foot on it there is no halting-place until you get to the bottom.

As for Chamberlain's proposed reductions of the tea and sugar duties, these duties should be abolished altogether. They were only put on to meet the needs of the war.

His peroration admitted the need for improvement in the national economy and laid special stress on the need for greater technical training. This, indeed, was to be a main theme in his speeches and Haldane's in the months ahead.

. . . do not let it be supposed that because we are driven to defend the citadel of Free Trade we, therefore, think that all is for the best and are content with a policy of folded hands. That there are disquieting features in our industrial as in our social conditions no honest observer, certainly no member of the party of progress, will be found to deny. We have seen industries in which we ought to have maintained our supremacy falling behind, and in some cases entirely taken away from us by our competitors. Defective knowledge, inferior processes, lack of flexibility or versatility, a stubborn industrial conservatism, these are the real enemies of British trade, and have done us infinitely more harm than all the tariffs and all the dumping syndicates that were ever created. Better education, better training, better methods, a larger outlook than for our primary needs — and it says little for our political sagacity that we should allow our minds to be diverted from them by quarrels as to the quantum of dogmatic theology that is to be administered to little children, or by demands to revive the fallacies of Protection. No, that is not the way in which we should improve our condition. True it is also that in spite of the continuous growth of our national prosperity we still have with us the unemployed, the ill-fed, the aged poor ; but here, again, let us look to natural and not to artificial remedies. Instead of raising the price of bread let us try to raise the standard of life. Temperance, better housing, the tenure and taxation of land, these are matters as to which we have allowed our legislation to fall deplorably into arrear. To take up the task in a spirit of faith and of resolute purpose is, I hope and believe, the mission of the Liberal party in a Liberal Parliament.

The Cinderford speech is a brilliant case for the defence delivered by a brilliant advocate. Chamberlain's inaccuracies on points of detail reflected on the validity of his whole case. If his assumptions were true, then his remedies were inadequate. Either the Empire was not breaking up, and in that case there was no need for Preference ; or it was, and much higher duties would be called for. Besides, Chamberlain's case was not proven. It was far from clear either that our trade was stagnating or that the Empire was disintegrating; of course there was room for improvement, but there was no danger to the economy which could not be remedied by more efficiency and technical education.   It was very skilful advocacy, though scarcely a match for Chamberlain's combined appeal to the interests and to the ideals of the nation.

VI

Chamberlain took Asquith's strictures on his statistics seriously, and we find him asking Garvin for a brief from which to prepare an answer.   From this time, moreover, he arranged for Hewins to provide him with a weekly digest of his opponents' speeches together with suggested replies.   Hewins begged Chamberlain to let him have his statistics checked by competent statisticians, but Chamberlain never adopted this suggestion.   He had his own way of 'getting up' his subject and would not change.[1]

Chamberlain has often been censured for his handling of statistics, and there is no doubt that he did make some glaring mistakes.   The following correspondence, however, shows that the fault quite often lay with the official statistics and that some of his points raised issues on which the most eminent authorities had no clear view.   Giffen had written to *The Times* challenging some of the figures used in the Glasgow speech

CHAMBERLAIN AND GIFFEN

J. C. to Giffen, 24 October 1903.—. . . I saw your letter in the 'Times', and have written as you wish to say that the figures are taken from the recent blue book and will be found in table 1, page 5. . . . If you have any corrections to make, and if, what I should still more value, you should give me any suggestions, I should greatly appreciate the opportunity of discussing them with you privately. . . . I know what pitfalls there are in statistics for inexperienced students, and in the present case the tables given by different authorities are so curiously arranged that I find it most difficult to deal with them especially when I desire to make accurate comparisons.

I imagine that no one doubts that certain general tendencies have developed themselves in the trade of this country during the last thirty years — that is to say, that we are on the whole doing less with the protected countries ; that what we are doing with them has somewhat changed its character and consists more of raw materials in proportion to finished manufacture than it used to do ; and that the trade with British Possessions has in the meantime greatly increased and has not been subject to this deterioration of quality.   But whether the figures that have been given to me, or that I have found for myself, and used as illustrations of these changes are the best that could be chosen I do not know.

If you can suggest to me any improvement, or any more certain line of argument, I should be infinitely indebted to you.

[1] W. A. S. Hewins, *Apologia of an Imperialist*, vol. i, pp. 72–73.

Giffen to J. C., 26 *October* 1903.— . . . Would you let me urge you as
an old friend always to give references when quoting new figures ?
Imports and exports we all know about ; they are all in the Trade Returns
as they are called ; but the figures you quoted were in a new Return
which I for one had not examined when you made your Glasgow speech.

May I say that I was quite bewildered by them and wondered for a good
while what you had got, especially as your figure was quite different from
those in the Monthly Trade and navigation accounts where the imports
of manufactures from all countries, Colonies as well as foreign countries,
are given in 1901 as £93,609,000 only, instead of £149,000,000, which
you stated as the figure for 1902 on the authority of another return which
I was not then acquainted with.   (I have not got the a/cs for Decr. 1902
by me, but I believe they show some increase on 1901.)[1]   What I had
in view when I suggested in the 'Times' your giving a reference was to
comment on the discrepancies in the official returns themselves, and on
statistical points of the kind, which have become rather serious.   They do
not concern you specially.

I am sorry to say I do not agree with you as to our exporting less to
protected foreign countries, and the change in the character of the business
generally.   There are some changes of course, but they would require
much investigation I think before that opinion could be justified.   I am
sorry to say the Blue book (C. d. 1761) to which you refer and from which
you quoted is not trust-worthy on the point, as the countries are often
'grouped', and it is impossible to see what the causes of change in the
currents of trade have been, for which it would be absolutely necessary
to look at the details, as these are not given.   It is evident, however, that
the increase of exports to the Colonies in recent years has been exclusively
to Natal and the Cape of Good Hope, the result partly of the gold development of the Transvaal before the war, and since that time of our expenditure and *loans.*   The question of protection or no protection, or of foreign
countries and Colonies, is not considered.   But whether these are right
inferences or not, it is a pity the Returns in C. d. 1761 are not in such
detail as to enable me to accept them without further inquiry.

VII

Asquith's speech at Cinderford was followed next day (9 October)
by Ritchie's explanation of the Cabinet crisis to his constituents at
Croydon.   The unhappy ex-Chancellor had some difficulty in getting
a hearing, and when he spoke of the danger of American reprisals if
we abandoned Free Imports, the audience drowned his speech by
singing 'Rule, Britannia'.   Passions were rising, and the same evening in the greater security of the Eighty Club, Lord Spencer, leader
of the Liberal party in the House of Lords, denounced Chamberlain
as 'one of the most ruthless and unscrupulous of statesmen who never

---

[1] See *Trade and Navigation Accounts for December* 1901, p. 67.

hesitated to use any weapon that could advance his cause'; a censure which Austen would describe as 'vulgar abuse' [1]

The attack was resumed after the week-end. On 12 October Sir Henry Fowler spoke at Glasgow. On the following day Rosebery denounced the new policy on the highest Imperial grounds. He had been attracted once to the idea of Preference but had had to abandon it as impracticable. Besides,

> I, as a profound and convinced Imperialist, do not wish our people at home at any time of scarcity . . . to weigh the interests of their material well-being against the conception of the Empire. It will be a bad day for Great Britain . . . when the artisan returning to a stinted meal . . . may say to his family 'Things would have been very different had it not been for this Empire for the preservation of which we are now so heavily taxed'.

Rosebery's speech was followed up a week later by further speeches from Campbell-Bannerman, Goschen and Morley.

All this time, Chamberlain received almost no support from any colleague of the front rank. Austen,[2] Onslow [3] and Lyttelton [4] defended him against personal attacks but they were inhibited by their position as Ministers from defending his policies to the full.

The lack of colleagues was a weakness, but it also brought into relief the tremendous impact of Chamberlain's personal popularity. There was something about this single-handed contest which appealed to the sporting feeling of the country. This feeling was growing daily at the expense of other considerations, as Wyndham saw:

> . . . The big political wigs are providing a good entertainment. If anything were needed to expose the folly of those who cried 'efficiency', and cried for 'business methods', it is that they no longer cry for these things, but sit down in the stalls to enjoy a down-right rhetorical hammer-and-tongs set-to between the big wigs. That is what Englishmen enjoy without your excuse of convalescence. The huge blue-book of statistics; the speeches by manufacturers, all that is expert or informed, the rival theories of economic schools, are bundled aside to a general 'Ah' of relief and satisfaction, punctuated by 'go it, Joey,' 'bravo! here's Rosebery in the ring!' Even the War Commission report is used only as a missile. South Africa, the Far East, Morocco, Ireland, the Navy may 'go bang'. Education was all very well; but, with Nonconformists who can't fight well, or won't fight fair, it pales before a classic campaign of renowned gladiators. 'Heavy pounding, gentlemen, and who can pound longest' is the one consideration.

[1] 12 October 1903.   [2] 12 October 1903.
[3] 14 October 1903.   [4] 15 October 1903.

This instinct of Englishmen is probably sound. You must drop building when the battle begins. I prefer building to fighting. But, once
fighting has begun, I believe in fighting hard in order to get it over and
get on to building again. Arthur's 'little Ministry' is not a bad 'fighting
unit'. Arnold-Forster and Graham Murray are good men on the platform. Austen Chamberlain carries weight, Selborne is useful. Stanley
can rally Lancashire.[1]

The success of Chamberlain's opening round stimulated the
Unionist Free Traders to renewed activity. Had Devonshire
remained in the Government, the Free Food League would almost
certainly have been dissolved. His resignation, however, gave the
more active members of the League — James, Goschen, Churchill
and Hugh Cecil — their chance. They determined to make the
Duke president of the League and in time, perhaps, prime minister
of a coalition government. The Duke, himself, was very reluctant
to take the lead.

DEVONSHIRE TO JAMES

7 *October* 1903.—I have made so many mistakes lately, at all events in
procedure, that I should not like to take any step, or send any message
which could become public, without further consideration.

. . . But I suggest to you privately and personally that there does not
seem to be any reason why Free Trade Unionists should be in a hurry
about taking up an attitude hostile to the Government.

The position, which is singular in many respects, is especially so in this,
that so far as I know the Government are not likely either before or during
the next Session to take any step or propose any measure to which any
Free-trader can object.

DEVONSHIRE TO GOSCHEN

10 *October* 1903.—I find myself, as usual, in a very difficult position.
In the first place, I am very unwilling to put myself at the head of a new
political movement at all. I am getting old, and I am rather tired of, and
disgusted with, politics. The question itself is difficult and complicated,
and I have never given any special study to it. I never read a speech or
an article upon it on either side to which I see clearly the answer, and I
shrink from going through all the labour of getting up what is to me
almost a new subject. In the next place, I am not sure whether you and
the other Free Fooders do not wish to take up a more hostile attitude
towards the Government than I, who have only left it after much doubt
and hesitation, wish to do, or could decently do. I told Beach yesterday
that nothing would induce me to take up such an attitude, and that all I
could do would be to use any influence I might have in preventing them
from being led or forced by their followers to go beyond the limits of their
definite declarations. . . .

[1] George Wyndham to his father, 15 October 1903.

But they left him no peace; and, in a letter of 15 October to Hicks Beach, he agreed to join the Free Food League on condition that the League should not oppose the Government in so far as its Fiscal policy was limited to proposing tariff legislation with a view to negotiating commercial treaties. The election of officers duly followed and Devonshire was elected President of the League with Goschen, Hicks Beach and Ritchie as Vice-Presidents and James as Treasurer.[1]

VIII

All this time Chamberlain was at Highbury. It was the season of the Birmingham music festival and he had a house party, mingling relations, music-lovers, tariff-reformers and Milner. On the second day of the festival, however, Chamberlain developed a sharp attack of gout and spent two days in bed 'feeling very miserable', 'and dozing most of the time'.[2] On the third day (15 October) Milner walked into Chamberlain's room to find him sitting in front of a tankard of champagne. 'Does your doctor approve of such a diet?' 'He wouldn't be my doctor for long if he didn't,' Chamberlain answered.[3]

The house party dispersed on 17 October and next day Chamberlain set to work on the speech he was to make at Newcastle on 20 October. That night, however, he had a return of the gout. Ballance, his Birmingham doctor who came to see him in the morning, advised him to cancel his journey to Newcastle. Chamberlain, however, insisted on waiting till the morning of the meeting. Early on the 20th, Vince, his agent, received a message to say that Chamberlain was leaving after all. 'I went to the station and saw him start', Vince afterwards recalled, 'he looked very ill, evidently in pain and almost unable to walk; he had to be supported as he crossed the platform and lifted into the carriage.'[4]

While Chamberlain was in the train, the annual conference of North Riding Liberal Unionist Association was meeting in Newcastle. A letter was read from Devonshire deprecating any attempt to define the position of the party on the Fiscal Question. Despite this advice, a resolution was moved by Pike Pease and Lord Grey strongly supporting the Chamberlain policy. As a result, Arthur Elliot and six of the most prominent Vice-Presidents resigned from

[1] 23 October 1903.   [2] Mrs. Chamberlain to her mother, 14 and 16 October.
[3] Mrs. Chamberlain in conversation with the author.
[4] Vince to Garvin, 22 April 1920.

the Association.   Grey's action is interesting, for although he supported Chamberlain's views on Imperial grounds, he had grave doubts on economic grounds.   Grey was to take the chair at Newcastle, and only a few days before had written :

GREY TO CHAMBERLAIN

12 *October* 1903.—. . . I am to have the honour and privilege of presiding, an honour I greatly value as I regard your action in resigning with a view to securing for yourself a free hand to work for the consolidation of the Empire with the greatest admiration.

I cannot however associate myself with your advocacy of Protection as an end desirable in itself, and I hope you will not take it in any way amiss if in the 2 sentences in which I introduce you to the meeting I make the blunt statement that, although I am a Free Trader, I am in the Chair because I attach more importance to the Empire than to Free Trade and because I believe you are the one Statesman living who can save the Empire — There are a good many men who take the same view who will be at your meeting, and I think there is more to be gained than lost by your having a Free Trade Chairman who is prepared to make sacrifices in the interests of the Empire.

Chamberlain reached Newcastle with a raging headache which grew worse as the evening advanced.   He limped off the station and was driven through cheering crowds — 'much cheering and very little booing' Mrs. Chamberlain records — to where they were to dine.

The Newcastle speech, delivered to a packed audience of over 5000, was primarily a reply to his critics — 'more like a House of Commons speech' was Mrs. Chamberlain's description.   One passage only need detain us.

At the beginning of his speech Chamberlain argued that where wheat and bread were concerned the danger to the working man did not arise from any conceivable import tax the Government might put on, but from the possibility of a shortage of supply and the consequent increase in price.

. . . if . . . these countries wanted their corn for themselves, which they will do some day, or if there were bad harvests which there may be in either of these cases, you will find the price of corn rising many times higher than any tax I have ever suggested.   And there is only one remedy for it.   There is only one remedy for a short supply.   It is to increase your sources of supply.   You must call in the new world, the Colonies, to redress the balance of the old.   Call in the Colonies, and they will answer to your call with very little stimulus and encouragement.   They will give you a supply which will be never-failing and all-sufficient.

In this Chamberlain was well ahead of his time.   It is only since the Second World War that there has come a general acceptance of the need to stimulate the development of alternative and additional supplies of foodstuffs and raw materials.

Chamberlain afterwards told Vince that at one point in his speech his headache became

so bad that everything he had in his mind to say suddenly vanished from his memory. Luckily he had just said something that elicited a long cheer, and was able to pull himself together before the applause subsided. Nevertheless, after getting through a long speech, he let himself be persuaded to go on to an overflow meeting, where he spoke for another half hour . . . Reporters told me afterwards that they had thought him below his usual form at Newcastle; but they had not suspected that he was ill.[1]

In the circumstances, the Newcastle speech must be judged a physical *tour de force*. Next day Chamberlain was 'no better but no worse'; [2] and he spoke with his usual force at the luncheon given in his honour at Tynemouth.

The Tynemouth speech began with an eloquent tribute to the leaders of the Fair Trade movement in the 80's. Here Chamberlain pointed out that 'whereas in 1883, or thereabouts, I was convinced of the extreme importance of, and advocated, free imports, at that very time my opponent was Mr. Ritchie who was advocating Fair Trade and Preference to our Colonies'.

The rest of the speech was mainly concerned with giving his version of the events leading up to the Cabinet crisis. But in the closing passages he explained in some detail the first steps which a Tariff Reform Government should take.

. . . All my policy is to be considered, as I have myself represented, as a broad outline. . . . It is not a cut-and-dried policy which cannot be altered in any detail. What is going to happen if I am successful? If I carry the people of this country with me, and, above all, if I carry the working classes, the majority of the voters — well, what is going to happen is that the Government elected on this principle will immediately have a series of negotiations to undertake. It will have to negotiate with the Colonies. For my part, I think it would not be bad if the then Secretary for the Colonies were to go to the Colonies and negotiate on the spot. . . . But not only have you to go to the Colonies, but you have also to go to the foreign countries that are concerned. They must negotiate each a treaty of their own; and lastly — and this, perhaps, is more important than all — if I had anything to do with such a thing, I would not consent to move a step without calling for the opinion of experts from every industry in the country. . . .

[1] Vince to Garvin, 22 April 1920.
[2] Mrs. Chamberlain to her mother, 24 October 1903.

Everybody interested — whether in thimbles, in anchors, or in anything else in the multiplicity of trades in this country — would, of course,
be glad to assist any commission which was attempting to make a tariff.
Their witnesses would be heard. Everything they had to say would be
taken into account, and then, and then only, could we say in detail, and
with absolute accuracy, what each article should pay, or what articles
might be entirely relieved.

George Hamilton spoke for the Free Trade side next day giving
his version of the Cabinet crisis. On 23 October the Unionist Free
Food League published their manifesto. On 24 October Asquith
followed Chamberlain to Newcastle. Meanwhile Chamberlain lay
at Highbury at work on the speeches he was to make at Liverpool
the following week. A letter of Mrs. Chamberlain's suggests he
was quietly confident of the success of his movement in the constituencies but beginning to be anxious about Balfour's attitude.

. . . the *intense* interest with which the audience listened to every word
exceeds anything I have ever seen in England — greatly as they have
cheered him on former occasions. It is very encouraging, and, though one
must not be too confident that the general opinion is coming towards
Joe's policy, there is no doubt that every week brings new adherents and
the tide is turning. If only the Prime Minister realized it ! I feel it is so
likely that he does not at present. Many of the younger men in and out of
the Government who sympathise with Preferential Tariffs feel that if this
goes on, it will hardly be possible to avoid fighting the next General
Election on them. . . .

Austen is a little disturbed in his mind between his desire not to go
beyond the prescribed limits and his growing belief that his Father's
policy might carry all before it ; and I find this feeling very prevalent
among the younger men. Lord Percy at Tynemouth, you will see,
expressed it as well as he could without exceeding the limits laid down in
Mr. Balfour's Sheffield speech. . . . [1]

Mrs. Chamberlain's opinion that the movement was gaining
ground received confirmation from more than one unbiased source.
Buckle of *The Times* had written just before the Newcastle speech :

BUCKLE TO CHAMBERLAIN

14 *October* 1903.—. . . Your action in resigning is certainly abundantly
justified by the freedom of speech which you have gained and the dismay
which it has thrown into the ranks of your foes. Your only difficulty is in
obtaining first class platform support, as your sympathisers within the
Ministry are bound to stop short of more than a general approval of your
aims and tendencies. . . .

[1] Mrs. Chamberlain to her mother, 23 October 1903.

I am surprised at the favourable manner in which your proposals have been received in the City. Even among the most convinced Free Traders a great impression has been produced ; and they are at last disposed to think that you may win. As you know, originally prejudice was very strong there against you.

A few days later Fitzroy noted in his diary :

17 *October* 1903.—. . . I met Winston Churchill at luncheon at Devonshire House, where he was arranging with the Duke the reconstitution of the Free Food League on terms which would secure the Duke's adhesion. . . . Churchill was very despondent about saving even a remnant of the Conservative Party from the contagion of Protection. In his constituency, and he believed in every other, the organisation and the popular feeling would be arrayed on the side of Mr. Chamberlain, and it was only by appealing to the Liberal opposition that they would obtain audiences.[1]

IX

On 27 October Chamberlain set out for Liverpool. Salvidge, as we saw, had promoted the invitation ; and the main meeting was to be held under the auspices of the Conservative Working Men's Association, a very powerful body in Lancashire. Chamberlain's correspondence, indeed, in the days before the meeting shows plainly that he intended to make the Liverpool speech a bid for Labour support.

Notwithstanding this democratic purpose, Chamberlain's visit to Liverpool was like a royal progress. The following memorandum from one of his secretaries gives some idea of his style of travel.[2]

With regard to the luggage . . . please note that the servants and *all* the luggage will travel in Mr. Chamberlain's train and will go direct to Liverpool and thence to Knowsley. The luggage should therefore be put in that portion of the train which will be brought by special engine from Wavertree to Liverpool.

The rain which had dogged him at Glasgow and Newcastle followed him to Liverpool. He was met on the station by four of the Liverpool members of parliament and a delegation of two hundred working men. Outside an escort of mounted police conveyed him to the Conservative Club through dense, cheering crowds. Despite the downpour, thousands waited for an hour or more to catch a glimpse of the famous little man in the astrakhan-collared travelling

[1] *Memoirs of Sir Almeric Fitzroy*, vol. i, p. 160.
[2] Stanley Salvidge, *Salvidge of Liverpool*, pp. 52–53.

coat, with the eyeglass and orchid. At the Hippodrome even ticket-holders had arrived as much as five hours before the meeting to make sure of their seats.

The meeting was probably the finest of the tour. Salvidge took the chair. Derby, Alfred Jones and half the great names of Lancashire were on the platform. When Chamberlain rose to speak, a storm of applause broke from the audience. It lasted for six minutes while he stood there, right foot slightly advanced and one hand grasping the lapel of his frock-coat. Then suddenly the cheering ceased and a deep hush fell on the crowd. 'He was in his best form',[1] and the speech he made that night was certainly the finest of the campaign — perhaps of his whole career.

Coming here at the invitation of a working-class association, I am going, as one principal part of my speech, to ask you to consider with me why the working man, and especially why trade unionists, should support my proposals. . . . If I am right, every class in the country will be benefited by reforms which will give increased work and increased employment to the poor, and I dare say increased profit to the capitalist. Now, why should you follow the advice which I tender to you? In the first place, because, thank God, the working men are now, as they have always been, patriots, because they, to whom every additional expense counts for more than it does to other classes, yet always put first in their creed the welfare of the kingdom and the welfare of the Empire.

This strong appeal to the heart was followed immediately by an appeal to the head and pocket. A patriotic policy was also in the best interest of the working class, and that interest could be summed up — and Chamberlain was the first statesman to say it — in the one word 'employment'.

What is the whole problem as it affects the working classes of this country? It is all contained in one word — employment. Cheap food, a higher standard of living, higher wages — all these things, important as they are, are contained in the word 'employment'. If this policy will give you more employment, all the others will be added unto you. If you lose your employment, all the others put together will not compensate you for that loss.

Having identified his policy with the ideals and interests of the Working Class, he went on to expose 'Free Trade' as a Middle Class movement.

. . . when Free Trade was carried, the working classes were neither represented nor consulted. I do not say that that makes Free Trade good or bad, but it is a fact that the movement was a manufacturers' and a

----

[1] Mrs. Chamberlain to her mother, 30 October 1903.

middle-class movement. The leaders of the movement . . . admitted that they thought it would enable wages to be kept at what they called a reasonable level. They thought that it would give cheap food, and that if the labourer had cheap food he could afford to work for lower wages . . . it is worth remembering that long after Free Trade was carried . . . Mr. Bright, in writing to a friend in America, and protesting against the doctrine of Protection, points out to him that, if the Americans made Protection their policy, they would have to give higher wages to their working classes — higher wages and shorter hours. I do not think that that would be a disadvantage. But what I want to point out is that, rightly or wrongly, the leaders of the Free Trade movement believed that the big loaf meant lower wages. . . .

He went on to invoke the shades of Feargus O'Connor and the Chartist Movement.

At the time of the Free Trade agitation, what was the action of the Radicals in those days? The Radicals of those days were represented by the Chartists. The Chartists were entirely opposed to the Free Trade movement. They said that they alone had the right to speak for the unrepresented classes, that Free Trade was a red herring drawn across the path of electoral reform, and they invited their followers to spurn and scorn the action of the Anti-Corn Law hypocrites.

Since then the Working Class had won the franchise. They were the master. No decision could be taken over their heads.

You have the franchise; you have the majority of votes; and you can say 'Yes' to this policy or you can crush it. The responsibility, therefore, is yours. It no longer rests upon the minority. It does not rest upon the aristocracy or the House of Lords. It does not rest upon the middle classes. It rests upon the shoulders of the workmen. There is, indeed, still one responsibility which rests upon those of us who call ourselves statesmen. We have been, by your votes, selected for the position of leadership. It is the duty of a leader, if he has come to any conviction, to express that conviction as clearly and as plainly as he can to those who are indeed his masters, but who ought to listen to the leader whom they have chosen. It is his duty to do this, even though in doing it he may lose any little popularity that he may have gained, even though in doing it he puts an end to his political life. I have the satisfaction of thinking that in attempting to do this you will, at all events, recognise my good intentions. I have an idea that the working classes of this country are on this question more advanced than many of their leaders. If so, we shall win. I care not who is against us. The Cobden Club may rage furiously in all the languages of the civilised world. The 'Free Fooders' may imagine vain things — but we shall win the victory.

He now appealed to the working men against the Trade Union Congress:

Ah! but it is said, 'How can you expect to do that when the Trade Union Congress has passed a resolution against you?' It is true that some of them have declared against us, but I recollect that there are many trusted leaders of the working men, both of trade unions and of other organisations, who do not share the views of the Trade Union Congress; and therefore, great as is their authority, I humbly venture to appeal against them to you, to appeal against the officials to the men who appointed them and gave them their power. . . . It is rather an extraordinary thing that these trade union officials, acting apparently on the instigation of the Cobden Club, have prepared a manifesto, circulated through the Cobden Club, against the proposals to which I am asking your attention. Why should they do it through the Cobden Club? The Cobden Club was formed to honour the memory of a man whom we all know to have been a sincere man, whether he was right or wrong, and always deserving of the respect of his fellow-countrymen. Yes, he was all that; but he was not a friend of trade unions, and now you have the trade unions in the arms of the Cobden Club. Mr. Cobden himself, speaking of trade unions in 1844, just before the reform of the Corn Laws, said: 'Depend upon it, nothing can be got by fraternising with trade unions. They are founded upon principles of brutal tyranny and monopoly. I would rather live under the Dey of Algiers than a trades committee.' Surely to use a Club founded in memory of a gentleman who held those opinions is a strange thing for trade unionist leaders of to-day. . . . The Trade Union Congress was not always of the opinion of the Congress that met this year. In 1888 the Parliamentary Committee offered a report, in which it said this: 'The demon of cheapness' — the present Trades Congress makes a god of cheapness; the Parliamentary Committee in 1888 spoke of it as a demon — 'the demon of cheapness has pervaded our whole social system, and while the cheapness of goods has been a matter of wonder, purchasers seldom or never give a thought to the human blood and muscle that have been ground up in the production of the article.' That is admirable, and if I had time I could preach a sermon from it, and I think it would be well to preach that sermon before the present Trades Congress. My first point, therefore, is this — that it is not only the consumer you have got to consider. The producer is of still more importance; and to buy in the cheapest market is not the sole duty of man, and it is not in the best interest of the working classes.

He went on to argue that in the strict sense of the terms, 'it is absolutely impossible to reconcile Free Trade with Trade Unionism'.

. . . what are the legitimate objects of trade unionism? In my opinion there are five. In the first place, to enable working men by union and combination among themselves to meet employers on equal terms. . . . Then . . . to secure the highest wages which are consistent with the conditions of each trade — to raise the standard of living and to prevent unfair competition — to insist on proper precautions for the health and safety of those employed; and, lastly, to provide for those of their comrades, who owing to temporary illness or misfortune, are deprived of their means of livelihood. Those are legitimate objects, in my judgment, and I heartily approve of them. . . . But one thing is certain. While we have done much to secure these objects . . . and have passed legislation such as the Factory Acts, the Mines Acts, the Truck Acts, the Compensation to Workmen Acts, the Fair Wages Clauses, the Prohibition of Prison Goods, and a number of other minor Acts of the same kind, every one of these measures is opposed to the strict doctrine of Free Trade. Free Trade says you are to buy in the cheapest market. Free Trade says you are not to interfere with the freedom of independent men, not to prescribe to an employer what he shall or shall not do, but to leave him free to bargain as he likes with his workpeople, and, on the other hand, you are not to make combinations which tend in the slightest degree to destroy the liberty of the workman to sell his labour just as low or just as high as he pleases. Those are the doctrines of Free Trade ; and all these doctrines we have put aside now for twenty years in our endeavour to benefit the condition of the working men and to raise the standard of living. Is it not a little too much now to come down and tell me that I am a heretic, that I ought to be put out of the congregation, forsooth, because I will not allow to be sacred and inspired the doctrines that those who accuse me have abandoned long ago ? But there is another most important point which I want working people to consider. Grant all this legislation, and much more of the same kind, I warn you it will be absolutely futile unless you are prepared to go farther. What is the good, I ask, in the name of common sense, of prohibiting sweating in this country, if you allow sweated goods to come in from foreign countries ? . . . Limitation of hours . . . precautions for security . . . all these things add to the cost of production, to the difficulties of the manufacturer in selling his goods, and unless you give him some increased price, some increased advantage in compensation, then he cannot carry on competition any longer. . . . I say, then, that if it were possible to calculate exactly what these precautions cost over and above similar precautions taken in the other countries with which we are competing, we should be justified, without the slightest infraction of the true principles of Free Trade, in putting on a duty corresponding to that cost.

At the end of this passage he returned to the theme with which he had begun — the importance of securing full employment.

Now, what is the conclusion of this branch of the matter ? If protected labour is good, and I think in many ways it is — that is to say, the fair protection of labour — then it is good to protect the results of labour ; and you cannot do the one without the other, or else in trying to do good to labour you will do it much more harm than good. And if it be good, as I think it is, to support the object of trade unionism, then, I say, those objects can only be secured, can only be permanent in our system as long as we can offer to the bulk of our workpeople, to all those who are willing to work, constant and remunerative employment. As long as we have got large numbers of people who would work if they could, but cannot find work to do, so long it is useless to talk of raising wages or restricting the hours of labour, or putting on to manufactures additional cost which they cannot afford to pay. The only result will be that you will still further lessen the amount of your employment. Now I hope to give you more

employment. I hope to do so by keeping, in the first place, a firmer hold
upon home markets ; I hope, in the second place, to do so by encouraging
the best of our trades, the trade which is most possible to us in proportion
to its size, the trade which is increasing most quickly, the trade which we
have it in our power to stimulate most greatly — I mean the trade with
our own kith and kin across the seas.

The rest of the speech was devoted almost entirely to applying
these general ideas to Liverpool's greatest interest — shipping.
Britain still led the world in shipping, but other countries were
catching up.

It is not what we have now, but the question is, How long we keep it ?
And how much shall we keep of it ? We are like a man in a race. He
starts with a great advantage ; he has been given a hundred yards,
perhaps. In the first lap he loses thirty ; in the second lap he loses fifty
more ; and then he is seen by an observer from the Cobden Club and the
Cobden Club says, 'That is my man ; he is still ahead.' I think we know
better.

Foreigners subsidised their shipping heavily. Should we not subsidise ours at least enough to compensate for the cost of such safety
regulations as the Plimsoll Line. France had reserved the Madagascar trade and the United States the Cuban trade on the ground
that these were 'coasting trades'. Should we not regard our trade
with the Colonies as 'coasting trade'.

The peroration was one of his finest :

. . . it is for that power of bargaining, and, if necessary, of retaliation,
that Mr. Balfour has asked, and that I have asked. And, after all, if there
be any difference between us whatsoever, it is only that I go farther than
he does and that I ask, not in the future, but to-day, for the Preference to
our Colonies which will bind them and us together. . . . One of the most
strenuous advocates in the press of the views which I oppose declared the
other day that the great issue between us was no mere party question, but
it was a conflict between Imperialism and Little Englandism. Yes, he is
right. He is a little Englander. I am an Imperialist, and the conflict is
between us. This is now to me the urgent and the present issue.
You are called upon in this generation to a greater responsibility than
ever before. It is on your decision that this tremendous issue rests. The
balance hangs, but I know what your forefathers would have said. I know
what they did. I know how they endured burdens and sufferings to which
our sacrifices, if indeed sacrifices there be, are as nothing but as a drop in
the ocean ; and I know how, with half our population, with one-tenth of
our wealth, with Ireland hostile, under conditions of which we have no
conception, they nevertheless, and at times almost alone against the world,
bore themselves bravely in the titanic strife with Napoleon and came out
victorious. What is our task to theirs ? It is a mere trifle ; it is only for
us to keep the fruits of the victory that they have won. I commend this

issue to your consideration, and if indeed we are called upon to give up some antiquated and nevertheless dearly beloved prejudice or superstition, if indeed we are called upon for more than that, let us show that prosperity has not corrupted our blood — that it has not weakened our nerve or destroyed our fibre.

The ovation after the speech was even more prolonged than the welcome before it. Within a few minutes special editions of the *Liverpool Courier* were on sale in the streets. They carried the full text of the speech, 'electro-phoned' to the newspaper office while Chamberlain was speaking. Meanwhile, in the Hippodrome, a dark young man had risen on the platform to move the resolution. He made a brilliant speech. Chamberlain eyed him with undisguised amazement and whispered to Salvidge, 'Who on earth is this? He will go far.' Salvidge answered that he was a young man called Smith. A later generation would know him as Birkenhead.

X

There was no lack of public interest on the second day of the visit. The sun came out, and the Derbys were astonished when they drove in with Chamberlain from Knowsley at the warmth and familiarity of the crowds. He lunched with the Lord Mayor and afterwards addressed his fellow guests as a 'businessman speaking to business men'. It was not an easy speech to make: for, during luncheon, a vast crowd had gathered on the Exchange flags outside; and even inside the banqueting room his words hardly carried above the sound of the cheers and patriotic songs.

After the speech, Mr. and Mrs. Chamberlain went out onto the balcony and showed themselves to the people. Next came the presentation of a casket from the Working Men's Association. Another full-length speech was now required. This third Liverpool speech was primarily an appeal to Lancashire's interests and grievances. The watch-making trade of Prescot, the plate-glass industry of St. Helens, the wireworks of Warrington had all been hard hit by foreign competition :

'What does it matter ? You have lost all those trades. You are losing others, but there is something that remains. The men who made watches are doing something else.' Yes, and what do they do ? Here is a man who makes a watch. For that he required a fineness of touch that often is hereditary, which can only be obtained after years of work, obtained only in youth and never obtained in after-life ; and the moment the watch trade ceases, or does not continue to employ the same number of workpeople, this man, who has acquired the special gift that is worth much to himself and his family, has to throw it away, to destroy it. He has to go and act as a porter or a dock labourer, or to sweep the streets, and if afterwards we restore to him his trade he would be no longer able to take advantage of it. He is dropped into the ranks of casual employment, dropped down into the 13,000,000, be they more or be they less, who are always on the verge of hunger.[1] I say that the personal equation of suffering which all this transference of trade involves is the sort of thing which some political economists never think of at all, and the Cobden Club treats it as if it were of no consequence. It is, I say, of the utmost consequence. Even if it could be proved in the long run that the country did not suffer in wealth, that there had been a transfer from one trade to another, still I should say, when you count up the families that have been reduced to misery, all the heart-burnings, all the suffering that has been caused by these changes to the individual, when you think of the honest men who have gone to the workhouse and can never be brought back again to the ranks of continuous labour — when you think of all these things, then I say, even if the country were enriched, its wealth would have been dearly purchased.

The third day of the visit was spent quietly at Knowsley, save for a visit, with Sir Alfred Jones, to the Tropical Diseases Hospital. Even then 'crowds gathered wherever we stopped, and as our visit was unexpected it was wonderful how they sprang out of the ground'.

The warmth of Liverpool's reception was a great encouragement, and increased Chamberlain's confidence in the success of his cause.

All through the visit, indeed, he seems to have been in the highest spirits. On the first night at Knowsley

he discarded all reticence in describing the relations between himself and his late colleagues, and declared that all the present Cabinet were with him heart and soul, except Londonderry, 'who does not count.' Lord Derby, who was brought up in an older and statelier tradition, was not pleased, and had some difficulty in concealing his scanty appreciation of such methods. Chamberlain is also very violent in his denunciation of the Board of Education, whose 'rotten' policy he holds responsible for much of the Government's unpopularity, which he foresaw and predicted.[2]

On the last night at Knowsley, Chamberlain argued at length the case for Tariff Reform. As they retired for the night, Derby said to him: 'Almost thou persuadest me'. 'Almost, Almost': Chamberlain replied, 'That might be the motto of the Stanley family'.

Derby's presence on Chamberlain's platform, indeed, led some to believe that he might have secured the support of the Stanley

[1] The estimate given by Sir H. Campbell-Bannerman.
[2] *Memoirs of Sir Almeric Fitzroy*, vol. i, p. 163.

influence. Chaplin, indeed, considered asking Derby for a contribution to the Tariff Reform League. The real attitude of the Stanley family, however, is best shown by the following exchange:

STANLEY TO CHAMBERLAIN

31 *October* 1903.—*Confidential.*—I am rather disturbed to find from Alice that you are under the impression that I have pledged myself *never* to vote for a tax on food. . . .

What I have said is that while I can go heart and soul with the 'retaliation' policy, I am not at present prepared to support the 'preferential' — I supplemented this declaration, by saying that the electors were not now being asked to support the latter policy — as it was not the policy adopted by the Government, but that it would still be a matter for Education — or enquiry — on which they could keep an open mind — as I should myself — I added that I would pledge myself not to vote for a tax on bread or meat — without their consent — but that if I changed my present opinion — and came to the conclusion that 'preferential' taxes were necessary — I should not hesitate to support the policy, but only after I had submitted myself to my constituents for re-election.

In other words: I am completely in accord with Arthur Balfour's present policy — and I hold myself perfectly free to support the preferential part of your policy — but only after I have discussed the question with my constituents — and submitted myself for re-election.

I think the course I have taken is under the circumstances the right one to adopt, and I am sure you will agree it is very far from the one you are under the impression I have taken. I can assure you that if I find I can support you I shall not hesitate to say so.

STUMPING THE COUNTRY

(*October–December* 1903)

The Birmingham Speech — Churchill and Hugh Cecil's Raid — Balfour and Hicks Beach at the Dolphin Banquet — Hicks Beach Accepts Retaliation — Chamberlain's Optimism — The Cardiff and Newport Speeches — Dissensions among the Unionist Free Traders — The By-elections Show a Swing to Chamberlain — The Leeds Speech — Balfour's Speech at Manchester Disappoints — Chamberlain's Exchanges with the Canadian Leaders — Deakin Invites Chamberlain to Visit Australia — The Tariff Commission: its Terms of Reference and Composition — The Guildhall Speech Ends the Campaign — Personal Sidelights.

I

THE demagogic flavour of the Liverpool speeches, and their increasingly aggressive Protectionism provoked the Free Traders to retaliate. On 30 October Asquith at Paisley touched Chamberlain on the raw by declaring that the Colonies 'showed not the faintest inclination to respond' to his proposals. But it was an ill-timed gibe. The same day, the High Commissioner for Canada and the Agents-General for the other self-governing Colonies, when presenting the new Colonial Secretary with an address of welcome, pointed out that there was a strong feeling in the Colonies, as in England, that closer bonds of union were now necessary to make the structure of the Empire more secure. They also observed that trade relations within the Empire had been improved by the abrogation of the German and Belgian treaties and by the preferential tariffs of Australia and Canada.

Next day, at Rawtenstall, Harcourt thundered a denunciation of Chamberlain's attack on Cobden and the anti-Corn Law League. He recalled his own youth in Preston in the days of Protection when starving mobs roamed abroad and the police shot people down in the streets. Meanwhile the Free Food League had undertaken a nation-wide propaganda campaign and plastered the hoardings with posters contrasting the large Free Trade loaf with a shrunken Protectionist loaf. 'Do you want the big loaf or the little loaf?' was their slogan.

Back at Highbury, Chamberlain was busy with the affairs of the

Birmingham Tariff Committee, the Tariff Reform League, and the Liberal Unionist Association. Pearson, Monkbretton and Powell Williams came to stay. He also had to prepare the speech he was to deliver in Birmingham on 4 November.

Chamberlain's way in preparing his speeches was still much the same as when he first went into the House. The day would have been devoted to interviews and current business. Work on the speech was, therefore, almost always left till after dinner. He would begin by making notes and then write out the text in longhand. If the flow of his ideas should 'wobble' he would stop work and read something light — a French novel for preference — for half an hour or so. He would then go back to his desk until the draft of the speech was completed. He would then read it through two or three times making endless corrections, and afterwards condense the main points to one or two sheets of writing paper. It was from these notes that the speech would finally be delivered. He often discussed his ideas with others before preparing a speech but he never seems to have shown its text even to his closest associates.

Chamberlain was 'very gloomy' at the prospect of his Birmingham speech. He would be speaking to his own townsmen and they would expect great things of him. Yet it was difficult, almost impossible, to introduce a new theme into the Fiscal controversy. As so often, he fell back on his old recipe 'when in doubt, always attack'.

10,000 people waited at the Bingley Hall on the evening of 4 November.

a wonderful crowd — as far as the eye could see — and so well behaved, so good-tempered, so interested, so intelligent and so enthusiastic, that one could not have had a better audience. For once Joe was a little disturbed as we drove down. So much was expected, so great would be the disaster did he not rise to the occasion, and he was not altogether satisfied with his notes. . . . As I walked on to the platform with Mr. Collings, the sea of faces, all eager and upturned, which met the eye was an extraordinary sight. After giving me a welcome, they broke out with a measured cry, short and sharp : 'Where's Joe ?' 'Where's Joe ?' — which broke into round upon round of cheers as he followed a moment afterwards.[1]

He began by pouring ridicule on Harcourt's account of the 'hungry forties'.

Is it true that at the time when Free Trade was introduced and the Corn Laws were repealed we were in a state of destitution and misery and starvation ? Is it true that, under the protection which prevailed before, this country was going down in the scale of nations or losing its prosperity

[1] Mrs. Chamberlain to her mother, 5 Nov. 1903.

and losing its trade ?   No, absolutely no.   The exact reverse was the case. In the years preceding the repeal of the Corn Laws — and I will take especially the years from 1830 to 1841 — there was a time of great prosperity in this country under Protection.   I do not mean to say that the country was as rich or as great as it is now, but comparatively with other nations it occupied a better position, was absolutely in the first rank.   It had conquered, under Protection, the absolute commercial supremacy of the world, and although trade was less then than it is now it was increasing with a rapidity, a proportionate rapidity, which has seldom been exceeded since.   But in 1841 we had in this country one of the crises which occur in every country from time to time, whether they be Protectionists, or whether they be Free Traders.   We had a time of bad trade and small employment. . . .   This was the time — in 1841 and 1842 — to which Sir William Harcourt referred in his speech which was made on Saturday last.   He went back to the memory of his youth, and said that at that time he was at school — I think at Preston — and had been, I understood him to say, a witness of riots in which some of the people had been shot down by the military.   He went on to say that nothing of the sort had ever happened since.   Well, sir, this is a very small matter, but I think his memory deceives him, bcause I think in later times — I believe, I have not had time to check it — I believe he was Home Secretary, people were shot down in a Midland mining district, and a special commission was appointed by the Government to inquire into the circumstances.[1]

His own version of the events leading to the repeal of the Corn Laws was followed by sharp attacks on Asquith and the Unionist Free Traders.   Then as in his other speeches, he gave examples of Birmingham industries depressed by foreign competition : jewellery, brass, pearl buttons, bicycles.

All this was good platform stuff.   But Birmingham wanted something more.   They needed, and he gave them, a 'stunt'.

You know that during the last few weeks the walls of Birmingham have been covered with a poster, a flaming poster which is intended as an advertisement for a London newspaper which made itself notorious for its pro-Boer sympathies during the late war, and for the ready credence which it gave to every calumny on our soldiers or upon our statesmen. That poster shows you the big loaf bigger than any I have ever seen — I should think it must weigh about eight-and-twenty pounds.   It shows you a little loaf, smaller than any I have ever seen, and which, I suppose, might weigh a few ounces.   And it tickets one 'The Free Trade Loaf', and it tickets the little one 'The Zollverein Loaf'.   The placard has no other object than to induce you to believe that if you adopt my policy of Preference with the Colonies it is this little bit of a loaf to which you and your families will be reduced, and you will have sacrificed the mammoth loaf which appears in another part of the poster.   Now, I have had the curi-

[1] The Featherstone riots.   Mr. Asquith was Home Secretary and Sir W. Harcourt Chancellor of the Exchequer at the time.

osity to inquire what would be the exact difference in the size of the loaf
if the whole tax which I propose to be put upon corn was met by a corresponding reduction in the size of the loaf. I asked my friend Mr. Alder-
man Bowkett to make me two loaves in order to test this question.

At this point Chamberlain unwrapped a parcel on the platform
and produced two quartern loaves. He held them up, one on either
hand, and continued :

I do not know whether your eyes are better than mine, but I admit that
when I first saw these loaves I was absolutely unable to tell which was the
little one and which was the big one. I know there is a difference, because
I know that in the smaller one a few ounces less flour have been used in
order to correspond to the amount of the tax. But it is still, I think, a
sporting question which is the big one and which is the little one. What
is to be said of a cause which is supported by such dishonest representations as the one to which I have referred ?

This homely demonstration was the making of the speech. The
audience 'roared and shrieked with delight and called again for the
loaves to be held aloft'. 'You are the only man who could do it'
was Powell Williams' comment, to which Mrs. Chamberlain added
'and only in Birmingham'.

II

The Bingley Hall speech was subjected to the usual barrage of
Liberal criticism. In the next few days Rosebery, Asquith, Fowler
and Campbell-Bannerman all returned to the charge. Rosebery, in
a curious passage, declared that what the economy of the country
needed was 'not fiscal reform but commercial repose'.[1] More
significant, however, was his appeal to Liberals to forget past differences and unite in defence of Free Trade. Campbell-Bannerman
responded warmly when he spoke at Frome ten days later. This
exchange marked the public sealing of the reconciliation between
the main factions of Liberalism. Suspicions and antagonisms would
remain but from this time it is possible to speak of a united Liberal
Party.

The Unionist Free Traders were even more active than the
Liberals. The three ex-Chancellors of the Exchequer all took the
field against Chamberlain: Hicks Beach at Manchester (5 November), Goschen at Liverpool (6 November) and Ritchie at Thornton
Heath (13 November). Meanwhile Churchill and Hugh Cecil
raided Birmingham itself.

[1] Leicester, 7 November 1903.

MRS. CHAMBERLAIN TO HER MOTHER

11 *November* 1903 and 15 *November* 1903.—To-morrow the great Free Food Meeting of Lord Hugh and Mr. Winston Churchill takes place. I only hope that it will go off quietly. It is rather significant that though a Conservative (who has always been a cross-grained person and a personal opponent of Joe's) Mr. Moore Bayley is to take the Chair for them, the Conservative and Liberal Unionist Associations refused to have anything to do with the meeting and they have had to go to the Liberal Association to print their posters and distribute their tickets, and no doubt to supply their audience. I have heard from people who have seen them that they are much annoyed by it and consider themselves badly treated, and that if Joe had raised his little finger there would not have been all this trouble. That is one way of looking at it. If they choose to come to Birmingham to attack his policy I do not see that he can be held responsible for the fact that his friends in Birmingham seem to have very little sympathy with their efforts to get a hearing.

15 *November* 1903.—The Cecil-Churchill Meeting went off quietly — a vast crowd outside, but no attempt at serious disturbance I am glad to say. The audience was almost exclusively Liberal, so it can hardly be claimed that they found many Unionist Free-Fooders in Birmingham. I hear that Winston's was by far the most taking speech and that Lord Hugh was so dull and solemn, that when a pause came a gentleman in the audience called out 'Amen!' I do not think they will have helped their cause much, though I daresay they are congratulating themselves on having bearded the lion in his den.

More significant for the cause of Tariff Reform was the joint appearance of Balfour and Hicks Beach at a banquet at Bristol (13 November). A month before Balfour had described the line he intended to take at the banquet as follows:

BALFOUR TO HICKS BEACH

14 *October* 1903.—Your very friendly letter has given me great pleasure. As at present advised I do not propose to speak on Tariff Reform at Bristol — but *if* I do I shall certainly not go beyond my Sheffield speech.

If I am not mistaken the chief fiscal difference between us is that I am much more drawn towards a Colonial arrangement than you are. I feel real and deep anxiety about the protective policy of our Colonies both in its commercial and its Imperial aspects : and, *if* I thought it practicable, which (as at present advised) I do not, I should not shrink from some sacrifices for the purpose of keeping important channels of trade permanently free and open to British Commerce. I gather that you have so little hope of this, or rate the value of it so low, that you hardly think the matter worth serious thought.

Balfour did speak on Fiscal Reform, but kept well within the limits of the Sheffield speech. He described his policy as that of a Fiscal reformer, by which, he said:

I mean a man who, looking at the whole circumstances of his time and of his country, feels that some change, some deep and genuine change, is required in our fiscal system in order to enable us to deal with a situation which was not in existence when our present system was planned by our fathers and grandfathers.

What the change should be, he declined to say, but characterised as ridiculous the Liberal suggestion that all we needed was more technical education, as if any amount of education could help our exporters to sell their goods over 80 per cent duties imposed by foreign countries.

Hicks Beach replied, agreeing that we ought to have the power to negotiate and to be in a position, when other nations treated our exports unfairly, to retaliate if expedient. He was still definitely opposed to Chamberlain's proposals, which he described as 'the unauthorised programme'. He was prepared, however, to support Balfour's policy of 'a genuine change' as being a wiser policy than simply holding uncompromisingly to the old lines.

Hicks Beach described the purpose of his speech as follows:

HICKS BEACH TO HIS SON

11 *December* 1903.—. . . I have tried my best to keep Balfour to the lines of his Sheffield speech, which of course was only possible by supporting him. So when I heard he was going to the Dolphin dinner at Bristol, I wrote to tell him that I would go there to support him, if he stuck to his own policy; which he promised to do. The Bristol people were rather astonished at my coming and afraid I should say something disagreeing with him — but of course I shouldn't have gone if I'd intended to do that —; and they were proportionately delighted when I supported him. . . .

Campbell-Bannerman, who had counted on the support of 'Michael and his angels', read the speech as an indication that most of the Unionist Free Fooders would now rejoin the Balfourian fold. Devonshire was despondent and attributed Beach's action to the pressure of his constituents. At Highbury, Mrs. Chamberlain, at least, regarded the event as a distinct gain for the cause of Fiscal Reform.

MRS. CHAMBERLAIN TO HER MOTHER

13 *November* 1903.—Much interest centres tonight in the fact that Mr. Balfour and Sir Michael Hicks Beach are both to be present at the Colston banquet. The latter has announced his adherence to the Sheffield programme, and it is hard to see how he can remain a leader of the recalcitrants.

17 November 1903.—. . . Was not Mr. Balfour's speech at Bristol good ? — from his own point of view and also from ours. . . .

24 November 1903.—. . . I had a brief talk with Mr. Balfour, for which I was very glad, for I wanted to congratulate him on his Sheffield and Bristol speeches. . . .

Contemporary opinion generally regarded Hicks Beach's support of Balfour as a sign that Chamberlain was winning. Hicks Beach, himself, was inclined to believe that his speech had been in vain. 'I fear it is all no use', he wrote, 'for it looks now as if Balfour would not be able to stand up against Chamberlain.'[1] Looking back we are inclined to take a different view. Hicks Beach's support may well have encouraged Balfour in the view that he still had something to gain by keeping his own policy distinct from Chamberlain's.

It was certainly the general view that Chamberlain was gaining ground. Fitzroy noted in his diary :

14 November 1903.—I saw the Duke at the Travellers'; he fears Chamberlain is making headway, and, no doubt, so far as his influence with the Liberal Unionists goes, he has captured two-thirds of them, both in Parliament and in the country.

19 November 1903. —I was between the Governor of the Bank of England and the President of the Royal Academy : another instance of the variety of one's experience at these functions. The Governor of the Bank, strong Liberal and Free Trader as he is, was constrained to admit that Chamberlainism was increasing in the City, and Austen, who gave me a lift back, professed to be extremely well satisfied with the way his father was making in the country.[2]

Chamberlain seems to have shared this confidence, though he was irked by the lack of support from the Unionist leaders.

CHAMBERLAIN TO ONSLOW

11 November 1905.—. . . It is a great disadvantage that I am deprived of the active cooperation of the members of the Cabinet, who with an entirely free hand, would have carried the war over a much wider country. But even in spite of that, the success hitherto has astonished me.

He certainly put on a bold face in public. At a farewell speech to the Colonial Agents-General he spoke of his 'hope and just now almost assured conviction' that his policy would soon carry. We get some impression of his outward mood from the following vivid if unfriendly account of his deportment at the royal banquet given at Windsor for the King and Queen of Italy (17 November) :

---

[1] Hicks Beach to his son, 11 December 1903.
[2] *Memoirs of Sir Almeric Fitzroy*, vol. i.

I am told that Chamberlain at Windsor last week was splendid. He was the man of the hour, and carried himself as if he knew it. Dilating to high and low on fiscal policy, summoned to explain it at this moment to Kings and the next to Queens, proclaiming to everyone, with an easy conviction, his certainty of success, he left with the belief, as he boasted on his way up to London, that he had converted the whole Royal Family, and that the Queen was an ardent Protectionist. It is said that, when wanted to talk to the Queen of Italy, he could not be found for some time, and was at last discovered in a small room concluding an animated peroration to an assembly of certain minor royalties.

Sir Frank Lascelles, who does not share the enthusiasm of Society for J. C.'s schemes, admits that public feeling in Germany is keenly excited, not to say apprehensive, on the subject, but particularly careful not to give criticism a provocative air : to this extent he believes in the possibility of something resulting to the benefit of the British export trade, as the Germans are so determined to hold the advantages they at present enjoy that they will make some concessions to avert a tariff war. He mentioned one very amusing incident, which shows the extraordinary readiness of the German manufacturer to avail himself of domestic circumstances abroad, in order to push German trade. The Bavarian Minister at Berlin reported that a clockmaker in Bavaria had produced a clock surmounted with a figure of Chamberlain making a speech, which emerged when the clock struck : one sample of this having been bought and taken to England, the enterprising clockmaker has now received orders for 22,000 clocks of similar pattern.[1]

III

Chamberlain's next major speech was at the Drill Hall in Cardiff (20 November), the centre of the coal, iron and steel, and shipping of South Wales. He made the most of Balfour's speech at Bristol and mocked the divisions among the Unionist Free Fooders. The passage we quote below gives some idea of his power to attack :

. . . I hope you have all read the admirable and convincing speech that was made by the Prime Minister the other day at the Colston banquet in Bristol. . . . That speech was a development of the previous speech of Mr. Balfour at Sheffield, and it is absolutely consistent with it. After that speech it is impossible for any honest man to pretend that he does not know what the Government's policy is . . . Mr. Balfour . . . has said that the Government is entirely in favour of fiscal reform. . . . That is then the policy of the Government.

But Mr. Balfour was followed by Sir Michael Hicks Beach — (*cheers*) — and he made a statement which, under existing circumstances, is perhaps, even of greater interest. He said : 'Free Trader though I am, and always have been, yet I am prepared to support the policy which the Prime Minister laid down at Sheffield, and again in his speech to-night.' That

[1] *Memoirs of Sir Almeric Fitzroy*, 23 November, vol. i, p. 170.

is a remarkable declaration. (*Cheers.*) I accept it with gratitude — (*hear, hear*) — otherwise, without note or comment, even though Sir Michael Hicks Beach goes on to say that he is steadfastly opposed to the unauthorised programme — by which, I suppose, he means Preference and reciprocal treatment in the case of the Mother Country and the Colonies. But I am thankful to have half a loaf rather than no bread. (*A laugh.*) Sir Michael Hicks Beach is heartily with that branch of our policy which is represented in the policy of the Government. I commend that to the Members of the Free Food League, and I want to know whether they are prepared to follow their founder in a similar declaration. (*A laugh.*)

There is my friend and former leader, the Duke of Devonshire. The Duke of Devonshire resigned his place in the Government the other day because he did not agree with the Sheffield speech of Mr. Balfour, which, however, Sir Michael Hicks Beach is prepared most heartily to support. Well, things move quickly nowadays. (*Laughter.*) May be the duke is also moving with them. His last intimation was that he was not opposed to the Government, but he hoped to be a drag upon the wheel. That is a curious ambition. (*Laughter.*) Here we are, in the crisis of our lives ; here we are with burning questions for which we have to find a solution. I should have thought that the time had come for statesmen of some energy and initiative — (*loud cheers*) — and for some foresight. (*Cheers.*) Pitt — the great Pitt — was toasted, and is even now known to history, as the pilot who weathered the storm. (*Hear, hear.*) I do not think I should much care to go down to posterity as a drag on the wheel. (*Loud cheers.*)

The rest of the speech was devoted to local illustrations of the danger of foreign competition. Even coalmining was in danger, he argued. The United States, Germany and France were developing their own coalfields. Besides, if the great home industries that depended on coal were depressed, the coalminers' living would be threatened too.

From coal he passed to tinplate. The McKinley tariff had destroyed the tinplate exports of South Wales to the United States. They had been saved from the full consequences of this loss of trade ; but only by the increased orders from the Colonies and particularly from South Africa.

From tinplate he passed to steel and to the dangers of American 'dumping'.

The mischief at present has not gone far. But you have begun with the dumping of 250,000 tons. Do you suppose it will stop there ? In an address he delivered to the students of St. Andrews University . . . Mr. Carnegie repeated a statement which he said had been made to him by Mr. Schwab, at that time the Manager of the great Steel Corporation. Mr. Schwab said that in a very short time one third of their production would be dumped in this country. If ever one third of their production is dumped in the United Kingdom, Heaven protect *our* trade !

Then came a caustic riposte to Rosebery.

. . . What does the Opposition say ? . . . I must not do them an injustice. I had almost forgotten that they have a leader, a new leader. When I say a new leader, I mean an old leader become a new leader. They have Lord Rosebery — (*laughter*) — who after being excommunicated and having excommunicated, after having retired so many times to his tent that we were tired of seeing it, now comes out to offer a hand to those who have denounced him, and to say, 'Whatever we do, whatever we think, let us fight this policy with an alternative'. And what do you think the alternative is ? 'What we want,' says Lord Rosebery, 'is commercial repose' — (*laughter*) — Rest, and be thankful. (*Laughter and cheers.*) Go to sleep, gentlemen, and forget your troubles. (*Laughter.*) Are you in anxiety, do you fear danger, have you nightmares ? (*Laughter.*) Then try Lord Rosebery's specific. (*Laughter.*) Try the famed soporific pills — (*much laughter*) — and you will have a wholesome slumber. No, gentlemen, it is not commercial repose that we want, it is commerical activity. (*Cheers.*) It is time to change our system.

The closing passage gives some idea of the historical proportions in which he saw his own role :

What Washington did for the United States of America, what Bismarck did for Germany, it is our business and our duty to do for the British Empire. We are here forty-two millions of persons. But outside, scattered, indeed, but still, with one heart and mind, there are some eleven millions more. We can begin with an Empire of between fifty and sixty millions of the British race, and over and above that we have hundreds of millions of those native races for whom we have made ourselves responsible. (*Cheers.*) And to bring them together is our task. It is not enough to talk platitudes about Empire. We have to make it and to strengthen it.

Chamberlain still had two speeches to make during the Welsh part of the tour. He had found it a strain at Glasgow and at Newcastle to prepare two speeches in advance, and to have the second on his mind while delivering the first. At Liverpool, therefore, he had decided not to begin work on the second speech till the first one was over. After the Cardiff meeting, however, he was too tired that night and the following morning to work at all. The next two speeches were thus wholly unprepared.

The first was delivered at a business men's lunch in Cardiff, and was an excellent appeal both to the interests and to the patriotism of the Middle Classes. £1100 were subscribed at once by the guests to the funds of the Tariff Reform League.

In the evening, he spoke at Newport, with Lord Tredegar in the Chair. At Cardiff his invective had been mainly reserved for the Unionist Free Traders. At Newport it was the Liberals' turn.

s

When I propose a reform I expect that the first argument of my opponents will be that no reform is necessary. I am not disappointed. Every speaker on the other side tells you that the country never was so rich, never was there so much income-tax paid, never were there so many cheques passed through the clearing-house, never was there such a satisfactory state of affairs with regard to the condition of the working man ; and if you would only get rid of a certain pestilent ex-Colonial Secretary — (*laughter*) — why, then, you might be happy ever afterwards (*laughter*) — and you would have nothing to wish for . . . Well, if you are satisfied, . . . if you think that everything is for the best in the best of all possible worlds, that we have reached the conclusion of all reform and all change, and can afford to stand still while all the rest of the world is moving, I might as well sit down. But . . . Are we so prosperous ? . . . Here is Mr. Asquith telling us that you cannot improve your situation, that everything is so prosperous, and so satisfactory, that really it is almost wicked on the part of anybody to suggest an amendment ; and here is Sir Henry Campbell-Bannerman, who goes down to some place in the North of England and says that there is one-third of the population of this country who are underfed and on the verge of hunger — thirteen or fourteen millions of people, according to Sir Henry Campbell-Bannerman, who are on the verge of hunger ; and yet everything is for the best.

Now, ever since Sir Henry Campbell-Bannerman made that statement he has been trying to wriggle out of it. He used it for his own purpose in order to create a prejudice against me and in order to be able to say, ' Here are these thirteen millions actually on the verge of a precipice, and here is Mr. Chamberlain who is going to add to the cost of their living and to shove them over the precipice.' That is what he wished to say, but he has very often forgotten that there are two sides to an argument of that kind. . . . if there be thirteen millions of people to whom such a trifle as one-eighth of a penny upon a two-pound loaf would make all the difference between living and starvation, then I say there is something rotten in the state of Denmark — (*laughter*) — and it is time for someone to put it right. (*Cheers.*) . . . It doesn't matter to me whether they be thirteen millions or whether they be three millions. It is quite enough to know that in this country, in which we are told that everything is so prosperous, there are still so large a number, counted by millions, of our fellow-citizens and fellow-creatures in this deplorable condition.

Then our opponents have a second statement to make. They say, ' Oh, yes, that is true, but it is their own fault. It is due to their idleness, their thriftlessness, or their drunkenness.' It is very easy from a comfortable position to denounce those who have never had the same advantage. (*Cheers.*) I don't doubt that drunkenness and thriftlessness are great evils, and that many people suffer from their own fault ; but I know — I have had experience enough to know — that all these things are connected ; that drunkenness, for instance, is not always a cause, but is sometimes a consequence. If you take a man in constant employment at good wages, and take that employment from him at middle age, he can find no other employment, and he drops into the class of the casual worker, and gradually finds himself sinking further and further. Do you wonder that sometimes he takes to drink in order to forget his misery ? (*Cheers.*)

We are not reading now a sermon to the poor, but let us all take to heart the general fact that when people are comfortable there is much less temptation to do wrong — (*hear, hear*) — and for myself I should never be satisfied until in this country there is full employment at fair wages for every decent, honest, and industrious man.

Asquith, Harcourt and other Liberals had taken the line that foreign 'dumping' was really to Britain's advantage. Chamberlain dealt faithfully with that argument.

We are the only free country that admits . . . dumped goods, and we become in consequence the dumping-ground and the dust-heap of all Europe and America. ('*Shame*') . . . Mr. Asquith has devoted himself to this subject of dumping, and still has a good deal to learn. He has made some astounding discoveries, which I am sure will surprise you very much. He is satisfied, and I think that others who follow the same line — Sir William Harcourt and other members of the Opposition — they have come to the conclusion that dumping is a positive benefit, that it is really a good thing that you should have sent over to this country goods below any fair cost price. . . . These gentlemen believe that foreign countries are making us a present when they dump their goods below our cost. Now, is not that rather silly ? Here are these people, the Americans and the Germans, the keenest men of business in the world, the most intelligent, as intelligent as any — do you really think they are spending millions of money in order to promote our interests ? (*Laughter.*) Do you think they are ruining themselves in order to make us a handsome present ? No, they are doing nothing of the kind. The whole defence of this system is based on an utter misapprehension of what this is. They can afford to dump because it does not cost them anything ; but we, who have to take the dumped goods — it costs us our employment, our profit, our trade. (*Cheers and a Voice: 'Let us alter it; it's time.'*) Now, Mr. Asquith said the other day : 'Suppose there is some dumping done by the foreign country. It is at a loss, and can't go on for ever.' But that is pretty poor comfort. (*Hear, hear.*) I don't suppose I can hold Mr. Asquith's head under water for ever — (*laughter*) — but I can hold it there long enough to drown him. (*Loud cheers and laughter.*) . . .

Now let us come home to Newport. (*Hear, hear.*) Let us ask how is this matter affecting you in this present year, 1903. It is estimated that 250,000 tons of steel bars, billets and blooms will have been imported into Newport alone ; at all events, into South Wales. . . . What is going to be saved to anybody by that 250,000 tons of steel ? . . . Suppose that the whole is put down at 10s below the lowest English price. They say the manufacturers that use the bars and the blooms and the billets will profit to the extent of £125,000 a year and that is what Messrs. Harcourt and Asquith are always dwelling upon. They dwell upon the profit. Somebody or another gains the £125,000 a year by buying billets so much cheaper. Yes ; but how much is lost ? (*Hear, hear.*) Do you know how much wages there are in 250,000 tons of this stuff, if you take the cost of

what has to be done in order to make the bars ? If you supposed that they
were made in this country from the ore we should get from abroad. . .
that 250,000 tons would involve £500,000 worth of wages — wages alone
paid to the workmen. . . . Every man employed on each stage — the
miner, the over-ground workmen, the furnacemen, the roller — every
man employed in every branch of this industry from beginning to end
would have a share in the advantage, and the total sum in wages gained
by the country would have been £500,000 a year, which you are throwing
away for the sake of a profit of £125,000 to a particular trade. . . .

I ask on all these occasions where does the individual come in ? (*Hear,
hear.*) What becomes of the men who lose their employment ? They are
always supposed, on the happy-go-lucky theory of Mr. Asquith, to find
other employment. Well, they do not. (*Hear, hear.*) In many cases the
only employment they find is at the workhouse. (*Hear, hear.*) In other
cases they emigrate. In others they go into inferior employments. The
other day I had a story told me by a railway servant, and it seemed to me
rather pathetic. He was at a station near Birmingham, and he saw three
men unloading trucks, and the trucks contained German wire. As he
passed, one of the men said, 'This is rather hard ; we used to make these.'
These were men who had been in Birmingham or elsewhere as wire
makers. They formerly got good wages, and had acquired a special
aptitude, but they lost their employment, and then, according to Mr.
Asquith's beneficent theory, they have been transferred to other employments, being now engaged like common labourers — all their skill thrown
away and no longer of the slightest advantage to them, as they worked at
unloading German wire. Who profits by this ?

The speech, unprepared as it was, fully deserved the tribute paid
by *The Times* next day :

Nothing bears more eloquent witness, not merely to his physical energy,
but to the mastery of the subject and the abundance of the resources on
which he draws, than the way in which he is thus able, time after time, to
follow up one remarkable utterance with another, perfectly new in
character, and not less impressive.

It had been a good day's work and Chamberlain might leave
contented for an appropriately Disraelian week-end at Weston, the
home of Lord and Lady Bradford. There next morning he received
the news that the New Zealand Parliament had passed the Bill giving
Preference to the United Kingdom. Stout old Seddon would write
his own account a few days later.

SEDDON TO CHAMBERLAIN

Wellington, 2 December 1903.—I have read with delight the great achievement of your life at Glasgow. Going into the stronghold of free-trade and
carrying a Glasgow audience with you, must have given additional
strength and confirmed you in the conclusion that you are doing the right
thing. No wonder at your having spread dismay amongst those erratic

men who will persist in doggedly holding on to that will o' the wisp, Free-Trade. Their persistency is almost as senseless as those who adhere to the handcart or bullock dray for the removal of their goods in these days of the locomotive. But the old stage coach has disappeared, and so should the existing fiscal conditions of the United Kingdom.

I noted with pleasure the great reception they gave you at Newcastle, and there you will have the main body of the people with you, but the leaders of the miners and of the labour organizations at home, as here, seem to be behind the men they are supposed to lead.

Your reception at Liverpool, being a Lancashire man, pleased me very much. Lancashire will be evenly divided upon the issues submitted — they are a very obstinate and self-willed people. I have noticed that the Oldham electors are not in touch with Churchill their member, and in this as in other manufacturing parts of the country I am inclined to think that they will support your proposals; if not, they will rest upon that nice soft bed of down prepared by Mr. Balfour for those who want a half way resting place.

You will be pleased to learn that the New Zealand Government succeeded in carrying through the Coastwise laws Bill, thus preventing foreign ships participating in our Coastwise trade.

We have also passed the Naval Agreement and Preferential Trade Bills. The former was passed almost unanimously, and the latter, in the 3rd reading, was carried by 50 votes as against 16.

. . . I purposely delayed bringing down the Preferential Trade Bill till towards the end of the session, as I was given to understand that it was going to be made a party question, which I endeavoured to avoid. However, after I moved the Second Reading, the leader of the Opposition challenged the Government by moving that the second reading of the Bill should be postponed until next session. On the division he was beaten by 46 votes to 23, so that with a majority of two to one our position, as a Government, may be considered fairly safe, and the desire of this Colony for preferential trade with the United Kingdom, and that forthwith, has been amply demonstrated. The general feeling of the people of this Colony is that you may succeed. Of course, we have here, as you have at home, little Englanders, but the one feeling permeating the breasts of the great majority is a united Empire.

Above all else, I hope your health will bear the terrible strain which the self-imposed task must entail and that you will succeed in your great undertaking. I feel that the righteousness of the cause will lead to success, and ultimately ensure a united and prosperous Empire, for, with the Colonies and the United Kingdom cemented together by preferential trade as well as the ties of kindred, the combination will be so powerful as to impel other nations to come to heel, and thus prove the efficacy of retaliation.

IV

The campaign had been in progress for nearly two months and still public interest showed no sign of flagging. Each new speech of Chamberlain's raised the temperature; and his opponents' replies only added fuel to the flames. If they could have ignored him, if they could have raised some new issue of their own, Chamberlain's campaign might have faded out like the Fair Trade movement twenty years before. But the opportunity to the Liberals to close their ranks and divide their opponents, the natural desire of the Unionist Free Traders to justify their resignations from office, and, above all, Chamberlain's own personality kept the initiative in his hands. Then, as on previous occasions, his opponents did more than anyone to keep his ideas before the public. He made them do his work for him.

The Cardiff and Newport speeches were no exception to this rule. On 24 November the Free Food League staged a great Demonstration in the Queen's Hall in London. Devonshire was in the chair. Goschen, Hicks Beach, Ritchie, Northbrook, Cowper, Churchill, Hugh Cecil and a galaxy of lesser notables graced the platform.

The Duke, in his presidential address, justified his decision to resign. He then replied to Chamberlain's attack at Cardiff.

Mr. Chamberlain says that I am content that my name should go down to posterity as the 'drag on the wheel'. If he will allow me a slight modification of the phrase I am content to accept it. A brake is an important and sometimes necessary part of the mechanism of a locomotive. More than ever it is necessary now, when the engine-driver has got down and allowed another to take his place, and when that other is running the locomotive at full speed down the line and against all the signals. More important than how my name will go down to posterity is the question what the leaders of the Unionist party are going to do with this policy. To me it seems that they are rapidly allowing the guidance of the party to fall from their hands. I trust it will not be long before they tell us whether they intend to join their late colleague in his retrograde career, or how long they intend to sit still as silent spectators or listeners while their colleague assumes all the duties, privileges, and responsibilities of leadership.

Goschen, who followed, dilated on the plight of the working class in Protectionist Germany who were driven to eat horseflesh. The general tone of the meeting was hostile to Balfour, and it was noted that Hicks Beach did not speak. The final resolution, however, expressed readiness 'to consider any Government proposals for mitigating the effects of hostile tariffs in certain cases', while maintaining uncompromising opposition to any taxation of food or any preferential or Protectionist policy.

In a speech next day (25 November) at the Surrey Theatre, Rosebery went so far as to admit that there might be cases where retaliation could be justified. This was generally interpreted as an overture for an alliance between himself and Devonshire.

Further Free Trade speeches followed in the next few days; among them one from Asquith (25 November), and one from Campbell-Bannerman, who followed Chamberlain to Newport (30 November). We catch a glimpse of the Liberal leader's private feelings at this time from the following letters.

CAMPBELL-BANNERMAN TO HARCOURT

27 November 1903.—There never was such a strange 'controversy'. Joe countered on all points : his blunders shown up, his errors exposed : but he never acknowledges, excuses or explains anything! He trusts to vulgar, ignorant applause of the 'strong man', and to the selfish interests of particular trades. The Duke of D.'s speech is a huge help : but what a feeble lot are his followers — time-servers almost to a man.[1]

CAMPBELL-BANNERMAN TO MR. BRYCE

Belmont, 7 December 1903.—. . . I doubt whether — barring individual manufacturers, speculators and loafers — Joe is making much way ; I should add fine ladies and 'swells' generally. But these were probably all Protectionists at heart already, so far as they have hearts and any knowledge.

There is a good deal of doubt what to do with the Free Fooders.

Tweedmouth is full of a scheme for half a dozen voting with us on the Address, resigning their seats and standing as Liberals. A little melodramatic for John Bull's taste ! And after all Winston is hardly worth any increase of complications.

I had a tremendous time at Newport — I never saw anything like it ! I do not think Joe has captured S. Wales.[2]

But now Chamberlain began to receive his first reinforcements. On 27 November Chaplin wrote to say that the elections to the executive of the National Union of Conservative Associations had given a considerable majority to the Chamberlainites. On 29 November the *Sun* newspaper, which had a considerable circulation in London, declared for Chamberlain and published a letter from him across the whole front page. A few days later, on 7 December, Selbourne, though still a Minister, came out strongly for Colonial Preference in a speech at Edinburgh. Two days later (9 December) the Council of the Chamber of Agriculture passed a strong resolution in favour of the full Tariff Reform policy. Next day, the veteran Field-Marshal Wolseley announced his support for Chamberlain.

---

[1] Gardiner, *Sir William Harcourt*, vol. ii, p. 559.
[2] J. A. Spender, *Life of the Rt. Hon. Sir Henry Campbell-Bannerman, G.C.B.*, vol. ii, p. 131.

The following extracts suggest that it was now the general view that Chamberlain had captured at least the bulk of Unionist support.

3 *December* 1903.—I had a serious talk with Haldane this morning about the progress Chamberlain is making. He quite admits it, and is greatly disquieted. He fears the country being rushed into a revolution of its fiscal system, and, the first results not answering popular expectation, a growing demand for still stronger doses of Protection.[1]

11 *December* 1903.—So far as the upper and middle classes are concerned, the great bulk of the Unionist party has either gone over to Chamberlain, or is quite ready to go. . . . When the general election comes, the Unionist party may be simply Chamberlainite — in which case I should retire from Parliament, for even I should have no chance as a Unionist Free-trader, and I can't join the other side. At the same time much may happen before an election. The whole Protectionist cry really depends on Chamberlain. It would collapse without him.[2]

13 *December* 1903.—It becomes every day more apparent that the force of the current in favour of fiscal reform is setting in the direction of Mr. Chamberlain, and that the Prime Minister's formulae make no way in the constituencies.[3]

Matters now moved to their first major test. Five by-elections were pending: Dulwich, Lewisham and Norfolk which were regarded as marginal Unionist seats: Ludlow a safe Unionist seat; and Ashburton a Liberal stronghold: Dulwich and Lewisham were both to poll on 15 December.

The Unionist candidates in both constituencies were requested by the Central Office not to go beyond the Balfour policy. They began by taking this advice. But strong counter pressures were applied both by the Tariff Reform machine and by their own supporters.

CHAMBERLAIN TO PARKER SMITH

12 *January* 1904.—. . . It is always a question whether we should force the pace, or openly declare that, as the candidate does not accept the policy of the Tariff Reform League, we repudiate him and will take no part whatever in the election. Then, if he loses, it is his affair and not ours.

You may be aware that this was the line taken by both the 'Daily Mail' and the Tariff Reform League in the Dulwich and Lewisham elections, with the result that both candidates were stiffened and came out strongly on our side. Pearson told the agents of the candidates that, unless the latter made a strong declaration, the whole Tariff Reform machinery would be removed, the offices closed, and the meetings abandoned.

[1] *Memoirs of Sir Almeric Fitzroy*, vol. i, p. 172.
[2] Lady Victoria Hicks Beach, *Life of Sir Michael Hicks Beach*, pp. 200–201.
[3] *Memoirs of Sir Almeric Fitzroy*, vol. i, p. 173.

MRS. CHAMBERLAIN TO HER MOTHER

11 *December* 1903.—Another M.P. on our side has died, which makes five elections pending. The Government candidates have been placed under some pressure by their would-be constituents — and the Conservative Organisation will, I think, finally come to the conclusion that if they are to hold their own or to win they must not follow the policy of restriction, which they have undoubtedly hoped to maintain. We hear of pressure having been put on Members and candidates all over the country to keep to the Government Programme pure and simple — and there is no doubt, and it is not unnatural, that the party officials are more Balfourite than Mr. Balfour himself. In fact, we know that to be the case, for Mr. Balfour does not intend that the support of his plan shall exclude sympathy with the broader policy. But now an idea is getting abroad that Joe's policy is so much more popular than that of retaliation only that the constituencies care nothing for the latter, unless it means the possibility of the former. ''Arf and 'arfers' do not appeal to the working man. Two of the elections come off in a few days. Oh dear me ! what if they do not go well, and Joe has to speak at Leeds the day after they are declared ?

In the face of these different pressures both candidates yielded and declared for the full Chamberlain policy. As a result they gained the support of the *Daily Mail*. They also received a letter of endorsement from Chamberlain, as well as the customary letter from the leader of the party.

The decision of the Unionist candidates at Dulwich and Lewisham to declare for Chamberlain, placed the Free Food League in a quandary. What advice should they give to their supporters in these constituencies ? A meeting was held on 10 December at Devonshire House to decide the answer.

The Duke . . . presided . . . Beach, to his infinite discomfort, took part in the deliberations, and though he expressed his own preference for a Protectionist rather than a Radical, failed to impress his views on the meeting, which included Goschen, Ritchie, and George Hamilton, and was in favour of making common cause with the Opposition in all constituencies where the Unionist organisation had been captured by J. C.

Winston Churchill, who can find no platform on which to address his constituents, except the box-seat of a cab, asked the Duke's opinion whether he should accept an invitation to speak for the Opposition candidate in Ludlow ; but for this His Grace declined to make himself responsible.

Some forty to fifty Unionist Members of Parliament were present, and those whose seats are hopeless were all for the most violent courses. Hugh Cecil flatters himself he may retain Greenwich by the aid of the Radicals, but admitted that the Education Act created a serious difficulty.[1]

[1] *Memoirs of Sir Almeric Fitzroy*, 13 December 1903, vol. i, p. 173.

S 2

The upshot of the discussion was embodied in a letter published on 12 December and signed by the secretary of the Free Food League. This stated:

The Duke of Devonshire, as President of the Unionist Free Food League, is of opinion that an elector who sympathises with the objects of that League would be well advised to decline to give his support, at any election, to a Unionist candidate who expresses his sympathy with the policy of Mr. Chamberlain and the Tariff Reform League.

Hicks Beach regretted the Duke's decision. 'It all disgusts me more than I can say with politics', he wrote to his son next day, 'for I cannot support Protection, nor can I change my Party.' Ritchie, however, along with Balfour of Burleigh, George Hamilton and Goschen all publicly supported the advice given by the Duke. The two by-elections had thus become an open contest between the opposing tendencies inside the Unionist party.

Mrs. Chamberlain described the result as follows:

MRS. CHAMBERLAIN TO HER MOTHER

15 *December* 1903.—I have just come from the telephone, and am feeling much cheered by my conversation with the Midland Express, which announced that we have held our own at Dulwich and Lewisham — and the latter at all events by a good majority of 2,001. . . . As the prognostications had got gloomier and gloomier as the days went on this is very satisfactory, and we will hope will have a good effect on the other two elections which are pending, as well as on the Unionist Organisations and the country generally. To me it is, in addition to all this, a personal comfort that Joe will make his speech to-morrow at Leeds after a victory instead of a defeat, for in both cases the candidates have supported his policy as well as that of the Government. . . .

Fitzroy, who as we have seen, was no friend to Tariff Reform was equally convinced that the result was a triumph for Chamberlain. Here is his analysis noted in his diary next day:

16 *December.*—The elections in South London have gone in favour of the Government candidates by majorities which, having regard to the character of the constituencies, are disquieting evidence of the spread of Chamberlainism. In both Dulwich and Lewisham people with very modest fixed incomes are a preponderant class, and here, if anywhere, you might expect a large falling off in the Unionist vote, as both candidates declared themselves in sympathy with Mr. Chamberlain. It is true that this has happened to some extent in Dulwich, but local circumstances and the antecedents of Rutherford Harris had a good deal to say to it. Still, on a poll of 78 per cent, he has been returned by 1,400 votes: the clerks and small villa people being apparently prepared to take the risks of anything the Chamberlain policy may produce.[1]

[1] *Memoirs of Sir Almeric Fitzroy*, vol. i, p. 174.

Chamberlain's own judgment was clear enough. 'The two by-elections', he wrote, 'exceeded my most sanguine expectations.'[1] He now felt he had a right to expect more open support from Balfour and the official Unionist organisation. For some time now, he had been irked by the efforts of party officials to keep candidates to the limits set by Balfour.

CHAMBERLAIN TO COCHRANE

10 *December* 1903.—I understand that the complaints of interference by Conservative agents have been general. Mr. Goulding spoke to Mr. Balfour about it the other day and was told that it was entirely contrary to his wishes. I have no doubt that all will come right in time. . . .

The following extract from one of Mrs. Chamberlain's letters to her mother is probably a true reflection of Chamberlain's own mind.

These last elections show very clearly that it is his advanced policy which excites enthusiasm. As at the Sheffield Conference, the bare Government policy is acquiesced in in a half-hearted way, but the moment the wider plan is touched new life is infused into every meeting. At last I hope it is beginning to penetrate the somewhat obtuse minds of the Whips and Party officials. Their prophecies, or rather those of their underlings, that any attempt to push anything further would be fatal have been completely falsified — and I hope and believe that they begin to realise that the popular mind grasps broad ideas more easily than fine drawn distinctions.

V

Chamberlain spoke at Leeds on 16 December.

MRS. CHAMBERLAIN TO HER MOTHER

18 *December* 1903.—Leeds was as successful as all the other 'engagements' and I look back with wonder and admiration at Joe's powers of endurance and versatility in presenting a different phase of the same subject to each audience in turn. . . .

We did the usual thing and dined in Leeds before the meeting. As on the previous journeys crowds gathered at the stations and we received many salutations on the way. On arriving at Leeds to our surprise nobody was on the platform to receive us, though an enthusiastic crowd quickly sprang out of the ground, and then as we walked along the platform to the hotel at the end it gathered in such numbers that the two stalwart policemen in front were quite unable to stem the tide — and we were so closely pressed by friendly admirers that I began to wonder whether we should be carried off our feet. . . . We arrived and were shown to our rooms, and still no 'Reception Committee'. In a few minutes they began to appear, full of profuse apologies. . . .

[1] Chamberlain to Lady Jeune, 30 December 1903.

The meeting was very good and Joe, as the Duke of Sutherland (who has become an ardent supporter) said, in 'excellent form'. His voice, which I sometimes thought tired in South Africa, has been in wonderfully good condition.

Chamberlain began by taunting his opponents :

I am not so much impressed as perhaps I ought to be with the authority which they carry. It is true that Mr. Ritchie has called my attention to the fact that there are four Chancellors of the Exchequer among them, and that one of them is himself. (*Laughter.*) I have a doubt whether the magnificent robes which the Chancellor of the Exchequer wears upon occasion carry with them all the virtues and all the wisdom of all his predecessors — (*laughter*) — and I am quite unable — with no disrespect to him — to accept Mr. Ritchie as a great financial authority, because he happened to be under the tuition of the permanent officials of the Treasury for the space of a few months.
. . . I heartily rejoice that Mr. Haldane — by no means the first in the field, but still welcome, however late — (*laughter*) — should lend his influence and advocacy to the formation of Charlottenburg schools all over the country. There is no institution in Leeds to which I more heartily wish success than your University which you are about to establish — (*cheers*) — but when Mr. Haldane tells me that Charlotten-burg schools are to be a cure for dumping — (*laughter and cheers*) — then I decline to learn business principles at the feet of this Gamaliel. (*Cheers.*)

Next came a passage in which we find Chamberlain groping for a word to define what we now call the Commonwealth.

When I say Colonial trade, you will understand I mean the trade with our British possessions. (*Hear, hear.*) I wish — I know it is impossible, but I wish — we could find some word which did not imply possession, but which did include every Crown Colony. Lack of it leads to so much misunderstanding. I saw the Duke of Devonshire the other day declared that I had omitted — that I had not taken into account — the Crown Colonies and India. It is, perhaps, a want of clearness on my part, but when I speak of the Colonies I think of the whole Empire — (*cheers*) — I think of them not in a possessionary sense, as if they were ours and belonged to us to do what we pleased with them. No, that is fatal to the ideal of Empire ; but I think of them as States, co-equals, in a sense partners with us — (*hear, hear*) — equal, at any rate, in the local independence, equal, as I believe, in their patriotism and their loyalty.

After some discussion of the local interests of Yorkshire, he took up the charge that the Colonies were not really interested in Preference.

Again and again, in spite of the proof that is before their eyes, my opponents say there is no evidence of a demand from the Colonies. . . . It is really a monstrous misrepresentation. Do they really believe in their hearts that I have invented this thing? Have they forgotten all that has passed ? Have they forgotten the Ottawa conference, the second conference in London, the third conference in London ?   Take the last alone.   A resolution was passed unanimously — every Premier of every self-governing Colony was present — urging the British Government to take into consideration the question of mutual Preference, and if possible to give a Preference to the Colonies in return for Preference given by them on every article of our production upon which they already put, or might hereafter put, a duty.   Well, what more proof do they want than that ? (*Hear, hear.*)   They want — it is so childish that I cannot understand how they can put such a matter forward — they want me to produce not merely this indication of the desire of the Colonies to negotiate with us, but a cut and dried result of the negotiations.   (*Laughter and cheers.*)   Let them send me — (*loud cheers*) — as ambassador to the Colonies — (*more cheers*) — with full powers, and I am perfectly willing to risk my reputation on my being able, not merely to satisfy the Colonies that we have something to give them which is worth their acceptance — (*hear, hear*) — but also to secure from the Colonies equal measure in return.   (*Cheers.*) Meanwhile, here is something.   I received a letter a day or two ago from Mr. Fielding, the Finance Minister of the Dominion of Canada. . . . Mr. Fielding, in writing to me, after regretting that this matter had been made, to a large extent, one of party politics — a regret which I entirely share with him — (*hear, hear*) — states :   *We need not* [meaning the Canadian Ministers] *refrain from stating emphatically in reply to some of the statements which have appeared in the Press, that the position taken up by the Canadian Ministers at the Colonial conference last year in favour of Imperial preferential trade is cordially endorsed by both of the great political parties of this country.   That some difficulties might arise in the arrangement of the details of so large a scheme is to be anticipated, but surely it is not too much to believe that if the principle be approved the intelligence of British and Colonial public men may be relied upon to overcome these, and to put the project into practical form.*

The closing passage was one of his best, caustic and yet inspiring.

You would be without a spark of imagination if you did not see what a chance it is which you are asked to throw away, if you did not see that they are endeavouring to frighten you with what is only an infinitesimal possibility of an imperceptible sacrifice.   ('*Hear, hear,*' *and laughter.*)   If you are, as I said before, called upon for sacrifice — perhaps you may be, although I think not at present — you will do something, I believe, to show your appreciation of the action of those who have not been slow in recognising the duties and responsibilities of kinship.   Are we so mean that we can rejoice in the assistance of our Colonies in our time of trial and then leave the sentiment with a sneer, and ask that they should go their own way and work their own salvation on their own lines, and that when they tell us what they want is to move one step farther in the direction of the political union which alone can save the Empire, then tell them that is sentiment on their part and that it will cost us a farthing on the 4 lb. loaf? . . . Union of the Empire !   It has been played with by some ; by others it has been considered a beautiful dream.   Dream it may be ; a nobler aspiration has never come to statesman.   Let us all feel that we have a responsibility connected with it, and that it is our duty to do all in our power to make it a reality. (*Hear, hear.*) It is not impossible. Let us feel that we, at least, have not been deterred from taking our part; that we, at least have not been driven from the field by craven fear of possible opposition, by antiquated prejudice, or by any comparatively mean and contemptible party or personal interests. (*Loud cheers, renewed again and again, the audience rising and waving handkerchiefs.*)

The speech was followed by an overflow meeting: 'strangely heavy and stolid' Mrs. Chamberlain called it, with 'many opponents present' who showed a tendency to interrupt.

The streets were thronged when we came out, and the students of the Yorkshire College were in attendance in large numbers and escorted us by torchlight through the town. Really a great ovation. The Chief Constable told us that over 100,000 people were in the streets and we drove through closely packed streets, crowded windows and cheers and enthusiasm, which was more like the Birmingham torchlight procession than anything we have seen — and so we drove for nearly an hour.

The approach of Christmas imposed a truce on the war of speeches. Chamberlain thus had the last word before the holiday. Meanwhile the tide continued to flow in his favour. On 19 December the Protectionists carried the day in the Federal elections in Australia.

On 23 December the Unionist candidate, a Chamberlainite, held Ludlow in the by-election, despite Churchill's support of his opponent. On the same day, Lord Cowper, one of the leading Unionist Free Fooders, wrote to *The Times* deprecating Devonshire's advice to Unionists to withhold their support from Tariff Reform candidates. The same week, the Mansion House conference on unemployment, the publication of *The Times* enquiry into the increase of pauperism and a great meeting of Lancashire Cotton manufacturers and operatives held to express concern at the state of the industry, all seemed to point to the validity of Chamberlain's conclusions. If there were still any doubts over the attitude of Unionists in the constituencies, these were dispelled a few days later when both Lord George Hamilton and Winston Churchill were repudiated by their constituency associations.

At the annual Jewellers Dinner (11 January) Chamberlain 'was received with the utmost enthusiasm, people waving their napkins'.[1] The speech followed familiar lines; but we may mark one phrase. He referred to the new tendency of Unionist Free Traders and even Liberals to accept retaliation in certain circumstances, but never preference. 'But', he said, 'it is no use putting off your old faith in fractions and then shivering on the brink of a new one. You cannot

---

[1] Mrs. Chamberlain to her mother, 12 January 1904.

find a safe place on the fence.' In the context the words are plainly aimed at the Liberal leaders. Were they really intended for Balfour?

Balfour was to speak in Manchester the same night. It was incidentally his first meeting in his constituency since he had become Prime Minister eighteen months before.

Balfour's speech was important. It was his first opportunity to comment on the progress of Chamberlain's campaign. But Chamberlain, warned by Austen, does not seem to have expected any new move on Balfour's side. Austen had drawn Balfour's attention to Devonshire's letter of 12 December advising Unionist Free Traders not to support Tariff Reform candidates at any election. He had suggested that in view of this, Balfour would do well to go beyond his Sheffield position. Balfour was in Scotland and had let his brother Gerald reply that Sheffield had preserved the party from many defections and that to do this remained more important than ever now that there was the threat of a Liberal-Unionist Free Trade Coalition.[1]

Soon after the Leeds meeting Chamberlain had written to Chaplin, setting out what he regarded as the three main obstacles to the success of his movement. He seems to have regarded Balfour's attitude as the chief of these. There is no trace of Chamberlain's letter but Chaplin's reply suggests its drift.

CHAPLIN TO CHAMBERLAIN

31 *December* 1903.—. . . As to your 3 difficulties. I agree — and if Balfour should adhere to his present plan, it is our greatest in my judgment. But will he? I cannot think it. From all he has said to me at any time, especially at Balmoral, just when you had left him, he made no secret that his sympathies were with you — and that he only refrained from openly supporting you on the ground that the country then wasn't *ripe.* He emphasised this more at Sheffield than he did to me, but that I take it was for the purpose of keeping Hartington.

Victor Churchill, who was here till this morning, tells me too, — and he is Whip in the H. of Lords you will remember — that reports are pouring in at Headquarters from all parts, so strongly in favour of your policy that he considers A. J.'s conversion only a question of time.

This must have its influence and will probably do its work best left alone. My only doubt is whether something might not be said to him before he speaks at Manchester, — and if I could come across him casually, I shouldn't hesitate to do so — against saying anything there to damp or check the movement that undoubtedly is going on in your direction. I forget whether I told you before, but I saw him for a moment before I spoke at Ware. He told me then he should ignore Hartington altogether.

[1] 26 Dec. 1903, Austen Chamberlain Papers 17/60.

In the event Chaplin's confidence proved misplaced. Balfour's speech at Manchester certainly did not go beyond the Sheffield programme. He argued that to secure a closer union of the Empire through Preference would require two things : that Canada should modify her Protectionist policy ; that Britain should accept a tax on food. He did not believe that either country was yet ready for such changes. The rest of his speech was an appeal for party unity. Balfour renewed this appeal at a lunch next day and went so far as to urge the party to show consideration for the feelings of 'the weaker brethren' who had not yet understood the full necessity for Fiscal Reform. He also spoke of the opportunity of fostering Imperial Unity by co-operation in Defence.

We do not know what Chamberlain thought of Balfour's Manchester speeches. But they must have been a profound disappointment. Despite the undoubted success of his own campaign, despite the victories at three by-elections, here was the Prime Minister still saying that opinion was not ripe for a tax on food, appealing for consideration for the feelings of the 'Free Fooders', and suggesting that the best approach to closer Imperial Unity might be found in the field of Defence.

The Manchester speeches gave rise to the belief which first began to find expression about this time that Balfour was 'drawing away' from Chamberlain.

VI

At Leeds Chamberlain had read out a passage from a letter written by Fielding, the Canadian Finance Minister. He had done so in support of his claim that the Colonies were with him in his campaign. We must probe the origins of this letter.

From the beginning, Chamberlain had sought to extract some gesture of support from the Canadian leaders. We can see his mind on this subject from a letter which he drafted but did not send to Colonel Denison, and which remains among his papers.

CHAMBERLAIN TO DENISON

11 *November* 1903.—. . . I think that the time has now come when the Colonial authorities ought to take some notice of my proposals.

You may have observed that Mr. Asquith has stated again and again that the Colonies do not want Preference, that they have not offered to negotiate, that they will give us nothing of equal value to what we are asked to concede, and that 'they have not responded in any way to my proposals'.

This line of argument has also been taken by Lord Rosebery and by Sir Michael Hicks Beach. It has undoubtedly produced an effect. If it were true I should give up the agitation. But it is not true.

I think the leaders ought to say something definite on the subject. Of course they are not asked to pledge themselves to details, but they know exactly what are the concessions that I propose, and they could at least say that this was in accordance with their own Resolution at the Conference asking the Mother Country to consider the question and that if it were accepted by this country they would be prepared to reciprocate in a generous and not in a huckstering spirit.

I may add that before I spoke they had confined their request to a drawback on the shilling duty. As I am proposing a drawback of 2/-, besides a Preference on Meat and Dairy Produce, I am offering a great deal more than I expected; and if they really wish to see the policy adopted it is almost a necessity that they should say so in words that cannot be misrepresented.

Of course I should like a statement from the leaders of both parties — Sir Wilfrid Laurier and Mr. Fielding on the one side, and Mr. Borden on the other. If a statement could also be made by Mr. Tarte so much the better.

If they agree to do this it might take one of two forms — either a public statement made in Canada or a communication addressed to me through the High Commissioner.

. . . I believe that with proper support I can carry this country with me, but I am powerless if the Colonies do not officially respond.

This letter, as we said, was not sent. It is, however, clear that similar messages from Chamberlain reached Canada through Minto, through Strathcona and through Gilbert Parker who was in regular correspondence with Laurier. What was the Canadian response?

From Chamberlain's point of view, political circumstances in Canada were unfavourable. A General Election was at hand, and Laurier needed the support of Quebec where anti-imperialist sentiment tended 'to read into Preference several things such as contributions to defence — conscription of men to fight England's foreign battles — taking away Fiscal rights and having a general (*i.e.* imperial) Parliament'.[1] For electoral reasons too, Laurier was unwilling to arouse the suspicions of the Protectionist manufacturers in Ontario who feared that a Preference policy pursued by a Liberal Government might take the form of reducing duties in Britain's favour rather than of increasing them against the foreigner. There was also a serious though short-lived disturbance in Anglo-Canadian relations. On 20 October the Alaska boundary award was given against Canada, the British Commissioner voting with the Americans

[1] George E. Foster to J. C., 30 December 1903.

against his Canadian colleagues. 'The Alaska award was bitterly resented throughout the Dominion',[1] and for some months it was out of the question for any political leader of the front rank to give a lead in an Imperial sense.

The following letters, from Minto and from Borden, the leader of the Opposition, give some idea of the attitude of the Canadian leaders in these months.

MINTO TO CHAMBERLAIN

14 December 1903.—. . . Towards the close of the session in response to hints from me that something might be said to express at least goodwill to your proposals, he (*Laurier*) told me that he was averse to a resolution of the House in that direction, but that he intended during the last days of the session to take an opportunity of speaking in that sense, also that Mr. Fielding had drafted a letter to you intended for publication, which he told me was an excellent letter as expressing the views of his government . . . and he has always maintained in conversation with me that he absolutely adheres to the resolutions on Imperial preferential trade adopted at the Colonial Conference. Then just as the session was ending came the Alaska award, and for the moment all other questions disappeared. But I have repeatedly enquired after the fate of Mr. Fielding's open letter to you ; I have asked Fielding himself about it, but getting no decided answer either from him or Sir Wilfrid have come to the conclusion that for some reason it is not to see the light.

. . . I saw Sir Wilfrid yesterday evening and told him that . . . I could not but think, indeed that I had reason for thinking that though you quite understood the difficulties of his position a word of support from him would carry great weight, and that it was not encouraging to you to hear it stated, as I thought you very possibly had, that he was opposed to your proposals. I also again reminded him of Mr. Fielding's letter to you, and of what he had told me of his intention to speak in your support at the end of the session. He replied that he hoped very shortly, in two or three weeks, to speak at Toronto when he should refer distinctly to Canada's position . . . but he said 'after all, our opinions at the Conference were made public [*i.e.* the resolution on Imperial preferential trade] though I know how soon things pass out of the public mind' and then went on to explain what he considers to be Canada's position, in the sense I have indicated to you in former letters — viz. that Canada does not want to appear as a beggar, asking a favour from the Motherland . . . that she does not want to interfere in what is becoming a party fight at home . . . that the matter is one which the Old Country must first settle for itself, and that then Canada will know what to do . . . that Canada believes that preferential trade between the Motherland and herself would be advantageous to both parties but that the former with whom the decision rests must not put herself in the position of making or appearing to make sacrifices for Canada, etc., etc. . . . The above is Sir Wilfred's position as far as I know it. . . .

[1] Minto to J. C., December 1903.

BORDEN TO CHAMBERLAIN

26 September 1904.—. . . In 1903, after you had laid down the seals of office and devoted yourself to this great question I went privately to Sir Wilfrid Laurier and asked him to introduce a resolution of this character and promised him the unanimous support of the Conservative party. My idea was to strengthen your hands in this way. Sir Wilfrid Laurier declined very abruptly and gave as his reason that Canada had no right to interfere in a question which had become a subject of party controversy in the mother country. I pointed out in reply that we would be merely expressing the willingness of Canada to negotiate; and further that Canada had not been backward about interfering in 1900 with respect to matters in South Africa and on more than one occasion with respect to the Home Rule question. I said I would not move a resolution which would be voted down because I did not wish to prejudice the cause in Great Britain, but I said I would at least discuss the subject on motion for Supply. He asked me not to do so but I adhered to my intention. Before I could carry it out, however, the Alaskan Boundary Award was made and public opinion became somewhat excited so that I judged it inexpedient to touch the matter at that time.

Fielding's letter to which Minto had referred duly arrived. It was never published, apart from the one short passage Chamberlain had read out at Leeds. Here is the full text with Chamberlain's reply :

FIELDING AND CHAMBERLAIN

Fielding to J. C.—4 *November* 1903.—I have observed with surprise that some of the writers on the fiscal question now engaging attention in the Mother Country have represented that Canadian public opinion is opposed to the movement in which you have recently taken such a prominent part. I am sure that I am in a position to give such statements a most emphatic contradiction. On the principle of Imperial preferential trade there is practical unanimity in this country. Where dissent from your views is expressed, it is in nearly all cases founded on misconceptions of what the movement contemplates. In one quarter, we hear that your proposals should be condemned because they involve complete Free Trade throughout the Empire, and the consequent ruin of established Canadian industries. In another, we hear that the adoption of your scheme would necessitate the surrender of that constitutional independence which the greater Colonies achieved after many years of agitation. In another, the cry is that the adoption of your views respecting preferential trade would be accompanied by a demand for large colonial contributions for military and naval purposes in which the Colonies would have no voice. But all these, as I well know, are unwarranted and erroneous interpretations of your proposal ; and therefore any conclusions based on them must be set aside.

The Canadian view of the question was very clearly set forth in the papers submitted to the Colonial Conference of 1902, and everything that has occurred since has confirmed what was then said by the Canadian Ministers as a correct expression of the public opinion of this Dominion.

Our fiscal questions are usually discussed in the Canadian Parliament in the Budget debate. In the Budget Speech of this year I reviewed the proceedings of the Colonial Conference and gave prominence to the documents touching the question of preferential trade. It is not too much to say that, while other features of the policy of our Government were criticised, there was practically no dissent from the position taken at the Conference by the Ministers on the trade question. There may be some difference between the two political parties in Canada as to the extent to which they are prepared to go in granting a Preference to the products of the Mother Country. Subject to the need of revision from time to time, consequent upon changing conditions in this young and fast growing country, our Government have been disposed to adhere to the rates and terms of the present Canadian tariff. The Opposition, who are more favourable to high protective duties, have been and are still disposed to insist on higher duties than we now levy on British goods. Neither political party is willing to make the rates of duty under the Preference so low as to imperil existing industries in which are involved interests of capital and labour which could not be disturbed without serious consequences. Both, however, are willing to give a considerable advantage to the British manufacturer over his foreign competitor. Inasmuch as Canada imports largely, that advantage is one of material value. At a time when foreign markets are being closed as far as possible to his wares, can the British manufacturer or his workmen afford to be indifferent to the offer of admission to the rapidly enlarging Colonial markets, not on equal terms with foreigners, but on terms of substantial Preference ?

On one point some of the writers in the British press do injustice to Canada. It appears to be argued that if Canada fails to receive the Preference in the British market which she has sought, she will become less loyal and less devoted to British institutions. No Canadian would be content to have his loyalty measured in that way. Whether the Preference be granted or not, Canada will continue to play her part as one of the most loyal portions of the Empire. She may not be able to continue the Preference which for some years she has given to the products of the Mother Country. Nobody is authorized to say that the Preference will be withdrawn. But there are influences against it that must be reckoned with. Many of the Canadian manufacturers have always viewed it with disfavour, because it admitted of some competition between them and the British manufacturers. Many Members of Parliament have sympathized with the manufacturers' views. Many have contended that the Preference should only exist on reciprocal conditions. Canadian trade has been penalised in some quarters abroad because of the Preference granted to Great Britain. There are foreign countries with which we wish to trade — for we desire a world-wide commerce — which we have reason to believe would be disposed to deal more liberally with us if we would put them on an equal footing with Great Britain in our markets. Other things are occurring to raise questions concerning the Preference. A Government with the strongest desire to maintain the Preference might find these forces too powerful to be resisted. If under such circumstances, the existing Preference should be withdrawn, could our friends in the United Kingdom complain ? We should be sorry to find anybody supporting the preferential movement in Great Britain upon the ground that if no Preference be granted the Colonies will cease to be loyal to the Motherland. But while we say this, may we not be permitted to hold that if the people of the Mother Country can see their way clear to the adoption of a trade system which will give to the chief products of the Colonies a Preference over the products of foreign countries, a new and strong bond of union will be created ?

From the Colonial point of view, it is to be regretted that this great question has become to a large extent one of party politics in the United Kingdom. I feel that it would be unseemly for Colonial Ministers to take an active part in the contest under such circumstances. Our desire is that Canada, her people and her institutions, shall stand well in the eyes of the people of all parties and all classes in the home land. We therefore hesitate to press our views on this question as strongly as otherwise we might. We are free to say what we think is the best policy for Canada. Perhaps we are not so free to urge what we think would be best for the Mother Country. On that part of the question we must acknowledge the right of the people of the United Kingdom to decide for themselves. *But we need not refrain from stating emphatically, in reply to some of the statements which have appeared in the press, that the position taken by the Canadian Ministers at the Colonial Conference last year in favour of Imperial preferential trade is cordially endorsed by both of the great political parties of this country. That some difficulties might arise in the arrangement of the details of so large a scheme is to be anticipated. But surely it is not too much to believe that if the principle be approved the intelligence of British and Colonial public men may be relied on to overcome these and put the project into practical form.*[1]

J. C. to Fielding.—10 *December* 1903.—*Private.*—I received with very great pleasure your letter of November 4 and beg to thank you for it. It is perhaps inevitable that in the discussion of so great and complicated a question as our fiscal system there should be some misunderstanding and misrepresentation, and you are, of course, entirely justified in contradicting the statements to which you refer as having gained currency in some quarters.

It is true that I should like to see a much greater approach to Free Trade throughout the Empire, but I have fully explained my reasons for recognising that this is, at present at any rate, impossible, and that I confine myself therefore to suggesting such mutual Preference as may be given with great advantage both to the Colonies and to this country, and which will in no way interfere with the industrial progress of any part of the Empire.

I have never believed it to be either possible or desirable that there should be the slightest interference with the constitutional independence of the self-governing Colonies, nor have I ever connected my present proposals with the question of Colonial contributions for military and naval purposes. Some day or another I hope we shall be able to work out a

[1] The passage shown in italics is the one read out by Chamberlain at Leeds.

complete system of Imperial defence, and I think I see the way to an arrangement which would be acceptable to the Colonies and which would conduce to our mutual security without diminishing in any way local independence; but that is another question altogether and I have no intention of mixing it up with the fiscal discussion.

I ought perhaps to add that, while I should be opposed to any arrangement which would interfere with the industrial progress of Canada or of any other Colony, I think that an agreement would not be complete or entirely satisfactory to this country if it were absolutely confined to a Preference over the foreigner; but when you were in England we discussed this matter and I think we both came to the conclusion that there were many articles which for years to come would not be the subject of interest to Colonial manufacturers on which the duties might be lowered so as to develop British trade. I understand that you discussed this with the Board of Trade and that although nothing was decided it was mutually agreed that there was room for changes in this direction.

As regards the future I am sanguine that the principles of my proposals will be before long adopted in this country. Meanwhile I have never spoken of Canadian loyalty as if it were dependent on my success. What I do believe is that unless, to use Mr. Rhodes' words, we can invent some practical tie to prevent separation, the Colonies and the Mother Country may in the future drift apart.

Meanwhile I understand that if we are unable to give reciprocal treatment we shall run the risk of losing our present Preference.

The statement of the case contained in the concluding sentences of your letter is quite satisfactory to me, but in view of the extraordinary assertions of some of my opponents that the Colonies are not responding and will not respond to any such Preference as I am seeking to give them, I think the time has come when great good would be done by some more formal declaration on the part of your Government on the main principles at stake. Details must be left to the future, and I for one believe that there will be no difficulty in overcoming them; but my hands would be strengthened by a declaration on the part of Canada that she would gladly meet us on the lines I have laid down with every hope of coming to a mutually advantageous decision.

The last paragraph of Chamberlain's letter evoked no response; and some weeks later we find Chamberlain commenting:

CHAMBERLAIN TO GILBERT PARKER

5 *January* 1904.—. . . Laurier's . . . letter is not satisfactory in tone. I am much disappointed with his action, or rather his inaction. After all he and Fielding said at the conference of Prime Ministers, I think they might have backed me a little more strongly. However it is only one of the difficulties which must attend any great movement.

On the whole we have made more progress during the last year than I could possibly have expected, and if we go on as we have begun we may attain a victory earlier than any of us expected.

Gilbert Parker wrote back defending Laurier and reaffirming his conviction that the Canadian Government would prove perfectly loyal. Chamberlain replied drily :

CHAMBERLAIN TO GILBERT PARKER

22 January 1904.—I am glad that you are sanguine as to the position of the Canadian Government and hope that you are right. I can only say that up to the present they certainly have not given me much useful assistance.

The attitude of the Canadian Government was certainly not heroic. But it was not unnatural. The Liberal party to which the Ministers belonged and the interests which they represented had always been at least lukewarm to the Imperial idea and at times even actively separatist. They regarded Preference as a valuable concession to the Prairie provinces and as a makeweight against the growth of American economic influence. But they had not seen it, as Chamberlain did, as the key to a United Empire. The very vehemence, indeed, of Chamberlain's advocacy of Preference on Imperial grounds tended, if anything, to put them off. Accordingly they waited, hoping for Chamberlain's victory but not prepared to take risks for what they never regarded as a matter of life and death.

Meanwhile an unexpected initiative came from the other end of the Empire. Deakin, the newly elected Australian Premier, telegraphed on behalf of his government inviting Chamberlain to visit Australia.

DEAKIN TO CHAMBERLAIN

30 December 1903.—The Prime Minister of the Commonwealth and his colleagues on behalf of the people of Australia invite you to visit us at the earliest convenient opportunity. We do not overlook the incessant demands made upon your time and strength by public duties in Great Britain, but conceive that this distant continent possesses a title to consideration as one of the intending partners in your proposed agreements for preferential trade. The issue is imperial in every sense. You have powerfully advocated the special advantages of this policy in the chief centres of the Mother Country. The same convincing exposition is desired here. No one could so effectively impress upon our citizens broad views of the beneficial influence of those closer commercial relations which it is your aim to establish between the several parts of the Empire, making for their development and the stability of the whole. You would also acquire personal knowledge of our resources and circumstances that must materially reinforce your policy and promote its practical application in our case. The preferential trade Leagues in course of formation in Sydney and elsewhere would receive an immense impetus from your coming. We, therefore, earnestly urge upon you, as the harbinger of commercial reciprocity between the Mother Country and her Colonies, the acceptance of this invitation, confidently assuring you an unanimous and enthusiastic welcome in all the States of Australia.

Reluctantly Chamberlain declined. He could not leave England till the issue was decided. Besides there was no one to whom he could have delegated the leadership of the Tariff Reform Campaign. It has been, perhaps, a tragedy for the development of the British Commonwealth that the aeroplane was not invented and developed fifty years earlier.

CHAMBERLAIN TO DEAKIN

31 *December* 1903.—Am deeply grateful to you and your Ministers for your flattering invitation and for the assurance you give of a cordial welcome from the people of Australia.

I recognize the advantages and pleasure to myself of such a visit as you suggest, but in this stage of the great campaign for the unity of the Empire, in which I rejoice to have your sympathy and support, I think I can best serve our common cause by devoting myself to its promotion here, where the Motherland is called upon to say what answer she will make to the advances of her children across the seas. I do not doubt she will be ready to meet in no grudging spirit all proposals for strengthening the bonds between us, but until her mandate has been given I cannot leave for a lengthened absence.

At a future time, I hope not far distant, I may be able to avail myself of the invitation so generously given ; and meanwhile, I accept it as a great encouragement and as evidence that the Commonwealth of Australia is not indifferent to the duty cast on all of us, in the present condition of the World, to weld together the Empire which is our common heritage — won for us by the sacrifices of our fore-fathers and only to be maintained by the devotion of their descendants to the same ideal.

For the public at large, these telegrams and the extract from Fielding's letter provided convincing proof that in this at least the Free Traders were wrong. The Colonies were solidly behind Joe.

We may close this section with an extract from a letter of Chamberlain's written not long before the Leeds meeting. It is, perhaps, the clearest statement he ever made of what he regarded as the next step after preference.

CHAMBERLAIN TO GIFFEN

4 *December* 1903.—. . . The further I go in the matter the more I recognise the difficulty of arguing from figures alone, and the more I am inclined to depend upon certain great principles which affect human action and national policy.

My ideal is a united Empire with some sort of Federal Council. We may possibly never be able to accomplish this result, but we ought to try in every conceivable way.

When we get any kind of commercial bond we should probably start with a Council to consider from time to time all the points connected with it. Beginning with commercial matters we might refer other questions to the same or a similar body, and ultimately rise by slow degrees to a full Imperial Council.

Those who have made up their minds that this is impossible, or who are unwilling to take any risk or to make the slightest sacrifice to secure it, must I suppose continue to oppose me, but in that case I am convinced that slowly but surely the Empire will become a dream and we shall have to accept our position as one of the inferior states of the world.

VII

At Leeds Chamberlain had made a major announcement :

. . . We are told that we cannot make a scientific tariff. . . . Now we are going to try to do it. I am going to make a proposal of some importance, as I think it will prove in the future . . . under the auspices of the Tariff Reform League. . . . We are going to form . . . a commission — not a political commission, but a non-political commission — of experts — to consider the conditions of our trade and the remedies which are to be found for it. This commission will comprise leading representatives of every principal industry, and of every group of industries, representative of the trade of India and the Crown Colonies and the great self-governing Colonies. It will invite before it witnesses from every trade, and it will endeavour, after hearing all that can be said, not merely in regard to the special interests of any particular trade but also in regard to the interests of all the other trades which may be in any sense related to it — it is going after that to frame a model tariff.

The origins of this Tariff Commission deserve our attention. In his speech at Tynemouth, Chamberlain had explained that the precise structure of his proposed tariff would depend on the outcome of consultations with the British industries concerned and of bilateral negotiations with the Colonies and with foreign countries. The prospect of such a series of consultations and negotiations consoled many Free Traders. Chamberlain might secure a mandate for his policy ; but there would be endless opportunities for obstruction and delay before it could be put into practice. The Government departments were quite unprepared for so great a business as the framing of a Tariff. Differences would develop between industries, between officials, perhaps even between Ministers. At least a year, possibly two or three, would pass before a scheme could even be submitted to the House of Commons.   Here again the opportunities for amendment and diversion would be endless.   Meanwhile the new policy would have lost its *élan*.   Other issues would have arisen.   It might even be too late to apply a Tariff before another General Election had taken place.   Hewins was impressed by the danger which these possibilities presented to the cause of Tariff Reform.   He discussed them with Caillard and Pearson on the night of 2 November and stressed that the framing of the tariff must be a long business.

Pearson went to Highbury two days later for the Bingley Hall speech.   Afterwards he and Chamberlain sat up late discussing the problem to which Hewins had drawn their attention.   Chamberlain realised at once that he could not afford to wait till his policy was accepted.   He would set up an unofficial Tariff Commission at once.   Given members of sufficient prestige and the necessary finance, such a commission could command all the information necessary to frame a detailed tariff.   Chamberlain would thus have a cut and dried scheme to present to Parliament as soon as there was a mandate for the new policy.

The decision was taken there and then.   Next day Pearson invited Hewins to become secretary of the proposed Commission.   He agreed at once and drafted his own terms of reference as follows :

It should be clearly understood that the aim of the Committee is to work out in detail the first draft of a practicable scheme.

The outline already submitted to the country by Mr. Chamberlain should be taken as the basis of the inquiry.   This supplies perfectly definite points upon which the various trades can be consulted.

Invitations to serve on the Committee should, if possible, be signed by Mr. Chamberlain, or at any rate issued in his name.

The Committee would be far too large if it included representatives of all even of the important trades.   But it should be as far as possible National, or rather Imperial in character.

It is of the greatest importance that representatives of Colonial interests should be included.

The inquiry should proceed by trades, not by commodities.

The trades should be grouped as far as possible in the order of their organisation ; schedules of the commodities which will be affected should be worked out for each complete group ; and the effect, cumulative and in detail, of the suggested duties can be examined.

All trades, if possible, should be examined.

Much relevant information which must be abstracted and considered by the Committee is contained in British and foreign official reports, economic works, trade journals and reports.

Evidence must further be obtained by the issue of properly constructed forms of inquiry.

The construction of such forms involves some preliminary examination of the trade and interest concerned and consultation with experts.

In this connection it is of the greatest importance that all the members of the committee should be acquainted with the technical features of different trades and businesses.

Wherever there is a trade organisation it should be consulted and its co-operation invited.

Witnesses should represent such authoritative organisations and typical firms.

On certain points valuable evidence can be given by trade unions, co-operative societies, etc.

Evidence should be obtained both for and against the proposed policy.[1]

Chamberlain accepted Hewins' proposal 'without any important modification',[2] and the formation of the Commission began. Invitations to join were issued over Chamberlain's signature as follows:

The enclosed memorandum develops in some detail a scheme which I have suggested to Mr. Pearson, the Chairman of the Executive Committee of the Tariff Reform League.

I attach the utmost importance to the investigation which I desire shall be set on foot. It will enable us to show how the principles of the League may be put into practical operation with the least disturbance of trade and the greatest advantage to our Home and Colonial industries.

In no other way can we check our proposals by the opinions of experts representing all the varied industries concerned, and thus be in a position to propose a final scheme in which all these interests will have been taken into account.

I shall be very glad if you can give the necessary time and are willing to serve on this Commission as one of the representatives of the . . . industry.

Pearson had suggested that Leverton Harris should be Chairman; but Chamberlain's choice fell on Sir Robert Herbert, a former permanent under-secretary at the Colonial Office. Others who accepted membership included: Sir George Ryder, who had just resigned from the Chairmanship of the Customs Board: Sir John Cockburn, a former Prime Minister of S. Australia; Sir Alfred Jones, the shipping magnate, and Charles Booth, the well-known social worker.[3]

[1] See *Apologia of an Imperialist*, by W. A. S. Hewins, vol. i, p. 75.   [2] *Ibid.*
[3] The full membership of the Tariff Commission was as follows:
Colonel Charles Allen, Mr. Frederick Baynes, Mr. J. Henry Birchenough, Mr. Charles Booth, Mr. Henry Bostock, Mr. S. B. Boulton, Mr. Richard Burbidge, Sir Vincent Caillard, Mr. J. J. Candlish, Mr. Chaplin, M.P., Sir John A. Cockburn, Mr. J. Howard Colls, Mr. J. G. Colmer, C.M.G., Mr. William Cooper, Mr. J. Arthur Corah (Leicester), Mr. J. W. Dennis, Mr. Charles Eckersley, Mr. Francis Elgar, Sir Charles Elliott, Mr. Lewis Evans, Mr. George Flett, Mr. Thomas Gallaher, Mr. Vicary Gibbs, M.P., Mr. Alfred Gilbey, Mr. W. J. Goulding (Dublin), Mr. W. H. Grenfell, M.P., Mr. F. Leverton

The adherence of Charles Booth was obtained by Hewins.[1]   It was a great strength to Chamberlain, for Booth's prestige was immense, particularly in Labour and 'progressive' circles.   He had devoted years of his life and thousands of his own money to social reform and his support of Chamberlain was an earnest that Tariff Reform was not directed against the interests of the Working Class. We see something of the stir which Booth's decision caused in the following diary note made by Mrs. Sidney Webb:

> 20 *December.*—The effect created by the accession of Charles Booth to the protectionist ranks proves what power, nowadays, is wielded by a non-party expert who is free to throw himself on one side or the other, and who is widely known to be personally disinterested, if not, indeed, philan-thropic in his ends.   Intrinsically, I do not attach much importance to C.B.'s opinion on the fiscal question — he has no special knowledge, a great deal of prejudice, and by no means any marked capacity for intricate reasoning.   But for the world at large his credentials are 17 volumes, a public life of 30 years' service, and a great expenditure of private means for public objects.   A platform which even a more powerful politician might well envy.   Such a position is the sort of thing I aim at for Sidney.[2]

Chamberlain was probably justified in describing his commission as 'the most wonderful representation of British industry that has ever been brought together'.[3]   It was equally strong on the Imperial side.   Agriculture was less well represented; inevitably, perhaps, for the farmers were far less organised in those days than they are today, and the very diversity of British agriculture made it difficult to find a single spokesman for their different interests.   To overcome this weakness, it was decided to appoint a special subcommittee on which the different agricultural interests could all be represented.   Another criticism was that there was no Labour representation on the Com-mission.   By modern standards this might seem a grave omission; but we must remember the circumstances of the time.   The Trades Union Congress and the Labour party had declared against any

Harris, M.P., Mr. J. Mitchell Harris, Mr. W. Harrison, Sir Alexander Henderson, M.P., Sir Robert Herbert (chairman), Sir Alfred Hickman, M.P., Sir Alfred L. Jones, Mr. Arthur Keen, Mr. J. J. Keswick, Sir W. T. Lewis, Mr. I. Levinstein, Mr. Robert Little-john, Mr. Charles Lyle, Mr. A. W. Maconochie, M.P., Mr. Henry D. Marshall, Mr. W. H. Mitchell, Mr. Alfred Mosely, C.M.G., Sir Andrew Noble, the Hon. Charles Parsons, Sir Walter Peace, Mr. C. Arthur Pearson, Sir Westby Perceval, Mr. C. J. Phillips, Mr. Joseph Rank (Hull), Mr. R. H. Reade (Belfast), Sir George Ryder, Sir C. Clementi Smith, Sir Charles Tennant, Mr. Francis Tonsley, Sir John Turney, Mr. S. J. Waring, jun., and Mr. W. Bridges Webb.   The secretary Mr. W. A. S. Hewins, and the assistant secretary, Mr. Percy A. Hurd.

[1] See *Apologia of an Imperialist*, by W. A. S. Hewins, vol. i, p. 78.
[2] *Our Partnership*, ch. vi, p. 279.   [3] J. C. to Lady Jeune, 30 December 1903.

change in the Fiscal system. Chamberlain, therefore, could hardly turn to them. He could, no doubt, have secured one or two dissi-dent Labour leaders but they would have added little to the work of what was primarily a technical and not a propagandist body. He preferred, therefore, to rely on the presence of social workers like Booth as a pledge that the interests of all classes would be truly considered.

The Commissioners had been chosen. The next step was to raise the funds to cover what must prove considerable working expenses. Pearson accordingly gave a dinner on 14 January. The following note by Sir Harry Brittain, then Pearson's personal assistant, shows what passed.

There had been several little discussions between Joseph Chamberlain and Sir Arthur Pearson, at which I was present, as to the question of ways and means.

The suggestion was made that a dinner might be the most effective means of bringing the right people together. I had the details to carry out and, speaking from memory many years afterwards, it was the Hyde Park we settled upon. The very best of menus was evolved together with the choicest wines — in fact the dinner was excellent.

It was arranged that Mr. Chamberlain should make his appeal and should then be followed by two distinguished citizens who were to start the ball rolling with specific amounts, the first being Alfred Beit who promised (I think I am right) £5,000, followed by Sir Alec Henderson (Lord Faringdon) who promised £2,000.

I took round the hat, or rather the Subscription List, and I remember I annexed names and promises up to £27,000 at that comparatively small dinner.

That gathering is what really launched the Tariff Commission on a practical business basis.[1]

The formation of the Commission was received with indignation by the Free Trade leaders. Harcourt described it in private as 'the most revolting thing I ever knew or dreamed of'.[2] *The Standard*, organ of the Unionist Free Traders, attacked it as 'a usurpation of the prerogatives of the crown' and 'an insult to the Prime Minister'.[3] On 15 January Chamberlain addressed the opening meeting of the Commission at the Hotel Metropole. We shall return to its labours at a later stage. Meanwhile the following letter from Caillard gives some idea of the spirit in which the members set about their work.

---

[1] The Chamberlain papers also show that Lord Strathcona sent a cheque for £5000, 8 January 1904.

[2] Harcourt to his son, December 1903, see *Sir William Harcourt* by Gardiner, vol. ii, p. 561.   [3] *The Standard*, 15 January 1904.

CAILLARD TO CHAMBERLAIN

19 *November* 1903.—. . . I shall not only be extremely glad to give the time necessary for service on the Commission which you propose, but . . . I consider it a high honour that you ask me to do so. I believe that the scheme which you have, in general principles, laid before the country, is essential both to the prosperity of the United Kingdom and to the welfare and union of the Empire taken as a whole.

All, therefore, that I can do to assist in working out that scheme in detail, and in carrying it to a successful issue I will do, I promise you, with all my might. It is my dearest hope that you should succeed.

VIII

The first tariff campaign now drew towards its climax and close. The Protectionist Press maintained an atmosphere of triumph, though a few clouds were gathering on the horizon. The Liberals had greatly increased their majority at the Ashburton by-election. On 15 January they captured Norwich from the Government. The Trade Returns for 1903 were now published. They revealed a quite unexpected upswing from the depression and seemed to belie Chamberlain's warnings. Meanwhile, Parliament would soon be meeting; and still there was no response from Balfour.

For all that, the preparations for the final speech went forward in a blaze of publicity. Intense interest was aroused and, for the first time in British history, arrangements were made to bring the speech almost simultaneously to a wider audience. The Guildhall was linked by electrophone to the People's Palace in the East End of London and to the Queen's Hall in the West End. Skilled shorthand writers would take down the speech at the Guildhall and phone it through section by section to the other halls. There it would be retranscribed and handed up to the platform to be declaimed before packed audiences by a well-known actor.

On 19 January Chamberlain drove with Mrs. Chamberlain to the Guildhall. It was his third speech in two years 'within those gray, historic walls'. It had rained all morning and the mud was ankle deep; but they were escorted by members of the Stock Exchange who marched in front of the carriage singing patriotic songs.

The hall was packed. The platform down one side held the few ladies who were present (including Lady Dorothy Nevill, who must be in the eighties, and the Baroness Burdett Coutts, who is ninety-one) and the notabilities, and in front were the seats arranged diagonally. All the rest of the space was filled with men standing. . . . After the Lord Mayor had proceeded into the Hall, and the Mace and Sword and he were duly in their places, Joe and I went in with members of the Committee. He had a great reception, both on his arrival and when he rose to speak, and even I was satisfied.[1]

Chamberlain first addressed himself to the Free Trade argument that any interference with Free Imports would injure the City as the centre of World Finance.

What are the arguments that I have addressed to my fellow-countrymen elsewhere, and which I am told will be inappropriate in this ancient hall ? I have pointed out that 50 years ago we altered our national policy, with a definite purpose, in order to secure free exchange with all the nations of the world. But we do not possess free exchange. (*Hear, hear.*) We have never had it. (*Hear, hear.*) We have free imports instead. . . . I have pointed out that . . . competition with our trades and manufactures has increased, is increasing, and that it has altered its character to our disadvantage. . . . Then I have urged that the future of this country as a country of production, as the creator of new wealth, and not merely the hoarder of invested securities . . . depends mainly on the continuance of its position as the centre and head of the Empire. . . .

But then I am told that this does not affect the City ('*Oh,*' *and laughter*) — that the City is the greatest distributive agency in the world, that whether it distributes home goods or foreign goods matters not to the City as long as they pay their toll and commissions. I am told that whether the goods which you handle have given employment to your own countrymen or to foreigners matters not to you. ('*Oh*') London is cosmopolitan. The City has nothing to do with patriotism. ('*Oh*') Yes, but that is the consequence of the argument. . . . Then, again, it is said that the City is the centre of the world's finance, that the fate of our manufacturers therefore is a question of secondary consideration ; that, provided that the City of London remains, as it is at present, the clearing-house of the world, any other nation may be its workshop. . . .

Now I ask you, gentlemen, whether — putting patriotism altogether on one side — that is not a very short-sighted view of your personal interests. (*Hear, hear.*) Granted that you are the clearing-house of the world, are you entirely beyond anxiety as to the permanence of your great position ? Are you as certain as, perhaps, a generation ago you might have been that your command of the financial world is as unassailable as it ever was ? . . . Is there any one among you, is there any one who knows anything about trade and commerce, or about the position of this City, who will seriously maintain that either its financial or its distributive position is a thing which stands alone, isolated from the condition of the rest of the country, independent of all the influences which affect the rest of the country ? Do you think it can support itself ? Do you suppose that it could be maintained in the face of any serious falling off in the industries of the country — in the face of any great change in

---

[1] Mrs. Chamberlain to her mother, 22 January 1904.

the comparative position of this country as compared with other nations, or any great change in its character. . . .

You are the clearing-house of the world. Why? Why is banking prosperous among you? Why is a bill of exchange on London the standard currency of all commercial transactions? (*A voice*, '*Free imports*.') Is it not because of the productive energy and capacity which is behind it? Is it not because we have hitherto, at any rate, been constantly creating new wealth? Is it not because of the multiplicity, the variety, and the extent of our transactions? If any one of these things suffers even a check, do you suppose that you will not feel it? Do you imagine that you can in that case sustain the position of which you are justly proud? Suppose — if such a supposition is permissible — you no longer had the relations which you have at present with our great Colonies and dependencies, with India, with the neutral countries of the world, would you then be its clearing-house? No, gentlemen. At least we can recognize this — that the prosperity of London is intimately connected with the prosperity and greatness of the Empire of which it is the centre. (*Cheers*.) . . . Banking is not the creator of our prosperity, but is the creation of it. It is not the cause of our wealth, but it is the consequence of our wealth ; and if the industrial energy and development which has been going on for so many years in this country were to be hindered or relaxed, then finance, and all that finance means, will follow trade to the countries which are more successful than ourselves.

He turned next to Campbell-Bannerman's claim[1] that the Trade Returns had knocked the bottom out of his case.

'Why cannot you let well alone?' (*Laughter*.)

This argument, which all reformers have to meet has been, in the opinion of the gentlemen who differ from me, triumphantly clinched and confirmed in the last week or so by the publication of figures by the Board of Trade which have shown an increase in the year 1903 in our imports and our exports. Yes, it is quite true that there has been a small increase in our exports and a large increase in our imports (*laughter*) ; and that, taken alone, I should be myself inclined to accept with satisfaction. But when a gentleman of distinction in politics like the leader of the Opposition (*voices* — '*Which one?*' '*Name*', *and laughter*) declares that these new figures entirely destroy and level to the ground the scaffolding which I have attempted to raise, I wonder how a man who is presumably sincere, who is presumably intelligent (*laughter*), can so entirely misrepresent and misunderstand the arguments of his opponents. Does he really think that I am disconcerted by those figures, which I have foreseen in the monthly returns ever since I began my mission? On the contrary I accept them with the greatest pleasure as the starting point for my future argument. I will take these figures as a basis and go into every town of the kingdom, if I am permitted to go there, and I will show that by comparing them with the figures of ten years ago, of 20 years ago, or of 30 years ago you will find exactly the same signs and tendencies to which I have called

[1] Speech at Maidstone, 13 January 1904.

THROUGH THE BIRMINGHAM LOOKING-GLASS
Off to Glasgow
'All my own invention'

6 October 1903

H. Chaplin

W. A. S. Hewins

Lord Selborne

George Wyndham

attention, and upon which I have based the whole of the argument which I have addressed to my countrymen. You will find, in the first place that there has been a decrease in the export of our manufactures to the foreign protected countries. Any one outside an asylum could have told you, not only that that was the case, but that it must be the case . . . the second point is that this decrease of the exportation of our manufactures to these foreign protected countries has been concealed hitherto and compensated by the increase of our exports of manufactures to our own countrymen in our own possessions. (*Cheers.*) And in connexion with this there is a point which fills me with alarm. As long as that continues, I do not know that we shall have much cause of complaint. If everything we lose with the foreigner we gain from our children I for one would be perfectly satisfied. But the point to which I call your attention, and which you will find emphasized in the figures for 1903, is that in our own possessions, in our own Colonies, there is a growth of foreign importation which in proportion greatly exceeds the growth of the exportation from the home country. (*Hear, hear.*) We are not even safe in our own Empire. . . . Meanwhile . . . the countries which are closing their markets to us, the countries which are burdened, according to the free importers, with a heavy tariff, in which, therefore, the cost of production must necessarily go up — who, therefore, are in a bad position to compete with us — they are doing more and more with us while we are doing less and less with them. (*Hear, hear.*) . . .

What are the conclusions which I say any impartial man must derive from these facts ? In the first place . . . he must see that, in order to maintain our position as a manufacturing nation, we must increase, or at any rate, maintain . . . the trade with the Empire, the trade with our own countries. (*Cheers.*) In those circumstances is it not our first duty to ourselves, to our own interests — to speak of no higher reason — to do everything in our power to encourage and develop this trade ? (*Cheers.*) Then, what is the second conclusion ? Unless we change our policy our foreign trade . . . will disappear. It has decreased in the last generation, the tendency continues, and there can be only one end. We want to deal with these great nations on better terms. (*Hear, hear.*) It is no use appealing to their mercies; they consider, and rightly consider, their own interests first. (*Cheers.*) They will give us nothing unless we have something to give in return. Again I say that it is our first duty — if we want to keep the variety of our trade — not merely to have Imperial trade, but foreign trade as well — to put ourselves, and to put ourselves immediately, into a position in which we can bargain and negotiate with those countries on equal terms . . . My opponents — seem to me to be intellectually shortsighted. They cannot see beyond their noses (*laughter*); and throughout this controversy they have failed to seize what I believe is the essential thing to keep in mind — namely, that the greatness of a nation is not to be measured by a comparison with its own past, but by its relative position in the councils of the world. (*Cheers.*) Will you consider this for a moment ? Will you again consult the teachings of history ? We are richer — there is no doubt that we are richer than we were ten years ago, or 50 years ago. That is undoubted. . . . Yes, but what of other

T

LIFE OF JOSEPH CHAMBERLAIN

nations? Take the case of Spain. I think in the case of Spain, and I am certain in the case of Holland, that there is more acquired wealth in these countries to-day than there was in the palmiest times of their history; but that is all: In spite of the growth of their wealth they have fallen from their high estate. The sceptre they once wielded so proudly has passed into other hands and can never return to them. (*Hear, hear.*) They may be richer, but they are poorer in what constitutes the greatness of a nation, and they count for nothing in the future opinion of the world. Is it wished that we should follow in the same lines? ('*No, no.*') But of what are we proud? Of our wealth? I think that is a contemptible form of pride. (*Cheers.*) Are we proud of our power? Are we proud of the use we may make of that power in order to influence the civilization of the world? Do we desire to be, as we have been in the past, one of the greatest of nations? Do we wish our voice to be heard in Europe? (*Cheers.*) Then, if so, do not let us be misled by those who would teach us that we can afford to stand where we are and yet wallow in comparative luxury that may, indeed, be greater than any we have enjoyed before.

. . . Now, there is something else in these figures. I have not done with them yet. Although they are no test of our comparative position, they might be — one might presume they would be — a test of our actual position. We sent out more goods last year than we ever did before. We ought, therefore, to be more prosperous. Are we? Here is a significant fact that cannot be got over — an official fact from the same Board of Trade which has given us the figures and statistics I am considering. During the year 1903 there has been a constant falling-off in employment in our greater trades, which are the subject of the statistics of the Board of Trade. In those trades the number of persons unemployed has increased by 40 per cent. as compared with a year or two ago. Well, is that a sign of prosperity? . . . Wages have been reduced. You have only to read the papers to see almost daily some trade or another has to submit to a reduction. That, then, is not a proof of boundless prosperity. It is a proof of comparative decline, and, in my judgment, the writing is on the wall, there to be read by every impartial man.

His peroration was a worthy finale to his great campaign.

. . . There only remains to speak of another branch of this great policy, the branch nearer to my heart, more important to you, and to this country more urgent than anything else. I ask myself, 'Do my opponents, does any one really believe that our present relations with our possessions abroad can permanently endure?' Is it not certain that we and they must draw closer or we shall inevitably fall apart? Is it possible my opponents are not alive to the tremendous consequences of either alternative? What is it? Are we to be an empire or are we to be only a kingdom? The great Napoleon said that 'Providence was always on the side of the big battalions.' Do you suppose that is not the same with countries as with armies? The struggle for life, the struggle for existence in future will not be between cities or even between kingdoms. It will be between mighty empires; and the minor States will come off badly if they are left to be crushed between the gigantic bulk of these higher organizations.

Our opponents see this truth dimly, because when we come to talk of the prosperity of America and Germany they say, 'Yes, that is natural. Are they not greater than us, are they not more numerous ?' Then, in a sort of despairing fatalism they seem to say, 'What can our little England do but fall a victim to the inexorable decrees of fate ?' I am not impressed by their pessimism. I refuse to despair of my country. Are not we also an empire ? Are we not as great in area and as great in population, greater in the variety of our products and opportunities than any empire that exists or that the world has ever seen ? Yes ; but our union is incomplete, and the question which to me is everything is : 'Will it attain to a higher organization ?' It is impossible that it can remain the same : it must either shrink or it must develop. Our greatest thinkers and writers put this problem clearly before us — Seely, Froude, Lecky. They also dreamed dreams and saw visions of a united Empire finding its salvation in new forces of attraction capable of counteracting the centrifugal tendencies of its present composition. Yes, and now is the time, now is the opportunity for us to do our part. What is the historical progression in the evolution of empire ? First a kingdom slowly consolidating itself, growing conscious of its strength, utilizing its surplus energy to conquer new worlds. Then there comes a time when the empire has been attained. Those who had the courage to gain it unfortunately had not the wisdom and experience which would enable them to keep it intact. They lost the greatest jewel that the British Crown has ever possessed. The United States left us for a separate existence. We profited by that experience. Again a new Empire rises from the ashes of the old, and once more at the end of the 19th century we have a dominion greater than any before. We have the dominion ; but the problem is not yet solved how to keep the heritage which is given to us, how to make it permanent, how to give it strength. In the last 50 years we have been groping for our destiny. We have been gradually becoming more conscious of our duty and of our Imperial responsibility. But it remains to the statesmen of the 20th century, to those now living and to those yet to come, to complete this great work, the greatest that has ever fallen to a governing race to perform. We have to apply the lessons of the past ; we have to build up the framework for the new Empire under the new conditions ; we have to conciliate local and Imperial interests ; we have to create new bonds of union. We ought to succeed. We have been tested in the past ; we have had hard tasks given us to do. We have done them ; those who have preceded us have done them ; we have the like spirit, the like courage, the like resolution, and we shall also do our share of the work. Is there anything against us ? Yes ; it is that we have still a too provincial, perhaps I should say, a too insular spirit. In the great revolution which separated the United States from Great Britain the greatest man that that revolution produced, according to my judgment, was Alexander Hamilton. He was soldier and statesman, and he left a precious legacy to his countrymen when he disclosed to them the secrets of union and when he said to them, 'Learn to think continentally.' And, my fellow-citizens, if I may venture to give you a message now I would say to you, 'Learn to think Imperially'. I ask from you no ruinous sacrifice. I ask you to be worthy of your past ;

I ask you to remember that the future of this country, which we all cherish so much, lies in the future of the British race. The Colonies and possessions — they are the natural buttresses of our Imperial state, and it behoves us to think of them as they are now, in their youth and promise, to think of them also what they will be a century hence when grown to manhood and developing beyond anything we can hope for their motherland. (*Cheers.*) Think of them as they are; think of them as they will be; share and sympathize with their aspirations for a closer union: do nothing to discourage them, but show your willingness to co-operate with them in every effort they make or propose. So, and so only, can you maintain the traditions of the past, the renown of this Imperial City, and the permanence of that potent agency for peace and for civilization that we call the British Empire. (*Loud Cheers.*)

IX

The campaign and all that went with it — committees, interviews, lunches, dinners and long hours spent preparing speeches — left little time for personal life in these months. All the same there are some bright flashes.

Shortly before his resignation the following letter reached him from his old friend Morley.

MORLEY TO CHAMBERLAIN

2 *September* 1903.—In three or four weeks you will find 3 volumes — each as big as the Bible — 'dumped' upon your table. I can easily imagine that if you were compelled to read it, you would rather set up a prohibition duty against the import of this manufactured market. But you can, and will skip.

The Life of Gladstone arrived, appropriately enough, just before Chamberlain started out for Glasgow. We may conjecture that he studied carefully the account of the Midlothian campaign.

Chamberlain's comments on the life are missing. His letter to Morley, however, must have touched old chords. It drew the following reply.

MORLEY TO CHAMBERLAIN

15 *October* 1903.—Your kind and cordial letter gives me most lively pleasure. None goes more to my inmost being, and I am much obliged to you. Thirty years since our fraternal relations opened under a star that seemed bright enough; it has been sometimes clouded but there is still a silver twinkle in it.

I wish you would take up some policy that I could agree with before I die?

We've taken a new house, to make believe that all our life is before us. I'm very sorry about your gout, and hope it will soon vanish.

Chamberlain's friendship with Morley was if anything strengthened in these last years. They saw each other more often, now that Chamberlain had left office.

In other quarters, however, the tariff campaign aroused as much personal bitterness as the unauthorised programme had done in its day.

CAMPBELL-BANNERMAN TO BRYCE

31 *December* 1903.—Is it not extraordinary how J. C. always plays up to the vulgarity and cupidity and other ignoble passions. Equally when he talks of ransom, when he promises acres and cows and pensions, when he annexes goldfields, when he bullies Kruger, when he Mafficks, when he promises preferences and tariffs and work. It is always the same ; and he uses the foolishness of the fool and the vices of the vicious to overwhelm the sane and wise and sober.

What a cheerful thought for New Year's Eve!

X

Leaving the Colonial Office was a wrench. The senior staff presented him with his old office inkstand suitably embellished, and the office as a whole entertained him to dinner.[1] 'The thought of it stirred him more than he would be willing to admit — for I could see it was on his mind for some days.'[2]

The whole pattern of his life was now transformed. The routine of the Office, Cabinets, and official interviews had become second nature. Now all that ceased. No more boxes came with the Foreign Office telegrams. Access to official information ceased. The service of a great department of State was no longer his to command. The variety went out of his life ; and though in some ways he had now less work to do, he had to supervise the details personally as never before. The flow of correspondence and of interviews increased continuously. He was dealing now with voluntary workers not his own officials. They had to be persuaded, encouraged, entertained.

Another major change in his life was Austen's removal to No. 11 Downing Street. Until this time, Austen had shared his father's house at Prince's Gardens. Most evenings they had come back together from the House and sat talking over the day's events and the morrow's plans. When not otherwise engaged they had taken their meals together.

[1] 7 December 1903.   [2] Mrs. Chamberlain to her mother, 7 December 1903.

Austen's letter to his father written the first night he spent in Downing Street is one of the most pleasant pieces in the Chamberlain Papers:

11, DOWNING STREET, WHITEHALL,
S.W.
11.1.4

MY DEAR FATHER,

I cannot close my first evening away from your roof in a house for the time at least my own without writing a line to you. It is so great a change in my life, and all about me is so strange, that as yet I hardly realize it.

But what I do realize is how much I owe to you, and how very dear to me is the close friendship which you have encouraged between us. I do not think there are many fathers who have been and are to their sons all that you have been to me; and my prayer tonight is that the perfect confidence which I have enjoyed for so long may continue unimpaired by our separation, and that I may do something to help you in the great work which you have undertaken.

It is at once a great encouragement and a great responsibility to be heir to so fine a tradition of private honour and public duty, and I will do my best to be not unworthy of the name.

Ever your affectionate son,
AUSTEN CHAMBERLAIN

Chamberlain and Mrs. Chamberlain were frequent visitors at Number 11; and Austen continued to treat Highbury as his home. But it could not be the same. Austen's position was not easy, and, with the best will in the world, he must sometimes have felt a conflict of loyalties between his father and his colleagues in the Government.

We may close this chapter with a glimpse of Chamberlain's mood, written as the year draws to a close.

CHAMBERLAIN TO COLLINGS

30 *December* 1903.—May all that is good attend you and yours in the New Year and in this wish Mary joins with me most sincerely.

What a year it has been! I do not think I could stand very many more like it — but then I am not likely to have the chance.

I am very well, but I want a holiday. The pressure is very heavy. I expect you are in the same position. Why is there so much work in the world to do and so few men to do it?

THE SESSION OF 1904

(*January–June* 1904)

Assessment of the First Campaign — Chamberlain Favours an Early Election —
He Strains his Heart — Death of Powell Williams : a Bodyblow — A Holiday
in Egypt and Italy — The Tariff Reformers Force the Withdrawal of the
Wharton Amendment — Chamberlain and Balfour Meet — Chamberlain
Looks to the Election after next — Churchill Crosses the Floor — Chinese
Labour — A Birthday Dinner — Struggle to Control the Liberal Unionist
Association — The Rift with Devonshire — Chamberlain Gains Control —
Negotiations with Lansdowne — The Albert Hall Demonstration — Kipling's
Verdict.

I

THE first campaign was over. We must now seek to assess its results.
Chamberlain had left the Government to be free to preach the full
programme of Tariff Reform and Imperial Preference. Balfour on
his side had given Chamberlain to understand that he would adopt
the new policy as soon as public opinion had been educated to
accept it. How far had the work of education gone? No precise
answer is possible. But there are three things to be asked about
any political campaign. Does it hold the interest of the public?
Does it arouse the enthusiasm of its supporters? Can it command
a majority among those to whom it is addressed? We may apply
these rough but practical tests to Chamberlain's campaign.

On the first count, there can be no doubt as to the answer.
Chamberlain's own performance and the counterthrusts of his
opponents had ensured the 'box-office' success of the campaign.
For three months or more, the leader of 'Imperialism' had carried
the fight single-handed up and down the country. The evasions
of Ministers only underlined his own power of leadership. The
array of great names who came out to do battle with him — among
them one former Prime Minister and four ex-Chancellors of the
Exchequer — increased his own stature. For three months, all the
lights had been turned on to this one man and all the talk had
been about his policy. He had held the country's attention to the

exclusion of any other topic. As Harmsworth's *Daily Mail* declared :
'In politics and the whole realm of national affairs it has been
Mr. Chamberlain's year.' [1]

How far had he won support for the new policy ? Here again
we may speak with some assurance. He had rescued Unionism
from the doldrums, endowed it with a programme and regained the
political initiative. His programme had won the enthusiastic support
of most of the local Conservative and Liberal Unionist Associations.
It had also rallied to the Unionist cause a number of men who had
never thought of taking an active part in Unionist politics before.
Beyond this, Chamberlain had created, with Pearson's help and
Harmsworth's, the most powerful propaganda machine ever seen
in British politics.

Was all this enough to win an election ? Here the answer is
much harder to give. The most that can be said is this. Had
Balfour, in his speech at Manchester on 11 January, declared for
the Chamberlain policy ; had he added the authority of the Government and weight of the official party machine to the enthusiasm
Chamberlain had aroused ; had he freed the other Unionist leaders
to join in the campaign ; and had he then gone to the country in
February immediately after meeting Parliament or without meeting
it at all — then there is at least a chance that the Unionists might
have prevailed a third time. Haldane and other Liberal and Free
Food leaders feared this at the time. And Chamberlain, looking back
some months later would write : 'We might have won if Balfour
had been able to go the "whole hog" last autumn.' [2]

For our part, we are inclined to doubt whether anything could
have brought about a Unionist victory at this time. The passions
aroused by the Education Act, the general reaction against Imperialism that followed the Boer War, the trade depression, and the
almost certain loss of a score or more of Unionist 'Free Food'
seats — all these things must have been enough, given the natural
swing of the pendulum, to bring the Liberals in. But the Unionists
would have been in a very strong position. They would have been
united in support of a clear and popular policy. They would have
had a strong representation in the House of Commons as well as
control of the House of Lords. The Liberals, by contrast, would
have been in a very weak position. They would scarcely have had
time to settle their personal feuds let alone to unite on a programme

[1] *Daily Mail*, 31 December 1903.
[2] Chamberlain to Northcote, 25 December 1904.

of legislation. They could only have governed with the help of the Irish vote. At any time, the House of Lords might have forced another election on them. Such a Liberal Government could scarcely have been more than a transient phantom; and the Unionist reign might then have been prolonged into the next decade with immeasurable possibilities for good or ill in a world that was stumbling towards catastrophe.

Chamberlain seems to have discussed the merits of an early election with his friends. Certainly Campbell-Bannerman would write at this time 'you have heard the story of Joe advising a friend to be prepared for a general election in January! But how is it possible? What excuse is there?'[1]

There is nothing in the Chamberlain Papers to show whether the issue was ever squarely put to Balfour. There was no meeting between him and Chamberlain before the House met. Nor do any letters seem to have passed between them. Austen must have acted to some extent as an intermediary. But he lacked authority with Balfour. Besides, though the most loyal of men, the new Chancellor of the Exchequer can hardly have been enthusiastic for a dissolution before his first Budget. The probability is that the idea of an early election was discussed at Highbury but never pressed. Chamberlain's physical weariness from the campaign and Austen's career all argued the other way. And yet, here was perhaps the last real opportunity to carry the Tariff Reform policy and to save Unionism. This indeed was 'the tide in the affairs of men' for Chamberlain and for Balfour. There is nothing to show that either of them so much as guessed the measure of the moment.

The chief responsibility must attach to Balfour. Chamberlain had played his part and played it brilliantly. It was for Balfour, both as Prime Minister and as the Conservative leader, to play his. But Balfour was curiously detached from the main political currents. He always claimed to be the trustee for his party; but in fact his grasp of party interest was weak. When he spoke of 'party unity', as he often did, he meant keeping together the men he knew in Parliament. Not losing Beach or keeping Devonshire tended to be his standard. He never grasped that the real threat to Unionism lay not in the defection of influential leaders but in the defection of the electors. The real threat to Unionism was in the constituencies where new popular forces were gathering. To keep the party together meant to keep these forces behind Unionism. If they once

[1] Campbell-Bannerman to Bigle, 29 December 1903.

T 2

deserted to the Radical camp they would become the most thorough-going opponents of the existing order.

But Balfour did not want an election. There were certain definite things he still wanted to do while he had the power. The Education Act was law but not yet enforced. He was determined that it should be a final solution. He planned a Licensing Bill which would bring an equally lasting settlement of the Temperance question ; and, in this, he succeeded. He believed that Wyndham's Irish Land Settlement Bill would complete his own earlier work as Chief Secretary and place the Union on an enduring foundation. He had just set up the Committee of Imperial Defence and was awaiting the Esher Report on which he hoped to base a reform of the Army. There was the Cawdor programme for the Navy.[1] Above all he was determined to bring the negotiations with Japan and with France to a successful conclusion.

Balfour had no confidence that the Liberal leaders would or could continue his defence and foreign policies. He knew them to be opposed to his domestic measures. He doubted their grasp of the great issues abroad. He, therefore, came to consider his Government as indispensable at least until the things he wanted done had been done. And done they were, though in the process he lost most of the goodwill accumulated by his party over decades.

Where Tariff Reform was concerned Balfour felt no enthusiasm. He saw its possible advantages as a means to the closer unity of the Empire. But he never regarded it, as Chamberlain did, as the indispensable step towards that goal. On the contrary, he was half inclined to believe that his own defence measures might prove more effective in the long run. He was also very conscious of the possible disadvantages of the new policy. He was becoming convinced that Colonial Preferences to Britain would all take the form of increases in the Colonial duty on foreign goods, rather than reductions on British goods. He doubted how much we should gain in practice. He saw Chamberlain tending more and more towards Protection. In all this, he was far more sensitive to the criticism of friends and of the men he knew personally, than to the enthusiasm of the masses he seldom saw.

The personal issue must also be faced. What had been the nature of the compact between Balfour and Chamberlain, when the latter had resigned ? Both men had agreed that Colonial Preference was

---

[1] Admiral Fisher to Balfour, 12 December 19 : 'I hope you will hang on like grim death till the autumn of 1906.'

desirable. Both had agreed that public opinion was not yet ready to accept a tax on food. Both had agreed that Chamberlain should leave the Government to educate the public and that Balfour should support his policy as soon as public opinion had matured to the right point. No attempt, of course, had been made to define what this point should be. Balfour was thus perfectly free to come on or to hold back as he chose. The whole tenor, however, of their correspondence, and Austen's continued presence in the Cabinet all suggested that Balfour would approach the question in a positive spirit. Especially was this so, when Devonshire's resignation had removed the last brake on the Cabinet's freedom of action. It had been Chamberlain's expectation and that of the general public that Balfour would declare for Preference as soon as he reasonably could. In these circumstances there was plainly an obligation on him to consult with Chamberlain before he spoke at Manchester or before he decided to meet the House. We cannot accuse him of deceiving Chamberlain ; but he was certainly not acting in the spirit of their compact.

When Balfour accepted Chamberlain's resignation in September, he may well have been genuine in looking forward to joining forces with Chamberlain once more when public opinion had been sufficiently educated. But the course of Chamberlain's campaign must have raised, on personal grounds, a question mark in his mind. For three months Chamberlain had bestridden England like a colossus. If Balfour now declared for the full policy ; if he joined hands with Chamberlain, if he accepted the support of the Tariff Reform League and the Pearson-Harmsworth press, if he went to the country on Chamberlain's slogans — he would be leader only in name. It may well be that the very success of Chamberlain's campaign — the extent of his personal triumph — made Balfour less inclined than ever to admit it.

II

Balfour's speech at Manchester had been a rebuff to Chamberlain. The latter might have 'educated' the whole strength of Unionism in the constituencies, but it was in vain so long as he had not 'educated' the Prime Minister in whose hands the decision lay. Now, with the meeting of the House, the situation which had seemed so favourable to the Tariff Reformers at the New Year was transformed, greatly to Chamberlain's disadvantage.

The influence of public opinion, in England, is decisive at election time. Between elections it is parliamentary opinion that counts. Once Balfour had taken the decision to meet the House he was a prisoner of parliamentary arithmetic. The Unionists had a majority of about 90 in the House of Commons. The bulk of Unionist members were Fiscal reformers, supporting the Chamberlain and the Balfour policies in roughly equal numbers. There were, however, between 40 and 50 Unionist Free Traders. If these changed sides and voted against the Government, the Unionist majority of 90 would be wiped out. Balfour would be unable to carry on the Government. He would then have either to face the election he did not want or to make way for a combination of Liberals and Unionist Free Traders under Rosebery or Devonshire. The Duke's biographer has expressed doubt whether Devonshire would ever have accepted the lead in such a combination.[1] But the following diary note of Fitzroy's relating a conversation with Balfour's secretary, Sandars, has an authentic ring. It refers to a conversation between the Prime Minister and the Duke early in the New Year:

19 *January*.—... I had an interesting conversation with Sandars; ... the Prime Minister deplores very strongly the line recently taken by the Duke. When the Prime Minister was at Chatsworth he had many talks with his host on the subject; nothing could have been pleasanter than their relations; but the Duke left no doubt in his mind that he was going over to the Opposition, even to the length of being ready to assume the Premiership as a means of uniting discordant forces.[2]

But there were many obstacles in the way of such a combination. Men like James and Goschen, in the Lords, and Churchill, Seely and Poynder in the Commons were quite prepared for what Churchill called 'the reconstitution of the Liberal Party in its old power and integrity'.[3] But the greater part, men like Hicks Beach and George Hamilton, were not prepared to side with Radicals if they could possibly avoid it. We gain some idea of the weakness of the Free Fooders and the inadequacy of their leader from the following letter.

DEVONSHIRE TO LEONARD COURTNEY

3 *January* 1904.—I have a meeting at Liverpool on the 19th and another in the City soon after the meeting of Parliament, and I do not think that I can undertake any more until I see how things are going. Our

[1] Bernard Holland, *Life of the Duke of Devonshire*, vol. ii, p. 332, footnote.
[2] *Memoirs of Sir Almeric Fitzroy*, 19 January 1904, vol. i, p. 180.
[3] Churchill to Devonshire, 6 October 1903.

Free Traders are extraordinarily weak, and I think by that time I may be left almost alone and represent nobody but myself. Strongly as I feel on the subject, I find a great difficulty in speaking about it. It is too big, and my political economy is not strong. What do you think is the best line for a man who does not profess to be a political economist? I am sure that more ought to be made than has been made of the Colonial and Imperial side of the question; but then I do not know much about the Colonies either.[1]

Nor was there any great enthusiasm for a reunion with 'the Whigs' on the Opposition side. Liberal Imperialists like Rosebery and Grey might have welcomed it; but the Radicals saw clearly enough the risk of concessions over Education and Ireland and the postponement of their own plans for winning Labour support. Already before the House met, we find Campbell-Bannerman pouring cold water on overtures from James.

CAMPBELL-BANNERMAN TO HERBERT GLADSTONE

26 *December* 1903.—We are to withdraw candidates wherever our local people will allow it, in order to save the skin of the Free Traders.

In return the Free Traders are most of them to run away or join the enemy on any amendment to the Address.

I fear our people will hardly see it.

James does not seem to recognise that they are in a cleft stick, and that the time comes with the opening of Parliament which will show how many of the 53 are really in earnest and have the courage of their opinions; and when all who take refuge in such shallow devices as these may as well march into Joe's camp at once.

In short, we are under no necessity to go to them, and indeed cannot go to them: it is they who must come to us. This need not be proclaimed, but it is the essence of the situation and cannot be ignored.

A few weeks later (11 February) we find Dilke taking counsel with Lloyd George, Redmond and Ramsay MacDonald to consider the 'risk of the speedy formation of a Whig Administration dominated by the Devonshire influence'.[2]

These hesitations both in the Free Food ranks and among Liberals were Balfour's opportunity. He could not keep all the Free Fooders. But, fortunately for him, the more extreme of the Free Food leaders were in the Lords — Devonshire, Goschen, James. The more moderate — Hicks Beach and George Hamilton — were in the Commons. His aim now became to keep Hicks Beach. If he succeeded, his majority would be safe. He, therefore, pursued much

[1] Gooch, *Life of Lord Courtney*, p. 493.
[2] Gwynn and Tuckwell, *Sir Charles Dilke*, vol. ii, p. 459.

the same tactics as he had followed in the Cabinet crisis. This could only mean one thing: the postponement of a reunion between Balfour and Chamberlain.

Chamberlain was thus left with a difficult hand to play. The campaign in the constituencies was over. He could not force the Government's hand in the House without risking its defeat or a permanent breach with Balfour. He had, therefore, to accept some loss of momentum and to concentrate instead on building up parliamentary support for his movement. For this purpose he must show his loyalty to the Government whenever he could and at the same time gradually push his own ideas to the fore. This would have been hard enough at the best of times. It is one thing to carry out a platform campaign single-handed; quite another to confront the House of Commons alone, with no right of reply. The task was made doubly difficult by personal considerations. At Highbury, Austen's future had become almost as important as Tariff Reform. He was now in line for succession to the Unionist leadership. His first Budget was just ahead.

In the circumstances, Chamberlain judged it best to go away. He would attend the opening of Parliament and deliver his resignation speech in the debate on the Address. He would then go abroad for a much needed holiday, leaving his affairs in Powell Williams' capable hands.

III

The Guildhall speech drew the usual crop of replies from the Free Traders. In the next ten days Morley, Bryce, Campbell-Bannerman, Asquith, Goschen and Hugh Cecil all returned to the charge. This time, however, Chamberlain had rather more support. Austen, Bonar Law and Lyttelton all spoke in his defence. So did the economists Ashley and Cooper. The Tariff Reform Movement also gained a significant new recruit in the Duke of Bedford. The by-elections, however, continued disappointing for the Government; the Liberals holding Gateshead and winning Ayr. There were few tears shed at Highbury over Ayr, for the candidate had taken the strict Sheffield line and refused the support of the Tariff Reform League.

All this time Chamberlain was at Highbury. He was busy with arrangements for the conduct of the Tariff Reform movement while he was away. There was friction between the Birmingham Tariff Committee and the Midland Unionist Association to be ironed out. There were deep differences with Devonshire which we shall presently consider. Then there were local demands.

MRS. CHAMBERLAIN TO HER MOTHER

29 January 1904.—... Yesterday Joe had the Court of the University to preside at — to-morrow a short speech in the Town Hall, at which he is now slaving. This is to acknowledge a tribute from his Constituents, who have put up a clock in West Birmingham to commemorate our visit to South Africa. After the Town Hall we are to drive to it and I am to unveil it. . . .

Last night Mr. Pearson and Mr. Powell Williams were here — and so it goes. Each day with its claims — and it is time we broke loose from it all. . . .

Just before this letter was written Chamberlain had a bad attack of gout and neuralgia. He saw his Birmingham doctor, Ballance, who diagnosed a strained heart. The diagnosis was confirmed in London by Broadbent, the eminent heart specialist.

CHAMBERLAIN TO COLLINGS

9 February 1904. *Private.*—Before I came up to town Ballance examined me and found that I had overdone matters and had got something a little wrong with my heart.

Sir W. Broadbent saw me here, and confirmed Ballance's opinion, but said that if I would take immediate rest I should be perfectly right again.

In fact Broadbent's view was rather more serious than this letter suggests.

BROADBENT TO CHAMBERLAIN

2 February 1904.—While I feel confident of your recovery, when once you are out of the turmoil and under favourable climatic conditions, your heart would not stand indefinite work and strain without change and rest, and I begrudge every day's delay.

Broadbent asked Chamberlain to take four months consecutive holiday. This would have meant being out of action till mid-June. To this Chamberlain would not agree. He would take two months at once and promised to take a further holiday in the autumn. He also agreed to advance his departure from 16 February to 11 February. This should just give him time for one speech on the fiscal question.

Parliament was to meet on 2 February. The night before 'a big party at Lansdowne House took the place of the one which has been held at Devonshire House for years'.[1] The report of the Esher

---

[1] Mrs. Chamberlain to her mother, 6 February 1904.

Committee had been published that morning and Esher was very much the hero of the evening. 'I have seen all the ministers', he wrote two days later (3 February) :

and they said very friendly things, but the warmest congratulations came from Chamberlain, whom I met at Lansdowne House. He shook hands very warmly and said : 'It very seldom falls to the lot of any man to be able to do such good service for his country.' This is a phrase I can never forget.[1]

The sensation of the evening, however, was the news that Balfour had been taken ill just before his official dinner to Ministers. He would not be able to go to the House next day, and so it fell to Austen to speak for the Government. Austen was in a difficult position as he had to be loyal both to his father and to the Prime Minister. His speech was a fitting start to what would soon be known as 'the dismal session of 1904'.

3 February.—The selection of Austen Chamberlain to represent the Government yesterday afternoon proved a dismal failure. It is perhaps futile to seek the causes, but nervousness and inexperience seem the most obvious. He was disconcerted just before he got up by upsetting an ink-bottle over his trousers, but that hardly accounted for his inability to get any grip of the substance of his task. One explanation is that he realised the impossibility of touching the fiscal problem without giving the Prime Minister or his father away, and heroically resolved to sacrifice his reputation as a debater by taking refuge in incoherence. On this theory, he performed his self-allotted role with great courage and adroitness; but I am told it was one of the most painful incidents in recent parliamentary history.[2]

Chamberlain was naturally distressed by Austen's failure and inclined to blame it on lack of support from the backbenchers. The next evening he dined with some of his closest supporters in the House and urged them to combine and back each other up. Parker Smith left a note of his table talk that night :

Dined at H. of C. with Griffith Boscawen to meet Mr. Chamberlain. Present — Chaplin, Sir A. Henderson, Pike Pease, Duke, Pearson, L. Harris, White Ridley, Goulding, Gilbert Parker, and self besides Mr. Chamberlain and Boscawen.

General talk through dinner — after which Boscawen proposed Mr. Chamberlain's health in very pleasant terms. Mr. Chamberlain replied, speaking I suppose nearly half an hour.

He was going away, not because he was ill but had been warned there was danger of his breaking down if he did not. He wanted his friends to take an active part in the coming debates though he would not be

---

[1] *Journals and Letters of Viscount Esher*, p. 41.
[2] *Memoirs of Sir Almeric Fitzroy*, vol. i, p. 184.

there. He strongly urged them to *sit together* — to gather round the benches below the gangway. It was the only way to get attention in the House. H. of C. was a curious place — always up or down. When he first got in he felt that one day everybody was happy and confident from some good speech ; the next every one despondent and miserable because something had gone wrong. The only thing that steadied him was that he used to go down every week to Birmingham — and there he found they did not care a brass farthing what had been happening in the House of Commons. They had returned their party to power, and they meant them to go on carrying out what they had been sent there to do. — But if men were to be heard they must combine, — Austen had been treated very badly the day before. He had had no support from his friends. — If it had not been his own son he would have led cheers himself, and when a man is getting encouragement that makes all the difference. There is many a bad speech turned into a good one by cheers.

We had sat listening to all C.B.'s little jokes and points like gentlemen, and then when A was speaking *they* all were jeering and laughing at him and our men did not defend him. We must form together, must sit together, and must back each other. If it is a good speech cheer it, and if a bad speech cheer it louder.

The H. of C. had altered greatly of late years owing to the methods of Irishmen. The other side try to break a man down. If they see he is nervous they try all the harder to break him down. People used to listen, not to laugh or cheer ironically unless real openings were given. — Support meant confidence.

Chamberlain followed up this advice, next day, with an active lead. The Liberals had put down an amendment bringing up the report of the South African War Commission. Robson, in moving it, censured Chamberlain and Balfour in rather violent terms. Towards eleven in the evening, Chamberlain rose to reply. He spoke from the corner seat of the third bench below the Gangway.

'The rising of Mr. Chamberlain,' wrote the *Daily Express* next day, 'was the occasion for a remarkable demonstration. Cheers rolled over the Unionist benches, some members rising to their feet ; and these cheers were met by counter cries from the Liberal side of the chamber. Mr. Chamberlain, in faultless evening dress, stood the while in Mr. Chaplin's "corner" and there he continued to stand until the rival sides of the Household exhausted their emotions. But it was cheer against cheer for nearly three minutes.' [1]

Of the speech itself we will only say in Mrs. Chamberlain's words : 'Joe spoke in splendid form. He was in his best fighting mood. It encouraged and roused our men and I hope he has given the Government a real lift.' [2]

[1] *Daily Express*, 5 February 1904.
[2] Mrs. Chamberlain to her mother, 5 February 1904.

IV

On the Friday morning, 5 February, Chamberlain conferred at
length with Powell Williams at his room at the House of Commons.[1]
Together they made the final arrangements for the conduct of
Chamberlain's affairs during his absence abroad.

Powell Williams had been one of Chamberlain's few intimates
in recent years. He was a Birmingham man, had graduated like
Chamberlain from the Council to the House of Commons, and had
sat for South Birmingham since 1885. He had first attracted
Chamberlain's attention in the Home Rule crisis when he had acted
as a kind of unofficial Whip for the Liberal Unionists. Chamberlain
had secured junior office for him in the 1895 Government but he
was a poor speaker and had been dropped in 1900. 'Powell
Williams', Chamberlain had written at the time, 'cannot get hold of
the House of Commons. But I think he is the best political organiser
living.'[2] Ever since he had been Chamberlain's shadow; a hench-
man perhaps rather than a colleague, and yet knowing Chamberlain's inmost mind and acting for him in the most important affairs.
With Chamberlain's resignation, their relationship had grown still
closer. He had become the Chief of Staff, doing for Chamberlain
what Austen and the Colonial Office had previously done.

Chamberlain now placed in Powell Williams' hands the direction
of the Tariff Reform group in the House of Commons, of the Tariff
Reform League, of the Birmingham 'machine' and of the Chamberlain element in the Liberal Unionist party. It was a heavy responsibility, but Powell Williams was thoroughly conversant with
Chamberlain's interests in these several spheres.

After this conversation, Chamberlain returned to Prince's
Gardens. Morley had tabled an amendment on Fiscal policy. This
would be called on the Monday, and Chamberlain would have to
intervene at an early stage. It would be an important speech;
for it would give the lead to the Tariff Reform members for the
period of Chamberlain's absence. Chamberlain had a dinner
party at Prince's Gardens on the Friday night. His guests were
busy speculating on the significance of another dinner then in
progress at Wimborne House where leading Unionist Free Traders
were meeting the Liberal leaders. Their discussion was interrupted
by the news that Powell Williams had been suddenly taken ill.

[1] He was allowed the continued use of a room, partly as leader of the Liberal Unionists
and partly on personal grounds.   [2] J. C. to Selborne, 6 November 1900.

MRS. CHAMBERLAIN TO HER MOTHER

5 *February* 1904.—A heavy blow fell this evening, in the sudden and serious illness of Mr. Powell Williams, who, after taking part in the division, had an apoplectic attack in the lobby of the House. Joe had just made all arrangements with him about the things to be done in his absence, and he is his right hand man — in fact, the only person whose experience and whose comprehension of political needs can meet the demands. The Liberal–Unionist Association, Tariff Reform League, and Imperial Tariff Committee all were in his hands. What Joe will do without him I cannot imagine and yet his services cannot now be rendered or asked for.

In the morning, Chamberlain went to Westminster Hospital and saw Powell Williams. He was conscious but too weak to speak. All day he hung between life and death but rallied somewhat in the night and sent on Sunday morning for Chamberlain. Chamberlain went with Mrs. Chamberlain to the hospital but when they arrived, Powell Williams had become unconscious. They waited all morning and about lunch time Chamberlain was summoned to the sick-bed. 'It is my fault,' he said to his wife as he left the waiting room. 'I have worked him to death.' Powell Williams had again fallen into a coma before Chamberlain reached his room. They waited through the afternoon but he died without regaining consciousness.[1]

Chamberlain was broken by the incident. The personal loss and the blow to his cause were too much for him. At first he talked of cancelling his holiday. There was no one now to whom he could entrust his affairs. Then a complete sense of hopelessness overcame him. He wrote that night to Collings.

CHAMBERLAIN TO COLLINGS

7 *February* 1904.—I am cut to the heart by Powell Williams' death. To think that it was only on Friday that we were chatting together and planning for the future. I can do nothing and think of nothing else. I shall not go to the House again before I leave England and I think I should have given up my trip altogether if it were not that the doctors say I must rest, and I owe it to Mary to obey them.

But the light has gone out of public life. What a good fellow he was! I never knew a more loyal or more unselfish.

I was at the Hospital all this morning, but he did not know me and he was unconscious till he died. He recognised me on Saturday morning but could hardly speak.

What a damned hard thing life is sometimes. You and I are the

[1] From a note of a conversation with Mrs. Chamberlain.—J. A.

only older ones remaining now. Austen was everything that was good and thoughtful and I believe that he helped Mrs. Powell Williams and the family.

Politics seem a miserable little thing beside these great mysteries.

Morley's amendment on Fiscal Policy was called next day (8 February). But Chamberlain could not bring himself to go to the House.

CHAMBERLAIN TO LEVERTON HARRIS

8 *February* 1904.—Powell Williams' death has made me useless for the time. It is the close of twenty-five years' friendship with the most loyal, generous, and unselfish of men.

I am not coming to the House again before I leave, and if I am to do any more work at all I had better get away as quickly as possible.

It is right that you should speak in the debate. I suggest that in my absence you should ask Chaplin to mention it to the Speaker.

The debate went forward without him; and so the resignation speech on Fiscal policy was never made. The House understood his absence; and Morley in his opening speech said of him that 'he possesses in a most marked and peculiar degree the genius of friendship.'

Chamberlain planned to go to Birmingham for Powell Williams' funeral, but Mrs. Chamberlain was so disturbed by his condition that she called in Dr. Broadbent.

CHAMBERLAIN TO COLLINGS

9 *February* 1904: *Private*.—Today Mary insisted on my seeing him again and he now says that the shock of Powell Williams' death has made matters sensibly worse, *although still quite reparable*, and that I cannot go to Birmingham without real risk.

I am very much troubled at being unable to pay this last mark of respect to my dear old friend, but I am not alone, and of course I must consider Mary.

So I telegraphed to put you off today, and this is the explanation.

It is an awful blow and I feel all the fight knocked out of me. It is not only a personal loss to me — for one does not pick up 25 years of friendships every day — but it seems to take all the life out of the cause.

He was such a good, cheery, unselfish, splendid fellow, and I cannot reconcile myself to a political life without him.

We start for Egypt on Thursday and I suppose it is the best thing to do but I feel depressed at the idea of leaving and generally good for nothing. I am afraid I am an awful anxiety to Mary, although you must clearly understand that there is *no danger* at present and if I have luck and complete rest I shall get all right.

I suppose I shall not see you again before I leave, so goodbye, old fellow, and mind you take care of yourself. I was not pleased with your looks last Friday and I wish you would take some rest too.

What is the use of killing yourself over this damned politics?

I know you must feel Powell Williams' death almost as much as I do.

V

Chamberlain left with Mrs. Chamberlain for Marseilles on 11 February. They sailed thence to Port Said and spent four days with Cromer in Cairo. The voyage had done Chamberlain good and he had a good talk with the Khedive.

From Cairo he went to Luxor. Cromer's son was there and took the elder statesman to see the excavation of a well. He would afterwards recall the boyish excitement with which Chamberlain watched the different statues and fragments drawn up as out of 'a lucky dip'.[1]

At Luxor, the Chamberlains were joined by Sir Hamilton Gould Adams, governor of the Orange River Colony. Together they proceeded by steamer as far as the first cataract.

On 13 March, Chamberlain left Egypt for Italy. He spent a few days in Sicily and towards the middle of April started homewards by way of Florence.

The journey greatly restored his strength. But its effects did not last. Looking back, Mrs. Chamberlain felt it had been a fatal mistake not to take the full four months' holiday.

VI

For the rest of February and the early part of March, Parliament was mainly occupied with the Fiscal question. The debate on Morley's amendment lasted a full week. The object of the amendment had been to split the Free Fooders from the main body of Government supporters and, in this, it achieved some success. The Ministers who intervened found it extremely difficult to speak with one voice. Gerald Balfour, who opened for the Government in Balfour's absence, made a speech which rather pleased the Free Traders. Under intensive questioning from both sides, however, he admitted that he did not regard preference as altogether impractical. Later in the debate, Lyttelton aroused the deepest suspicions of the 'Free Fooders' by pleading earnestly that the door

[1] The second Lord Cromer in conversation with the author.

should not be closed upon Preference. On the Unionist back benches, the Chamberlainites had the best of the debate by weight of numbers; and at the weekend there were rumours that the Free Fooders would all vote against the Government. On the last day (15 February) Akers-Douglas, the Home Secretary, wound up for the Government. He made a clear statement that the Government was opposed to any duty on raw materials or food. But this was not enough to restore Party unity. On the division, the Government majority fell to 51 ; 27 Unionists voting with the Opposition and 12 abstaining or away unpaired. But for the absence of a number of Irish members, the Government's majority would have been in the twenties.[1]

The Unionist defections in this debate strengthened Balfour's reluctance to go beyond the Sheffield position. As Sandars wrote to Balfour a few days later (21 Feb. 1904) : 'The issue, therefore, is this. If we avoid frightening or irritating these 25 (Free Trade) Unionists we shall carry on. If . . . we alarm or annoy them on the fiscal question they can turn us out at a moment's notice.' [2]

A few days later, there was a fiscal debate in the Lords. The hesitations of the Balfour policy were an easy target for peers of all persuasions; but the event of the debate was Devonshire's resignation speech. In its concluding passages, the Duke moved further into Opposition to the Government than he had done before. He had already advised electors not to vote for candidates who declared for the Chamberlain policy. He now urged them to exact a pledge from every candidate to oppose 'Protection in whatever shape' and to make their support conditional upon this pledge.

Devonshire's speech naturally gave rise to renewed rumours of a Free Trade coalition. Balfour, just risen from his sick-bed, took fright and nearly upset the Government in his efforts to conciliate the Free Fooders. On 9 March, Pirie, a Liberal member, introduced a resolution 'that this House, noting the continued agitation in favour of preferential and protective tariffs, which is encouraged by the language used by certain of His Majesty's Ministers, deems it necessary to express its condemnation of any such policy.'

The object of the resolution was to draw a declaration of policy from the Government which must alienate either the Free Fooders or the Chamberlainites. Balfour determined to avoid the trap and arranged, through the Whip's office, for an amenable backbench

[1] Sandars put the number of deliberate Unionist abstentions at 7.
[2] B.M. Add. MSS. 49762 (Balfour Papers).

member named Wharton to put down an amendment 'approving the explicit declaration' of the Government 'that their policy of fiscal reform does not include either a general system of Protection or Preference based on the taxation of food'.

This amendment was not one which the 'Free Fooders' would be likely to oppose; and, indeed, at a private meeting of their group the prevailing opinion was in favour of going no further than abstention. But the amendment went much too far for the 'whole hoggers'. 112 members met, in a Committee room upstairs, under the chairmanship of Sir Herbert Maxwell. They decided that if the amendment were pressed to a division, they might no longer be able, then or later, to support the Government. The Whips were duly informed. The Wharton amendment was withdrawn. Twenty-four 'Free Fooders' voted for the Liberal resolution; a number more abstained; and the Government's majority fell to forty-six.

But Balfour's attempt to placate the Free Fooders had one significant effect. It convinced Hicks Beach that the Prime Minister did not mean to follow the Chamberlain policy, and he accordingly voted with the Government. Having voted against so many of his 'Free Food' colleagues Hicks Beach now offered to resign from the Vice Presidency of the League. They begged him not to do so and he relented, but made it clear that he could not side with the Opposition.

HICKS BEACH TO DEVONSHIRE

18 *March* 1904.—I felt it unpleasant that my name should appear as a V.P. of the F.F.L., and that I should attend their meetings, while I voted against them, so I suggested that I had better resign; but as they all objected, I said I would let matters remain as they are for the present. As to the future, I fear it is very possible that you may be right, and that the general election may see the Unionist party committed to Preference and Protection, for our 'Retaliation' candidates don't seem to have better luck in the by-elections than the Tariff Reformers.

I am utterly disgusted with the prospect, and (as I think I have already told you) shall simply stand aside, for while, in such a case, I should disagree with my party on the great issue of Protection, I remain in agreement with them on other questions, and could not bring myself to join the Opposition — a position which to me, who have stuck to my party for 40 years, would be simply intolerable.[1]

Balfour would have one more 'close shave' that session, but from this time on Hicks Beach would act as a dissolvent among the 'Free Fooders'.

[1] Lady Victoria Hicks Beach, *Life of Sir Michael Hicks Beach*, p. 203.

Now other issues moved to the fore. The struggle against the Education Act was approaching its climax. In the previous year more than 7000 summonses had been issued against persons who 'passively resisted' payment of the Education rate, and in several hundred cases the authorities had resorted to distraint of property. In the early months of 1904, the agitation spread like wildfire and in Wales was even supported by the local authorities.

The same Nonconformist sentiments which inspired the opposition to the Education Act were further aroused by the news that the Government were contemplating a Licensing Law.

Besides these domestic issues, major developments in the foreign sphere drew attention away from the fiscal question. War had broken out in the Far East between Russia and Japan. What was now the position of Japan's ally, Britain, and Russia's ally, France? The danger that the conflict might spread from the principals to the seconds was one of the decisive factors which led, at the beginning of April, to the Entente Cordiale.

Chamberlain, as we saw in another volume, had played a leading part in the preparation of both the Anglo-Japanese alliance and the Entente Cordiale. Since his resignation he had had no time to spare for questions of foreign policy. Nevertheless foreign Governments were busy speculating on his attitude to the Crisis in the Far East.

At the end of the year, as the war clouds thickened over Manchuria, Holstein drew a strangely misleading parallel.

One remembers involuntarily the beginning of *the Crimean War*. At that time the Aberdeen Cabinet was disinclined to take part in a Russo–Turkish war, but the English people thought otherwise. Lord Aberdeen was overthrown by a vote in the Lower House and replaced by Palmerston who at once declared war.

Just so today, if the English people is less peaceful than the Cabinet *Balfour might suddenly be replaced by Chamberlain* from whom the same might be expected as from Palmerston in his time.[1]

In Washington, Theodore Roosevelt suspected Chamberlain of planning to take advantage of the Russo-Japanese war to declare a British Protectorate over Southern China. 'Chamberlain,' he said to the German Ambassador, 'is quite unreliable and might jump into the Yangtse valley at any moment.'[2]

Both these opinions were wide of the mark. British opinion was

[1] 23 December 1903, *Die Grosse Politik*, vol. 19, p. 74. Translation.—J. A.
[2] 27 September 1904, *Die Grosse Politik*, vol. 19, p. 542. Translation.—J. A.

at its most peaceable; and the German Ambassador in London was much nearer the truth when he wrote, 'if all the signs are not misleading England is in full reaction against the Jingoism of the Chamberlain epoch.'[1]

Bernstorffs's judgment was confirmed in these days by the beginnings of an agitation which was to upset Chamberlain's plans and Balfour's. On 11 March, Lyttelton yielded at last to Milner's urgent pleas and authorised the Transvaal 'Chinese Labour Ordinance'. We have already watched the beginnings of this question and Chamberlain's attitude towards it. We shall have to return to it again. Here it is enough to say that within a month, the Government's decision had led to heated debates in both Houses and to a mass demonstration in Hyde Park.

Tariff Reform no longer held the field alone.

VII

Chamberlain returned to London on 15 April. 'He looks wonderfully better' his wife wrote, 'and is very well, but time is needed to confirm the gain. He would laugh at this view!'[2] He spent the weekend at Highbury, and was back in the House on 19 April to hear Austen open his first Budget.

Austen's Budget was as complete a success as his speech on the Address had been a failure. 'It could not have been better' was Chamberlain's proud comment. Austen added a penny to the income tax, raising it to 1/- and slightly increased the revenue duties on tea and tobacco. He thus succeeded in striking a wholly orthodox balance between direct and indirect taxation. Congratulations poured in from both sides of the House; and an attempt by McKenna to argue that the Chancellor had been improperly influenced by the Tariff Commission was a transparent failure.

Thereafter for a full three weeks, Chamberlain was outwardly inactive. Harcourt believed that 'the Chamberlain flurry has failed and all his bombast has fizzled out'.[3]

Fitzroy thought him self-muzzled.

21 *April* 1904.—The impression gains ground, and is strengthened by Austen Chamberlain's speeches, that his father has subscribed to a self-denying adherence to the fiscal formula adopted by Ministers. Some

---

[1] Bernstorff to Bülow, 16 April 1904, *Die Grosse Politik*, vol. 20, p. 14. Translation.—J. A.
[2] Mrs. Chamberlain to her mother, 20 April 1904.
[3] Gardiner, *Sir William Harcourt*, vol. ii, p. 562.

may say that Mr. Chamberlain's parliamentary self-restraint does not afford any very firm grounds for confidence; but the interest he has for the moment in gaining time may serve to repress dangerous ebullitions.[1]

In fact the next stage in the Tariff Reform campaign was now crystallising in his mind.

From Naples, on his way home, Chamberlain had written to Balfour as follows:

Naples, 8 *April*, 1904.

My dear Balfour,

I expect to be in London on Friday evening. I think there would be some advantage if I could have a talk with you and learn your views on the situation and on future policy before I see any one else. If therefore you are in town on Saturday I should be glad to call on you at any time in the morning most convenient to yourself. In the afternoon I shall go to Birmingham for Sunday.

I hope you have now entirely got rid of the effect of that infernal influenza. I gather that you have had rather a rough time of it and that the House and Country are not quite so sensible of the blessings of a Unionist Government as they ought to be. Well! let them have a turn with the Radicals!

Meanwhile, I congratulate you on Army Reform and, as far as I understand it, on the French arrangement.

You have not lived in vain if you carry through these two great affairs.

Ever yours,

J. CHAMBERLAIN.

P.S.—Please drop a line to 40 Princes Gardens and say if and when you can see me.

In the whole correspondence between Chamberlain and Balfour, from the beginning to the end of their acquaintance, there are only two letters in which Chamberlain departs from the formal 'Yours very truly'. This is one of them.

Chamberlain saw Balfour at Downing Street on the morning of 16 April. It was their first serious talk since Chamberlain's resignation, eight months before. We know nothing of what passed at this meeting, though Mrs. Chamberlain described it in a letter as a 'pleasant and satisfactory talk'.[2] The two letters, however, which we print below show how Chamberlain's mind was moving only a few days later:

CHAMBERLAIN TO NORTHCOTE

22 *April* 1904: *Private.*—I do not expect, and indeed never have expected, to carry the country with a sweep at the next election. *All my efforts and hopes are directed to the election after next.* I expect the Unionist

---

[1] *Memoirs of Sir Almeric Fitzroy*, vol. i, p. 199.

[2] Mrs. Chamberlain to her mother, 20 April 1904.

Party will be defeated next time although possibly by a small majority. *We cannot get a clear issue for Preference* and the result will be complicated by a number of other questions which have made the Government unpopular with different sections. Besides that, the division in our own Party militates seriously against immediate success. My object is, first, to unite the Unionist Party on the policy of fiscal reform and Colonial Preference. *This will, I believe, be accomplished at the next general election where the so-called free-fooders will go to the wall.* Their defeat will mean Liberal successes in many constituencies, but at the following election, and with candidates in accord with the general feeling of the Party, we shall retrieve our position. The swing of the pendulum will then be in our favour instead of against us, and the Radicals will have shown their incapacity to fulfil the numerous and extravagant pledges that they have given.

The worst thing that could happen for me would be that our Party should win by a small majority. In that case we should be powerless, and fiscal reform would be indefinitely delayed.

Of one thing you may rest assured, and that is that the seed of reform is fairly sown, and nothing will choke it, although it may be some time before it bears fruit. The country is really suspending its judgment, but the feeling in favour of some change is decidedly growing and when purely party issues are out of the way it will make itself felt in Parliament and legislation.[1]

CHAMBERLAIN TO DENISON

22 *April* 1904: *Private.*—Many thanks for your interesting letter which I have received since my return from my holiday. The rest and change have been of great advantage to Mrs. Chamberlain and myself, and I hope to be able to continue my work with renewed energy; but I should like to warn you for your own information that I am confirmed in the opinion I have always held that we cannot carry the country at the next election. This is due to political causes external to the tariff question. The Unionist Party have been practically in office for eighteen years, and there is a vague desire for a change in 'personnel' which indeed is almost essential if the practice of our party system is to be preserved. The issues will therefore be complicated and the result will largely be decided by questions of local politics such as Education and Labour policy, while the Tariff Question will only be one of many considerations Also the division in our own Party must inure to the advantage of the Radicals.

I think that every so-called Free Trader on the Unionist side will lose his seat, but it will be filled by a Radical, at the next election. My expectation is that a Radical Government will soon become desperately unpopular owing to their incapacity to fulfil the numerous extravagant pledges that they have given, and my whole efforts will be directed to securing a united tariff reform party to fight on that issue in the general election which will follow the next after a short period of Radical rule.

On the whole, therefore, I regard complete success as improbable —

[1] My italics.—J. A.

almost impossible — for two or three years ; while I believe it to be certain at the expiry of that period if the Colonies play up fairly in the game. The continued repetition of the statement that they will make no concession, and that they do not want Preference, has of course influenced many people. What you are doing to show that this is not true is of great assistance to me, and I hope that Canadian Ministers will bear in mind the difficulties with which I have to contend and will do all that they can, without seriously damaging their own political position, to support my contentions.

These letters suggest that Chamberlain no longer expected the Government to come out openly for his full policy. He does not say so in so many words, but the impression is left that Balfour's indecision would continue until, at the next election, the Free Fooders were eliminated. Only then would the Party unite in supporting Tariff Reform and Preference.

Chamberlain's task, as he now saw it, was to convince his supporters that they would win in the long run. It is no easy thing for a political leader to anticipate defeat and tell his followers to prepare for the next election but one. It was characteristic of Chamberlain that he did so publicly and got away with it.

On 12 May, a year almost to the day since he had launched his Fiscal thunderbolt, Chamberlain addressed the Grand Committee of the Birmingham Liberal Unionist Association. After a tribute to Powell Williams, he asked his audience to assess the results of the Tariff Reform Campaign up to that date.

I asked for a full and impartial discussion. (*Cheers.*) We have had a good deal of discussion — (*laughter*) — more, perhaps, than even I myself expected. How far it has been impartial — (*laughter*) — I will not attempt to determine. But I think it may now be useful, twelve months later, to take stock of the result. . . .

. . . I was not cast down when on my return from a short holiday the other day I was assured by my opponents that my new programme had fallen flat, and that the issue I had raised had already been decided against me — decided against me by the overwhelming logic of the Free Food League, by the romantic arithmetic of the Cobden Club, and by the colossal imagination of the Radical Press. (*Laughter.*) Well, but, gentlemen, are not these persons a little premature? Are they not in too great a hurry? Does their study of political history teach them that a question which has aroused so much and such deep interest, so much real enthusiasm, so much support from all classes in the country — does their study of history teach them that such a question can ever die? Believe me, it is not to be disposed of by the waving of old rags or the clattering of worn-out pans. (*Laughter.*) They will find their mistake. The question will remain until it is no longer a question, but a fact. (*Applause.*) I never expected — I never desired — that the settlement of this question should be unduly hastened. I hold that a great change — and no one has recognised the importance of this change more seriously than I do — should not be carried hastily without full consideration, without a great mass of public opinion behind it. I do not think that a year, or even more, will be wasted in preparing a secure foundation upon which the new policy can safely rest. (*Hear, hear.*)

Meanwhile we reformers have a great deal to congratulate ourselves upon. After all, it is only twelve months since this question . . . was raised. And since then what has happened ? One of the great political parties in the State (and in our constitutional system it is necessary to proceed by parties) has at all events advanced to the point of recognising that the existing system cannot continue, that a change must be made, that we are not going to remain for ever a football to foreign nations. (*Great cheering.*) . . . The Unionist party almost unanimously in the House of Commons — even more unanimously in the country — is pledged at least to endeavour to recover that power of retaliation the loss of which farseeing statesmen regretted fifty years ago . . .

. . . But if we intend success we must not rest upon our oars. We have much to do. My appeal is, as it generally has been, not to dignitaries and powers, but to the people at large. (*Loud cheers.*) Parliament is the executive of the nation's will. I do not appeal to the Executive. I appeal to the makers of Parliament.

He now led up to the prospects at the next election.

It is unfortunate, I have often thought, that in our Constitution there is no such admirable arrangement as exists in the United States of America, in Switzerland and in some other places, and which is there called the referendum. . . . I wish this country could take to-morrow a referendum, a plebiscite, a vote of the people of this country as to whether or not they would have the change in our fiscal system which I have proposed to you. (*Cheers.*) Honestly I believe that by a great majority they would vote in favour of the change.

But will that be the issue at the next general election? (*A voice :' Yes'.*) Well, I wish I were equally certain. (*Laughter.*) A general election is determined by a multiplicity of considerations — by the popularity of the Government of the day, by the judgment which people form of its past policy, by a number of different, complicated issues, and it is very difficult indeed to get a clear and definite decision upon a new point. Now the general election is not coming just yet. (*Laughter.*) *But it is coming within a reasonable time —* (renewed laughter and cheers) *— and I do not myself think that it ought to be delayed beyond a reasonable time.* (*Laughter.*) What are we going to fight it upon ? Are we going to fight it upon the Education question ? . . . is the election next time to be fought upon Chinese labour ? . . .

. . . Is that the issue . . . or is it to be fought on the Licensing Bill ? . . .

. . . But, after all, these matters are a little beside the main thread of my argument. *What I want to lay before you is the difficulty of securing at the next general election a fair test of the opinion of the people on the question which to my mind is of the greatest importance of all. We must be prepared for that.*

We cannot alter the Constitution; we cannot affect the instrument with which we have to work; we will make the best of it. If it does not serve us well this time we will keep it in reserve for the next. Every Government in turn has to spend its popularity. But, gentlemen, although there may be some delay, I am not certain that the great issue will not be hastened by a change of scene, a change of actors, by putting on a new piece which will not last long (*cheers*) — and which will soon be hissed off the stage. (*Great cheering.*)

Now came the clearest political conclusion. The party must go all out for the full programme.

Meanwhile we shall gain nothing by shirking the great issue. Bye-elections, I am told by timid people, by those who are always looking to see how the cat is going to jump, have been unfavourable to the Union-ist party. I do not deny it. I do not attach overwhelming importance to bye-elections. At the same time I am perfectly ready to admit the significance of any signs of the kind. But they have not been unfavourable to the policy of fiscal reform. Since 15 May, when I last addressed you, the turnover of votes in these bye-elections, great as it has been, has been considerably less on the average than it was before. Where we have won our greatest successes has been in London, in Rochester, in Shrop-shire, and, above all, in South Birmingham; where we have had candi-dates who have had a little courage, and who have dared to call their souls their own — (*laughter*) — who have supported with all their might whole-heartedly the policy in which they believe, and who have earned and deserved to earn, the result of their courage. Victories in politics are like victories in war : they are won by enthusiasm; they are lost by timidity. It is not, after all, good policy — to say nothing at all about morality — it is not good policy to sit upon a fence. (*Hear, hear.*) Now, I say, at the next election, whatever its result is to be, let us hold our banner high — (*cheers*) — and we shall have plenty who will come to the standard. Let us fight, if we must fight, for something worth fighting for. I do not much like the modern political nomenclature, and I will not use it; but I will say that on the whole I believe that those who take 'Thorough' as their guiding motto will be much more likely to be successful than those who are half-hearted and weak-kneed and trying to catch a breeze that will never come.

Chamberlain's speech dispelled overnight any idea that the movement for Fiscal Reform was dead. He had given his audience a progress report which, as *The Times* pointed out, showed much greater advance than Cobden could have claimed at any time in the first six years of the Anti-Corn Law League. But this Birming-ham speech of 1904 did more than take stock. It gave practical political advice for the future. Unionists must avoid being put on the defensive over Education, Licensing, or Chinese Labour. Let them get off the fence. Let them go into battle under the banner of the full programme. In this sign they would conquer if not at the first election then at the next. Here was something for the constituency associations up and down the country to bite on. In the autumn, Chamberlain had given Unionists a platform. Now he had given them a plan of campaign.

VIII

On 18 May, within a week of the Birmingham speech, the Fiscal question was again debated in the House, to the considerable embarrassment of the Government. Black, the Liberal member for Banffshire had put down a resolution that 'This House, believing that the Protective taxation of food would be burdensome to the people and injurious to the Empire, welcomes the declaration of Ministers that the Government is opposed to such taxation'. This was really the Pirie resolution of 9 March in another form; but, this time, the Tariff Reformers decided not to wait for the Government to move. Chamberlain gave notice of an amendment:

That this House, taking note of the opinion expressed by the Prime Minister in favouring a change in our fiscal policy and of his declaration that such a change cannot be advantageously undertaken in the present Parliament, expresses its continued confidence in His Majesty's Government.

The terms of the amendment were conciliatory enough. But the Free Fooders could not bring themselves to support any proposal standing in Chamberlain's name. At a private meeting, on 16 May, with Devonshire in the chair, they agreed unanimously — Hicks Beach included — to vote for Black's resolution.

Black's resolution was not a motion of censure. The fate of the Government, therefore, was not directly involved. It was, however, at least questionable whether Balfour could continue to govern if the bulk of his supporters were put in a minority even on an abstract resolution. At the last minute, therefore — and this time in agreement with the Preferentialists — he put down a further amendment: 'That this House considers it unnecessary to discuss the question of fiscal reforms and the declaration of the Prime Minister at Sheffield on 1 October, in regard to which His Majesty's Government have announced that no proposals will be laid before the present Parliament, and, expressing its continued confidence in the present Administration desires to proceed with the business proposed in the gracious speech from the Throne.'

This amendment, standing in the name of the leader of the House, took precedence over all other business and, of course, raised the question of confidence. The debate which followed was unusually heated. A Unionist 'Free Fooder' seconded the Liberal resolution; and the Government were accused of pursuing a policy of 'sham, shuffle, and shout'.

Hugh Cecil 'made a most violent speech — a deliberate and virulent attack upon Joe, accusing him of physical cowardice'.[1] He compared Chamberlain to Bob Acres, whose courage oozed out when he had to fight and accused him of not daring to test in debate the arguments which he put from the platform.

Chamberlain replied in difficult circumstances. He had dined at 11 Downing Street before making his speech. There, Mrs. Chamberlain had told him of his younger brother Herbert's sudden death. The news seems to have taken some of the fight out of him. His reply to Hugh Cecil was dignified and well argued but it lacked his usual joy of battle. His main theme, reasonably enough, was that to debate abstract resolutions was to waste the time of the House. He was not afraid to have his policy debated, but he preferred to keep to the platform until he was in a position to bring down definite proposals for legislation.

Hugh Cecil's speech had gone too far even for the 'Free Fooders'. Not even Chamberlain's worst enemies had ever accused him of cowardice. The tide turned in favour of the Government; and their victory in the division was ensured by Hicks Beach who declared that, though he would have voted against Chamberlain's amendment, he was quite prepared to support Balfour's. In the event only five 'Free Fooders' went so far as to vote with the Opposition. The majority abstained and Balfour carried his amendment by 55 votes.

IX

4 June 1904 witnessed the centenary of Cobden's birth. This was the occasion for demonstrations and counter demonstrations of Free Traders and Tariff Reformers. Chamberlain's proposals were still the leading issue of the day; but only just. The agitation over Education, Licensing, and above all Chinese Labour made increasing inroads on the Government's popularity.

When the House met again after Whitsun, Churchill and two or three of his friends crossed the floor and, for the first time, took their seats on the Liberal benches. 'If I had had my way,' Chamberlain

---

[1] Mrs. Chamberlain to her mother, 18 May 1904.

THE DORMOUSE WAKES UP

(A sequel to the mad tea-party.)

11 December 1903

'MARCHING IN FRONT'

'We, the Liberal Unionists of the country, appeal to our Government and promise them our support if they will march in front of us to victory.'

exclaimed, 'Winston would have been with us.'[1] He was thinking of his own suggestion to Balfour that Churchill should be given junior office in the Ministerial reconstruction of 1902.

The following week brought further reverses. The Liberals held Market Harborough with an increased majority and captured Devonport. Balfour, indeed, thought the future of his Government so uncertain that he discussed with Esher what course the King should take if Ministers were defeated in the House. He even had a memorandum prepared setting out precedents.[2]

Throughout the session, Chamberlain remained punctiliously loyal to the Government. The Licensing Bill was awkward for him since it brought him into conflict with many of his Nonconformist supporters, in much the same way, though on a smaller scale, as the Education Bill had done. By way of aggravation, his brother Arthur was one of the leaders of the agitation against the Bill. For all that he went out of his way to defend the Bill not just in Birmingham but in debate in the House (4 July).

It was the same with Chinese Labour. In the previous volume we noted Chamberlain's stubborn resistance to Milner's proposals on this score. He had always maintained that he could not agree to the import of the Chinese coolies until there was 'incontrovertible proof' that this was what public opinion in the Transvaal desired. He had also sensed from the first the political danger in Milner's proposals. 'It is at least doubtful,' Asquith wrote in his memoirs, 'whether Mr. Chamberlain would ever have given his sanction to this short-sighted and ill-judged experiment.'[3] We are inclined to doubt this judgment, seeing that both Milner and the Chamber of Mines were at one in their decision for Chinese Labour. We cannot help feeling, however, that Chamberlain would have taken greater care to prepare public opinion for the proposal.

Once the Government had taken their decision to bring in the Chinese, he gave them full and consistent support. Immediately after his return from Italy, he made the following statement for publication.

21 *April* 1904.—During my absence I have seen very little of the discussion which has been going on in regard to Chinese labour, and I have not yet had time to make myself fully acquainted with the facts.

While I was still Colonial Secretary I laid down the principle on which I proposed to deal with the question — namely, to offer no opposition

[1] Chamberlain in conversation with J. L. Garvin, from a note in the Garvin papers (undated).   [2] *Journals and Letters of Viscount Esher*, 20 June 1904, p. 55.
[3] *Fifty years of Parliament* by Lord Asquith, vol. ii, p. 22.
U

on the part of the Imperial Government to the employment of Asiatic labour if it were clearly shown that such employment was desired by the great majority of the white inhabitants of the two Colonies.

I stated that in all matters in which Imperial interests were not directly affected, I considered that the only safe and proper policy was to treat the Colonies as though they enjoyed self-government, the concession of which is only a question of time.

I assume that the Government have satisfied themselves that the condition I laid down is now fulfilled, and that the feeling of the white inhabitants is strongly in favour of the proposed employment.

In this case, I think it would be disastrous if we allowed any objections which might be felt to the policy of such employment to override the convictions and wishes of our fellow-subjects on the spot.

I understand that the arguments put forward against the introduction of Chinese are as follows :—

(1) It seems to be thought that their labour will come into competition with that of white men. This is absolutely contradicted by the experience of all who know anything about South Africa, where unskilled labour has always been performed by the coloured people, while the work requiring skill and intelligence has been undertaken entirely by the whites.

The two forms of labour are mutually dependent, and without the coloured man there will be no employment for whites, who will not undertake the inferior kind of labour. It is, therefore, absolutely certain that if the employment of Chinese or other Asiatic labour is successful, it will pave the way for the introduction of a much larger number of British workmen than could, under any other circumstances, find occupation in South Africa.

Such an increase of British labour is eminently desirable, both on political and social grounds, and I believe that the vast majority of British workmen already in South Africa are prepared for this reason, to welcome a great addition to the number of unskilled labourers at present in the country.

(2) It has been urged that South Africa is a white man's country and that the introduction of Chinese will alter and lower the character.

I am convinced that this opinion is wholly unfounded. It would only be true if the Chinese came to stay, but, under the conditions of their employment, they will be temporary residents, and will return to their own country at the expiry of their engagement.

(3) It is pretended that the Chinamen under these conditions will be practically slaves. The statement can only be honestly made by persons who are entirely ignorant of the facts. The Chinaman is quite intelligent enough to take care of himself. He will know the terms on which he is engaged, and he will not accept them unless they are to his advantage.

Any ill-treatment would be impossible under the supervision proposed, and, even if it were possible, it would be the worst policy on the part of those whose object is to attract the Chinaman and to be able to count on his continued assistance.

When I was in South Africa, I went carefully into the condition of the natives already employed under similar regulations at Kimberley and elsewhere, and I came to the conclusion that their position was quite as good as that of any other coloured labourer in any other part of the world.

That they themselves were contented with it was proved by the readiness with which they make re-engagements after a full experience of the conditions of their employment. Under these circumstances I do not think that there is any ground, either moral or political, for the opposition which has been started, largely for political reasons, in this country.

Whether the employment of Chinese will be an economic success is not to my mind so certain; but in all such matters I feel that the opinions and experience of those on the spot are a better guide than any formed here upon imperfect information.

He developed these arguments later in the year (21 July) when he came to the support of the Government with a powerful speech in the debate on the Colonial Office abstracts.

All this time he was heavily committed in the direction of the different aspects of the Tariff Reform campaign. On his return from abroad Mrs. Chamberlain had written: 'This year we hope that Joe's greater freedom will enable him to play truant more often.' In fact his diary shows a continuous grind of committees, lunches, dinners and even weekend parties almost all in aid of Tariff Reform. He moved, breathed, ate, drank and slept continuously in this environment.

17 *June* 1904.—We lunched yesterday with the Chamberlains — to introduce the Irvines — others there were the Bonar Laws and a certain Sweet-Escott, Governor of British Honduras. I sat on one side of my old friend and we talked without constraint. He is obsessed with the fiscal question — has lost his judgement over it — refuses to think or talk of anything else. He looks desperately unhealthy, rather thin too; a restless look in his eyes, bad colour, and general aspect of 'falling in'. But I should imagine that there is plenty of force in the man yet; an almost mechanically savage persistence in steaming ahead.[1]

So much for the outward impression. The following letter shows well enough his inward mood and direction.

CHAMBERLAIN TO LADY DOROTHY NEVILLE

20 *June* 1904.—Many thanks for your note. The Primrose League is as timid as the other wire pullers. They do not see that the new policy is to take the offensive and they allow their opponents to force them to fight on the defensive against Chinese Slavery, Education, Licensing and all the rest of it, whereas their new policy should be to carry out a

[1] *Our Partnership* by Beatrice Webb, p. 292.

flank attack with fiscal reform. However they must go their own way to destruction !

Market Harborough and Devonport have turned out exactly as I predicted. Good Lord ! What fools they be !

> In politics the only strategy is attack.

We saw how, on his return to England in April, Chamberlain had set his sights on the election after next. By the end of June, this general idea had crystallised into more definite and practical form.

CHAMBERLAIN TO NORTHCOTE

2 *July* 1904: *Private.*—The situation here is interesting, but perhaps not easily understood away from the centre. The popularity of the Government has undoubtedly declined and can hardly be said to exist. Each measure in turn offends some of their supporters while the gratitude of those who are benefited is not a real asset in politics. Chinese labour, grotesquely misrepresented by the Opposition, is a formidable difficulty in elections, as the more ignorant of the working-class are made to believe that it portends the general introduction of cheap labour into this country. The Nonconformists are still violent against the Education Act, and the temperance people in a fury of fanaticism over the Licensing Bill.

We have nothing in the future to look to to counteract these prejudices ; and I regard it as absolutely certain that, whenever the dissolution comes, the Opposition will obtain a large majority. I hope, and still believe, that the Government will get through the present session. In that case they ought to meet Parliament next year with a single measure of Redistribution and either carry it or go out upon it. In the former case a dissolution would follow the passing of the Bill and an appeal to the new constituencies.

All this applies to the position of the Party as a whole. Our position as fiscal reformers, although necessarily involved in it, is quite different. The official and wire-pulling element has always been against us. They are always timid, always opposed to new ideas, and incapable of trusting to the enthusiasm which new reforms can excite. They have been working against us under ground without, I believe, any instructions, and indeed against the wishes of the Prime Minister ; but we find that the candidates put forward by the Central Association are all wobblers and half-hearted. Their defeat is a foregone conclusion. They have to bear all the attacks of the Opposition with their hands tied behind their backs and with no aggressive policy to meet their opponents. Personally I rejoice in their defeat and have come to the conclusion that no progress will be made until the Opposition have had a term of office. Then there will be a great reaction, and with the ordinary swing of the tide the Unionist Party will come in again with a big majority. The only practical question is : Will they come in as free-traders or as fiscal reformers with my full policy? I am convinced that the latter will be the case. The great majority of the Party and all that is vigorous and enthusiastic is with me. They are kept back and controlled by a small but noisy minority. The election will rid us of most of these and those who return will be chastened and will be obliged to come up to the party mark.

I think that if the Government had been bolder and had frankly declared their sympathy with my views, and their intention to give effect to them if they were returned again, they would have had a chance of success in spite of their unpopularity on other grounds. As it is, it is too late to expect this now, and my hopes are turned entirely to the election after next.

Meanwhile my avowed object is to secure a united party in favour of fiscal reform. In a few days the great meeting of the Liberal Unionist Association will be held, and will, I believe, pronounce strongly for me. Later on the same question must be raised at the National Union of Conservative Associations. The party divisions cannot be conciliated and one side must give way to the other. I am determined that the minority shall yield to the majority, and I believe that the majority is to an overwhelming extent on my side. If I am wrong I must accept my defeat. If I am right the cause will profit by my victory.

This letter still shows some illusions about Balfour's purpose, and though Chamberlain speaks in it of the Liberals securing 'a large majority', there is no hint of the magnitude of the disaster facing Unionism. But his plan was now clear. He would press for an election early in 1905. Meanwhile his main purpose would be to capture the Liberal Unionist and Conservative party organisations.

This purpose was advanced by the rapid decline in the Government's popularity. There is a natural tendency in all political movements to turn to extreme courses as their fortunes decline. So it was with Unionism. With the mounting danger of electoral defeat, Unionist members everywhere began to realise that there was no safety in explaining away Chinese Labour, justifying the Education Act or keeping an open mind on Colonial Preference. If the Party was to survive, its members must be armed with a positive policy and take the offensive. They, therefore, turned increasingly to Chamberlain.

This trend was clearly demonstrated a few days later. On the initiative of Maxwell, Chaplin and other supporters it was decided to give a dinner to Chamberlain on his birthday.

The dinner, however, was not to be a mere convivial affair. Those taking part were limited to Unionist private members 'who are in general sympathy with his [Chamberlain's] policy of preferential trade within the Empire'.

How many members would accept this designation? In July of the previous year, Chamberlain's active supporters were put at between 50 and 100. In March 1904, 112 members had insisted

on the withdrawal of the Government-inspired Wharton amendment. When Chamberlain had returned to England in April,
Savile Crossley, the Liberal Unionist Chief Whip, had given him
a list of Preferentialist members numbering 132. At that time,
therefore, Chamberlain still commanded the active sympathy of
less than half the Parliamentary party. The balance now swung
in his favour. Exactly 200 members attended the dinner at the
Hotel Cecil as co-hosts. Chamberlain could now claim the support
of a clear majority of Unionists.

The significance of this demonstration was plain to all. Chamberlain gave added point to it in the closing words of his speech to the
assembled company :

> We must seize this opportunity to take the first step towards the
> erection of that great edifice which we hope will endure until the ages
> come to carry to distant posterity the glory of the British Empire. (*Loud
> cheers.*) And, believe me, in such a policy as this, boldly adopted, boldly
> advocated, in an appeal to the patriotism of our countrymen, be they
> rich or be they poor, be they high or be they low, we shall find a force
> which will raise an enthusiasm which will always be denied to those
> who fear to give effect even to their own convictions, but who play for
> safety by sitting upon the fence. (*Loud cheers.*)

X

Within a week of the demonstration on his birthday, Chamberlain
scored a major success. He secured undisputed control of the
Liberal Unionist Organisation. The struggle which led to this
victory had been in progress for several months. To understand it,
we must now look back a little.

On 20 October 1903, the day of Chamberlain's speech at Newcastle, the Northern Area conference of the Liberal Unionist
Association had passed a resolution in support of Chamberlain's
policy. This resolution, as we saw, had been passed in spite of an
open letter from Devonshire deprecating any attempt to define the
party's fiscal policy. It had been followed by the resignation of a
number of prominent Liberal Unionist Free Traders from the
Area Association.

The Duke and those around him concluded from this that they
might soon find themselves at the head of a party committed throughout the constituencies to Tariff Reform. To resist the Chamberlain
influence in the constituency associations seemed hopeless. On the
other hand, to lend the weight of their names and, worse still, to

subsidise from their central fund associations pledged to Chamberlain seemed a gratuitous proceeding. The danger of a renewed
Home Rule agitation seemed remote. The danger of Tariff Reform
was immediate. They accordingly judged that their best policy
would be to dissolve the Liberal Unionist Organisation altogether.
This would relieve them of any responsibility and would prevent
the Liberal Unionist Party as such from becoming an instrument
of Chamberlain's policy.

DEVONSHIRE TO CHAMBERLAIN

23 *October* 1903.—You will remember that we had in May last a short
correspondence on the subject of the position of the Liberal Unionist
Association in reference to the Fiscal question, and that we had subsequently a meeting of the Committee of Management in Great George Street.

The time seems to have now come, having regard especially to the
proceedings of the Conference at Newcastle, a report of which you may
probably have seen, when the subject will have to be further considered.

I have looked a little more closely into the operations and finance of
the Central Association, and I find that one of its most important functions is the distribution of grants to local Associations, over the policy
and action of which little or no control can be exercised from Great
George Street. It is obviously inconsistent with the neutral position
which we agreed to endeavour to maintain, that we should continue to
subsidise local Associations which have, like those represented at the
Conference, taken up a decided position on the question of Tariff Reform,
but it is very difficult to see how under the present system of management
at the Central Office this is to be prevented.

It must have occurred to most of us that it is almost impossible with
any advantage to maintain under present circumstances the existence
of the Liberal Unionist Organisation, but before taking any steps in the
matter I should be very glad to know your views.

What makes my position in the matter still more difficult and responsible is that the expenditure of the Liberal Unionist Association
largely exceeds its income, and that such operations as it carries on are
only made possible by grants made from time to time from a fund which
in no sense belongs to the Association but was collected by me, and
entrusted to me personally, as the Leader of the Liberal Unionist party,
to be applied at my discretion for political purposes.

Chamberlain had no intention of agreeing to the dissolution of
the Liberal Unionist Association. He had been quite prepared to
go on acquiring control of it piecemeal without a showdown with
the Duke. But, if the latter were determined to obstruct him, then
he would have the issue out in a full meeting of the party. His
reply pinned on the Duke the responsibility for proposing the
break-up of a historic organisation.

CHAMBERLAIN TO DEVONSHIRE

26 *October* 1903.—The question you raise as to the future of the Liberal Unionist Association is one of great importance and I have been considering it for some time.

I should preface my answer to your letter by expressing my extreme astonishment that you, who are the President of the Association which has done so much to organise and strengthen Unionist opinion in the United Kingdom, and which is still one of the great barriers to the adoption of a policy of disruption, should be the first person to suggest that it should be violently broken up — not because the members desire it, but because you fear that the opinion of the majority on a question which is not at present a party question may be found to differ from your own.

I must say that, although I am deeply interested in that question, I have not hitherto been inclined to destroy our organisation against Home Rule because of my differences with some of its members on the question of Tariff Reform.

The main object of the Association has, of course, always been to prevent the return of a Home Rule Government, and in that respect matters remain unchanged. In the course of the last seventeen years the Liberal Unionists have, however, followed the Party leaders in regard to many other questions not connected with Home Rule. The greatest blow struck at their influence has been, as I always warned you it would be, the introduction of the Education Act for which you were in a special degree responsible, and which has driven from our ranks many of our most energetic Nonconformist supporters. But that is now past history.

The question now is what position does the Central organisation hold with regard to the local Liberal Unionist Associations. As far as I know neither in the case of the old Liberal Association, nor of the Conservative Association, nor of our own, has there ever been any pretence to control the decisions of the local associations in regard to matters outside the immediate party programme. Again and again these bodies have passed resolutions with which we may or may not have agreed, but which certainly have affected subjects not at the time officially recognised as belonging to the category of practical politics. We have supported them, even in spite of opinions which some of us may have considered heterodox, on the ground that they still served their main object and gave their support to the official programme of the Unionist Party. I have not heard that any of them have refused to do this; and in many cases, if they are not provoked to a contrary course of action, the services of the official organisation would be offered to a Unionist against a Liberal even if the views of the former on fiscal policy should differ from their own; and I do not think that there is any fear that they will follow the bad example of the Free Food League, of which you are also President, which professes to support the Government and yet allows its literature to be largely used against one of the Unionists, as happened in the case of the Leamington election.

I should have thought, therefore, that on all grounds it was better to let sleeping dogs lie and to allow each local association to pass what resolutions it pleases in regard to unofficial questions.

If, however, you mean to create a new test of Unionism, following the recent example of Lord James of Hereford, and to excommunicate any local association which passes any resolutions with which you do not agree, it is evident that a very serious situation will be created.

I should not myself be willing to break up the Association without a struggle to retain it in existence to continue the work which it has hitherto so admirably performed. It is undoubtedly my conviction that a vast majority of the rank and file of the Liberal Unionists are with me, and therefore against you, on the question which I have raised, but at present of course I have taken no steps to test this opinion.

If you think that it ought to be tested I should be prepared to approve of a general meeting of delegates from the Liberal Unionist Associations throughout the country to be held in London in the Spring, when Resolutions might be submitted which would raise the point of difference. If the majority agreed with you, you would of course retain your position as President and would deal with the funds and the policy as you thought fit. In that case my friends and I would retire, and would have to consider whether or not it would be our duty to form another Liberal Unionist Association in agreement from the first with our views. If on the contrary, the majority were on my side, it would of course be open to you to review your position in connection with the Association.

I quite appreciate your feeling of responsibility in connection with the Funds which you say have been entrusted to you personally as Leader of the Liberal Unionist Party; but I think you are under some misapprehension on this point, as I am informed that a considerable portion at any rate was subscribed by friends who share my views or who contributed for the objects of the Association without making you in any sense personally responsible for the distribution of the money. In any case you are aware that under our agreement when the National Liberal Union was merged in the Central Association, it was arranged that I should make no separate effort to collect funds, and that everything should be left to the Central Association. I think, therefore, that it would be difficult to say whether those who contributed to the Central organisation would desire that their money should be differently appropriated if the Association were committed to either of the two opinions of which you and I are the representatives ; and I can only suggest that if you think it necessary to take a formal vote in order to discover whether the Liberal Unionists throughout the country favour your views or mine, you should, after their decision has been given, and whichever way it goes, communicate with the subscribers to the Fund and inquire whether they would wish any change in the appropriation of the money they have contributed. Of course a large portion has been already expended on the objects for which it was given, but the proportion which remains might either be returned to the subscribers or applied to any other political object which they prefer to support. It does not appear to me that it would in any case be justifiable to dispose of the funds for any other object than the general support of the Work of the Liberal Unionist Association without consulting each subscriber individually.

You will understand that I do not urge this course upon you. Personally I think that we might go on as we are with a neutral Central organisation dispensing its funds impartially and, as before, to those local associations which are in need of them and which continue to support the Government, without reference to the views they hold, whether expressed or unexpressed, on the fiscal question. But, if you think otherwise, I am quite prepared to meet you and to take a formal vote of the representatives of Liberal Unionism throughout the country as to our future policy.

In a postscript to this letter, Chamberlain added :

I have not marked this letter private as if a meeting of Delegates has to be called I think that this correspondence will best explain the reasons for the action taken.

The Duke's letter of 23 October had not been marked 'Private' either. He realised at once that he had been seriously outmanœuvred. Anyone comparing the two letters would conclude at once that the Duke's proposal was a high-handed attempt to dictate to the constituencies on a question which had been in no one's mind when the Association had been formed. He accordingly drew in his horns.

DEVONSHIRE TO CHAMBERLAIN

31 *October* 1903.—I certainly did not intend in my letter of the 23rd to suggest that the L.U. organisation should be violently broken up, though on referring to it again I find a sentence as to the impossibility of maintaining it under present circumstances, with any advantage, which may have implied more than I intended.

What I had in mind was that the neutrality on the fiscal question on which we agreed is difficult to observe and if strictly observed almost paralyses us.

However I had already asked Powell Williams to see me which I hope he may do next week when I shall try to find with him some solution of the difficulties which seem to need consideration. Till then I will not make any further reply to your letter ; and I do not think that if it should be necessary to publish our correspondence this need be included.

The Duke does not seem to have seen Powell Williams as he proposed. Nor did he see Chamberlain. In the course of November, however, he made certain proposals to Selborne for transmission to Chamberlain. For some reason, Selborne did not report these proposals to Chamberlain personally but through Powell Williams. This multiple use of intermediaries led to a total misunderstanding. We have three versions of the Duke's proposals, and must record them if only as an example of the part which accident, inattention and inaccuracy so often play in human affairs.

DEVONSHIRE'S VERSION

I saw Lord Selborne in November and read to him a suggestion as to the future proceedings of the Liberal Unionist Association which he undertook to convey to you. The Memorandum from which I read is as follows :—

'The Liberal Unionist Association will continue to maintain a position of neutrality in reference to the fiscal question. It will not therefore withhold its support from any Liberal Unionist candidate on account of his opinions on that question. With reference to the choice of candidates, the Central Association will not attempt to influence the decision of the local Associations, but it must be understood that it cannot continue to aid financially or otherwise, local organisations whose action may involve any attack on the position of sitting Liberal Unionist members. The Committee of Management will consider and deal with individual cases on these principles.'

SELBORNE'S VERSION

Admiralty, 5 February 1904

My Dear Duke,

What you proposed to me and I passed on to Powell Williams in connection with the Liberal Unionist Association was as follows

(1) That it should continue to exist in a semi-dormant state taking no part in the fiscal controversy, and managed by a Committee of four, two representing your views and two Mr. Chamberlain's views.

(2) That no contribution should be made to the expenses of a Liberal Unionist candidate or branch Association who adopted or favoured Mr. Chamberlain's fiscal programme, on the other hand no branch Liberal Unionist Association was to be allowed to act for the Free Food League and receive a subsidy.

You gave me nothing in writing but this is exactly how I understood you.

CHAMBERLAIN'S VERSION

I do not think that formally any proposal was made to me and I had no communication with Lord Selborne, but I heard through Lord Selborne and Mr. Powell Williams that the Duke had suggested that the position might be regularised by our declaring that in no circumstances would one spend any money, either in the way of contributing to a Local Association or in assisting a Liberal Unionist candidate, in any case in which either that Association or that candidate had expressed any opinion favourable to the views which are connected with my name in regard to preferential tariffs.

Devonshire's proposal, as he himself described it, would presumably have been acceptable to Chamberlain. It would have meant a return to the situation prevailing before the Duke's letter of 23 October and was in fact exactly what Chamberlain asked for in his reply of 26 October. Selborne's version, however, and still more that which Chamberlain received from Powell Williams were plainly unacceptable. Chamberlain said so to Powell Williams; and on 21 December, Selborne informed the Duke that his offer had been turned down.

There is no need to shed many tears over this imbroglio. Before Chamberlain's reply reached the Duke, the latter had taken a step which was in complete contradiction with the spirit of his own proposal. On 11 December, as we saw, he had written a public letter advising the electors not to vote for candidates supporting the Chamberlain policy. In doing so he had violated that neutrality of the Central Organisation which was the basis of his proposal. He was after all President of the Liberal Unionist Association, and, though he had the same right as Chamberlain to campaign for the policy he favoured, he could hardly advise electors to vote against Liberal Unionist candidates on fiscal grounds without a breach of the fiscal neutrality of the organisation over which he presided.

In Chamberlain's eyes the Duke's action coming as it did on top of Powell Williams' account of Selborne's version of the Duke's offer added insult to injury. He sent him what was virtually an ultimatum.

CHAMBERLAIN TO DEVONSHIRE

22 *December* 1903.—In the absence of your promised reply to my letter of October 26 I had ventured to hope that you had accepted my suggestion that the *modus vivendi* previously arrived at between us with regard to the Central Liberal Unionist Association should be maintained, and that the Association should continue to carry on its original objects without interfering with the opinions of its members on subjects outside the official programme of the Party.

In these circumstances it is with the greatest regret that I have seen your recently published letter advising Unionists who agree with your views on the fiscal question to refuse to support any candidate differing from them in this respect, even though he may be pledged to support Unionist principles and had been chosen by the local Unionist Association.

Your action has created a new situation which is embarrassing to all of us and cannot be maintained. It is calculated to assist the cause of Home Rule and it is directed against the majority of your colleagues in the House of Commons who have followed you loyally during the last seventeen years, but who are unable to share your objection to a policy of mutual Preference between the different parts of the Empire.

I think that you must admit that, unless you have taken this step with the intention of breaking off all relations with the Liberal Unionist Association, the position can only be regularised by a vote approving your action and passed either by the council of the Central Association or by delegates from the Liberal Unionist Associations throughout the country, as suggested by me in my previous letter.

I am prepared to accept the decision of either of these representative bodies and, if you approve and will indicate which method you prefer, I suggest that you should name some gentlemen to meet Mr. Powell Williams in order to arrange all the details of such a Conference.

As I am leaving England after the Address for a short holiday I should be much obliged if the date could be fixed before February 15th.

The Duke sent an interim reply on the 29 December pleading for delay. He must, he said, consult his friends. Chamberlain, however, was in no mood for delay. 'I am corresponding with the Duke.' He wrote to Collings. 'After his letter, we must deal with him. I want a meeting of the Association to choose between him and me.'

His suspicions were further aroused by a letter from Powell Williams, written from the Liberal Unionist headquarters.

POWELL WILLIAMS TO CHAMBERLAIN

30 *December* 1903.—*The Duke is evidently consulting his friends.* Today comes a letter from Arthur Elliot to Boraston asking for 'the most recent list of members of the L.U.A.' Also for the Rules of the Association. The Duke writes Anstruther saying that there is now no prospect of an agreement with you as to the future working of the Association, and asking A. to pay all obligations to the end of the year, and then transfer the balances. A. has very properly reminded him of his (A.'s) obligations for rent, etc., and in respect of shares in the R. World, and has enquired what arrangements are to be made in respect of them. No answer so far.

It seems to me that too much licence in the way of time should not be allowed to these gentlemen, and, that, before long, a public movement against them, and an attack on their position should proceed from you, if they do not make up their minds to face the music.

Chamberlain acted at once on Powell Williams' advice.

CHAMBERLAIN TO DEVONSHIRE

31 *December* 1903 : *Private.*—I am much obliged by your letter of the 29th inst. I was just telegraphing to you as the delay is most unfortunate and is interfering with my arrangements for a holiday. I fully recognise your claim to consult others before giving a final reply, but I may remind you that my first letter, which practically raised the same issue, was dated October 26 ; and I had hoped, therefore, that you would have had full opportunity beforehand of deciding on your action.

Now I learn that you have written to Anstruther to pay over the balance of funds in his possession to you at the end of the year. Surely this is anticipating matters, and I must repeat my protest against any dealing with these funds on your part.

I do not admit that you have any moral or legal claim to use them, or any part of them, for any other purpose than that of the general work of the Association ; and if a general meeting should decide in my favour, or if it be your intention to sever your connection with the Liberal Unionist Association it would become my duty, having regard to the interests at stake, and especially to the liabilities of the Association incurred on the supposition that these funds were available for its general objects, to take steps to test the matter.

I have carefully considered how this may best be done ; and, as it would be obviously undesirable to appeal to the law courts, I venture to suggest that we should agree to a friendly and private arbitration which might decide between us.

It is with the most sincere regret that I recognise that future political cooperation between us has been made impossible. I am not unmindful of the great services you have rendered to the Unionist cause, nor of the many kindnesses that I have experienced at your hands, and I heartily reciprocate your good wishes for the coming year.

On the question of the funds Devonshire yielded to Chamberlain. He declined, however, to submit the difference between them to the Association itself.

DEVONSHIRE TO CHAMBERLAIN

2 *January* 1904 : *Private.*—I have given no instructions to Anstruther but merely asked him for information as to how it is held, etc.

He has suggested that the two sets of subscriptions now standing in Selborne's and his, and his and L. Cavendish's names should be transferred to the names of Selborne and L. Cavendish, and to this I have no objection, but I think that until a final arrangement is made, I ought to be informed beforehand of the amount and objects of the donations from their Fund to the L.U. Association. Of this I have only hitherto had an annual account from Anstruther. I have never had any idea of disposing of their funds under present conditions without consulting the subscribers, and I agree with you that if any difficulty should arise as to their ultimate destination, it may be disposed of by private arbitration.

2 *January* 1904.—You are aware from the private communications which have passed between us, that the delay in replying to your letter of Oct. 26 has been due to an attempt on my part to find some solution of the difficulties, apparently considerable, in the way of continuing the operations of the Central Liberal Unionist Association, on the basis of neutrality affecting the fiscal question agreed to by us last May.

As a result of interviews between Mr. Powell Williams, Lord James and myself, and subsequently between Lord Selborne and myself, I made certain suggestions to Lord Selborne which he undertook to communicate to you. These suggestions appeared to me to embody the minimum security I thought I had a right to require in order to prevent the Association, of which I am president, from becoming actively identified with the support of a policy disapproved of by me, and it was not till Dec. 21 that I heard from Lord Selborne that you were not prepared to concur in the course proposed by me to him.

I have thus, I think, done all that was in my power to avert the violent disruption of the association, the suggestion of which you imputed to me in your letter of Oct. 26.

I now find, from your letter of Dec. 22, that you consider that the course taken by me in reference to recent bye-elections renders that disruption inevitable, for whatever might be the result of the procedure which you suggest, it is certain that, after the discussion and vote proposed by you to be invited, either you and your supporters, among whom are some of those who have taken the most active part in the work of the Association, or I and those who agree with me could no longer continue to be members of that body.

I agree with you that the situation is embarrassing, but I do not desire to discuss in this correspondence whether this is due to your action in raising a question of the highest political importance on which you knew that the opinion of Liberal–Unionists must be divided, or to mine in giving the advice which I thought was called for under the conditions created by your action. What is certain is that the course now proposed by you must bring about disruption in its most violent form.

Deeply as I regret, I do not question the conclusion at which I assume you must now have arrived that the continuance of the existing Liberal–Unionist Organisation is no longer practicable or possible. I have always considered that you have underrated the gravity of the issue which you have raised, and your assumption that it is one upon which men might be content to differ, and yet act together, seems to me untenable. I would also observe that so low an estimate as you thus appear to form of the importance of the relative merits of Free Trade and Protection seems hardly consistent with the sacrifices you have made and the exertions you are putting forth in favour of one aspect of the controversy.

You state truly that the main object for which the Association was formed was to prevent the return of a Home Rule Government, but I cannot agree with you that in that respect matters are unchanged.

Your agitation has made it certain that the issue before the country at the next election will not be Home Rule, but that of Protection against Free Trade, and many of us are not prepared to surrender the principle of Free Trade because at some future time the Home Rule policy, to which we are as strongly opposed as ever, may be revived. The differences between us are certainly not less vital or urgent, as questions of practical politics, than those which separated us from Mr. Gladstone in 1886.

The natural consequence of this situation would appear to me to be that the Liberal Unionist Association, which has done its work in averting Home Rule, and has helped to maintain a Unionist Government in power for the greater part of seventeen years, should recognise that under present conditions its existence is no longer necessary, and should be dissolved with as little recrimination or bitterness as may be possible. It can no longer be as it has been in the past, and as its name implies, an association which includes all Liberals attached to the Union ; and a majority, on whichever side of the fiscal question it may be, no more than a minority, would have a right to retain that name.

While, therefore, I shall be willing to enter upon a fair and friendly discussion of the arrangements necessary for the dissolution of the Association, I cannot be a party to a proceeding which can have no other effect than that of dividing it into sections neither of which will have a right to assume to represent Liberal Unionist opinion; and if this course be insisted on by any section of the party, I shall have no other alternative than to resign the office of president and leave to others the responsibility attaching to such a course.

Chamberlain replied with two letters, one for publication, the other a private remonstrance. Both are worth quoting.

CHAMBERLAIN TO DEVONSHIRE

4 January 1904.—As you decline to join with me in consulting the members of the Central Liberal Unionist Association as to its future policy, it appears unnecessary that I should trouble you further by discussing the other points raised in the letter containing your decision.

I must, however, point out in order to avoid misconstruction, that you are quite wrong in assuming that I have arrived at the conclusion that the continuance of the Association is no longer practicable or possible.

On the contrary I believe that its existence is still necessary to the success of the Unionist cause, and for this reason I should strongly deprecate its dissolution.

In any case the decision is in my opinion clearly one for the Members themselves, and ought not to be forced upon them by any official action.

I propose, therefore, on my own responsibility, to call a general meeting at as early a date as possible, in order to consider the situation and decide as to the course to be taken.

If the meeting should resolve to continue the operations of the Association, I do not feel with you that the resignation of some of its Members, however much to be regretted, would deprive it of its representative character.

5 January 1904: *Private.*—I have gone through your last letter and find that all the corrections you desire were made in the original sent to me.

I take the opportunity of saying that although I did not wish to deal in public with what I may call the personal side of the question, I think you could hardly have expected me to anticipate beforehand such a 'disruption' as you now contemplate, seeing that you voted with me on the proposal to keep the Corn Tax and give the 1/- Preference to Canada; *that you also heard without objection of my intention to raise the whole question in the country — and that your remark to me on that occasion was — 'Well! I suppose I shall have to take my name off the Cobden Club'.*

All this was not calculated to warn me that you would consider an attempt to secure mutual Preference as a heresy only comparable to Gladstone's Home Rule Bill.

This is by the way and I do not expect any reply but only desire that you should know that I was certainly misled as to your personal opinions.

XI

This struggle for control of the party organisation had hitherto proceeded in private. On 11 January, however, an edited version of the correspondence quoted above was published by mutual agreement. The crisis was now public property.

Fitzroy who liked the Duke and never cared much for Chamberlain knew at once that the latter had won the day.

15 *January*.—The publication of the correspondence between the Duke of Devonshire and Mr. Chamberlain is another illustration of the last-named's smartness in controversy. He sees very clearly the advantage of preserving the L.U. organisation, which he has already captured, for the purposes of his new campaign, and is determined at all costs to keep it alive, so that whatever prestige it enjoys should be at his service. He accordingly contrives, with great astuteness, to impart an air of detached concern for the views of its members, which are in danger of being ignored by an autocratic and irresponsible President. The Duke, on the other hand, objects strongly to the transfer of the good-will of an association, of which he has been for nearly twenty years the corner-stone, to the furtherance of a policy he has abjured, and thinks dissolution the only alternative if neutrality cannot be observed. From his point of view, it is altogether improper that an organisation called into being for a special purpose, and largely maintained out of funds of which he is sole trustee, should be utilised for ends outside the scope of that trust, and, to those who do not believe that everything should be sacrificed to the success of Mr. Chamberlain's schemes, there is a great deal of force in his contention ; but the turn given to the controversy by J. C.'s dexterity has lent the Duke's action the appearance of being dictated by a desire to proclaim himself the Alpha and Omega of Liberal Unionism. Mr. Chamberlain is an excellent judge of the uses of the long spoon, and has made the most of the Duke's candour and indifference to dialectical subtlety.[1]

Speculation centred chiefly on what the Duke's followers would now do. Churchill wrote to him : 'No doubt Chamberlain had an advantage in your correspondence in being able to appeal to a majority ; but, notwithstanding this, your last letter has equalised matters. I am glad the correspondence has taken place and hundreds of Liberal Unionists all over the country will silently resort to Liberalism.'

Would the Duke now make common cause with the Opposition ? A dinner and reception were held at Wimborne House on 5 February. The leading Liberals and the foremost Unionist Free Traders sat down together. Nothing came of it.

[1] *Memoirs of Sir Almeric Fitzroy*, vol. i, p. 179.

Meanwhile Chamberlain had not let the grass grow under his feet. He summoned a meeting of the Liberal Unionist Council. On 3 February, 84 out of 120 of its members met at the Westminster Palace Hotel. Chamberlain was in the chair.

The conference had been carefully prepared by Powell Williams. Four resolutions were passed.

The first proclaimed that 'the existence and activity of the Central Unionist Organisation should be maintained'. This was a straight rebuff to the Duke's proposal to dissolve the organisation. It was carried with only two dissentients.

The second instructed the Central Organisation 'to assist as heretofore all Liberal Unionist candidates and Liberal Unionist Associations that are prepared to support a Unionist Government without regard to the personal opinions of such candidates upon the question of Fiscal Reform'. This resolution, which was carried unanimously, must have barred the Duke, as President of the Central Organisation, from advising electors to vote against Liberal Unionist candidates on the ground of their fiscal opinion.

The third resolution authorised the Committee of Management to prepare new rules for the Council which would provide 'for the fuller representation of the Liberal Unionist party'. Chamberlain had decided not merely to drive the Duke out of the party but to revise its constitution so as to break the hold of the Whig influence upon it. Henceforth he would be the master. This too was carried unanimously.

The final resolution, with unconscious irony, instructed Chamberlain to inform Devonshire of what had passed.

The Duke now realised he had fallen between two stools. The resolutions of the Central Organisation confirmed that the overwhelming majority of the party were against him. The dinner at Wimborne House had discovered no satisfactory basis for a coalition with the Liberals. In the circumstances the Duke's instinct was to play for time. He may have hoped that, with Chamberlain away and Powell Williams ill,[1] events and his friends might work a change of heart in the Liberal Unionist Party. Equally he may still have thought there was a chance of a combination with the Liberals. If so, it was essential to keep his followers together, so that they should secede from the Government side as a body and not merely as individuals. Chamberlain's speech at the Council had brought to

[1] The Duke's letter asking for delay was written on 6 February — the day after Powell Williams' stroke and before his death.

light the discrepancy between Devonshire's offer of the previous November and Selborne's report of it. Here was a legitimate handle for delay. The Duke accordingly wrote to Chamberlain explaining the terms of his November offer and concluding 'under the circumstances I think it desirable to take further time to consider the Resolutions'.[1]

Chamberlain could not well refuse. For one thing, it was now clear that there had been a major misunderstanding on the central issue. For another, Chamberlain was leaving the country the following week and was virtually incapacitated from business by the state of his health and the death of Powell Williams. The matter accordingly was allowed to rest for over two months.

Chamberlain returned to England in mid-April to find the situation in the Liberal Unionist party unchanged. The Tariff Reformers were undiminished. The Free Traders had not come to terms with the Liberals. In one respect, however, the Duke had departed still further from the fiscal neutrality which he professed to regard as the proper attitude for the Central Organisation. He had ended his resignation speech in the House of Lords (19 February 1904) with these words:

I have been reproached with disloyalty to the Unionist Party for having advised free traders to vote against protectionist candidates. I have given that advice. I have never advised anyone to vote against candidates who were pledged to the policy of negotiation and retaliation — partly because, as I have already said, I do not know what that policy means. But I do advise every man who professes Free Trade opinions, and does desire that freedom of exchange should not be diminished but increased, to exact from every candidate who seeks to represent him in Parliament ... to exact a pledge from the candidates that they will vote against Protection, and that they will oppose protective taxes on food, that they will oppose the imposition of a protective duty upon foreign manufactured goods; and I will advise that, failing this pledge, he will refuse to support a candidate even if he professes to be a supporter of a Unionist Government.

Chamberlain saw the Duke in London on 22 or 23 April. Fitzroy was afterwards told that they discussed the misunderstanding over the November proposals 'in the friendliest spirit; but the divergency of feeling in the constituencies has grown too marked to permit things now being arranged on the suggested basis'.[2] It is clear, from what passed subsequently, that the continuing ground for disagreement between them was the Duke's advice to electors quoted

[1] Devonshire to Chamberlain, 6 February 1904.
[2] *Memoirs of Sir Almeric Fitzroy*, 11 May 1904.

above. The Duke would not, indeed could not, with honour withdraw from this position. Chamberlain would not let the matter rest unless he did.

In the absence of agreement, there was no more to be done until the annual meeting of the Liberal Unionist Council. This was to take place on 18 May. The main business of the meeting was to confirm the resolutions adopted at the extraordinary meeting of the Council of 3 February and a further resolution submitted by Chamberlain 'that the Liberal Unionist Council be reconstituted on the basis of a fuller popular representation of the party and that the draft rules now submitted be adopted in the place of those now governing its organisation and functions'.

The following letter exchanged just before the meeting shows the attitude of the protagonists.

DEVONSHIRE AND CHAMBERLAIN

Devonshire to J. C., 14 *May* 1904.—It may be convenient to you that I should give you some outline of the course, which as at present advised I propose to take at the meeting of L.U. Council on Wednesday . . .

. . . I propose to make a short statement referring to our correspondence, to the meeting held on Feb. 3 and the Resolutions proposed at it, and also to the misunderstanding between Selborne and myself. I should then refer to the Resolution of which you have given notice, and state that having regard to the opinions expressed in my correspondence and to my unchanged opinions on the subject of the Union, I could not offer any opposition either to the Dissolution of the present Council and Association, or to their proposal on a constitution in a combined form. But I should add that in view of the difficulties which I saw in the way of the conduct of the affairs of such an association on the neutral basis indicated, I could not undertake any responsible position in connection with it. My tenure of Office as President of the two bodies will lapse with their dissolution and re-constitution, and it will be for the new body to appoint its Officers. As to continuing or renewing my membership or advising my friends to do so, it must depend on the success with which under its new organisation the Council may be able to maintain a strictly neutral attitude on the Fiscal question, but personally I should be unable to continue my membership, if it was held to debar me from giving such advice in regard to the choice or support of candidates professing Unionist opinions as might seem to me called for in the circumstances of each case. I should endeavour as far as possible to avoid controversial expressions, and to limit what I have to say to a bare statement.

J. C. to Devonshire, 15 *May* 1904.—I am much obliged by your letter of yesterday and concur with your proposals as to the order and conduct of business on the 18th.

Assuming that the new Rules are carried I think the business of this meeting would then terminate and that Boraston acting under instructions from the existing management Committee must summon a meeting of the New Council some time in July to confirm the rules, elect officers, and transact other business.

I gather from your letter that you reserve to yourself the right to advise your friends to vote against Liberal Unionist candidates, duly selected by the local Associations, if their views on the fiscal question are not approved by you. If this is so, it is not *neutrality* but *war to the knife* with all who hold my opinions.

I do not complain as I like a clear situation, but it does seem to me that your decision to this effect must necessarily prevent common action in the future.

I am very sorry that this should be the case, mainly on personal grounds, but if we must part it will be on my side at any rate with no diminution of the respect and regard I have always entertained for you.

The Council met in the long room in the Westminster Palace Hotel. Besides Chamberlain and Devonshire, Austen, Lansdowne, Selborne, James and Arthur Elliot sat at the President's Table. Devonshire and Chamberlain both made personal statements on the lines of the correspondence we have already considered. At the end of his statement, however, Chamberlain showed his plain intention of turning the Liberal Unionist Association into an instrument of his fiscal policy :

I propose to create a great representative authority, as to whose right to express the opinion of the Liberal Unionist party there can be no possibility of doubt. (Hear, hear.) You have stated, my lord duke, that you considered the party — I forget the exact words — but they seemed to imply that the party was divided in something like equal proportions on this subject of fiscal reform. That may be so. In my opinion, however, it would be more correct to say that of the rank and file of the voters 99 per cent go one way — ('No', and 'Hear, hear') — and the minority is not more than the fraction that remains. But I do not assert that. I merely express my opinion. The proof will be in our hands. The new association, if it be created, must in its representative capacity and after full discussion come to a conclusion upon this matter.

At the end of his speech, Chamberlain moved the adoption of the new rules. Various attempts to refer the rules to a sub-committee or to adjourn the meeting were defeated. The members of the council grew impatient and called for a division. The new rules were carried by a large majority.

Devonshire did not renew his membership of the Association. Most of his friends followed his example. 'Lord James of Hereford' Chamberlain wrote soon afterwards 'has retired shaking the dust from his feet.'[1] Chamberlain had won the day; and the new rules ensured that his control would be undisputed.

So ended one of the strangest relationships in English history. Devonshire and Chamberlain were poles apart in background, temperament and outlook. In the days before Home Rule, they had represented the extreme antagonism between Whig and Radical opinions which Gladstone had striven in vain to reconcile. Then a great cause, the union of the Kingdom, had thrown them together. Their alliance which most men had thought too incongruous to last a week had proved one of the most formidable combinations in political experience. Together they had crushed Home Rule and broken the Liberal Party. Together they had guided their Conservative allies exercising an influence out of all proportion to their numbers in Parliament or in the country. Then suddenly their old antagonism had re-emerged. The Duke's refusal to join Chamberlain in crushing Balfour's Education Bill undermined the foundations of their power in the country. The Duke's championship of Free Trade wrecked Chamberlain's attempt to carry the Cabinet for Tariff Reform. The antagonism became a head-on clash. The fight between Whig and Radical was fought to a finish; and the Radical prevailed.

XII

Chamberlain had captured control of the Liberal Unionist Association. But it would be a hollow victory unless he could reconstitute it with powerful backing. Otherwise, he would be left as the leader of a fraction of a faction.

He determined to take the Presidency himself. Selborne was persuaded to become one of the Vice Presidents. So, after some hesitation, was Lansdowne. Next he planned a mass demonstration at the Albert Hall. He would make the key speech. A resolution would be moved expressing support for his own policy. Lansdowne would be invited to reply.

CHAMBERLAIN TO LANSDOWNE

16 *June* 1904.—I have been trying my hand at a resolution for the great meeting at the Albert Hall to be held after the Conference of Liberal Unionists on July 14.

Will you look at it and say if you approve or if there are any alterations or additions you would suggest?

---
[1] Chamberlain to Selborne, 3 June 1904.

The idea is that the meeting should open with an address (half hour) from the Chairman — then that the resolution should be moved and seconded in two speeches of 10 minutes each and replied to on behalf of the Government by yourself in a speech of any length *not less* than half an hour and better if three quarters or one hour.

You will see that it would be open to you to devote most of your time to Foreign policy and the general idea of Imperial Union, and that the Fiscal policy is intentionally left in a vague way. But it may easily be possible to alter and improve the wording, and on this I beg for your advice.

Resolution.—That this meeting expresses its continued confidence in His Majesty's Government, and especially congratulates them on the recent agreement with the French Republic which has removed long standing causes of difference and will tend to promote the friendship and good understanding between this country and her great neighbour which will make for peace and civilisation throughout the world.

This meeting also recognises the continued efforts of His Majesty's Government to promote a closer union between the different parts of the Empire, and will support them in any well considered proposals for securing this object by arrangements intended to develop commercial intercourse on terms of mutual advantage between the Motherland and her Colonies and Dependencies.

Lansdowne was very close to Balfour; and the correspondence which follows suggests that he had accepted the Vice Presidency of the party in order to act as a brake on Chamberlain. He was to play the part Balfour had originally assigned to Devonshire. Chamberlain was conciliatory about the form but adamant about the substance.

CHAMBERLAIN AND LANSDOWNE

Lansdowne to J. C., 22 *June* 1904.—Please forgive me for having kept you waiting so long for my answer as to the Albert Hall Meeting. I thought it desirable to confer with my L.U. Colleagues and I have had some difficulty in getting at them.

We feel strongly that whatever is now decided should be decided in such a manner as to create as little difficulty as possible for H.M. Government in the House of Commons. The tactical policy required for the House of Commons may no doubt not be well adapted to the Constituencies, but for the moment, so far as we are concerned, it is the House of Commons policy which must prevail. While therefore we desire not to absent ourselves from the Albert Hall meeting, we feel that harm would be done to the L.U. party and cause, which is yours as well as ours, if our attendance at the meeting or the nature of the proceedings were to add seriously to our Parliamentary difficulties or even contribute to the defeat of the Government. We therefore welcome the desire which you have shown to consider our views and to bring the proceedings so far as possible into harmony with them. I gather from what Austen said to me after the last Cabinet that, if we attend, you will be careful to pitch your speech in a tone which will not alarm the moderate members of the party, and I trust that we may assume that other speakers will maintain a similarly cautious attitude, and that any resolutions which may be offered will be conceived in the same spirit.

With regard to the main resolution of which you kindly sent me a draft I venture to suggest a slight modification of the wording of which I hope you will not disapprove. The resolution should, I think, contain a distinct expression of approval of the policy which we have accepted as well as of any future efforts which we may make to promote a closer union between the different parts of the Empire.

Lyttelton and Arnold-Forster, as well as Selborne, will I hope, also be invited to the meeting.

J. C. to Lansdowne, 24 *June* 1904.—I agree as to the objects which we should keep in view, and am quite ready on my part to do all in my power to prevent anything at the great meeting at the Albert Hall from being a cause of embarrassment to the Government.

My feeling is that it is most desirable that the Government should be closely connected with and represented on the new Association, and I am therefore desirous that all the Liberal Unionist Ministers should be present.

It would be clearly out of place in such a case for me to go into details about my policy, although I suppose that general expressions as to the importance and necessity for closer union with the Colonies could not be objected to.

I do not think that there will be any difficulty on this score, but I must ask you to reconsider the Resolution, your alterations in which are really of the first importance. You will recollect the old saying that *inclusio unius* is *exclusio alterius,* and in your version you have definitely expressed approval and support for the establishment of the Committee of Defence as a means of common action, and of the intention of the Government to defend the Colonies against attack by foreign powers on their fiscal independence.

Now I do not think that the Committee of Defence, with the occasional presence of a single Colonial at special meetings, is likely to do much by itself to bring the Empire together; while the promised defence against foreign powers has not been afforded in the case of either Canada, against whom Germany still imposes differential rates, nor India, against which Russia took action the other day.

In my opinion the Government is quite right in not taking notice of these two cases, but under those circumstances we can hardly bring into prominence its readiness to do so under some circumstances which have not arisen and may never arise.

Again, you ask us to approve of the Fiscal Policy of the Government. What is its Fiscal Policy? If it is confined to Retaliation we do not approve of it except as a stepping stone to higher things.

Still I would stretch a point for this, although I should like a more definite reference to the statements of the Prime Minister which expressed sympathy with Commercial Union and contemplated the adoption of Preference under certain conditions.

Having regard to all these difficulties, I have tried my hand at another draft which I hope may be satisfactory and not be held to commit you one atom further than you wish to go. Of course, as you are asked to acknowledge a vote of confidence, and not to move it, you are not really committed to the actual words although you must be supposed to accept the general spirit.

New Draft.—Further this Meeting approves the Fiscal Policy of H.M. Government, which will enable them to deal with hostile tariffs and the practice of dumping; and, being deeply impressed with the necessity of promoting a closer union between the different parts of the Empire, and of maintaining and developing commercial intercourse between the Mother Country and her Colonies, welcomes the sympathy expressed by the Prime Minister at Sheffield with these all-important objects.

Lansdowne to J. C., 25 June 1904.—Many thanks for your letter of yesterday. I have communicated with my L.U. colleagues, and we accept your amended draft. Selborne is away, but I do not suppose he would object.

The first meeting of the reconstituted Liberal Unionist Council was held in the Imperial Theatre, Westminster, on 14 July. The same day, as it happened, another stubborn antagonist, Paul Kruger, died in Switzerland. The adoption of the new rules and the election of officers went forward as planned. In the evening came the great demonstration in the Albert Hall. Lansdowne, Selborne, Lyttelton, Austen, Chaplin and a host of other dignitaries were on the platform. A great banner stretched across the middle tier of boxes proclaimed 'Learn to think Imperially'. Every space in the building was filled.

Chamberlain's speech was short and unusually vigorous even for him. He began by reminding his audience that the union of the Kingdom was still in danger. Nevertheless, a purely defensive policy was not enough.

We do not think that there is anything in present circumstances which would justify us in laying down our arms or in relaxing our vigilance. We believe that there is still a necessity for every strong arm and every patriotic heart to join in defending the very citadel of the Empire which is threatened by foes without and by traitors within. (*Cheers.*) But no great political party can live upon a negative alone — (*cheers*) — ... while I confidently appeal for a favourable verdict upon our past services, it is not upon them that I am going to rest our claims as a party for future support. The political party which confesses that its work is done, the party which admits that the time is come to rest and be thankful is a party of the past. (*Cheers.*) It must make room for those who still find in the changing circumstances of the time opportunities for further usefulness and further reforms. (*Cheers.*) Progress is a law of our being. Finality in politics is as impossible as finality in science. We do not seek change for the sake of change, but a change of policy is inevitable if we are to keep pace with the times in which we live. (*Cheers.*)

That ought to be a platitude, and yet in the last twelve months we have seen that the suggestion of a change in a policy established sixty years ago has been received as if it were a heresy deserving the pains and penalties of the Inquisition. (*Cheers and laughter.*) And one great party in the State, the party, forsooth, which boasts of its progressive aspirations — that party has refused even to inquire into the origin of its faith. . . .

The Liberal Unionist Council . . . the rank and file from every district in the United Kingdom — from the north and the south, the east and the west, met today. . . . They have passed resolutions by an overwhelming majority approving of the demands of the Prime Minister for further power in order to enable the British Government to deal with hostile tariffs — (*loud cheers*) — and with unfair competition. They have appealed to the Government to see whether it cannot yet be possible to draw the Empire closer together by commercial bonds of union based on reciprocity and preferential conditions. (*Cheers.*) That policy may be right or wrong but it is a living policy and not a dead superstition — . . .

In the second half of his speech, Chamberlain turned on the Opposition. He showed his audience how to fight the election when it came.

Before I sit down I should like to ask you for a moment to consider what is the alternative. There is another party anxious beyond measure — (*laughter*) — to occupy the seats that we now fill, to displace the Government that we now follow. What are they going to do for us? (*Laughter.*) Are they agreed? (*Laughter.*) To me it is almost a matter of cynical enjoyment to see the agonised expectation of a party that has been so long excluded from office. (*Laughter.*) We are told — no doubt truly — that they are at last a happy family. (*Laughter.*) And apparently in the political Ark in which they reside the animals have ceased to claw one another. (*Loud laughter and cheers.*) They are waiting patiently for the feeding time. (*Renewed laughter.*) Is it not amusing to see Lord Rosebery effusively embracing Sir Henry Campbell-Bannerman? — (*loud laughter*) — and Sir Henry Campbell-Bannerman coyly repelling anything in the nature of a too-exuberant emotion? (*Roars of laughter.*) But there is a point of interest to us; which is the predominant partner in this union of hearts? (*Laughter.*) Will the Irish Nationalists be entirely satisfied by the protestations of devotion to their cause which have recently been given by Sir Henry Campbell-Bannerman and Lord Spencer? And do the Liberal Imperialists imagine that they will be strong enough to take care that these protestations are not followed by any active or practical measures? (*Laughter.*) I should be sorry myself to leave the fate of the Union to those stalwart defenders, the Liberal Imperialists. (*Laughter.*) In my experience, they have been always magnificent in professions, but very mediocre in performance. And, again, are the passive resisters going to resist no longer? Will the wicked cease from troubling, and the weary be at rest? (*Cheers and laughter.*) Will their consciences be satisfied when they have their own party in office? — (*a Voice: 'Yes'*) — or will they, on the other hand, demand their pound of flesh, ask for the performance of the pledges with which their support was gained? And if they do this, what price is the Radical party to pay in order to conciliate the Irish Roman Catholics? (*Cheers.*) ... In this approaching millennium of Little Englanderism, we shall repudiate any appeal to the Imperial instincts of the race. We shall neglect and snub our friends for fear we give offence to our competitors. (*Cheers.*) We shall resist the tendency to draw closer together the British race, lest in the process we fall to blows among ourselves. ... Their policy is below contempt. (*Prolonged cheers.*) It is a policy of shreds and patches, of provincialism in the Empire, and of selfishness in the individual, and they will march to victory — (*laughter*) — under the inspiring music of parodied hymns — (*laughter*) — and the noble and elevating cry of 'Chin Chin Chinaman'. (*Laughter.*) It is a sordid bond that holds them together, and sooner or later this nation, which responds so readily to what appeals to the instincts of an Imperial race, which rises nobly to the conception of an Imperial mission, and all the duties involved in Imperial privileges — sooner or later this nation will judge, as it deserves, this factious and fortuitous combination.

Lansdowne, in his reply, spoke mainly on Foreign Affairs. Towards the end of his speech, however, he turned to the Fiscal proposal in the resolution: 'I am here to tell you', he said, 'that Mr. Balfour's sympathy is unabated. And, indeed, is it conceivable that any of us should regard such a proposal without sympathy? I can myself conceive no greater, no more stirring ideal than that which Mr. Chamberlain has put before you this evening.'

The *Daily Telegraph* commented next morning.

Without abating one jot or tittle of his attitude upon the fiscal question, Mr. Chamberlain has reappeared as a critic of general politics, and he has electrified one of the greatest political gatherings for twenty years by one of the finest fighting speeches of his life. ... The speech has carried the war, with the aggressive genius, with the old distinctive audacity, into the heart of the enemy's camp. Unionist strategy has recovered the initiative. ... If the protagonist of the campaign has his way, the General Election cannot be considered lost one moment before it is decided; ... Mr. Chamberlain is convinced that the cause of Imperial union upon a preference basis can save the Unionist party, and that no other cause can.

XIII

Lansdowne's and Selborne's acceptance of office in the new Liberal Unionist Association gave the Opposition just the opportunity they had been waiting for. They could now challenge Ministers in a form which the latter could no longer evade. In the House of Commons, Campbell-Bannerman put down a motion of censure calling attention to and condemning the action of certain members of the Government 'who have accepted official positions in an association which has formally declared its adhesion to a preferential fiscal policy involving the taxation of food'. For procedural reasons Campbell-Bannerman's motion could not be called for another ten days. We shall return to it in a different context. Meanwhile Devonshire had given notice of a similar motion in the House of Lords. This was called on 21 July. The Duke's speech, according to Fitzroy:

was delivered with a good deal of emphasis and some bitterness, and Lord Lansdowne was not very successful in removing the impression that there was a good deal of ambiguity about the situation. Indeed, it is becoming more apparent every day that Mr. Chamberlain holds the key of the citadel, and can force the Government at any moment into an acceptance of his terms.[1]

The same evening, Chamberlain rubbed in the lesson of his Albert Hall speech when he addressed the first annual meeting of the Tariff Reform League. It was a notable utterance both for its implied criticism of Balfour and for the confidence which he showed in the progress of his movement.

The Anti-Corn Law League was formed, I think, in 1838 or 1837, and seven years later, when Mr. Cobden brought forward his annual motion in the House of Commons he could only find 120, or a few more, members to support it, and yet he had funds at his disposal which make our mouths water. He had everything to assist him, and yet seven years after the agitation began, if it had not been for what I may call the accident — the incident of the Irish famine, and the somewhat unexpected conversion of the then Prime Minister, Sir Robert Peel, he seemed to be as little advanced at the end of that time as he was at the beginning.

We have only been in operation for twelve months. We, more fortunate than Mr. Cobden, have always enjoyed the sympathy of the Prime Minister and his colleagues. (*Hear, hear.*) I wish it had been a little more than sympathy — (*laughter and 'Hear, hear!'*) — but everything comes to him who stands and waits. (*Laughter and cheers.*) We have the support of 200 members of the House of Commons. (*Cheers.*) We have the aid of the most powerful and influential portion of the Press — (*hear, hear*) — and we have the enthusiastic approval of the vast majority of the Unionist party. (*Cheers.*) That has been indicated by recent meetings, and I venture to say that at the present moment you cannot call a popular open meeting of Unionists, whether they be Conservative or Liberal, in which the vast majority of the rank and file will not be in favour of our proposals. (*Cheers.*) I have said that we have the sympathy of the Prime Minister. I hope we shall retain it . . .

[1] *Memoirs of Sir Almeric Fitzroy*, vol. i, p. 212.

... Well, under these circumstances, although I think he would be a very bold man who would predict the hour of our victory, I think we may confidently predict that success will be ours at no distant date ...
... We have to choose. Ours is a positive policy — (*cheers*) — theirs is a negative policy. (*Hear, hear.*) Ours is a constructive policy; theirs is a destructive policy — (*hear, hear*) — and I venture to think, after some experience of my countrymen, that although there may be some hesitation, although there may be some difficulty all at once in meeting the misrepresentation to which we have been subjected, that the constructive policy will win in the long run. (*Cheers.*) A fighting policy will have the best chance — (*hear, hear*) — and, if I am to use the slang of the day, the whole-hogger will beat the half-hearter. (*Cheers.*)

All in all, July had been a month of uninterrupted success. Chamberlain had rescued Tariff Reform from the doldrums in which it seemed for a time becalmed. In a few days the House would rise and the second great campaign would begin. Meanwhile, in *The Times* of 1 August, Rudyard Kipling published these verses:

And Joseph dreamed a dream, and he told it to his brethren; and they hated him yet the more! — Genesis xxxvii. 5.

Oh ye who hold the written clue
To all save all unwritten things,
And, half a league behind, pursue
The accomplished Fact with flouts and flings,
Look! To your knee your baby brings
The oldest tale since earth began —
The answer to your worryings:
'*Once on a time there was a Man.*'

He, single-handed, met and slew
Magicians, Armies, Ogres, Kings.
He lonely 'mid his doubting crew —
'In all the loneliness of wings' —
He fed the flame, he filled the springs,
He locked the ranks, he launched the van
Straight at the grinning Teeth of Things.
'*Once on a time there was a Man.*'

The peace of shocked Foundations flew
Before his ribald questionings.
He broke the Oracles in two,
And bared the paltry wires and strings.
He headed desert wanderings;
He led his soul, his cause, his clan
A little from the ruck of Things.
'*Once on a time there was a Man.*'

Thrones, Powers, Dominions block the view
With episodes and underlings —
The meek historian deems them true
Nor heeds the song that Clio sings —
The simple central truth that stings
The mob to boo, the priest to ban ;
Things never yet created things —
' *Once on a time there was a Man.*'

A bolt is fallen from the blue.
A wakened realm full circle swings
Where Dothan's dreamer dreams anew
Of vast and farborne harvestings ;
And unto him an Empire clings
That grips the purpose of his plan
My Lords, how think you of these things?
Once — in our time — is there a Man ?

BOOK XXV

TARIFF REFORM:
THE SECOND CAMPAIGN
(1904–1905)

CHAPTER CXII

THE APPEAL TO AGRICULTURE

(*July* 1904–*January* 1905)

Chamberlain Turns to the Country Districts — The Welbeck Speech — Do the Colonies Want Preference? — Chamberlain Proposes a Conference — An Exchange with Rosebery — A Formula to Unite Chamberlain and Balfour? — Negotiation with Balfour — Balfour Goes Halfway at Edinburgh — Chamberlain Replies at Luton — The Southampton Party Conference — India and Tariff Reform — Chamberlain's Irritation with the Government — 'I could not bring out one' — The Limehouse Speech and Alien Immigration — The Preston Speech — Balfour's 'halfsheet of Notepaper' — Ethel's Death — The Gainsborough Speech.

I

T H E day after his triumph at the Albert Hall, Chamberlain wrote:

CHAMBERLAIN TO SELBORNE

22 *July* 1904.—It will not be easy to make an Empire and it is well that all who desire it should know the difficulties.

But they are not greater than those confronted by the makers of the United States.

They *can* and they *must* be overcome if we have as much faith, determination and courage as Washington and Hamilton.

Sometimes I think we are of inferior fibre — and then only do I despair.

A few days later we find him writing to his most intimate friend.

CHAMBERLAIN TO COLLINGS

25 *July* 1904.—I did not get to Highbury yesterday but spent Saturday and Sunday with Gerald Balfour from whom I heard much that was encouraging as to the opinions of himself and colleagues.

Thus despair alternated with determination and, underlying all, a growing repugnance to the drudgery of the task. It was in such a mood that Chamberlain entered on what came to be known as his Second Tariff Reform Campaign.

The programme was rather lighter than in the previous year. There would be only five major engagements instead of seven and

X 601

only one speech at each, not two or three as in 1903. The main object of the second campaign was to reach the agricultural districts, omitted altogether in the first. Meetings were, therefore, to be held at Welbeck and Luton — the first two in the campaign; and at Gainsborough — the last. There would also be speeches at Limehouse, regarded as the poorest district in the country and at Preston, Farrer Eckroyd's old stronghold, but also a centre of the strongly Free Trade cotton industry.

It was eighteen months since Chamberlain had launched his fiscal thunderbolt at Birmingham. From the beginning, public excitement had been aroused by the novelty of the proposals and the standing of their author. Then had come the break-up of the Cabinet and the first nation-wide campaign. By December 1903 it had seemed to many as if Chamberlain might carry all before him and sweep the Unionists back into power on the crest of a new Imperialist wave. But when the crunch came, Balfour had refused to commit the reserve. The last chance of victory had been lost, and ever since the Unionists had been in full retreat. Other issues had arisen, exposing other flanks to attack. Trade had improved and the atmosphere of economic crisis was no longer there. Meanwhile the Prime Minister's continuing hesitation had made fiscal reform a bone of contention between Unionists rather than the main dividing line between the opposing parties.

In such circumstances many men would have retired in anger to their tents. That had been Rosebery's way more than once. It could never be Chamberlain's. He had sacrificed everything to his cause and was determined 'to win or die' in the attempt. To have diminished the agitation at this stage would have been to admit defeat and to demoralise countless enthusiastic supporters. He must go on or give up.

But to preach fiscal reform on a rising market was to double stakes on a losing game. There was a real risk of a 'flop'. Would the audiences still pack out the meetings? Would opponents keep the debate going? No effort was spared to draw them. Every device of stage management was employed. Vast funds were spent on propaganda. *The Times*, the *Daily Telegraph*, the *Daily Mail* and the *Daily Express* gave their full support.

It was uphill work all the way, but it succeeded beyond expectation. Despite every adverse circumstance, Chamberlain brought the fiscal question back into the forefront of politics by the middle of July and kept it there till the House met again in February.

The second campaign could not succeed where the first had failed. It would not carry the country. But it would seal the triumph of the new policy in the Unionist Associations up and down the country.

II

On 4 August, before the House had risen, the first demonstration of the campaign was held at Welbeck, the palace of the Dukes of Portland. The meeting was held in the Riding School on 'a piping hot afternoon'. The audience, mainly agricultural labourers, numbered over 12,000. A host of magnates and political leaders adorned the platform. They included four dukes who had come to support the Birmingham tribune — Portland, who took the chair, Newcastle, Sutherland and old Rutland, the John Manners of Disraeli's 'Merry England' days. It might, indeed, have been a scene out of a Disraeli novel.

It was no easy task, in those days before the microphone, to hold an audience of 12,000. Chamberlain began well enough. But suddenly there came a storm; and for ten minutes or so the noise of the thunder and of the rain falling on the glass roof of the riding school drowned the speech altogether. Meanwhile three or four thousand of the audience who were standing at the back of the school began shuffling on the wooden boards and talking among themselves. The storm ceased as suddenly as it had started; but, with the shuffling and whispering at the back, Chamberlain remained inaudible to many of the audience till near the end of his speech. The Tariff Reform League had attempted too much. But though a quarter of the audience at Welbeck might not have heard the speech, newspaper readers had every word before them at breakfast next morning.

Chamberlain began by a description of Balfour's policy of Retaliation. Then as the storm subsided, he turned to the position of agriculture.

Well, ladies and gentlemen, that policy of Retaliation is a very good policy as far as it goes. (*'Hear, hear' and a laugh.*) But where does agriculture come in ? (*Hear, hear.*) The policy will help the manufacturer of this country to recover and to maintain his position, but how does it help the farmer and how does it help the labourer ? Yet, if you look, it is the farmer and the labourer who have suffered more than any other classes from the system to which I have referred. (*Cheers.*) . . . Our opponents will tell you that you have nothing to complain of. Mr. Morley at Manchester the other day said that owing to Free Trade the farmer was able to hold up his head and the labourer was in a superior position. I am very glad to hear it. I should be still more glad if it were true. (*Loud laughter.*) If that were the case I should not be wanted here. (*Laughter and cheers.*) If you are well you need not call in the doctor. (*Hear, hear.*) But is it true? (*Cries of 'No'.*) Are those the facts? In the last 30 years the acreage in corn in this country has lessened by three millions of acres, the green crops have lessened by three-quarters of a million, much land has gone out of cultivation. What is of much more importance, an enormous amount of land has passed from arable to pasture; and although that may not matter much to the farmer it matters a great deal to the labourer (*hear, hear*), because there is less labour required upon the land. The stock of the country has on the whole diminished by something like two millions of head, and the farmers' capital, according to Sir Robert Giffen, has diminished by something like 200 millions sterling. Well, but what is the consequence of all this? The consequence is that there has been less labour for the working man to do, and the number of people cultivating the land has decreased by 600,000 in the last 30 years; and if you go back for 50 years it has decreased by something like a million. What would you say if something of that kind was told you about any other business? If you were told that the returns had diminished, that the capital had been lost, and that the number of workpeople had been decreased, would you see in all that any evidence of great prosperity? I think you would be justified in saying that under such circumstances a change had become necessary. . . . Are you not justified in claiming the same justice for your industry which the Government has promised for manufactures? Is it possible that either the farmer or the labourer can be satisfied with the existing state of things?

Then came an appeal to the interests of the farmer and still more of the farm labourer.

As to the farmer, I am pretty well aware of what answer he will make. The other day a duty, a moderate duty of a shilling, was placed upon corn. It is a very small duty. It had no effect upon the price of bread. It could not be said to have given any substantial advantage to the farmer. But he welcomed it; and if he welcomed that, still more is he likely to welcome the much greater advantages that I promise to him. (*Cheers.*) I do not believe that I have to preach to the farmer. It is rather to the labourer that I have to address myself.

And the first thing I say to him is this, that now, as never before, he is being consulted as to this matter. Free Trade was carried into effect without any reference to the agricultural labourer. He had no votes. He was of no importance. Nobody thought it worth while to ask his opinion. But now he is in a different position. He has the vote; he can make his voice heard; he can carry elections in many counties. If he is not convinced, if I cannot convince him that what I am proposing is to his benefit and advantage it ought not to be successful. . . . I have been 30 years in politics, and during the whole of that time I have had a special interest in the condition of the agricultural labourer (*cheers*), and I have taken that interest because, of all the working classes in the country, he is the least fortunate, because he in the general progress has gained less than any other class. I took an active part in securing for him the franchise; and when the franchise was obtained, . . . free education for his children. . . . Then, the next thing we did — I say 'we' because it was with the approval and assistance of my friends Mr. Chaplin (*cheers*) and Mr. Jesse Collings ('*hear, hear*'), and others who have always shown themselves to be friends of the labourers — it was with their assistance that we were enabled to obtain legislation which facilitated the acquisition of small holdings and allotments, and . . . the result has been that at the present day 100,000 labourers at least have got allotments who never had allotments before. . . . Why do I remind you of all this? Not to boast of it, but to say that, while we had very little assistance from those Radicals who now ask for your votes, we have shown by our past history that we have some right to call ourselves friends of the labourers. (*Loud cheers.*)

My opponents say that I am going to reduce you to famine and starvation because I propose to put a tax of 2s. a quarter upon corn. I do propose to put on that tax. (*Cheers.*) But . . . let me . . . impress upon you the fact that those who try to induce you to believe that everything depends upon the price of corn are deceiving you. (*Hear, hear.*) What you have to find is employment (*cheers*) — plenty of employment and the best wages you can get for that employment. (*More cheers.*) If you want an illustration, let me take it from two very different examples: If the Radicals are right when they come and tell you that even a small increase in the price of your food would be ruinous to you, then the happiest countries in the world must be the countries where food is cheapest; and what countries are those? China (*laughter and cheers*) — China and India. (*Renewed cheers.*) Well, ladies and gentlemen, in China and India, although food is cheap, wages are only a few pence a day, and I should be very sorry to see any of you emigrating to China or to India with any idea that you could better your position. (*Cheers.*) But then look at the other end of the scale — look at America. In America the price of food and the cost of living are higher than in England. I do not know how much higher — probably 10 or 20 per cent. But then, as the agricultural labourer in America has wages of 4s. or 5s. a day, he has a much larger margin than you have, and he is much better off. So that my point is this — and I beg you to consider it — what you have to do if you want to improve your position is to see what system, what policy, will give you most employment and most wages. (*Hear, hear.*) Now, has Free Trade given you more employment? (*Cries of 'No'.*) No, it has driven from the land half the labourers who used to work upon the land, and where have they gone? They have gone to foreign countries, away from their homes and the people whom they hold dear. They have gone into the towns already overcrowded, into insanitary conditions, or they have gone to the work-house. ('*Shame*'.)

The effect of Free Trade upon the labourer of this country has been disastrous. (*Cheers.*) But has it raised your wages? Yes, to a certain extent the wages of the labourer have been raised. But mark this — of all classes in the community, that of the agricultural labourers is the one in which wages have been raised least (*hear, hear*) ; and that is the consequence of the system which I am condemning. I see from the great Blue-book which was published the other day that, while the average wages for the five years ended 1902 in the case of all other industries had risen 17 per cent above the wages 20 years ago, in the case of the agricultural labourer the increase was only 6 per cent. (*Hear, hear.*) Now, I ask the labourers, Is it worth your while to give your vote for a system under which you are still the worst paid labourers in the United Kingdom, and under which your rate of progress has only been one-third of that of other classes?

There followed a long passage in praise of French agricultural policy.

I cannot help thinking that our neighbours in France manage these matters better than we do ourselves.

Then came a hint that the tax on corn and meat might be offset by reductions on tobacco as well as on sugar and tea. Altogether there would be a saving of

4½d. a week to every labourer's family ; and although that is not a great deal, I venture to say it is a great deal more than anybody else has ever promised you (*laughter and cheers*).

He closed this passage with a slogan for agriculture :

The watchword of the new policy . . . the watchword in the agricultural districts is this 'more profit for the farmer, more employment for the labourer, and cheaper food for his family'.

It was a powerful appeal with a Radical as well as a patriotic ring. Yet, we can see, in reading it, why Chamberlain had refused to visit the agricultural districts in his first campaign. He could not preach the new policy to an agricultural audience without stressing his proposals to tax food. Besides, advocacy of a tariff on imports of foreign foodstuffs very swiftly crossed the dividing line between Retaliation and Protection. In the Welbeck speech, a passage on the milking industry and another in praise of French and American agricultural policy showed Chamberlain's policy in a more protectionist light than ever.

III

From Welbeck Chamberlain and his wife paid a short visit to the Duke of Rutland at Belvoir. They then returned to London, where Chamberlain sat to Furse for his portrait, waiting for the House to rise.

The next six weeks were spent at Highbury save for a long week-end at Burghley, the great house of the Exeter Cecils. On the whole it was a time of relaxation. Morley came to spend a few days; and Churchill spent a night to discuss the proofs of his life of Lord Randolph. There was no escape, however, from the burden of correspondence. His secretaries estimated, about this time, that the daily postbag was never less than 200. There were occasional committees too; and, this year, he made a special effort to bring some of his friends in the Government to support his campaign.

CHAMBERLAIN TO SELBORNE

16 *September* 1904: *Private.*—We are promoting meetings for the autumn in the Midlands district, and I write to ask whether you could give me say a couple of speeches if we make all the arrangements? By 'we' I mean the Midlands Liberal Unionist Association.

In this district, as you know, we are all Fiscal Reformers and I do not see how that part of our programme can possibly be omitted from the speeches, but unless circumstances have materially changed since I left the Government, you and other Cabinet Ministers are free to express your own personal opinions on the subject without any suspicion of disloyalty to the Party or to your Leader.

Hitherto I have fought the battle almost alone, and I hope that in view of the coming election, I may now have some assistance from those who are in full sympathy with my views.

CHAMBERLAIN TO SELBORNE

26 *September* 1904: *Private.*—The Resolution we should propose to submit would be one of confidence in the Government with the addition of the Resolution passed by the delegates at the morning conference of Liberal Unionists in London. It would therefore run as follows :—

'That this meeting expresses its full confidence in H.M. Government, and believing that the time has come for a complete reform of our fiscal system, approves of the demand made by the Prime Minister for increased powers to deal with hostile tariffs and the practice of dumping, and further expresses its earnest hope that the ties of sympathy already uniting the British Empire may be strengthened by a commercial union with the Colonies based on preferential arrangements between them and the mother country.'

Selborne sent a staunch reply. Since Powell Williams' death, Chamberlain now looked to him more than anyone; and he proved a good friend. Lyttelton also agreed to speak for preference. So, of course, did Austen whose early hesitations were by now completely dispelled. Meanwhile a new transaction was afoot. To understand it we must go back a little.

IV

Chamberlain had secured a nationwide audience for his new proposals. He had built up strong support for them in the House of Commons and in the constituencies. His second campaign would, no doubt, carry this process still further. Yet where would all this lead? There could be no question now of carrying the country at the General Election. The most that could still be attempted was to prevent the coming electoral defeat from turning into disaster; and, if the Unionists went to the polls still divided upon fiscal policy, disaster was certain. The political problem, therefore, was to find a common fiscal platform on which the party could unite.

Chamberlain did not regard his Glasgow programme as sacrosanct, but there could be no question of abandoning the preferential policy. Balfour on his side showed no disposition to move a step beyond his Sheffield speech. Could they, perhaps, find some intermediate formula on which they could agree? Was there some practical next step which they could join in proposing, without in any way retreating from their respective positions?

Two things may have pointed to the formula which presently took shape in Chamberlain's brain. The first was the persistent claim of Rosebery and other Free Trade leaders that the Colonies were not prepared to give Britain any substantial concessions in any preferential agreement. The second was good news from the Colonies themselves. In opening the Canadian budget (7 June), Fielding had made a most helpful statement. He had declined an Opposition proposal to move a resolution in support of Chamberlain's policy, on the ground that this would be interference in the internal affairs of the United Kingdom. But he had nevertheless declared:

I think I am justified in saying that, practically, the two great political parties in Canada are a unit today in favour of the principle of preferential trade.

Fielding had followed up this declaration with similar statements and had been fully supported by Laurier. Even Minto, always inclined to be suspicious of his Liberal Ministers, had written that these statements 'appear to me very clear and a direct contradiction to the belief apparently existing at home that Canada is lukewarm'.[1]

Meanwhile Watson, the Australian Labour Premier, and Deakin

[1] Minto to J. C., 16 July 1904.

then in opposition had both made encouraging statements in favour of the Chamberlain policy.

The first indication we have of Chamberlain's new plan dates from the end of June. On 27 June, he entertained Harmsworth, Granby and Amery to lunch at Prince's Gardens. Afterwards, Amery jotted down the following note of their conversation.

J.C. unfolded plan of getting A.J.B. into line by device of declaring for Colonial Conference which A.J.B. was to announce at Southampton.

His idea was that Balfour should propose a conference to discuss with the Colonial Governments whether preferential arrangements mutually satisfactory to Britain and the Colonies could be worked out in practice. Chamberlain never doubted that the verdict of such a conference would be in his favour. But Balfour and others could go into it uncommitted and free to adopt or reject the policy of Preference in the light of the conference's results. Here was a practical way of resolving the differences among Unionists. If Balfour would declare for it, at the Conservative Party Conference at Southampton, then the whole party could unite behind him. Whatever their inward reservations, Preferentialists and Retaliationists could join hands; and even Free Fooders would have a good ground to suspend judgment. Such a proposal, moreover, could not fail to embarrass the Liberal leaders. Having denied that the Colonies really wanted Preference, they could hardly oppose putting the matter to the test. Yet if they agreed to such a conference, they would have to concede that food taxes were 'discussable'.

Chamberlain seems to have revolved this idea for some weeks. At the banquet given him by Unionist members on his birthday (8 July), he had made a cautious step towards it.

This is a critical and creative time. You cannot play fast-and-loose with your destiny. . . .
I think I am not vain when I say that I know what I am speaking of. I know that you have an opportunity of which you can now avail yourselves, which may never recur. I think the Colonies will never want for suitors; and if you do not pay your court to them, while still they are willing to receive your addresses, you will find that in the time to come they will have made other arrangements, and you will no longer be welcomed in the house of those who are now your greatest friends. I believe they are prepared to meet you, and in no grudging or halting spirit. I believe they will make concessions at least equal to any which you will be called upon to make. I believe that they will recognise that no agreement can be permanent and satisfactory which is not beneficial to us as well as to them . . .

X 2

All this constitutes the present position. Yet we are told that they have shown no readiness, that they want everything for themselves, they ask everything from us, and will give nothing in return. I wish I could look upon these statements as merely for home consumption. Then they would not do the harm they are calculated to do, and arouse the feelings they are certain to create. But if, in spite of all the evidence which has been brought before us, in spite of the declarations of Ministers, statesmen, Legislatures, and public bodies of every kind, they (the Free Traders) still profess to disbelieve in the willingness and the readiness of the Colonies to make arrangements which shall be substantially beneficial to all the parties concerned, then the test is easy. There will be no difficulty for them or for any one to secure a result which cannot be contested. Call the Colonies to your council, bring their representatives into communication with yours, and then let us see if we cannot together make some arrangement, mutually beneficial, which will indeed develop our trade with our best customers, which will at the same time people and make prosperous the whole Empire, and which will divert into British channels that great stream of emigration and of trade which has done so much for the prosperity of other countries, all of whom, at any rate, have not been equally friendly.

That is the test which I should like our opponents to apply.

Chamberlain discussed his idea fully with Austen who seems to have taken Lyttelton into his confidence. It is also probable that Chamberlain sounded Gerald Balfour on the subject when he visited him in the country on 23 July. It was not, however, till 1 August that he made a public and concrete proposal. The occasion was the vote of censure moved by Campbell-Bannerman on the action of Lansdowne and Selborne in accepting official positions in a reformed Liberal Unionist Association pledged to the taxation of food.

The course of the debate need not detain us. Despite a heavy abstention on the part of the Free Fooders, including Hicks Beach, the Government received a majority of 78. Chamberlain's speech, however, deserves our attention.

After some chaff at Hugh Cecil's expense, he defined the difference between his position and the Government's.

It is not for me to speak for my right hon. friend [Balfour]. If there is no difference between my right hon. friend and myself, why did I leave the Government? There was absolutely no necessity for my leaving the Government except this — that I held with sincerity the views which I have subsequently placed before the country. I recognised that my right hon. friend did not go as far as I wished to go, and that my continued presence in the Government would mean either that I should embarrass him or that I myself should be unable to speak freely. Therefore, I went to speak freely to the country on a matter to which I attached so much importance. What my right hon. friend said from the moment I left his Government was that he sympathized with the great aspirations which I have put before the country ; that he sympathized with the idea of preferential terms between the Colonies and ourselves even though those terms may involve a slight addition to our duties on food. . . . He assured me of his sympathy, but at the same time he said that, in his opinion the policy was not at the present time a practicable one, or one likely to be accepted by the people of this country. There probably is the difference which existed then, and which I fear still exists between my right hon. friend and myself. I myself think that this policy is ripe, at any rate, to be submitted to the people of this country.

I do not say that the people of this country would accept it at the first offer. I have never pretended — I have been perfectly frank with the country and with my supporters — I have never pretended that a great change of this kind could be expected hastily to be accepted by a people who for 60 years had been going on under a totally different system. But that it will be accepted I am as certain as that I am standing here. As the consummation which I desire will come all the sooner, the sooner the proposal is made to the country, for that reason, so far as I am concerned, the sooner the election comes the sooner I shall be pleased. Of course, if my late colleagues had accepted that view, which perhaps is a wrong one, there would have been no occasion for me to leave the Government, but as they did not accept it they are perfectly right in saying that they do not propose that policy to the present Parliament, and in saying that as to what they or any one else will propose to another Parliament is a thing which it will be quite time enough to discuss when that time comes.

He then turned to the Opposition :

I put this question for consideration before the Opposition. You condemn the Government, not because they are doing anything, not because they are proposing anything but because you suspect, or suspect at all events, some members of them, of sympathy — of what you called concealed sympathy, although I think it is open sympathy — with this idea of Preference. You can only do that by yourselves frankly and definitely declaring that you have no sympathy with it, and will not look at it under any conditions. Now, is that your position? Is it your position as responsible people who may very shortly be occupying office your-selves, is it your position that, no matter what the Colonies say to you, no matter what offer they make to you, no matter what advantages or concessions they will offer you, that you will shut the door in their faces and tell them, 'No. We are opposed to Preference'? We wanted to hang one Prime Minister because we suspected him of it ; and, of course, we should ourselves be ready to commit hara-kiri if we had sympathy with it. Though I put the question I do not ask for an answer, because I should be sorry to have it as positively given as I think it must logically be. But if you say, on the other hand, 'No. We are prepared to meet an offer from the Colonies if it is good enough', then I should ask you another question — Will you agree to call the Colonies to your councils?

In the closing passage he summed up his own position and made his definite proposal.

I have been satisfied loyally to accept and support the position taken up by the Government in this matter. So far as their policy of Retaliation goes, I entirely approve of it in principle. As to the details, I am content to wait till I see them. But I admit that, to my mind, the policy of Preference is more urgent and important than the policy of Retaliation. The policy of Retaliation might, I think, be adopted at a much later stage, although, perhaps, with less chance of advantage than at present. But the opportunity for the policy of Preference is sliding away. If it be not accepted within a reasonable time, the offer will no longer remain open. I go, therefore, one step further than I have ever gone before in connexion with anything that this Government may do, and I urge my right hon. friend the Prime Minister especially to consider whether, in view of the importance of this question, of the primary importance of knowing what it is that the Colonies really wish, and what it is that they are prepared to do, he should not ask them both questions and should not call a conference from the Colonies, a conference of representatives to meet and consider this subject in order that the House and the country may discover whether in what I have said on this subject I have based myself upon real knowledge and experience, or whether those are right who from the first, almost before they knew what my policy could be, determined to oppose it on purely party grounds.

Chamberlain's proposal led to an interesting correspondence in *The Times* between him and Rosebery. Rosebery, with typical impetuosity, was at first inclined to welcome the idea of a Conference. Then he saw the danger — or others pointed it out to him — and he drew back.

ROSEBERY AND CHAMBERLAIN

(to *The Times*)

ROSEBERY : 3 *August* 1904.—Under certain limitations to be stated in this letter, I welcome Mr. Chamberlain's proposal of a colonial conference to consider whether fiscal union be practicable, though it cannot be described as particularly startling, for colonial conference is the one sure base of Imperial union. The only wonder with me is that the proposal was not made long ago.

Had it been made in May, 1903, the Conservative party would have been preserved intact, much opposition would have been silenced, and what is infinitely more important, the Empire would not have been flung into the arena of party.

The country would not then have been told that the country was turning its back on an offer which we are now officially informed has never been made.

The very avoidance up to now of this obvious suggestion has been one of the main causes which have tended to throw doubt on the genuineness of the policy, and to associate it rather with party exigencies than Imperial ideals.

The proposal of a conference should in fine have been the base and starting point, not an afterthought.

But, Sir, if a conference is to be summoned, we must remember that it is a two-edged instrument, for if it be abortive it may do much more harm than good. If the delegates assemble in the expectation that Great Britain is prepared to tax or narrow its supplies of food, it is very likely to lead to disappointment and to reaction. Nor, indeed, can it do good unless it be desired by the outer Britains as well as by the home country.

It would, indeed, be best that they should signify an anxiety for such a conference before it be summoned.

Further, there should be a clear basis for the conference, drawn up in conjunction with the Colonies, a basis agreed to by both parties.

And lastly, the British representatives should be not merely partisan or official, but men of national weight.

Even under these conditions, a conference, it is obvious, cannot undo the evil of the last 14 months, but with the suggested safeguards it should bring the controversy to a practical issue. Only let me repeat my firm conviction that, unless it be desired by the Colonies, and assembled on a plain basis arranged beforehand, and freed from the party taint, it may do more harm than good.

CHAMBERLAIN : 4 *August* 1904.—I welcome the letter of Lord Rosebery in your issue to-day as indicating another change of front on his part which will carry him back to the patriotic attitude adopted by him in 1888, when he was ready to die for the cause of Imperial federation, and when he did not believe that 'you can obtain the great boon of a powerful Empire encircling the globe with a bond of commercial unity and peace without some sacrifice on your part'.

I observe that Lord Rosebery complains that what he calls the obvious suggestion of a conference was not made before ; but he does not explain why, in view of my neglect, he did not himself supply the deficiency. I admit that it seemed to me desirable in the first place to test the opinion of the country on the offer which, in spite of Lord Rosebery's denial, I still maintain was made by the Colonies on the occasion of the Conference of Premiers at the time of the Coronation.

This point, however, is not of importance, since I hope that we have now arrived at the same conclusion on the main proposal. But I am afraid that Lord Rosebery is still imperfectly informed as to the real issue. I entirely agree with him that the wishes of the colonists themselves should be an essential condition, and I trust that when these wishes have been expressed, whether before or at the conference, he will be prepared to give due weight to them. In this case, however, he must not at the outset bar out of consideration what will certainly be the main object of the colonists if they accept the proposal — viz., to see whether or not, in return for the Preferences they have already given and are prepared to give to us, we, on our part, are ready to make that sacrifice of our economic orthodoxy which Lord Rosebery contemplated in 1888, and to reciprocate with a Preference on those products of the Colonies, including corn and meat, the sale of which they desire to extend in this country. To suggest a conference on Preference, while rigidly excluding all reference to taxes on food, would be in present circumstances a childish and almost an insulting proposition.

ROSEBERY: 5 *August* 1904.—I see that my welcome was premature. Mr. Chamberlain — as the Duke of Devonshire said on a memorable occasion, only changing the name — 'Mr. Chamberlain and I do not mean the same thing'.

I am glad to have elicited his letter; the air is clearer, though he has killed his own proposal.

The conference would have been suggested before, it appears, had it not been desirable to test the opinion of the country on Mr. Chamberlain's policy. He has now had enough of testing, and, finding the results almost uniformly unfavourable, he harks back to a conference. Now, one point stands clear as a result of that testing — that the country will not tolerate any taxation of its food supply. Yet Mr. Chamberlain regards a conference which excludes taxation of food as a mockery. Why then should he desire to summon a conference? Nothing has happened since the conference of 1902, except the question put to the country whether it will tax its food and the emphatic negative of its reply. Surely then to summon a conference in order to discuss the taxation of food with the Colonies is, to use Mr. Chamberlain's expression, a 'childish and insulting proposition' — childish as regards practical result, insulting to the people of this country who decline to be parties to such a scheme.

So far, as regards this country; now as to the Colonies. I do not now ask what their representatives would bring with them in the shape of offers; 'the preference they ... are prepared to give to us' — that is an important though not the most urgent matter. But could Mr. Chamberlain's scheme be carried out? Who could appear as delegates for Great Britain to discuss the taxation of food with the Colonies? Whom would they represent? Whence would be this mandate? It is obvious that after what has passed nothing but a general election, giving an overwhelming majority to the food taxers, could confer such a mandate. Could there be a more 'childish and insulting proposition' to the Colonies than to invite their statesmen to come thousands of miles to discuss the question with delegates without authority or national credentials in the teeth of every indication of public feeling in Great Britain?

It would almost seem as if this is the second string of a broken bow.

A few days later (10 August), Howard Vincent put down a question to the Prime Minister, enquiring whether he proposed to summon a Colonial Conference. Balfour replied that he did not intend to take any steps 'at present'. Three days later, the House rose and the protagonists separated.

V

Towards the middle of August, Austen went to see Balfour. The main arguments he then put to him were repeated by Austen in a letter to Balfour of 24 August, written from Highbury. We print them below, in their different sections along with some explanatory comment.

Austen began with an analysis of the political situation as it appeared to him. He did not apparently consult Chamberlain before writing, but he knew his mind better than anyone.

Everything therefore tends to confirm me in the opinion which I expressed to you at our last meeting — that it is time that we had a change of Government. I do not think that we have credit or parliamentary strength sufficient to overcome so many difficulties. I do not think that we can in any case last long enough to reach better times, and I do not believe that we shall gain strength or live down unpopularity (earned or undeserved) by attempting to carry on administration through another session.

But, if this is a correct view of the position — and it is at any rate the view taken by so shrewd an observer as Douglas [1] — it is more than ever important that we should use what little time we have left to bring the Party together, to unite it on a common policy which will be our platform for the future, to awaken its enthusiasm and to prepare it and the electors for the fight in which we shall shortly be engaged.

At the present time the Party viewed as a whole is timid, undecided, vacillating. It has no constructive policy. It does not know what is to be its future. It is exposed to a most active and dangerous attack and it stands timidly on the defensive. Now, no party can win on these lines, and as things stand now, we are already disastrously beaten and every month's delay will only make our case worse. But there is no reason why we should thus sit still and let the tide of disaster swamp us. We cannot win now but we can lay the foundations of future victory, and even now we may profoundly modify the results of the next elections.

What is needed to work this revolution in our fate is only that our leaders should be united, and united in support of a positive future policy. You know what I think that policy should be. It need not be my father's. I am convinced that you and he could carry in a shorter period than most people suppose the whole of the Glasgow programme; but I can quite believe that though in general sympathy with his objects, you are not prepared to adopt all his methods, and I do not propose for your adoption anything to which I anticipate that in principle you can have any objection. Let it be your own policy announced by you at Southampton, distinct from his wherever you think a difference necessary,

[1] Right Hon. A. Akers-Douglas, then Home Secretary and for many years Chief Whip of the Conservative Party, afterwards 1st Lord Chilston.

but let it be one on which he and his friends can unite with you. I undertake that you will not find him unreasonable. You would not expect him to pretend — and it is not desirable that he should pretend — that you had given him all he asked or all he wanted. He may still think his own line the best, but I am certain that for the sake of unity, and, above all, for the sake of keeping in close touch with you, he will accept less and loyally work for it.

But, if we are to do any good we must get together quickly. We must plant our batteries at once and open fire on a concerted plan this autumn. I do not think that you have any conception of the results which would be achieved by such combined action even now, though you must see the disastrous effects which will follow from our silence or our half-hearted and discordant utterances during the next few months. The danger is in a nutshell: if we don't now get together, we shall inevitably and fatally drift farther and farther apart. It is a prospect which fills me with consternation on every ground — political and personal. And please allow me to say without offence that you have some personal responsibility in the matter. You encouraged my father to go out as a 'pioneer'; you gave your blessing to his efforts for closer union with the Colonies; you assured us who remained that we too thus served the interests of Imperial Union and we were thus induced to leave him at the time almost single-handed at his Herculean task. He undertook this work believing in your sympathy, believing that, when he had proved that the obstacles were not insuperable, you and your Government would be prepared to make some advance; and had he not been led to believe this, I think his course would have been different, and with however profound a regret at seeing so great an opportunity lost, I believe he would never have set out on a course which in such a case could only result in bringing him in conflict with old friends and particularly with yourself.

Are we now to tell him that we can do no more? That because some forty Free Fooders still hesitate, we are unable to move? You know that I cannot take that line, and believe me, there are many of your colleagues and more of your followers who are in almost as great a difficulty as I am.

Cannot you make a bridge for us all and yet do nothing and say nothing which is not in accordance with your most profound convictions? I think that you might; and it is in the hope that you will, that I give both you and myself the trouble involved in writing and reading this long letter.

Austen then put forward a definite plan based on Chamberlain's proposal for a Colonial Conference.

I tried to suggest the other day what such a policy might be. The main feature of it would be to announce that, if again returned to power, you would summon a conference of Colonial and Indian representatives to consider the question of Imperial trade and that, if you were satisfied by the result that other portions of the Empire would do their share, you would then propose to Parliament such measures as are necessary to fulfil our part of the common policy.

In this way and in this way only can your doubts as to the attitude of the Colonies be resolved; and please remember that all the members of the late Cabinet, except those who have since resigned, agreed to consult the Colonies and that we were only prevented from doing so by Ritchie and Co.

If the result is not satisfactory, you will not proceed further. If our doubters like Lytton and Maxwell[1] think it unsatisfactory, they will be free to act as they please. If the Colonies are unreasonable, I and others who think with me will have to recognise facts. We must surrender our hopes and we, at any rate, shall give you no further trouble.

I put this point first because it is the concession which I ask of you — a concession not of principle, but of policy only.

On the other hand, you might fix the limit of the duty on *wheat*. You might reduce it to 1s. if you think 2s. too high. You might reject the idea of a 'scientific tariff' if that frightens people, and you might substitute for it a fixed 10 per cent. or 7½ per cent. to provide the necessary revenue; you might have a fixed addition of 5 or 10 per cent. for retaliatory purposes where needed, or you might deal with each case separately; and you might graft on any such plan whatever proposals for dealing with dumping seem best to you. In short, in all these matters I think I may safely say that we should all desire to fall into line with you and to meet your wishes in every way.

This is not the Glasgow policy — still less is it the Glasgow policy in its later developments; but if you would put forward some such policy as this, closely in harmony as I believe with all you have ever said or thought, you would rally all our scattered forces, and we should go to the country united and zealous instead of divided and half-hearted.

At this point in their discussion Balfour seems to have put forward a counter proposal. He accepted the idea of a Colonial Conference to discuss fiscal policy; but subject to two reservations. He would want a mandate from the electorate before he entered on the conference. He would also feel bound to submit the conclusion of the conference to the electors before acting upon them. Two elections, would, thus, have to take place before a preferential policy could be introduced.

Austen seems to have demurred at this suggestion but asked for time to consider it. His written reply was a clear negative.

. . . I beg you not to proceed with the suggestion you made to me in Downing Street. It will not do to propose a second referendum after the Conference. The more I think of this suggestion, the less I like it; but one practical objection is I think sufficient to cause you to reject it on further consideration. You cannot ask your followers to work hard and long if the only result of success is to be that the fruits of victory are at once to be put to the hazard of a fresh election. No party can be kept together by a policy which promises at best but a succession of dissolutions, and candidates will not be forthcoming if the only result of their election is to be, that, within a year or so, they are to be involved in all the chances and expense of a fresh election.

But such a policy as I have tried to sketch, if put forward by you, would give us all the opportunity we want. It would change the issue. It would be your policy, not my father's. It would make the way easy for all those who wish to rejoin the ranks, and it would be received with enthusiasm by all those who have never wavered in their allegiance to you. And if we are once united I do not think you would have occasion to complain of lack of enthusiasm or of any difficulty in getting unpaid workers. We can get them here[1] though you know how peculiarly the Education Act has hit Unionists and especially Liberal Unionists in these parts. And we should get them elsewhere if we had a definite constructive policy to inspire zeal and evoke effort.

We doubtless may lose a man or two here and there, and the Party agents may always dwell on the danger of such losses. But in such matters they are the worst advisers. They think only of the few whom they know and forget the many whom they don't know. They never consider the enormous accession of power that comes to any party which can raise a great ideal and touch the spirit of the nation. They overlook the importance of acting on the offensive and substituting an active policy of the future for a mere passive defence of the past. In short, they think only of possible losses and not also of the certain gains.

Mind, I do not say that even on these lines we shall not lose seats. We must lose them after nearly twenty years of almost continuous success; but please observe that we have had no worse defeats since May of last year[2] than we had at Woolwich and Rye before that date; that we have fared no better where our candidate has been a 'half-hogger' than where he has been a 'whole-hogger'; and that both Bridgeman at Oswestry and Touche at Lanark think they would have done worse with the more restricted policy, and the former (while blaming most of all the lack of organisation) says that he attributes his defeat mainly to Education and cannot after careful enquiry find out that the labourers were influenced by dear food, though at first he was inclined to suppose that they were.

Do, I beg you, give your most favourable consideration to these suggestions before the Southampton meeting. If you cannot see your way to a policy which will unite the Party, then we are not only beaten at the next election — we are ruined. Beaten we shall be in any case; but surely what we have to do is to prepare the way for future success. And, if you will raise the standard at Southampton, we can all close up during the autumn, and instead of our present confusion and lethargy, you will inspire us with new life and courage.

It is you and you alone who can work this change and now is the time to do it.

[1] i.e. in Birmingham.
[2] When Chamberlain first raised the question in his speech in Birmingham Town Hall, 15 May 1903.

I cannot tell you how deeply I feel all this. It is my only excuse for writing, and if you knew how I hate writing, you would be able to measure the reality of my concern by the length of my letter.

I think we are on the brink of disaster. I know that you can save us, and I cannot rest content without at least trying to convey to you some part of my conviction and of the reasons which inspire it.

Sandars comments on Austen's letter throw a revealing, if rather sinister, light on the climate of opinion in Balfour's immediate circle.

SANDARS TO BALFOUR [1]

September 1904.—I take it that Austen's letter is the result of discussion with his father . . .

But first of all I demur strongly to some statements of fact.

1. *You did not* encourage Joe to go out as a pioneer. Joe was anxious to get out of office. Evidence of this is overwhelming. Having decided to retire all you could do was to wish him success . . . but it is outrageous to say that you encouraged him to leave the Government on this mission. (2) Again, it is equally unfair to say that you induced Austen to leave him for the time 'single handed in his herculean task.' You did nothing of the kind. We did not want Austen to go out . . . but he knew perfectly well the terms on which he remained . . . Really one rubs one's eyes, and begins to wonder whether this injured individual after all did start a policy of his own last summer year, fully aware that he was breaking up the Unionist party which your tact and skill still preserves in some fighting strength. . . .

Austen now calls upon you to make a bridge. For whom? Not for the great mass of our party . . .

Personally I think, it may be wrong, that . . . Joe has failed. Austen's letter shows that he knows he has, and that he wants to save what he can at some price. But why should we damage ourselves by paying that price? What Austen does not realise is that the main body of the Unionist party cannot swallow either taxation of food or naked protection. . . .

Austen made it clear in his letter that he was going abroad soon after 10 September. It was not till 12 September, however, the day before he left for the Continent, that he received Balfour's detailed reply.[2] This was cordial enough but did not yield an inch.

BALFOUR TO AUSTEN

10 *September* 1904: *Private*.—The agreement between your views and mine on the present political situation is so nearly complete, that the one difference which *seems* to divide us obtains perhaps an undue prominence. I hold as strongly as you do that — apart from old age — our weakness

[1] *Balfour's Burden* by Alfred Gollin, p. 232.
[2] There was an earlier acknowledgment.

in the country is due chiefly to our divisions on the fiscal question. If it were not for the fact that the elections seem to have gone as much against us before as after these divisions made themselves felt, I should indeed have regarded them as the chief cause of our weakness. But, whether they stand first or second in order of importance, their importance is at all events certain.

Now for your remedy. You think, and I agree, that there is nothing very inspiring in the 'Sheffield' programme. 'Liberty of negotiation' with foreign countries would, I am convinced, be a great gain. But it does not lend itself easily to popular treatment, and such merits as it might otherwise possess from a merely electioneering point of view have been largely discounted by the fact that both 'protectionists' and 'Free Fooders' have conspired to represent it as a 'compromise' or as 'a half-way house' on the road to something else. This is not an accurate way of putting the case, since the Sheffield programme is logical and self-contained. But even if it *were* accurate, it is not obvious why it should be damaging. There are many occasions on which a compromise is exactly what the public wants. The present occasion, however, is probably not one of them : if only because it requires considerable skill to 'take the offensive' from a position of compromise, and this skill the majority of the Party do not possess. Indeed, they find it hard even to 'take the offensive' quite apart from the fiscal question ; and so it must always be when one Party has done much, and the other nothing, for nine years. The latter find themselves naturally in the position of assailants, the former are apt to lapse into a position of mere defence — always a dissipating one except for the best trained troops.

How, then, is this state of things to be remedied? Remedied completely it cannot be till we have been some time in opposition. But what partial cure can be found for it? You say, in effect, that what we want is a policy on which, with all due reservations, the Party can agree ; and a policy which, when agreed to, will tap deeper springs of enthusiasm than can ever be reached by the Sheffield programme taken *simpliciter*. Holding the views which you and I share with respect to our Colonial Empire, there can be no doubt that it is in *that* direction we must search for what we want — even if we fail to find it.

There are other reasons lying altogether outside party politics which tend in the same direction. It seems quite impracticable to leave the Colonial question exactly where it is. The possibility of new commercial relations between Canada and the U.S.A. ; the awakening of Australia to her increased need for the protection of a powerful, and therefore Imperial fleet in the face of a victorious Japan ; our ignorance as to how far the Colonies are ready to make genuine gaps in their protective wall of tariffs for our benefit — an ignorance which paralyses effort on this side of the water in favour of closer fiscal union, and tends to make Imperialists rely unduly on protectionist support ; — all these considerations point to the extreme desirability of having a full and free discussion with our Colonies on the present position and future organisation of the Empire.

Such a discussion may of course be abortive ; but, unless it is 'full and free', it is, I think, sure to prove abortive. No relevant subject should be excluded from debate; no preliminary fetters must be imposed either on the Colonial or the British representatives. The Colonists must not come here precluded from discussing Imperial Free Trade in any of its various degrees; the British must not lay down as a condition precedent to discussion that this or that article of consumption must in no case be taxed. Liberty of suggestion, and (I should be inclined to add) privacy of discussion, without which liberty of suggestion is almost certain to be a mere sham, are essential to any fruitful result.

But if I have carried you with me so far, you will see why I do not think it possible to say, as you would wish me to say, that we must go to the country pledged, if we are returned to power, not merely to summon a Conference but also to carry at once into effect any conclusions at which it may arrive, provided they are, in our opinion, reasonable. I do not for a moment believe that the Colonies would enter into a Conference if *they* were required to give any such pledge. Their Ministers would say, and with much reason, that they could not ask their respective electorates to give them a majority which might be used to carry out some new, and, at present, wholly unthought of, plan; that if the Conference and the various Governments concerned were to settle the matter without any further reference to the electors, then each Government must lay down beforehand the general limits beyond which it would not go, and the delegates both of Great Britain and of each Colony must be tightly bound by their instructions to refuse even to discuss any scheme by which those limits would be transgressed. Once anything like this occurs, there is an end of 'full and free' discussion; and an end also of all the benefits which such a discussion will, I believe, confer on the cause of Imperial Unity.

And is there reason to think that any greater acceleration of Colonial Union would be obtained by your plan than by mine? I doubt it. I think yours would frighten the Colonies; and it would certainly frighten an important section of opinion in this country; — a reflection which brings us back to the strictly domestic aspect of the problem we have to solve. Would then, such a scheme as I have thus sketched not do more to unite the Party in respect of fiscal and Colonial policy than any possible alternative? The true protectionists would not much like it; but then I am afraid that, so far as I am concerned, I can propose nothing they *would* much like; and, in any case, they would probably prefer it to mere Cobdenism. The bigoted Free Fooders would regard even the permission to discuss food taxation as trafficking with the 'accursed thing'. The pedantic Free Traders would regard the removal of even the greatest obstacles to freer trade as too dearly purchased if it involved the imposition of a single customs duty unbalanced by an equivalent excise. But surely the great mass of the Party who belong to none of these sections would not only approve the motives of the policy, but would think it well worth fighting for — the reasonable 'whole-hogger' and the reasonable advocate of 'Sheffield-but-no-further', while not abandoning their views would be glad to have the whole subject examined in a broader spirit, and with an increase of knowledge which is impossible so long as

the Colonies are no parties to our discussions, and so long as those discussions rise but rarely above the level of mere platform recriminations.

My idea, therefore, would be to take the very earliest opportunity I
can find of (1) reaffirming the Sheffield programme, both on its positive
and negative side, *i.e.* saying that, if returned to power, we will at once
endeavour to make this change in our fiscal policy, but will in the next
Parliament make no other; at least, none involving bread taxation;
(2) saying that, in our opinion, the Colonial question cannot be left
where it is; that we will summon a free and full conference, with power
to consider *any* proposals which it may think likely to conduce to closer
union, fiscal or other, between different parts of the Empire; (3) it would
go without saying that if satisfactory proposals could be devised, we would
do our best to induce the country to accept them, and the Party to
embody them in its programme; (4) the Imperial and Colonial question
thus dealt with to be explicitly dissociated from protection (true protection), with which, indeed, it has no connection, logical or sentimental;
protection to remain what it has long been, a doctrine largely held in
the Party, but with no place in its official creed.

It seems to me that this scheme is in substantial harmony with your
father's views. It differs, perhaps, from some suggestions which he has
thrown out from time to time in the course of his Imperial propaganda.
But, unless I am much mistaken, these suggestions are not of the essence
of his policy, but are in the nature of (as the schoolmen would have said)
more or less 'separable accidents'. What he has fought for, what he
has done more than any man to promote, is *Union* — fiscal union, military
union, naval union, Union, in short, of every kind which is compatible
with the self-government of our free Colonies. I believe that my plan
for attaining this great object is the best which can at present be devised,
both considered in itself and considered in relation to the future of the
only party in the State which is capable of taking a lead in what I hope
will one day be a National policy. At present we can hardly hope to
carry both parties with us; but at least a great end will have been gained
if one of them could be induced to accept it with zeal and without
producing serious schism in its ranks.

Austen regarded the delay in Balfour's reply as evasion. He was,
pardonably, annoyed and wrote back with unaccustomed bluntness.

AUSTEN TO BALFOUR

12 *September* 1904: *Private.*—I cannot help regretting that the very
important reply which you have sent to my letter of 24 August only
reached me today on the very eve of my departure. I had hoped from
what you said that I should have heard from you in plenty of time to
allow both for careful consideration of all you might say and for further
communication with you if necessary. As it is I must content myself
with giving you briefly my first impressions on reading and re-reading
your letter.

They are not cheerful. I am afraid that the difference in our points
of view is greater than I had thought or than you suppose.

I believe in the policy of Colonial Preference. I believe it to be the greatest object to which we in our time can devote ourselves not only for itself but for all to which it may lead and which we cannot realise without it. I believe it to be worth great immediate sacrifices, if such were called for, both from the Party and the nation for the sake of the future advantages it promises. But I do not believe that in reality such sacrifices are necessary from the Party, for I think that the mass of the Party and of the nation have a true and sure instinct in this case as in so many others, and that such doubt and hesitation as prevails is due not to the question itself but to the divided counsels of its leaders and the hesitation of its parliamentary chiefs.

Believing this, you must forgive me for saying that I think your policy wrong alike from the national and the purely party point of view; and though it pains me deeply to have to say so, if this is your last word, I do not see how I can possibly come into line with you at the next election.

Looked at from the standpoint of party, I fear that the policy you sketch means further disunion, a prolongation of the present uncertainty, a controversy over and therefore a hardening of our views, wherever we disagree among ourselves. The struggle in the Party will continue, and each section will try, and will be bound to try, to make itself as strong as possible, by enforcing pledges and capturing associations and seats. As to the ultimate result of such a struggle, I have no doubt. But meanwhile it involves the Party in serious divisions, in perpetual controversy and parliamentary impotence.

For the nation it means, I fear, that this great question is put before them not as a noble cause worthy of all that is best in us, calling for great efforts and justifying every sacrifice; but timidly, hesitatingly, amid circumstances of doubt and indecision which obscure the greatness of the issue, which take off the edge of effort, and kill enthusiasm.

Lastly the Conference itself, so summoned, will in my opinion meet, if it meet at all, in circumstances the least favourable to a successful issue of its deliberations. Whether the Colonies would accept an invitation couched in such terms is, I think, doubtful; but that such a Conference could be successful, is, I fear, more than we have any right to hope. I grant you that Colonial statesmen are timid, but what then? We must have courage for ourselves and for them too. We must know what we want and how we mean to secure it; and whilst willing and active to meet their difficulties in every way possible to us, we must go into Council with clear and decided views both of the end and the means, and we must feed them with our strength and our enthusiasm. If we show doubt and hesitation we are lost, and with us goes the last chance of the permanent union of that Greater Britain of which we are still the centre and the heart.

It is because the policy you sketch appears to me, and will I fear appear to others, timid and uncertain, that I think it will be fatal to us and our cause. I cannot bring myself thus to postpone the great issue. I do not think it wise and I do not think it right. I cannot sit still while colleagues in the Cabinet — Londonderry or another — put such glosses on your utterances as he did in his speech in the north a fortnight ago. I have done my best, believe me I have done my best and under very difficult circumstances, to keep the Party together and to give you all the loyal support which my position under you makes it a pleasure to me to render. What the future has in store, it is now too soon to say. My position in regard to autumn speeches must in any case have been difficult. It will be doubly so now. I will continue to do what I can for you, if you wish it, while this parliament lasts; but its days are numbered and your letter deprives me of the hope that when the election comes I can issue an address indistinguishable in point of policy from your own.

P.S.—It is hardly necessary for me to add that I write without consultation with anyone as I wrote before. Before leaving B'ham, on my last evening at home, I told my father what I had already written to you without his knowledge. I found as I had expected that he would have acquiesced in such a compromise as I suggested, but you cannot expect him to view more favourably than I do the proposals you intend to make.

Balfour's answer was a 'brush-off' though friendly enough. A stronger man than Austen might well have taken offence.

BALFOUR TO AUSTEN

22 *September* 1904.—I will not be so unkind as to mar your trip abroad by a fiscal discussion ! But I am obstinate in believing that our differences (if differences they are to be called) are neither as great nor as irreconcilable as you suppose. Time will show it. I speak in a few days at a dinner in Edinburgh — and in the sense I told you. But I do not believe that either your father or you will take exception — or at least not serious exception — to anything I have to say.

I hope you will enjoy your holiday — you have most certainly deserved one.

Sandars' comments are often revealing of Balfour's own thinking.

SANDARS TO BALFOUR

13 *September* 1904.—. . . . Austen writes as if his policy would bring the party together, whereas he says of yours that it will continue the struggle within the party . . . I am sure that neither he nor his father have any counsellors beyond the Tariff Reform league, and that they know nothing of the sober steady forces of our party outside Birmingham . . .

The error of Austen's position is that he lumps together the general feelings which prevail in favour of Colonial Preference with the convictions that Colonial Preference can be attained . . . but the difference of opinion arises when particular methods are recommended. Time is wanted for the examination of these methods. At present the electors are very shy in view of food taxation. I am convinced you are right in suggesting that time should be allowed for opinions on methods to ripen both here — and indeed in the Colonies. . . .

You must let Austen go his own way. It cannot be helped. A good many things may happen in the interval : none of which can have a detrimental effect upon your plan ; they might have upon his. . . .

The postscript to Austen's letter of 12 September is interesting. It is quite probable that he had written to Balfour without actually submitting his letter to Chamberlain. It is unthinkable, however, that he should not have informed his father of the substance of Balfour's reply. We must presume, therefore, that Chamberlain knew what was in Balfour's mind by the middle of September.

It is unlikely that the news came as a great shock to him. He had Balfour's measure by now. We know that he wanted the earliest possible election but he was already expecting that the Parliament would run another year. 'The election,' he had written before the rising of the House, 'cannot come till the spring of next year and probably will not come till the autumn.'[1] Meanwhile his mind was mainly focussed on the Conservative Party Conference which would meet in Southampton in October.

CHAMBERLAIN TO PIKE PEASE

8 *September* 1904.—As regards the future, I consider that the future of the Party both at the election and afterwards depends mainly on what is done at Southampton. I am not without hope that Balfour will make a decided advance, but in any case the Association ought to speak out. The hesitation and timidity displayed up to the present time have done infinite and irreparable mischief.

Chaplin was to be in charge of the Tariff Reform interest at the Party Conference. He had been away in Austria for a cure but wrote to Chamberlain on his return. His tone was scarcely sanguine.

CHAPLIN TO CHAMBERLAIN

26 *September* 1904 : *Private.*—Among other things, we shall have to decide on our course at the meeting of the National Union at Southampton on the 28th and 29th of October which I shall attend.

I do not anticipate quite the same feeling that was evoked last year — but I have no reason to doubt that the Delegates will depart in any way from the line they took there.

Unless some understanding is come to before the election and Balfour makes some move towards you I am more than ever convinced that we shall have a smash.

Have you heard anything from him since I've been away? When I last saw him (as I think I told you) I understood that he meant to ask you to see him, as soon as you'd both had some rest after the Session.

---

[1] Chamberlain to Amery, 9 August 1904.

And, if anything is to be done, it should be if possible before the meeting of the National Union.

The Executive Council meets at 3, on the 13th October, to consider the Resolutions sent in and to decide which to put forward. The Resolution usually adopted is one which has been previously approved at Headquarters — and the General Council meets the next afternoon to finally decide it.

I have seen the resolutions already sent in, since my return and hope to have copies on Wednesday — but I am not particularly enamoured of any of them. They can still be sent in till the 29th or the end of the month — and in any case amendments can be moved should it be necessary.

What are your views as to the most fitting resolution under the circumstance? Have you any suggestion to make? And what do you think of the policy of approaching Balfour again, and seeing if it be possible to get him to agree to a resolution that we could accept?

My last experience was not encouraging — but if there was a chance of doing the slightest good — I should not hesitate to try again. The Full Text of Balfour's Report on Food Supply is just circulated. He makes the recommendation I wanted — but in the most half-hearted way — and a more inconsistent or more milk and water Report I never remember.

Chamberlain's reply shows the importance he attached to the Conference. He enclosed a model resolution and threatened that, if the Conference went against him, he might well abandon his task.

CHAMBERLAIN TO CHAPLIN

27 *September* 1904 : *Private.*—Welcome back again! Arthur Balfour has *not* asked to see me. I did not think he would. I hear from several sources that more than one of his colleagues have been pressing him to make a move forward. He listens — he is most conciliatory — but he gives no promise or sign of change. He will go his gait and we must go ours. I look on the Southampton meeting as one of the most critical stages in the campaign, and for the first time in my life I wish I had been born a Tory in order that I might be present and help you in what I foresee will be a difficult task.

If all those who agree with us will stand firm we shall win, but will they? It is a test and if *we* or they give way they will do perhaps irretrievable damage to the cause. I shall wait with *great anxiety* for the result as I am confident that Wells and the machine will leave no stone unturned to defeat us. Appeals for union, for loyalty to the Chief, etc., will be worked for all that they are worth to secure an adverse, or at least an evasive, verdict.

We know that the vast majority are everywhere with us but the object of the wire-pullers will be to induce them to conceal and withhold their real opinions.

I hope all our friends will avoid the net spread for them. If we fail at this meeting, I shall consider myself justified in reviewing my position for no leader can be of any service if the army will not follow him.

I enclose the Resolution passed at the meeting of the delegates of the Lib. Unionist Association. It may be altered in words but in substance it is the least for which we ought to ask. In dealing with the subject remember that the chief object of such popular representative gatherings is to inform thier leaders of thier views and wishes — not to *dictate* to them — but to let them know what policy would be most warmly supported by the rank and file. If such a meeting is afraid to express its opinions, the whole thing becomes a farce.

Hitherto, the leaders — Lord Salisbury for instance — have welcomed the expression of opinion, although they have not always followed it.

What will be the result of a decision? If it is unfavourable the position of Tariff Reformers in the House and the Country will be intolerable. If it is on our side it will strengthen the *friendly pressure* we desire to bring to bear on the Government. We know from their own lips that they 'sympathise'. If they do not go further it is for tactical reasons — because they fear that the Party (*i.e.* the Free Fooders) will not follow them. Let us show them that the great majority of the Party *will* follow them enthusiastically and then, surely, they will not sacrifice the majority to a few irreconciliables of whom some, at least, have other motives for opposing them . . .

I hope I have made clear the immense importance I attach to Southampton.

If money is wanted to pay travelling expenses, etc., it ought not to be spared . . .

P.S.—I see that I have omitted to say that I have some slight reason for hoping that A.J.B. might be induced to say at Southampton or elsewhere that he will ask for a mandate to summon a Colonial Conference and if the results are satisfactory to submit the decisions arrived at by the delegates to the new Parliament.

This would be a great advance, but the promise would be worthless unless it contained the second clause about submission to Parliament. Otherwise the Colonies would probably refuse and I do not suppose that members of Parliament would like to fight an election and then if they succeed to be told that after a Conference nothing practical will be done until a new mandate has been asked for and a second election gone through.

The postscript to this letter shows Chamberlain's unaltered opposition to the idea of deferring the introduction of Preference until a second General Election after the proposed Colonial Conference. His irritation with Balfour must have been steadily increasing, and his closest friends at Birmingham fed fuel to the flames.

COLLINGS TO CHAMBERLAIN

29 *September* 1904.—I was interested and a little uneasy at the conversation last Monday about Balfour's problem. Not from any fear of your yielding but lest in your desire to meet him in any way you might

let fall some phrase on which the enemy and the weak-kneed might found a statement that the 'extinguisher had taken fire'. We don't want at the present time to have any cross scent to confuse the real pack. I have felt all along that your separation from Balfour — unless he came round — was inevitable. It was only a question of when. I believe at his next utterance, if he voices his present position, will be the time. The proposal for a colonial convention cannot be taken as a policy. Such a conference can only be inferred to as a matter of course incident con-sequential to the adoption of the complete scheme. Otherwise it would be worse than a proposal for a Royal Commission. Everyone must see that a conference with the Colonials would be the natural thing after full powers were secured, as would be negotiations with foreign countries. The present position is in no way parallel to that of Home Rule. Balfour is a charming personality to those around him but he is not in touch with the people or a force with them. You are both and increasingly so. I question if he truly realizes that there are such people as agricultural labourers. If he sticks to the Free-Fooders, and says so, then it seems to me there is no alternative but a public separation, and for the country to take sides. You did not leave the Government in order to preach your full programme and at the same time to recognize — beyond a certain time — a party who disagree with it or accept only half of it. I believe if you were to drop the subject tomorrow that as far as the industrial centres are concerned the seed you have sown will spring up and bear fruit. It can't die now. A hard winter would ripen it rapidly.

For Chamberlain, a public separation from Balfour was, at this time at least, out of the question. His object was to win over the Unionist Parties to his policy and nothing could be more dangerous to this than a direct challenge to the leader of the Conservatives. If Balfour were to separate from him, that would be another matter; but that was not Balfour's way.

Meanwhile he had made a last attempt to prevent Balfour from committing himself to the idea of two elections. The opportunity had arisen unexpectedly. In his efforts to mobilise Ministers to join in his autumn campaign, Chamberlain had written to Lyttelton. Lyttelton in his reply volunteered his own opinions on the con-ference. The tone of his letter suggests that he had seen Austen's letter of 12 September to Balfour with its implied threat of resigna-tion. Lyttelton's letter was written from Balfour's home in Scotland.

LYTTELTON TO CHAMBERLAIN

21 *September* 1904: *Private.*—I think Austen knows how I have striven to get A. J. B. a little further along the road and have at any rate with Gerald's aid got him as far as advocacy of a Conference. Cannot we all keep for the present absolutely together on that platform. We shall no doubt be beaten at the gen.-election — but if we fight on that issue

we place our opponents in an impossible position, and we commit our-selves impliedly but inevitably to readjusting our food taxes if the Colonies make a reasonable offer. No doubt the opposition will endeavour to force a definite declaration from A. J. B. that if the Colonial offer is satis-factory he will support food taxation. And I confess that I am personally strongly in favour of a definite and categorical statement on the matter. The Briton above all wants to know indubitably from his leaders what they mean. But if A. J. B. will not and I very much fear that he will not go that length — you will appreciate how impossible it is for me to ever myself force him. If these matters are not brought so far forward as we should wish, is it not better that we should all unanimously go for a Conference with all subjects open than to be divided in the very face of the enemy. If a Conference takes place and it has been advocated by all of us, how will it be possible if the Colonial offers are reasonable to resist meeting them by some concession on food taxation. The resisters would plainly be open to the charge of countering the Conference out of pure wantonness.

Above all however a unanimous effort for a Conference would enable all of us who are in favour of Preference to get a free hand this autumn to advocate it. No doubt we shall be beaten at the Election, but in opposition A. J. B.'s hands would be freer, and solid and mature progress might be made in the matter.

Chamberlain sent a detailed and firm reply, evidently intended for transmission to Balfour.

CHAMBERLAIN TO LYTTELTON

24 *September* 1904: *Private.*—What you say about the situation is very important. I am anxious and uneasy. You know how much I value my co-operation with Arthur and how greatly I have desired that we should not drift further apart; but, in leaving office, and in devoting myself to the promotion of a new policy, I am bound to put its success in the first place, and if I am confronted with a final decision from the Prime Minister such as recently I have had reason to fear, I do not see how I could possibly accept it without some protest or declaration which would indicate a greater divergence than I have hitherto contemplated as possible.

I should be ready to do a great deal to prevent this, although my position has been made much more difficult by the undercurrent of opposition which I have encountered from the Conservative Party machine and by such speeches as those which have been made by London-derry lately.

There are two points to which I would specially direct your attention :—

(1) What is to happen at the Southampton meeting of the Conserva-tive Association? No doubt a motion similar to that which the Association has passed again and again in the past times without observation or objection from the leaders will be proposed on behalf of the Tariff Reformers. Will the Association be allowed freely to deal with such a Resolution, or will they be urged in the name of the Prime Minister,

and on the grounds of loyalty to him, to reject the Resolution and to go back from the position which they have previously taken up? or will they be allowed to make a frank expression of their opinion for the information of their leaders, although, of course, it will have, and can have, no binding effect?

(2) What will Balfour himself say on the occasion? Will he make any kind of pronouncement, or will he reserve anything of the kind for his election address?

If, on either of these occasions, he is willing to go, as part of his programme, for an open conference with the representatives of the Colonial Governments, I should welcome the declaration on the same grounds as those stated by you.

But I want to know how far this is going to carry us. We know that we shall be beaten badly at the general election, but we cannot go into the fight with a statement to this effect as a justification for not stating our intention in case we succeed. Suppose, for the sake of argument, that we win the election: that then we call a conference, and that the Colonies make to us proposals, which, in our opinion, including that of the Prime Minister, afford ample justification for some alteration in our food taxes, and the probable substitution of a tax on the food imports which we produce ourselves, coupled with a corresponding reduction on the imports of the articles of food and necessity which are not produced in this country.

Then, on this assumption, will the Prime Minister at once propose legislation to the then Parliament, or will he repeat his present policy and refuse to proceed until he has obtained a second mandate?

In other words, will he at the general election ask for a mandate to call a Conference, and, if the Conference justifies such a proposal as I have suggested, proceed to submit a plan to Parliament; or, will he after the success of the Conference go again to the country for a second mandate on what is practically the same question?

The practical difference between these two is enormous. If the latter course is adopted I do not think the Colonies will consent to a Conference, and I should say they would be very foolish to do so. They will regard the whole matter as insincere and will decline to show their hands if the only result is to have the question open for an indefinite time afterwards with all the possibilities of the intervention of other issues. Of course representatives at any conference cannot pledge their respective Parliaments, and it would be understood that all of them would only be committed to submitting the decisions of the Conference for approval or rejection by the several local Governments.

We should be just as limited in this respect as any of the Colonies; but it has hitherto been the foundation of every conference, whether with a Colony or with a foreign country, that the decisions arrived at being the decisions of the governments existing at the time, should be submitted with their authority to the confirmation or rejection of their respective legislatures. It has never in such cases been proposed that a further appeal to the constituencies should be taken before the Parliaments were consulted.

Of the two courses possible to us the first would mean business — the second would be only political tactics, and would in my judgment result not only in great delay but also in discrediting our sincerity.

I may add that the second course would do us great harm at the next election. It would lay us open to all the misrepresentations of our opponents who would say that it was an unworthy manœuvre, intended, however, to lead to Protection and a food tax. On the other hand, it would be regarded by our warmest supporters as an evident evasion and they would put no heart into a struggle which could only have an inconclusive result.

I have marked this letter private, but I have no objection to your showing it to Arthur if you think fit.

Lyttelton duly sent on Chamberlain's letter to Balfour. He had no doubt received Balfour's comments before he sent the following reply.

LYTTELTON TO CHAMBERLAIN

3 *October* 1904.—Many thanks for your letter which I sent after consideration to Arthur. He speaks to-night and I have the best reason for thinking that he will advocate a Conference. I agree with all you say about the inferences which must be drawn from this attitude and had put it in substance with Gerald's aid to him before your letter arrived. But I am not vain enough to think we had put it so well. When Arthur sees the inferences which will in fact be drawn by both friend and foe our arguments will I trust gain additional momentum.

I recognise the force of what you say on the 2nd election point, but I think Arthur's position much stronger there. Some of his best friends assure him (tho' I am not of their number in this) that he conveyed clearly at Sheffield that at this election he would not ask for powers to tax food, and this affects him greatly. But he also thinks and I am not sure that he is not right, that a very cautious advance here is probably the most likely to succeed, and in as much as we all know that in fact 2 elections must occur before we get another chance of office I beg you to think well before you partially dissent from him on this point which after all I venture to believe is not one of principle and is at most one of only secondary importance. Colonial Preference is a great object but I doubt if we can carry it for many years unless we are united with the exception of the Free-Fooders.

To-night Arthur speaks and the situation will be clearer afterwards.

VI

On the evening of 3 October, Balfour addressed a dinner at the Scottish Conservative Club in Edinburgh.

His speech was entirely devoted to the fiscal issue. He began by reaffirming the position he had taken up at Sheffield.

The first observation I have to make upon the fiscal question in its present aspect is that, so far as I am concerned, I have seen nothing to

alter in what is now known in the technical language of political controversy as 'The Sheffield Programme'. (*Cheers.*) I still believe that the
recommendations that I then made to my countrymen with regard to
an alteration in the traditional fiscal policy of this country were sound
recommendations. I still believe that they are consistent with the most
scientific teaching of political economy, as well as with the instincts of
practical statesmanship . . . I would venture to point out that the fiscal
policy that I recommended at Sheffield is not a compromise and is not
a halfway house. It is a logical, self-contained whole, defensible in itself,
sound, and not carrying within it the seeds of any development in a direction which either protectionist or free-trader may either hope for or fear.

He went on to deny that his policy was one of Protection : 'A
protection policy as I understand it is a policy which aims at
supporting or creating home industries by raising prices.'.

His next passage was a clear warning to the Party not to press him
too far.

I now proceed to say that I individually am not a protectionist.
Protection, in the true sense of the word, in the sense of the word in which
I have just defined and explained it, has always been, and is now, in
my judgment, an admissible doctrine in the Conservative party. The
Conservative party, indeed, after the Peelite split, was a protectionist
party. It was based upon Protection. That ceased, no doubt, in the
fifties, and the official programme of the Conservative party since then
has not been a protectionist programme. But there has always been an
admitted legitimate set of opinions in favour of true Protection in the
party. I do not share those views individually . . . I am of opinion, and
I desire to say it with very great distinctness — I am personally of opinion
that for this country in its existing circumstances Protection in the true
sense of the word, Protection as I have endeavoured to define it and
describe it to-night, is not the best policy. It is not one I have ever recommended, directly or indirectly, either to my colleagues in the Cabinet,
to the House of Commons, or to the country. It is a policy which I do
not believe to be expedient under existing circumstances. I should never
think of diminishing the zeal and earnestness of my support of a Conservative and Unionist party should that party take up a protectionist
line. But I do not think that I could with advantage in such circumstances
be its leader. A man can only lead his party if he believes in the party's
policy ; and although I do believe in the general scheme of politics
which we in this room represent, I think I should have to leave it to others
to deal with a policy of true Protection, if the country should decide that
such a policy was in its opinion expedient at the present time.

He then turned to the Colonial aspect of the question. Rosebery
had denied that the Colonies were seriously interested in Preference.
Chamberlain had affirmed that they were.

But, whether Lord Rosebery is wrong, whether Mr. Chamberlain in
his estimate of colonial opinion is right or whether he is wrong, whether

I, who, in this respect, entirely agree with Mr. Chamberlain, am right or am wrong, surely the question ought to be decided; and it cannot be decided merely by wrangling in the House of Commons, or by disputes or rival speeches at public meetings.

Well, how is it to be decided? In my view we have got to a point when the only possible way of moving out of the *impasse* in which we now find ourselves — an *impasse* dangerous to the Empire as a whole — is to have a free conference with those self-governing Colonies and with India which would enable us to determine, one way or the other, in the first place, whether these great dependencies desire an arrangement, and, in the second place, whether an arrangement be possible or be not. What are the conditions under which such an interchange of ideas as I have suggested could take place? Having given it the best thought I can, in my view we should meet — by we I mean the representatives of the free governing Colonies, with India and ourselves in this country — we should meet in order to talk out this subject in the freest possible manner, without being bound by special views or special instructions, knowing that we have to face a complicated problem, knowing that the fiscal views on the economic case of the Colonies differ from the fiscal views and the economic conditions of this country, knowing of the hampering effect of old traditions and new prejudices on one side or the other — that we should meet free and unfettered to discuss with each other, in the first place, whether this ideal of fiscal union is one which commends itself to us; in the second place — for I have no doubt as to what the answer to the first question will be — in the second place, to consider how it shall be carried out. Please observe that the very essence of the scheme which I am suggesting is that the delegates or representatives — call them what you will — who are to discuss this question should discuss it with an absolute freedom. I understand that Lord Rosebery made a suggestion, or threw out some time ago an idea, that such a conference might do good provided the representatives were bound strictly not to do this or that and were limited in this direction or that direction. I do not believe you could get any result out of a conference of that kind. Freedom in this case, free interchange of ideas, is of the very essence of success, and, without it, success I believe to be impossible. But then observe, if I am right in this view, I do not believe you will induce either this country, or Canada, or Australia, or New Zealand, or India — I do not think you will induce them to join in such a conference unless these various self-governing communities have the right to appeal to their respective electorates as to any scheme which may be hammered out. Of course, if they claim that liberty, as I am sure they will, that liberty, that necessity, must be equally claimed by us. My view, therefore, is that the policy of this party should be, if we have the power after the next election, to ask the Colonies to join in such conference and plainly intimate to them that those whom they send shall come unhampered by limitations in this direction or in that direction, but that, as a necessary corollary, an inevitable set off to the complete freedom of discussion, any plan, or, at all events, any large plan for Imperial union on fiscal or other lines, ought not to be regarded as

Y

accepted by any of the parties to the contract unless their various electorates have given their adhesion to the scheme. I can conceive no objection to that policy except the one that it may take, and indeed must take, some time to carry out. Is that a grave objection? For my part, I am so hopeful that an arrangement would be come to, and I am so fearful if it be come to without having behind it the public opinion of all the free-governing communities concerned, that I do not desire, as I long ago said at Manchester, to see this matter hastily forced upon public opinion. We want it to be permanent. What we are aiming at is the consolidation of the British Empire. The British Empire was not born yesterday. It is not a thing of to-day. It will not die to-morrow. What we should all aim at is to proceed to this great end with the wisest caution, which will enable every man concerned to feel that he is not building some temporary structure which a wave of public opinion or a temporary majority may overset, but that he is building for all time a great edifice which neither the wind nor the waves can affect, which shall be solidly based upon the common consent of the great self-governing communities, having no particular or selfish ends in view, but looking forward to being members of a great and consolidated Empire — based not upon special interests but upon a common desire for a great end. That then is the policy I would recommend to the Unionist party.

Balfour's meaning, so often obscure, was this time unmistakable. He had deliberately committed himself to the plan for two Parliaments — to the one thing in fact on which Chamberlain had begged him to remain at least unpledged.

VII

Chamberlain was furious. But, he was also powerless. For all its reservations, Balfour's proposal was a step forward. It could never be made a ground for a public separation.

CHAMBERLAIN TO LYTTELTON

4 *October* 1904: *Secret.*—Arthur has spoken. We asked from him one thing, namely, that he should not commit himself, at all events at present, to a scheme of two Parliaments and two mandates. Nevertheless he has put it forward.

I most deeply regret it, but I will make the best of it. I am convinced that it is thoroughly impracticable and when it is understood will be laughed at.

But the time has gone by for argument and I can only attempt to minimise the difference.

Nevertheless, Chamberlain felt bound to reserve his own position. The following day (5 October) he was to speak at Luton. His speech was awaited with intense interest, and a strong force of police was needed to enable him to get through the cheering crowds to his train at Birmingham station. 'Give Rosebery beans', 'Good old Joe' and 'Balfour's with you', were among the shouts that greeted him.

As at Welbeck, this second meeting of the campaign was held in a Disraelian setting. Chamberlain with his wife and daughters, Ida and Hilda, were entertained at Woburn, the palace of the Dukes of Bedford with its wonderful private zoo. The meeting itself took place in a temporary hall, specially built for the occasion at a cost of £4000 and pulled down a few days afterwards. Seven thousand people were accommodated; this time with seats for all. Bedford took the chair and among the magnates on the platform, Somerset provided yet another ducal recruit to the Chamberlain cause.

Chamberlain's speech, directed again at the agricultural interest, followed much the same lines as the speech at Welbeck. The passages, however, which attracted attention were those in which he commented on Balfour's speech two days earlier.

Mr. Balfour spoke at Edinburgh on Monday night, and his speech marks a stage in this great controversy. Mr. Balfour at Sheffield some time ago, laid down a programme which the whole party, with the exception of one or two superior persons, whom I am afraid we shall not see much longer in the House of Commons — which the whole party with those exceptions has adopted.

But at Edinburgh he went much further. It is true he dealt not with the question of principle, but with the question of procedure, but it is a most important part of the whole programme. He said that if he were again returned to power at the next election 'he would at once call an Imperial Conference with representatives of the self-governing Colonies and India', and, as I hope and I think, no doubt with representatives also of those great Crown Colonies which are equally entitled to attention. He would call such a conference in order to ascertain, in the first place, whether they were really desirous of the commercial union, and, in the second place, to see what terms could be made between them and us which would be satisfactory to them and also satisfactory to us.

In the last Session of Parliament I begged the Government to consider this project of a commission. Now I heartily welcome the decision at which they have arrived. I see in it the certain precursor of a victory which will give us the closer union essential to our future greatness. (*Cheers.*)

He then made his protest against Balfour's suggestion of a double mandate.

There is only one point — it is perhaps a point of tactics — in Mr. Balfour's speech which I hope he will be ready to reconsider. If we expect the Colonies to come to a conference with us, they will expect from us that we shall give to them the usual terms and conditions. Wherever such conferences have been held, there is not a single case in my belief in our whole history in which we have entered upon negotiations, either with foreign countries or with the Colonies, where it has not been an understood thing that if the representatives came to an agreement, that agreement should at once be submitted to the Parliaments and the Legislatures of the separate States concerned. Mr. Balfour seems, however, to have considered that it might be necessary to take a second election. I cannot understand what is the necessity for a second plebiscite, involving, as it would do, two mandates, two General Elections on the same subject, coming within a few months of one another. I think it would be very inconvenient and very unpopular, but it is more serious than that. If, after coming to an agreement, with your fellow-subjects, you are then to postpone the matter until every Legislature in every one of the Colonies and at home has been re-elected for this particular purpose of carrying out an agreement, the principle of which had previously been accepted, if you are going to do that, how long is it going to take? How long? For many of these Parliaments will have other business in hand. Will they be content to dissolve and to take again the opinion of their constituents? The result will be delay. Delay may mean the introduction of some new issue.

If that part of the scheme were to be insisted upon, I think the Colonies would be justified in accusing us of insincerity, and of saying — 'No, we will not come to a conference where we shall have disclosed our hands, where we shall have taken all this trouble, where we shall have expressed our willingness to make these sacrifices, and then find that nothing is to be done until after a number of doubtful events have taken place, over which we shall have no control and the performance of which may take many years.'

I have thought it right to mention that as the only blemish which I see in a plan which in all other respects I heartily welcome, and which I believe marks a great advance in the programme of the Unionist party. ('*Hear, hear*' *and cheers.*)

If this plan is carried, then all of us may live in hopes that we may be spared to see the realization of this great idea of union.

Having entered his protest Chamberlain determined, for public consumption at least, to make the best of the new position. He would disregard Balfour's reservations and concentrate on the proposal for a Conference. The Unionists were bound to be beaten at the next election and, by the time they came to the election after that, Balfour's pledge would no longer be binding. All the same, Balfour's disregard of his repeated advice altered their relationship. Hitherto, Chamberlain had regarded himself as still a colleague of Balfour's. Henceforth he would feel no such obligation towards him. 'On this and all else,' he wrote to Chaplin, 'I am inclined to put my own interpretation on Balfour's words and to accept them in the sense which I give to them.'[1]

---

[1] Chamberlain to Chaplin, 29 October 1904.

The following letter to Cochrane written on his return from Woburn shows the general course he proposed to take.

CHAMBERLAIN TO COCHRANE

7 *October* 1904*: Private.*—I am glad that you were pleased with my speech. There were, of course, points in the Prime Minister's address which I do not altogether approve, but I have felt that it is my duty to avoid magnifying differences and if possible to continue cordially to co-operate with him. I have therefore endeavoured to emphasise the matters on which we seem to be in entire agreement.

The question of delay I hope is not finally settled. The proposal to have a dissolution in order to confirm a Treaty seems to me not only indefensible but also unconstitutional. It is giving away the treaty making power of the Crown with a vengeance, and substituting a plebiscite for the approval of Parliament. It would be an example, which, if generally followed, would force on a dissolution of our Parliament every year, for hardly twelve month passes without some treaty or another being arranged.

You may see by the telegraphed opinion of Mr. Reid that he who is of course an opponent uses it as an argument to show that the whole matter is in the air, and this would be, I think, the general view of the Colonies.

Still, if Balfour rests satisfied with what he has already said, and does not carry the discussion further, I think we may also leave the final decision to the future.

I have not, therefore, pressed my friends to carry the question further at Southampton, as that might bring us into sharp collision. I hope that the officials will be equally considerate and that we may unite on a Resolution supporting the points on which we are agreed without raising any question on which we differ.

On 8 October, Chamberlain left England for a six-weeks' holiday in Italy. The day before he summed up the events of the past year as follows :

CHAMBERLAIN TO NORTHCOTE

7 *October* 1904*: Private.*—Here the situation has become once more most interesting. After the great campaign which I carried on last autumn I took a holiday, and having fully opened my attack, thought it undesirable and unnecessary to keep the agitation on a sensational scale, although in the six months that have elapsed there has not been a week in which I have not in one way or another raised the question.

My opponents, however, pretended to assume that the agitation was dead and the attempt to raise the people had proved a failure. For your information I may say that, whether they were sincere or not, they were utterly wrong. The question is still alive and is making undoubted progress both amongst the people and amongst the politicians. But, whatever the result of the next election may be — and I think myself it *must* be unfavourable to us — the Unionist Party of the future will consist almost, if not absolutely, of fiscal reformers.

We shall be beaten on other issues — education, Chinese labour, and so on, but when the reaction comes and we return with a big majority we shall be pledged up to the eyes to carry out the policy that I have advocated. It is, therefore, only a question of time — and I think of a short time — before we are finally successful . . .

Balfour has now pledged himself to a conference, and unless I am entirely mistaken, whenever the conference is called, it will result in an arrangement which the majority of the people will insist on carrying out.

My wife and I leave to-morrow for a short trip in Italy, but, when I return, I have a number of engagements to fulfil which will, I hope, keep the heather alight.

VIII

The preparations for the Conservative Conference now went forward under Chaplin's guidance. Before leaving for Italy Chamberlain had personally settled the terms of the resolution. This expressed agreement with the Prime Minister that the time had come for a revision of fiscal policy, cordially supported the proposal to deal with unfair competition caused by the practice of dumping and welcomed his intention, if returned to power, to call a Colonial Conference to consider the question of Imperial Fiscal Union. It was Chaplin's business to secure the acceptance of this resolution by the council of the National Union and later its adoption by the Conference.

We may leave his letters to tell the tale.

CHAPLIN TO CHAMBERLAIN

6 *October* 1904.—I read your speech in the 'Scotsman' today — and Arthur's at Edinburgh — on getting here from the West Coast yesterday. I agree with you. It is a great advance and it practically pledges him to all that any of us want — barring his stipulation as to the different electorates and a second appeal — which will have to be got over some-how when it arises.

It seems to me that it must make my position in the National Union next week much less difficult — and I shall be disappointed if I do not get the consent and adhesion of the Council to the Resolution which you have suggested.

At all events I propose to do all I can to get it accepted first by the executive and then by the general council and to have it moved at Southampton.

22 *October* 1904.—I have been so tremendously pressed I couldn't find time to write to you before. I have no secretary and the strain is tremendous. But I carried the Resolution at both meetings of the Council and omitting one word of no importance — unanimously —, and Wells assured me he would do his best with his side to secure its acceptance without opposition at Southampton.

That remains to be seen. I am suspicious of the Primrose League who are rotten — whom I never affected — and who are holding a gathering of their own down there the day before. Still I have no doubt we shall carry it.

27 *October* 1904.—Just a line to keep you informed how matters go . . .

To-night I go to Southampton. I have no reason to change my view as to the resolution being carried there — and in order to avoid all controversial matter at Southampton I said all that I had to say about Protection and Preference at Lincoln.

A Treasury man told me, E. Hamilton, he fancied Arthur had some idea of Subsidies for the Transports bringing Colonial food to this country, but that would make a row here at once, where they already complain of unfair foreign freights. Anyhow the time is coming when he will have to say what he means.

28 *October* 1904: *Private.*—I have just come back from Southampton; caught Austen at the House and suggested to him to wire to you the result of the meeting.

Nothing could have gone better and I carried the Conference completely with me. C.B. spoke at Norwich on Monday and his speech gave me the chance which I took advantage of.

I got out all that I wanted in the straightest and plainest manner in reply to him — not a word in reply to Arthur — and delighted the delegates by attacking the former. After lunch the Free Traders were idiots enough to move an amendment deleting the first part of our resolution and substituting a clause approving the whole of the policy in the Edinburgh speech.

I warned them in private and public, knowing the Meeting was with me, what was certain to happen if they persisted. They did. I flatly refused to accept it and pressing it to a vote they got exactly thirteen votes out of the whole of the meeting, a whole forest of hands going up for us with tremendous applause and cheering. The main Resolution was carried intact immediately afterwards with two only against it.

This is better than any one could have expected, for, as a matter of fact, though I did everything I could to prevent a division, what the idiots have succeeded in doing is to get the Conference to negative a resolution approving of the policy laid down at Edinburgh, with this result, that the only part of that policy which they approve is what is embodied in our resolution and the rest is condemned.

There is no doubt that outside the Conference with the general public who won't understand the folly by which it was all brought about that it can't fail to have a very considerable effect, but they have only themselves to thank for it.

2 November 1904: *Private.*—There was practically no report of the two speeches I made at Southampton, due to the war matter, though I never made more effect on an audience. But I made it absolutely clear without mentioning you that the Resolution had the full support of the Chamberlainite Party and I gave that as my principal reason for refusing the amendment. The one I knew would be universally accepted just as it stood, the other I couldn't answer for.

I was warned by one or two of your best friends on the Council whom I took into confidence to be very careful in submitting the resolution about its original authorship.

There was a good deal of jealousy, I was advised, and it would tend with some of its members to prejudice its acceptance and certainly prevent its being unanimous.

I am inclined to think that myself, and that with a view to the future, when the full support of the Council may be wanted again, it is wiser to say nothing about it.

The conference was a triumph for the Tariff Reformers and made all the more so, as Chaplin's letter of 28 October showed, by the action of their opponents. The Conservative party had in fact, singled out for approval those declarations of its leaders — and only those — which conformed with Chamberlain's policy. In July, the Liberal Unionist Association had given Chamberlain its full backing. Now the National Union of Conservatives had followed suit. Chamberlain's leadership of the rank and file of the party was thus confirmed.

In other circumstances, the conference would have put Balfour in an embarrassing position. But only a few days before, the Russian Baltic Fleet, on the first stage of its journey to the Far East, had attacked British fishing trawlers on the Dogger Bank. The attack had proved to be a total error; the order to fire had been issued in drink. Nevertheless British opinion was deeply stirred by the outrage and for some days there was talk of war. At the conference, therefore, Balfour devoted his entire speech to the Dogger Bank incident. It was one of his best and most forthright; and it was not till after he sat down that the audience realised he had never even referred to their fiscal resolution.

IX

Chamberlain and his wife, meantime, had travelled to Innsbruck and thence to Verona. Austen and Beatrice joined them there and spent ten days with them, leaving them at Bologna. Chamberlain and Mrs. Chamberlain then continued their journey visiting Perugia, Orvieto, Siena, Pisa and Milan.

Meanwhile Ministers had begun to speak their minds more freely on fiscal questions. Austen spoke out strongly in favour of Preference. Salisbury on the other hand dismissed Chamberlain's plan as 'a great Imperial dream which it is at present quite impossible to realise'.[1] Ridley had written to *The Times* to protest at this utterance. Chamberlain read both the speech and the letter. His comments are worth printing.

CHAMBERLAIN TO RIDLEY

Siena, 18 November 1904.—I must send a line to say how opportune and effective I think your letter to the 'Times' which I have just seen.

Lord Cranborne has rather hastily assumed the airs of a Jack-in-Office, after his promotion to the Cabinet, and characteristically expresses his lordly contempt for those impulsive outsiders who, like you and me, humbly assume that a great party ought to have some sincere beliefs and to be prepared to risk something to maintain them.

A Unionist Government is no doubt a valuable instrument, but if the sword is always to be kept in the sheath and we are never to use it except to cut bread and butter for the hacks, we shall do quite as well without it.

So, if Lord Salisbury is anxious to dispense with our assistance I am inclined to tell him that we can get on without him but that he cannot exist without us.

The Prime Minister has rightly, in my opinion, given great latitude to members of the Cabinet to express their personal views on the different aspects of the fiscal question, but I cannot believe that he meant to authorise subordinate members of his Government to speak contemptuously of the action and the support of the majority of his party. The situation is at all times difficult enough but the Salisbury clique will make it impossible — and therefore I heartily welcome your most useful hint.

One letter which reached Chamberlain at this time is of interest. Chamberlain was often accused of forgetting India in his tariff proposals. He was sensitive to the charge; for there was something in it. He had accordingly asked Curzon for his views on how the new policy might best be applied to the Great Dependency. The Viceroy sent his views a few days before leaving for India on his ill-fated second term. They may well have had some influence both on the Cabinet and on the Departments and deserve a place here.

CURZON TO CHAMBERLAIN

13 *November* 1904: *Private.*—When I dined with you, you asked me to set down sometime what I thought was the point of view from which India regarded your fiscal proposals, and what would be the best method of approaching her. I had hoped to do this at some length in the course

---

[1] 10 November at Horsham.

of the autumn but the terrible illness of my wife and the harassing strain that it has laid upon me have rendered this quite impossible, and I must leave England with the intention unfulfilled.

This, however, may be said. India's point of view is inevitably and deeply coloured by the fact that she is a dependency not a self governing colony. She would enter any conference or scheme or plan with no freedom but with her hands tied behind her. When a Conference is talked about, her cooperation is vaguely alluded to as though it were to be on the same footing e.g. as Canada or New Zealand. We know well from experience that it would be nothing of the sort. Our fiscal interests would be subordinated as they always have been (notice the Cotton duties — a most scandalous episode) to Lancashire or other British exigencies. We should never be allowed to stand up against the U.K. as a Colony may and does. Therefore India, though possessing very strong protectionist inclinations, would prefer to be left with her present Free Trade Tariff, modified only as it is for revenue purposes, to exchanging it for any new plan which might result in her interests being again subordinated to those of England.

Our own view of the way in which India ought to be treated in any matter in which her interests do not entirely coincide with those of the predominant partner, seemed to me to be shown by a remark that you let fall in a speech in the House of Commons about S. African labour in that the Government of India who were trying to make reasonable terms for themselves when lending their labour ought to have been over-ruled because their views did not coincide with those of the Imperial authorities.

As a matter of fact our proposals were those which Milner had agreed to give, but has subsequently receded from. We fear exactly the same argument and the same conclusion in tariff disputes. I think that is the Indian case in a nutshell. Our fiscal autonomy is a very thin shade as it is. We don't want to see it entirely dissolved.

By this time the fear of war with Russia which had temporarily raised the Government's prestige had evaporated. The Dogger Bank outrage had been referred to an International Commission of Enquiry. Meanwhile the by-elections and the local elections continued to favour the Opposition. More serious, Campbell-Bannerman in two speeches at Norwich (26 October) and Edinburgh (3 November) had begun to outline an election programme for the Liberal party. It was still negative and tentative but it should have been a clear warning that the chance to exploit Liberal disunity was almost passed.

Chamberlain's views on the possibility of war appear from the following letters to Chaplin and Austen. The former shows how complete was his obsession with the Tariff question. The latter, despite its qualifications, reveals a mood of contempt for the Government. He could not sympathise with them, still less praise them even when he knew they had taken what was probably the wisest course.

CHAMBERLAIN TO CHAPLIN

29 *October* 1904.—Here, I only get Italian reports of the Russo–Anglo situation which however looks serious enough. If the Russians do not give way I hope we shall sink their fleet with that drunken ruffian the Admiral on board. But in this case I take it there will be an end of our agitation for some time. It will not be much use holding demonstrations in favour of fiscal reform during a time of war.

On the other hand a great deal of money must come from additional indirect taxation. Will it be protective? I hope and think that it must be although the necessities of finance may prevent us from making it preferential.

If we have to fight I hope we shall call on all the Colonies for assistance but this time, if I were Col. Sect'y, I should let them know that while we would most gratefully accept their aid, we would not pay for the Colonial troops employed. There were reasons in the Boer War too long to explain which made this necessary, but I should use a European war as a test of what the Colonies will really do in money as well as in men.

I think they would come out well. They might send fewer troops but they would be better and I believe the Colonials in this case would tax themselves for their support. I suppose we should only fight on land for the protection of India.

We are living in interesting times anyhow. If war *should* be declared I shall come home at once to attend the meeting of Parliament.

CHAMBERLAIN TO AUSTEN

12 *November* 1904.—I do not see how you could have declined the reference to a Hague Commission if it was proposed by either Russia or France but I doubt if it was right for the Government to propose it themselves. War has been avoided and that is a good thing but I feel sure that, whatever the report of the Commission, the greatest international outrage of my time will go unrevenged and unpunished. It is not altogether a pleasing reflection but somehow or another we always get the worst of it in negotiations.

Balfour's speech at Southampton was strong in its terms but it will compare badly, I fear, with the final result. I thought Lansdowne at the Guildhall decidedly weak but then weak words are the proper accompaniment of a weak policy. Understand that I do not blame the Government and if I had been a member I expect I should have adopted the same course, but I do not conceal from myself that our love of peace has once more placed us in a rather humiliating position.

His views on the situation in the Unionist party as reported in Chaplin's letters and Austen's were equally frank and critical.

We get some idea of them in the following extract taken from the same letter to Austen which we have just quoted.

As regards the Fiscal situation I do not like to hear on Gerald's authority that A.J.B. is inclined to 'wriggle' about the meaning of the Edinburgh speech. It is inconceivable to a plain man like myself that the P.M. can seriously contemplate a conference with the Colonies without being prepared to give immediate effect to any proposals agreed to at such a conference. It is certain that if properly managed it would result in offers from all the Colonies first to give us a substantial Preference against the foreigner which will enable us to increase — *and to keep* our existing trade. The last is important for we are certainly going to lose it if we do not get a Preference.

But secondly they will modify their general tariff in a sense favourable on the whole to British trade. They will not of course sacrifice their own principal industries but they *may* be willing to give terms which will prevent their unnatural and artificial expansion to our detriment.

For these concessions they will require the taxation of food — or rather the transfer of food taxation which I propose.

All this is known to every sensible man, and will be clearly in evidence if a conference meets.

Will A.J.B. accept and press such proposals? If not it is sinful to talk of a free conference, with a foregone conclusion not to accept its results.

In that case the Edinburgh speech would merit all the evil things said of it by the Opposition. It would be a dodge to unite the Party — one section of which must obviously be duped.

Chaplin thinks that A.J.B. has an idea of giving subsidies to shipping so as to favour Colonial goods. I cannot believe it and in any case it would be absurd. Fancy the farmers being told that not only were we not going to give them any advantage over the foreigner, who would continue to compete as before, but we were going to give the Colonial farmer a Preference over the Britisher and so to increase and stimulate existing competition.

As to domestic policy, *we* know that retaliation is a farce. It is a word — a device on paper — a philosopher's romance — but it is not a practical commercial policy as the P.M. will discover if ever he attempts to apply it. But having warned him, we need not press the matter further for the present.

I am very glad to hear . . . that your interest in agriculture is reviving. Do not give it up. It will always be to you what flowers have been to me.

X

Chamberlain returned to good news. At the beginning of the month Pearson had bought the *Standard*, hitherto one of the main organs of the Free Trade cause. The day after his return, a telegram from Lonsdale announced that Rigg, the Liberal member for Westmorland had 'come round to Chamberlain's views and retired

from his seat'. Meanwhile Chaplin had been successful in securing
the adoption of several Tariff Reform candidates in different parts
of the country. These things and his holiday no doubt contributed
to the excellent humour in which he spoke at the annual dinner
of the Birmingham Faculty of Medicine (30 November) :

Sir Frederick Treves gave us some conditional particulars derived
from the experience of the profession with regard to a gentleman who
appears to have been providentially perforated — (*laughter*) — in order
that scientific men might examine what was going on in his inside —
(*renewed laughter*) — and I must say the result appears to me to be alarming. . . . For what does Sir Frederick Treves tell us? He tells us that this
scientific examination showed that it was almost a miracle that any of
us were alive, for almost everything disagreed with us — (*Laughter*) —
and especially three things to which he called your special attention,
ices, smoking, and drinking. (*Renewed laughter.*) Now a little bit of
practical experience may be welcome to you even from a layman. For
at least fifty years of a life which extends considerably beyond that
period I have eaten ices whenever I could get them — (*laughter*) — penny
ices being barred — (*renewed laughter*) — I have smoked whenever I had
nothing else to do — (*laughter*) — and generally when I had something
to do — (*laughter*) — and I have consumed in moderation such alcoholic
fluids as I see before me, and I have found them to be beverages which
in my case cheer but do not inebriate. (*Laughter.*) Now, as a result of
this prolonged experience, I am happy to be able to assure you that my
digestion is as good as ever it was, and quite sufficient for my purposes,
and that in any case, in my instance, I do not think it would be necessary
to make any perforation.

But this surface joviality covered a further setback. Chamberlain
had returned hoping against hope that Balfour could be persuaded
to go to the country in the Spring. Talks with Austen, however, and
it may be with other Ministers soon convinced him that there was
no chance of this. The political situation had so far deteriorated
that even his strongest supporters in the Government were not
prepared to put out to sea in such a storm. They hoped, as Governments are always tempted to hope, that the run of luck might change
if only they held on.

Soon after his return, Garvin asked Chamberlain why he did not
force an election by bringing out his followers in the Cabinet. He
lifted one finger and with a sardonic smile answered, 'I could not
bring out one — not one !' [1]

About the same time (1 December) Fitzroy noted sardonically in
his diary :

[1] Note by J. L. Garvin of a conversation with Chamberlain dated 'end of November'.

... the Prime Minister ... has put to his credit three considerable achievements : he has dished Mr. Chamberlain, he has kept the Unionist Party, in the main, together, and he has prepared the country to accept with resignation Sir H. Campbell-Bannerman as his successor.[1]

XI

The certainty of another session killed Chamberlain's zest for his campaign. Now that there was no prospect of an early decision, committee meetings, interviews and above all the preparation of speeches became an intolerable drudgery. Will-power drove him on, but his speeches and letters in the next two months are heavy with a sense of effort.

His next meeting was to be at Limehouse. He could not get started on his speech. He had devoted himself so much to one subject that all his material seemed stale. Five or six times he tore up his notes and tried a different approach. It was not till the evening before the meeting that the depression suddenly lifted and he 'at last got his line'.[2]

Next day he travelled to London and was busy with committees and interviews up to the last moment before his speech. He had not prepared as much as usual and was depressed at getting no time to himself beforehand. For all that his speech, delivered in a full-blooded vein well suited to the audience was an immense success. He spoke for over two hours but never for a moment lost his hold on an audience of over 4000.

The East End of London was the main centre of foreign immigrants. Chamberlain raised the question of restricting alien immigration. This roused the passions as well as the interest of his audience.

Let us go to the root of the matter at the next general election. I do not know when it is coming — the sooner the better as far as I am concerned. (*Cheers.*) ... You are suffering from the unrestricted imports of cheaper goods. You are suffering also from the unrestricted immigration of the people who make these goods. (*Loud and prolonged cheers.*) ... The evils of this immigration have increased during recent years. And behind those people who have already reached these shores, remember there are millions of the same kind who, under easily conceivable circumstances, might follow in their track, and might invade this country in a way and to an extent of which few people have at present any conception ... But the party of free importers is against any reform. How could they be otherwise? If they were openly to admit that the

---

[1] *Memoirs of Sir Almeric Fitzroy*, vol. i, p. 228.
[2] Mrs. Chamberlain to her mother, 14 December 1904.

policy which I recommend ought to be adopted they would be giving up their whole theory. (*Cheers.*) Where would Mr. Cobden be? (*Laughter.*) Where would the doctrine of free imports be? Where would the doctrine of cheap goods be? (*Cheers.*) And yet they are perfectly consistent. If sweated goods are to be allowed in this country without restriction, why not the people who make them? Where is the difference? There is no difference either in the principle or in the results. It all comes to the same thing — less labour for the British working man. (*Cheers.*)

Next came a passage on the importance of the new policy to the working man.

This alien problem is only a part of a greater problem — the problem of the employment of our people. The free importers never will look below the surface. They lose themselves in a mass of irrelevant statistics; but they cannot be brought to grasp the true question. The true question is not whether this country is richer or poorer, the question is whether this country provides sufficient employment at remunerative rates for all who seek it. (*Cheers.*) ... I was reading a very interesting book by a German ... He says that England is still a great country; that it is growing richer every day; that it has a wonderful energy and prosperity. But, he points out, it now is going on new lines. Whereas at one time England was the greatest manufacturing country, now its people are more and more employed in finance, in distribution, in domestic service, and in other occupations of the same kind. That state of things is consistent with ever-increasing wealth. It may mean more money, but it means less men. (*Cheers.*) It may mean more wealth, but it means less welfare; and I think it is worth while to consider — whatever its immediate effects may be — whether that state of things will not be the destruction ultimately of all that is best in England ... I have never been able to see how a rich man — a man already rich — would be materially benefited by my policy. Of course if the whole country profited I suppose he would profit in like manner. But as he would probably have to pay more for his luxuries, I think it is possible he would lose more than he would gain; but to the working man it is life and death. (*Cheers.*) I say that of all the social questions that any man can interest himself with there is none greater, none more promising of valuable result than the question of how to increase the employment of the working classes ... You can reject the policy I put before you ... You can reject it or accept it ... Yours is the power, yours is the responsibility. My duty ceases when I have put before you what I have made some sacrifice in order to promote. (*Loud cheers.*) Do not mistake. I am not alluding to any sacrifice of personal advantage. I mean the sacrifice of congenial employment, and of the hope that I was doing something to introduce a great policy which would conduce to the greatness of the Empire and the prosperity of this country. But I have sacrificed this power and influence which office gives in order to be able to put before you this question of fiscal reform free and untrammelled by any party connexion. I say that I have done my duty; it is for you to do yours. What will you do? (*A voice: 'Make you Prime Minister', and cheers.*)

He then discussed the claim of the Free Traders that the Colonies were not really interested in preferential arrangements.

There is only one way. I said to the House of Commons, you will not take my word, or the word of the Prime Ministers themselves. There is only one way to convince your unbelief. Touch and you shall believe. Call a conference; allow the colonists to speak for themselves, then you will know whether they want Preference, and what they will offer in return. (*Cheers.*)

Since I began this work some 18 months ago, I have addressed a series of meetings, chiefly, of course, consisting of working men, larger I think than have ever been addressed before by a single man on the same subject. I have everywhere been received with kindness, with sympathy, and I think with some agreement, and yet week after week from the very beginning, almost day by day, I have been told by my opponents that my policy is discredited and defeated ('*No*', *and* '*The wish is father to the thought*'), and that I myself am demolished ('*Not yet*'), pulverized, smashed (*laughter*), and for ever by my own suicidal act excluded from any position, power, or influence in this kingdom. Pulverized! Do I look like it? (*Laughter.*) I do not know. Anyhow, it is amusing after all that to read a speech by Mr. Asquith to his constituents at East Fife the other day, in which he told them that the fiscal question still dominated the political issues of the times. That was pretty good for a cause which has been smashed and defeated. (*Laughter.*) . . . For myself, at any rate, I refrain from prophecy; but there is one thing that I can tell Mr. Asquith — one thing that I know, and that comes, therefore, within the region of fact rather than prophecy. I tell him that, whether he has a victory at the next general election or not, the question of tariff reform, once raised and introduced to the consideration of the people, will never die. (*Loud cheers.*) No victory, however decisive, no victory that he can contemplate or hope for in his most sanguine moments will be a really decisive victory unless it ensures that in the future the earnest and sincere endeavour shall be made for closer relations between our Colonies and ourselves, based on a system of Preference by which every man within the Empire shall have better treatment from his fellow-subjects than they give to the foreigners — (*cheers*) — by which the manufacturer of the United Kingdom shall be placed at least on equal terms with his foreign competitor, and by which the British workman shall be secured against what is now his urgent and most pressing danger — from being ousted from his legitimate employment by the unfair competition of underpaid labour. (*Loud and prolonged cheers.*)

XII

The Christmas holiday brought little respite. There were no meetings, but there was little break in the round of correspondence and interviews. 'The worst of it is,' wrote Mrs. Chamberlain, 'when Joe tries to get out of these interviews by saying he will not be in London, they all eagerly express their willingness to travel to Birmingham.'[1]

Yet there were some bright spots. Lyttelton, deputising for Balfour at a meeting in Glasgow (19 December) implied that the Unionists would only need one electoral mandate not two to hold the Colonial Conference and carry out its conclusions. Balfour was called on to confirm or deny this interpretation but never replied. It was this, perhaps, which led Chamberlain to take stock of his position in rather more optimistic terms.

CHAMBERLAIN TO NORTHCOTE

23 December 1904.—Balfour's declaration at Edinburgh constitutes a great advance. He is now pledged to call a conference if he is successful at the election; and the whole Party, I think, without exception, have accepted this policy, although many of them perhaps do not see where it will carry them. If the conference were held, and fair proposals were made by the Colonies and accepted by our representatives, I think it would be impossible not to bring them before Parliament at once, and they would be part of the future Unionist policy certain to be carried whenever we came in with a sufficient majority.

I think, however, that I have already told you that I do not look upon a Unionist majority at the next election as possible. We might have won if Balfour had been able to go the 'whole hog' last autumn. Now the hesitation and vagueness of the Government declarations have frightened the weak ones and to some extent discouraged our friends, and the issue must be complicated by the general unpopularity of the Government and the natural desire for change which affects democratic constituencies. As, however, the worst thing for our policy, and I think for our Party, would be a victory with only a small majority, I am now anxious to have the election as soon as possible to let the Opposition try their hand. I am sure that they will be unable to fulfil their pledges and will disappoint their friends, while they will arouse serious fears amongst all who hold Imperial ideas. The result will be a political reaction and another election after a year or two at which we shall again come in with a swinging majority.

Under these circumstances our friends in the Colonies must be patient. We cannot carry a great change in this conservative country without a great deal of delay. Cobden took nine years to carry Free-Trade, and would have failed then but for the accident of the Irish famine and the strange conversion of Peel. I hope and believe that we shall be much more fortunate, and I do not doubt that something like three years will see us through.

CHAMBERLAIN TO COCHRANE

25 December 1904.—Many thanks for the partridges and for your kind remembrances of me. It is good to know that one's old friends and fellow workers do not forget the past companionship. To be a pioneer has one

[1] Mrs. Chamberlain to her mother, 24 December 1904.

great disadvantage — it separates one, for a time at any rate, from old comrades, and sometimes I feel a little lonely in consequence. But, as you know, I am an optimist and I believe that all will come right in the end though I sometimes wish that some of our leaders were a little more 'impulsive' as Salisbury would say. After all there are more battles won by audacity than by prudence, and I fear we have lost a chance by depending too much on the latter virtue.

XIII

Chamberlain's next meeting was at Preston. 'These meetings are beginning to pall on him,' wrote Mrs. Chamberlain. 'Still his band is doing good work and there is a general feeling that things are more favourable to us than six months ago.' It was a difficult speech to make. Preston had been the constituency of Farrer Eckroyd — the father of Fair Trade. But it was also a leading cotton town. Lancashire, in those days, hardly thought of the danger of foreign competition in the home market. All eyes were on the export trade, and an industry so concentrated on exports felt its interests bound up with the cause of Free Trade.

His speech was made in the great Public Hall to an audience of some 5000 people. Much of it was a reply to a speech made by Asquith in Preston a short time before. He admitted that cotton was an exceptional case. The home trade, in those days, was only one fourth of the export trade. But, in a prophetic passage, he warned the industry that foreign competition would grow, that they would lose their main foreign markets, and unless they took measures now even the Colonial and the home markets would not be safe. It was a closely reasoned and moderate speech. Few opinions, perhaps, were changed by it; but he had shown the flag in Lancashire and his supporters there were heartened.

From Preston, Mr. and Mrs. Chamberlain went to Knowsley. Next day they attended a lecture on Tropical Medicine by Ross and visited the Colonial exhibition with Sir Alfred Jones. On 13 January they were back at Highbury. That night Mrs. Chamberlain wrote to her mother. She mentioned, in her letter, an unexplained anxiety over Chamberlain's daughter Ethel, who was convalescing in Switzerland. On 15 January came a telegram to say that Ethel was dead.

CHAMBERLAIN TO COLLINGS

15 *January* 1905.—Ethel died this morning at Adelboden. You will sympathise with me — it is hard when the young die first.

'Joe is very good,' Mrs. Chamberlain wrote to her mother, 'but the sorrow is what you know it must be to him. He is taking it very naturally and is well; but tired. He says to tell you what it is to him and to all to have me here.'[1]

On the day of the funeral (18 January) Chamberlain read the order of the Burial of the Dead in the library at Highbury. 'It was a great effort to him; but he wanted to do it . . .'[2]

Politics give little quarter to personal sorrow. Chamberlain cancelled his engagement to speak at the Annual Birmingham Jewellers' Dinner. This was his only concession.

On 26 January Balfour spoke at Manchester and replying to a challenge from Morley summarised his fiscal policy on 'a half sheet of notepaper':[3]

First, I desire such an alteration of our fiscal system as will give us a freedom of action impossible while we hold ourselves bound by the maxim that no taxation should be imposed except for revenue. I desire this freedom in the main for three reasons. It will strengthen our hands in any negotiations by which we may hope to lower foreign hostile tariffs. It may enable us to protect the fiscal independence of those Colonies which desire to give us preferential treatment. It may be useful where we wish to check the importation of those foreign goods which, because they are bounty-fed, or tariff protected abroad, are sold below cost price here. Such importations are ultimately as injurious to the British consumer as they are immediately disastrous to the British producer. Secondly, I desire closer commercial union with the Colonies, and I do so because I desire closer union in all its possible modes and because this particular mode is intrinsically of great importance and has received much Colonial support. I also think it might produce great and growing commercial advantages both to the Colonies and the Mother Country by promoting freer trade between them. No doubt such commercial union is beset with many difficulties. These can best be dealt with by a Colonial Conference, provided its members are permitted to discuss them unhampered by limiting instructions. Thirdly, I recommend, therefore, that the subject should be referred to a conference on those terms. Fourth, and last, I do not desire to raise home prices for the purpose of aiding home productions.

Balfour's definitions were regarded as evasive by Goschen in that they did not state whether or not he was prepared to put a tax on food. From Chamberlain's point of view, however, the 'half sheet of notepaper' was satisfactory enough. At least Balfour had not repeated the objectionable portions of his Edinburgh formula.

---

[1] Mrs. Chamberlain to her mother, 18 January 1905.   [2] *Ibid*, 20 January 1905.
[3] Morley had offerred a reward to any of his constituents who could write down Balfour's Fiscal policy on 'a (whole) sheet of notepaper.'

Chamberlain was to speak at Gainsborough on 1 February. He would have postponed the meeting had it been possible, but accommodation had been provided in a new-built factory, machinery was to be installed, large sums had been spent on advertising, over 7000 tickets had been sold. 'It cannot be postponed.'[1]

Personal sorrow is often the last straw. Chamberlain's temporary prostration after Powell Williams' death was the direct result of the strain on his heart of the 1903 campaign. Were the effects of Ethel's death a warning of the true physical deterioration beneath the varnish of vigour which his will-power had superimposed? Ten minutes before he was due to leave to make his Gainsborough speech, Mrs. Chamberlain found him in his room with his head in his hands. 'I can't do it,' he moaned. From him, of all men, this was appalling. 'Oh, but you will,' she answered; and he rallied.[2]

His speech, as it happened, was among his best. But it gave rise to a moment of anxiety. At one point Chamberlain ceased. The audience thought it a pause for dramatic effect. But Mrs. Chamberlain, sitting beside him, knew at once that it was a kind of blackout. She knew his arguments by heart and at once prompted the word missing in his brain. The flow of his speech resumed. For the rest, his voice held throughout — it had failed once or twice at Preston — and the argument was successfully sustained. The audience was predominantly agricultural; but the theme of the speech was imperial and social. It was a broad summing up of his whole crusade.

Little Englanderism is also closely connected with the doctrine of free imports. What one is in the financial sphere the other is in the political sphere. If you want an Empire; if you want influence in the world, I think you will find that free imports are inconsistent with it. But if you are one of those who hate the very name of Imperialism, as I think Sir H. Campbell-Bannerman said he did the other day — if you are one of those, then I agree that you are consistent — you are honest in saying that under those circumstances, you see no reason for a change in our fiscal policy. The two go together.

[1] Mrs. Chamberlain to her mother, 20 January 1905.   [2] *Ibid*, 3 February 1905.

THE SESSION OF 1905

(*February–June* 1905)

Chamberlain Opens Negotiations with Balfour — He Seeks an Early Election — By-election Tactics — Wyndham Resigns — Selborne Replaces Milner — Unionist Tactics in the Commons — A Difference with Austen — The Front Bench Walk out — Chamberlain's Memorandum — When to Hold the Conference? — Negotiating a Concordat — Balfour's Albert Hall Speech — Chamberlain at St. Helen's — His Disappointment.

I

Close and serious discussion between British political leaders has been the exception rather than the rule. The press of business, the way of life and a certain aloofness in the national character all tend against that continuous examination of positions and purposes which is the lifeblood of fruitful collective action. Nor is the need supplied by frequent but fleeting contacts in the House of Commons or round the dinner table. These sometimes provide opportunities for settling a piece of business but seldom for concerting a line of action or clearing up misunderstandings.

In the eighteen months since his resignation, Chamberlain had only had one serious talk with Balfour. This was on his return from Italy in April 1904. Austen, of course, had served as intermediary between them; but an intermediary was not enough. As a result the differences between them became magnified and they grew increasingly further apart. The process would continue with results equally disastrous for Balfour as for Chamberlain. Yet had they kept in closer touch from the beginning, had they acted up to their early professions that they were still colleagues, they might have achieved a greater unity and so limited the inevitable defeat ahead.

The blame, if blame there be, for this growing separation rests rather upon Balfour. Chamberlain was the most candid of men and very confident of his powers of persuasion. He would have rejoiced at any opportunity for frank discussion with Balfour. But Balfour made no move. Every conversation that took place between them after his resignation was on Chamberlain's initiative.

By the beginning of 1905, there were certain clear differences between Balfour's position and Chamberlain's. The first and most important was the form of the Colonial Conference to discuss mutual Preference. Was its summons to depend on the verdict of one election and the fulfilment of its conclusions on another? This was Balfour's position. Or would one election be enough, as Chamberlain maintained? Then there was the question of Retaliation. This was Balfour's part of the policy but he had never attempted to explain how he saw it in practice. Chamberlain, on the other hand, had already publicly declared for an all-round revenue tariff of ten per cent. Would Balfour agree to this? If not what would he propose instead? Finally there was the agricultural interest to consider. Its representatives were among the staunchest backers of Unionism. How were they to benefit from fiscal reform?

Just before the meeting of Parliament, Chamberlain made a last effort to treat Balfour as a colleague and bridge the differences between them in private discussion.

CHAMBERLAIN TO BALFOUR

12 *February* 1905: *Private.*—Since I resigned office about eighteen months ago I have only had one serious talk with you about the situation, which has necessarily changed somewhat in the interval.

Would it not be useful that we should have a free conversation very soon? Otherwise with every desire on both sides to co-operate, we may insensibly drift apart.

What I should like is that we should meet — either at your house or here, whichever is most convenient to you — at some time when we can be alone and *absolutely free from interruption.*[1]

A quiet dinner next Friday would be the best — if it is possible for you. I want to know your views about many points and it is no use attempting to discuss things while the House is sitting.

On the Friday (17 February) as proposed, Chamberlain dined alone with Balfour. 'I was so glad,' wrote Mrs. Chamberlain, 'for it is a long time since they have met in that way, and it is so much easier not to drift apart when one has opportunities for intimate and friendly talk together.'[2]

We can reconstruct the course of their conversation from a note Chamberlain made of it that night.

The first subject discussed was the proposed Colonial Conference.

---

[1] Chamberlain's italics.   [2] Mrs. Chamberlain to her mother, 22 February 1905.

Chamberlain 'urged Balfour not to commit us to two elections'. The delay involved might be indefinite, if the second election were lost. 'Parliament would not submit. The Colonies would object.' Balfour on his side argued that the country 'would never accept' a proposal which might lead to the taxation of food unless there were reserved to it a *locus penitentiae*, by which he evidently meant a chance to think again.

This topic as we shall see from subsequent correspondence occupied much of their time. Afterwards they passed to the question of Retaliation. Here Chamberlain began by asking Balfour how it would be 'carried out'. He went on to state his own plan, for an all-round revenue tariff. According to his note, there was 'no time for discussion' of this question. Seeing that the conversation continued for some time longer it seems likely that Balfour was evasive.

They then turned to the subject of 'recent [by-] elections'. Chamberlain spoke of the 'difficulty of candidates' who followed the Balfour line. They could not arouse the enthusiasm which the full Tariff Reform policy undoubtedly generated. At the same time their advocacy of retaliation laid them open to all the most unscrupulous attacks of the Free Traders. They were thus 'not able to defend themselves while incurring all the odium of false accusations.' He went on to deplore the influence exercised by the Central Office in London to persuade candidates to adopt the Balfour as against the Chamberlain policy. Balfour disagreed with this last point. He thought that 'in every case' the more moderate policy was 'forced on candidates by local not central influence'.

Before separating, they discussed the position of Hugh Cecil, who had been asked not to stand again by the Tariff Reform majority on his Committee at Greenwich. Balfour 'spoke bitterly of some of his attacks on Chamberlain, but distinguished between him and Free Fooders such as Elliot'. He had been asked for his opinion and 'would write . . . pointing out [that the] matter was for local consideration. But [he] thought of adding he hoped [Hugh Cecil] would not be opposed.'

The arguments on both sides, particularly on the question of the Colonial Conference, were further elaborated in the following correspondence.

BALFOUR TO CHAMBERLAIN

18 *February* 1905 : *Private*.—I feel moved to supplement by a few written words what I urged yesterday on the subject of a double election in connection with proposals for commercial union with the Colonies.

Let me begin by admitting that your arguments against this plan have great weight. The one on which I think you lay most stress, and which certainly appeals most powerfully to me, is that, in the event of a Government coming into power with a large majority pledged to deal with this question, it would be highly inconvenient, if a scheme were successfully devised by a Colonial Conference within the first year or eighteen months after the election, to oblige the Government of the day to appeal again to the country : that such a course would be so unpopular among the Members who had just successfully carried through an electoral campaign that it would be difficult to carry into effect : that, on the other hand, if the appeal were postponed for two or three years, the Government would inevitably have suffered from the diseases which no Government escapes ; its popularity would have waned : and the Colonial issue would be complicated by the innumerable petty subjects of criticism — just and unjust — to whose cumulative effect the so-called swing of the pendulum is due.

Now I agree that this is a most forcible argument against my scheme. Though I should have considerable confidence that any scheme, when it was once suggested by the Colonial Conference, and approved by the Colonial and British Ministers, would be practically safe from party attack. I do not mean that it would escape criticism, — but I think it highly probable that the Opposition would not find it pay to endeavour to prevent its ratification, but would turn the stream of criticism into another channel. The anxiety of the country for some colonial arrangement, having, by hypothesis, been demonstrated, they would shrink from taking the grave responsibility of wrecking a definite plan to which the Colonies had given their adhesion.

But, making all allowance for this and other analogous arguments, it remains true that so long as we concentrate our attention upon what is to happen when a Government pledged to a free Colonial Conference has been returned to power, your plan seems incomparably simpler, more convenient, and more effective than mine. And it has the further advantage of following the ordinary course adopted in respect of other Treaties, and avoiding a new constitutional procedure.

Why, then, do I urge so strongly that, in spite of all these shortcomings, the double election should be part of any plan aiming at commercial union? The reason is that a free Colonial Conference seems to me (and, I think, to you also) an absolutely necessary part of any machinery for arriving at an arrangement ; and that in my judgment, without a double election, no free Conference will be possible. A Conference will not be free unless it is at liberty to discuss the total abolition, and not merely the relative diminution, of some parts, at all events, of the tariff wall which the Colonies have raised against all external producers. Such a plan would be contrary to the whole spirit of colonial legislation ; and I am not aware that they have hitherto even suggested that they could do more for the Mother Country than put her in a somewhat less unfavourable position than they put the foreigner. They are not prepared with regard to any class of manufactures to give her equal advantages with their own manufactures, but only to impose upon her smaller disadvantages than they do upon the alien. I should therefore have supposed that, say, a Canadian Ministry would have some difficulty in obtaining leave to make an arrangement violating the whole Canadian fiscal tradition, without laying the general scheme, of which this was to form a part, before the Electorate of Canada. If I am right in this, Canada will insist on a double election as a prerequisite of a free Conference, and what Canada insisted on for *her* people we could hardly refuse to *ours*.

But I may be wrong in this estimate of Canadian feeling — a subject on which I do not profess to have any special means of forming a judgment. I cannot doubt, however, that analogous arguments will have enormous weight in England. Just as a free Conference requires the Canadians to go into it unpledged on the subject of Canadian Protection, so it requires the British representatives to go into it unpledged on the subject of food taxation. Now I have very grave doubts whether this end can be attained except on the double election plan. The prejudice against a small tax on food is not the fad of a few imperfectly informed theorists : it is a deep-rooted prejudice affecting the large mass of voters, especially the poorest class, which it will be a matter of extreme difficulty to overcome. I confess that it seemed to me last night that you underrated this difficulty. When I described the case of Candidates starting from a rather 'advanced' tariff reform platform, and finding themselves driven from it by local opinion, you seemed inclined to put this down to a weak yielding on their part to the local leaders, who, as you justly observe, are not always very safe guides. But my impression is that the local leaders, the squire, the middle-class members of the Association, and so forth, are as a rule, highly sympathetic to tariff reform, and, indeed, often hold protectionist views, which I am quite unable to share ; and that the obstacle with which the Candidate is confronted is not the opinion of the local leaders, but the absolute impossibility of inducing the mass of the voters to do anything which they can be made to believe would increase the price of bread. I do not think that you will get over this by any hypothetical presentation of the possible advantages to British trade of a colonial arrangement. But we *may* get over it if we can shew, in concrete form the merits of the bargain which is within our reach. But this cannot be shewn till a free Conference has devised a plan : so that a Candidate fighting on your scheme is necessarily deprived of his best argument. In other words, without the double election plan you will find Members pledging themselves under no circumstances to put the smallest tax upon foodstuffs, and, by so pledging themselves, rendering a free Conference extremely difficult. The double election will enable them truthfully to say to their constituents that, by assenting to a free Conference, they are not giving up their right to object to any tax on food : they are only postponing the exercise of their right till they see whether closer commercial union with the Colonies can be obtained without it, and, if not, whether commercial advantages obtained in exchange for it are, or are not, sufficient. In those cases, moreover, where a Candidate *has* pledged himself against a tax on food, a double election will give both him and his constituency a *locus penitentiae* if they desire to make use of it, — no small advantage, if, and when, a satisfactory arrangement seems to be within our reach.

To sum up in a word : if we could secure a free Conference on your terms, *your* scheme is the best. But in order to obtain a free Conference, *my* scheme is the best. And we probably differ, not because I rate lower than you do the advantages of your plan, but because I rate far higher than you do the difficulty of obtaining what is the essential preliminary to it.

CHAMBERLAIN TO BALFOUR

24 *February* 1905 : *Private.*—I am much obliged by your letter dated 18 February, but only received this morning. I have read it with great interest and I think I fully appreciate your argument. What you say about my reasons for pressing for a single election makes it unnecessary for me to add anything more on this score although I could add other arguments to those I have already submitted, but I gather I may take it for granted that you yourself would prefer my proposal if you thought it equally practicable with your own.

I confine myself therefore to some criticisms on your statement, and begin by agreeing that a Colonial conference absolutely free to discuss the whole question is a necessary part of the machinery for arriving at an arrangement. In saying this I am aware that, as every one in the least degree acquainted with the Colonial situation will agree, Free Trade between the different portions of the Empire is at present impossible. All we can hope to do is to make the nearest approach to it which we can secure at the present time.

I think, however, that you are entirely mistaken in supposing that the Colonies are committed to confine their concessions to some Preference as compared with the foreigners, but that they will make no reduction in their own tariff against Great Britain. On the contrary, at the time of the last Conference of Premiers the Canadians had already begun to discuss with the Board of Trade the possibility of reconsidering and altering in our favour their existing Tariff. No doubt their main hope of giving us advantages lies in an increase of the tariff against the foreigner. This they would do in two ways : (1) by increasing the present Tariff where the foreigner is concerned, and (2) by establishing a tariff against the foreigner where at present the articles are on the free list. But they were willing to go further, and, in cases where they have at present no important manufactures, to see if they could not reduce or place on the free list British manufactures.

I should hope therefore that the negotiations would result in a double advantage to British trade.

I did not gather from them at the time, nor did I understand from Mr. Fielding, whom I saw last week, that they considered it necessary to do more than submit any arrangement at which we may arrive to their Parliament. *On the contrary, Mr. Fielding objected to the delay which would be caused by any pledge to consult the electorate upon the subject. He pointed out that unless they could be sure of a speedy decision after the arrangements were made, it would be difficult for them to discuss freely the concessions they were prepared to make.*[1] Such a course would expose them to criticism or opposition from all the interests that might be injuriously affected, and this opposition would be working during the whole time that the fate of the treaty remained in abeyance. Members would not like to make enemies, even of a small minority, unless they were tolerably certain that the whole arrangement would be carried into effect before the opposition had time to gather, and would have a fair trial before it came — if it ever did — before the electors. The enthusiasm evoked by the idea of closer union, coupled with the advantages which the agreement would confer on a majority of the people, would be sufficient to overcome the opposition if no long delay took place.

Now, supposing that he is right, there will be no double election in Canada. On the other hand I concede to you that if Canada asked for it we might be obliged to give the same opportunity to our people which she claims for hers.

It remains to consider your second argument, namely, that the electorate in England will not give us a mandate unless they know beforehand that they will have a chance of rejecting, at a general election, any arrangement that we may have made. I do not think that this is the case. I admit the prejudice against a food tax, of which you speak, although I am convinced that it can and will be overcome, but where and so long as it exists those who entertain it will refuse the mandate under any circumstances, — they will not, as Campbell-Bannerman says, 'even touch the accursed thing'. The prejudice, however, has already largely disappeared among the artisan population, and even in agricultural districts I am sure that where a proper house to house education has been undertaken the labourers are open to conversion.

But the present position is the worst of all that can be conceived. Acting under natural feelings of timidity, the candidates who have been persuaded, or who have persuaded themselves, to declare against all food taxes, are at a treble disadvantage. In the first place they lose the support of the convinced tariff reformers. How serious this is may be gathered from many circumstances. At the last meeting of the Tariff Reform League I persuaded the meeting to stand aside entirely in the case of the Tewkesbury Division where Sir Michael Hicks Beach's son is standing. I did this out of feeling for Sir Michael and also because I believe that if his son gets in he will not prove irreconcileable. But I was assured that 9/10ths at least of the Unionist electors are dissatisfied with the candidate's position and have told him that he will certainly lose the seat. The feeling appears to be so strong that I doubt whether young Beach will think it worth while to continue his candidature. Similar feeling exists at Greenwich, at Gorton, at Durham, and in other places.

In the second place, that portion of the electors which is entirely '*free trade*' will have nothing to say to any compromise. They will vote against Retaliation and would not be influenced by any concession.

In the third place, while our candidate will have to suffer whatever the attack upon him from the Free Traders involves, he will be totally

[1] My italics.—J. A.

unable to put himself straight by bringing forward the very strong arguments by which we support our views. He and his canvassers cannot point to the advantages of closer union with the Colonies or the gain to be secured by the concessions they are prepared to make, nor can he argue that what we propose is merely a transfer of taxation by which the poorest will gain on the balance. All these things will be inconsistent with the position that he takes up if he rejects altogether the idea of preferential treatment.

These difficulties which will certainly be fatal in a large number of cases to our candidates will not be removed by your proposal. If, however, by boldly arguing the question they can convince the working people and the farmers (who will otherwise be inevitably estranged by a policy which threatens them with increased prices for all that they buy and gives them no corresponding advantage in what they have to sell) they will find that their supporters will desire that the new policy shall be put in operation at once and will just as readily give them a mandate to bring a satisfactory arrangement before Parliament, as for a plan which must involve indefinite postponement. In my experience the ordinary voter never cares for detail. He seizes upon a principle or a large issue and is quite willing to delegate to his representative all questions of detail and method.

On the whole, therefore, while I believe that we should not gain anything by dilatory tactics we should lose a great deal of the enthusiasm which alone carries great political changes.

I think I called your attention before to the interesting fact that while we have lost heavily everywhere in recent elections we have been much more successful in the case of the men who, like Mr. Banner at Liverpool, the other day, have openly defended the complete policy than in the case of those who have tried to trim.

I hope that when the tremendous pressure upon you is over we may have another talk on these points. I also want very much to know how you propose to carry out your own policy of Retaliation. At present I do not see how it can be worked in bits. There must, I think, be a complete scheme to secure the sort of backing which you want. If it is attempted to carry it out piecemeal the fight will be endless and the opposition will at the same time have a great tactical advantage over us, but as to this I do not sufficiently understand your scheme at present to speak with sufficient knowledge upon it.

It is important to be clear on the real meaning of the difference between Chamberlain and Balfour. The question of electoral sanction for the Colonial Conference was, at first sight, academic. Both Chamberlain and Balfour were convinced that they would lose the next election. But in another sense it raised very practical issues. The first of these and it is the one discussed in the letters shown above — was the question : which would be the better platform for Unionist candidates — one election or two ? On this question there can be little doubt that Chamberlain was right and

Balfour wrong. Chamberlain understood the constituencies. Balfour did not. But this is beside the point. The real difference between the two men never emerges in the letters. It is this. If the Colonial Conference and its results were to be subject to only one election, the Unionist party would be committed to the policy of Preference, provided satisfactory arrangements could be worked out. Balfour would in fact have to abandon the Sheffield formula that the taxing of food was not practical politics. He could hardly call a conference unless he did. But if the decisions of the conference were to be submitted to a further election there would be no real commitment at all. Now Chamberlain was determined to commit the Government, while it still was a Government, to the principle of Preference and to the principle of an all round revenue Tariff. This Balfour was equally determined to resist. To have admitted this would have been to go back on what he had said and written to Chamberlain at the time of his resignation. But it is clear that he had no intention of breaking with his Unionist Free Trade friends and the forces they represented. That he should have defended Hugh Cecil in his first serious talk with Chamberlain in ten months shows how his mind was moving.

II

The Government's prospects at the opening of Parliament seemed dark. Even Balfour's entourage and the Whips Office were pessimistic. Fitzroy noted in his diary:

31 January 1905.—Though Ministers in public and private avow their belief that Parliament will run out its ordinary course, my information goes to show that those with the best means of judging look upon the position as most critical. The ranks of the party are steeped in lukewarmness and discontent, a large number of members are not seeking re-election, some of them from disgust; many of the Unionist Free Traders would welcome the early defeat of the Government, and there is no driving power behind the formal machinery of the party. Such, at any rate, is the state of things described to me by Sandars today, and attributable, though he did not go so far as to say it, to the difficulties inherent in the course of events. In these views I take it Sandars expresses the opinion of Douglas and Alec Hood, who see further into the actual condition of things than most of their colleagues. . . . Sandars does not believe the Government can outlast the Session, and even thinks the catastrophe may be very near; but he admits the Prime Minister is more optimistic.[1]

[1] *Memoirs of Sir Almeric Fitzroy*, vol. i, p. 232.

If the Free Fooders wanted an early election, so did Chamberlain. He made no secret of it. 'It's all the time getting harder for Joe to support the Government,' wrote Mrs. Chamberlain. 'Better that the election should come soon, as the Government has no credit to gain by remaining in office.'[1]

Chamberlain had good reasons for wanting an election. Another session of Balfourian evasion was bound to demoralise the Tariff Reformers and weaken his movement. All this would add enormously to his own labours. Already, as his diary shows, he almost lived in the train between London and Birmingham controlling the activities of his two main organisations.

In Birmingham, staunch old Jesse Collings presided over the Imperial Tariff Committee. But as Mrs. Chamberlain wrote, 'he was no longer much help'. Chamberlain had hopes of some of the younger men, but none had sufficient authority to take his place.

In London, Pearson, overworked and fast going blind, had been forced to resign the Chairmanship of the Tariff Reform Committee. Chamberlain persuaded Ridley to take on the work. But this meant that he too would have to give more time to helping Ridley.

CHAMBERLAIN TO RIDLEY

18 *February* 1905.—I am not satisfied with the present position of affairs. I do not blame anyone, but undoubtedly mistakes have been made, and I do not think the control has been quite as complete as it should have been.

I propose during the sitting of Parliament a weekly meeting of the Committee which I will attend myself whenever I can possibly do so, and there are other alterations which I shall be glad to talk over with you.

It is especially necessary that we should have a chairman with leisure who can make himself fully acquainted with the work that is going on and arrange and conduct the business for the weekly meetings, and your experience in matters of organisation will be of the greatest service.

Then there were the Tariff Reform members in the House of Commons. To keep them together, he agreed to a system of twice weekly dinners which he would try to come to himself.

The sheer business of holding his movement together would make enormous drafts on his strength. Yet a dissolution would do more to put heart into his supporters than any number of speeches, or committees or private talks.

It was, moreover, only when a dissolution was decided that Balfour

---

[1] Mrs. Chamberlain to her mother, 22 February 1905.

would be free from dependence on the Free Fooders for his Parliamentary majority. Then, but only then, there would be at least a chance of agreeing a united policy.

Another consideration weighed increasingly with him. Each new evasion of Balfour's gave rise to doubts in the Colonies as to the sincerity of the Unionist Party. Each increased Chamberlain's isolation and weakened his authority in the Empire.

Above all he was convinced that the longer Parliament continued the lower the Government's credit would fall, and the greater would be the smash at the polls. Chamberlain was in his seventieth year and he wanted to see Tariff Reform in his time. He could hardly afford a full seven-year Parliament in Opposition.

He gave public expression to his wish for an early election in the debate on the Address (16 February), only two days after the opening of Parliament.

> . . . so far as I am concerned, dissolution has no terrors. I am quite content to trust my political fortunes with the working men who for 30 years have given me their confidence so generously. I will go further than this. I have no fear of a dissolution, whatever its result may be. I have said in the country, and I have no objection to repeating the statement here, that so far as I personally am concerned, so far as my opinion goes, the sooner dissolution comes the better . . . Now by the necessity of the case we are always on the defence. I look forward with unmingled satisfaction to the time, whenever it comes, when we shall be in a similar position to hon. members opposite. I have read with the greatest interest the letter of recommendation which was published the other day by a distinguished leader of the Opposition, in which was sketched, at all events, his personal idea of the policy which he and his friends would pursue. A close examination of that policy opens to me a vista which I confess makes everything now stale and unprofitable. I greatly desire, whenever the proper time comes, to exchange the responsibility of action for the joy of criticism (*laughter and cheers*). And now, speaking for myself alone, as a private member, dissolution has no terrors for me whatsoever. If it comes in the ordinary constitutional way, I say again the sooner it comes the better.[1]

He followed this up with an equally forthright restatement of his difference with Balfour over the form of the proposed Colonial Conference.

> I do not want to seem to have the slightest doubt or hesitation in regard to my own opinion . . . when the speech in Edinburgh was made, speaking at Luton almost immediately afterwards, I said that a question

---

[1] Chamberlain's contempt for the Opposition emerges clearly from a letter written to Harmsworth next day (17 Feb.). In this he says: 'six months' experience of a Liberal Government will work wonders.'

of method arose upon the last speech of the Prime Minister, and I ventured to criticize that method and to say that in my opinion if a conference were held, such as the Prime Minister proposed, and if the result of that conference were satisfactory, it would be impossible to withhold those proposals from the consideration of this Parliament and from their action if they were sitting at the time, and, if not, at the earliest possible moment. Very well, that is perhaps a difference ; in any case, it is on a point of method, and not on a point of principle. I think the time to discuss it will be after the principle is decided. The right hon. gentleman opposite — I think it was hardly worthy of him — actually made a point and occupied the time of the House for two or three minutes, of the fact that I spoke afterwards at Gainsborough and did not repeat that statement.

It is really childish to accuse me of having abandoned an opinion because I do not repeat it on every occasion. I repeat it when it is necessary. *I repeat it here in this House.* . . .

Chamberlain's frank statement on the need for an early election encouraged some of his more active supporters to contemplate forcing a dissolution by leaving the Government in a minority.[1] But the Tory party has a long tradition of loyalty to its leaders. Members of Parliament, besides, are nearly always reluctant to take the plunge. The ventilation of this idea provoked a reaction among some of the most influential Tariff Reformers.

HERBERT MAXWELL TO CHAMBERLAIN

25 *February* 1905.—As I am paired next week and shall be 700 miles from London, I am sorry that it is not in my power to attend the meeting of the Executive Committee of the T.R.L. on 3rd March.

I meant to have tried to get a word with you in the House this week but have failed to do so. I wished to have your views on a point upon which several men have spoken to me with some anxiety.

It seems to be the wish of some of our people, and is reported to be yours, to put an end to the present Parliament. Other men are of opinion that it is the plain duty of Unionist Tariff Reformers to support the present Government with all their might.

That is my own opinion — Balfour has advanced so far to meet us, that I feel he is entitled to our loyal support, and I, and those who think with me, will not do anything to bring about the fall of the Government, either by abstention or opposition. Of course, upon a direct motion involving the principles of Fair Trade v. Cobdenism, we should not hesitate to vote for the former, even should the Government oppose it, but that is not the way in which the Government could fall.

As a matter of policy affecting our movement, I daresay it might be better that a general election should come soon. In fact, I have heard you say that you wished it ; but I have told everyone who has spoken to

[1] See Chaplin on Joseph Chamberlain in the *Encyclopædia Britannica*.

Polling day 1906

H. H. Asquith

Walter Long

NO DIFFICULTY FOLLOWING BOTH
Of course there isn't! This is how it is done.

me on the subject that I am firmly convinced that you have no design of intentionally upsetting the present Ministers, and that Balfour has no heartier supporter than yourself. If that be so, and I have not a shade of doubt about it, it ought to be made clear to the Executive Committee on Friday, for you are being misrepresented as contemplating some action to accelerate a dissolution.

Apart from what I feel to be our obligation to the Government we were returned to support, I cannot but entertain mistrust of the result of precipitating a dissolution — the ultimate result, I mean, for we can't expect much from the first general election. To put it on the lowest ground — the anxiety of the Radicals to get in, makes it desirable to keep them out as long as possible.

Maxwell's letter is typical of the best type of Conservative back-bencher. There is the deep sense of loyalty, the readiness to interpret the leader's actions in the most favourable light and the strong determination not to let domestic differences play into the hands of opponents. Such men are very hard to move. They often act as a brake on 'rebellions' in the Tory ranks; though, once moved, they prove almost irresistible.

Chamberlain's reply shows that he never contemplated deliberately bringing down the Government. His letter, however, makes it clear that he would have viewed its defeat with complete unconcern.

CHAMBERLAIN TO MAXWELL

25 February 1905*: Private.*—Thanks for yours of today. I do not think that the subject referred to is one for the Executive Committee, and I should not myself introduce it on the occasion of the next meeting. Surely it is a matter entirely for Unionist members of Parliament who are also Tariff Reformers.

I know that there has been some misapprehension as to my views, and therefore I expressed them publicly in my speech on the Address. I still think that the sooner the present Parliament comes to an end the better for Mr. Balfour, for the Government, and especially for our cause, and I have reason to know that this is also the opinion of some important members of the Government itself. But I have never contemplated any opposition to the Government, and I think it would be bad policy to show any slackness in supporting them whenever they are attacked and require backing. Thus, in the case of MacDonnell, for instance, in which I think the action of the Irish Government indefensible, I nevertheless came down myself to vote and advised all my friends whom I could get at to do the same. I would on all occasions support the Government by my vote and presence on any question which amounted to a vote of censure. I should not vote *against* them on anything as at present advised, but I do not feel bound during the present session to attend as strictly from morning to night as I did in the last, and if the Government were

z

defeated on some snap division or trumpery question I admit that I should not be sorry. But this is a very different thing from working to bring it about. My feeling is that with the Party in its present condition you cannot force them to give up everything to prevent what two or three years ago we should have considered a catastrophe.

The situation is much the same as it was when Gladstone's Government fell in 1885. We were all pleased to be free and to give the then Tory Opposition a chance, but none of us so far as I know, worked for that result. It came about in the natural course as a consequence of the lack of enthusiasm, and the abstention of people who did not care to make the sacrifice required to maintain a permanent majority.

You are therefore perfectly right in saying that I have no design of intentionally upsetting the present Government, and that I am always entirely at Balfour's service if he requires it. Otherwise each man must do as he thinks right. I shall put no pressure on any of my friends further than to advise them most earnestly to support the Government on every question of confidence. If, as I understand, you would do, and as I know many others are prepared to do, they are willing to attend continuously whatever the sacrifice, I should certainly not intervene in any way. If, on the 'contrary, they incline to a little slackness I do not feel that I ought to interfere unless indeed Mr. Balfour himself asked me to use my influence to prevent it.

As to the desire of the Radicals to get in, I believe that they have got to such a condition that they would come in even if it were only for a day, and my conviction is that even a day's experience of them would gain for us a large number of fresh supporters.

Please treat this, as it is, a letter absolutely frank, and written to a confidential friend.

This exchange is important. Maxwell's letter was a warning to Chamberlain. He could count on the bulk of the party to support Tariff Reform but not to the length of openly opposing Balfour.

III

Chamberlain made no further reference to a possible dissolution at the meeting of the Tariff Reform League Executive (3 March). His speech, instead, was an appeal to candidates to go the 'whole hog' and not to limit themselves to the Sheffield policy.

We have just thrown away another seat. I am not surprised, and cannot profess any great regret at the result. The Unionist candidate was believed to be, and I think he expressed himself as being in favour of Preference to the Colonies, but he withdrew that statement, perhaps on account of the views of a small minority of his constituents. If he had stuck to his first position he might have lost some votes from the Unionists but I believe he would have gained votes from the other side to make up for them ; and he suffered as every one must suffer in an electoral campaign, if he is thought not to have the full courage of his convictions. Since this matter became a real political fight I do not think one single seat has been won by the Unionist party in which the candidate was half-hearted on the subject, and, on the other hand, in every case in which we have won the seat, we have won it with a candidate who was whole-hearted in the cause of tariff reform. That was true of Dulwich, Lewisham, Birmingham, Mile-end, Horsham, Rochester and Liverpool, and possibly others which I cannot remember at the moment. I have been in many agitations, and I do not say that what is happening now is at all strange to me; but I do say very emphatically that as time goes on there ought to be a certain stiffening of the backs of tariff reformers, in which case our ultimate success will be very much hastened. Meanwhile, I suppose that we may look forward to two or three years of the same kind of work as that which we have already undertaken.

The seat 'we have just thrown away' was North Westmorland, where the sitting Liberal member, Rigg, had retired, having come round to Chamberlain's views. The Unionist candidate, Noble, began as a Chamberlainite but was persuaded to change his position. The following letter from his election agent gives some idea of the results.

ABLEWHITE TO CHAPLIN

6 *March* 1905.—When I first went down into Westmorland, in Dec. last, Major Noble was a Chamberlainite candidate, and I spoke for him at Langdales, Shap and Brough, and was listened to with marked attention. We went the whole 'Hog', and two of these places, Langdales and Brough, I find *now* are very Radical, but they listened most attentively and we got a unanimous vote of thanks. Between these dates and the opening of the campaign, on the advice of Captain Bagot, M.P., and several other M.Ps., it was thought advisable to drop the Chamberlain policy, as they would never stand the 'dear Food cry'; and run as a *Balfour* or *Government Candidate*. This has been going on during the whole of January and February, and on my coming on the scene, it was all arranged that Major Noble was to be run as a Balfourian, his address was already prepared on these lines and the fight commenced. We beat the Radical candidate and his workers into fits; we were all over them with the general policy of the Government, e.g. Agricultural Rates Act, Aliens Bill, Education Bill, Army and Navy and, in fact, everything of a general character. But when we came to Fiscal Reform and retaliation only, this was not sufficient. They wanted to know more about it, and how it was going to affect them, the Farmer, Labourers, Granite workers, Lead miners, and Powder workers. They listened with the greatest attention, but the policy of retaliation did not satisfy them, and the candidate and speakers did all they could to explain Mr. Balfour's policy was *not* Protection. *The Free Trade League* came down and notwithstanding everything the candidate and our speakers said, preached the cry of '*Dear Food*' and '*Chinese Labour*', and told the most horrible and awful lies imaginable. They had 3 meetings a night, never reported and not announced until

the morning on which they were to be held. We had all the disadvantages of the work of this League and *no corresponding reply from our side*. It is quite hopeless to fight them with our ordinary staff of workers and speakers. They can only be tackled by the special men from the Tariff Reform League, and I go so far as to say it would be better if every one of their meetings ended in a *free fight*, than allow their statements to go uncontradicted. *It was the lies of the Free Food Leaguers that frightened the Farmers and Labourers and beat us during the last 3 or 4 days.*

Major Noble is an excellent candidate, to my mind, and he was badly advised to drop Chamberlain.

In an almost equally difficult seat, the Eastern division of Liverpool, the Unionist candidate, Harwood Banner, strongly backed by Salvidge, held his own by preaching the full Chamberlain policy.

CHAMBERLAIN TO SALVIDGE

9 *March* 1905 : *Private.*—Mr. MacIver (M.P. for the Liverpool Kirkdale Division) tells me of your action in the Liverpool election and I write a line to say how much I appreciate your pluck and resolution.

I am certain that it was the best policy and I have contempt for some of those shuffling people who are willing to swallow their pledges and convictions if even a mouse squeaks in the neighbourhood. I wish we had many more of your stamp.

Chamberlain was continually looking for a compromise with Balfour in the Parliamentary arena. But in the constituencies he gave no quarter. We have already mentioned his discussion with Balfour of Hugh Cecil's position. Cecil, it will be remembered, had been asked by his Committee not to stand again on account of his Free Trade views ; and shortly afterwards the Greenwich association had adopted another candidate named Benn. Cecil countered by announcing that he would stand if necessary as an independent Unionist. Faced with the danger of a split vote, Balfour had caused Acland Hood, the Government Chief Whip, to write giving the blessing of the Central Organisation to Hugh Cecil. Chamberlain was furious. He at once gave orders that the whole machinery of the Tariff Reform League should be put at Benn's disposal.

CHAMBERLAIN TO RIDLEY

13 *March* 1905.—I hope you will give special attention to Greenwich. I think we must do everything in our power to help Benn. We know they have been alarmed at the intervention of the Central and will require all the backing we can give them. My own suggestion would be to immediately issue a Manifesto by Benn stating the circumstances under which he comes out, and appealing for the support of all independent members of the Party and of all opponents who recognise that tariff

reform is the greatest question of the day. He should protest against the interference of the Central Office, and this Manifesto, which might be signed by him alone, or if thought better by the members of his Committee, should be sent round by post to every elector and followed immediately by a house to house canvass. If expense is a consideration, I am ready to find the cost from my private fund in addition to what I have already promised to Goulding towards the actual election expenses.

A few days later (24 March) Chamberlain followed up these private instructions with a letter to the Chairman of the Greenwich Association, Mr. Ronald Hill, in which he stated that he was 'clearly of opinion that the majority of the Unionist Party, whether in Greenwich or elsewhere, are not only justified but are required by their duty in a matter so urgent and important to make every effort to have their opinions fully represented in the House of Commons after the next election'.

In this same letter, Chamberlain, somewhat ill-advisedly, claimed that the late Lord Salisbury had been favourable to both Preference and Retaliation. This claim gave rise to a prolonged and not very edifying correspondence in *The Times* over the dead man's opinions. Speeches were interpreted; letters quoted; and private conversations recalled. It emerged clearly enough from these exchanges that Salisbury had had leanings in the 80's and 90's to both Retaliation and Preference but had not regarded them as practical politics. The new Lord Salisbury, his brother Hugh Cecil, and Hicks Beach, all claimed that in the last few months of his life, Salisbury had expressed to them his disapproval of Chamberlain's action in raising the fiscal question. On the other hand, Chamberlain had some evidence the other way.

CHAMBERLAIN TO PARKER SMITH

29 *March* 1905.—Cranborne's letter was a shabby trick — disingenuous if not untrue. Another member of the family in *confidence* assures me that it is untrue.

But I do not want a personal controversy over a dead man's opinions. If Lord S. *did* change it must have been when he had ceased to be himself.

Our Greenwich policy is unpopular, but I have gone through all this before. If we refuse to be frightened by their bluff and go steadily on they will soon change their note.

Meanwhile we must look for bad weather.

We may never know the exact truth in this matter. Salisbury, like his nephew Balfour, had the gift of being all things to all men without ever being convicted of complete inconsistency. But this controversy deepened the rift between Chamberlain and the Hatfield connection.

IV

The Government meanwhile had succeeded in offending some of their strongest supporters in another sphere : Irish affairs. Wyndham, despite a warning from Balfour, had chosen, as his Permanent Under Secretary, Sir Anthony MacDonnell, an Irishman, a Roman Catholic and a distinguished Indian Civil Servant. In accepting his appointment, MacDonnell had secured Wyndham's agreement that he should be allowed rather greater initiative than was usual in a civil servant.

At first the partnership prospered ; and MacDonnell played a leading part in the preparation and negotiation of the Land Purchase Bill. After that he began to investigate the possibilities of a constitutional solution to the Irish problem with Dunraven and other leading Irishmen who favoured a moderate measure of Home Rule or 'Devolution' as they called it. Dunraven and his friends founded the 'Irish Reform Association'; and MacDonnell helped them to frame a constitutional scheme which he drafted himself on Dublin Castle notepaper.

MacDonnell mentioned the progress of his negotiations with Dunraven to Wyndham and sent him occasional reports. But Wyndham was 'overengined for his build'. At this period of his life, he drank too much and worked off the ill effects in bouts of hard exercise. He often failed to read his official papers through to the end and did not always fully grasp what he was told. He certainly failed to understand the exact purport of the MacDonnell–Dunraven negotiations.

In the autumn of 1904, Wyndham went to Germany for a cure and there again neglected to read with any care the letters which reached him from MacDonnell. On his way home, however, he read in *The Times* the text of Dunraven's 'Devolution' scheme and a leading article attributing 'this insidious project' to 'an influential clique in Dublin Castle of which Sir Anthony MacDonnell is regarded by numbers of Irish Unionists as the head'. Wyndham wrote at once repudiating any connection with Dunraven's scheme. MacDonnell disassociated himself from the Irish Reform Association. But the damage was done. The Ulster members were seething with indignation and so were many other Unionists who regarded any move towards Home Rule as 'an unholy thing'.

Wyndham failed altogether to satisfy the anxieties of the House. His speeches were 'involved, unconvincing and prolonged . . . He wholly failed in the steadiness of plain sense which is the essence of political self defence.'[1]

Londonderry and Carson threatened to resign.

Oldfashioned Tories, who, in the whole course of their parliamentary lives had never entertained the thought of voting against their Party, now left the House swearing that nothing would induce them to stay and vote. They swept past the Whips at the doors, ignoring their presence or rudely repelling their efforts to detain them, till the Whips themselves deserted their posts in despair, and defeat was only averted by putting up stalwarts to talk against time.[2]

Wyndham accordingly resigned. His place was given to Walter Long who struggled for the remainder of the Parliament to govern Ireland 'with Lord Dudley as a Lord Lieutenant of profligate habits and expenditure and Sir Anthony MacDonnell who had been the undoing of his predecessor'.[3] Long's appointment gave rise to the jibe that 'the Government having failed in sending Don Quixote to Ireland now propose to send Sancho Panza'.

Wyndham returned to the House in May to make his resignation speech. Jack Seely who was in the House that day recalled that 'when Wyndham came to the passage in his speech exonerating Balfour from any part in the imbroglio, Balfour turned round and seemed to hypnotise him. It was like Svengali and the maid.'[4]

We shall meet Wyndham again sometimes sympathising with Chamberlain, more often stimulating Balfour against him. But his influence henceforth declined sharply. 'Up to this date', wrote Sandars,

he had been Balfour's most intimate friend. Their terms were of real affection. He was, moreover, the brother of Balfour's devoted Aspasia and had been one of the most popular figures of the Community of the Souls — his good looks fulfilling that necessary qualification for acceptance in that *dilettante* Society. Up to the time of his appointment as Chief Secretary there was no one who was so intimate in political confidence with the First Lord — no one upon whom Balfour relied more. But, when Wyndham received the Irish appointment, these close relations necessarily ceased, and he played no part of importance in the transactions of the Inner Cabinet. On the contrary, as time went on, their affections mutually declined, and his premature and tragic death was borne by his once cherished leader and friend with philosophic calm. Fortunately, his dying hours in Paris were soothed by one whose love for him was an idyll begun and maintained in the Salon of the Souls. He once said bitterly to

---

[1] Unpublished papers of J. S. Sandars.
[2] *Memoirs of Sir Almeric Fitzroy*, vol. i, p. 241.
[3] Sandars papers.   [4] Note of a conversation with Lord Mottistone.—J. A.

the writer : 'Put not your trust in Princes in whom there is no help.' . . .
It is interesting to recall that Balfour once volunteered that his two capital
errors of patronage were (1) in allowing Curzon a second term of office as
Viceroy, and (2) in recommending George Wyndham for the Chief
Secretaryship of Ireland. The confession was justified by the *finale* in
each case.[1]

Chamberlain supported the Government in the vote of Censure
over the MacDonnell affair. But he was deeply disturbed. With
all his memories of the sacrifices he had made to fight Home Rule,
he felt something like bitterness. 'Joe loathes "the taint" of Home
Rule.'[2] Was it for this that he was supporting the Government?
'The general impression of incredible muddle is straining the loyalty
of Tariff Reformers almost to breaking point.'[3]

Another change, weakening the Government and Chamberlain,
occurred about this time. Milner resigned his office in South Africa.
Selborne was appointed in his stead.

SELBORNE AND CHAMBERLAIN

Selborne to Chamberlain.—23 *February* 1905: *Private.*—I am going to
succeed Milner. It is still a secret as H.M. has not yet approved, but I
wanted you to know at once.

Chamberlain to Selborne.—23 *February* 1905.—My first instinct is to say
that your acceptance of the H.C.ship is one of the most patriotic acts I
have ever known. Yet there are few positions that I would sooner fill.

But you have an office you love — in which you have done splendid
work — and which places you in the first rank of our domestic statesmen,
so that you might feel assured that you would have equal opportunities
in every succeeding Unionist Government. If your new work could be
regarded as permanent and non party, like Cromer's in Egypt, it would
be a splendid opportunity to create a lasting reputation and to do service
to your country which would be worth almost any sacrifice — but in
the present state of the Opposition — soon to be essentially a Little
Englander Government — you may be hampered at every turn and your
position may be intolerable. They may not dare to turn you out but
they may force you to resign.

So you see I am torn between conflicting emotions.

There is no one I would sooner see in the position — no one who can
fill it better — but you risk for yourself a great deal and may find it
impossible to serve your new masters.

No one will more heartily wish you the success you deserve — no
one will follow you in your new career with more interest.

Your courage deserves reward — and of course generally is rewarded
— so, in spite of some evil auguries, I will have confidence in your star
and congratulate you on the fresh laurels you are going to win.

[1] Sandars papers.   [2] Mrs. Chamberlain to her mother, 1 March 1905.   [3] *Ibid.*

Back in England Milner might have strengthened Chamberlain's hand. He shared Chamberlain's broad views, but he needed a rest after his African work and would take no very active part. Besides as he once remarked he 'was a Tariff Reformer in spite of Mr. Chamberlain's speeches'.[1] Meanwhile Selborne's departure was a great loss to Chamberlain. After Austen, Selborne had been his most trusted friend in the Cabinet.

Lord Cawdor followed Selborne to the Admiralty ; an admirable choice as it proved but one which fully justified Fitzroy's comment when he heard the news : 'When it becomes known that the Prime Minister has had to go outside the ranks of active politicians to find a successor to Selborne the public will realise how exhausted are his ordinary resources.'[2]

'This poor Government,' wrote Mrs. Chamberlain, 'every few days faces a crisis. As Austen says "each time a little skin comes off".'[3]

V

On 8 March Churchill introduced a motion from the Liberal benches. This sought to commit the House to the view that 'the permanent unity of the British Empire would not be secured through a system of preferential duties based on the protective taxation of food'. He asked for a plain 'yes' or 'no' answer.

CHURCHILL TO CHAMBERLAIN

25 *March* 1905.—May I ask you to use your influence with the Government to secure a decision by the House of Commons, free from party bias upon a question, which you have repeatedly declared to be above party, and which the Prime Minister has stated is not within the scope of any policy which he will propose within the lifetime of the present Parliament?

Neither Chamberlain nor Balfour could agree. The motion was a direct challenge to Chamberlain's views. It also ran counter to Balfour's policy in that it sought to prejudice the very issue which, Balfour had declared, should be left to 'a free and unfettered' Colonial Conference. The fact remained, however, that on a straight vote on this motion, the Free Fooders would not have supported the Government and might well have brought it down.

Chamberlain favoured a straight vote and regarded the likelihood of defeat as a heaven sent chance to dissolve or resign. Balfour,

[1] Sandars papers.   [2] *Memoirs of Sir Almeric Fitzroy*, vol. i, p. 241.
[3] Mrs. Chamberlain to her mother, 7 March 1905.

Z 2

however, was determined to continue in office. Accordingly, after various fruitless attempts to draft an amendment which would have kept the whole party together, it was decided to meet Churchill's challenge by moving 'the previous question' and resigning if defeated.[1] Even so, the Whips, scared by the Party's mood over the Wyndham imbroglio, forecast a majority of not more than fifteen. It is hard to imagine a more humiliating position for a Government than to have to run away from the major issue of the day. But there was worse to come.

Churchill in opening the debate 'spoke extremely well, with great dignity and good taste, so that Joe paid him a little compliment on his manner of upholding the traditions of debate'.[2]

Chamberlain used the opportunity both to preach his own gospel and to identify the Government's position with his own. The pith of his argument is to be found in these extracts from his speech.

I accept the meaning and intention of the motion to be not only a challenge to my policy, but a challenge to the Government policy. What is the Government policy? (Ironical Opposition cheers.) To me it ought to be plain even to the meanest intelligence (cheers), for what is it declared to be? The calling of a Conference between the representatives of this country and the representatives of the Colonies and great dependencies of the Empire, which is to discuss any question that may be raised in that Conference by any of the parties attending it, and among others — this, of course, being an important matter at the present time — the prospect of a commercial union based upon Preference between the parts of the Empire and the Mother Country. That is the first thing. Is not that intelligible? (Ministerial cheers.) Here is the second point, which is equally important. It is that the Conference shall be open, absolutely open, that it shall not be committed beforehand ... Now, what would be the effect of the resolution? The effect of that resolution would be to muzzle the Conference in regard to the one subject —

Lord H. Cecil (Greenwich) — Why should it? (Cheers and cries of 'Order'.) — To muzzle the Conference in reference to the one thing upon which I am confident the greatest attention will be directed. (Hear, hear.) ... My noble friend said, why will it muzzle the Conference? Perhaps he will say what he thinks the intention of this resolution is. The intention of the other side is to put out the Government, but is that his intention? (Lord H. Cecil was understood to say 'No'.) No, he is a loyal supporter of the Government. Well, but in those circumstances the only practical effect will be that in view of a resolution of the House of Commons, if the Conference is held during the period of this House, the representatives of the country will go there practically with instructions given by this House that they are not to consider the question of Preference. Then I

[1] Royal Archives, 12. 26, no. 1, Balfour to the King, 21 March 1905.
[2] Mrs. Chamberlain to her mother, 10 March 1905.

should have thought that my noble friend, who has a very quick intelligence, would have understood that the result would be to muzzle the Conference and to prevent our representatives even from considering what I have said the Colonies would consider the most important part of the duty of the Conference. Now, Sir, am I not right in saying in those circumstances that this resolution is a challenge to the Government? The Government want an open Conference; those who support this resolution are in favour of a limited Conference. I confess that if I could have had my way, if I had the influence which the hon. member attributes to me, I would have invited the Government to meet this motion with a direct negative. (*Opposition cheers.*) That is my own opinion. I do not like a challenge to be thrown down and not taken up. (*Opposition cheers.*) I regret, though I entirely assented to it and am bound by it, the decision of the Government not to deal with this question in the present Parliament. I should have desired that it should be dealt with, as far as Parliament could deal with it, immediately. The Government, however, decided not to deal with it in this Parliament, and in those circumstances they are absolutely consistent in saying that this discussion is premature. (*Cheers.*) I think they are more than consistent in inviting their followers, myself among the number, not to commit ourselves to a decision with regard to this Conference until we know what it will bring forth. (*Hear, hear.*)

Chamberlain spoke with a heavy cold and Margot Asquith noted in her diary 'Chamberlain's fire seems to have gone and his speech was dull'. It is lively enough, however, to read; and Balfour, who followed him, described it as 'a speech of singular beauty and eloquence'. On the result of the debate we may quote the entry Fitzroy made in his diary next day.

9 *March.*—The Government majority, which nobody expected to exceed 20, reached 42, and for the moment Ministerialists are enjoying their triumph. The personality of Winston Churchill had something to do with the result, but the reluctance of the Free-Trade members of the party to vote against their leaders is the real explanation. Quiet abstention becomes very difficult when direct issues touching the existence of the Government are raised, and the old traditions of allegiance assert themselves with unlooked-for force. The Free Fooders did as well as they had hoped, so far as the actual number that went into the 'No' lobby was concerned; but the rallying power left still to the Government had been under-estimated. It resolves itself into a question of staying power, and Ministers' chances of surviving the Session will be determined by whichever side can keep its mobilised units for a longer time in the field.[1]

Chamberlain's cold now developed into a serious bout of 'flu, with the depression that often goes with it. His views, however, were kept prominently before the public in a signed article, 'Nelson's

[1] *Memoirs of Sir Almeric Fitzroy*, vol. i, p. 242.

Year and National Duty' which appeared in the *Outlook* of 11 March. It is too long and closely argued to quote here, but the following letter gives some idea of its impact.

LYTTELTON TO CHAMBERLAIN

12 *March* 1905: *Private.*—I cannot refrain from sending a word of strongly felt admiration for the striking and inspiring article in the *Outlook.* I don't think anything finer has appeared since the memorable Birmingham speech of many years ago. After all what does it matter if there are some obstacles — the spirit of greatness is in that ideal and to fail in it is worth most successes.

I believe the real heart of the nation is as ready now as ever it was to make sacrifices for great causes : but this only needs I think our closest thought viz. how to put the sacrifice on to the shoulders best able to bear it.

That really is the rub — but I do not believe that the problem is insoluble when once its conditions are all known and when we are all free to lend a hand in the vast labour of solving it.

Meantime our gratitude and thanks.

Chamberlain himself summed up the situation that week in a letter dictated from his sick bed to Northcote in Australia.

CHAMBERLAIN TO NORTHCOTE

14 *March* 1905: *Private.*—The political situation here is interesting but not satisfactory. Thanks to the loyal support of the Tariff Reform Party and the bad generalship of the Opposition the Government has got well through the three fiscal debates, viz., that on the Address, that on the sugar question, and the last one on Winston Churchill's motion. Still they are liable to be upset at any moment by a snap division, and, as I have already told you, I still think that an early dissolution would be the best thing for their reputation and for our cause. No-one, however, can predict with certainty in this extremely unstable political climate.

VI

It so happened that in the ballot for Private Member's time, the Liberals secured four evenings in close succession : 22, 23, 29 March, and 4 April. They determined on a fresh onslaught on the fiscal question and gave notice of four resolutions. We must transcribe these if the rest of our story is to be made clear.

Resolution 1, in the names of Ainsworth (Liberal) and R. Cavendish (Liberal Unionist) : '*that, in the opinion of this House, the imposition of a general duty on all manufactured goods imported from abroad not exceeding* 10 *per cent on the average and varying according to the amount of labour in these goods would be injurious to the commercial interests of the United Kingdom.'*

Resolution 2, in the names of Walton (Liberal) and Moulton (Liberal) : '*That, in view of the declaration made by the Prime Minister, this House thinks it necessary to record its condemnation of his policy of fiscal retaliation.*'

Resolution 3, in the names of Osmond-Williams (Liberal) and Denny (Conservative) : '*That, in the opinion of this House, grave injury would be caused to the shipping industry and to other industries dependent thereon by the adoption of the changes in the existing fiscal system proposed by Mr. Chamberlain.*'

Resolution 4, in the names of Sir J. Leese (Liberal) and J. Seely (Liberal Unionist) : '*that this House disapproves on principle of the taxation of corn, meat, and dairy produce as being especially burdensome to the poor and injurious to the welfare of the nation; and believes that no proportionable remission from existing duties on tea, sugar, coffee and cocoa would afford compensation for the imposition of such taxes; and declares its opinion that any Colonial Conference that is entered upon, except upon the understanding that this country will not agree to the taxation of corn, meat and dairy produce will result in failure.*'

These four resolutions between them effectively covered the whole range of Unionist proposals for fiscal reform. Resolution 1 was aimed solely against Chamberlain. Balfour could hardly put on the Whips to instruct his supporters to vote against it. Resolution 2, however, was aimed solely against Balfour. No policy advocated by Chamberlain was at stake. Resolution 3 again was aimed solely at Chamberlain, while Resolution 4 like Churchill's earlier motion was aimed at both Chamberlain and Balfour.

What line was the Government to take? At the time of Churchill's motion Balfourians and Chamberlainites had agreed to meet any similar attack by moving the previous question. The Whips, however, now reported that though this device might be employed for Resolutions 2 and 4 in which the Government were attacked directly or by implication, nothing would persuade the Unionist Free Traders and some of the Retaliationists to defend the purely Chamberlainite policy. The Whips, accordingly, recommended that Resolutions 1 and 2 be left to a free vote of the House. Balfour was disposed to agree. He was reluctant to throw over Chamberlain, but he was determined to avoid defeat.

Chamberlain, of course, soon heard what was afoot. He wrote at once, to warn Austen.

LIFE OF JOSEPH CHAMBERLAIN

CHAMBERLAIN AND AUSTEN

J. C. TO AUSTEN.—17 *March* 1905.—When W. Churchill's motion was
met by the Previous Question I understood that the Government had
decided to meet all similar motions in the same way. That appeared
to me at least logical and consistent. I understand the Opposition have
got three more Resolutions in hand, each dealing with bits of the Fiscal
policy :

1. Against moderate duties averaging 10 % on manufactured goods.
The words in this case are taken from a speech of mine.
2. Against Retaliation as proposed by Balfour.
3. Against Protection as it affects Shipping.
4. I do not know the terms of this but I am told its object is to emphasise
differences between Balfour and myself.

Now it would appear to me to be simple to meet each in turn by the
Previous Question, but Parker Smith and Boscawen have just been here
to say that A. Hood and Sandars are agreed that the Party should be
advised to 'go as they please' on No. 1.

I need scarcely point out the result of this — which would leave me
to fight against all the Radicals and the Free fooders combined, with
many of the trimmers, and I suppose part of the Government added.
Surely Balfour will not agree to such treachery. I am writing to him
quietly tonight but I thought you ought to know what is going on.

AUSTEN TO J. C.—18 *March* 1905.—Many thanks for your letter. I
am horrified by what you tell me. I had heard nothing of this change
and can only say '*Quos deus vult perdere!*'

I have not been able to see Balfour or Hood this morning but I must
try what I can do on Monday.

Chamberlain, as he had told Austen, wrote 'quietly' to Balfour
the same night. He made it quite clear that if Balfour let him down
on Resolution 1, the Tariff Reformers would not support the
Government on Resolution 2.

CHAMBERLAIN TO BALFOUR

17 *March* 1905 : *Private.*—When you decided to meet W. Churchill's
resolutions with the Previous Question, I understood that this decision
would apply to any similar resolutions by any other member.

This course would be consistent with what you have always said in
deprecating discussion on a question which is not a practical one in this
Parliament.

The other side have given notice of, I think, four more Resolutions,
the first of which comes in next week and is directed against the 'Tariff
Reform' part of my speeches as opposed to the 'Preference' part which
no doubt will be Churchill's motion.

The next Resolution is one directed against *your* policy of Retaliation,
and there is another to emphasise some alleged difference between you
and me.

I should have felt certain that they would all be treated by you in the same way, but that I am told this evening that Alec Hood and J. Sandars say that they advise that the 'party should go as it pleases'.

The effect of course in existing circumstances will be that the Resolution against my proposals will be carried by a large majority. *If Retaliation is afterwards to be treated on the same principle it will also be defeated, as the Tariff Reformers can hardly be asked to support it after they have been left in the lurch over next week's Resolution.*[1]

Surely this is bad tactics and I do not believe that you have been consulted about them. I am obliged to go to Birmingham tomorrow, partly for an important Committee, partly to get a change of air as I cannot get rid of a very troublesome attack of influenza.

I am very sorry that I cannot see you personally, as any change of policy now with regard to such Resolutions will be most serious, but I sincerely hope that there is not the slightest chance of it.

Chamberlain's letter opened an immediate crisis. Balfour was cornered. If he stood by Chamberlain on Resolution 1, he would be defeated in defence of the Chamberlain policy. If he let members 'go as they please' on Resolution 1, he would be defeated on Resolution 2 by a revolt of the Chamberlainite section. Balfour sent no reply to Chamberlain; but the following note of a talk between Fitzroy and Sandars gives some indication of his mind. Sandars would naturally have stressed the differences between Balfour and Chamberlain when speaking to Fitzroy, since Fitzroy was close to the Devonshire connection. Yet after making every allowance for this and for any personal bias on Sandars' or Fitzroy's part, the account in Fitzroy's diary is too circumstantial to be regarded as invention.

18 *March.*—While I was with Sandars he took the opportunity of unveiling the political situation with even more than his customary openness. Referring to the Cabinet Ministers I had met the night before, he said that very few of them knew how acute the situation had become. In fact, the relations between the Prime Minister and Mr. Chamberlain have almost reached breaking point. Some indications of it have been given to the world, or at least that portion of it who weigh what they read, in Mr. Chamberlain's recent declaration touching the imminence of a General Election, and in the attitude of undisguised indifference, not to say contempt, which the Tariff Reform League have recently assumed towards 'Retaliation'. The yoke of Chamberlainism has at last wrung the withers of the Prime Minister, and in Sandars' expressive phrase it will soon be a question with him 'whether it is worth while to strain the party machine any longer in order to maintain the present artificial equilibrium'. Chamberlain's temper and disposition have at last got the better of him, and the dexterity with which the Prime Minister has concealed the deep differences that exist between them is exhausted,

[1] My italics.—J. A.

having perhaps performed its task and secured that after the General Election the centre of gravity of the Conservative Party will not rest with fiscal heterodoxy. Sandars enlarged on the difficulty a man of Chamberlain's temperament had in abstaining from the direction of any movement, and the tendency, which sooner or later dominated him, to force the hand of those who were in part association with him. Up till now Mr. Balfour has had less trouble from the Tariff Reformers than from the Free Trade section of the party, partly, no doubt, as Sandars said, from motives of self-interest. With the one exception of the ultimatum to the Government over the Wharton amendment, they have been content to support Mr. Balfour ; but, unless they were prepared to pre-cipitate an appeal to the country, they had no alternative. This, it appears, it is now Mr. Chamberlain's intention to do, and the votes of some fifteen to twenty stalwarts which he can command, and perhaps more, place it in his power to act whenever he thinks the moment is ripe. There is an idea that parental pride may lead him to give Austen Chamberlain the chance of introducing a Budget of relief, but after April 10th the 'crash' might come at any minute. Austen himself has no illusions upon the spirit that is now animating his father, and does not, I understand, propose to mortgage his political future by standing in with him. The Prime Minister believes that, with whatever misunder-standing and suspicion his contemporaries may view his proceedings during the last eighteen months, the historian will do him the justice of admitting that by his patience and tact he has saved the Unionist Party from the permanent taint of Protection, and, feeling that this has been achieved, he may be advised to anticipate the blow Mr. Cham-berlain is meditating. He is very sore at the tortuousness that has domi-nated the other's policy : indeed, he is again being reminded of what all those who have co-operated with Mr. Chamberlain have found out sooner or later, that he has no conception of obligation in any fine sense of the phrase, and that his masterfulness and lack of restraint are sure to prejudice if not to ruin, any cause in which he is engaged. As soon as the Prime Minister diverges formally from Chamberlain, his tacit understanding with Sir Michael Hicks Beach, who dislikes the other as one who has tainted the Tory party with demagogue intrigues and fiscal heresy, will come into activity, and the breach be healed with all except the most violent asserters of Free-Trade doctrine in its extreme form. It will be seen from this summary of the situation, with what immense disadvantages the Unionist Party will enter upon the General Election, but it will be manifest that the responsibility of its ruin will rest with Mr. Chamberlain, and, so far as the event shows that the disaster has been frustrated, the honour and credit of the achievement will rest with Mr. Balfour.[1]

Resolution 1 was to be moved on 22 March, a Wednesday. The Cabinet would meet on the Tuesday to decide their line of conduct. Austen's position was a difficult one. What terms should he accept from Balfour ? At what point should he resign ?

[1] *Memoirs of Sir Almeric Fitzroy*, vol. i, p. 245.

Austen dined with Chamberlain on the Monday night (20 March). Several years afterwards he wrote the following note of their talk.

I dined with my father on the 20th and sought his advice. We were both much moved, but he felt and said that on this occasion he *could not* advise me. The responsibility was mine — our respective positions were so different, he out and I in the Government — I must take my own decision. It cost me one of the two sleepless nights that I have passed owing to politics. The only other occasion was when I had to decide my resignation on Mesopotamia.[1]

A man does not order his son out of the Cabinet. Every personal inclination of Chamberlain's must have led him to find a way by which Austen should remain in office. It is hard, therefore, to interpret Chamberlain's refusal to advise his son at this crucial moment as anything but a hint that the time had come to resign. In retrospect this was certainly Mrs. Chamberlain's view.[2]

At the Cabinet next day (21 March) a compromise was proposed, humiliating in the extreme to both sides, but equally so. This was that all Unionists should be advised by the Government to abstain on all four Resolutions. The Whips would only be put on if Balfour were directly censured. If this was not accepted, the Prime Minister would resign.

BALFOUR TO THE KING

21 *March* 1905.—Mr. Balfour with his humble duty . . . has respectfully to say that only one topic was discussed today in Cabinet :—namely the course that was to be adopted with regard to certain fiscal resolutions which are to be moved during the next few weeks by unofficial members of the Opposition . . . Mr. Balfour would treat it with contempt. Neither Mr. Chamberlain himself, however, nor Mr. Austen Chamberlain are inclined to take this view ; and they desired very earnestly that the 'previous question' should be moved and made a matter of life and death to the Government. This . . . Mr. Balfour absolutely refused to assent to . . . Mr. Balfour informed the Cabinet that he would, this afternoon, have placed his resignation in Your Majesty's hands. Finally it was agreed that it was not necessary on any of these fiscal motions to endeavour to repeat the struggle victoriously terminated a fortnight ago ; but that the proper policy was to treat with neglect these abstract resolutions which deal with no problems with which the present Parliament is concerned, and which are only designed by their framers to embarrass and if possible to divide the Government and the Party.

[1] Note written by Austen Chamberlain and dated December 1930. It is an endorsement on the letter from Austen to Chamberlain of 21 March 1905.
[2] Mrs. Chamberlain in conversation with the author : J. A.

Fitzroy made the following entry in his diary next day :

22 *March*.—The Cabinet yesterday marked a stage in the crisis, which gave another point to the Prime Minister in his struggle with Chamberlain. It had been a very grave question whether his determination to treat Mr. Ainsworth's motion condemnatory of Mr. Chamberlain's Tariff ideas as one which the Government would decline to have anything to do with, would be supported by a unanimous Cabinet or have the acquiescence of Chamberlain. Had there been any secessions, Mr. Balfour had resolved to go. In the result all his colleagues rallied to him.[1]

Immediately after the Cabinet Austen sent Chamberlain the following account and explanation.

AUSTEN TO CHAMBERLAIN

21 *March* 1905 : *Secret*.—The Cabinet has decided to advise all our supporters to abstain from taking any part in tomorrow night's division. I have acquiesced in this course on condition that the same advice shall be given when we come to next Tuesday's Retaliation motion, and that the Government and the Government's Whips shall take care that not only is the same advice tendered but that that advice has the same result and that the two Resolutions are carried in the same way, *nemine contradicente* so far as Government influence reaches.

The only exception that I admit to this bargain is a necessary, though it may prove an embarrassing one. If the Prime Minister or the Government is directly censured in next Tuesday's motion, when the terms are put upon the paper, it is obviously impossible that I or any member of the Government should allow such a censure to pass without objection. But if the two Resolutions are comparable in kind, the same treatment shall be accorded to both and it will be the business of the Prime Minister and of the Whips to secure that the same treatment produces the same result.

This is indeed drinking to the dregs the cup of bitterness, and I have consented to drain it with my colleagues. You and others may well ask *why*, and to you I can give my reasons.

There were many of us — I think without doubt a large majority of us — who would have preferred the 'previous question'. But we were all convinced — and I ask you to take it from me that it is a fact — that on the previous question we should be beaten.

None of my colleagues was prepared to take a defeat on this particular issue and at this time. They were agreed that rather than do that we should all resign today, though how we could explain our corporate resignation I think none of us were able to see without making, revealing and rendering permanent a disastrous schism in the party.

I might still have announced that I at least was unable to continue to hold office. God knows it was the easiest and simplest course for me to follow and would have saved me personally an infinity of mortification and humiliation. But if I did so, I took issue for our cause on the least

_____
[1] *Memoirs of Sir Almeric Fitzroy*, vol. i, p. 246.

favourable occasion. I blame myself for having left the Cabinet of a fortnight ago under a misapprehension of what our decision to move the previous question then meant. Had I conceived it possible that the same course was not to be followed on every fiscal Resolution this session, I would have resigned then and there, and I should then have joined issue on Colonial Preference and should have felt that, whilst freeing myself, I was also serving the cause.

But on this occasion our own people are not united and many of those who are really with us would have been perplexed and troubled if called upon to make tomorrow's Resolution the standard of secession. We should have given battle under circumstances which would not have allowed us to muster our full strength and which would have been altogether misleading to the country at large.

I do not think it would have been good for your cause and mine to break the party on such an issue. I may be right or I may be wrong; but I have not decided lightly and I hope I may never again be called upon to endure so great a humiliation. You and you only will know how great a sacrifice I have made. I would not have made it to save the Government, but I have consented to it because, with the best information I could get, I thought to resign now and on this occasion was to safeguard my own character and peace of mind at the expense of the cause for which alone I consented to remain in the Government when you resigned.

It is bitter for me to do this thing. It is bitter to write it to you and to think of your feelings as you read it. I have only one consolation that as we said last night nothing shall ever come between us and you will be my best friend as I shall be your very loving and devoted son.

The tone of this letter; Austen's note of his talk with Chamberlain on 20 March; and Sandars' statement on 17 March that Austen did 'not propose to mortgage his political position by staying in with his father', all point to a difference between Chamberlain and Austen. Certainly, when Balfour eventually resigned, Austen's sister wrote to him:

HILDA CHAMBERLAIN TO AUSTEN

5 *December* 1905.—. . . You have suffered much, I know, and in nothing so much, I think, as in feeling that it has prevented your walking absolutely side by side with Papa, and that by the necessity of the case you were forced to see things at times differently, from inside, from his outside view.

This must have been very trying, but it only shows still more strongly what an enormous help you have been as a link. When slight differences of thought arise, even between you and Papa, I feel how wide would have grown the differences if there had been no one in the Cabinet to make Papa feel he had someone to take his side, and how absolutely unavoidable a rupture must have been.[1]

---

[1] *Life and Letters of Austen Chamberlain*, by C. Petrie, p. 166.

The most diligent search reveals no suspicion of difference between Chamberlain and Austen save in the crisis we are now considering and which would continue till the end of May. But in this period, a shadow lay between father and son.

Whether Chamberlain or Austen was right is another question. If Balfour's threat to resign was seriously intended, the best course might have been to force his hand. Austen, however, believed that if he (Austen) resigned, he would resign alone. His action might force Balfour to dissolve ; but the rupture between Chamberlain and Balfour would then have been complete ; and Chamberlain would have been blamed for the inevitable crash at the Polls.

On one point, however, Austen cannot escape censure. He accepted a proviso which would have obliged him to abstain on Resolution 1 and yet to vote on Resolution 2, if Balfour's honour had been challenged that day. Fortunately for Austen's honour he was not put to this final test.

VII

On 21 March, after receiving Austen's letter, Chamberlain left for Folkestone, to recuperate from the 'flu and, no doubt, to avoid the humiliations Balfour had prepared for his party. The same afternoon, 80 of the Tariff Reformers met under Chaplin's Chairmanship to decide their attitude to the advice of the Whips. Parker Smith sent the following account of their meeting.

PARKER SMITH TO CHAMBERLAIN

21 *March* 1905.—I have not written you as you have heard everything from Austen better than I could tell you.

But I had better write and tell you of our meeting this afternoon where, of course, he was not present.

It was summoned at very short notice, and we got about eighty good men with Chaplin in the chair.

Boscawen gave them a very good account of the position, and of Arthur Balfour's intentions for tomorrow. Men wanted assurances that those intentions would be made absolutely clear by himself, that no distinction was to be made between tomorrow's Resolution and the reciprocity one next week, that the other sections of the party except Free Fooders would follow his lead, and so on.

On receiving assurances as to these, the general feeling of the meeting was clearly that the best course was to accept the lead of the P.M., though various of us said how reluctantly we did so, what punishment we expected both in the House and the country, and what a false position we felt we were in. — However only 5 hands were actually held up against a motion to abstain as requested, though several men did not vote.

But I think all the men (except H. Vincent) were willing to fall in with the majority. — Chaplin saw A.J.B., and was fully satisfied with his assurances.

Talking to men since I find nearly all taking the same line, that the policy is very damaging to us, and the longer continued the worse. Some attach more importance to one thing being completed before a Dissolution — Aliens Bill, Agricultural Rating, South Africa, and so on, and no one is anxious to have the credit of wrecking the Government or to see the bitterness between sections that would follow upon that, but I can find no one except the regular Government bonnets who wish the election put off longer than when they have got the special thing they want.

It was a very great loss not having you for the meeting, — but if you had been here I do not believe that you would have taken any different line to that which the men adopted.

Men were very jealous for you in their scrutiny of Balfour's pledges, and I believe that Austen got these on a quite satisfactory footing. I hope the occasion for a dissolution will arise soon, but I do not believe that tomorrow was the right occasion either by courting defeat or by resignations.

Next day, 22 March, after Resolution 1 had been moved, Balfour announced his intention of abstaining on this and the other three Resolutions. He advised his supporters to do the same and then left the chamber followed by all his colleagues on the Treasury bench. The Resolution was, accordingly carried by 254 votes to 2 with two Liberals acting as tellers for the two who opposed. Parker Smith reported the feeling in the Party as follows.

PARKER SMITH TO CHAMBERLAIN

23 *March* 1905.—There is an extraordinary diversity of opinion about last night's doings. Many men are thoroughly well pleased, say it was the right way to deal with the tricks and tactics of Opposition and that the country will be thoroughly pleased. Lots of men who are heartily with us — I should say the considerable majority take this line. Others (like G. Parker, Morpeth, Willoughby d'Eresby, Boscawen, Claude Lowther and myself) feel throroughly ashamed and like whipped curs to-day and some think we made a great mistake in not speaking and dividing even when we knew the Government were going to abstain.

Outside I hear just the same diversity of opinion. Pearson for instance whom I met to-day thinks it is doing us much harm.

I had another talk with Austen yesterday who urged me to go and speak myself to the P.M. I got an opportunity of doing so in the course of last night, and send you an account I wrote down just after what was said.

He seemed to me to have more immediately in his mind than I had expected the question of immediate resignation or dissolution, but was very largely occupied with the question of the probable *local* effects of an immediate or deferred Dissolution.

The account of Parker Smith's talk with Balfour is worth reproducing. It gives the feeling in the Party very clearly. The scene was Balfour's room in the House of Commons. No one else was present:

PARKER SMITH : 'I wanted to say to you that you are putting a very great strain on some of us by this policy.'

BALFOUR: 'How? I thought it was well accepted by your meeting.'

PARKER SMITH : 'Yes, there were a great many in favour and more who accepted — but, if you will let me, I would rather speak for myself — I know there are a number who feel with me but I would rather just speak for myself. I feel we are dragged through the mud by this. — How did you like what you got just now?'

BALFOUR : (shrugged his shoulders) : 'Oh ! that was nothing !'

PARKER SMITH : 'If it was bad for you it was much worse for us who have gone for the whole thorough policy. I feel we are cowards not to stand up for it.'

BALFOUR : 'You can't be called on to do that on unsuitable occasions. What else can be done? It would have been the worst policy to be beaten on this.'

PARKER SMITH : 'I have no doubt the previous question could not have been carried and this would not have been good to go out on. When we do go out I am most anxious that it shall not be by any split between ourselves or by any ministers resigning and bringing matters to a standstill, but all together by some cordite resolution.'

BALFOUR (looking at Parker Smith most cordially and nodding most emphatically) : 'Yes, that is right. But how are we to do it? I was willing to resign yesterday. I discussed resignation in Cabinet.'

PARKER SMITH : 'I don't think yesterday would have been a good or suitable time in view of the motion, but I don't think the hammering the party is getting is doing us good. You can mark a circle in chalk on your chest and say no hits outside shall count. It is all right if it is foils you are playing with, but to-night the swords are sharp.'

BALFOUR : 'No, they are only foils. I don't believe the country is affected.'

PARKER SMITH : 'They are feeling us cowards, and what I am much the most concerned for is Chamberlain's reputation. They are getting to say he is running away and hiding.'

BALFOUR : 'No, that is ridiculous ; that is impossible.'

PARKER SMITH : 'Yes, as soon as he appears that will be gone and vanished ; but I hate the feeling.'

BALFOUR : 'I know he is worried, much worried, I feel that, but there is nothing in the other.'

PARKER SMITH : 'The strain is very great upon us ; I hope it will not last long.'

BALFOUR : 'You mean a dissolution. Well, there are two questions, one the foreign and S. African question where I may flatter myself we are best for the country and I think time is wanted, and the other the local circumstances of different parts of the country. I am trying to find what men feel as to whether time would advantage them all through the country. I asked Lockwood who said he had asked twenty men at random, of whom nineteen had said they wanted a little time.'

PARKER SMITH : 'I talked to my Chairman that very morning who said Glasgow did not want time.'

BALFOUR : 'Yes, and the question is when to dissolve so that we may not be too hopelessly outnumbered but may come back strong enough to check them.'

PARKER SMITH : 'Redmond will take care of that. After his speech in reply to Rosebery he will throw the weight of his force into the scale so that the Radicals don't get a majority independent of Irish. Even at the last moment if the burghs were going too strongly against us he could do that in the counties.'

BALFOUR : 'Well, I don't know. We are improving in Education and Chinese labour.'

PARKER SMITH : 'Yes, in parts, but I am afraid of this hurting the party as a whole. It gives the impression we are trying to hold out too long.'

BALFOUR : 'That is very unjust.'

PARKER SMITH : 'Certainly as regards the individuals.'

BALFOUR : 'It is not the first time this has happened — things were much worse with Gladstone.'

PARKER SMITH : 'Yes, but the difference was Gladstone could make believe and you do not. He pretended up to the last that he believed the country was with him and you have said quite frankly a dozen times that we shall be beaten. Thank you for having let me speak freely.'

BALFOUR : 'Yes, I am very glad and I have talked quite openly to you. We have talked it out like old friends (holding out his hand), and I don't think we have found any very fundamental difference between us.'

(PARKER SMITH demurred somewhat to this, but took his hand).

BALFOUR : 'We shall do the same next week when it is Retaliation.'

PARKER SMITH : 'Yes, you made that perfectly clear — unless it is some personal attack on your honour that could not be let pass — but some of my colleagues would not agree.'

Some idea of the situation as it appeared in Balfour's camp may be gathered from the following entry in Fitzroy's diary:

25 *March.*—I saw Sandars in order to ascertain whether, the situation being apparently easier, it might be assumed that the King would not be called upon before Easter to hold a Council for a dissolution. He was jubilant over the success of the Prime Minister's action and the progress it marked in the gradual isolation of Chamberlain. Not that he expected him for long to acquiesce, but every point in the progress scored by Mr. Balfour was calculated to reduce the number of those who would in the last resort obey Chamberlain to the length of voting against Ministers, and therefore tended to strengthen the Cabinet in their policy of freeing

the party from the Protectionist taint. At the same time, it is certain that Chamberlain will not surrender his hold on it without a severe struggle, and the term of the Ministry's existence will synchronise with the moment chosen to put forth what power he has in reserve. As far as the immediate future was concerned, Sandars agreed that the position was much improved, the Prime Minister's success with the Cabinet having been more complete than he had reason to anticipate a week ago, and, so far as he could foresee, the King was free to leave the country for some weeks if his doctors wished him to do so.[1]

Chamberlain's own feeling on the situation emerges clearly in his reply to Parker Smith.

CHAMBERLAIN TO PARKER SMITH

Folkestone: 24 *March* 1905.—Many thanks for your two letters — both very interesting and especially the latter with your interview with A.J.B.

I feel entirely with you as regards the general policy. It is bad and it will certainly do us harm with the country which likes a square fight. But, with the Government agreed upon it, I do not see what you could possibly have done especially as our own people are so timid.

The fact is as I have frequently observed before that while members talk very boldly about dissolution the great majority always shiver on the brink and draw back at the last moment.

Personally I am by no means sure that Ainsworth's motion would have been bad to go out on, but I see that I am in a small minority in this. My idea, however, is that it would emphasise our question at the General Election and tend to force the issue on our lines. I am, of course, glad that it should have been decided to treat all fiscal resolutions the same way — but I do not believe that this will work. The Opposition will meet it by transforming their resolution against Balfour's policy into a direct vote of censure and then the Balfourians will declare that their — or A.J.B.'s personal honour is at stake and the Resolution must therefore be treated differently from the one directed against my policy only. It seems to me that the longer we go on, the worse the tangle is and unfortunately we cannot go back. *The right thing to have done would have been for Balfour — when accepting the Colonial Conference to have nailed his flag to the mast and called the Conference this year, pointing out that the delibera- tions would take time and that the results could not therefore be submitted to the present Parliament for effective treatment, but might be made the subject for a mandate at the General Election.*

Then we should have had the best tactical position. Will you refuse the offer of the Colonies with all its advantages rather than substitute 2/- on corn for 6d. on tea?[2]

I think this place is doing us good but improvement is slow. My wife suffers from neuritis and I from neuralgia, two of the most depressing ailments I know. I wish we could find candidates to oppose Lambton, R. Cavendish, and some others of the Free Fooders. They are being

---

[1] *Memoirs of Sir Almeric Fitzroy*, vol. i, p. 246.   [2] My italics.—J. A.

encouraged to take a more definite line against us, and if this does not injure their chances at the election the rot will spread.

However, it will come right in the end, although we shall have to go through the fire first . . .

We have printed one passage in this letter in italics. It marks the first appearance of a new version of Chamberlain's conference plan. Hitherto he had argued that the Unionists should seek a mandate to summon the Conference and then act at once on the Conference's recommendations. Accepting now that Balfour did not mean to dissolve, he proposed to reverse the plan. The Conference should be summoned at once and the Government might then go to the country on its recommendations. We shall see more of this idea presently.

Meanwhile Chamberlain's most immediate concern was with the fate of Resolution 2. He was convinced, as his letter shows, that the Balfourians would treat this as a vote of censure and had steeled himself to the prospect of seeing his own son defend the Prime Minister after abandoning his father's cause. In the event he was spared the final humiliation. The wording of Resolution 2 was a direct condemnation of Balfour's policy. The speeches with which it was moved reflected directly on Balfour's personal honour. He needed no pretext now to put on the Whips. But in every battle there is an element of uncertainty. Balfour had received sharp protests and warnings from Austen, Chaplin, Parker Smith and perhaps others. He did not know that Austen and even Chamberlain were, in fact, prepared to acquiesce. He accordingly played for safety and gave orders to persist in the policy of abstention. In so doing he lost what was perhaps his only chance of asserting his supremacy over Chamberlain without provoking an open breach.

Chamberlain received the news with relief. 'Last night's business,' he wrote next day, 'was a sorry farce; but under the circumstances it is the best thing for us.'[1]

The final humiliation came next day when Balfour was asked at question time why he had made no reply when changes reflecting on his honour had been made against him. He replied that he had not had time to read the newspapers. He, therefore, did not know what had been said in the debate. This was reducing the proceedings of the House of Commons to a farce.

The public reaction was damaging to the Government. The Radical press held the passage of Resolution 1 as evidence that

[1] Chamberlain to Parker Smith, 29 March 1905.

Balfour had broken with Chamberlain. 'Mr. Chamberlain thrown over'[1] was the headline in the *Daily News*. After the passage of Resolution 2 the same paper claimed that the country had now 'witnessed the process which reduces the Prime Minister and his economic policy to nothingness.'[2]

The Unionist press was if anything more bitter. 'The future prospects of the party,' wrote the *Daily Mail*, 'are being sacrificed for the immediate purpose of keeping the present Cabinet in office. What will result if the present incertitude is prolonged will be not defeat but complete and irreparable disaster.'[3] 'Mr. Balfour,' wrote the *Daily Express*, 'by eviscerating the policy has emasculated the party.'[4] The opinion of the man in the street, as far as it can be gauged, was entirely hostile to Balfour. People felt as if the batsman had claimed to retire to the pavilion because the bowling had got too hot.

Meanwhile Tariff Reformers were seething with indignation. After three of the resolutions had passed Griffiths Boscawen, one of Chamberlain's most loyal and active supporters, wrote imploring him to force a dissolution. He knew nothing, of course, of the difference in this issue which had arisen between Chamberlain and Austen.

BOSCAWEN TO CHAMBERLAIN

30 *March* 1905.—The state of affairs here is very unsatisfactory. We decided, after consultation with Austen, to fall in with the Government's plan of abstaining from their fiscal debates, and have done so, but I am convinced that it has done a lot of harm, not only to us but also to the Government — indeed mostly to them in consequence of their running away from the 'Retaliation' debate, and the absurd statement made yesterday by the Prime Minister, that he did not know what had happened the night before. I did not think so before, but am now convinced that every day they stop in, the party as a whole sinks worse into the mire. But we can't put them out by what would be an act of disloyalty so long as Austen and the supporters of your policy remain in the Government; that is really the crux of the situation. None of us want to act disloyally in any case, certainly not while the Government contains well known Tariff Reformers. The best solution would be for the Cabinet to decide to dissolve; cannot pressure be brought on the Prime Minister externally and internally in the Cabinet to bring this about? All sorts and conditions of people desire a dissolution. Yesterday Beach told me he was urging the P.M. to take this step.

In the meantime, when you return I think we ought to have a small meeting of the T.R. stalwarts, then to be followed by a larger meeting of all the supporters.

[1] *Daily News*, 22 March 1905.
[2] *Daily News*, 29 March 1905.
[3] *Daily Mail*, 30 March 1905.
[4] *Daily Express*, 7 April 1905.

We are keeping together very well by means of our Monday and Thursday dinners, but there is a very general feeling of discontent and dissatisfaction — failure almost. I think if you meet our friends and had a talk privately with them it would do good. Please agree in this suggestion.

The verdict of the country was given soon enough. On 5 April, Brighton, a Unionist stronghold, fell to the Liberals.

VIII

Chamberlain's political relations with Balfour were now very strained, though the two men remained on perfectly friendly terms. 'Joe looks and seems extremely well,' wrote Mrs. Chamberlain.

Yesterday he went down to the House to set his wheels in motion. The papers are full of dissensions between Mr. Balfour and Joe, which does not make it easier for either of them. But while Joe frankly tells him that he thinks it would be best for the country and the Party that a dissolution should come soon and thus differs as to policy in dealing with the affairs of the moment, it is, of course, absurd to say that they are no longer friends. Yesterday Joe and he had a pleasant and most friendly talk and on Monday we are both to lunch with him before Austen makes his Budget Speech.[1]

Chamberlain, however, as his wife noted, had 'set his wheels in motion'. Having loyally if reluctantly supported the Government through the humiliations of the fiscal resolutions, he was now determined to exact some reciprocity. The feeling among Tariff Reformers made it essential that he should take some action. Another consideration also weighed much with him. Fielding, as we know, had been to see him in February and had warned him of the growing pressure from the United States in favour of a Canadian-American reciprocity Treaty. At the beginning of April this warning was reinforced by a letter from Borden, the leader of the Canadian Opposition.

BORDEN TO CHAMBERLAIN

3 April 1905: Private.—Be assured that there is much which tends to bring Canada into closer trade relations with the United States. The vast immigration from the Western States to our North West Territories, the increasing investment of United States capital in the development of Canadian industries, the remarkably conciliatory and appreciative tone of United States statesmen, newspapers and business men towards everything Canadian — all these have a certain influence which may become very strong if our kinsmen in the British Islands continue to slumber.

---

[1] Mrs. Chamberlain to her mother, 5 April 1905.

Let no one forget that the strong attachment of Canadians to the British Empire is due in some measure to the strong dislike of Canadians towards their neighbours to the South. The United States for many years acted the part of the bully towards Canada. Their journals sneered at Canada and all things Canadian. Their leaders in public and commercial life affected to hold us in contempt. As the people liked the United States less, they became stronger in their attachment to the mother country. The statesmen, the journals and the people of the great Republic are now beginning fully to understand and appreciate the tremendous resources and possibilities of this country. The tone is entirely changed. They confidently expect and believe that Canada will become a part of the United States within the next twenty-five years and that this will be accomplished by a peaceable arrangement between Great Britain and Canada on the one hand and the United States on the other.

Let our friends in Great Britain therefore realise that more is involved in the policy of which you are the chief exponent than the mere economic feature of trade Preferences within the Empire. The continuance of Canada as a dependency of the Empire may be and probably is in question.

Hard on the heels of these warnings came a public statement from President Theodore Roosevelt, who stood in the United States for much the same things as Chamberlain stood in England.

Chamberlain drew attention to the danger from the United States in a speech at the Liberal Union Club (13 April) :

There is one point I cannot help referring to at the present moment. The President of the United States, one of the ablest, one of the strongest, one of the most courageous men that ever sat in the Presidential chair, as a patriot, has openly declared that one of his great objects and desires is to connect the United States more closely with Canada by means of a reciprocity tariff. I do not know what success he may have with his own countrymen, but certainly they are in a position to offer very favourable terms to the Dominion. If we reject the idea of a similar proposition made by Canada to us, is it too much to expect that Canada may turn in another direction?

Most of Chamberlain's speech that night was devoted to an attack on Devonshire and the Unionist Free Traders who had recently formed the Unionist Free Trade Club. Most observers had expected that Chamberlain would make some comment on the recent fiscal resolutions and his silence on this score was widely interpreted as a sign of weakness. Fitzroy wrote :

14 *April.*—Chamberlain has passed under the Caudine Forks : instead of turning out 'the best of all possible Governments' whose early doom he was prophesying a few weeks ago, he has in substance capitulated to the dexterous management of the Prime Minister, and has accepted a formula that emasculates Tariff Reform for all present purposes. The

natural annoyance excited by finding himself in a situation that admitted of but one alternative, has betrayed itself in a splenetic attack upon the Duke of Devonshire, whom he assails with a vehemence and inaccuracy all his own.[1]

In fact Chamberlain's silence was not due to any acceptance of the existing position but to a new initiative which he was in the process of developing. It was really a continuation of the negotiations he had opened with Balfour when the House met in February. His aim now as then was to commit the Government on three points : first, to the principle of an all-round Tariff on manufactured exports for revenue purposes ; second, to some concession to Agriculture, whether in the form of a Tariff on agricultural imports or of relief financed from the proceeds of the Tariff on manufactured imports ; third, to a Colonial Conference subject to only one General Election.

On 13 April, Chamberlain summoned a meeting of Tariff Reformers in a Committee Room at the House of Commons. 142 members attended. Chamberlain took the chair and submitted a memorandum to be sent to the Prime Minister for the approval of the group.

CHAMBERLAIN'S MEMORANDUM

13 *April* 1905.—As far as can be ascertained at present the Unionist party in the House of Commons is composed as follows :

(1) Preferentialists who have publicly expressed their support of the whole policy	172
(2) Preferentialists who would support the whole policy if it were recognised as being the policy of the Government	73
	245
(3) Retaliationists, many of whom would support Preference also, if adopted by the Government, but some of whom would refuse in any case to go further	98
	343
(4) Members totally opposed to any change in our fiscal system — most of whom are retiring at the next election	27
(5) Members who have not been included in this classification	4
Total	374

---

[1] *Memoirs of Sir Almeric Fitzroy*, vol. i, p. 249.

It would appear from this that the first group, who are commonly known as Tariff Reformers, constitute, with the second group, two thirds of the whole Party. The Tariff Reformers have loyally supported the Government on all occasions and especially at all times of difficulty when members of the fourth group have abstained or have even voted against the Government. They desire to continue this support and to follow the lead of the Prime Minister both in policy and tactics.

They feel, however, that the situation is critical, and that the prospects of the Party as a whole are seriously jeopardised by the unfortunate division of opinion on the fiscal question, and by the uncertainty which still prevails as to some parts of the Government policy. They recognise that the Prime Minister has strained every nerve to keep the Party together during the last two years, and especially to keep within the Party those who are still uncertain as to the course they will ultimately pursue.

This effort has, however, involved a system of compromise which has lessened the influence of the Government: and the Unionist rank and file, who have shown themselves overwhelmingly in favour of the views taken by Tariff Reformers wherever the issue has been clearly raised, either at the meetings of the Central Organisations or at the meetings of local Committees, have been more or less disheartened by the lack of a definite lead and are becoming mystified by reports, sedulously spread by the Radicals, of dissension both inside and outside the Government on cardinal points of fiscal policy.

It is impossible much longer to avoid the issue which has been raised within the Unionist Party, and any further delay in declaring the exact position of the Government as to the points in dispute is only likely to increase the dissension that already exists.

The declaration of the Prime Minister that no attempt would be made to alter our fiscal system during the present Parliament has been universally accepted, but it is felt that, in view of the possibility of an early appeal to the country, it is becoming increasingly necessary that some clearer indication should be given of the objects for which Unionists will be asked to combine, both at and after the election.

At the present time the party has no fighting policy, but is reduced to defending and explaining its past action. In this condition it arouses no enthusiasm, but leaves its opponents free to continue the attacks and misrepresentations which have been so unscrupulously employed in the bye-elections. A purely defensive attitude is as ineffective in politics as it is in war, and the only remedy for the situation thus brought about is the adoption and support by the Unionist leaders and the official organisations of some policy which will arouse the active interest of the mass of the Party. It would be much better to risk the defection of a minority of doubtful supporters than to go into battle with the bulk of the army dissatisfied and apathetic.

A fighting policy must involve a clear and simple issue, appealing strongly to all classes, and this can only be found in the reform of our fiscal system. To this reform the Government is already pledged, but it will never be an effective weapon until it is more clearly defined.

The Prime Minister at Manchester laid down the general lines of his policy in four propositions which may be summarised as :

(1) a distinct repudiation of protective duties when imposed only for the purpose of raising home prices :

(2) a demand for complete freedom of action in all cases in which the tariffs of foreign countries are seriously hurtful to British interests : and

(3) closer commercial union with the Colonies to be arranged after a free conference between their representatives and ours.

In principle, all Tariff Reformers are prepared to accept the policy thus indicated, but everything depends on the methods by which it is to be carried out. For instance, no information has been given as to the way in which the policy of Retaliation or Reciprocity will be applied. It is submitted on behalf of the Tariff Reformers that both theory and experience show that no such policy can be successful unless it embraces the system of a *general tariff* as adopted by all other countries which have accepted the principle.

Such a tariff would be a revenue tariff, moderate in amount, which could be reduced or increased by the Executive, according to the action of foreign countries, so as to prevent the practice of dumping and to offer the opportunity of treaties of reciprocal concession.

It is also submitted that in arranging such a fiscal system the interests of Agriculture must be taken into account either by including agricultural products in the general tariff or by concessions in the shape of a reduction of the burdens which now press with exceptional severity on this industry.

Again, it is uncertain how the Prime Minister proposes to deal with the results of the Conference for which he asks a mandate. It is understood that his principal object would be to ascertain whether or not treaties of commerce equally beneficial to the Colonies and the Motherland could be arranged on a preferential basis : and that if it be found that this cannot be done without imposing a small duty on certain articles of food the Prime Minister will not consider this condition any bar to an agreement.

The Tariff Reformers would, however, in this case press for a compensation to the consumer in the shape of a reduction of taxation on other articles of necessity or universal consumption.

They also urge that, if an agreement is come to, it should be immediately submitted to the decision of Parliament as they believe that any delay in this respect would throw doubt on the sincerity of the negotiation, and would make the acceptance by the people of this country of the decision of the Conference dependent on all the complicated issues which arise at a General Election.

The urgency of a decision on these points is increased by the action of the American Government in endeavouring to promote a reciprocity treaty with Canada which would, if successful, probably make impossible any satisfactory arrangement with this country.

The Tariff Reformers believe that on all these points an agreement might be come to which would be welcomed by the whole of the first and second groups referred to at the beginning of this statement, and which could be accepted by the great majority of the members forming the third group.

Failing such an understanding the party will have to face the election with no concerted action or inspiring cry. No section of the party will be enthusiastic or able to arouse any enthusiasm among their supporters. At the best the issue will be indefinite and evasive, and the result must inevitably be a defeat unparalleled in recent political history.

The further proceedings were described as follows in the communiqué afterwards issued to the press.

At the meeting of Tariff Reformers held at the House of Commons this afternoon over which Mr. Chamberlain presided, nearly 150 Members were present in addition to which a good many apologies for absence owing to ill health or other engagements were received. The Chairman, after a few opening remarks, presented for the consideration of the meeting a statement expressing the views of Tariff Reformers. The adoption of this statement was proposed by Sir Herbert Maxwell, and seconded by Mr. Halsey. After some discussion and with a few verbal amendments the statement was unanimously accepted by the meeting and a deputation was appointed to convey the statement to the Prime Minister consisting of the Right Hon. J. Chamberlain, the Right Hon. T. F. Halsey, the Right Hon. Sir H. Maxwell, Sir Alexander Henderson, Lord Willoughby d'Eresby, the Right Hon. H. Chaplin, the Right Hon. J. Parker Smith, Mr. Baldwin, Mr. Whitmore, the Hon. Arthur Stanley, Sir F. Banbury, Sir Howard Vincent, Sir Gilbert Parker, Mr. Goulding, Lord Morpeth, Mr. A. G. Boscawen, and Mr. H. Pike Pease.

Chamberlain was 'very much encouraged by the meeting which was in all senses most satisfactory '.[1] He led his deputation to Balfour next day (14 April) who promised to study it and reply in due course. 'The proceedings', wrote Mrs. Chamberlain, 'were most friendly.'

IX

During the Easter recess Balfour discussed Chamberlain's proposals with Wyndham. Their judgment seems to have been unfavourable. In retrospect, at any rate, Wyndham would describe the proposals as 'practically protection of manufactures plus a surplus revenue to be devoted to conciliating agriculture by *doles* and fostering advanced domestic legislation '.[2]

Chamberlain spent the recess at Highbury. The weather was 'odious and a bore . . . Joe has made no sacrifice of principle to

<hr />

[1] Mrs. Chamberlain to her mother, 15 April 1905.

[2] Wyndham to Balfour, 8 November 1905.

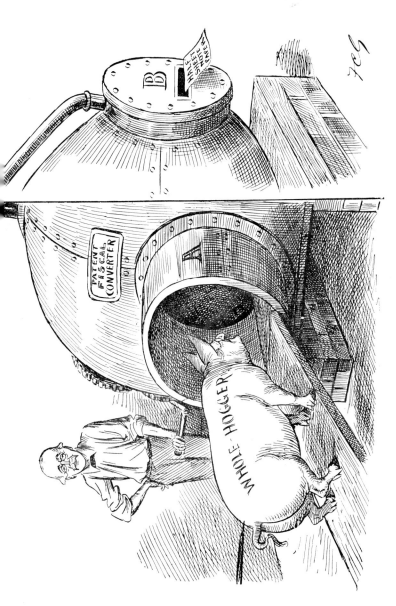

THE 'FISCAL CONVERTER'

Insert Whole-Hogger in opening A, turn handle and —— a half-sheet of
notepaper will appear at opening B.

17 April 1905

N.B. This process can be reversed. If Whole-Hoggers be desired, insert half-sheet at B, turn handle the other
way, and Whole-Hogger will emerge at A.

NO SURRENDER

How he would like to face the foe.

Mr. Balfour. If only the latter would follow Joe, the party would be practically united with the exception of about 20 out and out "Free Fooders". It is a pity to wreck the party for them . . . I have a feeling that there is an opportunity not to be lost, whether Balfour will use it or not remains to be seen.'[1]

On 2 May came the second reading of the Aliens Bill. Chamberlain spoke 'in hitting form'.[2] Next day, however, he caught a bad chill which was followed by violent bilious headaches. He was to address the Grand Committee of the Birmingham Liberal Unionists on 5 May. That day,

he was almost blind with headache and unable to do one thing in preparation for his speech this evening, for which he had only the roughest notes. Up to 7 o'clock, I did not see how he was going to address the meeting, but as usual he rose to the occasion and considering that his speech was insufficiently prepared and he had not been able to define the main line of his argument in his notes, he got through wonderfully. Of course, it was not one of his best speeches, but it did not matter, and as usual he had a splendid reception which Birmingham always gives him.[3]

On 15 May, Balfour asked for a private meeting with Chamberlain to discuss the Tariff Reform Group's Memorandum. We may let Herbert Maxwell take up the tale:

A meeting was fixed between these two for 4 p.m. on an afternoon in May (16 May) in the Prime Minister's room at the House of Commons. The previous evening Balfour came to me during a division and said he wished me to be present at the conference. I went to Chamberlain some time before the hour fixed in order to arrange our points, and found him very gloomy and rather cross.

'What do you expect to hear?' I asked.

'Precious little,' said he. 'I think things are going very badly.'

Well, we went to the Prime Minister's room. Lord Lansdowne, leader of the House of Lords, was the only other present. Balfour led off with a statement which made me rub my eyes, so far did it exceed my expectation. He said, that whatever happened, Tariff Reform, *including Colonial Preference*, must be *the* foremost article in the programme submitted by Unionists at the approaching General Election.

Next, he accepted as part of that programme, the principle of an all-round Tariff.

Chamberlain spoke next, cordially accepting in the name of the deputation what had been offered. It was then my turn. My object was to have explained what Balfour had said in Edinburgh, which, rightly or wrongly, had been understood by some of us to pledge him to appeal to the country before the Colonial Conference should be summoned,

---

[1] Mrs. Chamberlain to her mother, 26 April 1905.
[2] Mrs. Chamberlain to her mother, 5 May 1905.   [3] *Ibid.*

and again to appeal before effect should be given to the Resolutions arrived at by the Conference.

'Suppose,' I said, 'the Government were to remain in office to the end of 1906; the Conference will assemble automatically in the summer of 1906; will there then be anything to prevent the Government appealing to the country on the Resolutions of the Conference?'

The Prime Minister then sent for his Secretary, Jack Sandars, and bade him hunt through all his speeches to ascertain whether he had ever said anything to preclude him from acting on my suggestion of an appeal to the country and taking action upon the Resolutions of the Conference. Sanders came back in an hour to report that there was nothing so explicit as to prevent action being taken on the line indicated.

The same evening, Chamberlain sent Balfour the following note of what he and Maxwell understood had been agreed.

CHAMBERLAIN TO BALFOUR

16 *May* 1905: *Private.*—After our talk this afternoon, Maxwell and I agreed on the enclosed Notes (slightly altered by me for sake of clearness) as being what we thought the most important results. I think you ought to see them before tomorrow's continuation of the discussion in order that there may be no mistake.

We are agreed that we have made progress, and we are both hopeful on these lines of coming to a conclusion which will give entire satisfaction to the majority of the Unionist party — a majority sufficient to keep the Government in office if it is willing to remain.

NOTES

1. Agreed that the main, fighting, constructive issue for us at the next election must be Tariff Reform, including Preference as the question probably arousing most enthusiasm and being most urgent.

2. Assuming that it would not be inconsistent with the Prime Minister's public utterances, he would not object to the following programme:

(a) Dissolution not to be officially contemplated till autumn 1906.

(b) Meanwhile Conference with Colonials to be held automatically in spring of 1906 and to be free as to subjects of discussion.

(c) Report of proceeding and recommendations of Conference with views of H.M. on them to form important part of the reference to the Constituencies, who will then be asked for a Mandate to carry out decisions arrived at.

By the necessity of the case the result of the election will decide, whether or not, the decision of the Conference shall be carried out at once.

3. The Prime Minister has no objection in principle to a General Tariff although he would not pledge himself not to have recourse to special negotiation if that appeared to offer better chances of success in any particular case.

The negotiations were continued on the next evening (17 May). Here is Maxwell's account:

We separated, to resume next evening, when Chamberlain and I dined with the Prime Minister in Downing Street. Mrs. Chamberlain, Miss Balfour and Gerald Balfour were the only others present. Immediately after dinner, the Prime Minister, Chamberlain and myself adjourned to the Prime Minister's room at the House of Commons, where we were joined by Lord Lansdowne. During this second conference Chamberlain made a memorable proposal. He asked Balfour whether he would consider the expediency of re-admitting him to the Cabinet, without a portfolio and without salary. He said he was prepared to give up all claim to Colonial Preference as being his own plan and proposal, provided the Cabinet would adopt it and carry it through. His offer was not accepted. We sat till 11.30, when Chamberlain and I adjourned to his room, and wrote a memorandum of what had been agreed on — as follows :

1. Tariff Reform including Colonial Preference, to be *the* leading article in the Unionist programme at the next general election.
2. The basis of fiscal policy to be an all-round tariff.
3. Should the Government remain in office beyond the deliberations of the Colonial Conference, the result of such deliberations should be acted upon in preparing programme of legislation in the new Parliament.

We had obtained all we wanted! Chamberlain was in high spirits, but he warned Pike Pease and Parker Smith not to be too jubilant. It was a timely warning. The fact is that Balfour at this time was running, or attempting to run, with the Free Trade hare and the Tariff Reform hounds. I was informed by one of a Free Trade deputation that waited on him next day, that he assured them he had given us no promise. He certainly had learnt how to wrap up the truth in parti-coloured envelopes.

Maxwell was certainly right in believing that Balfour had given an assurance to the 'Free Fooders' that he had given no promise to Chamberlain. Ritchie would confirm this presently to Gilbert Parker.[1] Balfour also consulted Wyndham. His advice corresponds so closely to Balfour's eventual decision that it should, though rather involved, be quoted.

WYNDHAM TO BALFOUR

20 *May* 1905: *Private and Confidential.*—I will gladly look into your room for a talk on Defence and Fiscal position.

It may save time if I jot down my ideas on the latter. It is no longer a case of what this, or that, man wants. I want for example, retaliation and the *Imperial* side of Chamberlain's original propaganda, without Protection. But the question is now 'How to save the Party and for what objects?' I want to save the Party for Imperialism, for Religious Education, for the avoidance of class conflicts, for the maintenance of the Union (negatively as against constitutional experiments and positively

[1] Memo by Sir Gilbert Parker of a talk with C. T. Ritchie, May 1903.

to improve the condition of Ireland and the relations between the 2 countries) and to make Imperial *Defence* at once scientific and economic.

The danger which threatens the Party is the confusion in men's minds on the Fiscal question. That danger becomes immediate when stated in terms of the relation between a Conference and an Election.

It is said that Tariff Reform is the principal question before the country, and that you have not spoken clearly upon it.

The second proposition is untrue and may be dismissed: the first is misleading and requires examination.

Turning, first, to Parliament.—This Parliament is pledged not to deal with Tariff Reform and is practically debarred from modifying even the custom and routine of Budget-making. It cannot, e.g. reimpose the 1/- on corn; it can hardly embark on any new tax; it cannot Retaliate. Its attention *ought* to be engrossed on Redistribution and alleged 'clerical disorders!' Its continued existence postpones any attempt to consider the Fiscal question as a whole.

Turning, next, to the Constituencies.—Three separate questions, which are distinct, which cannot be easily adjusted, and which may prove irreconcileable, have been actively canvassed on the platform in a somewhat confused manner:—

1. Protection of British Manufactures of a character indistinguishable, in kind if not in degree, from Continental or American Protection.

2. A tax on corn and foodstuffs.

3. An aspiration towards closer Union with our Colonies including commercial union.

As I understand the matter:

On (1) *Protection*, you are opposed, but, with due notice before an Election — (already given) — you intend to resume in another Parliament the right to Retaliate, subject to House of Commons control, for two purposes: (a) to combat, or prevent hostile tariffs framed to injure this country or a Colony, (b) to combat, or prevent 'dumping'. This subject is almost exclusively domestic and specifically incapable of being dealt with prior to an election. Consequently it clashes with the project of a Conference, prior to an election, on the Imperial aspect of Tariff Reform.

On (2) and (3), *Food Taxes* and *Preference*, you have said (a) that the people at home, who look to the past, have a traditional aversion from any tax on food, (b) that our Colonies, who look to the future, exhibit some desire to protect their nascent manufactures even against the Mother Country though, no doubt, in a lesser degree than against foreign countries.

The aspiration towards closer Imperial Union remains, beset, however, in respect of commercial methods, by these two difficulties.

That being so, you have advocated a Conference at which all concerns common to the Empire and all methods for increasing Imperial Unity, including Tariff methods, shall be freely discussed.

The Party as a whole agrees on what shall be discussed. It may split on the date of discussion in relation to the election.

I think it *was* understood that you promised the electorate two electoral opportunities to decide on two questions—

(1) Yes, or no, will you refer all matters of Imperial concern, including Preference, to a Conference?

(2) If the Conference recommends, *inter alia*, Preference between the parts of the Empire then that recommendation may be accepted, modified or rejected *only by a second election*.

It may be said that 'Circumstances alter cases'; that this Parliament has lasted longer than was expected; that a Conference might, in any event, reasonably be called for 1906; that Preference was discussed at the last Conference and could not be excluded from the next, etc., etc. I doubt the force of these arguments and fear that they may lead to a disruption of the Party.

Let us assume, for the sake of argument, that this Parliament continues till the autumn of 1906. What would happen? You could not deal with Retaliation. The terms of reference to the Conference would be bitterly discussed. A section of the Party would complain that they had misunderstood the point of the 2 elections. Preference, in respect of the Conference, would become *for the first time* a question before *this* Parliament. The discussions at home would react unfavourably on the Colonies. And, with the Fiscal question thus revived, this Parliament, in order to continue, would be forced to *carry* Redistribution and discuss the report of the Commission on the alleged 'clerical disorders'. Confusion would, I fear, become worse confounded.

In order to stay in, you must proceed with Redistribution, you must postpone the question of Preference. Otherwise the Free-Fooders; the wobblers who seek safety in Redistribution alone; and the Opposition, will wreck you on the terms of reference. But, on the other hand, if you do postpone Preference, Chamberlain and his followers will, naturally, complain. In either event, one section, or the other, of the Party will — I feel pretty sure — say it has been misled. I can discover no workable middle term between (*a*) staying in for a year or more, solely to *carry Redistribution*, and (*b*) having an election in the Autumn on Conference, Defence, Retaliation, Home Rule, Religious Education, our Licensing Reform, readjustment of Local Taxation to Grants-in-aid and ultimate Redistribution.

The first plan will give offence to Chamberlain and only please the bulk of the Party until Fiscal inroads make it fail.

The second, though not very palatable either to Chamberlain or to the bulk of the Party, cannot be repudiated by either. It saves everybody's face and is truly applicable to the situation and probable results of any election. For it points to another Election in 3 years when views are matured on (1) Preference, (2) Redistribution, (3) Local Taxation. It fits the facts and all reasonable forecasts. But to mix up (1) a Conference *prior* to an Election with (2) Redistribution, and (3) a new Fiscal concordat tending towards mild protection of Home manufacture and away from Imperial aspirations, spells ruin and shelves *Defence*.

All the shortsighted people who desire *separately*, Protection or only *one Election before Preference*, or *Redistribution in order to postpone both*, may unite on a middle course of mere delay for a time. But when the smash comes, as I think it will, they will turn round and say that you ought to have foreseen it and that you were the only person with the power to avert it. I have no personal predilection for a speedy appeal to the country. I want the Conservative Party to continue as a force with you as its only and unchallenged leader. And I dread a confused middle course.

Yet, at first, the Government seemed to point the other way, at least in public. On 12 May at Farnham, Brodrick replying to questions after a meeting said that 'the subject of Preference to the Colonies had been reserved by the Government for consideration with the Colonies. They should call the Colonies into council and they proposed to confer with them *next year* on that very important subject.'[1]

Brodrick's statement led to enquiries in Parliament. Were the Government contemplating a Colonial Conference before the election? Balfour replied that the Colonial Conference was due to meet again in 1906. He denied that he was in any way prevented by his speech at Edinburgh or by Lansdowne's statements in the House of Lords from discussing the question of Preference with the Colonies if the Parliament was still in being when the Conference assembled. Campbell-Bannerman moved the adjournment of the House, and accused Balfour of breaking a pledge. Balfour put up Lyttelton to make the opening speech on the Government side. Extraordinary scenes ensued. The Opposition refused to give Lyttelton a hearing. They clamoured for Balfour. Balfour declined to intervene. After 50 minutes uproar in which Lyttelton failed to make two consecutive sentences heard, the Speaker was forced to suspend the sitting. Chamberlain, however, had every reason to be encouraged by Balfour's obstinacy.

CHAMBERLAIN TO TENNYSON

23 *May* 1905.—The answer of Balfour last night to the questions put to him on the subject of a Conference was entirely satisfactory to me and to the supporters of my policy. It does away with the necessity of a second general election which we have felt all along would be considered as an evasion by the Colonies and would cause so much delay and confusion that we could hardly hope to succeed.

CHAMBERLAIN TO HARMSWORTH

24 *May* 1905: *Private*.—I am glad to say that recent events have made a great difference in the position, and I am now very sanguine as to the result of my conferences with the Prime Minister. What seems likely is that we shall now both work to keep the Government in office over next year when the Conference will be held. If, as I believe, the Conference arrives at a satisfactory result we shall go to the country for it. In this way we get rid altogether of the difficulty of a double election which

[1] *The Standard*, 13 May 1905.

was from the first one of the most serious obstacles in the way of my agreement.

The exact form of this agreement is not yet settled, but I think it will deal with the whole subject, and will probably be announced in Mr. Balfour's speech on 2 June. I shall have the opportunity of acknowledging it when I speak the next day.

I have marked this private because we are on rather thin ice. If we say too much, and above all if my friends are too triumphant, we shall irritate the moderate Free Fooders, who might then join the enemy and turn us out at once. Some of the extremists will go in any case but as far as I can make out, they would not number more than half a dozen if we do not make ourselves offensive.

The scenes in the House, however, had one unfortunate effect. The Opposition decided to put down a Vote of Censure on the alleged breach of Balfour's pledges at Edinburgh. The Free Fooders let it be known that they would not support the Government if there were any question of holding a Colonial Conference to discuss preference in the lifetime of the present Parliament.

Negotiations between Chamberlain and Balfour were resumed on 26 May. Our only account of these is again from Maxwell, though by an accident he was not actually present at the meeting :

I went down to Cooper's Hill College in the morning. When I got back at 1.30, I found a telegram from Chamberlain asking me to meet him in Downing Street at 1. I was dusty and tired, and fancied it would be useless to go there an hour late. However, when I reached the House of Commons at 3.30, I found that Chamberlain was still in Downing Street with the Prime Minister, so I went there. Jack Sandars came out to tell me that the Conference was almost at an end, so I did not go in. In addition to Lord Lansdowne, Austen Chamberlain (Ch. of Exchequer) and Alfred Lyttelton (Colonial Secretary) were present. All had gone wrong. The Prime Minister had told them that owing to the construction put upon his Edinburgh speech by some of our party, he felt debarred from allowing the Conference to assemble before the General election. He explained that, when he made that Edinburgh speech, he had never contemplated the possibility of the Government remaining in office through 1906, and it was only when I brought that point forward at our first conference that it had presented itself to him as a possible, even probable contingency.

Well! here was a terrible discouragement. Chamberlain was much depressed. I sat with him in his little room in the House of Commons, trying to persuade him that, after all, we had been engaged in a negotiation, and had carried two points out of three. Was not that enough to justify us in supporting the Government on Tuesday following, when a vote of censure was to be moved?

'No,' he said emphatically ; 'I can't support them. I won't vote against them, but I'll walk out.'

Parker Smith came in after we had sat about twenty minutes. Chamberlain continued to talk despondingly. He said he would remain in London over Sunday, in case we had anything to suggest.

If Chamberlain walked out and refused to support the Government in the Censure debate, other Tariff Reformers would do likewise. The Government was, therefore, likely to fall on the Tuesday night. On the Friday night (26 May), after leaving Chamberlain, Maxwell decided to make a last appeal to him. Balfour, he argued, had conceded two out of their three demands, was it worth while breaking on this question of the Conference? It was after all an academic point. The Unionists would lose the election and their pledges now could not bind them thereafter.

MAXWELL TO CHAMBERLAIN

26 *May* 1905: *Private.*—I have to speak at Loughborough tomorrow night, but I shall return on Sunday in hopes of seeing you for ten minutes on Monday morning . . .

. . . Meanwhile, here is what I'd like to say after reflection upon what has happened today.

It seems scarcely possible that the Prime Minister, in consequence of the interpretation which some of his friends have put upon his Edinburgh speech, can postpone the Colonial Conference (which, I understand, was fixed to assemble in 1906) until after it suits him to appeal to the country whether it shall assemble or not.

If it assembles, it will be impossible to bar the question of preferential trade, and equally impossible to prevent the majority of the Unionist party advocating a settlement on that basis when the election takes place. Assuming the improbable, that the Unionists were to come back in a majority, Arthur would feel under pledge not to proceed with a Colonial trade treaty before the second election. The natural thing would then be that he would advise the King to send for you.

On the other hand, Arthur gave you and me an implicit and hearty assurance that Tariff Reform, *including colonial preference*, must be the foremost article in the programme submitted at the general election. I think that before deciding what line we are to take on Tuesday night, we should obtain a renewal of that assurance. If we get it — passed! there has not been much lost, for it is *not* likely that the Unionists will win the next election, and the slate will be clear of phantom pledges for what follows.

In the highest interest of the cause, I am most anxious that you and Arthur should hold together, for he has immense personal hold upon the party in the House, and you have an unrivalled influence upon those outside the House. The people believe you to be absolutely disinterested : I should lose my faith in human nature if I doubted your motives. — But if this minor point about the conference should prove insurmountable there is a section of our party who will suspect them. Do not give them nor the enemy this groundless cause to blaspheme if you can help it. If we can clinch Balfour and Lansdowne to the two points — Preference and an all round Tariff — surely that is so much more than we expected to get that we may waive the third point, which Arthur called academic.

Next day, the Saturday, Chamberlain consulted with Austen, Goulding and Parker Smith over lunch. Parker Smith brought with him a memorandum. In this he argued:

I have felt all along there was great difficulty in reconciling it (*i.e.*, *a free Conference before the election*) with the P.M.s answers to questions — unless he boldly took the line, 'I am not bound but am free to vary'.

That line is scarcely tenable for changes made during a Parliament, for value has been received in the shape of support.

But a General Election dissolves all pledges and gives a fresh mandate.

Parker Smith went on to suggest, therefore, that the Tariff Reformers should give way on the precise method of the Conference provided Balfour would make a statement on the following lines.

'I accept your construction of my pledges and adhere to them in the strictest sense for the present Parliament. I will therefore hold no Conference and do nothing before the general election, but I will go to the country with Tariff Reform and Colonial Preference as the main issues of the election, and will ask a mandate to hold a full Conference including India and the Crown Colonies, and I give notice that if I am returned I will act upon the results of that Conference should they be satisfactory according to the constitutional treaty-making power of the Government without the need of another appeal to the country.'

Chamberlain accepted this proposal. Wilson, his secretary, made copies of the declaration proposed by Parker Smith. One of these, it would seem, was given to Austen for transmission to Balfour. Chamberlain summed up their deliberations in a letter to Maxwell written the same evening.

CHAMBERLAIN TO MAXWELL

27 *May* 1905: *Private.*—Thanks for your letter of the 26th. You may rely upon it that I have one motive, and only one, and that is the success of the cause.

I have seen Goulding and Parker Smith. They agree that if Arthur would give on Tuesday the assurance which he has given to us that Tariff Reform including Colonial Preference will be the foremost article in the programme submitted at the general election, and that, after the next election, he will hold himself unpledged, we should accept his present policy which consists in declaring that under the circumstances he will postpone the 1906 Conference and take no steps whatever during the existence of the present Parliament.

It would not, however, be possible for him to make a statement as regards the general tariff on Tuesday as it is really irrelevant to the subject of a Conference.

2 A 2

Balfour's immediate reactions to Chamberlain's proposal were summed up in the following questions :

BALFOUR TO LYTTELTON

27 *May* 1905.—. . . if by 'Colonial Preference' is meant (as I suppose it is) close commercial union with the Colonies (as per halfsheet of note paper) and if by 'first item in my programme' is meant (as I suppose it is) that I regard it as the most important part (though the most difficult) of fiscal reform, and fiscal reform itself as the most important part of the Unionist policy, why should I not give the assurance asked for ? — and why should my colleagues resign ?

On Balfour's instruction Lyttelton turned this interrogative note into a positive letter to Austen, which Austen copied out in his own hand and gave to Chamberlain.

LYTTELTON TO AUSTEN

28 *May* 1905.—The P.M. is ready to announce on Tuesday that Colonial Preference, *i.e.* the adoption of closer commercial union with the Colonies in order to bring about freer trade between them and the Mother Country is the most important (though the most difficult) part of fiscal reform, and fiscal reform itself the most important part of the Unionist policy.

He is willing to make this (Colonial Preference) the first item in his programme subject of course to the proviso that it is not necessarily the first to be *carried* out because it is no doubt a problem of great intricacy affecting very widely separated countries, while Retaliation may be — at any rate in isolated cases — very speedily applied.

X

On the Monday, Chamberlain attended a full meeting of his Tariff Reform Group. We do not know what passed there. The censure motion was to be moved on the Tuesday. Balfour, however, now asked, on grounds of health, that it should be postponed till after the Whitsun recess. This was agreed.

The postponement of the Censure debate meant that Balfour's next major public engagement would be a speech in the Albert Hall to the National Union of Conservative and Constitutional Associations. Chamberlain, accordingly, asked Austen to insist with Balfour that his speech contain a statement of the three main points they had agreed in the conversations of 16 and 17 May. These it will be recalled, were :

1. Tariff Reform, including Preference, must be the main fighting constructive issue at the next election.[1]

[1] From Chamberlain's rough notes of the meeting of 16 May.

2. That the issue of Preference must be submitted to a free and un-fettered Colonial Conference.

3. The need for an all round Tariff on imported manufactures.

Austen accordingly went to see Balfour and 'assured him that if he would do this, he would make it much easier for my father to cooperate heartily with him'.

He readily agreed; indeed he drew from a drawer in his writing-table a couple of those long envelopes on which he was accustomed to make his notes and showed me that he had already jotted down two out of the three points which I had mentioned for incorporation in his speech. I reported to my father what had passed between us, who replied that if Balfour would do that, it would be very satisfactory and helpful.[1]

Balfour spoke at the Albert Hall on 2 June. We may let Austen continue the story:

My father rang me up on the telephone the morning after the Albert Hall meeting. 'Well,' he said, 'Balfour has let us down. He hasn't said what he told you he would say.'

'Oh yes he has,' I answered and recited the three points, adding that he had made them all, and I proceeded to read them out from the Times which lay before me. 'That's all right,' said my father, 'but where do you find that?' Alas! there was the rub. The first statement came near the beginning, the second in the middle and the third near the end of the speech. The effect which I had hoped they would produce was wholly lost in the mass of intervening matter.[2]

Here are the three statements:

1. Free-trader and protectionist may surely alike agree that our commercial interests are likely to be furthered by some power to negotiate effectively with those countries which have erected against us so high a tariff wall. That does not touch any of the prejudices of either one party or the other; it is an interest common to both, it is an interest consistent with the doctrines of both. Then, in Heaven's name, why cannot we agree upon that?

2. What I have said, about what is commonly known as Retaliation, I say with equal emphasis and with far greater feeling upon *that other great branch of Fiscal Reform*, which, while it is most difficult, is always most important, and *is one which stirs and ought to stir a responsive fibre in the heart of every citizen of the Empire*. It is to be judged, not on economic grounds alone, but on Imperial grounds. But whether you judge it on economic grounds, or on Imperial grounds, it is not, in my mind, in conflict with the doctrines of either of the two historic opponents — Free Traders or Protectionists.

3. What has been asked in respect of this, the greatest, the most important, and, for reasons based mainly on colonial sentiment, *the most urgent of all the great constructive problems with which we have to deal?* I have asked that a question which touches nearly the whole Empire should be

---

[1] Austen Chamberlain, *Down the Years*.   [2] *Ibid.*

dealt with by a Conference representing the whole Empire, that that Conference should be a free Conference, and that the inhabitants of these islands, as well as our fellow-subjects in the self-governing Colonies and in India, should suspend their judgment as to what can be done, as to what plan can be proposed by such a Conference until they see.

On the method of the proposed Colonial Conference, Balfour also took an important step to meet Chamberlain.

I have been told, I think, by Sir Henry Campbell-Bannerman that this plan of getting a mandate to summon a free Imperial conference and then submitting the results of that Conference to the suffrages of this nation — I have been told that that puts off the consummation of our wishes to some indefinite period through an almost innumerable series of general elections. (*Laughter.*) I do not know what that means. I have never suggested and I have never thought that the plan of a double election — I do not go into it now — should have any force or operation unless we were returned to power at the next general election, and Sir Henry Campbell-Bannerman tells me explicitly or implicitly on every decent occasion (*laughter*) that there is no chance of such a result. It therefore does not matter to him, and from one point of view does not matter to us. If he is right, and if we are not going to be returned to power at the next general election, the whole scheme which I ventured to adumbrate at Edinburgh of a double election of course falls to the ground. We deal with a new situation, under new conditions, and I see no reason to anticipate that any undue delay can in any circumstances result if we are beaten, though I admit that a scheme of double elections — though I believe it to be necessary if we are successful — would, in those circumstances, be cumbrous and lead to a prolongation of the controversy. I have never denied that, and I think it is perfectly true, but nevertheless, for reasons which I have given at length elsewhere; I feel that the balance of advantage lies upon that side ; but it does not carry with it the consequence, and cannot carry with it the consequence of this indefinite delay of a problem which I have agreed with all my critics, if critics I have, is the one which most pressingly requires the immediate consideration of every part and element in our Empire.'

Balfour closed his speech with a strong appeal for Party unity.

If your wishes and my wishes are fulfilled then, whatever be our fortunes this year or next year or the year after, howsoever the balance of the constituencies may wave from side to side under this or that impulse, one thing is certain — that a united party having not merely in its charge the unity of the United Kingdom and the great cause of Imperial defence, but having before it the great ideal of a closer union with the Colonies, the reform of a system, a fiscal system no longer adequate or fitted to our needs — a reunited party with these beliefs and these ideals is destined, and must be destined, to ultimate success.

The form of Balfour's speech was disappointing to Chamberlain. So was the lack of precision in his statements. But the Tariff

Reformers had carried their main point. Despite qualifying phrases, Balfour had admitted that Preference was the most urgent and important part of the policy of fiscal reform. There was no mention, however, of an all-round Tariff. The claims of Agriculture were ignored : and the compromise over the Colonial Conference, though better than nothing, was uninspiring. All the same, the Albert Hall speech was a step forward. It offered no ground for picking a quarrel. Chamberlain, therefore, decided to take half a loaf as being better than no bread. As he had written to Chaplin at the time of the Edinburgh speech : 'on this and all else, I am inclined to put my own interpretation on Balfour's words and to accept them in the sense which I give to them'. He wasted no time in doing so.

The day after Balfour had spoken, Chamberlain addressed a mass meeting at St. Helens in Lancashire. After developing the case for Imperial Preference and Tariff Reform, he gave his own version of Balfour's speech.

Last night there was a great and impressive meeting intended to do a well-deserved honour to the Prime Minister (*cheers*) and our leader. No man has better deserved the respect of all or the devoted affection of his own followers. (*Cheers and 'Bravo'.*) It was his business on that occasion to review the situation and above all to look forward into the future. Every loyal Unionist will be grateful to him for the lead which he was able to give us. We have now from his lips a clear exposition of official policy at the next election. I do not think even Sir Henry Campbell-Bannerman (*laughter*) will be able to misunderstand it. (*Laughter and cheers.*) What did Mr. Balfour say? He said last night, tariff reform will be the most important part of Unionist policy. (*Cheers.*) He said, Colonial Preference is the most important part of tariff reform. (*Cheers.*) He said, Colonial Preference will therefore be the first item in the future Unionist programme. (*Cheers.*) Then he asked all of us through that great audience that the question which, as he truly says, touches the whole of the Empire should be referred to the Conference representing the whole Empire. (*Hear, hear.*) He urged, lastly, that the Conference should be absolutely free, and he asked that all who were represented at that conference, the motherland as well as the Colonies, should be free afterwards to consider and to deal with the results, whatever they may be. (*Cheers.*) Here is the official programme to which I most heartily subscribe. (*Loud cheers.*) It is a clear and unmistakable issue ; and I cannot help thinking one of its merits is that it is entirely and absolutely opposed to the policy of the Radicals . . .

. . . But, in my view, I say that it will be impossible for you to meet the Preference which the Colonies have it in their power to offer you, which, I think, they will offer to you, and which, I believe, will enormously — very largely indeed — increase the trade of this country and the employment of the working men — it will be impossible for you to meet that Preference, unless you are willing to put some small duty on corn which comes from foreign countries (*hear, hear*), not, remember, in order to raise the price of corn — I do not think it will do it — but in order to transfer the trade of corn from foreign lands to lands under the British Crown. (*Loud cheers.*) Now, you may make that small transfer in such a way that it will not be felt by the poorest of our people. (*Hear, hear.*) You may do it in such a way that you may even reduce the cost of their living. (*Hear, hear.*) That is my own opinion. I state it as my view, after having considered this question from all possible aspects; but I have never asked any one to commit himself immediately and bow to my opinion. I have said what I believe will happen. I have asked my friends to wait and see. (*Hear, hear.*) I have said that if I find when the conference comes together that the representatives are not agreed that the Colonies will do anything for us, while at the same time they ask a great deal from us, then with all thanks to them for their coming and frankly putting their views before us, I should be the first to say that I cannot make a bargain which would be so one-sided. I do not ask you to pledge yourselves utterly beforehand, before you know the result which may ultimately be arrived at at the conference. I agree, there-fore, and it is no new thing, and it is another point in Mr. Balfour's declaration I hold with him, that all men should suspend their judgment. No one needs commit himself absolutely to put a duty on corn until he sees whether I am right in thinking the advantage to be derived is infinitely greater than any possible loss you can sustain. On the other hand, let no man commit himself rashly to the other side of the question. Let no man refuse to agree either to the taxation of corn, or to any particular method of securing this great result, till the whole transaction is before him. Let him avoid it lest he place himself in the position which is the position of the Opposition, as described by Mr. Balfour, in which he said they will not be able even with the best will in the world to carry out their duty either to the country or the Empire. Now this policy of Mr. Balfour's surely may be accepted by every loyal Unionist (*hear, hear*) who is not a bigoted Cobdenite. Of such men, of such extremists, there may be a few in the House of Commons; there are precious few in the country. (*Laughter.*) As to them all I would say is that if they were obliged by the introduction of this policy, as the policy of the party, to withdraw themselves from the party for a time, I should deeply regret it, but I should think it was much better than that they should remain to be a drag upon the wheel. (*Hear, hear.*) In parties, as in coun-tries, after all, the minority must yield to the majority, or nothing can get on. In this case it is a very small minority that in any circumstances could be asked to make the sacrifice, and meanwhile let us, the vast majority of the party, rally to the flag that Mr. Balfour has raised (*cheers*) ; and with a great party consolidated and a great issue to fight for, we will carry the standard to victory, and that before a very long time has passed.

Chamberlain's speech, as he had of course intended, 'put an interpretation' on Balfour's speech 'which has driven the Free

Fooders wild.'[1] On 6 June Devonshire asked the Government in the House of Lords whether Chamberlain's interpretation was correct. Lansdowne's reply must have delighted Chamberlain.

The noble duke referred to the speech delivered by Mr. Chamberlain on Saturday last, and he took exception to that speech as differing widely from the speech delivered by Mr. Balfour at the Albert Hall. I do not know that I have collated the two speeches with the same close care that the noble duke has bestowed on them. But I confess it seemed to me that Mr. Chamberlain had taken almost textually from Mr. Balfour. (*Cries of 'No, no'.*) Will the noble duke tell me where the difference is? The words attributed by Mr. Chamberlain to Mr. Balfour were that 'Colonial Preference is the most important part of tariff reform' — that appears to me to be a truism — and that Colonial Preference would therefore be the first subject dealt with by the conference. I do not know whether those are the exact words used by Mr. Balfour or not. I am sure that Mr. Balfour dwelt on the fact that perforce this subject of Colonial Preference which was to be referred to the Colonial Conference would assert itself and occupy the most prominent place in the findings and deliberations of the Conference. If I had known that the noble duke was going to compare these two speeches so minutely I would have taken more trouble to examine the two texts. But then I will say that in our proposals, whenever the time comes for going to the country, we shall certainly put in the forefront of our programme, in the first place, the policy of retaliation as described by Mr. Balfour at Sheffield, and in the next place the policy of calling a free and unfettered Colonial Conference (*laughter and ironical cheers*), at which the question of Colonial Preference will certainly be examined.

We are among those who believe that the relations between the different parts of the Empire are capable of improvement, and we implore your lordships not to prejudge the question, and not to assume as the noble duke assumes, that this Conference is predestined to failure. As for us, we shall abide loyally by the result of the appeal which will be made to the people of this country. If we are successful we shall not depart from the pledges we have given ; if we are not successful then we and our pledges disappear for a time.

Campbell-Bannerman returned to the charge in the debate on the Whitsuntide adjournment (8 June). Balfour, who spoke at the beginning of the debate, reaffirmed what he had said at the Albert Hall. As to Chamberlain's speech at St. Helens, he said :

I do not propose to deal with the question which has been raised as to the suggestions of the right hon. member for West Birmingham, because I wholly dissent from the principle . . . that my Right hon. friend is to be judged by my speeches and that I am to be judged by my Right

[1] Balfour to Lady Elcho, 5 June 1905 — quoted in Kenneth Young's *Arthur James Balfour*, p. 227.

hon. friend's version of mine. Those who wish to know the views I hold had better get them from my own speeches not from those of the Right hon. member for West Birmingham.

The sting in this comment was underlined by Balfour's reply to Dilke who had referred to Lansdowne's interpretation. 'Lansdowne', he said, 'has been misunderstood.'

Chamberlain had the last word on the Unionist side. He bluntly repeated his version of Balfour's speech and challenged his opponents to find 'any substantial difference in point of principle between myself and the Prime Minister'.

The debate on the Whitsuntide address marks the end of Chamberlain's attempt to secure a common front with Balfour. He had extracted as much as Balfour was prepared to yield; more no doubt than Balfour had intended, though nothing like as much as Chamberlain had hoped or wished.

On the evening of the debate on the Whitsun adjournment, he replied to one of his supporters who had made new suggestions for a statement of common policy:

CHAMBERLAIN TO FREDERICK MILNER

8 June 1905: *Private.*—After the debate of yesterday I am doubtful whether the Prime Minister would agree to anything in the nature of a joint declaration, and I am quite certain that no declaration that we could make would satisfy the Opposition or prevent them from attempting to discover minute differences between the Prime Minister and myself.

If that is so I am content to leave the matter where it is.

He summed up the situation very frankly in a letter to Northcote.

CHAMBERLAIN TO NORTHCOTE

13 June 1905: *Private.*—As regards politics here I have been hoping to send you something very definite as to the position. Negotiations have been going on between the Prime Minister and myself, and I have received privately very gratifying assurances, but it seems impossible for Arthur Balfour to dot the i's and cross the t's so that his own opinions and decisions can be understood by all alike.

I enclose some extracts from his last speech in the Albert Hall with my comments upon them made the next day at a great meeting at St. Helens. A discussion in the House of Commons took place on Wednesday upon these speeches, the Free Fooders on our side pretending, or perhaps really believing, that there was a discrepancy between us. I do not think that it is otherwise than a difference of expression which results from different temperaments, but I do wish that Arthur would come out clearly so that no possibility of misinterpretation could arise. The doubt as to his exact position has done infinite mischief in the constituencies and at the bye-elections. I believe that some seats have been lost entirely owing to the attitude of the candidates on what is of course the primary issue at the present moment.

They are afraid to risk a clear declaration, and hence have to fight with their hands tied; and, while their opponents denounce them as food-taxers, they offer no defence and allow the case against them to go by default. It is a weak policy and will make the defeat which I have contemplated as certain at the next election more serious than it need have been.

My own forecast remains what it has been from the first. We must be defeated chiefly owing to the defection of the Non-conformists who have been alienated by the Education Bill. When we are in Opposition I hope we shall come together again, and if we can have a really united party, even though we may have lost a few of its members, we shall be able to direct such a fire upon the new Government as will, I think, render their tenure of office a brief one.

There is no doubt in my mind that not only the Party but the Prime Minister himself have lost influence owing to the ambiguity of his policy. The man in the street is constantly complaining that he does not know where the Government are, but I am afraid that this unwillingness to make a clean breast of it and risk something for the sake of an absolutely plain issue is constitutional and that we may be forced to go into the fight when it comes without the definite declaration which I think is required.

Meanwhile I cannot hope that much more will be done in the Colonies until we can strike a clearer key note on this side.

I am sure that we are making way among the masses, and have been myself surprised at the indications of a change which have been given by a canvass made in all parts of the country of the Radical electorate. We have found in every case that a considerable fraction of the Radicals, not less than one sixth, report themselves as in favour of tariff reform and Preference, but I cannot rely upon them to vote until they are certain that the Unionist party are united in a thorough policy of reform and have thus made it a question of immediate practical politics. It is not worth the while of such men to break with their own party when the policy submitted on our side continues indefinite.

BOOK XXVI

THE LANDSLIDE
(1905–1906)

THE END OF THE GOVERNMENT

(*June–December* 1905)

The Strain and a Warning — Chamberlain for the War Office? — Tactical Problems — Chamberlain Attacks Balfour's Indecision — The Session Ends Badly — A Successful Holiday — Chamberlain Rejects Tennyson's Compromise Proposal — Balfour's Initiative — Chamberlain Calls for an Early Election — A Clash with Londonderry — Chamberlain Opposed to Gerald Balfour and Austen's Compromise Proposal — Chaplin's Victory at Newcastle — Balfour Appeals for Party Unity — Balfour and Chamberlain at Windsor — Chamberlain Demands Party Unity for the Glasgow Programme — Balfour Resigns — Austen's Home-coming.

I

To form a full picture of Chamberlain's life at this time, we have to remember the many and varied demands that were made upon his strength. They form a continuous background to his main work. There is no space, even in a full-length biography, to do justice to all his activities that spring and summer. Quite apart from the negotiations and speeches we have considered, there were a number of other speeches. In the House of Commons he spoke on the Brussels Sugar Convention (27 February), on Selborne's appointment as Governor General of South Africa (6 March), on the Aliens Bill (2 May), and on South African policy (24 May and 27 July). Outside the House, there were speeches on Tropical medicine (10 May) and at Birmingham University (13 May), where he entertained the aged Halsbury. On 17 May, he made a powerful speech at the Annual Conference of the Organised Labour Branch of the Tariff Reform League. On 21 June he spoke to the Women's Branch of the League, and on 27 June he delivered a heartening address to a deputation of Canadian manufacturers visiting Britain. To this list of public engagements must be added ceaseless committees in London and Birmingham, an honorary degree at Cardiff, and the exacting social round of the Edwardian season which this year included the State visit of the King of Spain.

These secondary activities enormously increased the strain of the main effort. But Chamberlain had little gift for the conservation of energy. And yet he had reached an age when rest was necessary. A man cannot live on his nerves in his seventieth year.

We have already seen how he had nearly broken down before his meeting at Gainsborough and how Mrs. Chamberlain had had to prompt him during his speech. At first the family thought it the effect of shock caused by Ethel's death. But the tendency grew on him. Vince, his chief agent in Birmingham, recalled that, about this time:

we observed one slight symptom of decay. His memory, which had always been extraordinarily good, sometimes failed him. At Committee meetings he would sometimes forget the name of a person he wanted to mention; a sort of lapse to which nine people out of ten are accustomed all their lives — but it evidently vexed him. Also he sometimes forgot a word during a speech, and Mrs. Chamberlain (with whom he had perhaps rehearsed the speech) prompted him in obedience to a little signal. She did it so readily and cleverly that generally no one, not sitting very near to them was aware of anything wrong.[1]

Attacks of gout, bad colds, and the 'flu became more frequent. Recovery seemed slower. We have seen how he was prostrated the whole day before his speech at Birmingham on 5 May by a bilious headache. On 1 June came a more serious warning. Mrs. Chamberlain had gone to Liverpool to meet her parents, arriving from the United States. Chamberlain had stayed in London. He was in the midst of negotiations with Balfour and had to prepare the speech he was to make at St. Helens in two days' time. Feeling slightly giddy he had rung to ask for a drink. But when the butler came in, Chamberlain found he could not speak. With some presence of mind he tried to write down his order only to find he could not write. The butler assumed that Chamberlain was finishing a letter and waited. A few moments later the power of speech came back to him.

On her return, Mrs. Chamberlain found him looking very ill and worried. He told her what had happened. She sent for the doctor, who ordered him to cancel the St. Helens meeting. Chamberlain replied, 'If I don't do it, I shall never speak again. I must and I will.'[2] He did. It was a triumph of willpower; but a clear warning of the danger ahead. Fortunately, the Whitsun recess came in the following week, and for ten days he was able to leave off all work.

[1] C. A. Vince to J. L. Garvin, 22 April 1920.
[2] Mrs. Chamberlain in conversation with the author.—J. A.

II

Parliament met again after Whitsun only to witness the deepening decline in the Government's stock. Enquiries into the disposal of surplus war material in South Africa suggested corruption. Ministers were accused of negligence, and a Royal Commission was appointed to clear up the scandal. In fact, Arnold-Forster had been less negligent than at first appeared. Chamberlain, however, was in no mood to take a charitable view of any of the Government's activities.

CHAMBERLAIN TO PARKER SMITH

24 *June* 1905: *Private.*—The Party is in a bad hole, but the blame is certainly not entirely Balfour's. As I understand matters I am afraid our friend A. Forster is the head offender. Nowadays the Prime Minister cannot look after everything and the heads of departments ought to save him from an unpleasant surprise such as this. The moment any insinuation — even the slightest of the possible existence of a scandal reached the S. of S. for War he ought to have made it his own principal and personal business to follow it up.

As regards Monday I am paired, and I have no intention of coming up. I am not in a position to defend the Government, believing that they have grossly mismanaged the affair from first to last — on the other hand it would be contrary to the policy I have laid down for myself from the first, that I should attack them, or give them a push now that they are toppling.

I wonder whether Arthur Stanley, and others of our friends who took his view, are now convinced that I was right when I said that the sooner the election came the better it would be for all of us. It has turned out as I expected, and while delay has not helped us in the least, it has brought us into a difficulty worse by far than any the Free Fooders could have made for us.

The fact is that the Government is worn out — they stumble at every step.

If you and others of our Tariff Reformers like to speak on Monday, I do not think you can do any harm — provided that you speak rather in sorrow than in anger and do not preclude yourselves from voting with the Government. Even I cannot see that a general election at this moment would be advisable and we had better scrape out of the Session somehow without a crisis.

It is a most disagreeable and depressing situation, but we have had no responsibility for it, and I do not see that we can do anything to improve it.

If I were in Balfour's place and got over this hedge, I should insist on prolonging the Session till all the Bills introduced were carried as well as the Resolutions for Redistribution. If my followers would not make the sacrifice, a defeat on any one of them would now be the best thing to fall on.

The War Office had throughout been the Achilles heel of the Unionist Government. Lansdowne had failed there. So had Brodrick. Arnold-Forster, whose industry and ability were matched by a total want of tact, fared little better. It is interesting to recall that at one time there was a move on foot to persuade Chamberlain to take the post. When the Army scandal first came to light, Chamberlain had received the following letter:

TENNYSON TO CHAMBERLAIN

29 *May* 1905 : *Private and Confidential.*—I feel bound to pass you on any important communications from Australia. Let me tell you that there is now a strong feeling in Australia and in other Colonies that Arnold-Forster's management of the War Office is making the Colonies fast disbelieve in Great Britain and in the Government, and I think that so greatly grows this disbelief (owing to him) that any conference that is held next year is likely to be more or less of a failure (if he stays where he is). It is pretty evident too that in Great Britain the Government is being disconcerted by Arnold-Forster's policy — Australia, and the other Colonies as far as I can learn, are most anxious that you should go to the War Office — and I think that you are so patriotic that you would undertake the task if by any chance at any time the post of Minister of War were vacant.

You would feel as the Colonies do, that the Tariff Reform and Preferential Policy would win much more favour with the conference and with the country, if you were once united with the Government as *War Minister.* I pray you not to cast aside this suggestion as idle. The future of Great Britain largely depends on your decision supposing that Arnold-Forster resigns the office he now holds — as appears to be the one solution of the present tangle. The Colonies from their very aloofness seem to me to see further into our domestic politics than those who are in the thick of them — and therefore I venture to send you this word of entreaty — based on the opinion which I and many of your and my friends hold — do not trouble to answer.

The idea of finding a ground to bring Chamberlain back into the Government occurs more than once at this time. Chamberlain however seems to have obeyed Tennyson's request not to answer. In the event Arnold-Forster survived the crisis, and nothing more came of this particular suggestion.

Hard on the heels of the Army scandal came the first public intimation of the feud which had opened in India between Curzon and Kitchener: 'antagonists', as Milner said, 'worthy of each other's steel or should I say, stiletto'. The matter was raised in the House on the Indian Budget and weakened the Government still further. A more adroit Minister than Brodrick might have effected an accommodation between Viceroy and Commander-in-Chief. In fact his interventions, so Sandars judged, tended to widen the breach.[1] Curzon's resignation was not announced till after the House had risen; but though he found few sympathisers it was another nail in the Government's coffin.

Another cause for anxiety which would grow in the autumn was the strong feeling aroused in Scotland by the Scottish Churches Bill. Here was the beginning of a new agitation. It would also go against the Government.

We can plot the decline in the Government's fortunes from the steady loss of seats at by-elections. On 29 June, the Government lost East Finsbury, mainly, so the Tariff Reform League believed, because the Unionist candidate had been persuaded to abandon the Chamberlainite for the Balfourian policy:

CHAMBERLAIN TO LEVERTON HARRIS

3 *July* 1905.—A little more of this and there will be an insurrection which, indeed, would probably be as good for the Conservative Party as it would be for the people of Russia.

In the course of July I think there ought to be another meeting of Conservatives to consider the whole question of their organisation.

Some consolation was provided by a Unionist success at Kingswinford on 4 July. But it also seemed to bring confirmation of Chamberlain's views. The candidate had gone 'the whole hog' on Tariff Reform.

III

From the Whitsun recess to the end of June, something like a truce reigned on the fiscal front. Balfour was hopelessly and inextricably entangled in a web of ingenuities of his own contriving. Chamberlain had failed to break through to him and ran the risk of being enmeshed in it himself. What should be his next move?

Balfour had never yet sent a formal answer to the memorandum signed by the 142 members on 13 April. Should he be pressed to do so? Or would this only widen the breach? So far Chamberlain had worked to win Balfour over to his policy. 'The alternative policy,' wrote Parker Smith, 'was always in his mind, to raise his banner and to say "Qui m'aime, me suive", but it was never carried out and became more difficult as time went on.'[2] It is

---

[1] Unpublished papers of J. S. Sandars.
[2] 'Memoirs of Joseph Chamberlain' by J. Parker Smith, in the *National Review*, May 1932.

doubtful, indeed, whether it was ever practical politics. Many of his staunchest followers, men like Maxwell and Chaplin, accepted his lead on policy but would not have followed him against Balfour. He opened himself on this whole question at the beginning of July in a talk with Parker Smith who had come to discuss his next speech with him. This account of their conversation is based on a rough note made by Parker Smith immediately afterwards.

I went in accordance with Mr. Chamberlain's note to his house at 9.15 (p.m.) and found him alone in the dining-room. After telling him the progress of the afternoon debate, I gave him the substance of Gilbert Parker's memo as to his conversation with C. T. Ritchie.

CHAMBERLAIN : 'All this raises another question viz. whether it would be wise to press Arthur Balfour for a definite answer to the Memo. of the 142. None has yet been given, and several men have pressed me as to this. On the other hand, comparatively few of the 142 are excited about it, and I am quite sure they are all prepared to leave it in my hands. Arthur Balfour is an unwilling witness, and lawyers all say that it is unwise to press such a witness. Supposing I went to Arthur Balfour with an ultimatum — and suppose we got an unsatisfactory answer, what would happen then. We could not take it lying down, and the breach would be between us and the main body — which is what I have been trying all along to avoid. No third party has ever lived in this country. It was different over Home Rule where the split from one party brought us into line with the position of the other. A breach in fiscal policy would only put us into the wilderness.

'We have made enormous advances in the last two years. Don't let us be in too great a hurry. We have dragged Balfour along with us far beyond his original position. It isn't a satisfactory way of leading, but there it is.'

PARKER SMITH : 'It's rather like the comic opera, where the chief character rushed after the crowd, shouting, "I am their leader — I must follow them".'

CHAMBERLAIN : 'Exactly. Is it wise to try and force him along too fast? It is his nature. Of course, if I had been in Balfour's place, when I put one construction on his speech and Ritchie followed immediately putting a diametrically opposite one, I should certainly have risen and disclaimed one or the other — but that isn't Balfour's way.

'My main hope at present is in the scheme for capturing the organisation, which I suggested at the T.R. Executive Meeting. I talked to Balfour yesterday — he gave me an opening by congratulating me in the lobby on Kingswinford. I spoke to him of the rottenness of the Conservative organisation — and found him very conscious of it. I urged him to have a meeting to invite the ablest party agents to luncheon by themselves, and consult them on the matter.

'I am finding this speech very difficult to make. What line should I take? I have thought of and abandoned many. To seem to doubt Balfour's full acquiescence would be a case of he who excuses himself accuses himself. The other side are always trying to make differences and mischief, but in their hearts they know the strength of our party. To reassert this and not be unduly hurried is the best game. It would be the greatest mistake to risk a breach while we still have a chance to carry everything. Our own men, even many of the best, feel this very strongly, from all sorts of motives, not only selfish but unselfish. To smash a great party is a serious thing. I don't doubt that I'm strong enough to smash Balfour and the party if I chose; but on every ground, friendship, loyalty, and the interest of the cause, such a thing is not to be risked short of the last necessity. Besides what can you say on such a matter in the Albert Hall? In every speech you have to think of your pulpit. The relations of the various sections in the party can be discussed in a Committee room but not before a vast audience.

'The situation is very like that of 1885, when the unauthorized programme received such enormously exaggerated importance. Mr. Gladstone hated that programme, and tried with more or less success to keep the peace between myself and Hartington. Gladstone once said in 1885 that he thought the Irish question would swallow up all the others. I did not at the time fully appreciate the remark as I did not realise then that Gladstone would go for Home Rule.'

On 7 July, Chamberlain addressed a mass meeting of the Tariff Reform League in the Albert Hall. Yet another ducal recruit, Argyll, took the chair. Despite the cautious tone of his talk with Parker Smith two nights before, the speech was the most forthright he had yet made and must be considered in detail. It was a hard-hitting and devastating attack on Balfour's indecision.

He began by making it clear that the League would not be deflected from its task:

We have kindled a torch which not all the puny efforts of all our opponents can extinguish. (*Loud cheers.*) We have raised an issue of no ordinary importance ... of absorbing interest to the people of this country. There is no question today which can command such great audiences in every part of the country, audiences which in a way almost unknown in our time come willing to listen and anxious to learn (*cheers*). ... Our opponents would be wise if they would assume in the future that we, who have promoted this great cause in the fullest conviction of its importance, are not going to be driven from our point; are not going to abandon the task that we have undertaken (*cheers*) however heavy it may be. They would do well to accept as a fact that we will not go back one step (*hear, hear*) until all the essential attributes of our policy have been successfully accomplished.

This was followed by a powerful restatement of the aims of the League: more employment at home; closer union with the Colonies. Then came a first attack on the trimmers, the half-hearted, the Balfourian section of the party.

We do not only exist for inquiry (*cheers*). We are not where we are merely to ask questions — we are determined to carry inquiry into action (*loud and prolonged cheers*).

Let no man join us under any mistake. We are a fighting force (*renewed cheers*). We have a definite and a constructive policy. Let no man join us who does not agree with the whole of it (*prolonged cheering*). It is our desire to put that policy before our people, so that it shall be understanded of all of them. There is no object in concealing anything. We do not shrink from the logical consequences of the action we have undertaken (*cheers*). Why are we an independent association? In order that we may be independent, that we may speak our minds. In the resolution which is to be proposed to you later in the evening . . . we have endeavoured to put before you, and through you, before a much vaster audience, the policy which, in our opinion, will promote the interests of the masses of the people, and will secure the union of the Empire. We believe that the clearer this policy is — the more definite — the more it will appeal to the people (*cheers*).

I am a politician — with all the faults of a politician, and I know if I was speaking and acting as a politician alone I should recognise the value in politics of a discreet obscurity (*laughter*). I am not speaking to you to-night in that capacity, and while what I say may not be universally popular, I cannot help believing that in the long run it will be the wisest course to take even for a hardened politician (*laughter*). I know very well there are men on both sides of politics who, when some forward movement is in progress, are led by their excessive modesty to creep to the rear (*laughter*). They are the men who tell you that rapid advance — too rapid advance — should be avoided. They are the men who are afraid to commit themselves prematurely (*laughter*), and it is only when the battle has been fought and won (*cheers*), that they emerge to congratulate the victors (*laughter*).

Gentlemen, I say that we, a political association which is not a party association, are independent of the considerations which move these people. We are outside mere party considerations. We have all of us committed ourselves to a policy which we believe to be right and true. We care nothing for what is, perhaps, the ordinary object of personal and party ambition, unless with the power which we seek we can carry with us the cause to which we have devoted ourselves (*cheers*). We cannot afford to be obscure. It is not our business to gain adherents even to our cause by leaving any doubt upon the minds of any living men as to what we are aiming at, as to what we intend to gain.

We are pioneers (*cheers*). I have never pretended to offer any opinion as to how long a period may elapse before we win the victory, but this I do know, and when we win it (*a Voice: 'When?'*) and we shall (*cheers*), it shall be a victory complete and final. We will not have the fruits of our victory frittered away by the belated discussion of details which ought to be settled now (*cheers*). We want the Bill, the whole Bill, and nothing but the Bill (*cheers*).

I say we cannot afford to be obscure. Why? Are we to waste the rest of our lives in striving for a victory which will be bootless when it is gained? I hear with some amusement speeches in the House of Commons by those who avowedly remain within our party in order to be a drag upon our wheels — who accept in name the policy that we have put forward, but with the thought concealed that they will take care to make that policy ineffective, even after it has been carried (*'Shame'*). We are not babes in political controversy. We will have a clear understanding as to every point of our policy (*cheers*). We will not allow these gentlemen — I think myself the constituencies will not allow them (*cheers*) — after having done everything in their power to thwart us in the commencement, to come back after our victory as nominal supporters, but with the full intention — the amiable intention — of preventing us from securing what ought to be the natural results . . .

Next came his own definition of Retaliation. It was not to be an academic philosophical concept like Balfour's, but a practical all-round Tariff on manufactured goods.

Our policy is the policy of the vast majority of the Unionist party (*cheers*). It is the policy of Retaliation and Preference (*cheers*). But let us be careful that we understand each other as to what we mean by words. Retaliation is an excellent text — so is Mesopotamia (*laughter*). What do we mean by Retaliation? We mean an effective engine to force a fair trade policy upon the nations with which we exchange our products. Or, failing that, to take up our own independent position, and if we cannot exchange our goods with friends to keep for our own people our own demands (*cheers*).

We want the big revolver when we meet men who are armed at all points — the big revolver (*A Voice: 'Well loaded'*). I agree with that interruption (*laughter and cheers*). That is the whole point of my argument (*renewed laughter and cheers*). What is the use of a revolver which is not loaded? (*cheers*). *We will load our revolver with a general tariff* [1] (*cheers*). That tariff may be moderate — must be moderate, in my opinion (*cheers*). It will be a tariff principally for revenue (*hear, hear*) — it will be a tariff which contains a large free list of articles which are necessary for the spread of our commerce, and on which, therefore, we should be foolish to put any duty. It must be a scientific tariff (*cheers*), and when we have it we must have power — we must ask at the same time for a mandate from the electorate of this country that the revolver is not given to us as a toy (*cheers*), but that it is meant for use — that its charge — this general tariff of which I speak — may be turned at a moment into a penal tariff in the case of those nations which will not meet us on equal terms. And we may ask also that it may be turned into a perfectly innocent weapon when we find others who are ready to grant us reciprocal concessions.

Why should we go into this great negotiation and then find when we appear to have been victorious that we have no power to carry out the mandate which will have been given us. No, ladies and gentlemen, make no mistake. If we are successful and I think we shall be, we will accept no success which is not immediately effective.

[1] My italics.—J. A.

The revenue raised by the Tariff could be devoted to the relief of agriculture and to social reform. He did not mention Old Age Pensions specifically, but the implication is clear.

People argue, our opponents argue, as though every tax was a burden. That depends upon what you do with the tax. I have pointed out before that money which would come into the Exchequer under a system of this kind cannot be buried in a stocking (*laughter*). The Chancellor of the Exchequer must do something with it (*cheers*). I would like to live long enough (*cheers, and a Voice: 'You will'*) to see one Chancellor of the Exchequer who should have this opportunity. Under such circumstances he would be able, from the surplus which would thus be provided, to lower the cost of living to the poor (*cheers*). He would be able to deal, in some way, at any rate, with the burning question of the pressure of rates (*cheers*), especially on the industry which once was the greatest industry in this country, and which suffered so much from our policy of free imports. He would be able still with the surplus to carry forward some of those great social reforms which at the present time we cannot afford to contemplate, because our resources are so limited.

He then turned to the Preferential side of the policy. This he told his audience bluntly would mean a tax on wheat.

There is the question of Retaliation ; there is the question of Preference. Again, let us have no ambiguity. What do we mean by Preference? Surely we mean absolute fair play as between our Colonies and ourselves (*cheers*). They do not want a one-sided bargain ; neither do we (*hear, hear*). They can give us if they like to-morrow a Preference which would throw into our hands something like thirty millions of trade, which now goes in ever-increasing proportion to our competitors on the Continent and elsewhere. Are we going to ask them to give us this, and are we going to tell them at the same time that we will give them nothing in return? (*No, no.*) We must have a reciprocal Preference. If they give us a Preference on the goods which we manufacture we must give them a Preference on the goods which they produce (*hear, hear*).

But I, for one, am not going — I never have attempted — to conceal that this policy almost necessarily involves a small tax upon wheat (*cheers*). But the effect of this tax, if we consider it, must be inappreciable. At the very outside, if the consumers of wheat do pay every farthing of it, it would only amount to a farthing on a loaf, or less than a farthing. . . .

Now came the open advice to the candidates and Unionist associations to go 'the whole hog'.

Not a day passes in which you do not see in the newspapers the announcement of an alteration in the price of bread, which amounts to a halfpenny or a penny a loaf. These things of everyday occurrence pass absolutely unnoticed. But when I, who, unfortunately, happen to be in public life, put forward a case for a rise of even a farthing, I am told that my deliberate intention is to reduce the condition of the poor to that which they held in the hungry Forties — to bring the labourers of this country to absolute starvation.

Well, I have never known throughout my somewhat stormy life (*cheers*) such gross, such scandalous, such unworthy misrepresentations (*cheers*). But do you think that misrepresentation of this kind is to be accepted as a reason why we should not do the thing that is right? (*No, no.*) How do you expect to meet misrepresentation? By facing it boldly (*hear, hear*) ; by nailing those lies to the counter (*cheers*). There is no candidate, on whatever side he stands who will do any good to himself or to his party by ignoring this question, and trying to put it behind him (*cheers*).

It is no use for a man to go down into the country and to profess to be an advocate of Preference with the Colonies, to put forward the importance of the union of the Empire, and at the same time to boast that he is unwilling to pay the price (*hear, hear*). It is not a large price, but he will find it better policy to face all the difficulties of the situation than to attempt to escape them, as I am sorry to say some politicians have done. I think they do not do justice, either to the intelligence or the patriotism of the people of this country. It is quite true that our electorate — now that the electorate has been so widely extended — it is quite true that they do not follow very closely philosophical argument. They do not understand the complication of statistics and facts, but they do understand a simple issue. They do honour the man who has the courage of his convictions (*cheers*), and they know how to treat at its proper value the shilly-shally of those who have no convictions at all to speak of (*laughter*).

We do not know what were Balfour's feelings when he read the speech. It is likely enough that he would have agreed with the comments Wyndham sent him the next day.

WYNDHAM TO BALFOUR

8 *July* 1905: *Private and Confidential.*—I have read Chamberlain's speech. Certain features in it — declared to be cardinal — will revive discussion and precipitate conflict. Those which strike me most are :

(1) There is to be a *general* Tariff. This is stated to be a necessary part of the policy.

(2) This General Tariff is to be used 'at a moment'. That can only mean a power of increasing taxation on particular items — already taxed in the general Tariff — by Executive action released from *existing* Parliamentary control. Some other form of Parliamentary control may be contemplated. But, obviously, departures from the Budget of the year by the executive are contemplated in the first place.

(3) This general Tariff employed as a 'datum level' for increases against unfair competition and decreases for benefits received, is in itself to be of such a character that it will provide a *large surplus*.

(4) That surplus is to be used for experiments in social legislation, for the relief of rates and specially for relieving rates on Agricultural Land.

This programme is highly contentious.

Other members of the Party will be struck, rather, by the renewed emphasis on the necessity of taxing wheat. Nearly all will deplore the militant tone; the reference to offers of cooperation having been made to the other side; the unfortunate phrase 'we fell back' on the Unionist Party; the gibes at 'ambiguity' and 'shilly-shally'.

Proposals (1), (3) and (4) have never been advocated in any speech which you have made, and the taxation of wheat — to which I attach less importance — has been made specifically conditional on the result of a 'Free Conference'.

The speech seems designed to draw the maximum of fire from all quarters.

The cumulative argument against the proposals may be stated thus: Employment is more important than cheapness even at some cost. Imperial Unity is vital even at some cost. Retaliation is necessary, even at some cost. Yet the machinery for effecting these objects, at the risk of three separate occasions for cost, is, in addition, to extract surplus millions. And these millions are to be dispensed by a future Chancellor of the Exchequer in promoting social experiments and endowing Agriculture by relieving it from Rates.

When this is understood I am convinced that the Middle Classes will rebel. Yet all are invited to accept the proposals in their entirety at the peril — if they demur — of being stigmatised as timid timeservers who seek the Palm without the Dust: unless, indeed, for the purpose of blowing into the eyes of the public in the form of ambiguous evasions.

Chamberlain, quite possibly does not mean all he says. Yet this is a different matter from Retaliation and a Free Conference.

It will be called Protection of Manufacture *plus* doles to Agriculture. It will be defeated in the towns by reference to the second proposition and in rural districts by reference to the first.

Chamberlain escaped for the weekend to Batsford Park, Lord Redesdale's house. His speech and its excellent reception by the Unionist press had left him in high spirits. Esher who was also in the party wrote:

... Chamberlain had aged. He was 69 yesterday. But he is *in talk* as vigorous as ever. He is dead keen for the Government to go out. He thinks that once in Opposition, Arthur [Balfour] cannot fail to take up the line along which Chamberlain desires to see him move. Mrs. Chamberlain is quite as much *au courant* of politics as her husband.[1]

At the end of the month (28 July), Devonshire raised the question of Chamberlain's Albert Hall speech in the House of Lords and sought to carry a resolution condemning it. Marlborough, speaking for the Government, followed the Balfourian line of refusing to comment on other people's interpretations of the Prime Minister's statements. Chamberlain's position was vigorously defended by

[1] Viscount Esher, *Journal and Letters*, p. 90.

Ridley and by Minto who took occasion to explain the strong support for Preference which existed in Canada. The previous question was moved and Devonshire's motion defeated.

Minto might well have proved a powerful ally to Chamberlain. He could have led the numerous but not very vocal band of Peers who had embraced Tariff Reform. But this was his one and only chance to intervene on Chamberlain's behalf. Within six weeks Curzon had resigned the Viceroyalty and Minto would be his successor.

IV

In the month that elapsed between the Albert Hall speech and the rising of the House, the Government sank still deeper into the mire. On 11 July, Ministers published their Resolution on a proposed scheme of Redistribution of the constituencies. This would have had the effect of increasing the English and Welsh constituencies by 18, increasing the Scottish by 4, and decreasing the Irish by 22.

Balfour had hoped that the scheme could be debated as a single resolution and would take only one debate, spread no doubt over several days. The Speaker, however, ruled that it must be divided into eight or nine parts to be debated separately. It was certain that the Irish would oppose each Resolution with the utmost resourcefulness and the whole Parliamentary timetable would be wrecked. Balfour, accordingly, withdrew the Resolution and announced that he would proceed by Bill in the next session.

Next day (18 July) the Prime Minister addressed a meeting of the Unionist Party in a committee room upstairs. He urged them not to be despondent about the withdrawal of the Resolution and again undertook to bring in a redistribution measure in the next session. He also took occasion largely on grounds of foreign policy to deprecate the idea of an early dissolution. He ended with an appeal to members not to relax their effort or attendance in the weeks before the House rose.

Notwithstanding this appeal, the Government was defeated only two days later (20 July) on the vote for the Irish Land Commission. The defeat was solely due to slack attendance and there was no question of resignation. All the same it was a stinging little reverse.

Chamberlain was by now strongly in favour of an autumn dissolution. The Government had suffered a net loss of twenty seats since 1902. There was no prospect of anything turning up

2 B

to their advantage. Above all he could not endure the thought of another session in which Balfour would again have to keep in with the Free Fooders in order to maintain his majority in the House. He urged the wisdom of dissolving on Balfour. Balfour appears to have said that he would take soundings in the Party before reaching a decision. For some days Chamberlain was inclined to be hopeful.

CHAMBERLAIN TO GARVIN

1 *August* 1905.—In spite of the semi-official statement in the *Daily Telegraph* I still believe in a dissolution this autumn and in the extreme unwisdom of meeting the House of Commons. I must not, however, be quoted as holding this opinion, but I will explain the situation to you when I see you.

A few days later, however, his tone was more pessimistic. He had learned that a number of his own supporters, Chaplin among them, were against an autumn election.

CHAMBERLAIN TO GILBERT PARKER

7 *August* 1905.—I agree entirely with your view as to the advantage of a dissolution in the autumn, and I have most strongly urged this course upon Mr. Balfour. I doubt very much whether he intends to give effect to my recommendation, and if he does not, while I think that he will make one of the greatest mistakes of his life, yet he will be to some extent justified by the action of Tariff Reform members many of whom I notice have written to urge him to meet the next session of Parliament.

By this time Chamberlain had shaken the dust of London off his feet. Tired and depressed, he had paired with Morley for the rest of the session, and had gone off to Highbury, taking Morley with him for the weekend. There the news reached him, doubtless through Austen, that Balfour had decided to meet the House again :

CHAMBERLAIN TO PARKER SMITH

15 *August* 1905.—As I told you, I believe the Government have decided against my view as to dissolution. They base this entirely upon the preponderant opinion of their followers including of course those who favour my proposals of tariff reform. I am afraid they are right, and that our own people are chiefly desirous of putting off the inevitable.

I cannot express myself stronger than I have done, and I must leave them to take their own course.

CHAMBERLAIN TO LEVERTON HARRIS

15 *August* 1905.—I am discouraged to find that the Government have practically decided to go on for another session. It is a deplorable mistake and means the waste of a year for our cause. They justify them-

selves on the ground that there is a preponderant opinion in favour of this course even among those who are described as tariff-reformers. There seems to be an extraordinary desire on the part of Members of Parliament to postpone the day of execution, but I am certain that the longer we remain the worse will be the result.

However, I have given my advice in the strongest terms and can do no more, though it is discouraging to see with how little wisdom our proceedings are controlled.

Next day, before setting out on his holiday, he sent another of his situation reports to Northcote in Australia. It may serve as a summary of the mistakes of this disastrous session and shows his own mind on the need for an autumn election.

CHAMBERLAIN TO NORTHCOTE

16 *August* 1905: *Private and Confidential.*—You may like to hear a word or two about matters here. Balfour has at last managed to struggle through the Session which has been from all points of view the worst for the credit of Parliament and the most humiliating to the Government that I have ever known. My own opinion, which I pressed very strongly on Balfour, was that they should ride for a fall at the beginning of the Session. I felt that they would do no good, that nothing was likely to turn up which would improve their position, and that the best thing which could possibly happen was that the other side should be made to take the responsibility of office and to attempt the fulfilment of the pledges they had made. In this case I thought they would have a short term of office and we should return after a brief experience of opposition as strong as ever. But Balfour was determined to go on, and events have, I believe justified my prediction. The Party stands much worse with the country now than it did at the beginning of the year.

Before the Session closed I again pressed Balfour for an autumn election, but again, I think, he will pay no attention to my advice and will go on to another Session.

I cannot understand how any man of his refinement can stand such a position as he occupies. He has certainly lost ground in the country where he is suspected of clinging to office for office's sake. He is also thought to be playing with the Fiscal question and really to have no strong principle to guide his political action.

The attempt to reform the Army has failed with Brodrick first and now even more so with Arnold-Forster. The appointment of McDonnell to Ireland alienated the Ulster men. Education and Chinese Labour are still stumbling blocks with many Unionists.

Legislation has been almost at a standstill and in fact the only thing which has brought any credit whatever to the Government as a whole has been its foreign policy, which is undoubtedly popular.

I fear that another session will be thrown away and of course our ultimate victory postponed at least by that period.

The situation is discouraging, but I have been in contests before which have appeared hopeless and yet with patience and resolution have been successfully won.

Whenever the election does come you must look out for a bigger smash than we have ever had before. It will not be owing, however, to the merits of Fiscal Reform although the tactics adopted in regard to it have weakened the confidence of the country in the Unionist party.

V

By the time the House rose, Chamberlain was physically exhausted.

'His condition at that time', Neville Chamberlain afterwards wrote, 'occasioned us the gravest anxiety.'[1]

He had been persuaded to try a cure at Aix-les-Bains and left London on 19 August. Mrs. Chamberlain, Neville and Mrs. Chamberlain's parents, Mr. and Mrs. Endicott, went with him. On arriving at Aix, 'he complained of giddiness, but though we begged him to lie down he refused'.[2]

The cure did good and after three weeks at Aix, he left for an after cure of a week on Lake Geneva. Then, for a fortnight, he travelled through the Auvergne, returning to Paris on 3 October. Austen and Ida joined him there. Ten days later they were back in London. Family and friends agreed alike that Chamberlain had come back a changed man. For some months now there was a full return of the old vigour. Looking back, Mrs. Chamberlain would always regret that they had not discovered Aix before.[3]

VI

Chamberlain returned to England, still convinced of the need for an autumn dissolution. Austen was of the same mind,[4] and they must have discussed the whole question while they were in Paris together. The Anglo-Japanese Treaty had been signed at the end of September, and there was now no serious reason for postponing the election. Nevertheless, on 5 October, Gerald Balfour spoke at Leeds in terms which were generally interpreted as notice that the Government would meet the House again. The same day, Chaplin sent an account of a talk with Alec Hood which pointed to an election in the spring.

[1] Neville Chamberlain's recollections of his father, dated July 1914.
[2] *Ibid.*   [3] Mrs. Chamberlain in conversation with the author.
[4] Petrie, *Life and Letters of Austen Chamberlain*, p. 161.

CHAPLIN TO CHAMBERLAIN

5 *October* 1905: *Private.*—I had a long interview a few days ago with Alec Hood. His home is near here, a delightful place within a drive, and he asked me to go over and see him a day or two after I arrived. I did so, and we discussed the best time for a Dissolution, for ¾ of an hour after lunch. I told him that the Japanese Treaty, which by the way has only been published since my return, had profoundly modified my views as to the date of an appeal to the country. That I was all for an election soon — as soon as it could be fittingly engineered, and that I should write this to Arthur, which I have done since then.

His chief difficulty about an immediate appeal to the country was this. He still wanted time to find candidates for a certain number of seats, not a very great many I gathered, in which the Radicals are still unopposed. Beyond that, I could see no insuperable difficulty or practical reason against an election before Xmas. I urged an Autumn Session if possible and if not, the meeting of Parliament as early in January as possible — and as to resignation as against dissolution — which he favours himself — the difficulty he said would be to prevent, not to arrange a defeat, the moment that Parliament met. He added that many of the men had been informally told that an autumn election was very improbable. My impression was that he would prefer it in spring and that that is what they are aiming at.

Chamberlain's own opinion at this time appears from the two extracts we give below.

CHAMBERLAIN TO SAXON MILLS

18 *October* 1905: *Private.*—I think that the political situation is very unsatisfactory. As you know I have pressed the Government to dissolve, and I think the delay has only made things much worse than they were. We shall, I fear, come out very badly at the General Election, but the sooner it is over the better and the sooner the tide will begin to turn. It is clear the country is tired of the present men and wants a change.

CHAMBERLAIN TO GARVIN

23 *October* 1905.—I have to speak very shortly to my constituents. I do not know yet exactly what I shall say, but I must, I think, speak against the hesitation & weakness of the official position. It is rather difficult sailing as I do not want to quarrel with the Government or to put Balfour with his back against the wall. The delay, however, in the election is most provoking and the worst possible tactics. The situation is much worse for the party than it was two months ago. I do not know whether it can further deteriorate, but the present official tactics are certainly as bad as they can be.

Meanwhile, whatever the Government might do, he was determined on an active autumn campaign. He needed help and sought to enlist Wyndham for the cause ; only to meet with a decided rebuff.

WYNDHAM TO CHAMBERLAIN

28 *October* 1905.—I ought not — possibly — to trouble you with any further statement of my political position. But you say : 'I have, I hope rightly, always counted on you as one of the strongest supporters of my proposals while you were in the Cabinet' — and that constrains me to add a few words ; for I am loath to adopt — even in appearance — the attitude of one who waits on events, holding himself free to advocate any opinions which may in the long run prove popular.

I am anxious, now as in 1903, to work towards a closer unity throughout the Empire, embracing, if that should prove feasible, some measure of commercial unity. I deprecate, now as I did then, any actions or words which may repel our Colonies and hinder such a consummation. But, on the other hand, I am no more persuaded now than then, that anything in the nature of a general tariff imposed for the double object, first, of giving employment to those engaged in manufacture and, secondly, of providing a surplus revenue of some millions for the relief of Agriculture and Social legislation, is expedient.

I should but ill repay the kindness of your letter if I dilated in my reply on such points of divergence. But, in view of the sentence I have quoted, I felt it right to state that such a measure of divergence does exist.

Thanking you again for the kind terms of your letter, and trusting that you will understand my reasons for withholding from an agitation which would I fear — at least in my hands — serve only to accentuate differences in the Party on the eve of an election.

It would not be long before Wyndham changed his tune. About the same time, Chamberlain received a further compromise proposal from Tennyson. It is not clear whether it was really inspired by Balfour but it is interesting as an example of the kind of scheme that was being discussed at the time.

TENNYSON TO CHAMBERLAIN

23 *October* 1905*: Strictly Private and Confidential.*—I have been asked by a very prominent Member of Parliament to tell him your private opinion if possible whether, if Mr. Balfour adopted the platform which I venture to suggest to you for the coming election — you would go into the fight with him simply and solely on this platform — and so adopt a programme likely to consolidate the Unionist party.

My suggestion, if you recollect, was 2½ p.c. preferential revenue tariff for the purpose of local defence (that is to be devoted to the popular cause of Volunteers and Militia) on all foreign imports other than cotton and raw products.

This would be a substitute for the average tax of 10% on foreign manufacturers' imports, and obviate the necessity of the compensatory remissions of duties on tea and sugar.

According to what I can ascertain this would bring in about 7 millions, but, if compensatory remission were still needed, most of the sum might be absorbed and nothing appreciable left for the purposes of Local Defence.

The proposed preferential revenue tariff would be imposed — leaving the other parts of the Empire to respond or not as they pleased.

Australia, as I cabled to you when Governor-General — (for Barton was sure of it) — would be content with even 6% duty on corn in favour of the Colonies.

I shall treat your answer as confidential unless you allow me to communicate it direct to Mr. Balfour and not through any third person.

I would rather not intermeddle at all, but I have (more than once) been prompted by the question 'Have you submitted your plan in a definite form to Chamberlain and Hugh Cecil?' and I seemed to see a gleam of hope in the way that the suggestion has been privately taken up.

Tennyson's letter drew a frank reply. The last sentences show that Chamberlain was no longer concerned with compromise. There was no longer any room for a middle position. Balfour must choose between the Free Fooders and himself.

CHAMBERLAIN TO TENNYSON

24 *October* 1905 : *Private.*—I am much obliged by your letter of Oct. 23 which I will endeavour to answer frankly and at the same time as concisely as possible.

In starting the Tariff Reform movement it was necessary to lay down some kind of skeleton scheme so that the public might understand what the practical result was likely to be if the policy were adopted. Accordingly this was done in my speech at Glasgow on October 6 1903, but neither at the time nor since have I ever presumed to regard this scheme as more than a skeleton or as a definite and final proposal. I have felt that, if the general principle were adopted by the Party, the exact method of application must be left to the Government elected to carry it out, and, providing that the principles were fully accepted, and that I considered the plan finally adopted adequate, they would be assured of every possible support, whether in or out of the Government, that I could give them.

Although, however, under these circumstances, I do not consider myself pledged to the strict letter of the scheme which I have advocated, I am convinced from long political experience that it would be most unwise for me in any way to change it while the question is in the preliminary stage of agitation. The old proverb against swapping horses whilst crossing a stream holds good, especially in such a case as this, and therefore, where friends have suggested alterations or improvements, I have invariably declined to commit myself to them, and have pointed out that, while it is open to them or anybody else to urge them on their own responsibility, I cannot as leader of the movement lay myself open to the charge, which would certainly be brought against me, of not knowing my own mind and of being ready to alter my programme in order to catch votes from all quarters.

I might stop here, and ask you to accept the above as my answer to your proposal, but I think that I owe it to you, whose opinion and support I much value, to say that as at present advised I do not think that your suggestions would be easier to carry than mine, or that they would form a practical solution to the question. It is not the *amount* of the change to which my opponents object, but *to any change at all*. They would oppose 2½ per cent as much as 10, and, from their point of view, they would be right, as such an arrangement could be considered only as a first step. On the other hand it would give me too little to be able to satisfy the bulk of my own followers.

I have chosen what I think to be the minimum on which the new plan can be worked. The subsequent investigations of the Tariff Commission tend to confirm this, although it is possible that the average rate of duty which they recommend will be somewhat less than I originally proposed; but their inquiries go to show that any uniform rate would work out injuriously to British trade. This is so complex that a 2½ per cent might seriously hamper some great industry while it would be an absolutely insignificant protection to others.

I am also of opinion from information received that 2½ per cent would not be a sufficient margin on which to work a preferential arrangement with Canada.

I think I am right in supposing that you, like myself, are most strongly interested in what I may call the Imperial side of the question, and especially in Imperial Defence. I am, however, coming more and more strongly to the conclusion that we have in the past not sufficiently appealed to local patriotism in the case of the Colonies. The idea of a tribute to the mother country is fatal to success, and the Colonies would never continue to pay over large sums to be spent in England by the British Admiralty or War Office. On the other hand it might be possible to get them to accept advice and conference with us as to the character and numbers of the Army and Navy which they themselves shall provide.

Once secure an expenditure adequate to their share, for say a Canadian Navy, and it would, I think, be easy to ensure that the Government should work with ours whenever any part of the Empire were attacked.

This is a big subject, and I can only suggest the general idea in correspondence.

In conclusion I may add one thing. The controversy has now gone so far as to disclose plainly the issues, which, as between myself on the one side and Lord Hugh Cecil for instance on the other, are irreconcileable. We have different objects, and no compromise could possibly bridge over the divergence of opinion. The Unionist party must adopt one view or the other.

Any attempt to find a road on which we can all travel would be as futile as Dunraven's attempt to unite Unionists and Nationalists. The Prime Minister has to choose, and it is his anxiety to avoid this necessity which has led to all the ambiguity and indefiniteness which is the root of the present political impotence of the Unionist party.

I have troubled you with a longer reply than I intended, but I hope I have made my meaning clear.

VII

Balfour, meanwhile, seems to have felt the time had come to consult with Chamberlain upon election tactics. Towards the end of October, he wrote, out of the blue, from Scotland.

BALFOUR TO CHAMBERLAIN

October 1905.—I am just off to London — and hope to see Austen soon — we have not met since Parliament prorogued. I only mention this because I would rather write to you on the future *after* seeing him than before.

What an incalculable element this Russian revolution must introduce into International relations!

This strange missive was followed a few days later by a very full analysis of the alternatives open to the Government. By this time, Balfour had reached London but had failed to find Austen.

BALFOUR TO CHAMBERLAIN

2 *November* 1905: *Private and Confidential.*—I had hoped to see Austen on my arrival here; but I find that he is in the middle of an electoral campaign; so that I must write to you upon the Dissolution question without having had the preliminary advantage of a discussion with him. This would have been valuable, because I think he does not wholly agree with me.

As regards the past, Dissolution either in June or in August would have been very undesirable in view of the Japanese Treaty; while the latter date had special objections of its own connected with the time of the year. So far most of those who have had to consider the question are in agreement. Controversy begins in connection with the proposal to resign, or dissolve, in the Autumn.

For my own part I should have liked this course, not merely because, on personal grounds, I am very anxious to get out of office, but because the chapter of accidents is always *against* a Government; and while some untoward event might cause us fresh embarrassments, it is beyond the ordinary range of possibility that any event, either at home or abroad, would add to our strength. Some of the arguments, indeed, of those who favour this course do not appeal to me, e.g. the argument based upon bye-elections and 'dignity'. Bye-elections have, and must have, a great indirect effect upon the fate of the Government and its Parliamentary position: but they ought not in themselves to be regarded as a governing principle in determining the time, or occasion, of a Dissolution.

However this may be, I thought, and still think, that October would have been a very fitting period at which to have sought a termination of the present state of things.

The main reasons why the idea was abandoned were three in number, the first two being, comparatively speaking, subsidiary.

2 B 2

LIFE OF JOSEPH CHAMBERLAIN [BK. XXVI–1905]

(1) Walter Long, from the point of view of Ireland, implored me in the most urgent manner not to have an Autumn election, which, according to him, would have been regarded by our Loyalist friends as a gratuitous abandonment of their interests, which he hopes, partially at least, to safeguard during the next few months.

(2) The second is a similar appeal from Selborne, as there are certain matters of policy which he thinks he can carry through while we are *in*, but not after we go *out*.

I find it very hard to estimate at their precise value these two appeals. There will probably always be found *some* part of the British Empire which would like to defer any risk of change, although it were but for a short time. Yet, especially in the case of Long, the appeal has been made to me so repeatedly and so earnestly that I thought, and think, that it ought to count for something in the decision arrived at.

A much stronger argument, however, and the one which really over-bore my own predelictions, was the great preponderance of party opinion in favour of postponement. I rather gather that Austen is disposed to dispute the fact; but I think there can be no doubt about it. I did not rely merely upon the reports of the Whips, although they derived a special importance from the fact that A. Hood, like myself, would have preferred an Autumn resignation. I took particular pains to make en-quiries of my own. For example, I discussed the problem in the utmost detail with Arthur Stanley, who himself took my view about October, and begged him to make enquiries among his friends to see what view they took. He returned to me, and informed me that, to his surprise, and somewhat to his disgust, he found that the great preponderance of opinion was *against* an early resignation or Dissolution, that Parker Smith and one or two others, whose names I forget, took a different view, but that they were in a very small minority.

I also found that the majority of our Chairmen and Agents were in favour of postponement, although, as it happens, the Chairman at Manchester — a most competent man — took the other view.

Altogether, I was forced, very reluctantly, to the conclusion, not merely that the Party were opposed to the October policy, but that they would have regarded it in the light of a very serious and gratuitous injury to themselves. Some may conceivably have been influenced by the desire to retain the letters 'M.P.' after their name for yet a little longer; but this certainly was not the prevailing motive and I got appeals in the same sense, not merely from Members, but from candidates.

You will perhaps ask me whether I ought to have been diverted from the course to which I was inclined on its merits, by the views of our Party. My reply is that on many subjects I have to ask them to take my judgment rather than theirs, and to support us in the faith that we know more about the matter in dispute than they do. But I confess that I shrank from any such exercise of authority in this particular case. Had there been any reasonable prospect of our winning the election, dis-content would no doubt have been swallowed in victory. But where no great principle or public interest is at stake, I really could not force upon my followers a course to which each unsuccessful candidate would have attributed his defeat. It is not merely that I should have been violently abused for such a proceeding (to this we are all too much accustomed to pay much attention) ; but I think it would have damped the ardour of our forces, and have greatly imperilled any usefulness which I may have in directing Party counsels.

So much for the past. Now for the future. October being once over, I do not think that the two remaining months in the year afford a fitting opportunity for a change. If I dissolved (to which there are objections, on which I shall have something to say in a moment), I should certainly be attacked for dissolving on a decrepit register, and also for having chosen a period at which the English register was at its *oldest* and the Scotch register at its *newest*. If, on the other hand, I found an excuse for resigning, the other side certainly would not have dissolved until the middle of January, and the whole country would be, till that date, in turmoil as bad as those of a general election. The question therefore is narrowed down to *what* ought to be done, and *when*, after the middle of January. My own view is this — that we should call Parliament together on the last Tuesday in January, or the first Tuesday in February, and take the earliest opportunity of resigning. If I rightly interpret the signs of the times, that opportunity will probably occur in the first week : for I shall not think it necessary to wait for a defeat. It would be perfectly constitutional for me to say on the first Amendment to the Address on which I did not receive adequate support that I did not think that I could, under these circumstances, with advantage attempt to deal with so large a problem as Redistribution, the principal measure of the Session. I should in that event resign ; C.B. would form his Government, announce his programme, and dissolve. I may say (of course, in the strictest confidence) that the King who would, I think, greatly dislike an un-motivated resignation or Dissolution, is quite prepared for this course.

There is no suggestion here of 'riding for a fall'. I am confident that a sufficient *approach* to a fall will come without any riding at all.

The difference in date between the latter half of January and the first few days of February is in itself insignificant. But I think the difference between resigning and dissolving is *not* insignificant, and it does not seem very easy to find an excuse for resigning while Parliament is prorogued. I never worked out any satisfactory method by which this could have been done in October, had the October plan been otherwise practicable ; and I think it is even more difficult when Parliament is on the eve of re-assembling.

You may perhaps think that I exaggerate the advantage of resignation, and I quite agree that the broad result of an election is not likely to be profoundly modified by any difficulties the other side may have in framing either a Government or a policy. But these difficulties are real and great. And they are increased by personal differences and jealousies, which will make the next Cabinet an eminently unfriendly collection of friends. I should infinitely prefer getting them 'into the open' before the fight begins.

In any case, I do not mean to have another Session like last one. In the middle of August I thought my weariness of office might be attributed to mere physical fatigue. But it is not so. I have had my holiday. I am perfectly well and cheerful; but I find that ten years of leading the House of Commons has given me an unutterable desire for a change; and I never go upstairs to bed without thanking Heaven that, in a very brief period, I shall have left my official residence and gone back to the comfort and repose of my own house!

Balfour's intention, thus, was to meet the House in the New Year and to resign almost immediately. From Chamberlain's point of view, this plan offered marked disadvantages and no apparent advantage.

If Balfour once met the House, he could not escape a fiscal debate either before his resignation or on the initiative of the new Government. Such a debate could only weaken the Unionist Party unless it was preceded by a firm agreement between himself and Chamberlain. On the other hand, if such an agreement could be reached — and Balfour would have to throw over the Free Fooders to reach it — there would be no need to meet the House. Two speeches or an exchange of letters would be enough to seal the reunion of the Party.

The same day that Balfour's letter reached him (3 November 1905), Chamberlain spoke in Birmingham. His speech was in effect a public reply to Balfour's private letter.

He began by re-emphasising his belief in the need for an early election.

We have reached, ladies and gentlemen, a very interesting, even a critical, stage in our political history. We are engaged in an autumn campaign which has commenced rather earlier than usual, and appears to be likely to be continued with more than ordinary energy. We are almost in the throes of a general election — (*hear, hear*) — and yet the election continually recedes into the background. (*Laughter.*) I myself had hoped when the date of this meeting was fixed that we might actually have found ourselves in the act of deciding this party issue which lies before us, and I have never concealed my own opinion that every month's delay was to our disadvantage. (*Hear, hear.*) You have seen, perhaps, in the papers, some ridiculous and absurd reports invented by the Opposition press, with what object you can divine. You have seen that I intended to force this election upon the Government. Well, really, this does not do much credit to the judgment and intelligence of those who invent reports of this kind. I could not force it upon the Government if I desired to do so, and I would not force it upon the Government if I had the power. (*Cheers.*) Not because I do not hold, as every man in my position has a right to hold, my own opinion, but because, after all, this is a question of tactics, and it is the Government, and the Government alone, that ought to decide it. (*Cheers.*)

But I have a right to give the reason for the faith that is in me. I wish an election because the great Unionist party is marking time when it ought to be fighting the enemy — (*hear, hear*) — and the sooner we get into close conflict with our opponents the better I shall like it.

Then came an open criticism of the leadership of the Party in the last session.

I accept the policy of the Prime Minister — (*hear, hear*) — in the words in which he himself states it, and I am prepared to give it every support in my power. (*Cheers.*) But there is this difficulty. At the commencement of this great campaign we — and I say we because I myself was a party to the decision — we decided that during the present Parliament we would not take any steps to secure the practical accomplishment of the policy to which we have devoted ourselves. We thought then that time was necessary in order that the country might consider all that was involved in a policy which touched every man and every woman amongst you. Gentlemen, I still believe that that self-denying ordinance was justified at the time, but I also think that we have given a sufficient opportunity for this discussion and enquiry, and that now we ought to regain our freedom as quickly as we can. (*Applause.*) We offered a sort of armistice to our opponents, but while we put our swords in their sheaths, our opponents drew their swords and refused to accept the truce that we offered. And what has been the result? It is to be seen in the proceedings of the last session of Parliament, which, to my mind, were more humiliating to ourselves, to a great party, than I can recollect in the course of my political experience. We, who boasted a majority of 80 in the House of Commons, left the field to our opponents; we allowed them to carry, without opposition, resolutions to which the vast majority of our party were entirely opposed. I am convinced no such strain will ever again be put upon the loyalty of our party. I do not like running away from our political adversaries — (*applause*) — and I am perfectly prepared to join issue with them at the earliest possible moment. (*Cheers.*) Why should any of us fear an appeal to the country? (*Hear, hear.*) If we are victorious, well, then we shall once more be free men. We shall be rid of all those pledges; of those embarrassing restrictions upon our action; we shall be able with renewed strength, with definite and aggress-ive policy, to go forward to the accomplishment of our purpose. (*Cheers.*) But suppose we are beaten. Well, we have been beaten before now. (*Laughter.*) We don't expect to be always victorious, and I cannot for the life of me see that we should be any the worse off, even if we were beaten — (*hear, hear*) — for a time. (*Laughter and cheers.*) I do not propose, ladies and gentlemen, that we should remain in a minority for ever, but I say to you I would infinitely rather be part of a powerful minority than a member of an impotent majority. (*Cheers.*) We shall, in the case that I have suggested, resume the initiative of attack. We shall no longer be on our defence. We shall be able to submit the proposals of our opponents to what they have taught us to consider legitimate discussion. (*Laughter.*) Somehow or another it seems to me to open to us an agreeable prospect. (*Laughter.*) We shall, and this is the most important thing, shake off the apathy which has been born of timorous counsels and of half-hearted convictions. (*Hear, hear.*) If the Radicals win — let us project ourselves into the future — I do not think that their lot will be a happy one — (*laughter*) — or their life a long one. (*More laughter.*)

Chamberlain went on to attack recent speeches by Rosebery and Asquith. Then came the statement of his own positive policies.

I think that after so long a period of hard work we perhaps need a little repose — (*laughter*) — only we must take care to use the opportunity that will be afforded to us to close our ranks and agree upon a definite, constructive fighting policy — (*applause*) — to secure the unity of our party, not by ignoring our principles . . . but on the contrary by enforcing them with all the energy and ability at our disposal, and by securing their ultimate adoption.

Our policy can be understanded of the people, both what it is, how it is to be attained, and what it means. In the first place we want to secure more employment for the industrial population of this country. (*Applause.*) . . . any policy which will increase the employment of the working people of this country would be the greatest social reform which has ever been known. (*Cheers.*) . . .

Our second object is no less important. It is to strengthen the ties of unity between this country and the sister States which are rising daily into greater importance beyond the seas. (*Applause.*) . . . these two objects are closely connected. They stand together. You cannot, in my opinion, secure the results which you desire without adopting both of them.

What are the means by which we seek to secure these objects? They also are simple. We want the power of retaliation — (*hear, hear*) — against those who treat us badly — (*cheers*) — and we want the power of preference to those who treat us well. (*Renewed cheers.*) . . .

Now, I say to you I am well content with the progress that has been made. (*Applause.*) We might have done more if we had been thoroughly united — if some of those who ought to have been loyal had not dissevered themselves from the policy which shortly[1] became the policy of their party — if there had been more courage, and a little less playing for safety. (*Hear, hear.*) But in spite of that, what we have done? We have shaken to its base the idol of our opponents — (*hear, hear*) — of the free importers.

The speech had one immediate result in Birmingham. It provided the *Birmingham Post*, hitherto hostile to Tariff Reform, with an opportunity to change its mind and prepare to give full support to the Unionist candidates in the coming campaign.

It was also notable for another reason. On 1 November, Londonderry, the Lord President of the Council, had spoken at Sunderland.

---

[1] 'Shortly' — Chamberlain seems to have used the word in the sense of 'for a short time', referring presumably to the attitude of the party immediately after the 1903 resignations.

After referring to the 'dangerous split' in the Unionist Party, he had gone on to say that the forecast made by Chamberlain in 1903 had not been borne out by subsequent trade figures. As a result, he had continued, many who had been attracted by the glamour of the Tariff Reform policy were now flocking back to the banner of the only man qualified to speak on behalf of the Unionist Party, and that was the Prime Minister. The whole question of Fiscal Reform, he had argued, should be approached with the greatest caution. Meanwhile, both Tariff Reformers and Free Traders would do well to keep the Union of the Kingdom in the forefront of their programme and give only the second place to their economic views.

Chamberlain could hardly allow such a statement from a member of the Cabinet to go unanswered.

. . . no Government ever lives upon its past merits. It must always have, if it is to retain the confidence of the country, some great object, some inspiration for the future. I consider that we have such an object and such an inspiration.

I find it in the words of the Prime Minister himself — words which seem to me to have been insufficiently understood and insufficiently remembered. I am going to give them to you verbatim, as they were spoken at the end of the last session in the House of Commons. Mr. Balfour then said : '*Fiscal reform stands in the forefront of our constructive policy — and of all the branches of fiscal reform, that connected with drawing closer the commercial bonds between us and our Colonies is the most important part of our policy.*' That is the policy of the Prime Minister. That is, therefore, the policy of the Government. If there be any member of the Government who differs from that policy I cannot understand how he can honourably retain his place in the Ministry. (*Hear, hear.*) And under these circumstances I confess that I read with some surprise, and even with a little indignation, a speech made only two days ago by Lord Londonderry at Sunderland. Lord Londonderry is not one of the oldest — I would even say he is not one of the most important — members of the Cabinet. (*Laughter.*) He owes his position entirely to the Prime Minister. He has continually boasted of his loyalty to Mr. Balfour, and yet we find him supporting the Free Fooders, who are the bitterest enemies of that policy, and apparently desiring that the policy itself should be put into the background, should be subordinated to other considerations, when it may be forgotten altogether by his lordship, and when he may no longer be required to make up his mind on a question which his chief tells us is in the forefront of the constructive policy of the Unionist party. (*Applause.*) I understand loyalty in a different sense. (*Hear, hear.*)

Austen followed up his father's stinging rebuke with a firm letter to Balfour asking him to repudiate Londonderry. Something close to a Cabinet crisis ensued. Once again, Fitzroy's diary gives the best account.

4 November.—Chamberlain was at his best last night. . . . His smashing rejoinder to Londonderry, in referring to him as the creature of the Prime Minister, who yet misrepresented his policy and was disloyal to his aims, was instinct with savage contempt. The speech, however, is not an auspicious introduction to the appearance of the Prime Minister at Newcastle, whither he goes from Wynyard the week after next, and serves to illustrate the incompatibilities that it is Mr. Balfour's present task to reconcile.

Meanwhile, the Unionist Press, with one consent, advocates an early dissolution, and it will be seen whether Ministers are to justify Lloyd George's epigram that they will die with their drawn salaries in their hands.

6 November.—The materials for a crisis are all at hand. The amenities that have passed between Londonderry and the Chamberlains, have, it is believed, been followed by a temperate but strongly worded representation from J.C. to the Prime Minister asking for an early repudiation of Londonderry's assumption that he keeps the fiscal conscience of the Prime Minister and is better informed upon his views than Mr. Chamberlain. Without giving this communication the character of an ultimatum, it acquired particular significance, seeing that the Prime Minister's first opportunity for declaring himself will be at Newcastle next week, whither he goes to address the Conservative Association's annual gathering from Wynyard itself; and Sandars was no doubt right when, in conversation yesterday, he indicated that the outcome of the next Cabinet Council, which is to be held on Wednesday, will probably determine whether Ministers are 'men or mice'. Londonderry, having rushed blindly into an attack on Mr. Chamberlain, is now in consternation at the effect of his interference, and is telegraphing to his private secretaries instructions in which defiance is curiously mixed up with contradictions of some of the statements that have been made on his own behalf.

8 November.—A Cabinet crisis has been averted. The Prime Minister's ingenuity has again been equal to reconciling the irreconcilable. He saw Londonderry before the Cabinet met and treated him to a full measure of the dulcet charm which none can exercise so well as he. His indiscretions were dealt with very lightly, and in reward for reticence in the future he was promised that things should be made as easy for him at Newcastle as was possible. When the Cabinet met, Londonderry and Austen Chamberlain had an angry altercation across the table, but, after they had been permitted to blow off sufficient steam, the Prime Minister pointed out that there was still a residuum of principle upon which they could act together, and appealed to his colleagues not to destroy the edifice he had so laboriously built up, with, he might have added, approaches from all sides and ways of retreat in every direction. In the end Ministers were content to remain bound in the gossamer web of their chief's dexterities, and Austen will have to make the best of the situation with his father.[1]

---

[1] *Memoirs of Sir Almeric Fitzroy*, vol. i, p. 266.

Chamberlain's private views are shown in the following caustic note:

CHAMBERLAIN TO RIDLEY

8 November 1905: Private.—I confidently expect dissolution the beginning o, February, and we cannot make changes till after it is over.

I hope we shall make a great coup at Newcastle. Londonderry has done something to clear the situation but he is so stupid that he does not know it.

I expect they will have a hot time at the Cabinets, but I imagine that L. is not one of the resigning sort and I suppose they will go on somehow or other.

VIII

In his speech at Birmingham, Chamberlain had been outspoken in his censure of official Party policy in the previous session and had stressed the need for a definite programme. He had, however, been less categorical about the terms of such a programme than in his speech at the Albert Hall in July. He had made no reference, for instance, to the all-round tariff and had spoken only in passing of the need to tax wheat. These apparent omissions may have encouraged the Balfourians in the Government and some of the moderate Free Traders to make a last search for some compromise proposal on which the unity of the Party could be re-established before the election. The crisis caused by Londonderry's speech may also have had something to do with it. Whatever the immediate causes, Chamberlain now received an interesting and detailed proposal. It originated from Gerald Balfour who had been encouraged to take this initiative by talks with Balfour and with Goschen. Austen acted as intermediary.

AUSTEN TO CHAMBERLAIN

9 November 1905: Private.—Gerald Balfour dined with me last night. He has had some talk recently with the P.M. & with Goschen, & the result is that he asks the question can nothing be done even in the few weeks that remain to us to bring the party together?

I said he knew how cordially I desired this result, but I did not believe it to be possible now to unite all members of the party on any programme.

Gerald said of course some few were gone for good — Arthur Elliot or St. Loe Strachey for example & now that the end of this Parliament was so near he did not think the P.M. would have the same objection as earlier to 'shedding some'. In the course of the conversation he repeated this phrase more than once. 'He might now be willing to shed some.' But Gerald believes, partly from his talk with Goschen & partly from what reaches him from other sources, that many of the Free Fooders, and among them some of the most important, are ready for a compromise.

What has frightened them most in your programme he believes is not Preference or even a corn tax, but the idea of a *graduated* duty on manufactured imports. This, they think, is real Protection & it is against this idea of a graduated import tax that they are really fighting most keenly.

Gerald therefore suggested the following basis which he had in conversation mentioned to the P.M. & to Goschen. He could not say they would accept but 'neither of them had rejected it'.

1. Raw materials free.
2. A fixed 5% duty on manufactured imports.
3. This 5% duty to be doubled, or increased in any proportion, decided upon, by simple resolution of the House of Commons wherever required for retaliatory purposes.

This is a great improvement on any suggestion I have yet got from him for practical retaliation. It gives an automatic tariff for purposes of retaliation enforced by a single resolution of Parliament instead of by Bill. It is not as good as saying 'Our tariff is 10% or 20% but you can be admitted by agreement to our conventional rate of 5%, but it is at least practical & workmanlike & would give us all that is necessary.

4. The Corn Tax to be a *real* open question till the results of the conference are known.

This condition I elucidated more fully by questions. It means that we are not to pledge ourselves to a corn tax till we know what we could get for it, but it also means that we accept it as a possibility & that we openly state that a corn tax is permissible, that we have no objection to it in principle & that if it is proved at the Conference that

(a) such a tax is necessary in order to obtain a Colonial Preference &
(b) that by it we can obtain a satisfactory Colonial Preference, we shall then propose Preference on this basis. The rallied Free Fooders would therefore have honestly to abandon all declarations against a Corn Tax or a Corn Preference as such and would undertake to support the tax if the above two conditions were fulfilled.

I pointed out that Beach would not accept this proposition as his objection was to Preference in any shape & not to a tax on corn. Gerald agreed, but thought most 'Free Fooders' would come back to the fold on these terms. He even believed he might get back the Duke.

I cannot believe that the Duke would take these terms which are in fact all that you have asked of others since you opened your campaign, but Gerald was sanguine and, encouraged by me, promised that he would make a determined effort to get the P.M. to adopt them & negotiate upon them with the Free Fooders. He thinks that these gentlemen are seriously alarmed by the growing weakness of the Unionist party & by the very socialistic views which prevail among the Opposition, & that they would really be glad to accept such terms as he suggests.

I did not tell him *how good* I thought the terms — they are in fact very nearly what I proposed last August twelvemonth — but I did tell him that I thought his suggestion a very good one & that if the P.M. would adopt it, I felt confident that Tariff Reformers could be rallied to that standard.

So he will now make his 'determined effort' with the P.M. I am not sanguine of his success, but *nous verrons*!

Had there been any chance of a Unionist victory at the elections these proposals might well have been acceptable to the Tariff Reformers. But, in Chamberlain's view, there was no such chance. In these circumstances, Gerald Balfour's proposals raised a number of questions. Was it any longer in the interest of the cause of Tariff Reform to try and reunite the Party? Did Chamberlain want to get into a position where he would have to work with Goschen in an Opposition Shadow Cabinet? Was there anything to be gained by any concession at this stage which would make up for the sacrifice that would be asked from his supporters? Above all was the proposal sincere? or was it merely a device to bring the two sections together into a round table Conference which might restrict Chamberlain's freedom of action in a critical period? Chamberlain's reply dealt both with the merits of the proposal and with the political realities underlying it.

CHAMBERLAIN TO AUSTEN

10 *November* 1905.—I have your letter of the 9th for which I am very much obliged. It is not, as you know, a new proposition. Your guest made it to me a year-and-a-half ago when I stayed with him, and Percy, who was there — and who may have been the original author of the suggestion — said that he thought that some of the Free-Fooders would accept it. It was to be submitted to the Prime Minister, but I never heard anything more about it.

I should add that I think that at that time it was stated that the general rate might be anything from 5% to 10%. Of course circumstances have much altered since then, and it does not follow that a proposition which both sides might then have accepted as a compromise would now be equally agreeable to either. Personally I do not believe that any compromise of the kind is possible now. Just consider how it stands with both Parties:

(1) The Free Fooders. They, as their name implies, have relied on the prejudice against a food tax to defeat us. You remember Goschen's dishonest '*mot*' about 'gambling with the food of the people'. If they now give up this, not only would they be very inconsistent, but their agitation, such as it is, would be further weakened. They must also feel that such an arrangement could only be accepted by us as a preparation for more drastic proposals. It is the first step down the Niagara of which the Duke spoke. Accordingly if they took up the idea at all, it must be because they know they are beaten but want to save their faces, and I don't think the strong men among them have come to that yet.

(2) Now look at it from our point of view. In the first place the inquiries of the Tariff Commission seem to show clearly that no general

rate, the same for all manufactured goods, would be practicable. Even 5 % would be too high in some cases and on the other hand it would be much too low in others. An announcement that this was our programme would dissatisfy and discourage that very large number of supporters who, whatever Balfour may be, are undoubtedly Protectionists; not, of course, in the sense of wishing to go back to the system before Free Trade but with the honest conviction that some Protection is absolutely necessary if we are to retain our position in the home trade. No strength that the Free-Fooders could bring us would in any way compensate for the loss of what is undoubtedly the majority of our supporters. Again, the line taken by Free-Fooders such as Hugh Cecil has deeply offended our people. They would disapprove any compromise to which he adhered, and unless he and others like him are 'shed' we should lose the confidence of our friends. If such men go, what remains? There are the veterans like the Duke and Goschen who are worn out and useless, and there are also a much larger number who are not Free Fooders at all but only sitters on the fence and who will come to us whenever we have clearly proved that ours is the only popular policy.

(3) The plan sounds simple, but is it so in reality? Suppose that it is passed — what are we going to do? Are we to negotiate separately with each protected country, or are we going to clap on the additional duty at once, raising the 5 % to 10 % or 20 % until any of the protected come to us with an offer of a reciprocal arrangement. If we had the 'graduated duty', as you call it, to begin with it would of itself be sufficient to have an immediate effect and we could afford to wait for the separate negotiations which would then, I suppose, proceed simultaneously with other Powers. A fixed 5 %, however, would disorganise trade and, as I have pointed out, would operate very differently in different cases. Our plans in practice would, I think, discourage the people who would have returned us to power, and the clamour for further alterations would begin immediately.

I have said enough perhaps to indicate my objections, but you are quite right in entertaining the proposal and seeing what will come of it. We want to secure the Prime Minister clearly on our side and we might lose influence with him if he thought we were irreconcilable.

I expect it will be a Round Table Conference, which, as experience has shown me, is a very difficult and delicate business. We must listen to everything, but not commit ourselves prematurely or without the most careful consideration.

I think if the matter goes further, it must be made clear that the proposition comes from the other side. No doubt any advance from that quarter would help us for the same reason that if it were supposed to come from us it would be considered a weakness.

I had the opportunity when in London of seeing a number of our friends. My speech has put them in good spirits and they are burning for a fight. They do not in the least mind being beaten and they are all for a strong policy. I have to hold them back rather than to push them on.

Have you considered another point? If a formal reconciliation were patched up, some of the leading Free-Fooders would have to be brought into the councils of the party while in Opposition, and to be treated as probable members of a future fiscal reform government.   Are there any of them whom you could trust?   Would you like Hugh Cecil, for instance, in such a Cabinet?

I send you my first impression of the suggestions and hope I may have an opportunity of fuller discussion when I come to London next week.

Chamberlain's letter makes plain that though he did not wish to seem irreconcilable, in fact he was.   He did not want a reunion with the Free Fooders.   He wanted to force Balfour to choose between them and him.   Austen's grasp of the political realities was much less sure.   He wanted a reconciliation between his father and Balfour for its own sake more than in the interests of Tariff Reform.   He continued, moreover, to think in terms of the existing sections of the Party in Parliament as if another election would confirm the existing pattern of Unionist representation.

AUSTEN TO CHAMBERLAIN

12 *November* 1905.—I hope you will not lightly close your mind to all idea of compromise, especially if the 'compromise' is of the kind I take Gerald's suggestion to be.   It seems to me that if that scheme is the policy of the Party, we should have won the battle.   I don't care the Duke of Wellington's favourite coin for the Free Fooders, but I care enormously for getting Balfour onto your platform; & if he could be induced to lay this down as his policy, it would be an immense practical advance on anything he has yet said.   It would turn abstract theories into concrete proposals.   It would directly negative all the real free-food propositions & it would consecrate the idea of a general tariff.

There would be enormous gains for us, & if more were necessary, it would be bound to follow when once we had secured such a foothold.

It is just for these reasons that I don't believe real Free Fooders will ever accept the policy.   If they do, they are captives of your bow & spear, & you can do with them as you wish.   But I think a good many who are not real Free Fooders at heart would be glad of anything which enabled them to join up, & that Balfour will be more ready to 'shed' some of the party if in so doing he can reunite others solidly.   The real reunion that I want is between you and him.   The rest may go hang.   He is the fish for whom my hook is baited !

I admit that the fixed 5% revenue tariff is not perfect or scientific, but I do not think it would discourage any of our people.   Surely all of them would regard it as a great victory, & if calling it a 'revenue' tariff eases the consciences of some weaker brethren, the name won't make whatever Protection it embodies less protective or less worth having.

As regards retaliation, of course the best development of the fixed 5% policy would be to impose at once a fixed 10% duty on all foreign goods & to admit them to the 5% rate by negotiation.   But it would be infinitely better to have it clearly laid down that we could refuse the

5% & impose the 10% *by resolution* & on *all* their manufactured goods than to have to devise & pass through all the usual parliamentary stages a special retaliatory tariff against each country separately & in turn, against French wines, & then against German toys & Italian silks or cottons & American pills! Such a policy, as you have seen from the first, is an absurd impossibility, but Balfour evidently leant to it in his Blue Notes & in his Sheffield speech; & though I have converted Gerald I am not clear that Arthur B. has even yet definitely abandoned this policy in his own mind.

It is not, however, the retaliation side of your tariff scheme which has frightened the people of whom I spoke. It is the average 10% duty 'graduated *according to the amount of labour* in the goods' (I quote from memory) which sticks in the throats of some of those who are or might be our friends. They have misunderstood the phrase which occurred in your Glasgow speech & make mountains out of a mole-hill. In the Cabinet discussions last year on (I think) Winston's motion, I had great difficulty about these words, which seemed to me to indicate quite clearly the very simple idea that the rate of duty should vary with the stage reached in the manufacture of the goods — completed goods having a higher rate than the half worked material, e.g. steel rails a higher rate than billets or iron girders than pigs. But even Gerald & Alfred Lyttelton stumbled over them, & I think Selborne, who traced in them some obscure heresy in regard to labour. It was, I believe, really more a question of words than anything else, but it made a real difficulty.

You must also bear in mind that there is a considerable body of opinion very favourable to reform but genuinely afraid of opening the door to a 'scramble of interests'. I never quite know how far Hugh is sincere when he gets on this ground, & how far he plays on his own fears & purposely frightens himself. But I am sure that a good many people are genuinely moved by this argument & afraid that we should make the House & its Lobbies a den of thieves. It is very foolish, but the fear is there. Charles Booth for instance takes this line & presses for this reason for three fixed scales of duties:

(a) the normal, say a 5% which would give not Protection in the old sense but 'a turn' in favour of home industry.

(b) a lower rate or free entry for all Colonial wares.

(c) a higher, but also fixed, rate for retaliation.

Surely the establishment of such a tariff would spell victory for us. I anticipate that whenever we impose a tariff there will be a momentary reaction & complaints of the disturbance to trade will be rife. We must live these down as the Republicans lived down the outcry that prevailed in America when we were there in 1900. But with such a tariff as I have sketched, I should not have any fear of the ultimate result. We might have to alter, but we should never abolish, the tariff; & meanwhile we should be gaining experience of both trade & administration which would powerfully help us in any future steps to a more scientific solution of the problem. I confess that I a little shrink from the thought of attempting as our first essay in reform the elaboration of a tariff on the German model, & should like to fight the first great parliamentary battle of the tariff war on a simpler issue where we should expose a smaller front to the enemy's attacks.

When all is said & done, I confess to the fear that Gerald's scheme will come to nothing. But I don't want *you* to bring it to naught. The very fact that both you & I feel that the Free Fooders cannot accept it, shows how favourable it is to our views.

There's a Sunday sermon for you! Forgive it & don't bother to answer till we meet. I shall not have occasion to say or do any more in the matter for some time, I expect.

All your friends are delighted with your last speech. I hope you saw & appreciated *Punch*'s prophetic picture — 'Hounds or no hounds, I start hunting today'. Well, you will have a good pack when you show them such sport.

Chamberlain's reply showed that he would do nothing to hinder the formulation of the compromise proposals. He agreed with Austen on the tactics of the situation and was content to leave it at that.

CHAMBERLAIN TO AUSTEN

13 *November* 1905: *Private.*—I agree with you in great measure and will certainly not interfere by any premature speech or action to bring the discussion which you have raised to a close.

Like yourself, I am not at all sanguine as to the result, but I would prefer that the failure, if it comes, should be evidently due to the unreasonableness of others.

I shall watch with the greatest interest the proceedings at Newcastle which will constitute another stage in the controversy.

There the matter rested. Nothing more was heard of Gerald Balfour's proposals. Balfour himself was clearly doubtful about them.

BALFOUR TO GERALD BALFOUR [1]

10 *November* 1905.—Not only am I reluctant to put forward on the platform detailed plans of fiscal change, but I view with some apprehension any pledge to put a general import duty upon manufactured goods. It is quite true that, if revenue had to be raised, such a duty would be quite consistent with my economic views. But, surely, if we were to announce it when the necessity for additional revenue is not demonstrated, the universal inference would be that the tax was put on, not to raise revenue, but because it would afford some protection to manufacturers; while if I were to supplement the proposed declaration of policy, as I should have to do, with a statement that such injury to the agricultural consumer as this import duty might inflict would be made good to him by using the proceeds of the tax to relieve his rates, should I not go near to Joe's methods of bribing each class of the country in turn?

[1] *Arthur James Balfour* by Kenneth Young, p. 251.

IX

The next major event in the political calendar was the Conservative party Conference. This was to meet at Newcastle on 13
November.

As in 1903 and 1904, Chamberlain had prepared the ground
carefully with Chaplin's help. Together they drew up a resolution.
This embodied a number of carefully selected extracts from Balfour's
speeches by way of preamble and called for a declaration from the
conference in favour of

a readjustment of taxation which, without increasing the cost of their
food to the poorer classes of this country, will tend to secure fairer treatment of British manufacturers by foreign nations, will prevent the practice
of dumping and will largely increase reciprocal and preferential trade
between the different parts of the British Empire.

Chaplin tested the mood of the party at an Area Party Conference
on 23 October. He moved a Chamberlainite amendment to a
motion embodying the Balfour policy and carried it unanimously.

CHAMBERLAIN TO CHAPLIN

24 *October* 1905.—I . . . congratulate you on the success of your action.
It confirms all that I have said as to the absolute safety of an appeal
to the rank and file. It is the wire-pullers only and the purely official
section who are against us and stand in the way of an active, definite
and aggressive programme.

I hope and believe that all will come right at Newcastle. Do not forget
that we must get you into the chairmanship and that you must be
supported by a majority on the governing body.

Next day Chaplin was able to report that their resolution for
the Newcastle conference had successfully passed the meeting of
the National Union Executive and Council.

CHAPLIN TO CHAMBERLAIN

25 *October* 1905: *Private.*—The Resolution, with the addition of eight
words in one of the quotations, was unanimously accepted by both
Executive and Council this afternoon as it stood.

The only rock ahead now is the possibility of the vote being delayed
and shut out till after Balfour's Speech by motions on organisation, of
which there are now 2.

I think however I shall be able to get round that somehow. The Central
Office are in a funk for the feeling of the party everywhere is very strong
— about the conditions of the organisation. If Hampstead is lost it will
be for that reason again.

In fact the discussions on Party organisation were the occasion of a preliminary victory. Chaplin threatened a direct attack on the Central Office. Wells, the Chief Agent, who was rightly or wrongly regarded as a stumbling block to the Tariff Reformers, resigned his post in consequence.

At Newcastle, Chaplin duly moved the Chamberlainite resolution. An amendment was proposed asking the Conference to declare instead

its cordial support of the policy of the Prime Minister . . . as detailed by him on a halfsheet of notepaper, the text of which has been issued as a leaflet by the Publication Committee of this Association.

This was rejected by an overwhelming majority after which Chaplin's resolution was carried with only two dissentients. The meaning of the Conference was unmistakable. The delegates preferred Chamberlain's interpretation of Balfour's policy to Balfour's own.

CHAMBERLAIN AND CHAPLIN

Chaplin to Chamberlain: 14 *November* 1905

My dear Joe,

A veritable triumph I think today. The resolution carried intact and *unanimously* after an amendment . . . had been defeated by a crushing majority . . .

I am just off, but you may be satisfied we have done a real good day's work, and the whole conference is delighted.

Neither Londonderry nor Hugh Cecil phoned, though in the town.

Chamberlain to Chaplin: 16 *November* 1905

My dear Harry,

. . . I telegraphed congratulations to you at Blagdon as I did not know your address.

I agree that the proceedings were a great triumph and fully justified your and my anticipations. The Free Fooders were evidently afraid to try conclusions. They must know that they are in an infinitesimal minority.

Henceforth Chamberlain and Chaplin would be 'Joe' and 'Harry' to each other; a degree of intimacy which Chamberlain neither gave to nor received from anyone else on the Unionist side.

Balfour's speech at the Conference was anything but the clear lead Chamberlain had called for. In parts, indeed, it was a reply to the Birmingham speech. The Prime Minister went out of his way to defend the policy of abstention from the fiscal debates of March as necessary in the interests of Party Unity.

'I was not afraid of the Opposition,' he said. 'I was afraid of my friends.' He made no reference to the resolution carried by the Conference but urged all sections to rally to his fiscal policy which, he implied, should be acceptable to them all.

The speech was coldly received. It pleased neither section. James noted in his diary:

13 *November* 1905.—Notwithstanding the protests made by the Duke of D., Goschen and myself, A.J.B., when speaking at Newcastle-on-Tyne today, appears to have deserted Free Trade. His speech was most unsatisfactory, especially to us Free-traders. He only begs us not to raise the question, and so would leave a free field to Chamberlain. This cannot be, and I shall do all I can to bring our forces into the field.[1]

To Chamberlain, the speech seemed 'very poor' and he praised Chaplin for criticising it at a subsequent meeting. Mrs. Chamberlain wrote:

At Newcastle, Mr. Balfour's speech in the evening elucidated nothing. He appealed for a United front and announced that, as the leader, he expected to be followed. The result of course has been Tariff Reform dissatisfaction and Free Food suspicions.[2]

X

After the Conference, Balfour was still undecided when to bring on the election. On 15 November, he was still discussing various alternatives. Esher noted this next day.

While I was waiting to see Sandars in Downing Street, Bob Douglas came in. The P.M. was to go to Windsor by the 6.30 train, but he wished to have a discussion first about the date of a resignation of the Government.

He sent Sandars in to say that he would like me to be present, and began by analysing the situation. There were two courses:

(a) to resign in the middle of December.
(b) to call Parliament together early, i.e. January 16th, and resign after the first Division.

The former possesses tactical advantages, as it forces the opposition to show their hand, but it is inconsistent with the attitude adopted by the P.M. all along, and would be unpopular with the Party.

While the latter is full of unpleasant difficulties, especially the necessity of introducing a Redistribution Bill, Acland Hood and Douglas nevertheless favour the latter course, and Sandars favours the former. The P.M. asked my view, and I said I knew nothing about politics, but of the two courses I preferred the latter, as it left his reputation for consistency and straightness unattacked.

---

[1] Lord Askwith, *Lord James of Hereford*, p. 288.
[2] Mrs. Chamberlain to her mother, 15 November 1905.

But I could not see why he should not dissolve on January 2nd. The idea that it is necessary to put your opponents in to dissolve is a superstition, unless they have to remain some time in office prior to dissolving. In the present case an appeal to the country would come constitutionally and properly from a Minister whom the Opposition have been unable to turn out, when the term of the Parliament itself is approaching finality.[1]

A few days later, on 13 November, Balfour again travelled to Windsor. This time he shared a first-class compartment with Chamberlain and Mrs. Chamberlain. They had been asked for the weekend to meet the King of Greece who was on a State visit.

In the train, they had 'a very frank conversation, civil but unsparing'. Chamberlain urged the overwhelming reasons for an immediate dissolution.

'I tell you, Arthur, you will wreck the Party if you go on. You should have dissolved two years ago.'

Balfour seemed at last, though not easily, convinced that an election must be faced, and remarked finally: 'Well, I suppose you are right.'[2]

This frank conversation seems to have improved relations between the two men. The weekend gave them further opportunities for discussion. We have no record of these further talks, though Mrs. Chamberlain has given us some idea of their atmosphere.

Saturday night.—As soon as dinner was over we adjourned to the Waterloo Chamber which had been turned into a theatre. ... I sat at the King's table, with Lord Roberts as my cavalier and Mr. Balfour on my other side as he had been at the play. He was delightful — the little *gêne* quite gone which I sometimes thought he had — or rather the tinge of shyness.

In fact all through our visit it was non-existent, and the old camaraderie and intimacy of political talk so complete that it would have given food for reflection to some of our 'friends', and certainly made me feel that one still belonged to the Cabinet circle. I am speaking now of myself, for it gave me much satisfaction, and with Joe it was the same as always. Their personal relations were of the most cordial, and they had one or two talks together which I think were good for both. I attach so much importance to meetings of this kind that I was very glad the opportunity presented itself. At the present juncture it was especially useful, for this week we have been in the throes of a 'new political crisis' according to the papers.

Sunday.—As I and Joe and Mr. Balfour were going along the corridors after church we encountered the King and Queen of Greece. They at once stopped and the Queen took hold of Joe's arm and turned him

[1] Viscount Esher, *Journals and Letters*, p. 118.
[2] Mrs. Chamberlain in conversation.—J. A.

round to look at himself in the shape of a portrait of Pitt. The King of Greece had thought the bust was of Joe, and was much astonished when he found it was not.[1]

Contemporary opinion and most histories have attributed Balfour's decision to resign to the speech which Chamberlain made at Bristol on the following Tuesday, 21 November. This is almost certainly an oversimplification. Chamberlain always denied it.

'It is not true that the speech altered Balfour's attitude,' he wrote later to Parker Smith.[2] While four days after the Bristol speech, Balfour noted:

25 *November* 1905.—My own leanings towards a December resignation took shape before that speech (J.C. at Bristol).

They were communicated to the King last week at Windsor and to such of my colleagues as I happened to meet, hours or days before the Bristol speech. I do not, of course, by this mean to imply that the speech leaves matters precisely as they were.

Esher, who may well have had the news from King Edward, noted in his diary on the Monday:

20 *November*.—. . . I think the P.M. has made up his mind to see the King on the 15th and retire. He will be glad to be free from office.[3]

It seems probable, therefore, that the talks between Chamberlain and Balfour in the train and at Windsor led to a provisional decision on Balfour's part to resign before Christmas. If so, it was now Chamberlain's interest to make it difficult for Balfour to change his mind. He had had, after all, too much experience of the Prime Minister's hesitations and qualifications, to regard any agreement they might seem to have reached at Windsor as binding. The best way to clinch the position was undoubtedly to launch an all-out attack on the Free Fooders and the doubters. There could, then, be no further question of a sufficient Unionist majority to justify the Prime Minister in meeting Parliament.

The occasion of Chamberlain's speech at Bristol was the annual Conference of the Liberal Unionist Council. Most of the Liberal Unionist Ministers stayed away, but there was an immense demand for seats at the mass meeting. The following anecdote shows something of the popular mood at least in Bristol:

A.—I'm a poor man and can't afford to pay 10/– for a seat in the gallery.
B.—It's well worth a guinea just to see him say 'Free Fooder'.

---

[1] Mrs. Chamberlain to her mother, 23 November 1905.
[2] 30 November 1905.   [3] *Journals and Letters of Viscount Esher*, p. 120.

The Bristol speech was a clear reaffirmation of Chamberlain's own policy and a blunt refusal to heed Balfour's appeal for Party unity. He began by stressing the need for the leader of a political party to be in harmony with his followers. His words were plainly aimed at Balfour.

This afternoon the conference of delegates from all parts of the United Kingdom has been held . . . in order to exchange views upon the political situation, and to state their conclusions and impress these views upon the leaders of their party. . . . As the president, whom they have selected — (*cheers*) — I want to say how deeply I value such assistance as conferences of this kind can render to a leader ; in fact, it seems to me that no leadership, no successful leadership, is possible unless the leader is constantly in close touch with his party, unless he knows their views, and I will even say, unless he can honestly and conscientiously say that he shares these views. (*Cheers.*) Well, today the conference has discussed the greatest question of the time. They have spoken in no uncertain voice and with extraordinary unanimity, and I am glad to think that I am in absolute agreement with the conference . . . and that we are working together for the same object and with the same enthusiasm. (*Cheers.*)

But the passage which was to cause the greatest *furore* was Chamberlain's blunt rejection of Balfour's appeal for unity and tolerance between the Unionist sections.

Now, ladies and gentlemen, we are standing on the very brink of a general election. (*Hear, hear.*) There are many prophecies that have been made as to the result. I will venture on no predictions — (*hear, hear*) — but I will say this : If you want to win now or later — if your policy is to bring with it the full application of the principles which you have desired to establish, believe me you must have a forward policy — (*cheers*) — you must not suffer it to be whittled down by the timid or the half-hearted minority of your party — (*cheers*) — you must not ask the majority, be it nine-tenths, or, as I think, ninety-nine-hundredths — (*hear, hear*) — you must not ask them to sacrifice their convictions to the prejudices of the minority. (*Cheers.*) No army was ever led successfully to battle on the principle that the lamest man should govern the march of the army. (*Hear, hear.*) I say you must not go into the battle which is impending, with blunted swords, merely in order to satisfy the scruples of those who do not wish to fight at all. (*Hear, hear.*) I think that is understood. (*Hear, hear.*) The Liberal Unionist Council, in its unreformed condition, was insufficiently representative, and it halted between two opinions. What is the result? It was absolutely paralysed and impotent. Twelve months ago it resolved to join issue. It attended to the rank and file, it appealed to the constituents of the party, and what was the result? The vast majority of the army pronounced in no uncertain voice. (*Cheers.*) What happened? We lost some of the friends whom we would very gladly have kept if they had agreed with us — (*laughter*) — we lost a few score — it may even be a few hundreds; and thousands and tens of thousands have taken their places. (*Laughter and cheers.*) We have had every promise of support, we have formed new branches, apathy has given place to enthusiasm, we are stronger than we were a year or two years ago — infinitely stronger, because we have had the courage of our opinions, because we have dared to express them and to stand for them, because we are once more a united party, pledged to defend this country against disruption and to promote the union of the Empire. (*Cheers.*) There is the experience, the example of the Liberal Unionist organisation, for all to read. Is there any doubt that the position of the Conservative party is less clear or less decided? If there was, what happened a week ago at the great meeting of the National Union of Conservative Associations? You have there a resolution carried through with practical unanimity in favour of a strongly definite constructive policy. (*Hear, hear.*)

I see in papers, I hear in speeches, talk about the divisions in the Unionist party. Where are they? (*Hear, hear.*) There is a most grotesque exaggeration on the part of the people who make the divisions. (*Hear, hear.*) Of course, if there are a thousand people on one side and one on the other it is a division. (*Laughter and cheers.*) Now I say this, that after the two manifestoes of today and of this day week no reasonable, no honest man will doubt for a moment that the Unionist party is substantially agreed — (*hear, hear*) — upon the two main objects of the future constructive policy. We are agreed upon Retaliation — (*loud cheers*) — we are agreed upon Preference. (*Renewed cheers.*) I will add to that, because I am determined to withhold nothing in my appeal to the country — (*cheers*) — you can't have Retaliation, and the more you look at it the more it will be clear to you, without a general tariff; you can't have Preference — that is to say, you can't secure from your kinsmen abroad the advantages which will secure to you their trade, their ever-increasing trade, unless you think in the same spirit — (*cheers*) — unless you will treat them a little better than your rivals and competitors, unless you will give to them, in return for a Preference on your manufactures, a Preference on their chief product, even although that product may be described as a principal part of the food of this country. (*Hear, hear.*) It is useless to hide yourselves in the sand, and because our opponents indulge in the grossest misrepresentations and the most colossal lies — (*cheers*) — I say it is perfectly absurd for us to think that we can meet these misrepresentations by trying to hide what our policy is. Let us defend our policy. (*Hear, hear.*) My object is to make clear what it is. '.. It is 'more work for the people of this country — (*cheers*) — and a closer union between the different parts of the Empire'. (*Renewed cheers.*)

The Bristol speech did not go much further than Chamberlain's speech in the Albert Hall in July. But coming, as it did, in reply to Balfour's speech at Newcastle, it had immensely more impact.

Two days later, *The Times* and *The Daily Telegraph* both carried leading articles arguing that the speech left the Government no choice but to resign. *The Times*, which openly took Chamberlain's side, pointed out that Balfour's appeal to Unionists to cease from

recriminations and to unite behind his fiscal policy had met with
no 'adequate response from the Party as a whole'. Chamberlain,
it went on,

not only did not respond to the appeal but put it aside altogether and
made a different and incompatible appeal — an appeal to the Unionist
party to unite in accepting and fighting for his own fiscal policy.

The Daily Telegraph was more critical of Chamberlain. But it
admitted that Balfour's policy was no longer that of the strongest
elements in his Party and that, in the circumstances, he could not
carry on.

Mrs. Chamberlain had been delighted by the meeting.

It was a fine audience : he was in good form. The speech was delivered
in his best style ; and, for force and vigour, satisfied even me.

After reading the papers on 22 November, she wrote,

I begin seriously to think that the Government will not meet Parliament after all.[1]

The impact of the Bristol speech on the political world in London,
may be judged by the following extracts from Fitzroy's diary.

22 *November*.—London was scared this morning by ominous articles in
'The Times' and 'Daily Telegraph' intimating that after Mr. Chamberlain's
speech the Prime Minister had no choice but an early resignation. . . .
Both papers seem to assume that Campbell-Bannerman would have no
choice but to step into the breach and lose all the advantages that
obviously belong to the construction of a Cabinet after, rather than before,
a general election. The calculation seems to be that, Chamberlain
having failed to respond to Mr. Balfour's appeal for unity, has left him
no choice, unless he is prepared to see the party go to the country with
an avowedly Protectionist programme under the other's leadership.

24 *November*.—The Cabinet rose after more than two hours' deliberation, with no more definite resolution than to meet again next Friday.
Before they met I saw Linlithgow, who was very strong on the indignity
to which the Prime Minister had been exposed by the proceedings at
Newcastle and their sequel in Mr. Chamberlain's speech : circumstances
which in his opinion made an early resignation inevitable, as the only
course consistent with self-respect. I was a little surprised, however, to
hear from Londonderry, after the Cabinet was over, that not only was the
whole question postponed for a week, but it was still undecided whether
they would meet Parliament. It is clear that 'The Times' and 'Telegraph',
with whatever inspiration they may have acted, overdid their brief, as
newspapers are apt to do ; but for all that the situation remains much
as they described it, and resignation or dissolution present the only
possible alternatives.[2]

---

[1] Mrs. Chamberlain to her mother, 22 November 1905.
[2] *Memoirs of Sir Almeric Fitzroy*, vol. i, p. 268.

In the memorandum of 25 November, which we have already quoted, Balfour wrote :

I do not, of course, by this mean to imply that the speech leaves matters precisely as they were.

He did not explain precisely how in his opinion they were changed. In two respects, however, the speech must have been decisive. First, it must have clinched Balfour's provisional decision not to meet Parliament again. Second, it must have decided the manner of his going. It must be resignation not dissolution. Dissolution would have meant going to the country as a united Government. There was no chance, after the Bristol speech, of finding any formula on fiscal policy to which the different sections in the Cabinet and the Party could agree.[1]

XI

If the Bristol speech determined the manner of Balfour's going, the timing of it was suggested by an incident in the Liberal camp.

Irish policy had been almost as sharp a cause of difference among Liberals as fiscal policy among Conservatives. The Radical and middle sections of the Party leaned to Home Rule. The Liberal Imperialists, Rosebery, Asquith, Grey and Haldane, were sharply opposed to it. Since mid-September negotiations had been in progress chiefly between Campbell-Bannerman and Asquith to find a formula on Irish policy to which they could all agree. They settled on what came to be known as the 'step by step solution'. There was to be no Home Rule Bill in the next Parliament, though there might be a step in that direction which, if accepted by the country, might be followed by other steps in subsequent Parliaments until the complete goal was reached. Asquith, Grey and Haldane agreed to these *salami* tactics. Rosebery was away. Unaccountably his friends neither consulted him, nor even informed him of what had been decided.

On 23 November, Campbell-Bannerman gave expression to 'the step by step' solution in a speech at Stirling. He advised the Irish to accept any instalment of representative control 'provided it was consistent with a lead up to the larger policy'.

Rosebery, wholly in the dark as to what has passed between Asquith and Campbell-Bannerman, spoke at Bodmin two days

[1] Balfour seems to have told the King that it was his intention to resign and not to meet Parliament about this time. See the King's letter to Balfour of 26 November 1905 expressing his regret.

later (25 November). He denounced Campbell-Bannerman's decision to revive the policy of Home Rule and declared

I will say no more on this subject except to say emphatically and once for all that I cannot serve under that Banner.

Balfour, of course, had no idea that Asquith had forgotten Rosebery. He read the Bodmin speech as meaning that none of the Liberal Imperialists would accept Campbell-Bannerman as their leader. Given time they would, no doubt, overcome their differences. But, if Balfour resigned at once, it might well be that Campbell-Bannerman would be quite unable to form a Government. Here, so it seemed, was a chance to inflict a damaging blow on the Liberals, right at the start.

On 28 November, Balfour discussed the question of resignation in Cabinet. Esher wrote in his diary:

28 *November.*—Today saw the P.M. He has decided to resign on Monday. His Cabinet were divided ; but Lansdowne, Lyttelton, A. Chamberlain were on his side.

At Highbury, uncertainty reigned. But the next day brought a letter from Austen, hinting darkly that the decision was as good as taken.

AUSTEN TO CHAMBERLAIN

29 *November* 1905*: Private.*—Nothing is certain yet, but I have great hopes that *after* Monday next we shall each of us be able to settle our future plans for the winter with full knowledge of all the engagements we are likely to have to carry out.

I haven't felt so lighthearted for a long time. Heaven send that I am not even now living in a fool's paradise !

On the eve of the great decision Chamberlain wrote to Northcote giving his analysis of the situation and his forecast for the future.

CHAMBERLAIN TO NORTHCOTE

30 *November* 1905*: Private.*—Your letter reaches me in the midst of a sort of political crisis made so chiefly by the newspapers in search of a sensation and especially by the *Telegraph,* whose friendship for Balfour is often indiscreet. The inner history of the matter is as follows :

Balfour has for some time found his position almost intolerable and has held office against his own judgment because he felt that many of his colleagues and the majority of his party in the House of Commons were opposed to dissolution. Why they should be so it is difficult to understand. Probably, however, their feelings are akin to those of the child who postpones as long as possible his visit to the dentist. Now, I think, he has made up his mind, and as the responsibility and power are wholly

2 C

in his own hands, I expect that before this reaches you, and probably about the middle of next month, his resignation will be announced.

In that case the King will send for Campbell-Bannerman and I think he cannot well refuse to take office. He will have to form a Government and dissolve in January, so that the new Parliament will meet in the middle of February, when I expect stirring times and plenty of occupation.

The *Telegraph* has been declaring that Balfour's determination is due to differences between him and myself as evidenced by his speech at Newcastle and mine at Bristol, but there is no foundation whatever for this statement. Our respective positions are exactly as they were last year, and you may absolutely disbelieve any rumours or statements to the effect that our friendship has been affected or that I have or ever have had any idea of supplanting him. I do, however, earnestly hope that I may induce him to express himself a little more clearly and decidedly. If he were to do so we should lose the Free-Fooders headed by Lord Hugh Cecil. They are very few in number and I would much rather see them outside the party than remaining in for the sole purpose of acting as a drag upon the wheels. The rest of the party in the House of Commons and practically the whole of the rank and file would go enthusiastically for my policy if they were certain that Balfour and I were in the same boat.

Meanwhile another sensation has been created by Campbell-Bannerman's declaration in favour of Home Rule and Rosebery's emphatic repudiation of that policy. I do not think that the latter has any longer much influence with the Radical party, but his position as a candid friend must be most embarrassing to them. What they are really contemplating is the repudiation of any present intention of proposing a separate Parliament in Ireland, while they hope to satisfy the Irish by promising them Home Rule by instalments. The administration is gradually to be placed in the hands of the Home Rulers and by that time they hope and believe that the substance having gone there will no longer be any objection to allowing the shadow to go with it. It is not a very honest policy and they find much difficulty in explaining it in terms to be understanded by the people. I fancy that Asquith, Sir Edward Grey, and Haldane will shout with the biggest mob — in other words they will leave Rosebery and pretend to be satisfied with 'C. B.'s' explanations, but a party formed on such a programme and only brought together by ignoring differences cannot last very long whatever its apparent majority may be. I still think they will get a large nominal majority of 120 or 140, but even this will leave them in the hands of the Irish who can transfer 85 votes on an emergency from one side to the other and so leave them in a minority of at least 30. They have other difficulties of a serious character. They have denounced Chinese labour in South Africa, but I do not think they will dare to meddle with it. If they do, I am afraid that the feeling in South Africa will be very strong against this interference from England and will place them as the advocates of self-government in a very difficult position.

Then they are pledged to deal with education in a sense which must be objectionable to the Roman Catholics in England and also to the priests in Ireland. They have also promised large economies which can only be effected by a reduction of the Army and Navy for neither of which is the country really prepared.

Altogether I predict that they will find their position in authority as something very different from that of mere critics. I do not know what they will do about a conference. I hope that if one is summoned the Australian Government will take care to ascertain very clearly beforehand how far they are to be allowed a free discussion, and if Preference is to be tabooed I suppose that Deakin would not leave Australia for what must prove a barren meeting. I agree with him that negotiations for Preference between the Colonies would be a step favourable to our ultimate aims, and I think Dr. Jameson and the other South African Prime Ministers would meet him half way.

Next day a further letter from Austen brought the definite news Chamberlain had waited for so long.

AUSTEN TO CHAMBERLAIN

30 *November* 1905: *Secret.*—You may take it as certain now that Balfour will place his resignation in the King's hands on Monday next & that H.M. will accept it & send for C. B.

This, of course, will be known as soon as the P.M. goes to Sandringham, but it won't do to alter any of our engagements till after it has become public property.

Today, I see, is Thanksgiving Day in America — & here too, is it not?

In fact Balfour reported the Cabinet as still divided on its course of action as late as 2 December. But in the end the Prime Minister had his way, and on 4 December he tendered his resignation to the King.

So ended the great Unionist administration which had governed Britain almost without interruption since 1886. It could lay claim to immense achievements in Imperial, social and foreign affairs. Had its leaders gone to the country in the autumn of 1903 they might conceivably have secured a further mandate. As it was, two years of hesitation, internal strife and inability to grasp the new moods that were stirring had robbed it of all credit. The Administration which had added the South African Republics, much of West and East Africa and the Sudan to the Empire; the Administration which had kept the peace in Europe and Asia, and had concluded the Entente Cordiale and the treaty with Japan; the Administration which had introduced the Workman's Compensation Act and compulsory Free Education, was literally hooted off the stage.

Chamberlain spoke at Oxford on 7 December. He went out of his way to pay a tribute to Balfour. It was his answer to the rumours, not wholly unfounded, that he had forced the Government to resign.

One word I would ask leave to say for myself personally. It has been one of the privileges of my long political career that I have been associated for many years with Mr. Balfour, out of office, and in office. I have been proud to work with him in Opposition, I have been proud to work with him and under him in a Government (*cheers*) ; and during the whole of that time there has never come between us any difference which has in the slightest degree affected our personal friendship or our political relation. (*Cheers.*) Now, with little hope indeed that I shall convince those who do not want to be convinced, I repeat again what I have said on previous occasions, that, although we have had differences, as all men must have when they endeavour to co-operate, those differences have always been differences of detail, never differences of principle, and they have never interfered in any way, or could have interfered, with our perfect co-operation. (*Cheers.*)

Two minor consequences of the Government's fall are worth recording. Ritchie called at Downing Street to lay claim to a Viscounty. Sandars, as we have seen, was not particularly well disposed to Chamberlain. But he had a strong personal aversion to Ritchie and held him, besides, responsible for the miseries of the Government. He told him, rather rudely, that he deserved nothing ; and it is almost certainly due to his influence that Balfour only gave his ex-Chancellor a barony.[1]

The other consequence concerned Austen. He lost not only his job but his house. Mrs. Chamberlain wrote at once to welcome him back to their home.

MRS. CHAMBERLAIN TO AUSTEN

6 *December* 1905.—A headache yesterday prevented me from sending a few lines to you, but I cannot have you leave Downing Street without them.

Now that you no longer are a Cabinet Minister, and the end we have desired so long has come, I want to tell you once more how truly we have appreciated the difficulties with which you have had to contend, how great has been our sympathy with you, and how proud we have been of the way in which you have fulfilled the duties of your high office and the manner in which you have won the respect and affection of your colleagues.

Throughout the most trying times we have never doubted that you were doing just what your father wished you to do when he urged you to remain in the Government, and though I know you have had many moments of doubt and discouragement yourself, I hope and believe that later, if not *already*, you will feel no hesitation in acknowledging to yourself that your decision was the right one, and that you were able to accomplish what could have been done in no other way.

It is a source of the greatest satisfaction to your father and us all that you have been so important a member of the Cabinet, and that the

[1] Unpublished papers of J. S. Sandars.

honour came to you from your own ability and exertions younger than it does to most men. The thought that you were there to keep the road open between Mr. Balfour and your father has helped *me* through many a difficult stage in the two anxious years which have passed since he resigned.

Of course, the future is not easy, but I feel very hopeful that it may hold much that is good in store for us. It is natural that I should feel this more than you do just now. You have been too wearied by the stress not to feel that the difficulties appear well nigh insurmountable. *But I don't believe they are*, and after a little time of rest I believe some of them will vanish more easily than you expect, and with greater perspective the scene will become clearer.

I need not tell you how we shall rejoice to have you return to our roof tree. When you left it two years ago I felt it more than likely that you would decide you must have a nook of your own when you gave up your official house, and had you so wished I could not have urged you to do otherwise, for I should have understood. But as you have decided of your own free will to come back to such limited quarters as it is only in our power to provide for you, the welcome which we give you in our hearts will, I hope, be some compensation to you for the loss of freedom which is inevitable in giving up your own establishment.

I have missed you more than I can express, and am looking forward to the resumption of our old habits with the utmost pleasure, and your father has, I know, the same feeling that I have. Indeed, it would have been a bitter blow to him had it been otherwise, even though he might have approved.

Your being at home in London will, I think, make his House of Commons work both easier and more interesting to him. This you must not forget.

My few lines have expanded into a long letter, longer than I meant to trouble you with when you must be busy winding up your affairs, but that you will forgive me.

Difficulties lived through together but tighten and strengthen the bonds of true friendship, and sometimes one likes the friend to realize that one feels this.

P.S. Now I have your telegram saying to expect you today. I will not destroy my letter, but leave it on your table instead of posting it.

Austen had been asked to remain in the Cabinet after Chamberlain's resignation. His promotion to the Exchequer had made the proposal attractive. The belief that his father and Balfour were working for the same end made it acceptable. But as the rift between the two men grew, his position became increasingly invidious. Nor once involved, could he extricate himself. He was, after all, only an Ambassador — for all the trappings of his office — and was never free to take a line of his own. This in itself prevented him from ever exercising much personal influence over his colleagues in the

Cabinet. As his father's Ambassador he played his part honourably and efficiently. Only one thing can be reproached him. As a member of the Cabinet he was in close touch with Balfour and should have realised much sooner than he seems to have done how great was the difference of opinion and still more of interest between Balfour and his father. He would have played his part better if he had warned Chamberlain of the Prime Minister's fundamental indifference to the new policy or if he had sought to devise means for forcing Balfour's hand in the Cabinet. Instead he seems to have been primarily responsible for nourishing his father's illusions of Balfour's friendship and sympathy. It may be that he was taken in by Balfour's amiable professions. He had his own future, too, to think of. His star had risen like a meteor and, if a split in the Party could be avoided, he had every chance of succeeding to the Unionist leadership.

VICTORY IN DEFEAT

(December 1905–January 1906)

A Visit to Oxford — Chamberlain and Curzon — Plight of the Free Fooders — Chamberlain Rejects any Compromise — His Part in the Campaign — His Election Address — Campaign Speeches — The 'Smash' — 'We are Seven' — Post Mortem.

I

THE difficulties which attended the formation of the Liberal Government have been described by its principal members or their biographers. Some observers, at the time, judged that Campbell-Bannerman could not overcome them. His Liberal Imperialist colleagues certainly made determined efforts to push him 'up-stairs' to the House of Lords. Asquith at one time made this a condition of accepting office; and Grey was only with difficulty persuaded to serve in a Cabinet from which Rosebery was excluded. Nevertheless, within five days, the Ministry was complete. On 11 December the new team kissed hands; a slower process than usual, for there was a thick fog that day; and Ministers had to abandon their conveyances and grope their way to the Palace.

Soon afterwards, at a mass meeting in the Albert Hall (23 December) Campbell-Bannerman presented his Ministers to the world. Opinion was unanimous that, despite their differences, they were a stronger and abler Government than those who had ruled since the resignations of 1903. Campbell-Bannerman passed judgment on Balfour's Government that day. It is not the whole truth, but it represented the bulk of opinion at the time.

> . . . We were told — told emphatically and abundantly — that the method of their (the Government's) going would be a masterpiece of tactical skill. Tactics! Tactics! Ladies and gentlemen, the country is tired of their tactics. It would have been better for them if they had had less of tactics and more of reality. But they have lived for some years on nothing but tactics and now they have died of tactics.[1]

[1] J. A. Spender, *The Life of Campbell-Bannerman*, vol. ii, p. 206.

Chamberlain meanwhile had gone to Oxford where he stayed with Warren, the President of Magdalen. Two anecdotes from this visit throw a curious light on his personality.

The senior scholar at the college was a Birmingham man. His academic success had been outstanding and he was to be presented to Chamberlain along with the Fellows of the college. All were assembled in the senior common room, as if to meet royalty; all save the senior scholar. The thought of meeting Chamberlain face to face had been too much for him, and he had sent a message asking to be excused.

The same senior scholar, however, went to Chamberlain's meeting at the Town Hall. What he saw there confirmed the awe with which he regarded Chamberlain. During the latter's speech a rather drunken member of the audience got up and began shouting 'good old Joe'. The interruption, though friendly, became tiresome. Chamberlain stopped short and turned a withering glare on the interrupter. The poor man subsided, blushing with confusion and trembling all over.[1]

On his return to London, Chamberlain entertained Milner and Curzon to dinner at Claridges. It was the night the Liberal Ministers kissed hands (11 December). 'Joe', Mrs. Chamberlain had written before the dinner,

thought he would like to see Curzon soon, as, if it is possible, he is anxious to secure his interest in the question of preference.[2]

If these three had been prepared to work together, they would have formed a very strong Imperial group within the Unionist party. But the attempt proved vain. 'Curzon', Mrs. Chamberlain was forced to write,

is hopeless for Joe's cause. He is so full of his own grievance as to be absorbed by it. India, he says, is only a pawn in the game.[3]

Milner was more sympathetic but he shunned the limelight and had not yet recovered from the strain of his South African years.

II

It could now be only a matter of weeks to the election. The different sections of Unionism had accordingly to decide the policies on which they would appeal to the people. Balfour's resignation had

---

[1] I owe these anecdotes to Lord Longford, who heard them from the 'senior scholar' in question.
[2] Mrs. Chamberlain to her mother, 6 December 1905.
[3] *Ibid.*, 15 December 1905.

dissolved any semblance of collective leadership and, after various last-minute attempts at reconciliation, the different factions went each their own way.

The Free Food leadership was by now almost entirely in the Upper House. Devonshire, Balfour of Burleigh and Goschen had been there before the fiscal controversy. Ritchie and Hicks Beach now took peerages. Lord George Hamilton retired. Churchill and Seely had already crossed the floor. Of the Free Food leaders only Arthur Elliot and Hugh Cecil stood again. Their position and that of their followers seemed hopeless; and, soon after Balfour's resignation, they attempted to rejoin the Central section of the Party.

DEVONSHIRE TO BALFOUR

7 *December* 1905.—Some of our friends of a sanguine disposition are of opinion that there might be some possible advantage to the future of the Unionist party, if in the present changed circumstances there could be some further communication between us.

I am, however, afraid that the last two years have rather increased than diminished the difference of the views which we take on the only question which divides us, and that there is little hope of my being able to contribute to the restoration of that unity in the party which you desire. All that I can say is that, as I told you in my letter of November, the great object of many of us is to prevent the party being committed to Chamberlain's proposals, and that any declarations on your part tending to show the fundamental differences between your own proposals and his would, I believe, be received with very great satisfaction by many of those who have been more or less in agreement with me. I cannot hope that any declarations you may make before the election will relieve me or other Unionists whom you may deem irreconcilable Cobdenites from the necessity of criticism, but they might certainly modify the character of such criticism, and go far to satisfy many who are now in doubt as to your position.

If you thought it of any use to see me, I am available at almost any time to-morrow; but I really do not think that I can add anything to what you already know as to my views.[1]

Balfour's reply was hardly encouraging.

BALFOUR TO DEVONSHIRE

8 *December* 1905.—I shall certainly do my best to keep steady to the course on which I have hitherto steered, and to make it as clear as possible to all concerned. This will probably not relieve me of criticism from the Protectionist wing of the party; and, speaking for the Cobdenite wing, you tell me that it will not relieve me of criticism from *them*. These are not very satisfactory conditions in which to engage in a great contest; but we must make the best of them.

[1] Bernard Holland, *Life of the Duke of Devonshire*, vol. ii, pp. 391–92.

2 C 2

You talk of the last two years having 'rather widened, than diminished, the differences of the views which we take on the question which divides us'. I am not conscious of having altered my view on any really important point during that time, and I therefore hope that you have somewhat over-emphasised the diversions of our views upon the only topic on which either of us have been, or are ever likely to be, in different camps.

The next day Balfour spoke at Manchester, and James noted in his diary:

On Saturday, the 9th, A. J. B. addressed a meeting of his constituents at Manchester, explaining the reasons for his resignation. He did not mention Chamberlain and did not refer to his Bristol attack, nor to some most adulatory references J. C. had made to him in a speech delivered at Oxford the night before. No reference was made to the Fiscal question, and beyond saying that the dissensions in the party prevented any attempt to pass the proposed Redistribution Bill, the speech in no way dealt with the dissensions existing in the party.

. . . There is no tendency in Balfour to incline towards Free Trade, and so now, with the General Election immediately in front of us, we Unionist Free-traders have to go our own way. The exact position we must take up will have to be agreed upon and announced in a few days.

For myself personally, I attach so much more importance to the cause of Free Trade than to any other consideration that I shall certainly be disposed to act to a great extent in concert with the Liberal party. I certainly shall do so in the House of Lords . . .[1]

Balfour followed his line of compromise and philosophic doubt to the end. If anything he leant rather more to the Unionist Free Traders than in the past. He encouraged a transaction whereby the Central Office persuaded the Tariff Reform candidate in Marylebone to stand down in favour of his Free Trade cousin Robert Cecil. In a speech at Leeds (16 December) he seems to have tried to draw a line between his policy and Chamberlain's. He declared, 'I belong to the Free Trade section of my party'; though he praised Chamberlain, he argued that Protection was contrary to Imperialism and that Retaliation was consistent with Free Trade. On 29 December he went even further and appeared on a platform with Hugh Cecil, Robert Cecil and Hayes Fisher, a strong Free Trade group hardly counter-balanced by the presence of Arnold-Forster. Now that he had resigned the authority of the Premiership he seems to have felt it his interest and perhaps his duty to act as a rallying point for those Unionists who would not take the Chamberlain line.

Chamberlain's irritation at Balfour's tactics emerges very clearly from the following letters.

[1] Lord Askwith, *Lord James of Hereford*, p. 290.

CHAMBERLAIN TO CHAPLIN

11 *December* 1905.—. . . The officials are at their old game. Could they possibly do anything more provocative than put up Robert Cecil for Marylebone. I am sure we shall never have a fair course until the present gang have been cleared away.

Oxford was a great success and our friends there were delighted at the character of the meeting.

23 *December* 1905 : *Private.*—I expect to issue my address about Jan. 1st. and have prepared a draft which, while preserving our position will not, I think, provoke opposition from the Balfourites.

Arthur's speech was characteristic. I might easily pick out from it sentences which, put together, would constitute an admirable programme.

But then, unfortunately, there are other sentences such as 'I belong to the Free Trade Section of my party' which are eagerly seized upon by such men as Robert Cecil and enable him to say 'I am a follower of Mr. Balfour'.

The Marylebone incident is most annoying. Here is the safest Conservative seat in London. The Constituency and the late Member were Tariff Reformers to the backbone and yet by their mismanagement it is probable that it may go to a bitter enemy who will come in to the House expressly to upset us. We are doing all we can to upset the plot which has arranged this result. It is uphill work now and yet one strong man could have knocked the whole thing into a cocked hat if he had been on the spot when the little game was first opened !

Unfortunately Balfour's speeches give us no help in such cases. The fatal influence of the Hotel Cecil leads him to sacrifice the cause to personal friendship. He will not see that a great movement like ours can only be carried by a unanimous party and that Hugh Cecil and his few friends cannot run in harness with the majority of Tariff Reformers. He must take sides sooner or later and choose between the 9/10ths who have made up their minds and would support him through thick and thin in a definite policy — and the little knot of 1/10th or less who were always 'frondeurs' and who now give him lip homage in order that they may come in under his umbrella and then act as independents or even as open enemies in times of difficulty.

Various proposals reached Chamberlain for a last-minute reunion with Balfour. He dismissed them all as impracticable. It was too late now for compromise. The election would change the whole balance of forces in the Party. Then, perhaps, would be the time to reopen negotiation.

CHAMBERLAIN TO PEARSON

21 *December* 1905 : *Private.*—I do not see any good in approaching Balfour. He seems determined to do all in his power to maintain the Free Fooders as an essential part of the Conservative party. As long as this is so there can be no union, I interpret his emphatic statement

that he belongs to the Free Trade Section as intended rather to increase difficulties than to lessen them.

Of course I might say that I also am a Free Trader — indeed I did say so in my first speech on the subject, and have subsequently repeated that I am not Protectionist.

If Balfour had gone on to define Protection we might find ourselves in entire agreement, as a general tariff is no more necessarily Protection than a tariff of Retaliation.

But I am tired of this word splitting, and I think in my address and election speeches I shall do best to go my own way without referring to Balfour at all, leaving others to put their interpretation upon both our speeches.

It is a difficult situation and I do not see what the end will be, but during our term of opposition I shall have many opportunities of closer communication with him than I have had recently and in this way we may find it possible to hit on a new programme. I do not think there is any use in further discussion until after the election.

CHAMBERLAIN TO GARVIN

28 *December* 1905.—I want to show both that I am anxious for union and that at the same time I stick to my own proposals. I shall therefore repeat my views as to a general tariff, although I shall endeavour to show that it is not protective and not inconsistent with the freer trade which we seek to gain by it. In this way I shall play up to Arthur Balfour and try not to widen any difference that exists till after the general election.

If union were only to be gained by sacrificing our opinions, that is to say the opinions of at least nine-tenths of the Party, in order to satisfy a few Free Fooders, union would be impossible, but I do not think this is necessary, and I believe your line and mine would be identical. When we get through the election we must have a long conversation on the whole situation as it emerges afterwards.

I think that by resigning Balfour has placed us already in a better position and that the majority against us will be less than it would have been otherwise. My present estimate is that it will be something between 90 & 100 — of course with the Irish thrown in.

In practice, Chamberlain fought the election as if he had been the leader of an independent Tariff Reform Party. Most of his time in these last weeks before the campaign began was devoted to selecting Tariff Reform candidates. These were the days when Members of Parliament were unpaid, and when candidates were expected to make substantial annual donations to their Associations and to pay the whole cost of their elections, a sum amounting to about £1000. Hopeless seats were thus often left uncontested and even marginal constituencies were frequently not filled till the eve of the campaign. Chamberlain disposed of substantial sums both through the Tariff Reform League and through a private Fighting

Fund of his own. These sinews of war enabled him to help a number of his supporters who could not have borne the cost of the campaign themselves. He kept the control of the Midland region under his own personal guidance. Chaplin undertook the organisation of East Anglia and Lancashire. Ridley had to do the rest. There was no consultation with Balfour and hardly any with the Central Office. In a few cases, indeed, the Tariff Reformers deliberately risked splitting the vote to prevent the election of Free Fooders. Thus they ran candidates against Arthur Elliot at Durham and against Hugh Cecil at Greenwich. If there must be Free Traders in the next Parliament, Chamberlain was determined that they should not sit on the Unionist benches.

The following extracts from Chamberlain's correspondence show the kind of preoccupations which now engrossed him:

CHAMBERLAIN TO RIDLEY

14 *December* 1905.—I have pleasure in enclosing my cheque for £2000 which I am glad to place at your disposal to spend as you see fit for promoting Tariff Reform League principles at the next election.

I have seen Lord Powis' agent this morning in reference to David Davies' candidature. I am afraid they are asking more than Davies will give, but I have suggested a form of words which I might be able to press upon him.

18 *December* 1905.—I am afraid that the Bishop of St. Asaph and the Church Party lost David Davies by pressing him too hard about the Disestablishment question. I pointed out that it was really academical at the present time, as, if the other side brought it forward they would have a sufficient majority and it would matter very little whether it was increased by Davies' vote or not. If we came in of course, we should not touch the subject. On the other hand Davies would have been all right about Fiscal Reform and Home Rule. Now I am afraid he has gone over finally to the Radicals.

As regards Louth, I think this is a case where the money ought to be found by the Central Conservative Association in London. They have got plenty of money and the Fiscal Reformers ought to have their share of it. Otherwise I suppose it will go to such candidates as Robert Cecil.

CHAMBERLAIN TO MOUNT-STEPHEN

22 *December* 1905.—I do not know how sufficiently to thank you for the cheque which Mrs. Chamberlain has handed to me and for the kind letter accompanying it.

At the present time I have many calls for pecuniary assistance in the work of education and also in securing effective representatives of our opinions who will carry our flag at the election. Your munificent gift is therefore most timely and encouraging.

On the whole I am well satisfied with the progress made. We find a marked change in many places where formerly prejudice was so strong that we could hardly get a hearing.

I do not think now, and I never have thought, that we can possibly win at the next election, but we are making the ground sure for the time when another swing of the pendulum will take place and when our policy will be accepted by the whole Unionist party.

I do not wish to lay too much stress on details, but on the other hand I am anxious that when the time of victory comes we shall be prepared with a definite plan and shall not fritter away time and enthusiasm in squabbling over methods.

The Home Rule declarations of the Prime Minister will help us somewhat, but not as much as some of my sanguine friends imagine. The votes will as usual be decided by a positive policy rather than by a negative one. Offence is the best defence, and tariff reform will prove a better weapon than opposition to possible Home Rule proposals.

CHAMBERLAIN TO CHAPLIN

23 *December* 1905: *Private.*—My 'private Fund' is not a large one but it is entirely at your disposal. You ought not to be a sixpence out of pocket for the expenses at Newcastle. Let me know what Mr. Mantalini called the 'dem'd total' — that is every penny — and I will send you a cheque at once with pleasure. I wish that everything may be as well spent.

As to Brigg — yes certainly if you think it worth while I am good for £500.

I understand that Croft will not now want anything and that the above will be all you require.[1]

I am obliged to ask this in order that I may not over-run my credit, but I am all right at present with a few thousands to spare.

Dissensions over fiscal policy had wholly demoralised the Conservative Central Office. The Tariff Reform League, indeed, was the only national organisation on the Unionist side capable of fighting a serious campaign. And even the Tariff Reform League was hopelessly inadequate in funds, personnel and experience for the task. Far more efficient — indeed still the most efficient political machine in the country — was the Birmingham caucus; but its influence scarcely spread beyond the Midland area.

Powerful forces were engaged against the wavering Unionist ranks. The Cobden Club was at least as efficient as the Tariff

---

[1] Chamberlain had persuaded Croft (later Lord Croft) to stand as a Tariff Reform candidate against Charles Seely the sitting member and a strong Unionist Free Trader. This meant giving the seat to the Liberals, but as Chamberlain said to Croft: 'I much prefer an open enemy as member for Lincoln than a professing friend who will stab me in the back'. *My Life of Strife* by Lord Croft, p. 43.

Reform League and disposed of larger funds. For the last time in English history, the Nonconformist vote was delivered *en bloc* against Balfour and his Education and Licensing Acts. For the first time in English history, the whole weight of the Trade Union movement was thrown onto the side of the Liberal leaders who had promised a Trades Disputes Bill to relieve the Unions from the liabilities of the Taff Vale decision.

The Unionists were in full agreement on nothing save their opposition to Home Rule. On every side they were assailed by a propaganda denouncing 'Chinese Slavery', 'the Dear Loaf', 'Rome on the Rates', 'The Publican's Party', 'the enemies of the Trades Unions'.

III

The campaign began in earnest in January. Chamberlain was first in the field with his election address, published on 1 January. We print it below in full. It will do duty for the many speeches he made in the campaign and which it would be tedious to reproduce.

PARLIAMENTARY ELECTION
1906

To the Electors of West Birmingham.

GENTLEMEN,

On the unanimous invitation of the Joint Unionist Committee of the Western Division of Birmingham, I ask once more for the renewal of the confidence and support which on six previous occasions you have so generously extended to me.

For fifty years I have been proud to be a citizen of Birmingham, and for nearly a generation I have been, by your favour, one of its Parliamentary representatives.

This long service makes it unnecessary for me to dwell on the principles which have guided my political action. I have sought in domestic policy the greatest happiness of the greatest number, and I have endeavoured at the same time to uphold the greatness of our common country, and the unity of our Imperial dominion.

In my opinion, both these objects are threatened by the new Government which has lately taken office, pending an appeal to the people.

It is essentially a Home Rule and Little Englander Government. It seeks by tortuous ways to compass the disruption of the United Kingdom, although it dare not openly place Home Rule upon its programme. It must, however, exist, if at all, by the support of Irish votes, and by the help of those who have openly avowed that separation is their ultimate object. In its professed anxiety for peace it will not face the sacrifices necessary to maintain peace, and to enable us in face of the ever growing armaments of other countries, to defend ourselves and our Empire against unprovoked attack. Its members have shown profound indifference to the wishes of our colonial kinsmen for closer commercial union, and have deliberately made a party question of a great Imperial policy.

They now base their chief claims for support on their irreconcileable opposition to the slightest change in the fiscal system of this country, which was adopted more than fifty years ago, in circumstances which were totally different, and on the faith of promises and predictions that have never been fulfilled.

The Unionist party is prepared to join issue on all these questions, and I rejoice in the opportunity which is now given to us of obtaining the verdict of the nation.

I shall not insult you by supposing that you have in any degree altered the emphatic opinion which you expressed twenty years ago on the question of Home Rule. You refused then to march through rapine to the disintegration of the Empire, and everything that has happened since has confirmed the wisdom and patriotism of your decision. The Irish Nationalists have shown how illusory was the pretended union of hearts with which they sought to delude you. They have thrown off any pretence of friendship and consideration; they have declared that they will rest satisfied with nothing short of separation on their own terms; they have admitted that they hope to gain their ends by practising on your fears, and you are threatened once more with those methods of terrorism which were devised to place our loyal fellow subjects in Ireland at the mercy of the enemies of this country.

Whether in opposition, or in office, I will spare no efforts to defeat this conspiracy of violence and treason.

This is, however, only the negative side of Unionist Policy — the positive side is kindred to it. We who have hitherto preserved the union of the United Kingdom, find in the closer union of the Empire the natural extension of our efforts and aspirations, and at the same time the most urgent issue of the present election. If we do not avail ourselves quickly of the opportunity, now offered by our great Colonies, of a preferential arrangement by which trade may be transferred, to our mutual advantage, from those outside the Empire to those within; and by which the bonds of sympathy and sentiment now existing may be strengthened and multiplied, we may find in the near future that we have allowed the auspicious moment to pass, and that the sister states across the seas have been unable to wait indefinitely for our decision, and have been forced to enter into arrangements with strangers who will thus profit by our indifference and apathy.

The Unionists are pledged to call a conference in which all parts of the Empire will be represented, and which will freely discuss this question, and endeavour to come to a mutually satisfactory agreement. If, as I am convinced will be the case, this conference ends in such an agreement, I hope that the results will be immediately submitted to Parliament, where I shall be prepared to support them to the best of my ability.

I recognise that it is probable that the terms of any arrangement giving to our manufactures substantial Preference in colonial markets, in return for a corresponding Preference on certain principal products of the Colonies, will include provision for a small tax on foreign corn; but as both Home and Colonial corn will be free, and the Colonial supply is unlimited, it is certain that the price of bread will not be increased in the slightest degree. Meanwhile our working classes will gain an immense new market, and the relations between the great States of the British Empire will be enlarged and cemented.

The fulfilment of this task is the first item of the future constructive programme of the Unionist party. The second is closely connected with it, and is known as the policy of Retaliation.

For sixty years we have striven to promote Free Trade with other countries, by freely opening our markets to them, while they have responded by closing their markets to us. We have utterly and entirely failed, and now every Unionist who accepts the official policy of the party to which he professes to belong, is bound to support us in the effort to defend our trade against the unfair competition and the dumping which have already wrested from us our former supremacy, and which seriously threaten our future prosperity. If the country is not prepared to deal at once with this question, it will suffer by the delay, but the subject will only be postponed, and at no distant time the necessities of our people, the cries of the unemployed, and the miseries of the poor, will force upon us the only solution.

So far, I believe that the Unionist party is absolutely agreed, or if there be any dissentients they form so small a minority, that they cannot hope to affect the result. When we come to discuss methods there may be some differences, although I think that in practice they will be found to have been greatly exaggerated, and to be more a question of verbal distinction than of practical importance.

For myself, I have felt it desirable that in entering upon this policy, we should have clear and definite ideas of the means by which we hope to give effect to it. I believe that our objects can be fully attained by a moderate general tariff scientifically adapted to the existing conditions of our trade, and arranged so as to secure the largest amount of employment at fair wages for our own people. It would necessarily provide for the free admission of raw materials and articles which we do not make ourselves; while it would place a toll on the manufactures of those countries that do not treat us fairly, but strictly reserve their home markets for themselves, and take advantage, at the same time, of our open door to dump their surplus products here. The object of our policy would be to secure employment, and not to raise prices. It would not be protective but defensive, and it would not be inconsistent with the true spirit of Free Trade. It might indeed bring us nearer to the state of things promised by Mr. Cobden — but never realised — when he assured his supporters that in five years from the adoption of Free Trade by this country, every other civilized nation would be compelled to follow our example.

There may be other methods of realising our objects, although I do not know of them; but provided that there is no doubt about the ends in view, I feel assured that we shall all be able at the proper time to agree also as to the means.

Our policy is constructive and practical; the policy of our opponents is destructive and theoretical. To destroy the union of the Kingdom; — to ignore the friendly advances made to us by our Colonies; — to refuse to treat our best customers any better than our most strenuous competitors; — to give the foreigner all the privileges of our market without the smallest contribution to our expenses; — to welcome with open arms the alien sweater, while the British workman emigrates or starves; — to drive native industries abroad, while increasing the poor rates at home; — these things do not constitute a programme which will commend itself to Birmingham working-men.

I trust that you will strengthen my hands to resist it, and will once more join me in promoting a policy which has for its sole objects the increase of employment, the development of our resources, and the consolidation of the Empire.

I am, Gentlemen,
Your obedient servant,
J. CHAMBERLAIN.

Devonshire's address was issued the same day in the form of a letter to Arthur Elliot. James would describe it as 'moderate and statesmanlike but . . . not sufficiently specific in the advice given'.

Balfour's address, published next day, ranged over the whole field of affairs but said little on fiscal policy. On 5 January, however, he published a volume of his fiscal speeches and writings from 1880 to 1905. No one could accuse him of not expressing his opinion on the question; but, in the thick of an election, no one had time to read his neatly balanced arguments.

Campbell-Bannerman's address contained a singularly objective statement on the relationship of Chamberlain to Balfour.

Let me only add, in case I am told that it is unfair to identify the late Prime Minister, chief of the party of Tariff Reform, with the extreme proposals of his leading colleague, that I understand Mr. Balfour to be agreed in principle with Mr. Chamberlain, and also that the Unionist party is committed to the programme of tariffs and preferences put forward by Mr. Chamberlain. This being so, I conceive that the minor fiscal policy indicated by Mr. Balfour occupies in the estimation at any rate of the majority of our opponents, little more than a nominal place in the contest in which we shall shortly be engaged. It is the larger policy, therefore, with which we are confronted and which we are called upon to fight. Our concern in any case is with the results that must flow from the adoption of either of these policies, and not with the question of whether Mr. Balfour conceives himself to be a Free Trader, or a Protectionist, or both, or neither.[1]

[1] J. A. Spender, *The Life of Campbell-Bannerman*, vol. ii, p. 215.

Chamberlain spoke every other day of the campaign from 30 December to 22 January.[1] He made only two speeches in his own constituency; but, except for a meeting at Derby, confined himself to the Midland region. The programme seemed too arduous to his family and Neville

had a serious talk with him representing that he owed it to his family to observe some moderation in the strain he put on himself. He consented to give up two meetings but refused to do less than the ten or thereabouts that remained. ' I cannot go half speed ', he said, ' I must either do my utmost or stop altogether and though I know the risks I prefer to take them.' The risk to which he alluded was that of a stroke and we were in constant dread of this from this time forward.[2]

Mrs. Chamberlain's letters give perhaps the best picture of the campaign as it appeared from Highbury.

30 *December* 1905.—Mr. Balfour made a big speech in London last night — Lord Hugh and Lord Robert Cecil on the Platform and Mr. Hayes Fisher, the chief supporters (all Free Fooders), though Mr. Arnold Forster was also there, to redress the balance a little. He bantered the new Government with some skill, was very direct and pointed on the subject of Home Rule, and had the appearance of only touching on the Fiscal question in response to a voice in the audience. . . . Nothing will prevent the Fiscal question being the main issue, and so far as the Home Rule question goes it is a help to us and a hindrance to C.-B and Company. They are shrieking that we have raised the 'bogey', when all the time it was their own Prime Minister himself at Stirling.

On the whole there is a feeling that our prospects have brightened since the new Government came in, and we hear they are beginning to quake a little lest their majority will not be independent of the Irish . . .

Joe's election Address is, I consider, a masterpiece. Really even I am often surprised at his ability, and his wonderful power of putting his case. This, of course, is meant for a wider public though addressed to the electors of Birmingham (West). It contains all that he holds most dear, and avoids the shoals and quicksands with great skill and makes the most of the deeper current wherever it flows. It is to be published on January 2nd. You will be interested to hear that last night he was formally adopted as candidate for West Birmingham.

3 *January* 1906.—. . . The Jewellers' Dinner was a great success. Joe was at his very best and the audience was immensely interested and very enthusiastic. He spoke for just an hour. . . . It was a good beginning of the electoral campaign. The result is that it put him into good spirits and now he is getting into the thick of it, and if only he can avoid chills,

---

[1] Birmingham Jewellers' Dinner (30 December); W. Birmingham (2 January); Derby (4 January); Saltley (6 January); Wednesbury (8 January); W. Brighton (10 January); Wolverhampton (12 January); Nuneaton (16 January); Handsworth (18 January); Wellington (20 January); Halesowen (22 January).

[2] Recollections of Neville Chamberlain.

etc., all will be well. Last night there were two meetings in his own Division, held in two different Board schools. It is a great pity there is no really big hall there for the speeches were worthy of audiences of thousands. He spoke for an hour at the first, and for 50 minutes at the second. There was a certain amount of interruption and noise, as at all election meetings, but it was delightful to see the ease with which he mastered it and the ridicule which he so skilfully turned upon his opponents.

5 *January* 1906.—. . . Last night we went to Derby, going over and returning by special train which makes all the difference to our comfort.

We dined at the hotel with some of the local people and then went to the meeting, which was an immense one of between five and six thousand, hot as fury! and very crowded. Joe had been rather disgusted to find that the Committee had sent out invitations to an open meeting to all the electors, informing them that 'first come first served' will be the rule as there could not be nearly enough room for them all. He prophesied there would be trouble. His prophecy was fulfilled. After giving him a splendid reception, for the majority were his friends, he no sooner began to speak than it was evident that there were some hundreds there who did not intend he should be heard. He went on, and for a few minutes I thought he was going to master them — but they were concentrated at the back of the hall where no one could get at them, and while they did nothing serious they kept up an incessant noise and hubbub. He made a gallant attempt to make his voice carry, and it rang out strong and full and dominated the meeting as no one else's did, but no one voice could be heard far, while such a racket went on, and after a time he no longer tried to do more than address the quiet ones in front. . . . When he had laid down the principles and was going to drive them home by argument it had become certain that there was no hope of getting them quiet and we saw him put his notes in his pocket and deliberately wind up what he was saying without attempting to wear himself out by delivering a closely reasoned speech which no one could really follow with so much to distract the attention. . . . I am glad to day that the Radical papers expressed disapproval of their adherents for it. However, as you will see, he delivered a good deal of his speech and it reads wonderfully well. . . .

Beatrice has come splendidly to the fore in trying to help him and spends most of her days telephoning to his agent and others who are working for him and has helped to start Ladies' Committees at Moseley, King's Heath, King's Norton, Barnt Green, etc. She does not undertake any canvassing or outside work of that kind, but of course can give them invaluable assistance by her advice and can instruct the workers on political subjects. I have felt for some time that it was all very well for the women of the family to hold entirely aloof, but now that so much good work is being done by women more or less behind the scenes where it is very useful, that it was rather mean to stand aside and take no part while receiving help from others. This applies especially to a County constituency such as Austen's. I was saying to Ida, as she and I drove back from the tea party of the West Birmingham Workers, that I thought the time was coming when someone would have to help in Austen's constituency and that I thought her father would not object — when the next day the question came up. I encouraged both Beatrice and Austen, and found the latter would be only too glad to have her help, only he had not liked to ask for it, and that Beatrice was quite ready to do it, provided her father did not disapprove. Joe, as I thought, was quite ready to have her do it, only advised her to keep to the Committee work which she could do well and which would not bring her into the fray. It is that to which he objects. This Beatrice has no desire to enter. . . . Neville spoke last night for Mr. Collings.

9 *January* 1906.—The speech in East Birmingham (Saltley) on Saturday was a great contrast to that of Derby. So determined were they to have no repetition of that hubbub that at the very beginning when the Chairman was speaking and two rather mild individuals ventured to dissent, there was a cry at once of : ' turn 'im out ' and out they went with lightning speed, being lifted bodily out of their seats and ejected, to the great satisfaction of the audience, who remarked : ' this isn't Derby ! ' Then it settled down to listen to Joe, whose closely reasoned speech interested them intensely. It was well adapted to the community and they thoroughly appreciated it.

Again last night at Wednesbury he adapted himself with his wonderful facility to his hearers. He put it very simply and rather from the beginning, for they were more ignorant of the conditions and less well instructed in the subject. He spoke one hour and 20 minutes and was severely chidden in consequence for every extra five minutes, when the hour (which should be the extreme limit) is over it; adds, I think, greatly to the strain. However, I have nothing to complain of, for he is getting on splendidly and if a little tired it is natural fatigue that passes away with a night's rest . . .

13 *January* 1906.—Last night at Wolverhampton Joe made his eighth speech, and now two-thirds of his list is accomplished . . . The satisfactory part is that he is keeping very well and is in good spirits. Depression will begin to set in when the first polling returns come in, for though one knows beforehand that we must lose, the realisation of the process is never pleasant.

It was a huge meeting of 7,000 last night, happily very quiet and attentive, which was a comfort, for the slightest noise and disturbance would easily have made speaking impossible as the acoustic properties were very bad. The speech was different from the others and extremely good. Joe has an extraordinary faculty of giving variety even to such a well-worn subject.

It was delightful to see the welcome he received in West Birmingham on Wednesday night, so warm and enthusiastic, with a personal touch of affection for ' our Joe ', and a real grasp of the object of his policy . . .

Of Chamberlain's own feelings and expectations, we get a glimpse in a letter to Chaplin.

CHAMBERLAIN TO CHAPLIN

9 *January* 1906.—The row at Derby did no harm to the cause. It really was due to bad arrangements for the meeting. One of our candidates is new to election work and would not take the advice of his people. They are very sanguine of winning one or two seats.

Also we hope for one or two at Northampton and several in other parts of the Midland district.

I am not so sanguine, but I think we have a chance of winning as many as we stand to lose, and that on the whole we shall come out as we went in.

Almost all my correspondents are sanguine, but I have an instinct that they are wrong and that on the balance we must lose. Indeed it would be terrible if by any chance we were to win and have to take office again with the old lot and the old policy.

From what I see, however, I cannot help thinking that Tariff Reform is the one fight at this election. Balfour keeps on preaching about Education and Chinese Labour, but the audiences seem to care for nothing but fiscal policy.

I was at the Imperial Tariff Committee this morning, but they said they had not yet received your letter to the Labourers. Please take care that we have it as I agree that we might circulate it with advantage in the Counties round about here.

Austen is starting to speak but is really not fit for work. When the election is over I intend to take him away for a fortnight or so at the Riviera. We shall both be the better for the rest after the racket.

But now the returns began to come in. These were still the days of staggered polls and the results were announced over a fortnight. On 13 January, Balfour was beaten in Manchester. On 15 January, his brother Gerald and Walter Long lost their seats. Next day Lyttelton was defeated; and Lancashire even rejected Arthur Stanley. Catastrophe was at hand.

On 16 January, Chamberlain spoke at Nuneaton. At the very beginning of his speech, he reaffirmed his loyalty to Balfour.

. . . we have seen . . . the action of Manchester — a most fickle city — a city which in the old days, having secured the capacity and ability of Mr. Bright and Mr. Milner Gibson — all that they could give to them — nevertheless in a short time turned round upon them and sent them to seek elsewhere a secure confidence which they could not expect from Manchester. I know what I am talking about, since Birmingham welcomed with open arms a great statesman whom Manchester had dismissed with such slight ceremony. Now it has dismissed another statesman, and really, I cannot help thinking that statesmen will be forgiving persons if they think of Manchester again. It will be a place where no statesman need apply. (*Laughter and Hear, hear.*)

Now we all feel, I am sure, great sympathy, but, what is more important, the deepest regret, at the defeat of Mr. Balfour. (*Hear, hear.*) Mr. Balfour, in or out of Parliament, is our leader. (*Applause.*) Now that he is out of Parliament he is more our leader than ever. There is no other man who has deserved so well of the Conservative and Unionist party; there is no other man to whom we look with so much confidence to restore us to our old position when the present delusions of the people have disappeared. (*Applause.*) Considering how in the House of Commons, for so many years, he has held his place, with what good temper, with what courtesy to his opponents, with what ability and capacity, I cannot help thinking that even some of those who have most outrageously abused him and depreciated him will now feel a certain regret that even for a short time the House of Commons will not know him as a member. (*Hear, hear.*) It will only be a short time. (*Applause.*) We, his friends and followers, who have shown him loyalty in the time of his prosperity, will show him all the greater loyalty now that he has, at all events for a period, to go through the waters of adversity. (*Applause.*) It is not, however, a mere personal defeat that we have to chronicle. I see absolutely no good, now or at any time, in minimising the importance of facts. We have, in the last few days, as a party, been badly defeated.

Birmingham polled on 17 January. In the afternoon, Highbury was sunk in gloom. Mrs. Chamberlain wrote her inmost anxieties to her mother.

17 *January* 1906.—. . . Mr. Balfour's defeat on Saturday night was the signal and now we are being overwhelmed by a flood. Overwhelmed, not entirely swept away, I trust, but the successes of the Liberals must surprise even themselves I think. Really it is most extraordinary, they are carrying everything before them, and even in this district where we believed we should hold the fort, the popular wave is sweeping onward and it is hard to tell where it will stop. . . . It is, of course, a great blow to Joe to lose seats in the neighbourhood of Birmingham, and what is extremely exasperating is the feeling that if the Birmingham Polling Day had been fixed on Saturday it would have been likely to have a distinct influence on the immediate neighbourhood and would have been some offset to the general disaster which has overtaken the Unionist party. The stupid Lord Mayor, who is a very weak man, fixed a day which is the latest day but one on which the Borough can poll. . . . When Joe remonstrated with him he consulted the Liberals, who naturally took the other view, and he kept to the day. The result will probably be that the large majorities we hoped to secure will be seriously diminished and East Birmingham (Sir Benjamin Stone's seat) about which we have been extremely anxious, will probably be lost. The work there has been done by the Conservatives, who have no organization worth the name, and now at the eleventh hour the Liberal Unionists have had to come to their aid, but I fear that it is too late to save it.

The canvasses have been extremely good, and Joe's is most satisfactory, judged by the standard of all past elections. But this election appears to be quite different from any which have preceded it. While in Wolverhampton our men polled a larger number of votes than last time, which was a record, the Liberals have polled enormously bigger numbers and 90% of the electorate has voted, an unheard of proportion. The canvasses there were excellent, so they were also in Manchester, and under these circumstances we now feel anxious as to what may happen here, while a week ago we were perfectly confident of our success.

There seems to be a new element coming forward, which Joe has fore-seen would some time happen, for undoubtedly the working classes are showing their strength as never before and are returning large numbers of Labour members. We hear from various places, Manchester, Leaming-ton, and now, I am sorry to say, in King's Heath, that these Labour people are telling lies as to what they are going to do and have done. Miss Balfour wrote me that in Manchester they actually came into the Committee Rooms and volunteered the information that they had voted for her brother, when undoubtedly this was untrue, and the word seems to have passed round among them that this is one way of playing the game and deluding us.

Chinese Labour has had an enormous influence, without doubt, and while they shriek 'Slavery' what they really care about is the cheap labour, and nothing will make them believe that white men cannot do the work which the Chinamen are doing in South Africa.

Mr. Gerald Balfour, Mr. Walter Long and Mr. Lyttelton have all been defeated, and we begin to wonder who will be left to occupy the front Opposition bench. . . .

Mr. Hills has had a triumph at Durham, where he has defeated Mr. Arthur Elliot, who, as you will remember, was a Liberal Unionist Free Trader of the most virulent type. We never really expected Mr. Hills to get in, though he himself has been extremely hopeful. . . . We cannot but be pleased that an election which has been fought thoroughly and simply on the question of Tariff Reform has been so successful.

Also we won Hastings with a Tariff Reform candidate, and that at present is our only gain of a seat. We have shed Mr. Tommy Bowles, Mr. Seely and Sir Albert Rollit, all Unionist Free Traders. Among the Unionists who have managed to get themselves elected, there is a pre-ponderance of Tariff Reformers.

At the same time, one is obliged to face the fact that Tariff Reform has not done so much to save the situation as we hoped. In some places, as in this neighbourhood, it has been the issue, but in Manchester the people did not really want to hear about it, and, according to Miss Balfour, Chinese Labour was the great cry.

Evidently the Labour people are thinking of their own concerns and are unable to grasp the idea of anything in the nature of a big and comprehensive policy.

You can imagine what a strange sensation it is after all these years of feeling we had the country behind us to feel that we are now to be not only in a minority but probably in a small minority. . . . You must not for a moment believe that we are discouraged, though of course we are much depressed at the moment. I myself believe that it will purge the party of much that was undesirable and that the mere fact that the defeat has been so overwhelming will bring the leaders more closely together and will make their followers strong to uphold them. Long before this reaches you you will know our fate. We are rejoicing this morning in brilliant sunshine which, as the weather has been very bad up to a few days ago is a comfort, and I am especially glad because they have insisted on Joe himself driving through his constituency, a thing which he has not done for many years. We therefore are starting very soon. . . .

Joe is well, though he cannot be said to be in a very cheerful frame of mind, but we shall be out of our misery tonight so far as he personally is concerned, and I hope that Birmingham will stand by him. . . . I greatly fear that our plan of going to the South of France will have to be postponed. He feels that he would not have the spirit to go away and that it might be misunderstood and that as Mr. Balfour is without a seat in Parliament he may have the responsibility thrown upon him which he must be here to meet if required. I cannot believe that Mr. Balfour will be allowed to remain outside for any length of time, and I think it would be base ingratitude on the part of his friends if someone is not found to resign a safe seat in his favour. Joe wrote to him at once a really delightful letter and had from Mr. Balfour a charming reply. He has accepted his defeat with splendid spirit and dwells very little on the personal side of it. What he does feel is the danger to the country which this Labour Movement is indicating, but of course it must be a bitter blow to him and we feel great sympathy with him and his brother and all the family. Austen is carrying on his campaign and is getting through wonderfully well. I *think* he will be able to hold all the meetings but he comes home terribly tired and stiff and I shall be glad when they are over. . . .

Well, for three mortal hours we drove in the open carriage round West Birmingham this morning, visiting almost all of the Committee Rooms. The workers there were cheering and confident and said we were doing well. I cannot think there can be the slightest doubt of Joe's return with a good majority, though I no longer expect it to be like the last — well over 4,000. The people in the street gave him the usual enthusiastic welcome, 'there's Joey', 'there's only one Joe', 'keep up your pecker', &c., &c., from the crowd. It was rather an exhausting morning, and when at 3 o'clock we got home we were ready enough for our lunch.

Beatrice, Austen and Mr. Duckworth have just gone off for A.'s speeches. Neville is speaking at — I forget which place, so to-night Ida and I alone are left to sit with Joe at the end of the telephone and hear the Birmingham returns. It has not been an enlivening performance the last few evenings. Let us hope to-night we shall have more cheering news ! If we do, Joe will recover his spirits — if we do not — well, one must do all one can to help him to meet the disappointment.

In fact, the Unionists held every seat in Birmingham by increased majorities.

We may let Mrs. Chamberlain continue the tale.

19 *January* 1906.—. . . We had really been extremely anxious lest we might lose East Birmingham and had it happened I do not know what Joe would have done, for he had set his heart on keeping all, and the increased majorities in the other divisions would have been no compensation to him. As the day and evening wore on I could see that the iron

would enter his soul if there were any break in the representation of Birmingham, and I trembled lest it would come. At last after trying to amuse ourselves — in vain — and to divert our own thoughts — the returns began to come in, and we sat in breathless excitement as Mr. Wilson received them by telephone. One by one they came — huge majorities in our favour, crowned by Joe's of 5,079 ! (increase 801). Last of all came the East and we drew a long breath of relief to hear the seat was safe and that Birmingham had more than justified the faith which Joe had placed in its patriotism. Joe, Ida and I and Mr. Wilson joined in drinking the health of the Town which had so well upheld the Unionist Cause at a moment when the rest of the Country seems to have gone blindly on in quest of it knows not what — a change — anything and everything.

Then Joe sent a message :

'Well done Birmingham. My own people have justified my confidence and I am deeply grateful to all who have assisted in winning this grand victory. We are seven.'

This was telephoned to the Daily Gazette, and in a few minutes was displayed to the excited crowd. They opened the window for us to hear the cheers and they resounded through the room. . . . The enthusiasm and excitement knew no bounds — the streets were packed and the people were dancing with delight and beside themselves with joy.

Well, it was a great night ! Neville came back from Rugby, where he had been speaking, radiant with pleasure, and it did my heart good to see my husband's happiness and relief. We felt in our hearts that Birmingham must be true, but the demoralising effect of the three previous days had been very far-reaching and serious, and one could hardly have wondered if even Birmingham had been somewhat influenced by it. At all events one did not dare to express what a few days before we had been confident of. As it was, the only effect was to spur the people to greater effort, and they worked like Trojans and now have the reward of feeling they have won a real triumph. Its significance is not lost on the rest of the Country, and though C.B. ascribes it to an 'unwholesome influence' it is discomforting to the victors who are carrying all before them that they have not been able to weaken the defence of the stronghold of Tariff Reform !

You should see the telegrams and letters of congratulation which have poured in upon us. Mr. Wilson had a clothes basket full — 358 telegrams came yesterday and there has been a steady stream today. Even I have over 50 and we are in despair how to acknowledge them. . . .

No one is inclined to say that Tariff Reform has done any harm. It has not done the good we hoped but in some places, as in the City of London, where there was a majority of 10,000 and Birmingham where it was the clear issue, it has carried the day. Undoubtedly the Labour Movement is the significant thing and there has not been so great a defection from our side as we feared, since we have actually polled more votes than before and this in some measure appears to account for the fact that though we knew certain Labour candidates were coming to the fore the extent of the support they would receive was not foreseen.

There was a melancholy list yesterday and again to-day and I am afraid Birmingham came too late to help very much. Alas ! Mr. Chaplin is among the slain. We have been almost in tears over it for he has made such a gallant fight. For 37 years he has represented Sleaford where he was 'the Squire' and his own people have turned on him. He will feel it terribly and I am so sorry for him . . . other members of the late Government are likely to have the same fate to-day. At present, Joe, Mr. Arnold-Forster and Mr. Wyndham have the proud distinction of being the only ex-Cabinet Ministers returned. . . . Austen will just get through I think. . . .

Saturday.—It is as I prophesied, the rout continues. Two more of Mr. Balfour's Government have been defeated. If it were not so tragic one would have to laugh.

Ah me, if only Mr. Balfour had resigned in the spring of 1904, so much would have been saved. The Chinese question would never have arisen and at that time the Liberals could not have secured more than a bare majority. The other day Mr. Asquith was exulting over how the delay had played into their hands and I fear it is but too true. Joe's advice on that point would have been worth taking. However, it is too late to cry over spilt milk.

Chamberlain's last speech of the campaign was made at Hales-owen. He faced up frankly to the 'revolution' that had taken place, and the setback to his cause which flowed from it.

. . . We should be foolish not to recognise that a great political revolu-tion has been in progress under our eyes. . . . Speaking for myself I can truly say that I entered into this contest determined as far as in me lay to present to the people of this country a clear, a definite issue upon the greatest, as I think, of all immediate questions. (*Hear, hear.*) To my mind at this moment the question of the greatest interest for the people of this country is how these small islands, all most congested as they are with an ever increasing population, can secure for their people sufficient employ-ment at fair and reasonable wages ; and also how at a time when the position of nations is changing, when the dealings with the world is alter-ing, how the union of this great Empire can be maintained. (*Hear, hear.*) In all that I have hitherto said — in the many speeches that I have made in the course of this election — I have refused to turn aside, and to be driven from my path by the introduction of side issues, such, for instance, as the misrepresentation about Chinese labour or the misstatements about the effect of the Education Act. (*Cheers.*) I have appealed to the people on one main issue, and upon that I have been willing to stand or fall, and the verdict of Birmingham has at all events justified the policy which I have pursued. (*Hear, hear.*) But elsewhere people have been carried off their feet. They have been deluded by the most scandalous misrepresentations. They have failed to use their judgment and in-telligence, and for one reason or another, very often from totally incon-sistent reasons, they have failed us at this crisis, and have given a majority to our opponents. The first result, therefore, is that Tariff Reform with all that it involves, has been for a time at least postponed. Tariff Reform has been postponed while this Government lasts, and our business is to see that it does not last too long. (*Hear, hear.*) I want once more, now towards the end of the election, to put on record my determination to pursue to the end the policy which I believe to be demanded in the interests of the country and of the majority of its population. (*Hear, hear.*) Tariff Reform is not dead, and when the calumnies which for the moment have overwhelmed it, when they come home to roost, and when the side issues are forgotten, Tariff Reform will remain as the only practical remedy for the dangers with which our British trade and our British workmen are confronted. (*Cheers.*) It will come back, and meanwhile our duty is to keep the lamp alight and to send back at all events as many as you possibly can in order to assist us in this task. (*Hear, hear.*)

Chamberlain's personal campaign was over now; and next day came the news that Austen too was safe. The Birmingham dynasty at least had found victory in defeat. Mrs. Chamberlain gives the atmosphere of these last days.

24 *January* 1906.—Well, the election is over so far as we are concerned and we indeed have cause to feel that our part in it has been attended with success and encouragement so far as the personal side goes and the consequences which follow. Austen has come off triumphantly as well as his father and has a splendid majority of 4,366. You can imagine our rejoicing when the news came, and it was not long before the Union Jack was waving in the breeze over the house for the second time in a week.

Added to this, Handsworth returned Mr. Meysey Thompson (a great improvement on his brother) by 4,771, so the Birmingham district is picking up and the neighbourhood doing something to counterbalance the losses at the beginning.

I do not know how to be sufficiently grateful that the standard has been held so high ! for here, unlike other parts of the Country, the attempt to obscure the issue has failed and the fight has been on Fiscal policy. It can truly be said to be a victory for Tariff Reform and though the Unionist party will go back to the House of Commons a battered remnant it will be through no fault of Joe's, and though many of his friends have fallen by the wayside the little band contains a large number of men who are wholehearted in their adherence to his policy. Of course there are some inside and *many* outside who are still under the domination of the 'machine' and they will undoubtedly feel it is a hard fate that in the general débacle such laurels as remain have fallen to the Leader who is so uncomfortably active and progressive. Still I have great hope that that feeling may not be widespread though we all know it has always existed in the Unionist Party and that it will die hard. Naturally our *friends* are ready to tell us all that they hear of it by way of making it easier.

One thing is certain, Joe has lost nothing of his position in the Country and even the Daily News and some other Liberal organs are generous enough to say he has deserved it. Among my letters was one from Mrs. Birchenough who told me her sister 'went with a party of friends into the midst of the Radical crowd before the Daily Chronicle stand to hear what the working people were saying. They were entirely Radical and greeted all the Liberal victories with frenzy and talked as Radicals about everything. Then everybody waited for Birmingham and as soon as Mr. Chamberlain's name appeared on the sheet with the figures a perfect roar of cheering went up from one and all and was echoed along down the Strand and Fleet Street almost and quite — as if it were in Birmingham, for they explained to everybody all round, "He's a *man* he is, and he knows what he wants and here's three more cheers for him!" and off again then and over. It was striking from a purely Radical crowd who until that moment had rejoiced in every Unionist defeat. I could not resist telling you. My sister said that the sudden outburst of enthusiasm for Mr. Chamberlain was the most overwhelming and spontaneous demonstration she had ever seen and it travelled all along the city.'

Is not that an interesting account? And we have heard of several other similar incidents in other places — while in the Theatres and Music Halls where the returns were announced, the enthusiasm knew no bounds. Lady Radnor wrote that at the Lyric the audience rose like one man and for at least ten minutes there was a roar of applause. No dissentient voice was raised, though much to her amusement she heard two men behind her who had remained silent, say they thought 'that sort of thing in very bad taste'.

IV

The final results were:

Government

Liberals	..	..	377	
Irish	..	..	83	
Labour	..	..	53^1	
			513	

Opposition

Chamberlainites	..	109	$(102)^2$
Balfourites	..	32	$(36)^2$
Free Fooders	..	11	$(16)^2$
Uncertain	..	5	
		157	

Out of a total of 670 seats the Liberals thus had an absolute majority independent of Irish or Labour support.

The poll was the highest recorded, averaging 92 per cent over the whole country. The new members included 157 Nonconformists.

[1] 29 members of the Labour Representation Committee and 24 Lib-Labs and officials of the miners' unions.

[2] Figures in parenthesis are taken from Devonshire's speech of 6 March 1906.

The Unionist defeat was shattering and complete beyond even
Chamberlain's gloomiest forebodings. What were the causes?
They are easy enough to enumerate, but it is more difficult to assess
the exact importance of each. Let us begin by taking the opinion
of the protagonists.

Within two days of his defeat, Balfour replied to Chamberlain's
message of sympathy.[1]

BALFOUR TO CHAMBERLAIN

15 *January* 1906.—Your letter has given me infinite pleasure, and it is
like you to have written it. There *have* been moments when I, like other
people who have had almost too much Parliamentary and official life,
have asked myself whether I could not spend my life in other ways
more agreeable and quite as useful. But this is not one of those moments.
The Party is in deep waters: you and I are, I verily believe, the only
two people who can do much, *as leaders*, to help them: and nothing
would induce me at such a time to abandon my share of the work.

The Manchester elections are interesting. The facts as I know them
in my own division are as follows:

(1) Meetings are never good and usually bad.

(2) Street popularity — *i.e.* colours in windows — shouting women and
boys — on my side.

(3) A very careful canvass and cross-canvass which shewed, after all
allowances, a majority for me.

(4) Most curious of all — the number of persons who *volunteered* the
statement that they have voted for me seem to have exceeded the pledges
— i.e. a large number of voters not merely lied as to what they had been
going to do, but as to what they had done.

(5) My people got more and more confident of victory up to the
moment of counting.

(6) Chinese labour was to all appearance the chief stumbling block:
but the true cause must have lain much deeper.

(7) *I* do not think Fiscal Reform did me any harm — though my
opponent informed me that he thought Free Trade his best card.

(8) I believe the event to be due to a (temporary) alliance between the
Independent Labour Party and the ordinary Radical. In other words,
it is the Labour party in Lancashire who are winning the victories: —
Who is going to reap the fruits of them?

I hope to Heaven Austen is safe. I need ask no questions about you.

Fitzroy's diary confirms Balfour's view of the importance of
the attitude of Labour.

24 *January*.—I met Stanley, the first of the defeated ex-Ministers to
whom I have had an opportunity of talking. He attributes his defeat
and all the disasters in Lancashire to the uprising of Labour. Working

[1] There is no copy of this message in the Chamberlain papers.

men who had been his supporters for years, and had actually been working for him in the earlier stages of the late contest, suddenly transferred their allegiance to his Labour opponent on the direction of the Trades Union authorities. The solidarity of Labour through the length and breadth of the country had the most striking illustration, for whereever a Labour candidate stood no length of service or weight of personal influence counted for anything in the opposite scale. For ten years Labour has been working to this end, but the cross issues that were prominent at the General Election of 1900 assisted to mask what was going on and to prepare the present surprise.

Stanley does not believe the fiscal question as such had much effect, except in so far as the Labour organisations have for the moment accepted Free Trade as an article of faith : it was rather the conviction, for the first time born in the working classes, that their social salvation is in their own hands and the accident that this conviction happened to coincide with a period of Liberal reaction in the political sense, that gave any party significance to the defeat of Toryism in Lancashire.

26 *January*.—Tom Legh, with whom I had a long talk this afternoon, confirmed what Stanley had said about Lancashire, but with greater independence of the official standpoint. The uprising of Labour was no doubt the principal factor, as was strikingly exemplified in his old constituency of Newton ; but there were other circumstances which gave it opportunity and augmented its force. Arthur Balfour was with him the Sunday after his defeat, and seems to have been very candid as to its causes. The fiscal question was not prominent in Manchester except in Winston Churchill's division, which was no doubt won upon it ; but in the rest of Manchester it was Labour working on the lack of interest felt in the fortunes of the late Government. He told Newton he wished to dissolve in the early autumn, which comes as a curious confirmation of the view I expressed some months ago, but was prevented doing so by those who professed to read the feelings of the party. It is unhappily true that political wiseacres are the worst guides at critical moments, and purely party moves are thus born in miscalculation and fructify in failure.[1]

Seely, who had been opposed to the Chamberlain policy from the first and had gone over to the Liberals, would attribute his victory above all to the agitation against Chinese labour.

Most people think that the decision of the electorate was mainly against Mr. Chamberlain and dear food. I do not believe this. I think a far greater factor of the defeat of Mr. Balfour's Government was the decision to import Chinese labour into South Africa. If there had been no Chinese labour I believe Mr. Chamberlain would have carried the day for Colonial Preference, if not at once, at any rate within a year or two. . . .

But when it came to the Chinese labour controversy, of which I had special knowledge, for I may claim to have originated the agitation in

[1] *Memoirs of Sir Almeric Fitzroy*, vol. i, p. 279.

this country, the case was quite otherwise. While an overwhelming majority of the voters hated the idea, many of them with a passionate hatred, there was nothing but a tiny minority who really favoured the plan.

I am not dealing now with the merits of either controversy, but only with the effect upon the electorate.[1]

Chamberlain's own analysis and something of his feelings emerge from the following letters.

CHAMBERLAIN TO MRS. ASQUITH

23 *January* 1906.—You at least have the magnanimity the absence of which I thought I detected in our great Prime Minister. Many thanks for your congratulations. We have done well today in Handsworth and in Austen's division and altogether we are rather pleased with ourselves here.

But what a smash! For me, I was quite out in my estimate and it was only the interruption of Horace Farquhar at Windsor that has saved me sixpence that I was about to bet with your husband against his having a majority over the Irish.

Well, we shall see what we shall see. Your coach has about 12 horses and will require skilful driving.

You are quite right in saying that I agreed with you that every week we stayed in after the end of 1903 cost us as many votes — but even then I did not anticipate the Labour earthquake.

CHAMBERLAIN TO COLONEL DENISON

24 *January* 1906.—The election here is practically over and has been a surprise to everyone. I knew that we should be beaten and expected a majority against us of anything to one hundred. The actual result has astounded me and is due to causes the existence of which we had not appreciated. The swing of the pendulum, the personal unpopularity of the late Government, the abominable calumnies about Chinese labour employed by our opponents for political purposes, and lastly the disaffection of the Nonconformists over the Education Act, would in any case have accounted for a heavy defeat, but the new feature is the growth and strength of what is called the Labour organisation, the exact objects and programme of which are still unknown.

The nett result is on the one hand a combination of sections which as long as they remain united will be all powerful, and on the other side a small but, I hope, practically unanimous Party for Union and Tariff Reform.

I anticipate a reaction which will speedily manifest itself and am not discouraged as to the ultimate result.

A great deal, of course, depends upon the effect that our reverse will have in the Colonies. If they stand firm to Imperialism and Preference, all will be well although success will be delayed. If they give up the

[1] J. E. B. Seely, *Adventure*, p. 102.

Austen Chamberlain

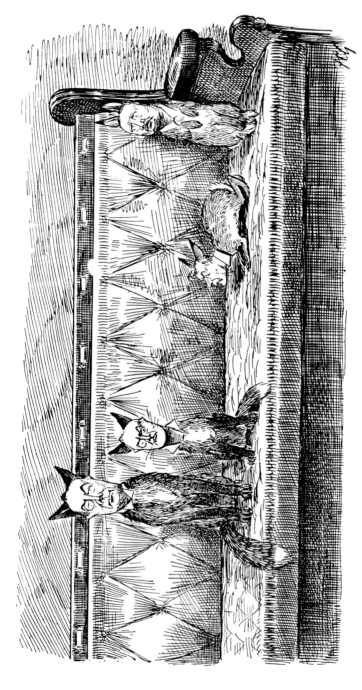

IN POSSESSION

The Front Opposition Bench

25 January 1906

struggle, the question of the tariff and of our future relations with our foreign competitors will remain, but the possibility of uniting the Empire by a Preferential Tariff will be greatly lessened.

It is too early to come to definite conclusions. I can only ask you at this moment to believe that I shall fight to the end and as long as life and strength are left to me.

CHAMBERLAIN TO PARKER SMITH

27 January 1906.—I need not tell you how sorry we were at the news of your defeat and how deeply we felt for you and your wife in what must be a very great disappointment.

The turn of the tide this time has been so phenomenal that almost everything has been swept away by it. I cannot see that Tariff Reformers have done much better than Free Fooders or Free Traders. Nothing has been able to hold up against this extraordinary storm. We must have time to think and to see if we can learn any lesson from the catastrophe. Personally I believe that the growing and underground feeling in favour of direct Labour representation has been enormously helped by the Chinese lies, not so much by the dislike of slavery as by the rooted prejudice against the employment of cheap labour anywhere.

But the opposition to the Trades Disputes Bill brought all the Trades Unions into line and helped to swell the Labour movement.

Besides this, we have in the English country districts the violent opposition of the Chapels and the Nonconformists, the effect of which I always felt would be very great. The Little Loaf has also done harm in agricultural districts where there has been no proper education. Oswestry is an interesting case of a division which was carried against us on Chinese Labour and the Little Loaf at a by election and has been won back by constant teaching carried on with admirable persistency by the candidate Mr. Bridgeman. What he did may be done elsewhere.

Scotland has been a great disappointment as I should have supposed the people were too shrewd to be taken in by the Chinese cry, while Education does not affect them.

I shall no doubt hear from you at your leisure with your review of the situation. Meanwhile there is nothing but patience and I hope clearer guidance than we have hitherto enjoyed.

The division in our Party and the uncertainty as to Balfour's views has handicapped us seriously and has prevented our new policy from being put forward with the conviction and earnestness which alone could have made it a strong steadying influence.

The *nouvelles couches sociales* will have their opportunity. What they will do I cannot imagine. I am afraid, however, they will have to do a great deal of mischief before they lose their present powerful position.

CHAMBERLAIN TO ROBERTS

27 January 1906.—. . . The disaster has been complete, but I agree with you that there must be a speedy reaction.

For the present we can do nothing but give our opponents rope. They

2 D

will be able to put their theories into practice and if we are right they will soon display their inherent weakness.

I still believe that the people are sound at heart, and above all are patriotic, although for a time they have been carried away by their desire for a change and their hope of certain material benefits promised them by the Radicals and Labour party. It will be a very interesting, but at the same time an anxious period to go through.

What is to be the verdict of history? In our view there were four major causes of defeat and we list them in order of importance.

First, the active opposition of the Labour movement, resulting from the total failure of the Unionists to remedy genuine working-class grievances or to develop a policy of social reform after the South African War. Chamberlain had sensed the danger and his Tariff Reform policy undoubtedly had a great appeal to the working classes. But even he had hesitated over Old Age Pensions. In other respects too he was out of date. He was frankly contemptuous of the Trade Union leaders and never made any serious effort to win over individuals among them or give them a prominent place in his movement.

Second, the alienation of the Nonconformists. The Unionist predominance over a score of years had been based on an alliance of Conservative Churchmen and Liberal Unionist Nonconformists. Balfour's Education Act had knocked out one of the main props of the great Coalition.

Third, Chinese Labour. This was not a deep-seated cause of defeat so much as a good cry to which Nonconformists, Trade Unionists and others simply wanting a change could rally. It is doubtful whether it turned many votes; but it played a decisive part in bringing the opponents of Unionism to the polls.

Far more difficult to assess is the part played by the Fiscal Question. Free Traders on both sides had every interest in attributing the Unionist defeat to the propaganda against the Dear Loaf. Yet nothing is more striking than the general admission of all sides that this was not the decisive factor. Some Tariff Reformers, indeed, went to the other extreme and claimed that the Unionists who survived had done so by going the 'whole hog'. Even Wyndham who had refused to join Chamberlain in the autumn now held this view.

WYNDHAM TO CHAMBERLAIN

13 *January* 1906: *Private.*—After our correspondence in October it is only right for me to tell you that I won *solely* on Fiscal Reform. I have fought on that ticket *within* the official programme. But I

served up the official programme 'piping-hot' with indignation against the foreigner & friendship for our Colonies.
The working-men polled right out for Fiscal Reform & the Empire. I won on that, & nothing else.

Chamberlain's own triumph tends to confirm this view, though in the Birmingham victories personality and organisation must have played as large a part as policy. Elsewhere in the country, such staunch Tariff Reformers as Chaplin, Bonar Law and Parker Smith went down. Nevertheless the fact remains that the candidate who had a policy was better placed than the men who had none. Hence the great preponderance of Chamberlainites among the survivors.

We have listed Fiscal Reform last among the causes of defeat. But in another sense it was the chief. The Dear Loaf cry may not have counted for much. But three years of divided leadership, humiliating Parliamentary tactics, and internal quarrels patched over by obscure declarations had completely demoralised the Party organisations and shattered the confidence of the public. Seen in this light Balfour's efforts to restrain what he regarded as Chamberlain's excessive Radicalism did more than anything else to ensure the triumph of the real Radicals.

Balfour's own verdict is given in a letter to Lady Salisbury. 'What has occurred has nothing whatever to do with any of the things we have been squabbling about over the last few years. Campbell-Bannerman is a mere cork, dancing on a torrent which he cannot control, and what is going on here is a faint echo of the same movement which has produced massacres in St. Petersburg, riots in Vienna, and Socialist processions in Berlin'.[1] All this was clear-sighted but unconstructive. Balfour failed to grasp the significance of Chamberlain's victories in Birmingham. These showed that the victory of Socialism was not inevitable. There was still a way to hold the working classes to their Tory allegiance.

[1] *Arthur James Balfour* by Kenneth Young, p. 255.

CHAPTER CXVI

THE VALENTINE COMPACT

(January–February 1906)

Chamberlain and the Unionist Leadership — He Demands Decisions on Fiscal Policy and Party Organisation — His Threat to Act Alone — Negotiations with Balfour — Division and Disagreement — Chamberlain Retires to Torquay — Balfour Accepts a Party Meeting — Further Negotiations — The Valentine Compact — The Lansdowne House Meeting.

I

THE election results of 1906 were no mere swing of the pendulum. They marked a revolution as complete in its way as that which followed the elections of 1832 and 1945. The old Tory party and its Whig allies were swept out of the constituencies. It was no mere accident that Balfour and Lyttelton were personally defeated at the polls, while Chamberlain held his own in Birmingham.

The Unionists were still strongly entrenched in the House of Lords. But if they were ever to break out of this last citadel and re-capture the British democracy, they must reorganise their party on a more popular basis and offer the electors a positive policy and a new theme. Someone must do for them — and on a larger scale — what Lord Randolph Churchill had done after the election of 1880. Never in the whole period between the Great Reform Bill and the Socialist victory of 1945 had the Unionists stood in greater need of dynamic leadership.

This problem of leadership was practical and urgent. Balfour was out. So were most of his friends. With the best will in the world, they could not win by-elections and be back on the front bench for the meeting of Parliament. Who, then, was to speak for the Unionists in the Debate on the Address? It would be a crucial Debate, setting the tone for the Opposition for several months ahead.

Of the survivors, Chamberlain was the senior and by far the most significant. His policy was the policy of the great majority of Unionists in the House and outside. These things marked him out as the natural temporary leader. But why only temporary?

796

Many Unionists, perhaps a majority, blamed Balfour's hesitations for their defeat. Still more felt that Chamberlain's aggressive and constructive temperament made him better suited to lead the forlorn hope to which the Opposition was reduced. In the last fortnight of January, letters began appearing in the newspapers urging that Balfour should give way to Chamberlain as Unionist leader. This correspondence seems to have been stimulated, in the beginning, by Pearson.[1] The first letters, certainly, appeared in *The Standard*. But the movement developed a momentum of its own and soon overflowed from *The Standard* to the columns of *The Globe*, *The Morning Post* and even *The Times*. Most of the letters appeared over pseudonyms such as 'Defeated Unionist Candidate', 'Unionist Chairman', 'Colonial' or 'Company Director'. But published, as they were, by reputable editors who must have known the identity of their correspondents, they could not fail to command attention. Here and there, in the correspondence, someone stood up for Balfour, but the overwhelming majority pressed Chamberlain's claims.

Some idea of the strength of feeling aroused may be gauged from the circumstances in which Balfour presently obtained another constituency. Alban Gibbs, one of the City of London Members, proposed to stand down in Balfour's favour. Alban, like his brother, Vicary, was an enthusiastic Tariff Reformer. So much so, indeed, that his personal relations with Salisbury, his cousin, were strained to the point that they communicated through an intermediary.[2] The City Unionist Association were by no means unanimous in welcoming Gibbs' proposal. Some objected to Balfour's lukewarm support of Tariff Reform. Others had no desire to hasten his return to the House of Commons.

Warned of the feeling in the Association, Chamberlain had used his influence with the chairman, Sir Joseph Lawrence — also a strong Tariff Reformer — to help secure Balfour's adoption. Lawrence proposed Balfour's name, but afterwards justified his action in a letter to *The Morning Post* in terms hardly flattering to the prospective candidate.

At the time, Balfour knew nothing of Chamberlain's intervention on his behalf. It might have been better for the relations between the two men if he had. Later, when his nomination had gone forward officially, Lawrence told him the full story.

[1] Sir E. Clarke, *Story of my Life*, p. 379.
[2] W. A. S. Hewins, *Apologia of an Imperialist*, vol. i, p. 164.

LAWRENCE TO CHAMBERLAIN

16 *February* 1906.—. . . Perhaps when you and Mr. Balfour next smoke a quiet cigar together, he may tell you what I said to him about you, personally. I extolled your chivalrous action and said you were a 'great gentleman' even in this City business; and I could see it touched him.

II

The feeling that Chamberlain should displace Balfour as Unionist leader was by no means confined to the outer fringes of the political world. Sandars wrote to Balfour (29 January) 'Alfred Lyttelton has just been here . . . He thinks Joe means business — *His policy* or *yours* with his *lead* or yours . . .' The Chamberlain papers certainly show that many of his closest supporters urged him to grasp the leadership himself and rid the Party machine of what they regarded as the dead hand of Balfour's circle.

RIDLEY TO CHAMBERLAIN

22 *January* 1906: *Private.*—(1) I am deeply convinced that it is quite impossible for Balfour to continue as leader. The present elections have in the main been a revolt against him and all that he stands for. He has undone all the good that R. Churchill began, and given Socialism a new impetus. I am not unaware of the feelings you have for him: and therefore I do not like to say or do anything, however feebly, without knowing more of your mind on the subject.

(2) The Tariff Reform League must be reformed. I have endured tortures with the present people there, who will not work *with* anyone and discourage all helpers, though they themselves have worked very hard.

(3) I think we might try and galvanise the House of Lords a little.

(4) I hear very distinct rumours that it is proposed to make J. A. Sandars head of the Conservative Office. This would be fatal to all progress and must be stopped. I have just written to Chaplin and hope to see him about it.

Chamberlain, himself, was determined from the beginning not to enter on a personal competition against Balfour. He felt that many Conservatives still regarded him as 'an alien immigrant' from the Radical camp, and that some even of those who agreed most with his fiscal policy would never back him in a personal challenge to their appointed leader. He was conscious, too, perhaps unduly so, of his own differences with the Conservatives over such questions as Education and Social Reform. We get a hint at least of these inhibitions in the following extracts from his and his wife's letters.

MRS. CHAMBERLAIN TO HER MOTHER

27 January 1906.—Judging by his correspondence and by what we hear from all sides and all the sections of the Party with whom we come in contact, there is a strong feeling that, if there is to be any hope of resuscitation, a clearer position must be defined, and that the policy of drift and shilly-shallying must be abandoned. All agree that the question of Tariff Reform has not been the cause of defeat — on the contrary both successful and unsuccessful candidates declare it to have been their best card.

Of course many of his correspondents and others urge that his attitude is the only one to command enthusiasm and that he should become the Leader, but on this point I feel as I always have done that it is not possible. He would not get the unreserved support of the Conservatives and, without that, leadership would be worse than useless and do his cause more harm than good. And so that is a thought which has no place in my calculations.

CHAMBERLAIN TO MRS. ENDICOTT

30 January 1906.—My special interest — that of Tariff Reform and Imperial Preference has not suffered I think so much as my opponents would like to make out, but its success is postponed indefinitely and there is still a big fight before me. Many of my friends, not always discreet, basing themselves on our victories in Birmingham would like me to compete with Balfour for the Leadership. But this I will not do, both on personal grounds and also because I feel that without his influence I could not hope in what remains to me of active life to restore the Party to its old efficiency and predominance.

I am therefore trying to secure agreement with him on a programme of more definiteness than he has hitherto been willing to adopt, but he is not easy to persuade and I do not yet know what will be the outcome of it all.

Hewins, who saw a good deal of Chamberlain at this time, attributed his 'unwillingness' to compete for the leadership to, among other things, 'a certain distrust of himself'.[1] This may well have been true of Austen at a later date. We must doubt whether it was ever true of Chamberlain, unless possibly on grounds of health.

His reluctance, indeed, to enter into a direct competition with Balfour did not mean that he would refuse the leadership under all circumstances. But he was determined that the issue if it ever arose, should turn upon policies not personalities. His main object was to have his policy of Fiscal Reform accepted by the Unionist party. If Balfour would accept it, he was quite content to serve under

[1] W. A. S. Hewins, *Apologia of an Imperialist*, vol. i, p. 164.

Balfour. If Balfour, however, would not accept it, then events, and the opinion of the Party, might compel Balfour to withdraw and so open the way for Chamberlain's own leadership. In the circumstances his choice was plain. If he staked a personal claim against Balfour he might well lose and would certainly split the Party. If, on the contrary, he staked everything on the policy, then either Balfour would come to terms and the policy would prevail, or Balfour would fight the policy and be forced to abandon the leadership.

Meanwhile, certain practical and immediate decisions had to be taken. Who was to lead the Unionists in Balfour's absence? Who would appoint the Whips? Who would give the usual dinner on the eve of the Session? Who should attend it?

Chamberlain, for his part, was not prepared to undertake these responsibilities except on the basis of the wholehearted acceptance by the Unionist Party of his Fiscal Reform policy. He was approaching seventy and felt there was little use in spending the next five years of his life supporting Balfour's formulas of compromise. He was not 'an old man in a hurry'. But there was one policy in which he believed passionately. He wanted to make it the main plank in Unionist policy from the start. He also wanted to gain control of the Party machine both to make it more efficient and to ensure its support of Fiscal Reform. If these things were refused him, then he would refuse the responsibility of leadership and take his place on the back benches.

The first step was to open a negotiation with Balfour. Here, he took the initiative. His main proposal was for a Party meeting to choose the temporary leader and give a mandate to his policy. For the rest the letter deals only with immediate and practical problems; but its tone is striking. He rubs in his own success at Birmingham. Balfour's leadership is not contested but it is certainly not taken for granted. At the end, Balfour is invited to Highbury.

CHAMBERLAIN TO BALFOUR

23 *January* 1906: *Private.*—I hope that you have had a few days comparative rest and that you are recovering from the physical fatigue of your recent exertions. I finished my electioneering work last night. Today we have retained Handsworth and Austen's seat in East Worcestershire, by largely increased majorities, and I hope we may win a seat in North Worcestershire on Thursday. In the present extraordinary situation we have reason to be thankful that Birmingham and the district have done so well.

We must now look forward to the immediate future and consider what is to be done when the House of Commons meets. I am anxious to see

you as soon as that is possible and should be glad to know your movements. We had intended to go to the Riviera for a fortnight, but that is
now impossible although my wife still hopes that we may get away for
a week's rest somewhere in England.

Austen has fought his election with splendid courage, but he is still a
victim to his sciatica and the sooner he is able to take at least a month's
holiday the better I shall be pleased.

Have any arrangements yet been made as to finding a seat for yourself?
What prospect is there of your being back in the House at an early period?
A great deal must depend upon this and meanwhile some arrangement
must be made for the interim. Who is to lead the House in your temporary
absence, and how is that question to be decided? A great deal depends
upon this matter, and personally it seems to me that there ought to be,
as soon as possible, a meeting of the Party to consider the subject. It is
not merely a question of persons that is at stake but also an indication
of future policy. Clearly no one, however ambitious, can desire to
occupy such a post even for a few days, and no one, I think, would be
wise to do so unless he had a clear mandate from the Party.

But who are to be considered as belonging to the Party? Are they
to be only the Unionists who have been returned to Parliament or are
other representative men, many of whom have fallen in the fray, to be
summoned to such a meeting.

Then, who are to take the office of Whips, and who is to appoint them?

You, of course, will have the decisive voice, but the interim leader,
whoever he may be, must be consulted.

Is there to be the usual Dinner of the Heads of the Party on the eve
of the assembly of Parliament to receive a copy of the King's speech?
Naturally you must be present either as host or principal guest, but there
should be a preliminary meeting of the principal leaders at an early
date when we must settle whether any amendment is to be moved to
the Address.

These are only some of the questions which naturally present themselves and which are so important that they ought not to be postponed
to the last moment.

Meanwhile, when and where can we meet? Is there any chance that
you and Miss Balfour would pay us a visit here? If not, when do you
go to London? I am sure that it is most important that we should have
a full private talk before any other steps are taken.

Chamberlain's letter reached Balfour in Scotland. His reply is
courteous but firm. Chamberlain, he thinks, must be the temporary
leader. He is very doubtful of the wisdom of calling a Party meeting,
unless, of course — and it is almost a challenge — 'the leadership
were in question'. He will give the traditional dinner, inviting
'members of the late Cabinet . . . *plus* you and George Wyndham'.
This last, a hint almost that Chamberlain would not attend as of
right. Finally he declines the invitation to Birmingham and suggests
instead, a meeting in London.

2 D 2

BALFOUR TO CHAMBERLAIN

24 *January* 1906 : *Private.*—You were quite right in thinking that we must have a very full talk upon the extraordinary state of affairs now prevailing.

Let me first say with what enormous relief I heard of Austen's victory. I had a sort of fear that the Birmingham influence might not extend to all the country seats in its neighbourhood, and that Austen might have trouble. I am immensely consoled and encouraged by the result.

I have not yet got a seat ; but I hope some arrangement may be come to which will enable me to join you in the House of Commons at the earliest possible date. Nothing that can be done, however, would enable me to be there at the beginning of the Debate on the Address, and it seems to me quite plain that there is only one man who can take my place — and that is *yourself.*

I am not absolutely clear that anything would be gained by a Party meeting. Dizzy had one in 1880 ; but nothing came of it. I do not see that much more would come of it now. Of course, if the leadership were in question, a Party meeting would be necessary, and it is quite possible that, after so great a disaster, there may be a feeling in the rank and file of the Party that some alteration should be made. I will try and find out whether there are any genuine indications of this being the case. Perhaps you will do the same. If it should prove that no such indications exist, I doubt a Party meeting being of much use ; but it does not follow that we shall not have to hold one, if only to satisfy men's minds that everything is being done that can be done.

As regards my plans, I did not think of going south till after the middle of next week. There will be nothing doing in the House of Commons till after the swearing-in and other formalities are accomplished, that is to say, not till Thursday, the 15th, at the earliest. In this case, the Parliamentary dinner would be on Wednesday, the 14th. I suppose I ought to give it ; and my idea would be to ask the members of the late Cabinet, whether in or out of Parliament, *plus* you and George Wyndham. There are objections to this, but I see no better course.

I do not think Alice can come to Highbury, much as she would like to do so ; for she will be getting Carlton Gardens, after ten years' vacancy, into some kind of order. Is there nothing which is likely to take you to London in the second half of next week, or later ? I am promised to Hatfield, but this is almost the same as London, and I could make any arrangement to suit you.

Chamberlain sat late that night with Ridley, talking over their plans. Balfour's letter must have reached him next morning. He replied at once, accepting Balfour's suggestion that they should meet in London but inviting Balfour to come to him for dinner on 2 February.

The rest of the letter is really the agenda of the meeting between the two leaders. Chamberlain insists on a Party meeting. He will not accept even the temporary leadership without a mandate from the rank and file of the Party for his policy. He does not seek to challenge Balfour's leadership but he insists on Balfour's acceptance of his fiscal policy and the repudiation of the Unionist Free Traders. Otherwise he will retire to the back benches. Finally, he aims at a reorganisation of the Conservative party on a more democratic basis and a union between it and the Liberal Unionist party. The letter is of cardinal importance.

CHAMBERLAIN TO BALFOUR

25 *January* 1906.—I have just heard with sincere pleasure that Gibbs gives way to you for the City. No better solution could have been devised. I regard an early conference with you as of so much importance that I will make a special visit to London next week. Will it suit you to dine with me at Prince's Gardens at 8 o'clock on Friday, 2 February? Austen will be there too, and if Miss Balfour is then in London we shall be delighted if she will join our family party.

I think there must be a Party meeting; and the more I consider it the more I believe that it ought to be called by you and confined to the Unionist members to the present Parliament. While I shall be glad to do anything that can assist you, I could not agree to take your place, even for a day, without a confirmation of my temporary position by such a meeting. No one can say as yet what are the views of those who are going to form the nucleus of our new Party, nor how far their views have been changed by the result of the elections.

I do not suppose that there will be any doubt as to the question of leadership. I have always held and declared, both in private and public, that you alone can carry us to ultimate victory, and I attach no importance to any difference of opinion which may or may not exist on this purely personal question; but my correspondence, which has been enormous, shows an almost feverish anxiety as to the policy which we are from the first to declare.

My correspondents are unanimous: (1) in desiring that our policy as a Party, whatever it is, should be made clear from the first, and (2) that if possible there should in future be no room for doubt that you and I are absolutely at one both as to the principles at stake and also as to the means which we are prepared to take to give effect to them.

Many of our old colleagues attribute their defeat to the fact that during the last two years there has been no definite agreement — that is to say no complete official policy to which you and I are alike committed.

Our defence against the misrepresentations of our opponents on the Big and Little Loaf has been weakened in consequence, and the education of the constituencies which must precede any ultimate victory has been delayed and confused because our men have themselves been uncertain, some going for what has been called, for want of a better name, 'the half sheet of notepaper', and others for what has been described most unsatisfactorily as the Chamberlain policy.

Surely it is desirable to ascertain at once whether the 150, more or less, who come back are agreed on either of these alternatives. Everything seems to me to depend upon it. For instance, if the great majority, or even a very large minority, desire that the policy of the Party should be modified in consequence of the election in the direction of minimising it, and if possible getting rid of any tax on Corn, it is quite clear that my leadership even for an hour would be undesirable if not impossible.

In such a case you would have to choose between Akers-Douglas and Walter Long, either of whom would no doubt admirably fulfil the temporary obligation; but in that case I must stand apart, at all events for a considerable time, and my present idea would be to take a back seat behind the front bench as an independent though friendly member.

On the other hand, it is possible that the conviction may have been brought home to the great majority of our present Party that a clearer acceptance of the policy laid down in my speech at Glasgow in 1903 is the only foundation for future action.

Can we in that case agree to work shoulder to shoulder or are our personal differences of opinion insurmountable?

Up to the present time I have hoped and believed that this is not the case, and that there was nothing between us on which we could not come to an agreement.

What I feel to be impossible is that we should go on as we have been doing for the last two years, allowing both sections of the Party to profess a separate loyalty to one or other of us while declaring disagreement with the other.

Nothing but union, clear, definite and publicly declared, can make of the forlorn hope that we have to lead an effective instrument in the future.

I am very willing to stand aside, but at my age it seems to be neither more nor less than folly that I should waste the rest of my life in struggling for a victory, which, when it was gained, would find us in the same position of doubt and division that has made us impotent for some time past.

I must not be understood as wishing to criticise in any way the policy of the past. There was much to be said for the manner in which you have endeavoured fairly to hold the balance, but in my judgment the time has come when you must decide between one or other section. Unless events have changed the views of men like Hugh Cecil and other Free Traders, it is really absurd to go on pretending that they and I are in the same boat. It is humiliating to both of us, and it disturbs the minds and weakens the enthusiasm of the rank and file who require steady and definite guidance.

From my point of view everything depends on the views of the majority of those with whom we have to work. If they are not prepared for a thorough and forward policy I shall accept their decision; and I do not think that I shall give much trouble to those upon whom in that case will fall the responsibility of carrying it out; but the question, which for me at any rate is a critical one, and which I now have to decide, is whether I am going to continue the active and strenuous fight which I have hitherto made, or for a time at any rate to fall back into comparative inaction.

Besides this crucial issue, there is a secondary matter of the greatest importance. Nothing can be worse than the present state of the Conservative organisation. It is not altogether the fault of the head office or of the officials. Their weakness has been partly due to the absence of clear and definite guidance from the leaders. Throughout there has been a sort of competition between the officials of the Conservative headquarters and those of the Liberal Unionist and Tariff Reform organisations. As regards the Liberal Unionists the time is coming when as a Party we shall cease to be of any importance. I shall have in the new House many more supporters among the Conservatives than of those who call themselves Liberal Unionists. The name and separate organisation must continue in special districts of which Birmingham of course is the principal example. In these places it would weaken us to give up our distinctive name and organisation; but I think it would be desirable that we should come closer together elsewhere and I contemplate as a possibility the union under the name of a Joint Committee of the two central organisations in London. I believe that one result would be that we should be able to democratise local Conservative associations by introducing our system of voluntary workers chosen from the working classes and getting rid of the existing system of privilege for subscribers and so-called men of influence who cannot be relied upon at a time of stress to do any actual work. Here again, however, everything depends upon a complete agreement between you and myself.

I gather from the newspapers that the House is to meet on February 13th for the election of a Speaker and that the King's Speech is to be postponed till the 19th. If so, the Party meeting which will decide the question of who is to take your place during the Address must be held before the election of the Speaker, and I think should be called for the 12th, which would allow time for the necessary arrangements after the decision of the meeting had been arrived at. I do not remember at what time the House meets under such circumstances, but I am afraid that it is too early to hold the meeting of the Party on the same day, otherwise that might be more convenient for the bulk of the members who will, however, no doubt come up on the 12th inst. if they are specially summoned.

Then the Dinner before the discussion on the Address would have to be held on Saturday, 17th. I quite agree that it should be given by you, and that the persons you name would have to be asked. We should not be a very united party, but I do not think that the minority could be omitted, and meanwhile if the course I propose is taken the Party will already have pronounced on the main issue.

As I shall have a number of private matters to settle which depend upon dates I should be very much obliged if on receipt of this you would telegraph to say whether you can accept my invitation to dine on Friday the 2nd.

This letter of Chamberlain's, unlike the first two, is not marked 'Private'. Chamberlain, indeed, made no attempt to conceal his views at this time. Quite the contrary. Next day (26 January), he wrote very frankly to Evelyn Cecil, one of his staunchest

Conservative allies, and to Boraston, the chief organiser of the Liberal Unionist party. This second letter, though marked 'private', was intended, as Chamberlain made clear, for the information of other Liberal Unionist leaders.

CHAMBERLAIN TO EVELYN CECIL

26 January 1906.—I have been so overwhelmed with work and correspondence that I have postponed my intended letter of congratulations to you upon your splendid victory at Aston, which with Handsworth has withstood so admirably the whirlwind that has overwhelmed so many of our friends.

I entirely agree with you as to the contest. Every single correspondent who has written to me on the subject says that our whole-hearted definite policy has everywhere been our sheet anchor, and although we have lost some of our strongest supporters — amongst whom I especially regret Chaplin, Goulding and Boscawen — I think the causes of their defeat are clearly to be sought for in other than Tariff reasons.

I have written to Arthur Balfour begging him to call a meeting of the Party, which must consider the temporary leadership and also the policy of the future.

The nucleus which will remain after the elections are over, and from which we have to create a new Army, must be animated by a single spirit. We must have no more nursing of the Free Fooders, and the minority of the Party must be content to bow to the majority or to stand aside.

At all events that is my opinion, and unless the majority are prepared to accept it I shall sit in the House of Commons as an Independent Member. I cannot take a place on the Front Bench to carry on for an indefinite time a policy in which I do not believe, and which I am convinced will never enable us to retrieve our old position.

CHAMBERLAIN TO BORASTON

26 January 1906: *Private.*—My movements are uncertain. I have given up going abroad but should still like a week's rest somewhere in the south if I can get it. All depends upon the necessary work before Parliament meets about which I have written to Balfour.

The Party, or its remnants, have to decide whom they will have as temporary leader, and whoever is chosen must have a clear mandate from the great majority of the Unionist members. I do not imagine that anyone is anxious to have such an unenviable position, but I have to consider the possibility that I may be asked to take it, and I say at once that I will only do so with a free hand to declare and promote in every way the policy on which I have fought this election. If Balfour and any considerable section of the Party prefer to go on on the old lines with the half sheet of notepaper and truckling to the Free Fooders I will have nothing to do with it — I will not sit on the front bench but will take my place as an independent member behind it.

I tell you this for your information in case our people want to know my intentions.[1]
I have not heard anything of what effect the election has produced
on Arthur Balfour's mind. I still think that he is the only leader with
whom we can hope to win, but we cannot win with him unless he is
willing to move to meet us.

If I were to be nominated as temporary leader you will understand
that I should regard it as solely a temporary appointment till he finds
a seat. I have no intention of setting up against him, but on the other
hand I will not join him again without a more definite understanding as
to policy. This is the critical time. What the beginning is, that will the
end be, and unless we start as a homogeneous organism with full vitality
we shall not, in my opinion, develop into a victorious party. The position
is what it was when Fiscal Reform first came up and when I said to
A. B.: 'if you and I stand shoulder to shoulder we may bring this thing
off.' He did not refuse, but as you know he has never heartily and clearly
worked with us.

It would be an absolute waste of my life to go on for another five or
six years to find myself at the end in the same sort of position in which
we have struggled during the last two years.

A postscript to the letter to Boraston asked him to summon a meeting of the Liberal Unionist Management Committee. Arrangements
were also made for a meeting of the Tariff Reform Commission.
The following extract gives some idea of the mood prevailing at
Highbury in these days. It no doubt echoes Chamberlain's table-talk.

MRS. CHAMBERLAIN TO HER MOTHER

27 January 1906.—I think, however, that after his success he must
take a slightly different attitude, for it is of no use to begin and have all
the same old difficulties and annoyances to thwart the progress of his
policy at every step as heretofore — and he is inclined to make propositions which will clear the air. If the Free Fooders are still to be pampered
at every critical moment he feels there is no use in his wasting time and
strength in helping to bear the brunt of the battle, and he would prefer
to be in an independent position. On the other hand, his greatest desire
is that the Opposition should show a united front and so far as such small
numbers permit be strong to fight. This, therefore, is his aim at the present
moment.

It is not clear at present how soon Mr. Balfour will be back in the House.
If not by the time the Debate on the Address takes place, somone will have
to lead temporarily and this naturally would fall to Joe. He will not,
however, consent to take Mr. Balfour's place if it involves any *real* leading
(as for instance replying to the Leader of the House on the Address) without
a clear expression of opinion from the Party itself that they wish him to
take the place until Mr. B.'s return, for if he is to speak he wishes to have
a free hand to express his own views if the occasion requires it.

[1] My italics. — J. A.

It is a moment when it is better to have a general house-cleaning and put things in order, for the situation has changed and at least so far as he personally is concerned he goes back to Parliament with an increased reputation, whatever his detractors may assert.

Mr. Balfour has not accepted our invitation here as I felt sure he would not, but proposes meeting in London. So we go up next week on Wednesday and he is to dine with us at Prince's Gardens on Friday when they will have a chance to have a good long talk and consider all the circumstances. I am glad he (Mr. Balfour) is to sit for the City of London, and hope that a constituency which is in such accord with the idea of Fiscal Reform will have an inspiring influence. At all events one feels he ought to have a dignified position and the slight which Manchester put upon him be wiped out. We have written to Torquay for rooms for a week on February 3rd. I am sorry to say we shall not leave work behind us as the Secretary is to be of the party . . .

III

Chamberlain's letter to Balfour of 25 January was firm and outspoken. But he was far from being Balfour's only outspoken correspondent at this time. Lansdowne, his most intimate colleague, wrote even more frankly and in a wholly opposite sense. He, too, looked forward to an early talk.

LANSDOWNE TO BALFOUR[1]

28 *January* 1906.—As soon as you come south I should like to discuss the situation with you. We shall have to consider very carefully the line to be taken in both Houses; and if Joe is to understudy you, I am by no means confident that his line will be that which I should approve.

I have received a summons to attend a Liberal–Unionist Association Council (Executive Committee) on Friday next. Joe will preside, and will no doubt produce a policy for our acceptance. I shall be surprised if it commends itself to your judgment or mine. From his speeches I infer that he will nail *his* colours to the mast, and invite us to set to work at once to convert the country to his fiscal proposals. This would, to my mind, be an egregious blunder. Many of your best supporters 'stretched a point' when they went as far as you did, and will absolutely decline to go any further. If Joe insists on pushing his views, the schism will become deeper, and the Unionist party will degenerate into two feeble and mutually suspicious groups. Surely we may, so far as the near future — certainly so far as this session — is concerned, relegate the fiscal question to the background of our political life, and devote our attention to the many grave questions which members of H.M. Government have told us will be taken up, and some of which will no doubt find a place in the King's Speech. With regard to these questions, there will, I hope, be a fair approach to unanimity amongst us, and I shall be disappointed

[1] Lord Newton, *Lord Lansdowne*, p. 348.

if, when they come up for discussion, some of the friends who have left us do not rally to *your* standard.

It is not necessary that we should recant our opinions as to retaliation or Colonial preference, but the country has pronounced decisively against them, and we must accept the verdict, whether the jury has been misdirected or not. With a majority of over 200 against us, we are — for the moment, at all events — relieved of the necessity of bringing forward a constructive policy of our own.

I particularly dislike the idea of tarring the H. of Lords with the brush of Protection.

If I am *not* likely to see you before the L.U.A. meeting, please write me a few lines to say whether you agree or differ. Two or three words by telegram would suffice.

I am delighted that you stand for the City.

Salisbury also argued strongly against holding a Party meeting.[1] Further evidence of the divisions in the Unionist camp came to light in a letter from Devonshire which reached Lansdowne next day. The Duke considered that differences over fiscal policy were so deep as to prevent him attending Lansdowne's eve of session banquet to the Unionist leaders in the House of Lords. He evidently proposed to invite the Free Trade leaders to a separate dinner at his own table.

DEVONSHIRE TO LANSDOWNE [2]

28 *January* 1906.—I do not think that the result of the elections has in any way modified my opinion that the distinction between Free Traders and all shades of Tariff Reform should be as marked as possible, and I am afraid, therefore, that we must dine apart. I do not understand Goschen's position. I wrote to him telling him that he would probably receive an invitation from both of us, and he will have to make his choice. St. Aldwyn I leave to you, but I think that Balfour of Burleigh, who I believe to be a strong Free Trader, should also have the option.

Chamberlain travelled to London on 31 January. Next day, he gave lunch to Northcliffe and, in the afternoon, addressed the Management Committee of the Tariff Reform League. We have no record of what he said but it was, probably, in keeping with the letters to Boraston and Evelyn Cecil which we have already quoted.

Gilbert Parker and Garvin came to dine that night at Prince's Gardens. In the telegram inviting Garvin, Chamberlain had commented on the leading article in the *Outlook*:

Wonderfully right. We want a change of policy and organisation not of leader.[3]

---

[1] Salisbury to Balfour, 28 January 1906.   [2] Lord Newton, *Lord Lansdowne*, p. 347.
[3] Chamberlain to Garvin, 31 January 1906.

Their talk at dinner, however, seems to have stiffened Garvin's attitude. His next leader, written the following morning, contained these words:[1]

the Byzantine theory of Unionist leadership — the theory of speechless loyalty to an hereditary succession — is at an end. As a Parliamentarian, Mr. Balfour has shown extraordinary gifts. But he has shown no power whatever of moving and holding the country. Unless the ex-Premier can show himself capable of receiving and communicating inspiration by rising to the height of Mr. Chamberlain's policy the Unionist party will never return to power under his leadership.

Next morning's post (2 February) brought a letter from Chaplin, giving the opinions of Akers-Douglas, Balfour's chief lieutenant, and of Walter Long, a figure now of some importance as, after Chamberlain, he was the senior Unionist Privy Councillor still in the House.

CHAPLIN TO CHAMBERLAIN

1 *February* 1906: *Private.*—I found considerable excitement in London — in reference to the position generally and the future Leadership. Ed. Lawson, of the D.T., came to see me twice yesterday on a fishing expedition apparently, and found me the 2nd time. I told him very little, except that it was manifestly impossible that we could continue to fight in the same party as Hugh Cecil and the Free Fooders. Afterwards I saw Bob Douglas and Walter Long. The former took the same line about a party meeting as Arthur, asking who was to summon it, and expressing the opinion that both Houses would have to be included, *if* it involved the Leadership of the Party as a whole — i.e., of course, the Members of each.

My reply was non-committal, but he had seen your correspondence.

Walter had seen no one. But Douglas told me they had all been hunting for him. I got first run however — in fact he came by appointment to see me at the Carlton. He was distinctly of opinion that there *must be* a party meeting, and that I fancy will be the prevailing opinion. But strongly as he avowed himself a supporter of yours and your policy, he was doubtful as to the expediency of requiring a mandate just now for the whole of your policy, especially on the specific duties on Corn. The Western Constituencies, which he knows well, he says would be very much put off. I reminded him that the original proposals had been put forward as tentative: that the Agricultural Committee of the Tariff Commission had not yet reported; and suggesting that our primary duty in the future was to organise and educate. I think he was impressed by my suggestion — that it was impossible to carry out that task effectually till we knew what we had to organise and educate for.

He is evidently much annoyed by something Arthur had said recently about the reasons for G. Wyndham's retirement, stating very clearly

[1] *The Outlook*, 3 February 1906.

that if it was repeated in the H. of C. he would hear more of it very plainly.

Touching your interview with Arthur and temporary Leadership — supposing you should not be forced by circumstances or the feeling of the Party into something more — I own it seems to me, that *if* you can come to anything like a reasonable arrangement with Arthur, it settles the question at once as to who is to represent the Party at any time, in case of absence, illness or anything else ; and also the reversion of the Leadership ultimately, if for any cause there was a vacancy later on in that position in the H. of C., and this no doubt you will carefully consider before you break off negotiations, unless for something you consider vital.

Chaplin's account of Long's views and his own final paragraph urging the advantage of an agreement with Balfour were a warning against pursuing too extreme a course. Nevertheless, Chamberlain seems to have spoken very firmly at the meeting of the Liberal Unionist Management Committee. Once again, we have no full report of what he said, but the following letter from Lansdowne shows how Chamberlain's words struck that section of the Party which Lansdowne represented.

LANSDOWNE TO BALFOUR

4 *February* 1906.—The situation as it developed itself at the Liberal Unionist meeting fills me with uneasiness. Is there any way out of it? Can we save the unity of the party upon terms which would not be disastrous to it and damaging to our own reputations? I wish I could answer these questions satisfactorily.

You are, I understand, to discuss with Austen the purely economical aspects of the problem. It is conceivable that by the exercise of much ingenuity and mutual forbearance you may discover a formula which will in appearance reconcile the two parties.

Armed with this formula we should, I suppose, summon the party meeting, and announce that henceforth we should be at one ; and when Parliament meets, Chamberlain would, as your deputy, explain in his own language the conditions upon which the compact has been signed. I gather that he and some supporters of his would move an amendment to the Address in terms which would clinch the bargain in the most unambiguous fashion.

I reluctantly express my conviction that any 'compromise' which the Chamberlainites are at all likely to accept would inevitably be regarded by the public and by your friends as a surrender on your part, and as an admission that we have been insincere when we have said and allowed our supporters to say that your policy was a self-contained one and that it differed from Chamberlain's.

And the public will be right, for it is, to my mind, certain that Chamberlain will not budge an inch from his position. It is you who will have to move towards him and to explain how it has come to pass that while, a few weeks ago, you resigned on account of the differences which existed within the Party, these differences have now been composed.

There are two conditions upon which Chamberlain will evidently insist :

1. The acceptance in principle of a scientific tariff, to be followed by an early promulgation of its details.
2. A complete severance of relations with Unionists who refuse to accept the full Chamberlain programme.

The first of these seems to me utterly unreasonable, especially having regard to our uncertainty as to the attitude of the Colonies. Chamberlain, no doubt, wants to have a tariff for purely protective purposes, but we are deeply committed against such a policy.

The second condition is, I venture to think, wholly inadmissible. At the Great George Street meeting, Chamberlain urged it with much bitterness. We are not only not to support staunch Unionists who are not whole-hoggers, but we are to repudiate them, and contradict them, when they suggest that they are our friends. Could any doctrine be more unpatriotic at a crisis such as that which confronts us?

It is founded upon the preposterous theory that we are concerned as a nation with one question and one only, and that at a moment when any of our institutions may be attacked, and before we know the quarter in which the attack may develop, we are to reject the assistance of our best soldiers because they differed from our military policy during the last campaign.

My own feeling is that almost any misfortune would be better for us than an alliance in these terms : I am, moreover, sure that if we made it, it would not last six months, unless we are prepared to follow Chamberlain still further into the quagmire. There would be renewed complaints, fresh recriminations, and the schism would declare itself in spite of all our sacrifices.

Only one word more, and I am not sure that I ought to write it. Your friends look upon you as the most valuable asset which the party possesses. The value of that asset will, to my mind, be heavily depreciated if, in your desire to maintain unanimity, you allow it to be said that Chamberlain has at last overcome your scruples.

If he wrecks the party, or what remains of it, let him accept the responsibility and the consequences. He must lead in the H. of C., and one of his men in the H. of L. If he persists in his views and we in ours, I don't see how he can refuse.

When this happens, I believe you will be surprised to find how many people there are who will rally to you.

IV

Chamberlain and Balfour met over dinner at Prince's Gardens at eight o'clock on 2 February. Mrs. Chamberlain and Austen were the only others present. They stayed in the same chairs till forty minutes after midnight, when Balfour took his leave. On the surface their relations were friendly enough, but the underlying tension between them was serious. A letter from Mrs. Chamberlain written a few days later[1] gives the background and atmosphere of their talk.

It is a difficult situation! and I do not quite see how it is to end. It has been enormously complicated by the indiscreet zeal of Joe's supporters as well as Mr. Balfour's and the very thing which I feared has happened. Their personal interview was too long delayed and the result is that much has been said which had better never have been said. Courses have been outlined which had better never been suggested, and altogether there is danger of a cleavage which could only do harm to the Cause and destroy much that is valued by both. It was because I feared this that I deeply regret that Mr. Balfour did not fix an earlier date for meeting. Joe wrote to him within a few days of his own return saying that he thought they ought to meet and discuss matters very soon and suggesting his coming to Highbury. He declined this and said he was not coming South for ten days or so and then Joe said he would go to London to meet him and the dinner was fixed. Meanwhile Joe was obliged to attend meetings of the Tariff Reform League and Liberal Unionist Council where of course he was obliged to speak of the results of the election and his view of what should now be done to meet the new conditions. Every newspaper in London had time to make its own surmises, all the Clubs were full of gossip, and by the time Mr. Balfour came to dine with us he had been besieged by his friends as Joe had been by his. And, if one may judge by the general tone of the latter as an example of what on his side Mr. Balfour probably had had to listen to, they were not calculated to make it easier for him to approach the conversation before him with that quiet consideration of the merits of the case which was desirable any more than it was for Joe. To their credit be it said they met with their old friendliness. It was however evident from the first that the advance which we hoped would be made was hopeless. On the contrary I think Mr. Balfour is more than ever convinced that the policy which he has pursued has been quite satisfactory and that he still adheres to his support of the principles of Fiscal Reform, but does not think it necessary to take any further steps to bring it about . . .

Within a few hours of the dinner, Mrs. Chamberlain wrote:

The interview was as I feared it would be — unsatisfactory . . . so I don't know what is to happen.[2]

Next morning (3 February), Chamberlain dictated a short account of his talk with Balfour. This was intended for Boraston for communication to other Liberal Unionist leaders.

Private and Confidential, for information, and not for publication.
I am afraid the results of the meeting must be considered as, from my point of view, very unsatisfactory and I see no prospect of any agreement.

[1] Mrs. Chamberlain to her mother, 6 February 1906.
[2] *Ibid.*, 3 February 1906.

Mr. B. is opposed to holding a Party meeting which he says would only make our differences public. He says that with a very small party, absolutely united on our opposition to the common enemy, our policy is clearly a policy of criticism and attack. The fiscal question is not a practical question for the moment and there is no need to bring our differences into the forefront.

I pointed out that it was impossible to pretend to ignore them as they would come into view from the very first in Parliament, and that if we pretended to shut our eyes the only result would be that we should go on without a definite aggressive policy either in the country or in the House, and even if we won at last, not on our own merits but by the mistakes of our opponents, we should then find ourselves in exactly the same position as we were before the Election and should break to pieces in the moment of victory.

I suggested that the election had shown that a half way policy was not popular — that we must be either free traders or tariff reformers.

He appeared to have hardened and to be inclined rather to magnify his statement of differences. *He is opposed to a general tariff*, and does not desire to put forward the Corn Duty except to the extent of saying that, if he cannot get preference without it and could get a *quid pro quo*, he would not see any difficulty in principle.

His views about organisation seem to me equally unsatisfactory. He was not enthusiastic at the suggestion of a union of forces, and indeed under the circumstances I cannot wonder. Why should he in any way weaken his control if he is determined to go forward on the present lines? He indicated a desire not to exclude anyone — in other words he would wish *to keep the Cecils and all that that means*.

Speaking generally I feel that every effort should now be made to make a Part(y) meeting essential and that those who believe in a definite policy should be prepared to say so emphatically at the meeting and to force a division so that we may know where we are.

I should then propose to form all those who support my views into a Parliamentary Tariff Reform Party. I do not think we need go as far as I at first proposed or refuse to receive the official Opposition whip, but we will have our own whips also, and weekly or fortnightly meetings in the House of Commons.

We must strengthen the organisation in the country and try and increase the Party as quickly as we can.

Two days later, he sent a rather fuller account to Garvin.

CHAMBERLAIN TO GARVIN

5 *February* 1906: *Private and Confidential.*—I think you will like to know exactly how things stand. My interview with Balfour was perfectly friendly of course, but most unsatisfactory from our point of view. I gather that the effect of the general election on his mind is entirely opposite to what it has been on ours. He still believes in the 'half sheet of notepaper' as the policy upon which he will ultimately win. He does not believe in the proportions given by the papers of the members returned

to support our views. He evidently counts on their loyalty to the machine and their unwillingness to separate themselves in any way from the official leadership. He is more definitely against a General Tariff than he ever was before. He does not wish to have a Party meeting, which he declares could have no practical effect. What he evidently desires is that Tariff Reform should be put entirely on the shelf during this Parliament when, he says, it cannot be practical politics. Why should we raise differences prematurely? He thinks that the Government majority is fissiparous, and that we are to be constantly knocking in small wedges all the time until we gradually disintegrate it. That will not be accomplished for some years, possibly for two Parliaments, and not till then need we raise any question of Tariff Reform.

The statement of some of the papers that I presented an ultimatum is of course untrue, but I pressed with much insistence for a Party meeting. I said that I could not agree with him as to a policy of delay which would result in our finding ourselves five or ten years hence with no settled policy in regard to what he himself had described as the first and most important item in a constructive Unionist programme.

I argued that we ought at the very beginning to adopt a definite programme, and that even if it costs us, as it probably would, some of our small minority, that would be of no present consequence, while in the future it would secure the absolute unity of the Party and would ensure that the candidates at bye-elections were all one way of thinking.

I also pressed for reorganisation, but he evidently was not prepared to give up the hold on the machine or in any way to interfere with its working which I think has been fatal to our success in the past.

Altogether I saw no signs of advance or of concession on any single point. He suggested that I might lead and he would sit below the gangway. I told him, as I have told everyone, that I absolutely refuse to accept a position of personal opposition to himself and that I still thought that he was the proper leader of the Party as a whole. I pointed out that one who has already been described by Hugh Cecil in the House of Commons as an 'alien immigrant' in the Conservative Party could not hope for that kind of personal loyalty which alone would make the situation possible.

I told him, therefore, that in the event of his standing, as he appeared inclined to do, on the old way I must attempt to organise a Tariff Reform group, and this is clearly what we are coming to.

I have, however, given up all idea of refusing the official whip. We shall be a group within the Party similar to the group of London members which existed during the last Parliament or the group of Ulster Unionists, but probably we shall be more active and more influential.

The suggestion has been made that Balfour should give way to Long. If he did, this would be for us a satisfactory present solution as Long is a convinced Tariff Reformer and I could work with him without requiring guarantees beforehand, but I entirely mistake Balfour if he will consent to anything of the kind. He believes in the Balfourian policy of delay and mystification, and perhaps at the bottom of his heart hopes to tire out his opponents and get rid of the subject altogether.

Of course under these circumstances I shall not represent the Party on the Address. I believe it will be wise for us to put forward either an amendment or a subsequent Resolution in favour of our scheme, after which we may be content to watch and wait for opportunities.

If I can get sufficient good and true men to join me I should propose to have a fortnightly meeting during the session to consider our proposals and to keep all our section in line. We should have our own organisation and should take care to be represented at the bye-elections.

Meanwhile our policy is to insist upon a Party meeting at the earliest possible date, to make clear our determination to oppose any attempt to shelve the main question, to point out that we part in sorrow and not in anger, and lastly I think it would be well to minimise rather than to magnify the importance of the separation as there are so many timid people, even among our own friends, who are afraid to detach themselves from the official organisation. It will be better in my mind to allow the point of difference to accentuate itself gradually rather than to emphasise it in the first instance. I want to get as large a majority as possible of Unionist members to join our group from the first and this can only be done by showing that their cooperation will not be incompatible with personal loyalty to the official leader.

The last paragraph of this letter seems of special significance, and particularly the phrase, 'it will be better in my mind to allow the point of difference to accentuate itself gradually rather than emphasise it in the first instance'. Chamberlain was not held back by any false or sentimental loyalty to Balfour. His restraint was dictated by policy alone. But if Balfour remained he was quite prepared to accept a widening of the gap between them until the point came when the Party would have to chose between personal loyalty and political principle.

The true nature of his attitude to Balfour is revealed by his readiness to accept Walter Long as leader, instead of Balfour, if that could be arranged. His views on this point became known to his friends and there were the beginnings of a Press campaign to make Long the leader. Long, however, sent a telegram to the Press declaring that he was not a candidate for the leadership. It was interpreted in some quarters as a rebuff for Chamberlain. This was almost certainly not Long's intention. Though perfectly loyal to Balfour, he was a staunch Tariff Reformer. Days later, when told how his telegram had been interpreted by some Tariff Reformers, he wrote to Chamberlain:

LONG TO CHAMBERLAIN

11 *February* 1906: *Private.*—I am told that my telegram has been misunderstood and that it has been read as referring to the suggestion

made by you and some of your friends. This is a mistake. I intended
to refer to the statements made in Daily News and other Radical papers
to the effect that I was intriguing to get the Leadership. This idea was
naturally extremely distasteful to me and hence my language. I need
only assure you that I was very much gratified by your suggestions
tho' I confess I feel it would be ridiculous for me to attempt to lead a Party
which contained you and Balfour. I hope I may have an opportunity of
a talk with you soon as there is much I should like to say.

I am most anxious that the Unionist Party should not be broken up
so long as there is any chance of keeping it together as a real fighting
force — but of course we must go on steadily with Tariff Reform :
there are many timid people who may easily be frightened into the Free
Food ranks, but who may also be very easily won over to our side if we
go carefully to work.

V

On the morrow of his dinner talk with Balfour, Chamberlain
left London for Torquay. Mrs. Chamberlain, Austen and the
private secretary went with him. All in all, Chamberlain had stood
up to the strain of the election surprisingly well. Mrs. Chamberlain,
however, was anxious that he should get a few days fresh air and
comparative rest. Austen, too, had been ill with sciatica and it
was hoped the change might do him good.

At Torquay, Sunday, 4 February, passed peacefully enough.
No letters were received or written. The sun shone ; and the elder
and younger statesman enjoyed the sea breezes and the Devon
coast. In London, by contrast, reports and rumours of what had
passed between Balfour and Chamberlain spread like wildfire and
threatened to be as destructive. Here is Mrs. Chamberlain's
contemporary account.[1]

As I told you, it was clear from the outset of their conversation that
Mr. Balfour was more rigid than he ever has been before — they got
no nearer each other and at the end of 4½ hours or more of talk he left
and we all (Joe, Austen and I) felt that it was as unsatisfactory as it
could be and it was hard to see any way out of the impasse.

We came down here the next morning and the newspaper world, the
Clubs, the Free Fooders, the retaliators, the Tariff Reformers, defeated
candidates, new M.P.'s and the many grades of opinion all set to work
to surmise, misrepresent, espouse one or the other, and attack each man
in turn till a most difficult and critical situation was produced.

Joe was on the whole the more abused of the two, or rather I should
say the more criticised. His expressed and emphatic contention that
there was no question of the leadership, that he was not a candidate for

[1] Mrs. Chamberlain to her mother, 9 February 1906.

it, was questioned and misrepresented and altogether there was a regular
hurly burly of clamour. Some of Mr. Balfour's friends openly denounce
Joe's attitude as an attempt to hold a pistol to his head, and some of
Joe's friends I have no doubt were equally indiscreet. Between them they
threaten to make the personal position as difficult for both as the political
one.

News of the widening breach between Chamberlain and Balfour
alarmed the more responsible Unionist leaders. Halsbury and
Long, loyal Conservatives but staunch Tariff Reformers, determined
to use their influence for peace.

HALSBURY TO CHAMBERLAIN

4 *February* 1906.—*I saw Balfour yesterday* and he communicated to me
the substance of what had passed between you on the previous evening
and I write to you because, though there is very much in what you have
said to him well worthy of consideration and negotiation and may I say
suggestive of concessions on both sides, there is one matter which seems
to me so urgent and important that I feel I must write to you at once
and put my views before you. I refer to your wish for a Party meeting
before the assembling of Parliament and, of course, before the programme
which must be indicated in the King's speech. Now I am probably the
only one of your colleagues who neither expects nor desires to be in office
again. I am a loyal adherent of the fiscal policy which you have ex-
pounded with such brilliant effect but I do deprecate as earnestly as I
can such a meeting.

I must say I have been present at a good many party meetings and I
cannot remember that we ever got much good out of any of them but
to have one now seems to me to render certain the shattering of the
Unionist party altogether. A number of angry men after an unprecedented defeat with nothing to discuss but their differences and the
various causes of the great disaster would be bad enough if it could be
kept 'confidential' but we all know that the substance of as many words
(probably angry and unadvised words) will be in the enemy papers the
same night.

Now present circumstances seem to me to render such a meeting
peculiarly inappropriate and would amount to washing our dirty linen
in public. The question of the leadership cannot be discussed in such a
meeting with temper and good taste and, if the correspondence in the
newspapers is a statement of what may be expected, I cannot conceive
what but the final extinction of all hope of joint action can be the result.

I have spoken to some of the heads of the party, I mean the old Conservative party (without of course mentioning you or your conference
with Balfour), and they agreed with me that a party meeting before the
King's Speech would be a fatal mistake in tactics.

The mere delay of a *few days* could not surely make such a difference
as to be injurious to any interest, while if held afterwards then the King's
speech gives us something to discuss and agree upon other than our
grievances against each other. I write to you freely. We have so often

agreed in Cabinet together and I feel you will not object to my saying freely to you what I think.

LONG TO CHAMBERLAIN

4 February 1906.—We want a strong united policy, but I feel strongly that you and Arthur ought to find a common platform — the country will not understand the split which I am horrified to think seems possible, and the Party will be split into fragments not to come together again I believe in 10 years.

It seems to me we want to unite to attack the enemy and defend our cause. Fiscal Reform must go in, but much *spade* work must be done, in the country, not in Parliament, and we must be cautious and careful. In Bristol, for instance, we can press the earlier policy, in the adjourning County divisions it is impossible at present till the spade work has been done.

You know how heartily I support Tariff Reform, how much I admire the great part you have played, and above all how deep and strong is my personal regard for yourself: and it is on this latter ground that I venture to appeal to you to make up your mind that a modus *shall* be found. If you do this the desired End will be accomplished. With Arthur and you leading us on the front opposition Bench we can do great Things, and I believe carry Tariff Reform in 5 years, or even less. With you two divided we shall be powerless and I confess I feel I should like to leave Parliament.

Forgive me for writing — the issue at stake is so tremendous.

These letters reached Chamberlain at Torquay on 5 February. He replied at once. His object, plainly, was to ensure that his colleagues had his version of what had passed as well as Balfour's.

CHAMBERLAIN TO HALSBURY

5 February 1906.–I will now try and put my views on the special point on which you lay so much stress.

I begin by saying that if 'mutual concessions' could remove our differences I hope that I should not be found unreasonable but as far as I can see there is no idea of anything in the nature of a concession on Mr. Balfour's part. On the contrary the result of the election seems to have hardened his mind in the opposite direction to ours, and he now speaks more decidedly on such questions as a two shillings duty on foreign corn and a general tariff than he has ever done before.

In fact he still believes that the 'half sheet of notepaper' is a gospel which all ought to accept and on which alone the Party can convert the country. Even this he would not put forward at the present time but would lay upon the shelf until by constant opposition we had worn down the enormous majority against us. In other words we are to have no distinct and definite policy ourselves except that of opposing the Government.

I believe this would be fatal both to the success of the Party, and also to the cause of Tariff Reform. The latter has been the only subject which has interested the people.

If it could have been put to a Referendum independently of the question of the existence of the Government, it might even now have secured a majority, and it is in my opinion the only constructive programme on which we can ever gain the support of the country.

I believe, although Balfour does not, that the great majority of those members who have been returned have been successful on these lines, and that they desire above all that Balfour and myself should unite in such a policy. They are not disloyal to Balfour personally, and if the issue were to be complicated by a personal question of this kind they would be placed in a very difficult position, and many might perhaps give up the policy sooner than to lose their present leader.

I should expect that a meeting of the Party would bring out these facts, and in any case it seems to me that we ought as soon as possible to get rid of uncertainties and mystifications and find out what is the real opinion of Unionists as a whole. Without this we have no solid foundation, on which outwardly to base our policy. It is true that a free Conference of the kind suggested would disclose considerable difference of opinion, but can we hope to hide its existence? Would it not be better to recognise it, define it, and estimate its importance and magnitude as a preliminary stage to subsequent agreement? Is not the present the best time, with a majority of nearly four hundred against us? Numbers are of no importance in comparison of clearness of object and expression. A minority of a hundred, knowing its own mind, will be a better foundation for our future army than one of a hundred and fifty in which differences are smouldering all the time.

I do not pretend that the exact date of such a meeting is a matter of supreme importance. All I plead for is a very early discussion.

What seems to me the most fatal of all alternatives would be to work for five years or more in order at the end, in the event of success, to find that the Unionist Party was again in the position occupied by it during the last two years in which the Party would be still divided and neither section would know the mind of the leader.

I hope that I have made myself clear and that we shall not be very far apart, but if you still think that I am wrong and have any further arguments to urge, please do so, and believe that I shall greatly value your advice in what is to me a most serious and critical moment.

Chamberlain's letter to Long is in very similar terms and it is enough to quote a very short extract even more emphatic than anything in the letter to Halsbury.

CHAMBERLAIN TO LONG

5 *February* 1906.—Balfour seems to me to have read the lessons of the election in altogether a different sense from what we do. He seems to me to have gone back and not forward in his views, and to be entirely wrong as to the real feeling of the Party as a whole. . . . In fact, he is

non possumus everywhere, and I confess I do not see my way out of the difficulty in which we are placed.

Halsbury's letter and Long's, the latter especially, were a warning to Chamberlain of the mounting anxiety felt over the question of the leadership. This warning was renewed next day (6 February), by a leading article in *The Times* stressing the personal rather than the policy aspect of the difference between Balfour and Chamberlain. Chamberlain was always inclined to be sensitive to personal issues; Austen almost morbidly so. Away from the centre of things, Chamberlain began to feel he was losing ground and in danger of being misunderstood. He decided, accordingly, to issue a full statement of his views on policy and organisation together with a frank disclaimer that he was a candidate for the Unionist leadership. This statement — it is a manifesto really — took the form of a letter to Ridley.

CHAMBERLAIN TO RIDLEY

6 February 1906.—I gather from a perusal of letters and articles which have recently appeared in the Press that there is still much misapprehension of our position as Tariff Reformers and even of my personal attitude, although I should have supposed that my public utterances would have made this at any rate perfectly clear.

I propose therefore in this letter once more to describe the situation as it appears to me.

In the first place I most strongly repudiate the notion that this is or can possibly become a question of persons or leaders. From the beginning I have made it absolutely clear that in no circumstances would I be a candidate for the leadership of the Unionist party — firstly because after having worked in the closest friendship with Mr. Balfour for over twenty years, I will not place myself in competition with him now; and secondly, because I entirely agree with those who say that the leader of a party seven-tenths of which are Conservatives, should be himself a Conservative.

All that is in question, therefore, is the policy which the Unionist Party propose to adopt in the future. It is absolutely untrue that any ultimatum has been presented to Mr. Balfour on this subject either by me or by anyone else. I have asked for a meeting of the Party in order that there may be frank and friendly discussion of the question, because to me, it has always seemed essential to successful leadership that the leader should be thoroughly and personally acquainted from time to time with the views and wishes of his followers. He need not necessarily accept them as a whole, but he ought at least to know what they are.

Now as regards Tariff Reform there appear to be three views held by different sections of our Party. The first is not unfairly stated in the leading article in yesterday's 'Daily Telegraph' and is based on the assumption that Tariff Reform cannot be a question of practical politics for some years to come, and the conclusion is that it should be dropped for the present as an active policy and that we should confine ourselves to harassing the Government, reserving all matters of difference till there seems some immediate probability of our being called back to power. If this view be adopted, Tariff Reform is to be placed on the shelf — all the enthusiasm and interest which it has created in the country is to be damped down — at bye-elections it is not to be mentioned — and the work of education, which all admit to be necessary, cannot be carried on since the teachers will not know what it is they are expected to teach and will have no clear guidance from their leader.

I need hardly point out that such a position would be entirely inconsistent with Mr. Balfour's language when he said that Tariff Reform was the first item in the constructive programme of the Unionist Party, and commercial union with the Colonies the most important and urgent branch of Tariff Reform.

The second suggestion is that, while not pressing Tariff Reform under existing circumstances, we are to unite, as among ourselves, on the programme known as 'the half sheet of note paper'. Between this programme and that of the more advanced Tariff Reformers there are two differences:

1. That we think that the probability of our having to place a moderate duty on corn from foreign countries in return for a substantial preference to be given by the Colonies to our manufactures should be frankly admitted and defended, and that we should make a full reply to the misrepresentations of our opponents in connection with the Big and Little Loaf. Mr. Balfour has more than once stated that he has no objection in principle to such a duty, but he has accepted without protest the statement of the Free Fooders that under no circumstances, whether after a conference or not, and whatever may be the offers made by the Colonies, will they assent to any duty on corn.

2. There is the question of a general Tariff, as to which it is necessary to say that in our opinion it is impossible without it to have any practical or effective scheme of Retaliation against the excessive duties imposed by foreign countries on our products. Mr. Balfour has never up to the present time attempted to put forward any alternative scheme although he has been pressed to do so both by Lord Hugh Cecil and by Tariff Reformers. I believe that he himself regards this difference of opinion as to procedure as insignificant, and I have hoped, not unnaturally, I think, that if he did not attach great importance to his own point of view he would be able, without any sacrifice of principle, to approach more closely to ours.

I see that it is stated by some of his supporters that an attempt has been made to impose upon him, as a condition of union, the exclusion from the Party of all who decline to accept the whole programme of the Tariff Reform League. Nothing of the kind has been suggested, although I have myself pointed out that it would be dishonest to pretend that the Free Fooders, who, while nominally supporting Mr. Balfour, were clearly opposed to his policy and would not accept his decision if after the Conference he proposed a preference on corn, were in the same boat as either the Tariff Reformers or the Retaliationists.

A further important point concerns the reorganisation of the party machinery. It is universally admitted that in its present form it has shown itself inefficient, and it seems to be desirable that, while the lesson of the elections is fresh, the Party as a whole should have an opportunity of considering how far a reform of the organisation has become necessary.

The issue seems to me the same as that which was raised by Lord Randolph Churchill in 1883, and involves the decision as to whether the Central Organisation is to remain an autocratic and non-representative body, or whether with a democratic electorate it ought not to be strictly representative and responsible to the Party as a whole.

I observe that the advocates of the existing system describe the proposal to popularise it as an attempt to secure the Party machinery for the furtherance of Tariff Reform and to get rid of the officials who have faithfully acted in accordance with the wishes of Mr. Balfour. It is evident that this statement involves the admission that if the organisation were popularised, and if the whole Party were consulted, they would vote for Tariff Reform and that consequently the policy and action of the organisation has been in the past in opposition to the wishes of the party. This however, is a matter which can only be decided by a party meeting and which would no doubt be one of the principal subjects for discussion on such an occasion.

Up to the present time I do not think that any of the lists which have been published purporting to show the composition of the Members returned as Unionists to the new House of Commons can be taken as authoritative. My own belief is that the great majority, if not all, are perfectly ready to accept Mr. Balfour's general leadership. I think it probable, however, that a majority would welcome a declaration by Mr. Balfour which would show clearly that Tariff Reform was not to be dropped and would indicate a definite and unmistakeable programme for the future to which they could all give their hearty support.

If, however, the majority should be in favour of the views expressed by the Free Fooders or should desire that the whole question should be left in abeyance, the Tariff Reform minority would in that case have to reconsider their position. After giving the matter full consideration, it does not appear to me that it would be necessary or wise that they should separate themselves from the Party as a whole or from the general leadership. They may, however, very properly constitute themselves into a Parliamentary group or Committee such as existed during the late Parliament. They would in the same way meet periodically *at the call of their own Whips* and would endeavour to agree as to their action and as to the occasions when they might properly bring forward their views in the House of Commons. These occasions will probably arise more frequently than is supposed.

The question of Social Reform for instance is intimately connected with the raising of the necessary revenue, and all proposals with regard to future and present taxation will suggest alternatives and may raise the points with which we are chiefly concerned. In this and other ways we shall keep the question alive and in conjunction with outside organisations shall secure continuous discussion in the country and shall take care that our views are fully represented at bye-elections.

I must apologise for this long letter, but I trust it will serve its purpose in making clear what I believe to be the views of all sincere Tariff Reformers. You will see that there is no question of repudiating the leadership of Mr. Balfour or putting undue pressure upon him to abandon his opinions or his friends. On the other hand Tariff Reformers sincerely believe in their principles and cannot be expected to put them aside to suit the exigencies of party wirepullers.

They are ready, now as ever, to work with their Unionist colleagues for common objects, but they cannot accept a policy of inaction and mystification with regard to the main object of their political life, honestly convinced, as they are, that in the acceptance of a full measure of tariff reform lies the best hope for the future success of the Party as well as of the cause.

Three things stand out from the letter. Chamberlain's disclaimer of any interest in the leadership. His frank declaration that he means to carry the Unionist Party for his policy or else form a group of his own. Finally, the pin-pointing of the issues on which he and Balfour were at odds: in the first place, policy, where acceptance of a general Tariff and a duty on corn are the test; in the second place, organisation, where democratisation is the test; in the third place, procedure, where Chamberlain insists on a Party meeting.

The same post that brought Chamberlain's letter to Ridley, brought an interesting mailbag to Torquay. There were further letters from Halsbury and Long, both urging that Chamberlain and Balfour were not as far apart as Chamberlain seemed to think. It is possible that they had also been pressing Balfour in the direction of agreement. Some substance is lent to this view by a letter from Balfour conceding Chamberlain's request for a Party meeting, and discussing its possible composition, venue and procedure.

BALFOUR TO CHAMBERLAIN

6 *February* 1906: *Private.*—This letter is not intended to re-open or continue our discussion of Friday night, as, where conversation has *for the moment* proved a failure, correspondence is not likely to prove a success. I only wish to ask your opinion upon subsidiary points.

You know how strong is my objection in ordinary circumstances to a Party meeting, and how reluctant I am to have all our differences dealt with in a manner which is certain to be public, and will probably be irritating. But, on carefully thinking over the whole situation, I have come round to your view that, *if you desire it*, a Party meeting must be held.

This decision, however, suggests several minor questions of considerable

THROUGH

31 January 1906

CAUGHT AT LAST

A Valentine – 14 February 1906

difficulty. Who is to be asked? Where are we to meet? What is to be the procedure?

As regards the place of meeting, I do not know that any place would be more suitable than Lansdowne House, supposing that provides the necessary accommodation. I will enquire of Lansdowne how many he can seat in his gallery.

The question of the place of meeting, however, must evidently in part depend upon the numbers who are asked. When I was dining with you on Friday, we agreed that the Party both in the House of Commons and in the House of Lords must have the opportunity of attending if they wished. Probably all the House of Commons who are not abroad, but only a portion of the Lords, would take advantage of the invitation. You then threw out a suggestion, which at first smiled upon me, that, in addition to the Members of the House of Commons, all unsuccessful candidates at the recent election should be requested to attend. There are subsidiary difficulties attaching to this proposal. Our figures would run up to a quite unmanageable amount. We can hardly expect it to be less than 800, and it may well be more. This is rather a formidable body in which to carry on a complicated and difficult discussion, and I do not know where we could find the necessary meeting-place. It is possible that Ellesmere's gallery holds more than Lansdowne's, and he might be willing to lend it; but I greatly doubt whether it would give us the required accommodation. I should be very reluctant to hire a public room for such a purpose, although I admit that I cannot give any very logical reason for my distaste.

There is, however, a more fundamental objection to asking candidates arising out of the fact that this practice has never been followed before, and could hardly be started now without setting a very inconvenient precedent. If it was desired to add to the one hundred and fifty and odd gentlemen who compose our Party in the new Parliament any unsuccessful candidates who had seats in the old one, we might ask *Privy Councillors* to attend who failed to obtain re-election. This would, of course, include many Members of the late Government, together with men like Billy Dyke, Parker Smith, H. Chaplin, etc. The line of division is a clear one, and would raise, so far as I can see, no difficulties either now or hereafter. But, on the whole, I think we should, on principle, refuse to extend invitations to the *general* multitude of rejected candidates.

The most difficult of the questions we have to settle, however, relates not to the composition or the place of the proposed meeting, but to the procedure which is to be adopted when it does meet. There is no case in history, so far as I am aware, in which a Party meeting has been summoned except to give emphasis and authority to a decision at which the Party have informally already arrived : still less is there an example to be found of a vote being taken at such a meeting. How then are we to proceed on the present occasion? Are you and I to agree upon some question on which the meeting can vote 'aye' or 'no' : if so, what is this question to be, and how is it to be formulated? And when it is formulated, how are we to make arrangements for a vote? These things puzzle me greatly, and I should be glad to have your opinion upon them.

2 E

As regards the time of meeting, I do not see how we can possibly have the meeting till next week, and I would suggest, at all events for consideration, that Thursday, the 15th, would be not unsuitable. If you agree generally, I would ask Bob Douglas to say the few necessary words from the Front Bench on the occasion of the Speaker's election. If neither you nor I are present, this commits nobody to anything.

Balfour's letter seems to have reached Chamberlain while he was writing to Ridley. He was acknowledging a telegram from Ridley about the publication of his manifesto and had gone on to discuss future organisation.

CHAMBERLAIN TO RIDLEY

7 *February* 1906.—Your telegram is just to hand. I am glad you approve of publication. Acland Hood and his friends have done their best to exacerbate matters and it is difficult to read without indignation the articles and letters which they have evidently inspired. This, however, is the natural course of wirepullers at all times.

I cannot help thinking that the democratisation of the Central Office will be popular in itself and may be kept separate from the fiscal question. It would be the best retort to Acland Hood's proceedings. In that case we ought to be prepared with the names of a Committee to be moved and carried at the Party meeting. If we could get a majority on such a Committee we might do much good, although I am afraid we cannot reckon upon any support from Arthur Balfour.

At this point, Balfour's letter must have arrived. Chamberlain read it; no doubt discussed it with Austen; and then continued his letter to Ridley telling him of Balfour's letter and of his own reactions to it.

Since writing the above I have received by express a letter from Arthur Balfour in which, while reiterating his objections to a Party meeting, he says that he has come round to the view that if I desire it one must be held, and he proceeds to ask several questions of which the most important are:

1. Who is to be asked? He urges that precedent requires that all Unionist M.P.'s and the Peers must be invited. Precedent is against any outsiders but he thinks he might ask Privy Councillors. He says to ask all Unionist Candidates would run up the meeting to not less than 800, for whom it would be difficult to find a meeting place and which would be unwieldy for discussion.

I propose to reply that I think we must either have all defeated candidates or none, and that the Party would object to what they would think a privilege given to selected individuals. Personally I am still in favour of asking all. A meeting of 800 is as easy to deal with as a meeting of four hundred. The circumstances are quite novel and we ought not to be bound by precedent.

2. He asks, are we to agree upon some question for discussion on which we can vote 'aye' or 'no', and how is it to be formulated and how is it to be voted upon.

I propose to reply that there will be two questions — firstly, a vote between the two policies, the 'half sheet of notepaper' and my policy. Secondly, a vote as to the reform of the Central organisation in order to secure in the future its representative and popular character.

If the necessity for reform is carried a Committee should immediately be appointed.

Let me know what you think of this, with any suggestions.

Chamberlain asked for Ridley's comments but did not wait for them before writing to Balfour. His reply, dispatched the same day, follows closely the intentions expressed to Ridley.

CHAMBERLAIN TO BALFOUR

7 February 1906: *Private.*—Your express letter has just reached me. I had previously sent a letter to Ridley for publication with the object, if possible, of getting rid of the exaggerations which indiscreet friends on both sides have been engaged in circulating during the last few days. I hope and believe there is nothing in it of which you would disapprove and that it may be useful.

Now as to your questions.

The circumstances seem to me entirely novel, and I do not think we could allow ourselves to be guided by precedent. There will be many new precedents made in politics during the next few years. I think the Party will not be satisfied without a meeting and that you have only two alternatives as regards its composition — either, that is, to ask the Peers and all the candidates, or to confine it to the Peers and the members returned. There will be great jealousy if you ask any class of privileged persons such as Privy Councillors, while excluding the rank and file.

Of the two possible alternatives I would greatly prefer the larger and more representative choice. The difficulty as to a meeting place, may, I hope, be got over. Besides the houses you name, I recollect attending a very large meeting at Stafford House where I should think nearly a thousand were present, although a number stood. Either of the others would do admirably if they have the necessary accommodation.

As regards discussion, a meeting of 800 is not more difficult than a meeting of 400 or 500. In either case discussion must be conducted by set speeches as in the House of Commons — only very small meetings can deal with any subject in a conversational way.

Lastly as to subjects: of course there will be no question whatever as to Leadership, but as I have already explained I think the Party as a whole should be asked to express freely their opinion as to the best policy for the future, and to vote as between the alternatives suggested.

I take it that, as matters stand, and assuming, *if I must assume* — that we can come no nearer, the choice lies between the 'half sheet of note-paper' and the Glasgow programme. We must find some words to describe the two programmes without using names. We ought to be able to devise something which will not be personal but will sufficiently describe them in general terms.

It will be clearly understood that the decision is not binding on the leaders or any of them, but is merely taken for information. It will secure what Salisbury has been trying to secure in a rather underhand manner by the issue of his circular letter of inquiry to Unionist members to give him information as to their opinions. That information, I suppose, he will use, and it will be, of course, contested : whereas a vote after discussion in a thoroughly representative meeting would furnish all of us with a really valuable indication of what is practicable as well as of what is desirable.

This would be the first matter for consideration.

The second would be a vote on the question that it is desirable to reconsider the organisation of the Party with a view (a) to bringing the existing organisations into closer harmony, and (b) of giving a more representative character to the Central Office and bringing it more closely into touch with the popular organisations.

As regards the time, a meeting on Thursday would do very well if all the preliminary arrangements can be agreed upon in time. If, however, we want more delay for previous consultation, I do not think a few days one way or the other will make any difference.

VI

We must now leave Chamberlain at the Imperial Hotel, Torquay, and take a railway ticket to London. At much the same time as Chamberlain was drafting his letter to Balfour, Gilbert Parker was speaking to him on similar lines. Parker's report of this conversation gives some idea of Balfour's mind that day and of the mood of the Tariff Reformers.

GILBERT PARKER TO CHAMBERLAIN

8 *February* 1906.—I had an hour and a half with Mr. Balfour yesterday, saying in effect on *your behalf* that many like yourself were determined to press reorganisation of the Central Office and citing instances of incompetency and of interference with the policy of Tariff Reform in the Constituencies. Also I said that we were determined that T. Reform should *not* be blanketed, should not be laid up for one Session or one month.

I said that if no one else did it, I would bring the question before Parliament in every possible way, and that there would be plenty or backing in such a cause, and that we would never submit again to the conduct of the Whips of last Session.

He said he realized our determination and would put nothing in the way. How much or how little that means I should not be predisposed to say or even to imagine.

I don't know whether the interview did any good ; but it did make clear that we were not to be smothered, and that, within the Party, we would fight for reconstruction and Tariff Reform.

Since writing you I have had notes from Ld. Ridley and Pearson, and Ld. R. has let me read your letter to him.

What you proposed in your letter to Mr. Balfour, is, in effect, what I said to him yesterday afternoon was inevitable. I said that Tariff Reformers were convinced that the Central Organisation should be started on a new basis. Mr. B. said that steps have already been taken to reconstruct the organization. My reply was that putting *one man* or *another* in a given position was not what we wanted; but such a Committee formed to supervise the Chief Organizer and his department as would insure the *policy* of the leaders being interpreted through effective *machinery*. He said he thought that the case against the organization was exaggerated, but there was truth in my main contention. He did not think, however, that this could properly be dealt with in a meeting of an hour and a half or two hours. My reply was that the *principle* of reconstruction and a Committee could be dealt with by a resolution. This he did not like at all — but he said little. I further said that we were bent upon getting the will of the meeting as to the future of Tariff Reform.

There ensued a *long* controversy, in which he quoted his speeches to show that there was little difference between us and that he did not *discard* a general tariff, but thought we could do without it, and get our ends in another way. To this I replied fully, and asked him what position he would take up if I moved a resolution (etc.) in the Commons embodying a general tariff. He said he could not vote with me because he did not think the General Tariff necessary for our ends. I replied that our ends were apparently not the same, since I desired *revenue* and the steadying influence on foreign competition in industry of a permanent tariff — a direct and an indirect benefit. Would he (for instance) object to an indirect benefit to an industry through a tariff for revenue? He replied that this was Protection and he was not a protectionist. My answer was that there was a *fundamental* difference between us, and not 'an infinitesimal and academic difference which keeps us apart' as he had said.

Forgive this long report, but I thought it better not to wait till Saturday, as my interview may throw some light on his attitude. He told me that he had written you on Tuesday and had suggested a day for the meeting. On the whole, as my previous letter indicated, the outcome was not satisfactory except that he was impressed by the clearness of our purposes.

Ridley, meanwhile, had duly received Chamberlain's manifesto of 6 February, and had passed it to Hewins to circulate to the Press. That night Ridley, Gilbert Parker, Granby and Pearson met and after some discussion felt that it would be prudent to eliminate from the manifesto the phrase that the Tariff Reformers, if baulked of their objects, would meet '*at the call of their own Whips*'. It was felt that anything which threatened a split in the Party would only weaken their position. Gilbert Parker explained the decision in a report to Chamberlain.

GILBERT PARKER TO CHAMBERLAIN

8 *February* 1906.—Last night Ridley, Pearson, Lord Granby and I took the grave responsibility of eliminating six or seven words from your letter as a matter of policy and tactics which I believe you will approve. On every hand I find — we all have found — a willingness to fight for Tariff Reform *within* the Party and to demand reorganization but no one will go into a separate Camp, and form, as it were a new party. It is perfectly hopeless to canvass men on that basis.

But on the other hand, there is a general desire that you should take the leadership if we pass our resolution at the Party Meeting. If we pass a resolution embodying a General Tariff and Mr. Balfour cannot accept it, and must perforce step down, *then* will you continue to resist the will of the majority? It is no competition. If he *resigns* I cannot see in that circumstance how you can decline the call.

I hope you will know that in speaking thus frankly to you, only my fidelity to your cause is responsible for the boldness. I also hope that you will think we acted with discretion in leaving out those few words, on the information we had.

Pearson was entrusted by the others with the task of ensuring that the necessary correction was made. 'Then that happened', Hewins wrote in his diary, 'which any fool might have anticipated.'[1]

Pearson was not aware of the method which the ever-suspicious Hewins had employed in circulating the manifesto. He communicated the correction to one Press Agency only, not to all as Hewins had done. As a result, the *Daily News*, the *Manchester Guardian* and some other papers published the full version including the offending phrase.

The letter was published throughout the National Press on the morning of 8 February. That there were two versions gave an impression of hesitation in the Tariff Reform group. Nevertheless, the general reception accorded to it was excellent. Chaplin sent some account of the comment aroused by it, and of the general situation as seen in the Carlton Club that day.

CHAPLIN TO CHAMBERLAIN

8 *February* 1906: *Private.*—I think your letter excellent and from all I hear just in the nick of time. Walter Long came in to see me yesterday, just after Ridley had been here to show it to me. I told him to look out for it next morning and wire me his opinion. Here is the telegram enclosed. — 'I think letter is quite excellent' — Long. — He talked to me very fully about the position. He is loyalty itself— and told me that he had been in correspondence with you. But while nothing would

[1] W. A. S. Hewins, *Apologia of an Imperialist*, vol. i, p. 163.

make him run counter to Arthur except absolute necessity, I am speaking now of Leadership — he is with you entirely in feeling, and thinks that if a breach or anything like one is avoided, we might carry it before 5 years are over.

Arthur, he tells me, is in a very peculiar frame of mind — very irritable and sore about the whole position, seeing all sorts of people with little claim to see him, and looking very ill and careworn. His father broke down very suddenly — and I've always been afraid, if he overdoes it, and he has had a tremendous strain, of even his endurance being over-tried.

I fully expect your letter will make a great effect in your favour again — among the members of the Party ; and although the Whips have been in the Club all day, I'm told, collaring every Member who comes up, some of my informants tell me (I've never left the house and been very bad since I saw you) with very little effect in a good many cases.

You remember in one of the letters I wrote last, I thought that if you could get any reasonable assurance of proper support, and I think you would do now — that there would be many advantages in your being temporary Leader if only for a very short time. It would settle the question on any future occasion — for any period of vacancy long or short — and personally I believe it would strengthen your position, especially with the younger Members of the Party, very considerably, unless you still consider the objections to it to be insuperable. After your letter they seem to me to be much diminished. It would certainly be the strongest visible and outward sign that there was no real split between yourself and Arthur — and might help to pave the way to a more favourable understanding as to organisation and policy when we come to a Party Meeting.

Walter holds this view I know and strongly — and he also tells me that, contest or no contest, Arthur can't be back in any case till the Address is considerably advanced. Will you consider this. I need not tell you I shall accept thoroughly whatever is your final decision.

Chamberlain, himself, was satisfied with the way his letter was received in the Press and accepted Ridley's censorship with good grace. He felt, by this time, that his supporters had pressed their attacks against Balfour too far. If anything, he may have exaggerated the reaction in Balfour's favour.

CHAMBERLAIN TO RIDLEY

8 *February* 1906 : *Private.*—I think the letter has on the whole been well received. In any case it had clearly become essential to define the situation.

Between ourselves, our friends in the Press put our position too crudely and provoked the opposition who were only too glad to try to make our differences personal and to appeal on personal grounds to the public.

In such a crusade as ours the less that is known or spoken of our intentions beforehand the better will be our chance of giving effect to them.

One thing must have been made evident to the hottest of the anti-Balfourites, viz. that, with such a Party as ours, my leadership would not have been possible for 24 hours.

I incline to think we shall now have to lie low in Parliament and to see what we can do with organisation (1) to reform the Central Council, and (2) whether we succeed in the first or not to go on with our organisation in the country.

The open quarrel is postponed but I shall be surprised if it does not arise again in another form on the bye-elections.

I quite approve of your omission in my letter. I had in mind the fact that we had our own Whips for our own special purpose in the last Parliament, but in view of the misunderstandings prevailing the re-assertion of our right at this time would no doubt have done harm.

VII

Next morning, 9 February, brought Chamberlain a decisive letter from Balfour. It was his reply to Chamberlain's proposals of 7 February. Balfour accepted Chamberlain's suggestions on the composition of the Party Meeting and agreed to appoint a Committee to consider Party Organisation. He made it clear, however, that he would regard confronting the Party with a choice between 'the half sheet of notepaper' and the Glasgow Speech as a direct challenge to his leadership. If the vote went against him, he could no longer serve as leader.

BALFOUR TO CHAMBERLAIN

8 *February* 1906: *Private.*—Though this is merely a business letter, I hope you will allow me to thank you for the very kind terms in which you have spoken of me in your communication to the public through Mat Ridley. I am sure that even were the differences between us much greater than they have ever been, or are ever likely to be, our friendship can suffer no dimunition.

Now as to the Meeting. It is clear that the members of the Party must have an opportunity of 'blowing off steam' on any subject they like, and the two subjects which they would most like are certain to be Fiscal Reform and Party Organisation. But is your idea of requiring them to choose between the Glasgow Speech and the 'half sheet of notepaper' really practicable? If they choose the Glasgow Speech, how can you refuse to become their Leader? If they choose the 'half sheet of note-paper', how can I continue to lead them? There is something amounting to absurdity in asking a Party to give an opinion upon an important question of policy, and, when it has given that opinion, perhaps against its titular leader, asking that leader to be good enough to continue his work on their behalf. This difficulty will not arise if the meeting occupies itself merely in hearing and expressing various opinions — if the difference between the Glasgow Speech and the 'half sheet of note-paper' is left an open question, and if, while Fiscal Reform is kept in its present position in the Party programme, differences between fiscal reformers are left an open question. But if, on the other hand, we take the course you propose, it seems to me that, should the vote go against *you*, your position will not be made easier : should it go against me, *mine* will become impossible, and you will have to reconsider your decision to 'refuse the leadership under all circumstances'.

As regards re-organisation, it is, of course, obvious that we must hear a great deal about this at the meeting. I shall, for my own part, declare a thorough reconstruction of our machinery as obviously necessary, and I shall propose that a small Committee be appointed to consider how this may be most effectively and expeditiously accomplished. On such a subject as this a large meeting can do no more than express general aspirations. I am making further enquiries about Lansdowne House and Stafford House.

I see your point about the composition of the meeting, and whether we keep to the old tradition or not, I have to admit, on further reflection, that, if we exclude candidates, we shall produce a considerable feeling of soreness among men, many of whom, no doubt, intend to fight again.

Balfour's letter was a serious check. Chamberlain had hoped to bring Balfour to accept his policy while retaining the leadership, or, failing this, to fight on the issue of policy leaving the personal question of the leadership to be decided later. He now had a plain warning that, if pressed too far, Balfour would appeal to the personal loyalty of the Party — the very issue Chamberlain had hoped to avoid. Whether this personal issue could still be avoided now seemed very doubtful. Chamberlain, however, felt it essential that he should first make every effort to bring about a compromise. If it came to a 'showdown' it must not be of his seeking.

So much was at stake that he sent only an interim reply to Balfour, reserving further comment until the next day.

CHAMBERLAIN TO BALFOUR

9 *February* 1906 : *Private.*—Let me say at once how heartily I reciprocate the opening words of your letter of yesterday. The profession of politics has many disadvantages but it becomes intolerable when it threatens such friendship as ours.

Your letter raises issues so important that I must ask for a few hours delay before answering it. I will, however, send a reply by express to reach you sometime tomorrow afternoon or evening.

I think I see my way to some suggestions which might materially lessen our difficulties, and I venture to think it is very important that you should have them under consideration before you speak on Monday. Will you, therefore, make arrangements to have the letters sent to you if you are going out of town?

2 E 2

There is only one point I need touch upon now, viz. the date of the meeting. I think undoubtedly the earlier it is held the better, and in no case should it be fixed for later than Saturday of next week. If all goes well it will smooth matters at the meeting of Parliament and enable us to agree on the temporary leadership during the first few days of the Addresses.

P.S. If you invite the candidates, as I think you will be wise to do, please take care that Tommy Bowles does not have an invitation. It would be very much resented. Otherwise there ought to be no exclusion, and particularly in the case of Greenwich, both Lord Hugh and Mr. Benn ought to be included. The latter, you will remember, polled by far the largest number of Unionist votes.

Chamberlain's first reactions after receiving Balfour's letter appear from two letters he wrote later that day commenting on what Balfour had said. Compared with the published manifesto and with earlier letters to Ridley they give a distinct impression of retreat from his earlier position.

CHAMBERLAIN TO RIDLEY

9 *February* 1906: *Private.*—I have today an important letter from Balfour the answer to which I shall postpone until tomorrow. In effect he says that a Resolution at the Party meeting which would raise definitely the question as between the Glasgow programme and the 'half sheet of notepaper' would, if it were carried against me, be embarrassing to me, and if it were carried against him would necessarily entail his resignation. He evidently would not continue to lead in such circumstances. He therefore suggests that the meeting should occupy itself in hearing opinions without a vote and while fiscal reform is kept in its present programme differences between fiscal reformers should be left an open question.

This as it stands would mean the *status quo ante* Election and would not be satisfactory. But I am inclined to try my hand at a Resolution which would reaffirm the importance of fiscal reform as the first constructive item of the Party policy and claiming that the idea of a general tariff and 2/- on corn should be left to the future without any premature committal.

You will see that the object is to prevent any wider severance between Balfourites and T. Reformers while putting in a wedge between Balfourites and Free Fooders who insist on committing themselves against a general tariff and against my tax on corn. We do not exclude them from the Party but we should be enabled to say that their views were not the official views. It is rather a delicate business, but I think it may be managed.

As regards reorganisation he will declare that a thorough reconstruction of machinery is obviously necessary and that a small Committee should be appointed to consider how it is to be accomplished.

This is alright, but evidently everything depends upon the composition of the Committee. As I hope to secure a Joint Committee of Conservatives and L.U.'s I have some claim to sit upon it which I am inclined to urge upon him and the meeting. We ought to be ready with a number of names. You must certainly be included. Chaplin has claims on account of his influence with the National Union. Goulding would be very useful. Ought there not to be one or two of the best Agents who can be relied on?

I should like to say in the Resolution that the object of reconstruction was to secure a more representative and democratic body. I think we should get support for this.

CHAMBERLAIN TO PEARSON

9 *February* 1906: *Private.*—I have another letter from Balfour deprecating a Resolution on policy at the Party meeting. He wants general expression of opinion but no definite vote.

I think under the altered circumstances he is probably right. We should hardly get a vote for a definite Resolution and probably the best thing is to lie low for the present.

He still wants me to take his place on the Address. There would be some advantages but I am rather doubtful. If the meeting is held first, its tone might enable me to decide.

He now says he is strongly in favour of reorganisation and proposes to appoint a small Committee.

In any articles on the subject I think we should avoid the slightest appearance of attacking persons. The Party is in a nervous condition and wants to keep up appearances. But our strong point is the unrepresentative character of the Central Office — to say that the popular body, viz. the National Union, should have control will please them and be difficult to meet; but please bear in mind that Randolph was wrong in asking for control of finance. A political association cannot publish its accounts. It must keep secret both the sources of its income and the particular purposes for which it is applied.

Chamberlain slept on Balfour's letter. Next day (10 February), he drafted an extremely conciliatory reply. He no longer pressed Balfour to accept the full Glasgow programme but proposed a resolution which he and Balfour might put forward together at the Party meeting.

CHAMBERLAIN TO BALFOUR

10 *February* 1906: *Private.*—I have now very carefully considered your letter & the whole situation. The artificial crisis, largely manufactured by the press, may be put on one side as of no importance. The real crisis will come when you and I find that we cannot possibly agree. There ought to be no reason to fear this. You only confirmed what I have frequently said when at Prince's Gardens you expressed your conviction that after all the differences which appeared to exist were only insignificant & academic. If that be true we ought to be able to find a thoroughly satisfactory *modus vivendi*.

Thank goodness! There is no personal question between you & me for such are always the most difficult to arrange. We both desire the same great objects and we are both ready to make sacrifices to secure them. There cannot or ought not to be any insuperable difficulty in coming to an agreement as to the way in which they can be most certainly attained.

I derived one conclusion from the recent election, viz: that amongst the principal causes of our defeat was the ambiguity of our policy and the impression created that there were two inconsistent policies promoted by different sections of our Party and indicating divided counsels among the chiefs.

Is it not possible now, in opposition, when some of the difficulties appertaining to ministerial responsibilities have disappeared to remove this suspicion of dual aims and to give to the Party a lead which will certainly be accepted by the great majority as an official policy while it will not exclude anyone who is not really irreconcileable.

I desire if possible to establish such a policy at the Party meeting. Your objections to the sort of Resolution I proposed are forcible and, indeed, are insuperable if you feel that a Resolution at such a meeting could not be treated merely as an indication of the prevailing sentiment of the Party but must be accepted by you as an instruction which you would have to accept or to reject.

On the other hand it seems to me that to have a sort of symposium with no conclusion at the end would leave us in a worse position than we were before the General Election. There would be no guidance for the organisation or the local associations. We should be at sixes and sevens at the first bye-election and our divisions would be equally manifest in the House of Commons.

Cannot you and I devise some compromise? What are our differences? As far as I know there is not a single word in any one of your speeches & declarations to which I take serious objection. If I differ at all it is because of what you have omitted to say rather than of what you: said but above all — and this is serious — I object to the interpretations of what you have said by those who are I think more Balfour than Balfour himself. For instance, you have said — 'I do not discard the idea of a general tariff, and I do not object to it in principle, but I refuse to commit myself until I have considered other possibly better alternatives'. Again you have said — 'I do not in principle object to a small tax on Corn, but I refuse to commit myself until I know the result of a free Conference with the Colonies'.

This appears to me a most reasonable attitude although, probably, I am more confident than you are as to what will be the ultimate result of the further consideration for which you reasonably ask.

But, basing themselves upon these statements of yours, a certain number of people, professing to be your loyal followers, have declared dogmatically against a general tariff and against the possibility of any tax on corn, however small, whatever may be the inducements offered by a Colonial Conference.

The public, who do not weigh the various utterances as we do, are confused. They attribute to you the conclusions arrived at by those who profess to be your followers, and no doubt in the same way they attribute to me the opinions which are expressed by some of those who profess to sympathise with my views.

This confusion must continue until we have some kind of joint programme or declaration to which both of us can agree and to which we can refer our respective adherents. Can we find an official policy of such a kind? If so, we could carry it at any meeting of the Party by an immense majority.

If, after such a declaration, any member of the Party expressed views inconsistent with our joint declaration we should not think of excommunicating him, but we should be able to say that his was an independent & not an official view. The official view would be the line of least resistance. The official organisations would accept it — the education of the Party would go on upon these lines and upon no other, and the individualists on either side would find themselves in so small a minority that their dissent would become of no importance.

Let me take an illustration. I believe that disestablishment would be a good thing for the Church & for religion, and several Bishops & many of the Clergy of my acquaintance agree with me : but that is not the official view. If I thought it necessary to press it — which I certainly do not — I should get no support from official candidates or organisations, and I should have distinctly to make it clear that I was speaking for myself alone. Still, unless I carried my advocacy so far as to oppose Unionist candidates who did not agree with me, or to raise an active agitation injurious to Party unity, I suppose I should still be allowed to remain a member of the congregation.

In the same way, Sir John Kennaway, for instance, might continue to delare his determination to vote against any tax on corn, however small, and even if it became after a Conference a part of the official policy. His support on all other subjects would be welcome — there would be no attempt to exclude him, provided he did not carry his opposition so far as to oppose official Unionist candidates or to carry on an active propaganda against the official policy.

In this long preface I hope I have made my meaning clear and have not wearied you.

Now I ask you to consider a form of Resolution which I have enclosed and which Austen & I have concocted between us, and which we think might be submitted to the Party meeting with your approval. I do not think that there is anything in it which may not be found almost verbatim in your speeches and declarations : and, although it is not nearly as definite and does not go nearly as far as the Glasgow programme, it *does* officially deprecate any premature decision against either a general tariff or a small duty on foreign corn.

If on examination you find in it anything which is inconsistent with any previous statement of yours, I should be very glad to reconsider the wording : if in substance you are able to assent to it, I see no reason why it should not constitute the charter of our co-operation during the existence of the present Parliament, and the basis of all instructions to our several organisations.

The proposed resolution ran as follows :

That fiscal reform is and must remain the first constructive work of the Unionist party ;

That the objects of such reform are to secure more equal terms of competition for British trade and closer commercial union with the Colonies ;

That it is at present unnecessary to prescribe the exact methods by which these objects are to be attained, but that amongst other means the establishment of a moderate general tariff on manufactured goods and the imposition of a small duty on foreign corn are not in principle objectionable and should be adopted if required for the attainment of the ends in view or for revenue.

The two letters printed below show what Chamberlain believed to be the significance of his letter to Balfour.

CHAMBERLAIN TO RIDLEY

10 *February* 1906 : *Private.*—I wrote a very long — and although I say it, a really persuasive letter to Mr. Balfour which I sent to him by express this morning. Its object was to suggest and press as an alternative to all other suggestions the adoption, with his approval, of the Resolution (a), copy of which I enclose.

It would, if agreed to, constitute the official programme of the Party, and while it would leave men like Kennaway free to advocate their own views it would place them in a conspicuous minority and would enable us to say that they were speaking only for themselves and that their policy was not the official policy.

I doubt, however, whether in his present mood Balfour will accept it. I think, however, he must in that case propose another alternative as I have pointed out that the Resolution proposed is practically made up entirely from his own speeches and declarations.

I send this proposal to you, but it is a delicate business and I think you had better not show it to anyone else though you can say in answer to inquiries that I am in correspondence with B. and trying to arrange some common foundation for our future action.

CHAMBERLAIN TO CHAPLIN

10 *February* 1906.—I believe that Arthur has at last agreed that all the candidates shall be invited and you will therefore get a summons. It is, I believe, the best course. The defeated candidates will be I think more independent than the elected members.

I have written a very long letter to Balfour proposing a *modus vivendi*. If he rejects it I think he will find it necessary to propose an alternative but there is no knowing how things will go at the last.

VIII

An unfortunate confusion now arose in the ranks of the Tariff Reformers. It suggests that the old saying, '*les absents ont toujours tort*' is particularly true of political leaders in time of crisis.

On the afternoon of 10 February, a dozen leaders of the Tariff Reform Movement met at Gilbert Parker's house. Chamberlain and Austen had decided to stay on at Torquay over the weekend and so were not present. There was some confusion in the minds of those attending the meeting. They were under heavy pressure from their Whips. They did not know the terms of the resolution Chamberlain had sent to Balfour — it was still in the post. Their leader was away. All they knew of his intentions was that he was preparing a compromise resolution — his letter to Ridley on 9 February told them that — and that he was not prepared to challenge Balfour for the leadership.

This last consideration was crucial. It is very difficult to follow beyond a certain point a leader who will not accept all the responsibilities of leadership. Chamberlain's self-denying ordinance on this score may have been inevitable, but it inevitably damped the ardour of his supporters and inclined them to play safe.

Seeing matters in this light, the meeting seems to have been struck by the contrast between Chamberlain's published manifesto and his letter to Ridley of 9 February. They feared, for a moment, that his suggested compromise resolution might give too much away. They accordingly drafted what they conceived to be their minimum terms, and, not having seen Chamberlain's text, drafted something much weaker. Even then they were uncertain whether this resolution should be brought forward at all and were rather inclined to put the emphasis on organisation.

The following reports of the meeting reached Chamberlain on the morning of Monday, 12 February.

GILBERT PARKER TO CHAMBERLAIN

10 *February* 1906.—At the meeting at my house today . . . we passed the enclosed resolutions. The second was meant merely to show that if *any* resolution at all on Tariff Reform was presented at the Party Meeting this would be, or should be, the *minimum* of our demands. We thought that you *might* think it worth while to test A. B. upon it, for it only embodies what he has not ruled out of possibility. We are aware that it may not be expedient to put or press a resolution on T. Reform; but this is the mildest form in which we would care to put our case. I am sure you will agree to that. But whether *any* resolution on T. R. should be put at all is a matter for your judgment. If A. B. *would* accept it beforehand, our cause would take a long step forward. As for reorganization I am *certain* we could carry our resolution.

I hope to enclose the list of names of those who have asked for a party meeting. We could only get at a certain number; but 59 have given their adherence, and about 20 others want the meeting but don't want to *petition* A. B., so rich is the milk of human kindness in their hearts ! If the list is not ready before post closes, I will forward it on tomorrow evening.

I am sending it to A. B. with a short covering letter, saying that it is merely expressive of a very general feeling.

Arnold-Forster did not write — he thought it better not.

EVELYN CECIL TO CHAMBERLAIN

10 *February* 1906.—At a small conference at Sir Gilbert Parker's this afternoon we drew up the accompanying Resolutions as a foundation upon which to act in view of the probable party meeting ; and I was asked to send them to you. They are intended merely to be submitted for your consideration, and not by any means necessarily to be moved or shown at the party meeting, though we were all agreed upon them. At the same time we thought we should like to leave it to your discretion whether they should be shown to Arthur Balfour before the meeting. It seems to me that if there is any chance of his agreeing to them and their being carried at the meeting, it might be desirable to show them to him, but if you think from your correspondence that he is likely to resist them, no useful purpose would be served by our attempting to carry them against him. Unless we can carry a definition of policy as strong as this, it is better at present not to carry one at all.

My own belief is that the first resolution is at least as important as the second, and that if we can get an adequate control or voice in the amalgamated organization, the rest will be comparatively plainer sailing.

The text of the resolutions was as follows :

1st *Resolution.*

That this Meeting is of opinion

(1) That the amalgamation of the Conservative Central Office and Liberal Unionist Organizations is desirable, and that a Committee to establish a Central Organization on a representative basis should be immediately appointed :

(2) That Mr. Balfour and Mr. Chamberlain be *ex officio* members of the Committee.

2nd *Resolution.*

That this Meeting desires that Tariff Reform should be actively maintained in the forefront of the Unionist policy in and out of Parliament, and considers that, in order to secure effective retaliation, and Imperial Preference, if it can be arranged through a Colonial Conference, a low general tariff on foreign manufactured imports for purposes of revenue is a necessary part of the policy.

These reports of the meeting were accompanied by the following comments from Ridley.

RIDLEY TO CHAMBERLAIN

10 *February* 1906.—I am more confirmed than ever in the view that any resolution at a Party meeting which seemed like another formula

would have a very serious effect on the tariff reform movement and would practically leave us where we are or a little further back. You will get by this post from G. Parker and E. Cecil what transpired at their meeting today and the kind of resolutions that they seemed to favour. As regards policy, I think their views may be described as in favour of pushing Balfour a little further if possible & getting him to accept some such resolution as the one forwarded to you : failing that, they were unanimous that it would be better to not bring up any policy resolution at all.

It seems to me possible that this latter course would be the best. If we can get the organization to act sensibly all is well : if we cannot do that it does not much matter what policy resolution is carried, as J. Sandars & Co. would disregard it in practice.

I suppose such a course would involve the separate T.R. Group in the House, and an active T.R. organization in the country. But if a compromise resolution is carried, and Tariff Reformers committed to it, both these actions would be rendered very difficult if not impossible.

The meeting at Gilbert Parker's had been animated by a fear that Chamberlain would give way too much to Balfour. But Chamberlain, on receiving their reports at Torquay, at once jumped to the conclusion that they — his chief supporters — were running out. Their proposed resolution was much weaker than his own. He thought they showed no stomach for a fight. The fact that they could only collect 59 signatures to petition for a Party meeting suggested that his following was dwindling. He wrote rebuking his followers for what seemed desertion.

CHAMBERLAIN TO EVELYN CECIL

12 *February* 1906.—Until I hear from Balfour I cannot decide anything, but it is evident that the Tariff Reformers are not prepared for a fighting policy at present, and of course I cannot go into battle unless I am perfectly assured of the approval and assistance of the rank and file.

CHAMBERLAIN TO RIDLEY

12 *February* 1906.—I have not yet heard from Balfour in answer to my last letter. I feel assured he would not accept a Resolution in the terms agreed to by Gilbert Parker's dinner party, nor do I expect that he will accept mine, at all events in the form in which it is drawn. I think, however, you will see that if he did it will not be open to the objection you take of an ambiguous formula. Assuming that he refuses anything, I gather that it is your unanimous advice that we should leave the question of policy altogether for the present.

Of course this is a defeat for us, but we cannot go into a hot fight unless our soldiers are inspired by the most determined enthusiasm. It is the old story, and the party machine is still great within the hearts of the Conservative Party and much too strong to be overcome by an independent reformer like myself.

Whether, however, in these circumstances, I can do any good by active work at the present time I much doubt, and I certainly hesitate to accept the responsibility even of a temporary leadership. What is the good of arousing the enthusiasm of the Party and earning their professions of confidence and support when I know that they are all conditioned on the abandonment of the one cause which actively interests me?

Mind, I am not complaining and I think the decision of my friends among the Tariff Reformers is probably right. But, if it is, Balfour is not only their best leader but their only leader, and should have the whole responsibility of a policy which is really in its effect hostile to any progress in the direction I desire.

Meanwhile we will certainly see what we can do do about organisation, although here also I expect the 'machine' will beat us and the Committee will be so manipulated as to end in nothing.

The confusion was finally dispelled by Ridley's reply. He made it clear that there was no weakening on the part of the Tariff Reformers but stressed the Achilles heel in their armour — their leader's refusal to lead the Unionist party.

RIDLEY TO CHAMBERLAIN

12 *February* 1906.—I am afraid I conveyed a wrong impression if I seemed to say that your friends were unanimously in favour of having no resolution of policy. Pearson was the only one who strongly favoured this. They were unanimous that the resolution must be a strong one: & unanimous that if the resolution could be construed by our opponents as a climb down it would be better to have none. But if the point had to be decided my impression is that a very large proportion of them would like a strong resolution put to the meeting even if we were to be opposed and beaten.

The great difficulty we are in now is largely caused by the fact that a large number of the House (*not*, I think, of the country) still hope to get real Tariff Reform from Balfour. If they were once persuaded, as some of us are, that there is no chance of that, the machine might not so easily claim them. And there is the further difficulty that you feel obliged to decline the logical sequence of pushing your policy — *i.e.*, leading the party yourself. In which opinion I am obliged reluctantly to acquiesce, though still convinced that once you were in the position your difficulties would not be so great as you imagine. With our party the power of the machine, as you say, is very great, & once you are in power the machine is yours, instead of theirs.

And I cannot help still hoping that the march of events may put you in the position where the country wants you. The one thing essential to that is that the public should think you are advancing rather than retreating. We know that you will not retreat : but to keep up the position we must let the public see we are advancing.

It is really, however, for you and Balfour to settle between yourselves, & I can only try to represent the news I gather : I am bound therefore to say that some of our friends, both in conversation & writing, feel very strongly that the weak point in your position is your refusal in any event to lead.

Surely what has transpired is enough to show there is no plot (I wish there were) to oust Balfour. But on policy, I for one should prefer you to move alone a full resolution at the party meeting. You would have certainly some supporters, & if it were clear that Balfour was immovable, very many. But if you stood alone (on policy) you must triumph in the end — and a short end. Now is the moment, I am confident, to strike harder than ever on your policy: & the party, bewildered as they are, must follow. Whatever resolution is carried at the party meeting must more or less bind *you* in the House as well as others.

Chamberlain and his party returned to London on the afternoon of 12 February. At Prince's Gardens, he found a cryptic letter from Balfour. This contained no comment of substance on his suggested resolution, urged him to read the speech Balfour was due to deliver that night, and invited him to a meeting next day. In its combination of mystery and naïveté it must rank as one of the more curious letters ever written by a responsible Party leader.

BALFOUR TO CHAMBERLAIN

11 *February* 1906[1] : *Private.*—Thanks much for your letter. Believe me, I fully recognise the cordial endeavours you have made in the draft Resolution to frame a formula which shall meet the difficulties of the case.

I venture to think however that we had better put off any decision as to the exact course to be pursued at the Party Meeting until we have had an opportunity of talking it over and until you have seen what I say to-morrow in the City. What that will be, I do not myself yet know — in the sense of having prepared a speech : but it will be my first utterance after the adverse decision of the constituencies and my last utterance (so far as I know) before the Party Meeting. It will therefore necessarily have a tactical importance, if no other ; and I think we ought to have it present to our minds before any final decision is taken. Could you see me on Tuesday afternoon, at, say, 5 o'clock? And would it not be a good thing that I should ask Lansdowne and Gerald to be present? By all means bring Austen, if he can come.

Chamberlain at once accepted the invitation.

Balfour spoke that night at the Merchant Taylors Hall dinner. The atmosphere was by no means wholly friendly to him. Sir E. Clarke, indeed, one of the City Members, who was also to speak, was advised that it would be well if he did not speak of Balfour as

[1] Mrs. Dugdale in her life of Arthur Balfour dates this letter as 10 February. But as the letter is clearly an answer to Chamberlain's letter of 10 February written from Torquay, 11 February seems more likely.

his leader.[1] Balfour's speech was, as his biographer has said, 'of the type which his contemporaries were apt to label "obscure",'[2] He suggested that 'the general tariff and the question of a small duty on food were questions of expediency and not of principle. He did not admit their expediency or reject them as in all cases inadmissible'.[3]

The speech disturbed Free Traders and gave 'great dissatisfaction to Tariff Reformers'.[4] Hewins sent Chamberlain the following analysis.

HEWINS TO CHAMBERLAIN

13 *February* 1906.—I venture to state to you as impartially as I can the impression Mr. Balfour's speech last night makes upon my mind.

(1) He puts *fiscal* reform in the forefront of the programme but it is clear from his argument that he has not made up his mind whether that involves a change of *tariff* policy or not.

I suppose he may have in view the possibility of dealing with present problems by a rearrangement of existing duties without ostensibly differentiating against any country or group of countries — as Gladstone did with the Wine Duties.

(2) He repudiates Cobdenism. But I cannot see that this throws any light on the policy he would be prepared to accept. I do not know a single orthodox economist who would not say the same thing.

(3) His object is the reduction of foreign and colonial tariffs with a view of extending our markets. But he comes to no definite opinion as to whether this does or does not involve a change of policy on our part. He is willing to consider any suggestion, without prejudice, and discusses several alternatives without approving or disapproving of any.

(4) The alternatives he has in his mind are apparently as follows:

(*a*) A General Tariff such as you have suggested, though in none of his speeches has he ever referred to the subject in a manner which would enable one to say what a general tariff is or what is its relation to preference.

(*b*) A General *ad valorem* Tariff 'to which even the present Government would be driven'. By this I presume he means a general duty of say 5 per cent. levied on imports, for revenue purposes. This is open to all the objections wrongly brought by the Free Traders against your policy. It is incompatible with (*a*).

(*c*) Retaliatory duties imposed *ad hoc*.
It would always be difficult if not impossible to make out a case, because the foreign country could rightly maintain that its tariff

---

[1] Sir E. Clarke, *The Story of my Life*, p. 380.
[2] Mrs. Dugdale, *Arthur James Balfour*, vol. ii, p. 26.
[3] Sir E. Clarke, *The Story of my Life*, p. 381.
[4] W. A. S. Hewins, *Apologia of an Imperialist*, vol. i, p. 165.

CH. CXVI–ÆT. 69] THE VALENTINE COMPACT 845

was carefully adjusted to promote its own interests, not in order to injure our industries.

Assuming we had powers similar to the German Customs Law, how could we apply them under our system? We could not without inquiry and consultation throw industries out of gear and extemporise tariff machinery.

This method of procedure would necessarily lead to high protection because you could not readily take off the duties when once they were on.

(*d*) Diplomatic pressure.

Mr. Balfour apparently attaches great importance to this — the only case in which he gives concrete instances, viz. Morocco and Madagascar. These, as far as I remember, are the only concrete illustrations Mr. Balfour has ever given in his speeches. They are not fiscal reform in any shape.

I do not see any basis for educating the electorate in this discussion of alternatives. Liberal Free Traders could accept it. There is not a single 'heterodox' proposition throughout Mr. Balfour's speech. I am afraid people do want to know whether the commercial union of the Empire involves a change of tariff policy, and if so on what general principles the tariff is to be constructed.

Balfour's adoption meeting took place in the City next morning. According to Hewins who had his account from Balfour's chairman,

Balfour was very nervous and hesitating, could not frame his sentences and trembled much. . . . Lawrence recommended his candidature in a Chamberlainite speech, interpreting Balfour's Monday speech in that sense, with which he says Balfour acquiesced by nodding his head.[1]

IX

The House met on Tuesday, 13 February, to elect the Speaker. Akers-Douglas spoke for the Opposition. It was announced that there would be a Unionist party meeting on Thursday, 15 February.

At 5 o'clock on the Tuesday, Chamberlain and Austen met Balfour, Gerald Balfour, Lansdowne, Akers-Douglas and Acland-Hood, the Chief Whip. Much time was spent on defining respective positions and registering such agreement as had been reached on the composition of the Party meeting and the need to appoint a Committee to consider the reorganisation of the Party machine. But on the main question of policy, there was no agreement. Chamberlain pressed for a resolution. Balfour argued that there was no precedent for such a course.[2] After an hour and a half no agreement

---

[1] W. A. S. Hewins, *Apologia of an Imperialist*, vol. i, p. 167.
[2] Unpublished papers of Sir Herbert Maxwell.

had been reached and it was decided to suspend discussions till the next afternoon.

Next day (14 February), St. Valentine's Day, the discussions were resumed at Balfour's house in Carlton Gardens at 4 o'clock.[1] Chamberlain still pressed for a definite resolution to test the sense of the Party meeting. He had put forward a suggested draft based on Balfour's own speeches. If Balfour did not like it, let him propose an alternative. Balfour still demurred at the idea of a resolution but

offered to embody in his speech the terms of the resolution proposed by Chamberlain. No thank you! It would have been so masked in periphrasis and so mystified in parenthesis that we should have been no further forward than before.[2]

After two-and-a-half hours' discussion in which Chamberlain 'showed wonderful patience and resource',[3] the position 'seemed hopeless'.[4] At this point, Austen took the initiative and suggested that an exchange of letters might take the place of a resolution. He offered to try his hand at a draft. Chamberlain does not seem to have placed much hope in this last-minute move. He strolled over to Stafford House and told Chaplin

that the position was hopeless, that it was impossible to prevent a Party split.[5]

Austen, meanwhile, had drafted a letter which was approved by Acland-Hood and Akers-Douglas. Sandars added a few qualifying sentences.[6] Balfour accepted it. Chamberlain, back from Stafford House, also agreed to it and wrote out a reply. The result was to be known as the Valentine Compact.

BALFOUR TO CHAMBERLAIN[7]

14 *February* 1906.—The controversy aroused by the Fiscal Question has produced not unnaturally an impression which I have constantly combated that the practical differences between Fiscal reformers are much deeper than is in fact the case. The exchange of views which has recently taken place between us leads me to hope that this misconception may be removed, and with it much friction which has proved injurious to the party.

---

[1] Lansdowne does not seem to have been present at this second meeting.
[2] Unpublished papers of Sir Herbert Maxwell. Maxwell dined with Chamberlain that night. His version is based on their dinner conversation.
[3] Mrs. Chamberlain to her mother, 17 February 1906.   [4] *Ibid.*
[5] W. A. S. Hewins, *Apologia of an Imperialist*, vol. i, p. 168.
[6] Austen Chamberlain, *Politics from the Inside*, p. 37.
[7] The draft in the Chamberlain Papers is in Austen's hand.

My own opinion which I believe is shared by the great majority of the Unionist party, may be briefly summarised as follows.

I hold that Fiscal Reform is, and must remain, the first constructive work of the Unionist Party;

that the objects of such reform are to secure more equal terms of competition for British trade and closer commercial union with the Colonies;

that while it is at present unnecessary to prescribe the exact methods by which these objects are to be attained, and inexpedient to permit differences of opinion as to these methods to divide the Party, I hold that though other means may be possible, the establishment of a moderate general tariff on manufactured goods, not imposed for the purpose of raising prices or giving artificial protection against legitimate competition, and the imposition of a small duty on foreign corn, are not in principle objectionable, and should be adopted if shewn to be necessary for the attainment of the ends in view or for purposes of revenue.

CHAMBERLAIN TO BALFOUR[1]

14 *February* 1906.—I cordially welcome your letter of today in which you have summarised the conclusions that we have reached during our recent discussions.

I entirely agree with your description of the objects which we both have in view and gladly accept the policy which you indicate as the wise and desirable one for the Unionist party to adopt.

In endeavouring to give effect to this policy and in defending all Unionist principles any services that I can render will be entirely at your disposal.

On leaving Carlton Gardens, Chamberlain called in again at Stafford House and told the astonished Chaplin, who was dressing for dinner

'that it was all settled satisfactorily and that he had the letters in his pocket.'[2]

That night, Chamberlain had invited a number of leading Tariff Reformers to dine. He had expected a breakdown in the negotiations with Balfour and had meant the dinner to be a council of war to decide tactics for the Party meeting next day. Instead, the dinner took the form of a victory celebration. Maxwell had gone to Prince's Gardens

expecting to find him in the dumps; for I knew that, until that morning no progress had been made. To my surprise I found him radiant.[3]

---

[1] The draft in the Chamberlain Papers is in Chamberlain's own hand.

[2] W. A. S. Hewins, *Apologia of an Imperialist*, vol. i, p. 168.

[3] Sir Herbert Maxwell.

The company sat at table till midnight.

All delighted. Mr. Chaplin considered it the greatest political triumph since the days when Disraeli captured the Conservative Party. He said no one but Joe could have done it.[1]

X

The Valentine letters were published in the morning papers of 15 February. They were widely regarded as marking Balfour's 'surrender' to Chamberlain; and there was much talk in Free Trade circles of the Unionist leader's 'moral degradation'. Tariff Reformers were jubilant — 'if anything a little too jubilant,' wrote Austen, 'giving us an almost embarrassing air of triumph'.[2] The success of the Party meeting, however, was now assured.

The Party meeting was held at Lansdowne House despite Lansdowne's regret that his home

should hereafter be associated with the memory of a discreditable and useless episode.[3]

Between six and seven hundred Peers, Members of the House of Commons, and defeated candidates attended. Balfour, who presided, 'appeared somewhat in the character of a captive'.[4] Chamberlain had a tremendous ovation as he passed to his seat.

Balfour opened the proceedings with a short speech delivered in an unusually 'stumbling and hesitating style'.[5] He urged the Party to give careful thought to its organisation and suggested the possibility of appointing a Committee. Devonshire hoped that the Party might act together under Balfour's leadership as 'a Constitutional Opposition'. He complained stubbornly, however, of the Valentine compromise and slowly read out Balfour's letter — a tactical error, as each sentence was greeted with cheers by the Tariff Reformers who were the overwhelming majority of the meeting. Hicks Beach, by contrast, declared that there was nothing in the letters definitely committing a Free Trader to any breach of principle.

Chamberlain had 'an extremely alert, smiling and triumphant air . . . the meeting was his and he could play with it as he liked'. . . .[6]

---

[1] Mrs. Chamberlain to her mother, 17 February 1906.
[2] Austen to Mrs. Endicott, 20 February 1906.
[3] Lord Newton, *Lord Lansdowne*, p. 348.　　[4] *Ibid.*
[5] W. A. S. Hewins, *Apologia of an Imperialist*, vol. i, p. 169.　　[6] *Ibid.*

He chaffed the Duke and declared that the Valentine letters were 'not a compromise but a definition'. This, Austen afterwards wrote,

'was not only the highest wisdom but has the further merit of being true. For the letters do not, indeed, contain anything which Balfour had not said before, but by bringing together in half a dozen lines what was scattered over ten times that number of columns in the newspapers, they give to his position that clearness and precision which was so terribly lacking in his previous utterances.'

At the end of the proceedings, the Duke of Norfolk and Saunderson moved a vote of confidence in Balfour. There was no opposition; but it was noticed that many of the Free Fooders moved off so as to avoid having to vote. Their feelings and those of many of Balfour's own friends were well summed up in the following letter received by Lansdowne and quoted by his biographer.[1]

A FORMER COLLEAGUE TO LANSDOWNE

I am afraid it has been a capitulation. Joe was able to say that he had surrendered nothing, that A.J.B. agreed with him, and that the result was the official policy; and amid the resounding cheers of Tariff Reformers, A.J.B. said nothing. What you said is, I believe, perfectly true, viz. that an agreement between him and Joe would be, in any case, considered a surrender by the former (i.e. Tariff Reform); and to make the thing certain, Joe dotted the i's, and A.J.B. and X. mutually congratulated each other that they have introduced some words of a limiting character in the precious resolution which Joe drafted.

The Liberals naturally interpreted it as a surrender to Tariff Reform and, at once, decided to oppose Balfour's candidature in the City.

Chamberlain's own verdict was one of sober satisfaction, mingled curiously with anxiety for Balfour's health.

CHAMBERLAIN TO CHAPLIN

16 *February* 1906: *Private.*—Reflection only confirms my satisfaction as to the result of our recent discussions.

I hope that the chapter of ambiguity and misrepresentation is finally closed and that we may go forward with the work of organisation upon a secure and common basis.

P.S.—. . . I do not like the look of Arthur Balfour. He is more tired than I have ever known him and I am really afraid of a nervous breakdown in his case also. Indeed we have all been overstrained the last few months. Those who can get away should take the first opportunity.

[1] Lord Newton, *Lord Lansdowne*, p. 348.

Chaplin, in his reply, spoke for the main body of the Unionist party.

CHAPLIN TO CHAMBERLAIN

18 *February* 1906.—You have every reason for satisfaction at the result of your recent efforts. It is the greatest personal and political triumph *I* ever remember, in the whole of my career, and has given, except to the Free Fooders, universal satisfaction I believe to almost the whole of the Party.

Some weeks later, at the annual meeting of the Liberal Union Club (11 May), Chamberlain summed up the significance of the Valentine Compact in these words:

Since our last meeting there has been a great deal of discussion to which I will not further refer than to say that it eventuated in a concordat, it eventuated in the letters, the correspondence, of February 14.

The result then attained may not be entirely in accordance with our opinions. I think myself that the great majority of the Unionist party might have wished that it had been even more definite than it was; but it was definite enough, and with much labour and with much consultation, and at the same time with a very general desire of conciliation on all sides, we have arrived at what is now the programme, the definite official programme of the party.

Let there be no mistake, there may be some of the party who still remain in the party and who refuse to accept this concordat. We do not excommunicate them; but we have a right to say to them, 'Gentlemen, you may call yourselves what you like, but you are not in accordance with the policy of your official leaders or with the official programme of the party'. We have a right to say — I hope we shall not vary in any word of expression from the shibboleth, if I may call it so, at which we have now arrived — but we have a right to put that shibboleth to every candidate for our favours, and to say 'Do you accept this? This is the official *minimum.*' If a candidate refuses, at least let it be understood that he is not on this point in unison with the vast majority of his party. If in spite of that his constituency, the constituency to which he appeals, chooses to elect him, then of course we shall welcome his co-operation on every other question; but the old state of things which existed when this club met a year ago has been changed. Then it was open for any individual to say 'My views are really the views of one of my leaders, if not of both; my views are the views of Mr. Balfour, or my views are the views of Mr. Chamberlain,' because neither the views of Mr. Chamberlain nor of Mr. Balfour had been brought together up to that time. Now they have been brought together, now we are absolutely unanimous; and I congratulate the Liberal Unionist Club and every Liberal Unionist organization on the solution at which we have arrived, and which will enable us to go either to a by-election or to a general election with a united official programme.

Lenin once epitomised the root problem of politics in the phrase 'Who? Whom?' In every political transaction, he argued, one element is the loser, the other the winner. How does the theory fit the Valentine compact?

Balfour had kept the leadership. He had also avoided the humiliation of seeing Chamberlain's policy supported by the Party meeting against his own. He had, however, been compelled to accept a stiffer dose of Tariff Reform than he had originally intended. Indeed, considering the extent of the concessions he had to make, we may well wonder why he fought so stubbornly and for so long. Chamberlain, on his side, had achieved as much as was possible while Balfour remained leader. He knew, however, that he had only won a battle, not a campaign. He would need all his skill, energy and tenacity to secure and exploit the fruits of this victory.

BOOK XXVII

THE LAST PHASE
(1906–1914)

CHAPTER CXVII

OPPOSITION AND APOTHEOSIS

(February–June 1906)

Leading the Opposition — Chinese 'Slavery' — The Kitson Resolution —
'Enough of this Fooling' — Chamberlain Defends Milner — Education Again
— His Efforts to Amalgamate Conservatives and Liberal Unionists — The
Struggle with the Free Fooders — Colonial Correspondence — Asquith's
Budget and Fiscal Reform — Holidays and Health — Birmingham Celebrates
his 70th Birthday.

I

THE Valentine compact was sealed by an official dinner given by
Balfour to the leaders of the Opposition on the eve of the session.
It was followed by a reception to the Unionist party at large at
Lansdowne House.

Sunday intervened. Then, on Monday, 19 February, the King
opened Parliament. The speech from the throne proclaimed the
general prosperity of the country in terms plainly designed to irk
the Tariff Reformers. There was an obscure hint at a possible
Land Reform and more definite proposals for an Education Bill,
a Trades Disputes Bill and a Workman's Compensation Bill.

In Balfour's absence, Chamberlain led the Opposition. It was
a trying task. The Unionists were not merely confronted by the
Liberals and their allies, but surrounded by them. Such were
their numbers that they spilled over onto the Opposition side of
the House as far as the gangway. The Unionists themselves, moreover, were demoralised and still painfully split. Lady Frances
Balfour told Salisbury about this time that she

. . . had never seen a party so disorganised, disloyal, dispirited and
ignorant what to do, as are the Unionists. Far worse than ever the
Liberals were. . . . the feeling against Arthur is strong, and, when you
take the dislike of Joe, it makes a queer business.[1]

Chamberlain's tactical approach to the situation was in keeping
with his own slogan 'always attack'. He would plead indeed, for

[1] *Ne obliviscaris,* p. 420.

855

continuity in foreign and Imperial affairs; but in social reform he
would do his best to outbid the Liberals. Mrs. Sidney Webb noted
in her diary before the House met:[1]

... We do not deceive ourselves by the notion that this wave of Liberalism
is wholly progressive in character — much of its bulk is made up of sheer
conservatism aroused by the revolutionary tariff policy of Chamberlain.
But it looms as progressive in its direction and all the active factors are
collectivist. Moreover, it is clear that Joe is going to try to outbid the
Liberals by constructive social reform. It is an interesting little fact that
a fortnight ago he wrote in his own hand to W. P. Reeves to beg him
to send all the Acts, and literature about the Acts, relating to old-age
pensions and compulsory arbitration (in New Zealand) — as if he desired
to convince himself of their feasibility as an adjunct to his tariff policy.
Whether or not this socialistic addition will make for the popularity of
protection, it will come at any rate as pressure on the Liberals to do
something for raising the standard of life of the very poor — it will bar
the way to a policy of the *status quo*.

Above all, Chamberlain was determined to prove the case for
Tariff Reform as a clear and constructive alternative to both
orthodox Liberal finance with its accent on retrenchment and to a
socialism which aimed to help the poor by raiding the rich.

In the day-to-day conduct of the Parliamentary battle, Chamberlain had to work closely with Acland-Hood, the Chief Whip. Hood's
secretary records:

Joe had to lead the Opposition. My Chief naturally had a great deal
to do with him . . . and was nervous as to how they would get on together.
Well, they got on very well indeed and I have most interesting memories
of Joe talking matters over with my Chief. . . . Joe missed nothing and
it was always facts, facts, facts and in every detail.[2]

Chamberlain led for the Opposition in the debate on the Address.
It was an excellent speech, traversing the whole political scene and
delivered in his most even-tempered style. He began by welcoming
the new Government's avowed intention of preserving continuity
in foreign policy. Continuity was no less important in Imperial
affairs. He hoped they might preserve it there. Turning to the
self-congratulatory paragraph in the Address on the extent of
national prosperity, he repeated his familiar question: How was
such prosperity compatible with the fact that a third of the population was underfed? Turning, in conclusion, to the Government's
proposals for social reform, he asked how these were to be financed.
The Unionists had a policy on this count and the Government

---

[1] *Our Partnership*, p. 330.   [2] L. Coles to L. S. Amery, 27 December 1948.

were much mistaken if they thought they had heard the last of Tariff Reform.

Campbell-Bannerman in his reply, declared that the exchange of letters between Chamberlain and Balfour had created a new situation by committing the whole Unionist party to a Protectionist policy. The Government would give time for a debate to elucidate the exact position of the Unionists. For the rest, he made it plain that the Education Bill would be the main feature of the legislative programme.

This bare account of the first day's debate gives no idea of the atmosphere in the new House. For this we must turn to contemporary evidence.

CHAMBERLAIN TO CHAPLIN

20 *February* 1906 : *Private.*—The first night passed off well, but we shall have a very different kind of House to the last. There will be a coarser tone although it was bad enough sometimes in the last Parliament ; but these fellows remind me of the behaviour of men in a second-rate County Council. The mover of the Address made the worst speech I ever heard in similar circumstances. Young Acland did very nicely.

We shall be, I am afraid, very weak in debate — there are so few of us — but I suppose we shall settle down after a little time.

MRS. CHAMBERLAIN TO HER MOTHER

21 *February* 1906.—. . . in Mr. Balfour's absence this week Joe is his substitute and leads the Opposition. He made an excellent speech in reply to the Mover and Seconder on Monday but the House is a hostile house to every Unionist who raises his voice and unpleasant to speak in. It was to be expected, but the composition of the Liberal Party is such that there are comparatively few among them who are alive to the dignity of Debate or the traditions of the House. They are flushed with their victory and there was an element of coarseness in their cheers and a readiness to be aggressive which was evident at once, and made it an extremely difficult assembly in which to speak. Our men have got to make up their minds that it will be a disagreeable task — that is all. In time it will settle down and the novelty will wear off — the Labour Members will learn how to listen to both sides and the corporate character which has been so marked a feature of the House will be restored.

Our remnant sounds very feeble when it cheers, but it is militant.

Next day (20 February), in the early part of the sitting, Chamberlain struck a blow for an old cause. He gave strong support to a Government decision limiting corporal punishment in the Navy and recalled how he had once co-operated with Parnell to put down flogging in the Army.

2 F

Despite this gesture to the Irish benchers, he was to suffer at their hands that same night. In the second part of the sitting — the House rose for dinner in those days — Saunderson moved an amendment from the Unionist benches to try and elucidate the Government's policy towards Ireland. Bryce, the Chief Secretary, made a speech strongly sympathetic to Home Rule. Unionist tempers rose. Nor were matters improved by a speech from Dillon, one of the Irish leaders and member for South Mayo, warmly praising Bryce. Chamberlain rose in a tense and angry House, to wind up for the Opposition. He was at his most aggressive.

The tension [a Member on the Government benches noted] was extreme when he rose to his climax. 'When the hon. member for South Mayo,' he drawled out slowly, 'congratulates and praises the new Chief Secretary for his brave speech, I am reminded of the boa constrictor who first slavers his prey before he devours it.' He paused for a moment of dramatic silence ; and in that pause a still small voice enquired from the Irish benches, 'Is that what yer did to Bhalfour?' The tension suddenly snapped — in Homeric laughter.[1]

It was one of the few occasions when an interruptor got the better of Chamberlain.

On 21 February the House debated Chinese Labour on an Opposition amendment. This regretted that Ministers should have brought the reputation of the country into contempt by describing the employment of Chinese coolies in the Transvaal as 'slavery', yet were not now prepared as was clear from the King's Speech to take action to end the system. The Unionists attributed their defeat above all to the 'Chinese slavery' cry, and feeling in the House ran high.

Churchill, who replied for the Government, admitted that the term 'slavery' could not be applied 'without risk of terminological inexactitude'. He was opposed to what had been done by the previous Government, but existing licences could not be recalled without inviting large and indefinite claims for compensation. The sudden withdrawal of Chinese labour might even bring about an economic collapse in the Transvaal. The system could only be ended gradually.

Churchill's speech was a bitter disappointment to many Liberal and Labour members who had taken the agitation against Chinese Labour seriously. There was talk of voting against the Government, particularly among the Labour members. When the debate was continued next day, Asquith

[1] Lucy Masterman, *C. F. G. Masterman*, p. 84.

rose and after many compliments to his young friend who had made such a clear and admirable speech, proceeded to 'restate' the Government's views. Winston looked distinctly restless and I imagine was smothering his feelings with some difficulty. To make a long story short, Mr. Asquith announced in very emphatic tones the same things, only with an important addition that no more licences would be granted.[1]

Asquith's speech rallied the Government supporters. Nevertheless its more aggressive tone gave Chamberlain just the opening he needed. He began by complimenting one of the Labour members who had spoken in the debate. He believed that the working classes had opposed the Chinese Labour ordinance from a fear that it marked the first step in the mass introduction of cheap labour into England to compete against British labour.

He went on to remind the House that he, personally, had never thought the introduction of Chinese Labour desirable. The arguments for and against were very finely balanced. These arguments, however, were not the subject of the debate nor had they been the issue at the election. The issue had been whether the ordinance had in fact legalised 'slavery'. Very slowly, he read out a description of Chinese Labour conditions from a speech by Dr. Clifford, the Nonconformist leader. Every sentence was loudly cheered from the Liberal benches. Very well, but if Clifford's description were true, it was intolerable that the system should be allowed to continue for a day. After all the allegations that had been made the only honourable course was to appoint a Royal Commission of enquiry to establish the facts about the conditions under which the Chinese worked.

The request for a Royal Commission of enquiry was for some months a main demand by the Unionist Opposition. It was never conceded.

There was an amusing sequel to this speech. At one point Chamberlain had accused Churchill of using very different language in the House from that which he had used in his constituency. This interchange followed:

Mr. Churchill: 'The words I used yesterday were almost word for word what I said to my own constituents in Manchester.' (*Ministerial cheers.*)

Mr. Chamberlain: 'But what you said in those words did not get you votes in Manchester. (*Ministerial laughter.*) What did gain the Under Secretary votes were the production of those posters and the parading of every street in his constituency by gangs of men dressed as Chinamen and accompanied by an agent got up as a slave driver.' (*Opposition cheers.*)

[1] Mrs. Chamberlain to her brother, 24 February 1906.

Churchill wrote indignantly denying the charge and inviting Chamberlain to withdraw it. But the efficiency of the Birmingham machine won the day. Vince soon supplied details of the Chinese posters used in Churchill's constituency. Chamberlain, jestingly, offered to publish the results of his enquiries, but did not press the point. It is only fair to add that Churchill was not personally responsible for the propaganda used by his ward committees.

On 27 February, Balfour was returned by a large majority for the City. As luck would have it, he and Chamberlain were both struck down with influenza on the day of the poll. Thus for the next fortnight the leadership of the Opposition was in commission.

Chamberlain had only been leader for ten days: too short a period to judge his qualities in that capacity. But there is little doubt that his leadership gave more confidence to his own followers and earned more respect from his opponents than would Balfour's. We cite, in support of this contention, two quotations, one from a Unionist[1] and one from a Radical supporter.[2]

I remember in 1906, after the crushing defeat of his policy at the polls, watching him lead the reduced Unionist Party in the House of Commons against overwhelming odds during the brief period when Arthur Balfour was without a seat. Bravely, sure of ultimate success, he fought every step, always on the offensive, and slowly placing on record every position won. And then one day, in the middle of a debate on Tariff Reform, Balfour, who had just been re-elected, entered the House, took his seat, and assumed control of the Opposition. Quickly the atmosphere changed, and the debate descended to a dialectical level, to which Chamberlain adapted himself.

... Mr. Chamberlain is listened to with respect and attention. Mr. Balfour, if he continues his present methods, will, I am afraid, be listened to not at all. Mr. Chamberlain's political position is entirely repudiated; but members seem to feel that he is fighting about real things, and that he cares. Mr. Balfour may care also, and he may be fighting about real things. But he has not succeeded in conveying that impression to the House of Commons ...

Nothing is more symptomatic of the political change that had taken place in England than the handling Balfour received from the new Parliament. Before the election he had been regarded as the greatest Parliamentarian of the day. Now he could scarcely command a hearing. 'It was not so much that they disliked him', Austen later wrote, 'as that they despised him, and contempt is

---

[1] Sir Fabian Ware, *The Post Victorians*, 'Essay on J. Chamberlain.'
[2] Lucy Masterman, *C. F. G. Masterman*, p. 72.

less easy to conquer than hatred.'[1] Soon after his return, Garvin asked Walter Long, 'Has A.J.B. become as powerless in the House as they say?' Walter Long replied, 'As if he was nobody. It's extraordinary. They laugh and jeer at him as if he was something let down from the skylight.'[2]

As the months went by Balfour slowly regained the ear of the House; but his old ascendancy never quite returned.

With Balfour's return, Chamberlain had to vacate the leader of the Opposition's room. He was relegated instead to 'a kind of unlighted underground lair, rather more dismal than the cell of a criminal in one of His Majesty's prisons. "This is the only place they have given me," he remarked with some bitterness.'[3]

II

Chamberlain's main concern in these months was to ensure that the day-to-day conduct of the Opposition should be in keeping with the spirit of his Valentine Compact with Balfour. The first indications were encouraging. Balfour of Burleigh was expelled from the Constitutional Club for having signed a circular supporting the Liberal candidate in Chelsea at the election. Meanwhile, in the City by-elections, Lawrence, the Chairman, had kept Fiscal Reform in the forefront of the campaign, and had given instructions that all posters and leaflets should carry the slogan 'Vote for Balfour: Fiscal Reformer and Anti-Home Ruler'.

Nevertheless, the long struggle for the soul of the Unionist party was not yet over. On 22 February, Devonshire initiated a debate in the House of Lords on the economic situation and took the opportunity to condemn the Valentine Compact.

I think the publication of this correspondence is a step far in advance of anything which we have hitherto heard from the leaders of the Unionist party, and as such it is deserving of the notice of Parliament. I do not desire to exaggerate its importance. . . .

It will be a very long time before these declarations can have any practical effect whatever. It will be a long time before the Unionist party and its leaders will be in a position to advocate any constructive policy. Much may happen in the interval, . . .

There is, therefore, so far as I can see, not the slightest probability that on many occasions those who hold my opinions will find themselves in a different lobby from my noble friend. At the same time, I, as a

[1] *Down the Years.*   [2] From a note by J. L. Garvin.
[3] Lucy Masterman, *C. F. G. Masterman*, p. 69.

Unionist, do not commit myself to any expression of general confidence in His Majesty's present advisers. I remain a Unionist, and I claim the right to remain a Unionist, irrespective of any opinions which I may hold on questions which are not connected with the Union. The Unionist party to which I owe any allegiance is a Free Trade Unionist party, if such a party may, by any possibility, be reconstituted in the future. As regards the constructive policy which by this correspondence has now been adopted in the name of the Unionist party by the leaders of the Unionist party, I decline altogether to admit any allegiance to the leaders or any responsibility for their action in regard to this policy, and I absolutely decline — I desire that it should be known that some of us, at all events, decline — to accept, as regards the future constructive policy of the party, the leadership of those who have accepted the principles which I find embodied in the letters to which I have referred.

Lansdowne replied for the official Opposition. His speech was perfectly loyal to the Balfour–Chamberlain Agreement; though, as was only to be expected, he laid the fullest stress on the qualifying phrases in Balfour's letter. The Duke, however, was not to be appeased. On 6 March, he presided at a meeting of the Unionist Free Trade Club, where Lord George Hamilton and Arthur Elliot moved a resolution condemning the Valentine correspondence. The Duke, in his closing remarks, declared that it was the duty of their club 'to oppose Mr. Balfour's present policy'.

The first major action after these preliminary skirmishes was the Fiscal Debate in the Commons promised by Campbell-Bannerman. The occasion was a resolution proposed by Sir James Kitson, a Liberal Member:

that the House, recognising that in the recent General Election the people of the United Kingdom have demonstrated their unqualified fidelity to the principles and practice of Free Trade, deems it right to record its determination to resist any proposal, whether by way of taxation upon foreign corn or of the creation of a general tariff upon foreign goods, to create in this country a system of Protection.'

This resolution was, of course, devised to split the remaining Unionist Free Traders from the official Opposition and, if possible, to embarrass relations between Balfour and Chamberlain.

The debate was to take place on 1 March, but was postponed, because of Balfour and Chamberlain's ill health, first to 8 March and then to 12 March. The Unionist leaders were glad of the delay. They were by no means agreed what line the Party should take.

The attitude of the Unionist Free Traders has been recorded by one of their number, Sir E. Clarke:[1]

[1] Sir E. Clarke, *The Story of My Life*, pp. 381 et seq.

As the day drew near it became incumbent on those who refused to support Mr. Chamberlain's programme to consult as to their action and a meeting was held in one of the committee-rooms, at which Mr. W. F. D. Smith presided over a gathering of about forty members. It was an interesting assembly. The son of the former leader of the House of Commons was in the chair, and with him were Mr. Hicks Beach, the son of the former Chancellor of the Exchequer, and Mr. Lionel Walrond, the son of the late Chief Conservative Whip. Sir John Kennaway, Sir Francis Powell, Mr. Percy Thornton, and Mr. Abel Smith, were four of the oldest and most respected members of the House. Sir William Anson and Mr. J. G. Talbot represented Oxford University, and Sir Philip Magnus the newer University of London. The Devonshire influence was represented by Mr. Victor Cavendish, and the Salisbury influence by Lord Robert Cecil, and the Durham influence by Mr. Lambton.

Mr. Rothschild and Sir Edward Sassoon, Sir Seymour King and Mr. Mildmay, coming from constituencies of widely differing character, were all opponents of the new Protectionist policy.

More than one meeting took place, and the question of concerted action was fully discussed. Eventually it was decided that no definite pledges should be given, but that if Sir James Kitson's resolution became the main question to abstain from voting in either lobby.

Chamberlain's views as to the line to be taken emerge clearly enough from the following correspondence.

CHAMBERLAIN AND PIKE-PEASE

J.C. to Pease, 3 *March* 1906: *Private.*—In my opinion there are two alternatives, the first is a simple negative. If that is objected to, then an amendment in the exact words of Balfour's letter to me. Having had all this trouble to get an agreement, let us stick to it in every particular and do not let us once more raise a confusion of which our opponents would be only too ready to take advantage. We have lost two years in finding a *modus vivendi*, and for Heaven's sake do not let us now lose what we have gained.

I see no objection in being a minority in the Division, but I should like to think that we can hold our own in the debate.

Pease to J.C., 4 *March* 1906: *Private.*—The suggestion you make as to an official Opposition amendment to Kitson's resolution is exactly what I intended to convey in my letter by the words 'embodying the substance'.

I appreciate very much being allowed to offer my opinion. To my mind the position is this — if it was decided to vote a simple negative:

(1) The amendments would come first to spoil the debate and the vote.

(2) There would be in our party those who considered that by opposing the resolution they were advocating Protection in its widest sense.

(3) There would be certainly a disposition among the timid members of our Party to stay away or pair. The latter nowadays, as far as

the effect produced is concerned, is much the same as the former because the public look at the number of Unionists who vote and not at the majority.

I submit that this matter is of the very greatest importance because an amendment on the lines of Mr. Balfour's letter is sure to be fought against privately by men like Sir John Kennaway. It appears to me that if you can arrange that an amendment is placed on the paper on Wednesday night in the language of Mr. Balfour's letter (and mentioning of course the possibility of a tax on corn and a general tariff), we should get a good result in the vote, if previously it is stated that there will be an official amendment.

The effect of Mr. Balfour's letter to you has been very great, but this would be accentuated by general party support being given to it in the House of Commons.

J.C. to Pease, 5 March 1906: Private.—This cursed influenza still hangs on me. I am ordered to Folkestone for a week. I have not seen Balfour, but Austen spoke to him and arranged that nothing should be done in the way of an amendment till we can meet, which will now be the beginning of next week. Meanwhile I have the *strongest possible* opinion that no Tariff Reformer can or ought to accept any other amendment than the exact words of Balfour's letter. That constituted the new treaty of alliance. If the parties to it are to break away a few days afterwards we shall never come together again.

I am wretched at having to be away at this time, but there is no help for it.

Chamberlain's plans for a week at Folkestone were roughly disturbed by the Liberal leaders. As soon as they heard that Balfour and Chamberlain meant to attend the House on the Monday (12 February), they declined to postpone the Fiscal Debate beyond that day. The Opposition had still to put down an official amendment and, since this had to be done before the House rose on the Friday, Balfour and Chamberlain were forced, much to their irritation, to come back to London on the Friday to decide its terms. That night, Mrs. Chamberlain wrote:

This afternoon they have been having a Conference (the ex-Cabinet, Joe and Mr. Wyndham), over the Opposition Amendment to the Fiscal Motion, and it has been settled after a long discussion. It is idle to expect that each occasion as it arises which requires definite assertion on the Fiscal Question will present no difficulties. Minds do not cease to work as they always have done, even when a policy has been defined, but the difference between the time before the last letters were exchanged and the present is that now there is the basis of those letters for the starting point. Anything which appeared in any way to weaken what is therein declared would stultify Mr. Balfour's position — and that everyone recognizes, even the least progressive of his colleagues. So it is much more satisfactory than it ever has been and as time goes on I have great hope that the different elements will draw closely together.

The amendment on which they agreed, and which was put down in Wyndham's name, invited the House to delete from Kitson's resolution the words directed against any proposal to introduce Protection by taxation upon foreign corn or by the introduction of a General Tariff. It went on to propose instead that the House, whilst recording its determination to resist schemes involving artificial protection against legitimate competition, should express a readiness to consider any scheme framed for purposes of revenue or to secure more equal terms of competition for British trade and closer union with the Colonies.

Chamberlain would have preferred a direct negative, but he could hardly complain of the amendment. It embodied Balfour's Valentine letter almost verbatim.

The Debate was the occasion of Balfour's return to the House. He rose as soon as Kitson's motion had been moved and seconded. 'Instead of discussing the large questions raised by the resolution,' one of his colleagues wrote'[1]

He described it as a vote of censure on the Opposition, and then proceeded to criticise its terms, and put five interrogatories to the Government, one being whether the Indian tariff was or was not Protectionist, and another being why the words 'or otherwise' were not in the resolution when first put on the paper and were in the resolution as moved. As he went on refining, and distinguishing, and inquiring, the cheers on his own side gradually grew fainter.

No Minister rose to reply to Balfour's questions. A brief consultation followed between Balfour and Chamberlain on the front bench. Chamberlain had prepared a full attack on the resolution. Balfour now urged him to move the adjournment as a protest against the Government's discourtesy in not replying to the questions of the leader of the Opposition. He agreed to do so, believing that he might still be able to intervene later in the Debate after Wyndham's amendment had been called.

Chamberlain's action in moving the adjournment stung Campbell-Bannerman to what was undoubtedly the speech of his life. He addressed himself to Balfour's questions:

The Right Hon. Gentleman is like the old Bourbons in the oft-quoted phrase — he has learnt nothing. He comes back to this new House of Commons with the same airy graces, the same subtle dialectics, the same light and frivolous way of dealing with a great question. But he little knows the temper of the new House of Commons if he thinks those

[1] Sir E. Clarke, *The Story of My Life*, pp. 381 *et seq.*

methods will prevail here. He has put some questions to me on this resolution. He has split it up and tortured it and pulled it to pieces, and he thinks that he has put some posers.

I put it to the House whether what I have said does not show how utterly unworthy of the occasion was the speech of the Rt. Hon. Gentleman. He first of all rides one horse and then he rides another — two horses perfectly incapable of being ridden together. One of his arguments contradicts the other. Then he says we are to stop the proceedings and this debate and his amendments are not to be moved until we have answered these terrible questions. In so far as I have referred to them I may have answered them incidentally. I have no direct answer to them. They are utterly futile, nonsensical and misleading. They were invented by the Rt. Hon. Gentleman for the purpose of occupying time on this debate. I say, enough of this foolery! It might have answered very well in the last Parliament, but it is altogether out of place in this Parliament. The tone and temper of this Parliament will not permit it. Move your amendments and let us get to business.

Chamberlain's motion for the adjournment was, of course, defeated by 405 votes to 115. The figures are important in view of the divisions that were to follow. He felt, himself, that his tactics had been mistaken.

I told Arthur Balfour [he remarked that night] that I wanted to hit them in the eye, but he said 'No, the right thing to do is to turn their flank'. So nothing was left for me to do but to make Campbell-Bannerman angry — which I did. Good enough for a Scottish Debating Society, but not what I wanted![1]

The debate was resumed by Austen, followed soon afterwards by F. E. Smith, speaking for the first time in the House. No more successful maiden speech has ever been made, before or since. Its theme was that the Liberal victory at the polls was due, not to dislike of Chamberlain's policy, but to misrepresentation on the subject of Chinese Labour and Education. It was 'begotten by Chinese slavery out of passive resistance'. Lloyd George wound up the first day's Debate for the Government, in a purely Free Trade speech.

When the Debate was continued next day (13 March), the Speaker called a private member's amendment moved by Stuart Wortley, which would have deleted that part of Kitson's resolution which claimed that 'in the recent general election, the people of the United Kingdom have demonstrated their unqualified fidelity to the principles and practice of Free Trade'. After some debate, this amendment was negatived by 445 votes to 118.

Wyndham then rose to move the official amendment, and after making a strong Tariff Reform speech, sat down shortly before the

[1] Sir F. Ware, 'Essay on Joseph Chamberlain' in *The Post-Victorians*.

hour for the suspension of the sitting. Campbell-Bannerman, reluctant to give more time for the debate and afraid that the resolution might be talked out, at once moved the closure, before Wyndham's amendment could be put to the vote. This closure move was carried by 471 votes to 123, including all Unionist members present. Wyndham's amendment was thus lost and the Speaker, accordingly, put Kitson's original resolution. Serious confusion now arose on the Unionist front bench. Here is Sir E. Clarke's account of the next five minutes.

I was sitting on the front bench next to Sir Alexander Acland-Hood, who told me he was not going to tell against the motion. The bells were ringing for the division, and he had scarcely told me this when Austen Chamberlain, looking very angry, came from his place to Acland-Hood, and said, 'What is this I hear, that you are not going to tell?' 'No,' said Acland-Hood, 'we are not going to — Forster and I must stand by what we told our constituents.' 'Well,' said Austen Chamberlain, 'I do not see how you can expect us to come down night after night and give you respectable divisions, if we are to be treated like this. Where's Arthur?' 'In his room.' 'Is not he going to vote?' 'I don't know.' Austen Chamberlain hurried off to find him, and before the Question was put the second time came back smiling, and said triumphantly to Acland-Hood, 'You are to tell. He says he wishes it.' 'Well,' said I to Acland-Hood, 'what are you going to do?' 'Oh,' said he, 'he is my leader, and if he tells me to do it I must, but ten minutes ago I believed he was not going to vote himself.' This choice of Whips determined a substantial number of votes. Akers-Douglas came in. Said I, 'What will you do?' 'Oh, I cannot desert my leader.'

Of those who had been present at Mr. W. F. D. Smith's meeting in the committee-room the large majority, and I among them, refrained from voting. Six stalwart Unionist Free Traders voted with the Government. They were Mr. Percy Thornton, Lord Robert Cecil, Sir Seymour King, Mr. Lambton, Mr. Walter Rothschild, and Mr. Gibson Bowles.

Nield and others fell into line, but 25 of those who had voted in the former division now abstained or voted for the motion, and only 98 went into the Opposition Lobby, while the majority numbered 474.[1]

Half a dozen Unionists had thus voted with the majority and a score had abstained. At first sight, this might seem discouraging, but it was a much better result, from a Fiscal Reform point of view, than the Whips Office had predicted. Acland-Hood, indeed, had worried that 'thirty might be expected to vote against Wyndham and forty in favour of the resolution'.[2] The final vote convinced Chamberlain that he had been right at the beginning in urging

[1] Sir E. Clarke, *The Story of My Life*, p. 388.
[2] Chamberlain to Balfour, 16 March 1906.

that the Unionists should not bother with an amendment but simply oppose the Kitson Resolution. We get some idea of his mood from the following extract:

MRS. CHAMBERLAIN TO HER MOTHER

14 *March* 1903.—After all the great Fiscal Debate over which we have expended so much tissue has proved a fiasco, and though Mr. Wyndham moved his Amendment no one spoke on it and it was not even voted on. The Government refused to carry on the Debate after the time originally allotted for it and, when they moved the closure, to everyone's astonishment the Speaker gave it. Our people had been confident that he would not give it before the Leaders had been able to speak on what was known to be the official Opposition Amendment, and consequently feel that the rights of the minority have not received that support from him which we are entitled to expect. Others feel that our tactics were not good — and as the event has proved they failed — but then no one could foresee the Speaker's action. It is however one proof more that the less direct course is misunderstood. Joe was very anxious to treat the whole thing more directly — in fact with a direct negative. But that was a view which he could not carry, and naturally he feels he was right and the others were wrong. However, perhaps the result will not do us harm and possibly new difficulties are avoided.

The action of the Unionist Free Traders provoked some resentment among Unionists outside the House. The Tariff Reformers in the City Association determined that Sir E. Clarke, their other Member, should pay for his speech and abstention. They moved that he had forfeited the confidence of his constituents. This proceeding was watched with some interest, for Balfour was the other City Member. He made no move, however, to save Clarke, and, at a public gathering a few weeks later, refused rather obviously to shake hands with him. Soon afterwards, Clarke gave up the struggle and resigned his seat. This incident was at least a warning that Chamberlain could no longer be flouted with impunity.

III

Fate now provided a fitting climax to the historic association between Chamberlain and Milner.

At the beginning of the Session (26 February), Milner had initiated a Debate on South Africa in the Lords and, in a maiden speech, had expressed grave doubts over the Liberal Government's declared intention of granting early self-government to the former Boer Republics. It was an impressive speech; and Elgin, the

Colonial Secretary, had paid tribute to it. The rest of the Debate, however, degenerated into a wrangle over how far the Liberal leaders had misrepresented the results of the Chinese Labour Ordinance. On this subject, Lord Portsmouth alleged a number of irregularities. In particular, he quoted from a statement by Mr. Evans, the Superintendent of Foreign Labour in the Transvaal, who had stated that he had sanctioned light 'corporal punishment' at the mines, that he had informed Milner of his action, and that Milner 'had taken no objection'. Portsmouth now asked Milner whether this was true.

Milner at once accepted full responsibility for what had occurred. He did not in fact recall the particular conversation with Evans, but he had full confidence in him, and so, accepted his version as correct. Looking back, he had no doubt that the decision had been a mistake. Abuses had come to light very soon after Milner had left; and his successor, Lawley, promptly forbade all further corporal punishment.

'I think I was wrong,' Milner declared, 'in not taking notice of this (*i.e.* Evans') statement; I regret that I did not do so.'

The Liberals seized on Milner's admission. Here was the heaven-sent reply to Chamberlain's charges of 'misrepresentation'. They determined to give the fullest publicity to Milner's mistake and tabled a private Member's resolution censuring his conduct. The Government agreed to provide time for the Debate. They at first intended to accept the resolution. At the last minute, however, at the instance of Asquith and Elgin, they put down an amendment censuring the flogging of Chinese coolies but inviting the House, in the interests of peace and conciliation in South Africa, to refrain from passing censure on individuals.

Milner considered the amendment as almost more offensive than the resolution.

MILNER TO CHAMBERLAIN

21 *March* 1906: *Very Confidential.*—I don't think much of the Govt. amendment, but still it is, I suppose, sure to be carried, therefore I must look to the speeches for my defence — not on the particular point on which I have put up no defence — but on that which everybody knows to be the real issue — my general character and conduct. I hope that the arrangement holds good, that you are to be my principal champion on these lines. If so, you may be interested to see the enclosed cutting from the *Daily Chronicle*, which, while deprecating the resolution, very frankly admits the true inwardness of the attack on me. I do not myself agree that my speech in the Lords was 'marked' in any degree by

'hostility to the Government now in power'. If I had wanted to attack *them*, I could have made a much more vigorous speech. But they and their followers choose so to regard it, and here we have the admission that it is *because of that speech* that many of them support the motion.

March 21 was appointed for the Debate. The temperature of the House was raised by the proceedings in the early part of the Session. Chamberlain renewed his demand for a Commission of Enquiry 'to report on the economic and moral effects of the system of indentured Labour at present in force in the Transvaal'. Churchill, in reply, made a bitter personal attack on Chamberlain. In his first speeches, he said, Chamberlain had sought to influence the Liberals by representing that the Government was not going far enough. Now he was exciting the feelings of the Colonists by conjuring up the danger of Whitehall interference. His conduct in this matter had not been 'wholly patriotic'. It was aimed at 'raising political capital' for his own side.

By the time the censure motion came on, after the dinner recess, the atmosphere was tense and stormy. Chamberlain rose as soon as the resolution had been moved and seconded. He was received with jeers.

The House of Commons [wrote Mrs. Chamberlain] today jeers at everything and in the beginning of Joe's speech was quite intolerable, laughing at every expression of conviction. However, he expected no quarter as he asked for none. He had it in control before many sentences were over. [1]

Chamberlain's speech was one of the most powerful he ever made in the House. He began by dealing with the resolution itself.

What is the proposal? In the absence, the necessary absence, of the person accused — for you have not called him to the bar of this House — you propose to call on the House to pass a resolution which can have no practical effect, and to inflict censure and humiliation on this man, of whose existence and work in our history, the people of this country will be proud. You ask the House to pass this censure on a man who is no longer in office, and for an error which you admit you know he had frankly acknowledged, and for which he has expressed regret. Where is the generosity? Where is the magnanimity for which we take credit when you can put aside all that you owe to this great and distinguished public servant in order to condemn him, and to inflict this unnecessary humiliation on him after he has acknowledged and regretted the error he has committed? The resolution is retrospective. It is vindictive.

Sir, let us have no cant about this matter. We all know, the country knows, that the object of this motion is to inflict humiliation upon a

[1] Mrs. Chamberlain to her mother, 24 March 1906.

person who is as honest and as sincere as any member of this House, but of whose policy honourable members opposite happen to disapprove; and for that and for Party reasons they pick up a single point in a long history of self-sacrifice and devotion. They pick it up because they have an admission; I am almost disposed to say an unnecessary admission — at all events it is a chivalrous admission — of the person concerned. They dare not question his policy as a whole, and they pick up the one point, the one little point, a comparatively unimportant point in the whole history of this great man's life. They pick it up because they have his own admission, and they cannot be contradicted; and they, accepting his regret, are not satisfied without the additional humiliation which they think they can inflict by a vote of this House, but which will recoil upon the heads of those who have proposed it, and upon those who may be ungenerous enough to support it.

After examining the facts of the case, he turned to the amendment.

Although the honourable member's resolution has been on the paper for a long time, it was only this morning that we learned the particular way in which the Government propose to deal with it. They have put down an amendment. Sir, it is a cowardly amendment. I would prefer infinitely the resolution of the honourable gentleman. At all events that presents a clear issue. I should vote against it with a light heart, but I should vote against it with some respect for the honourable gentleman who, with, I think, a mistaken impression of his duty, has put it down in clear terms. But the amendment! It is an amendment which insults Lord Milner, and at the same time accepts the substantial part of the resolution of the honourable gentleman opposite. They think to gain votes by distinctly pointing at Lord Milner, and at the same time with-drawing his name. That is party tactics : Liberal policy! Well, I must refrain. But there is something else. What is this 'conciliatory' amend-ment to do? It is proposed in the interests of 'peace and conciliation'. It is an amendment which a politician may accept, but which on its merits would be rejected by every honourable man.

Chamberlain went on to quote Disraeli's opinion that 'great services are not cancelled by one act, by one single error, however it may be regretted at the moment'. Then, lowering his voice, he raised the whole Debate on to a different plane.

Will the House allow me to try and bring before them the nature of the work which is imposed upon High Commissioners, Viceroys, and Governors of Crown Colonies throughout the Empire? These men are in a way autocrats, and that brings upon them all the disadvantages which autocrats have to suffer. They are responsible for everything, be it great or be it small, in the administration with which they are connected. They are answerable for the security of possessions for which they are made responsible. They are answerable for order, for legislation, for every detail of administration, for every act, be it great or small, of every member, be he important or otherwise, of the whole administration. For all these things these men are, technically, at any rate, responsible to their departments and to this House of Commons. They are not infallible. How can you expect to get infallible administrators under such circumstances? I do not believe they are to be found anywhere, but certainly you do not offer much temptation. I have never heard of any one in the colonial service who in these trying positions, having to submit, as he has to do, to this sort of ignorant and irresponsible criticism on the part of people who have none of his responsibility, has become a gold magnate, who has made a fortune, who has even been able to provide for those whom he has left behind him, by devotion to the public service, by his interest in the great work he is conducting from the highest motives. These men, some of them never rising to a great position, others occupying positions of the greatest responsibility, have continued to serve the country, and now you are placing a slight on the whole service in the person of one of its most distinguished representatives — Lord Milner.

It is admitted that before he occupied his position in South Africa, Lord Milner had done great service to the State — and that is to be considered. He had done great service to the Party opposite. But I put that aside. His great services to the country are his services in South Africa. During a great part of that time he was in a sense responsible to me, and as my colleague and friend a greater man I have never known. I have never known a great man who did not make mistakes. This man has given his life, he has risked his health, he has lived under conditions which very few in this House would be willing to sustain. Eight hours a day ! Why, eighteen hours a day of continuous brainwork very often fell to his lot. . . . under great stress and anxiety, . . . he has shown an ability, courage, and firmness that ought to commend itself to men who appreciate bravery at a time when his life might have been so much easier if he had shown weakness. Honourable members opposite may not agree with him, but I appeal with confidence to them to admire the character which he showed in difficult circumstances. . . . I want this House to consider the subject from that intimate point of view. Here is this colonial service of ours, which is known and admired throughout the world for its absolute integrity, its freedom from corruption, its ability, its humanity. It is only by these extraordinary qualities that what I may call the daily miracle of the successful administration of the British Empire is continuously carried on. But for them, how would it be possible for these two small islands of ours to administer so large a portion of the earth's surface and with so much distinction and general satisfaction? Sir, I ask the House to put aside every other consideration but that of their Imperial duty, the duty which they cannot escape, even those who least sympathise with the work, be they Irish, Scottish, or English, and look to those great considerations and principles which have made this colonial service undoubtedly what it is. I ask them to recognise the merits of this service, and I ask them to appreciate the difficulties under which every member of it lies, and not to discourage them when one of them has committed a mistake which he himself has freely acknowledged. I ask them not to discourage the whole service by harsh criticism of one of its most distinguished members.

Churchill's reply, from the Government front bench, was mainly addressed to his own side. He regretted his statement that Milner had been guilty of a 'grave dereliction of duty', and then proceeded to recall, in rather patronising terms, his past services to the country. Finally, he urged the House not to censure a retired civil servant who was now 'powerless, discredited and poor', but to vote instead for the amendment. This the House duly did by 355 votes to 135, a relatively low Government majority.

Next morning, Milner wrote:

MILNER TO CHAMBERLAIN

22 *March* 1906.—I must send you one line of warm personal thanks for the magnificent fight you made for me against a bitterly hostile audience and with a difficult case. I am sorry for all the trouble I have caused to my friends, but take some little comfort from the thought that the enemies of our work in South Africa have not done themselves much good by their recent tactics.

I am so glad the Opposition voted against the amendment, apparently to a man.

Chamberlain's own verdict on the Debate appears from the following letter.

CHAMBERLAIN TO SWETTENHAM

23 *March* 1906.—Independently of my friendship with, and great respect for, Milner, I regard the principle at stake as being of the greatest importance. The public service has a right to claim the support of its political chiefs against misrepresentations and injustice, and it is entirely a new departure that this support should be dependent on party or political considerations. The attack was disgraceful. The official comment was still worse; but although the mechanical majority is unimpaired, I believe that many of those who voted for the amendment were thoroughly ashamed of their action.

In their attack on Milner, the Liberal majority had overreached themselves. Churchill's speech, in particular, was bitterly resented by Imperialist opinion everywhere.

His patronising 'Defence' of Lord Milner [wrote Mrs. Chamberlain] was an insult and his manner of speaking intolerable.[1]

Counter-measures were now prepared.

On 29 March, Halifax moved in the House of Lords 'that this House desires to place on record its high appreciation of the services rendered by Lord Milner in South Africa to the Crown and the Empire'. The resolution was carried by 170 votes to 35. Next a

[1] Mrs. Chamberlain to her mother, 24 March 1906.

public address of recognition to Milner was proposed by Bartle
Frere and received many thousands of signatures. The climax of
these counter-demonstrations was a great banquet given in Milner's
honour on Empire Day, 24 May. Chamberlain presided, and so
had the last word in this burning controversy:

Considering how many men of great character and distinction we
have sent out from these shores to represent this country across the seas,
and what splendid services many of them have performed, it might at
first sight appear curious how casual and how slight has been any public
recognition of what they have done. It would not be difficult for any
of us to find many examples. I should not have to go further than this
company to find distinguished illustrations of men who have been amongst
the greatest names in our country and yet have been suffered, after their
term of office was over and they had put aside all the attributes and the
panoply of power, to come back home hardly with as much notice as
the captain of a cricket team or a champion football club. But I do not
know that any of us need regret the fact that we in England, in the
United Kingdom, have been so accustomed to take for granted and as a
matter of course the splendid performance of responsible duties that we
do not think it necessary to call any attention to it. The makers of our
Empire never sought popular applause. They have been content that
history and posterity should rightly appreciate their services.
But this is not an ordinary occasion. If it were, my noble friend at my
side would be the first to desire that he should be no exception to the
general rule. But we have an opinion in this matter as well as he; ...
to-day is Empire Day, ... than which no more appropriate day could be
found to recognise public and Imperial service. This great company,
than which I have never seen one more representative of every kind of
national character and expression, has been stirred to express its confidence to Lord Milner, and, as far as in it lies, to redress a great injustice,
and protest against the abuse of a temporary majority which has thought
fit to inflict an unmerited slight upon a great servant of the Empire.
Lord Milner has been censured by a majority of the House of Commons.
He was undefended by the Government, which, according to a great
tradition, is bound to support the servants, the Civil servants of the State
if they are unjustly attacked. He was insulted by a Minister who only
a few years ago beslavered him with fulsome praise; and he was deserted
by friends who hailed his appointment with shouts of applause.

Chamberlain went on to give the inside story, as it were, of much
of his collaboration with Milner during the war. The details have
long since been published; but, at the time, it was new and held
the audience fascinated.

After eight years of incessant, of untiring work, work that it is difficult
for any man who has not seen it to appreciate, he returned. And when
he left South Africa he could have boasted, if he had chosen to boast,
and we can declare for him, that he had restored the confidence of British

subjects in British power and British sympathy, that he had extorted from his adversaries the respect which adversaries always give to a brave man, that he had laid the foundation for a renewed and greatly increased prosperity of the country for which he had done so much, that he had marked out lines on which constitutional freedom might be safely extended. And this is the man — to-night he is our honoured guest — of whom it was said the other day with unctuous satisfaction and insolent commiseration that he was powerless, discredited, and poor. That is untrue. Lord Milner is rich in the only sense in which a man so disinterested would care to be opulent; he is rich in the admiration, the affection, the regard of those whose regard and affection are worth having. His policy is not discredited in the minds of those whose knowledge and experience give a right to express an opinion. If he is powerless in the sense that for the moment he holds no high official position, we hope and believe that his services will always be given when required, and that he remains now one of the great assets of the British Empire.

Milner in his reply paid a quiet but moving tribute to Chamberlain :

I am thinking of what we all owe him — all of us at least who look beyond the Empire as it is to the Empire as it might be — for the immense impulse he has given to the thoughts and sympathies and movements which make for a more effective union of the scattered communities of the British race. . . . The disappointment which one feels, as the years pass and one grows old and nothing happens, does not alter the fact that the idea is silently growing all the time.

Curzon followed, with a speech 'of ringing energy and stateliness . . . the ex-Viceroy marched over his subject with banners flying'. Many believed that this great gathering marked the dawn of an Imperial Revival. But, for all of its grandeur and pomp, it was only an afterglow.

IV

The legislative programme that spring revived many issues in which Chamberlain had played a prominent part in times gone by.

On 26 March, the Home Secretary introduced a Workman's Compensation Bill. This was an extension of Chamberlain's own act; and he welcomed it, though criticising certain details. His criticisms, we must admit, savour somewhat of tactics. He joined with Akers-Douglas and the more Conservative Wing in condemning the Government's proposal to shorten the period antecedent to compensation. He feared this might encourage shirking and absenteeism. On the other hand, he made a bold bid for popular support by complaining that there were too many exemptions from the Bill, and asking that its provisions should be extended to small works, clerks, shop assistants and domestic servants.

Next day (27 March), Lloyd George's Merchant Shipping Acts Amendment Bill came up for second reading. Its main purpose was to make British safety regulations compulsory for foreign ships entering British ports. Chamberlain had been a pioneer in the cause of safety regulations for Merchant Shipping in the far-off days when he had been Liberal President of the Board of Trade. He supported Lloyd George's Bill and welcomed it as an instalment of Tariff Reform in that it obliged foreign shipowners to accept the same obligations as British shipowners and so made competition between them fairer. He went on to suggest that in view of the unemployment among merchant sailors there should be a minimum proportion of British sailors in every British ship's company.

By the end of March, Chamberlain and Balfour were badly in need of a rest. Both had been ill and Balfour 'is only just well enough to do what is *absolutely* necessary'.[1] Balfour's doctors ordered him a complete rest. Chamberlain was persuaded by Mrs. Chamberlain to take a short holiday in the South of France. A letter written from Beaulieu gives his view of the first part of the Session.

CHAMBERLAIN TO CHAPLIN

4 *April* 1906.—I am very sorry I missed you when you were here. I should have been glad of a talk with you about all that has happened since we last met. I think that, all things considered, we have done pretty well and the Government, in spite of their colossal majority, have been a good deal battered and discredited. But from there to a defeat is a far cry and things will have to be worse before they are better.

Winston Churchill has done very badly as a speaker since he has been in Office. Lloyd George has lost his fire, and I am told is a bad administrator. C. B. is like a pettish old maid, and the only Ministers that have come out well are Haldane and J. Morley!

Thank goodness! The gilt is off the radical gingerbread!

The weather after being splendid for 3 days, has now become stormy and disagreeable again.

I looked in at the rooms at Monte Carlo the other day and put a Louis on for Mrs. Chamberlain *en plein.* It came up the first time, which is, I hope, a good omen.

V

The main business of the House when members met again after Easter, was the Education Bill. Education had been the theme of Chamberlain's maiden speech and it would be the occasion of his last intervention in the House of Commons. The issue played

[1] Mrs. Chamberlain to her mother, 14 March 1903.

such a large part in his career that we must consider in some detail his last stand upon it.

The Liberals were deeply committed to remedy certain grievances which the Nonconformists felt against the Act of 1902. These were first, that denominational schools were supported out of local rates as well as Government grants; second, that these schools were nevertheless not under full public control; and third, that in districts where there was a single school the children of Nonconformist parents received either Church religious teaching or none. This last grievance might easily have been remedied had provision been made that the children of such Nonconformist parents might receive separate religious instruction. The Unionist leaders, in 1902, however, had objected, illogically enough, that this would be unfair to the Church Schools unless the Board schools were equally opened to Church instruction on the same principle.

Birrell's Bill provided for the transfer of all elementary Denominational Schools to the public authorities. Schools not transferred would receive no further support from the rates or the Exchequer. In the transferred schools, as in other elementary schools, religious instruction in school hours would be limited to the Cowper-Temple formula. Denominational instruction could only be given in transferred schools, out of school hours, and not by school teachers. The only exception to this provision was to be in schools where four-fifths of the parents wished for the same Denominational instruction and where the children of the minority could be otherwise provided for.

The main feature of the Bill was that it made universal the Cowper-Temple teaching which the Church of England regarded as indistinguishable from most Nonconformist teaching. In the eyes of most Churchmen, this was an attempt to 'establish' Nonconformity as the official religion of the country.

Chamberlain's view of the Bill can be gauged from the following letter to a friend in the Church of England.

CHAMBERLAIN TO CARNEGIE

21 *April* 1906.—The Bill is a thoroughly bad one. It is unjust, confiscatory, and a complete surrender to the extremists on the other side. But having said this I must add that the situation seems to me a very difficult one. The majority which supports the Government can carry anything they like in the House of Commons. If you put your hope in the House of Lords, is it certain that a majority there will be willing to enter into a contest with the House of Commons on this matter? If they

do, and dissolution follows, are we yet able to look forward to a reversal of the last decision? It strikes me that before committing ourselves as a political party the Unionists must be prepared with an alternative. What is that alternative to be?

I can see only two systems that would be just. First, the education given by the State might be confined entirely to Secular instruction. Facilities might be given for the entrance to all the schools of religious teachers at a time outside the fixed hours and on the request of a fixed number of parents. Personally, I do not see why the teachers should not be free to give this teaching if they are willing and are invited to do so by the representatives of the parents. In this case, although they would be submitted to no tests on appointment as teachers, their fitness for giving the religious instruction would no doubt be inquired into by those who employed them and who would have to make some payment for the extra work.

This system worked out in detail would, I think, be absolutely fair as regards all the Denominations, but it is open to all the feeling regarding what is called a secular system. It was, as you know, tried in Birmingham and after three years was given up in face of objections, which came chiefly from the Nonconformists, although Dr. Dale strongly supported it.

The second alternative is practically concurrent endowment — in other words to arrange that every parent should be offered the opportunity of saying what religious teaching he wishes given to his children, and if there are a sufficient number of them to form a class that they should be taught this religion, whether Nonconformists, Church, Catholic or Jew by such of the teachers in the school as may be found fitted to give it.

The difficulty here, besides the general objection to concurrent endowment, would be to find teachers capable of giving the required education in single school districts, where the minorities would be very small and perhaps insufficient to justify the creation of a separate class.

I put this down roughly and do not know whether I make myself understood, but I should like to know what view you take of the matter, and whether you think it is possible for the Church, and for all who oppose the present Bill, to formulate an alternative which we could defend as just to the Nonconformist as well as to those who are described as Denominationalists.

I shall try to see the Bishop before I return to town, as I feel that the situation is critical and the whole character of our opposition in the House of Commons must depend on the extent to which we can agree about our ultimate objects. What I feel strongly is that negative criticism will not be effective by itself.

Chamberlain was clear in his own mind that it would be unwise to meet the Government's proposals with a direct negative. The Unionists must propose an alternative; and Chamberlain determined that it should be that system of secular education, with facilities for all denominations, which he had favoured in Birmingham in years gone by, but which had then been defeated by the scandalised opposition of the Church, the Wesleyans and the Methodists. After some discussion, the Archbishop of Canterbury and the Bishop of Birmingham were convinced. Balfour would not go so far but saw no point in opposing Chamberlain. Only Hicks Beach was publicly opposed to this new departure. Thus for some months, Chamberlain, Unitarian and agnostic, led the High Church party in a campaign for secular education.

Chamberlain proclaimed his alternative in a brilliant speech on the second reading of the Bill (9 May).

He began by recalling his part in the Education struggle thirty years before and summarised the view he had held consistently ever since.

I am a very old stager in the education controversy. More than thirty years ago I was chairman of the National Education League. At the same time, I was a member of the Central Nonconformist Committee, and a short time afterwards I was chairman for three years of the Birmingham School Board. I have had theoretical and practical acquaintance with these questions.

Thirty years ago, when I entered this House, I made my maiden speech, and it was on this subject, and curious it is to look back and see that the issue then was exactly the same as it is now. We have not progressed one atom, in my opinion, towards a final settlement, and until you come to some definite conclusion as to the principle to be adopted in order to do justice to all, you never will approach anything in the nature of a satisfactory settlement. I made two statements in that speech. The first was that if the clerical — ecclesiastical and ministerial — influence were withdrawn, there would be no religious difficulty. (*Ministerial cheers.*) But I am not certain, when we come to examine it, that the statement has helped, or will help, us much. My second statement was that the eternal principle of justice must be observed, and that the principles of the league, of the Nonconformist Committee, and of the Birmingham School Board, which involved not secular instruction, but an entire separation between the work of the State and the work of the individual or the denomination, seemed to me then, as they seem now, the only foundation on which you could permanently establish a fair and impartial system.

He admitted the genuine sense of grievance felt by many Nonconformists towards the Act of 1902.

The Government have attempted to remove that grievance . . . I do not complain of the attempt. I complain of the way in which they have done it. They have attempted to remove the grievance, the heavy burden which the Nonconformist felt upon his shoulder by sticking it upon the shoulder of the Catholic and Anglican instead.

Chamberlain proceeded to analyse the religious issue in education, showing a good deal of his old Radicalism. The Government benches hung on his words. The Tories were somewhat restive. Then came what one member described as the 'cleverest hit' he ever heard in Parliament.[1] Chamberlain was discussing a speech made by Lloyd George the night before:

What did the Right Hon. Gentleman say last night? The one sentence that will remain in our minds he quoted from a great Frenchman, and he said, 'Clericalism is the enemy'. (*Loud Ministerial cheers.*) Nonconformist religionists of different denominations cheered him (*more Ministerial cheers*). The Frenchman who used that expression had a different situation to deal with. He had to deal with a Clericalism which threatened the law (*Ministerial cheers*), which was considered to be opposing the law (*loud Ministerial cheers*), which was interfering in politics (*tremendous cheering from the Government side of the House*). Clericalism of that kind was thought to be an enemy of the State and for those reasons it was declared to be so by this great statesman (*prolonged and enthusiastic Ministerial cheers*).

We have your definition of Clericalism — those who interfere in politics (*further loud Ministerial cheers*), those who oppose the law.

Chamberlain paused dramatically; he dropped his eyeglass. The warm and persuasive voice became ice cold: 'Have you ever heard of Passive Resistance?'

'The general effect upon our benches', Masterman afterwards wrote, 'was that of a bowl of goldfish from which the water had suddenly been withdrawn.'[2]

Now came a frankly political threat. Was it wise to press a measure which the House of Lords might refer to the electors?

I ask you now, as politicians, do you think that this Bill will be a final settlement of the question? Are you not wasting your time if you think you are advancing our common object? (*Opposition cheers.*) You have a majority with which, in defiance of all minorities, you can, if you like, carry this Bill through the Commons without the slightest amendment. Well, under our Constitution, it will go elsewhere. (*Ministerial laughter.*) I am dealing with the practical situation. The Bill may be amended, but I ask you, whatever may be its fate in another place, whether it is ultimately destroyed there or destroyed by your refusal to accept amendments, do you think you will gain if there is another appeal to the people? On this question there is not the slightest doubt, practically, that at least one-half of the people are opposed to this Bill. (*Ministerial cries of* 'Oh, oh', *and Opposition cheers.*) You profess to think not. Wait for the election. (*Ministerial laughter.*) Whatever you may say for the purpose of cheering the spirits of this

[1] Lucy Masterman, *C. F. G. Masterman*, p. 84.   [2] *Ibid*, p. 74.

House (*Ministerial laughter*), there is not a man amongst you, in his heart, who has known anything whatever of political agitation in this country, who does not know, whatever happens, that if you went to the country on this Bill, you would come in with a smaller majority, and that would justify any action which might have been taken against you. There is only one way in which you can settle this question. You must settle it by some measure which will be recognised by the people of this country as inherently just. (*Opposition cheers.*)

Chamberlain now outlined the principles which, in his view, should govern a lasting settlement.

I say that the most logical, the fairest, the most reasonable, and the most easily obtainable of all systems is the system which separates the duty of the State from the duty belonging to the parent and the sect (*cheers*). One of the main objects of the Bill, it has been suggested, has been to prevent that system which has been described as a secular system — turning the Bible out of the schools, and bringing the children up in Atheism or irreligion. There is nothing substantial in that cry, like other cries with which we were familiar at the last election, but which are gone to the bourne from which no political cry ever returns (*laughter*). What we, who advocate this system, propose, is not secularism. What we all desire is not secularism, but a division of duty and conscience.

At this point, Campbell-Bannerman rose and enquired:

The Right Hon. Gentleman says 'what "we" desire'. On a previous occasion, we had to ask him what he meant by 'we', and he, then, said, 'the Unionist party', for which he was speaking. Does he still mean the Unionist party?
'On the present occasion', Chamberlain replied with mock gravity, ' "we" means those who agree with me.'

The reply brought the House down, and in the storm of laughter which followed, Chamberlain could be seen consulting rapidly with Balfour. He then resumed his speech, making the freest use of the word 'we'. At last, Campbell-Bannerman could bear it no longer. He again intervened and asked,

'Can the Right Hon. Gentleman say who is the particular we?'
Chamberlain smiled superciliously and replied: 'I have just consulted with my Right Hon. friend beside me (Balfour), and we agree that during the whole of this Debate, nothing has been expressed on this side of the House which conflicts with what I have said. If so, on this occasion, I may claim that "we" represents the Unionist Majority.'

Chamberlain gave further expression to his views on Education in the Debate on the Committee stages of the Bill. Maddison, a Government supporter, had moved an amendment that no religious instruction of any kind should be given in school hours or at the public expense. Chamberlain was against this provision, holding that this must encourage children to avoid religious instruction altogether. He would only accept Maddison's amendment if it were changed so that religious instruction would be given in and not out of school hours. He moved a sub-amendment accordingly, and collected 172 votes in its support.

His last intervention on the subject was in the Debate on Clause 4 (27 June). In this, he declared that the working classes of Britain were not as interested in the sectarian side of the question as many members supposed. What they wanted was to see justice done. He then referred to a recent speech by Dr. Clifford, the Nonconformist leader. Clifford had said, 'Everyone knows what Joey really wants'.

'If he means by that', Chamberlain now replied, 'that I want a general election, he is quite right.'

The Liberal Government had no intention of taking up the challenge. An election could only weaken them. Even when the House of Lords amended the Bill, they made no move. The Education Bill was then abandoned rather than face a General Election.

Despite their great majority in the Commons, the Liberal Government was paralysed by the power of the House of Lords to block all measures or force them to appeal to the country. Balfour had not been far wrong when on the morrow of his own electoral defeat, he had declared:

The great Unionist party should still control, whether in power or whether in Opposition, the destinies of this great Empire.

VI

The heavy casualties on the Unionist front bench as well as his own past forced Chamberlain to take a leading part in the day-to-day business of Opposition. Nevertheless, his dominant interest remained the cause of Tariff Reform.

The Valentine Compact with Balfour had secured the indispensable declaration of policy. The Unionist parties were now formally committed by written statements of their leaders. The next task was to create the necessary organisation to spread the gospel.

Chamberlain's chief lieutenants in this work were Ridley and Chaplin. Ridley was Chairman of the Tariff Reform League. Chaplin had considerable influence with the Conservative National

Union. Chamberlain, himself, of course, controlled the Liberal Unionist party and the Birmingham Tariff Committee.

The first aim of the Tariff Reformers in matters of organisation had been defined at the meeting in Gilbert Parker's house on 10 February.

> This meeting is of opinion
> 1. That the amalgamation of the Central Conservative Office and Liberal Unionist Organization is desirable, and that a Committee to establish a Central organisation on a representative basis should be immediately appointed.
> 2. That Mr. Balfour and Mr. Chamberlain be *ex-officio* Members of the Committee.

The difficulty here lay in the different constitutions of the two Parties. The Liberal Unionists, though entirely dominated by Chamberlain's personality, were on paper a democratic body. Their leader was elected by and responsible to the Party rank and file. The National Union, on the other hand, was controlled by the leader of the Conservative party, who was elected by a Party meeting in which the representatives of the National Union were in a small minority. It tended thus to be the instrument of the leader in the constituencies, rather than the voice of the constituencies in London.

Chamberlain's first aim was to put the National Union's constitution on a more democratic basis and so make it more responsive to public opinion. We may add that he had long been convinced that the more popular the basis of the Tory party the more likely it was to follow his lead and support his policies.

At the time of the Valentine Compact, Balfour and Chamberlain had agreed to set up a Committee to look into the whole question of organisation. The appointment was delayed first by Balfour's election and then by Balfour's and Chamberlain's illness. The following extracts give some idea of the progress of the affair.

CHAMBERLAIN AND PARTY ORGANISATION

Chaplin to Chamberlain: 16 *February* 1906.—we have a meeting of the Council of the National Union on Friday next, and I shall be up again early in the week.

You will remember that by a resolution at Newcastle, we are required to appoint a Committee to consider the question of reorganisation.

Meanwhile, I suppose you will have come to some understanding with Arthur & Co. upon that point — and if so perhaps you will let me know during the week before the 23rd when we meet. We shall then be better able to judge what course we had better take.

Chamberlain to Salvidge: 17 *February* 1906: *Private.*—Personally, I am anxious that the representative Associations of the Party shall now be reviewed, especially with the object of popularizing them and of securing the cordial assistance of the working-classes. They form the vast majority of the electors and they ought to have a prominent place in all our organizations. We have a great deal of popularizing work to do, but we have time before us, and, having satisfactorily determined the basis of our policy, we can proceed with confidence to secure a more efficient and democratic representation.

A small committee is to be appointed by Mr. Balfour and myself and we shall take evidence from different parts of the country as to the lessons of the election. I shall take care that you are invited to attend and to give us the advantage of your large and successful experience.

Chamberlain to Chaplin: 20 *February* 1906: *Private.*—As that imp Bowles has put Arthur to the trouble and expense of an election, I shall not be able to discuss organisation with him until it is all over. I am afraid it will take some time to manage satisfactorily.

Chamberlain to Chaplin: 4 *April* 1906.—I have heard nothing about organisation and I assume that nothing can be fixed till Arthur is about again. At any rate I have had no request to attend any Committee.

Preliminary contact was established between the seconds during the Easter Recess, and presently, Chaplin reported.

Chaplin to Chamberlain: 13 *April* 1906.—I got back just in time for the 3rd meeting of the Committee of the National Union — appointed in obedience to the resolution of the Newcastle Conference on Organisation — and at which we were to meet the Whip and 'the leaders' of the Party — and who do you think they were? Londonderry and Akers-Douglas ! ! !

I am glad I was there — our Chairman, though honestly anxious to give effect to the resolution which points to a representative element in the management of the Central Office — is not man enough for the job — is opposed to us on Fiscal — and overawed by the officials and the official element through whom he has been trying to come to an understanding. But they have no desire and certainly no present intention to agree to anything of the kind.

Douglas explained their position. There is no central committee of management at all in connection with the Central Office. The Central Office is really the Leader and the Whips, no one else — and in reality the answer was a '*non possumus*' in reply to the resolution at Newcastle, while on a number of subsidiary matters, such as lectures, publications, speakers and local organisation — they would be prepared to accept considerable changes.

The meeting ended by my asking Alec Hood to put on paper exactly what his proposals were and to let us have it before the monthly meeting of our Council, before the end of that week — and this he promised to do. But it was not forthcoming, owing to the pressure of his work in the House, and everything is now postponed till after Easter, in which I have gained exactly what I wanted. For that will give you time to discuss the whole subject with Arthur when he returns, and no good can be done till after that.

Many of our members objected quite as much as I did — to Londonderry and A. Douglas being commissioned to meet us as Leaders of the Party, and it was generally agreed that the only Leaders we desired to meet were Arthur and yourself.

Chaplin and Ridley pursued their discussions first with Akers-Douglas and Hood, then, later, with Balfour. At the beginning of May, Chamberlain received an invitation to discuss the whole question of organisation with Balfour. Ridley was hopeful about the outcome; but Chamberlain was sceptical.

CHAMBERLAIN TO RIDLEY

10 *May* 1906.—I have now an invitation to meet Balfour and Hood in Conference on Tuesday next (May 15).

I hope that you are justified in believing that you have gained substantially in the course of the discussion. Please remember, however, that any possibility of amalgamation with the Liberal Unionists depends upon the Conservative Committee selected having similar powers to those of our representatives. We have a really popular central body with full powers for electoral action and policy, and our people would not in any case give up these privileges in order to join a Committee whose functions were limited in these directions and who were under the ultimate control of any individual.

I should very much like to see you before I meet Balfour.

The first meeting with Balfour proved inconclusive and a second a few days later, almost equally so.

CHAMBERLAIN TO CHAPLIN

24 *May* 1906: *Private.*—I had another conference with A. B. about organisation — not much result, but Hood was requested to prepare a memorandum stating his objections. He is the real and only obstacle to a settlement, but I do not suppose he will give way or that A. B. will over-rule him.

The results of the Balfour–Chamberlain talks on organisation were evidently referred to the National Union on 25 May. The discussion seems to have gone badly for the Tariff Reformers.

RIDLEY TO CHAMBERLAIN

25 *May* 1906.—I am afraid that National Union affairs have gone very badly today; Mr. Chaplin & I have been giving the whole of our time to it: but now I fear it has all come to nothing, and that the constituencies will be bitterly disappointed.

The three representatives elected to sit with the Whips on the central committee are Imbert Terry, Granby, & Sir Walter Plummer. None of these will be of any use for anything. And the new organization committee appointed today consists mainly of all the useless old women who have always run the National Union.

A good deal of our fiasco has been due to the defection of Granby, who has been worse than useless : he has apparently come to believe in the notion (sedulously circulated by the Hood faction) that the lead Chaplin takes in the matter is unfortunate, as giving the impression that you are 'capturing our organization'. I am sometimes inclined to think that Chaplin has made his object a little too apparent, & that we might have got our own way more if he had not so frightened all the old women. As it is, his influence with the Council for the moment is nil : and it makes me very angry to see how these wretched people behave to him.

But our last resort is to smash the whole scheme if necessary, which I think we can do at a conference of delegates.

If you desire to hear more about it, I would gladly come to see you next week.

But till someone in the inner councils of the Party can move Hood I fear all will come to nothing : & that I shall have to withdraw from such profitless work & stick to the T. R. League only.

Chamberlain seems to have agreed with the last sentence in Ridley's letter. He took no further initiative that summer towards amalgamation between Conservatives and Liberal-Unionists. Instead, his main effort on the organisation side was directed to reconstructing the Tariff Reform League and to securing seats for friends who had been unhorsed at the election. The following letters on this subject are worth quoting. The first is of some historic curiosity. The other two give the constituency side of the continuing divisions in the Unionist Alliance.

CHAMBERLAIN TO CHAPLIN

10 *June* 1906: *Private.*—I arranged that your name should be put in the first rank of the suggestions for Worcester, but the local Committee who are a set of fools and want better guidance than any they have yet received, clamoured for a local man and finally selected Stanley Baldwin.

As to London our people will not take Curzon unless he gives pledges in writing — which he will *not* do. If he were brought forward as a Free Fooder they would fight against him even at the risk of a 3-cornered contest.

CHAMBERLAIN TO RIDLEY

14 *June* 1906: *Private.*—*Hartlepools.*—It really is most discouraging to find that our friends are so weak. Londonderry has openly declared his intention to get Hugh Cecil back into Parliament, and while I should be very glad to concur if the latter were to make any satisfactory advances

or to be content frankly to accept the Compact of Feb. 14, I recognise that without such a change on his part his return would be claimed as a great victory for the Free Food section. After Balfour's reply to Cecil at the Party meeting there ought to be no further attempt to bring him forward until he is ready to fall into line.

The situation was considered yesterday by the L.U. Council. Under the Compact we claim that this candidature belongs to us, and if that claim is admitted you may be quite certain that the candidate will be a Tariff Reformer. In no case will we accept a Free Fooder.

Storey has written me a strong letter saying that if such a candidate is adopted there will inevitably be a split and the Tariff Reform Association will work against him.

It is not safe to reckon upon a defeat, because we really do not know how far the reaction has gone. Furness has special influence, and now that Chinese Labour is out of the way and the Education Bill has become the principal matter of controversy, the Catholic vote might be transferred.

But if a Free Fooder were the candidate there is no doubt that his supporters would not recognise the true reason of a success or a great reduction of the majority, but would advertise it as a Free Food triumph. Such a candidature must be prevented at all hazards.

CHAMBERLAIN TO RIDLEY

18 *June* 1906.—I think Hartlepools is going all right, but it is most vexing to have these constant attempts to foist Free Fooders on the constituencies when so many of our people who are loyal to the Compact of Feb. 14 are still excluded.

VII

Despite the landslide against the Unionists, Chamberlain was still a powerful influence in the Empire. As the time for the next Colonial Conference drew near, the leaders overseas began to seek his advice. The following exchange with Deakin, Prime Minister of Australia, is the most interesting of many.

DEAKIN TO CHAMBERLAIN

14 *March* 1906.—Am just replying to an invitation from Lord Elgin to fix the date for the next Imperial Conference — which they will call 'Colonial' — and assume that it will assemble early next year. It is quite possible that in the present condition of parties here another Prime Minister may attend from Australia though there is no special reason for expressing that apprehension just now. While we remain as we are anything may happen and without notice. But in the chance of being present I have stipulated that my acceptance is based upon an assumption that the Conference will be entirely unfettered so that Australia may submit whatever proposals she thinks fit.

My present object in making that stipulation is of course to be free to propose *inter alia* any resolution relating to Preferential Trade within the Empire. It is upon the particular form that this should take that I am asking the favour of your counsel. Perhaps I ought to address this letter to Mr. Balfour but having regard to the fact that he is leader of a party including members who are not Tariff Reformers I have concluded that it is best at all events at the preliminary stage to address my inquiry to you directly. The intimate relations between Mr. Balfour and yourself will enable you to consult him at once if you so prefer or to advise me whether in any further communication I should address myself to him as well as to you. Not that this is an official letter demanding a party leader's official reply. Quite the contrary. But even in confidential correspondence, such as this necessarily is, I wish to avoid any implication that would be discourteous to either of you.

My own impression is that the chief object of discussing our trade relations next year will be in order to show that we ask no sacrifice from you, that we expect no bounty, that we are simply making a business offer to be dealt with upon national business lines. We are not suppliants for favours but are making a proposal which is only to be accepted if it be shaped so as to subserve the interests and minister to the advantages of both parties. We have no desire to interfere in your fiscal policy in any way — though we hold strong opinions on the subject — but we do claim the right to argue from and express our convictions that it will pay Great Britain as well as Australia to increase our commercial interchange, even at the expense of our foreign exchanges and partly on that account.

I shall be greatly obliged if you will be kind enough to criticise this attitude closely from an English political point of view and give me the benefit of your advice both as to the form and substance of any resolution we ought to table. Congratulating you upon your splendid win in Birmingham.

CHAMBERLAIN TO DEAKIN

26 *April* 1906.—I have duly received your important letter of March 14th, and hasten to reply to best of my ability. I think that as I am the undoubted leader of the movement for Tariff Reform and Preference in this country you are perfectly justified in addressing to me, in the first instance, any confidential communications or enquiries which you desire to make on the subject, and as I am on the best personal and political terms with Mr. Balfour, I shall be able to pass on to him all such communications. At the same time it might perhaps be better still if in all such cases you were kindly to address a copy of your communication to each of us direct to me as such direct communication may still more effectively ensure the full consideration which all such matters deserve. Before dealing with the main subject of your letter, it may be interesting to you to have in a few words my view of the present situation and of the fiscal question in this country. The result of the last election was, I think, a surprise to almost everybody, for, although it was well-known that the Unionist Government would be defeated, I am not aware that any responsible people foresaw the magnitude of the defeat.

Joseph Chamberlain and Austen, circa *1913*

THE BIRMINGHAM PET

'His blows are like the stroke of steel,
His words like burning wine.'
— Extract from the 'Celebration' song sung at Birmingham.

11 July 1906

It is true that under our present system the majority in the House of Commons is altogether disproportionate to the actual majority of votes secured by the Radical party, and the strength of the majority is therefore not to be entirely measured by its numbers. Whenever a further appeal is made to the Country a transfer from one side to another of a quarter of a million votes out of more than six million would reverse the situation in Parliament. Making all allowances, however, there is no possibility of minimising the completeness of the Unionist defeat. It was due to a combination of circumstances, and although there may be some controversy as to what were the main influential causes, no one will deny that more than one influence contributed largely to the result and that it was their cumulative effect which produced the abnormal majority.

Personally I should place them in the following order :

(1) General weariness of a Government which had practically been in power for twenty years, and had become stale, and the consequent apathy among its supporters and exceptional energy on the part of its opponents.

(2) Objection, especially in the rural districts, and among the Dissenters, to the Education policy of the Government.

(3) The intense feeling roused against the employment of Chinese Labour, partly due to misrepresentations as to the character of the system, but principally, as I believe owing to the prejudice against the introduction of cheap labour in any form.

(4) The fears of the Trades Unionists, constituting the organised Party of Labour, that their funds were endangered by a recent decision of the Court of Appeal and their determination to secure legislation to give them a privileged position.

While these causes were in my judgment the main elements in our defeat, the Liberals profess to believe that the proposed taxation of food and the Protection claimed for our manufacturers were also generally unpopular amongst the working classes. I am convinced that this is a mistake, and my information is uniformly to the effect that the new proposals for a change in our fiscal system were the only ones that excited keen interest and enthusiasm on the part of our supporters. Even among our opponents many were convinced of the necessity of a change, but they were not sufficiently won over to make it the sole issue or to vote with the Party to whom on so many other grounds they were strongly opposed.

In fact in my view the experience of the last Election justifies the predictions I made beforehand, viz. that we should be unable to obtain a definite decision until a second appeal to the country, when, especially if the trade of the country should then be less favourable than it is at this moment, I believe a very large majority will adopt the views of the reformers.

Since the new Government has met Parliament it cannot be said to have been very successful and its majority has shown clearly its heterogeneous character, each particular section pressing for its own share of the spoils ; and how long they will hold together it is impossible to predict with certainty, but I doubt very much whether they will last out their

2 G

full term, and all friends of Tariff Reform should be prepared for a further struggle in possibly two to three years time.

In view of this, the action of the Colonies and the discussions of the next Conference may have the greatest importance. The Government have tied their hands and are absolutely pledged to make no concessions inconsistent with Free Trade, but although no practical result can be anticipated at present the offers and opinions of the Colonial representatives will be followed with the greatest possible interest.

In spite of the declarations made both by Canadian and Australian Statesmen, the leaders on the ministerial side still profess to disbelieve in their sincerity or importance. They maintain the offers are vague and so qualified as to offer no prospect of benefit to this country; and, however inaccurate these professions appear to us, there is no doubt that they add to the hesitation on the part of our conservative people to undertake drastic changes.

Personally in all my speeches I have urged that the proposals are clearly for our mutual benefit, that each part of the Empire will gain; and the Empire as a whole will be strengthened: that the policy of the Colonies is largely governed by their Imperial patriotism although, of course, they must necessarily place their own interests in the foreground. These interests are not inconsistent with ours. Without serious sacrifice on either side, Trade within the Empire may be largely increased even though the trade of the Empire with foreign countries may be somewhat reduced. I have urged that the indirect advantages will be even more important than the direct and that no closer union can be successfully approached except by means of commercial treaties and agreements.

I do not imagine that the Government will dare to shut out discussion, but no doubt they will refuse to agree to any arrangement which would involve protective taxation. What I hope is that the discussion will clear the air, and may enable us, whether in the United Kingdom or in the States across the sea, to explain in detail the reciprocal nature of the offers made and the advantage that they may afford to all interested.

If I were proposing a resolution at the Conference I think I should be inclined to refer to previous Resolutions and to state emphatically and definitely the importance of preferential arrangements within the Empire, and as a practical result, to propose the formation of an expert Committee or Committees to draw up a scheme of reciprocal tariffs. I do not suppose that such a Committee could conveniently deal with the subject as a whole, but that it should be necessary to have a separate Committee for each group of Colonies. Thus, a Committee with representatives of Australasia would, with a corresponding number of representatives from the United Kingdom, endeavour, if it were appointed, to draw up a treaty of reciprocity and preference suited to the respective needs of the United Kingdom and Australasia, while similar Committees would be at work to deal with the cases of South Africa and Canada.

As we must anticipate that the present Government would refuse to accede to the appointment of such committees it would be an enormous advantage if the Colonies could nevertheless table something in the nature of a scheme or offer to which the friends of preference would afterwards be able to refer. Such a scheme would not only give the advocates of preference material with which to approach the different trades concerned, and enable them to point out the specific advantages which could be secured by a corresponding preference on colonial products, but it would be most useful in securing comments and criticisms and would pave the way for the final solution whenever the country should decide to give a mandate to a new Government on the question.

I have written somewhat fully on the subject and trust that I have made my meaning clear. I shall always be at your service for any further information or suggestions that you may desire.

VIII

Chamberlain's general view of the prospects for Tariff Reform at the beginning of the summer is well summed up in the following extract from a letter to Northcote.

CHAMBERLAIN TO NORTHCOTE

29 *May* 1906.—. . . we, who are tariff reformers, are not discouraged by the Election which we regard as taken upon false and irrelevant issues. Meanwhile the subject continues to interest public meetings everywhere, and I believe that it is already getting a strong hold of the people, and in the event of any falling off in trade it will come to the top immediately. Meanwhile the returns point to unexampled prosperity. I am not quite certain that the statistics can be relied upon, but in any case it is impossible to deny that they point to an exceptional boom. It is not a time for pressing anything in the shape of a sensational agitation, but the confidence of our friends in the policy has not, I think, been in the least shaken, and the Unionist party appears unwilling to accept any candidates who do not subscribe to the Concordat finally arranged on February 14th between Balfour and myself.

Asquith's first Budget presented an excellent opportunity to raise the fiscal question in the House. Austen, as the ex-Chancellor, should have replied for the Opposition, but he was away in Algeria recuperating from a sharp attack of sciatica. Chamberlain, accordingly, stood in for his son.

Asquith's first Budget was well described at the time as 'the last word of *laisser faire* finance'.[1] The Chancellor had inherited a surplus from his predecessor of just over £3,000,000. Of this he applied £135,000 for relief of necessitous school districts, £105,000 for improvements to the Postal Services and some £2,000,000 to the elimination of the export duty on coal, and the reduction of the duty on tea and on stripped tobacco. It was a pure Gladstonian

[1] *The Outlook*, 9 May 1906.

Budget of retrenchment. The only gesture made to the Government's Labour supporters was the announcement that a Committee would be set up to consider introducing the principle of graduation into the income tax.

Chamberlain intervened on 1 May, the second day of the Debate, in 'a brilliant and stinging speech'. He taunted the Government with the contrast between their promises of social reform at the polls and their austere performance in the Budget. In particular, he deplored their failure to take even a step towards the establishment of some kind of Old Age Pension. Instead of applying their surplus to measures of social reform, they had used it to reduce taxes which were of no inconvenience or perhaps of some advantage to the nation. The reduction of the tax on stripped tobacco would, he forecast, put some thousands of workmen out of a job. The reduction on the tea duty would benefit the wholesaler or perhaps the retailer, but it was too small to be of any advantage to the working-class consumer. The abolition of the export duty on coal could only advantage the colliery owners. The decision over the coal duty suggested another argument of some significance in relation to the Fiscal Debate. Asquith had told the House that its abolition would cost the revenue £1,000,000. This was an admission that it was paid by the producer. If so, did not this suggest that an import duty on corn would also be paid by the producer?

Chamberlain developed these points further in the second reading of the Finance Bill (16 May), and drew the moral. The financial policy of the country had reached a crossroads. Both sides wanted far-reaching measures of social reform. The problem was how to pay for them. One way was by a policy of confiscation, involving graduated income tax, higher death duties and the taxing of land values. This would be the inevitable result of persistence in a policy of free imports. The alternative was a policy involving a low general tariff and preference to the Colonies. This would provide a direct source of revenue and one to which the foreigner would contribute at least in part. More important still, it would promote home production, fuller employment and higher wages and so lead to a more buoyant revenue.[1]

Chamberlain reinforced the point a few weeks later (25 June). He was speaking as the guest of honour at the inaugural dinner of

---

[1] The same day, Chamberlain gave a warm welcome to Lloyd George's census of production Bill. This was an attempt to collect accurate statistics about home production and trade and was perhaps the first practical result of the Tariff Reform campaign.

the 1900 Club, formed to keep defeated and aspiring Unionist candidates in touch with their colleagues in Parliament.

We must not make the fatal mistake of thinking that we can or ought to ride back to power on a policy of mere negation. Speaking to you as a fighting club, I say, Give us or accept from us an effective, definite, fighting policy.

The policy of resistance, of negation, is not sufficient answer to that Socialist opinion which is growing up amongst us — the Socialist opinion the objects of which are, after all, worthy of earnest and even favourable consideration. But the means by which those objects are promoted are open to serious objection. We can only meet Socialism as that great republican in another country, M. Clemenceau in France, has recently done, by pointing out in all true sympathy the impossibility, the impracticability of the methods chosen, and by suggesting other and better methods for securing all that is good in the object sought for. That should be our policy also ; and as that policy, by whomsoever propounded, is a policy which means money, which means expenditure, it is closely connected with the third object of our party officially declared — that fiscal reform is the first constructive policy of the Unionist party. That is what you are all pledged to by your own rules and regulations. I need not argue the question now, but it is clear that, if great extension is to be given to social reform, the money can only be found by an extension of the basis of our taxation. It seems to me that it cannot be found in a less burden upon the people, a less interference with trade than by the moderate suggestions which the Unionist party have made. We are not called upon at this moment to press for fiscal reform ; no practical result would come from a discussion in the House of Commons ; but we are all committed to it. When we return to power we bring our policy with us. And, my lords and gentlemen, with fiscal reform, remember we bring preference also.

IX

We must interrupt our narrative for a moment to consider the personal side. Chamberlain's influence on the Unionist parties in the House and in the country depended on his personality as much as his opinions. His health and strength were crucial to the success of his cause.

The election campaign had tired him much less than he or his family had expected.

MRS. CHAMBERLAIN TO HER MOTHER

20 January 1906.—Really he has been wonderful ! He has gone through what after all is very anxious and very arduous work, speaking almost every other night for more than three weeks, with plenty to depress at times — though with much to encourage lately — without any more fatigue than a night's rest could banish. Now at the end he looks extremely well, is in excellent spirits and is already full of ideas and plans for the coming Parliamentary Session. Where most men would feel they must have a few days of repose he, with characteristic force and vigour, is already thinking of the future.

The cure at Aix had undoubtedly done good and Mrs. Chamberlain was determined that he should go there again. If there was any anxiety at Highbury it was rather on account of the sciatica which Austen seemed unable to shake off.

Nevertheless the strain of the first few weeks of 1906 was considerable. First there was the trial of strength with Balfour. Then the temporary leadership of the House. Next came a sharp attack of 'flu, from which he had to return too soon for the big Debate on Fiscal Policy. For the rest of March, the depleted strength of the Unionist front bench had made his presence in the House almost indispensable; and it was not till the beginning of April, as we have seen, that he escaped to the south of France for his first real holiday since the election campaign.

The holiday began well and on arriving at Beaulieu, Mrs. Chamberlain wrote, 'Joe is so much less tired than by our journey to Aix last year that it is delightful to see him'.[1] Once again, it was Austen who gave cause for anxiety.

Is it not too provoking? Austen started on Sunday meaning to break the journey at Paris and go to Algiers on Tuesday. On Sunday night he suddenly collapsed with a *new* sharp attack of sciatica and has been in bed there ever since. . . . He has had eight months of it.[2]

The weather, cold at first, improved. Chamberlain and his wife made excursions to Monte Carlo and Mentone. One day he was even tempted to take a walk, but the unusual exertion brought a sharp reaction.

MRS. CHAMBERLAIN TO HER MOTHER

13 *April* 1906.—On Sunday Joe and I took such a pretty walk, first along the sea, looking across the pretty, rather enclosed bay in which Beaulieu lies and along the coast with Mentone in the distance, then up among the olive trees on the ridge of the Cap Ferrat. . . . We sat there on a wall in the shade and luxuriated in it. Alas! there have been no more such expeditions — for on our return from Grasse on Tuesday he suddenly became lame and in the evening there was no doubt about it — he had an attack of gout. Is it not too provoking? just when I was congratulating myself on his excellent condition. He was looking particularly well and seemed like a boy in spirits. At first I thought it was only to be a slight touch. . . . Certain it is that last night it got worse and poor Joe is very miserable — and *bored* to extinction.

[1] Mrs. Chamberlain to her mother, 30 March 1906.   [2] *Ibid.*

The attack of gout proved unusually severe. It was followed by a sharp cold which caught Chamberlain as soon as he returned to Highbury and then a painful and irritating toothache. This bout of ill health was followed by a spell of unaccustomed frivolity.

MRS. CHAMBERLAIN TO HER MOTHER

5 *May* 1906.—Joe and I are going to sally forth to see some pictures and lunch in a restaurant. We have been quite dissipated the last two nights, for Joe suddenly announced his intention of going to the play. On Thursday we went to see 'Captain Brassbound's Conversion'. Then last night when we were to dine out, we were put off owing to our hostess having influenza, so off we went to the theatre again, this time a play by Pinero, 'His House in Order', which was extremely well acted and which we greatly enjoyed. Bernard Shaw's play reads better than it acts, we thought, and Joe, whose expectations were high, was much disappointed. Ellen Terry was rather a blow to him, for the years have told, and though she acts with much charm, it does interfere with the action that she constantly forgets her part. She covers it well — still, it is obvious.

Meanwhile, a happy and really unexpected development occurred. Austen, now over forty, had seemed a confirmed bachelor. A letter from Algiers announced his engagement to Miss Ivy Dundas.

MRS. CHAMBERLAIN TO HER MOTHER

21 *May* 1906.—Did not my cable take your breath away? It really is true and Austen is as happy as the day is long, says he feels 25 and as he walks along the street, thinks people must be saying : 'there goes a happy man'. Is it not a joy to have this come to him? He met Ivy in Algiers and then at Haman R'irha and was as quick about it as the Chamberlain men are. She is the daughter of a retired Army Officer, Colonel Lawrence Dundas, who has been Chief of Staff in India, Dublin and Gibraltar. Her age is 27, tall, fair, graceful and distinguished looking and Austen adds he thinks her pretty, certainly her photographs are most attractive looking. . . . Was it not a good cure for sciatica? . . . Joe is delighted and I am so happy for him that his *precious* son is to be married at last . . .

Chamberlain's own feelings can be judged from his report to Collings.

CHAMBERLAIN TO COLLINGS

14 *May* 1906.—Since I told you 19 years ago that I was engaged to Miss Endicott I have had nothing so good to tell as today when I am able to announce Austen's engagement to Miss Ivy Dundas, daughter of a retired Colonel in the Army. We are all *delighted*. She is 28, nice looking, and according to Austen, who is in the 7th Heaven, perfect.

They return to England towards the end of this month. The sciatica is gone, and possibly the engagement has done more for the patient than all the baths.

The first fortnight of June was filled with the business of the House and the round of Edwardian social life. Then on 16 June, staying at Taplow with Lady Desborough, Chamberlain complained of unusual tiredness. Another sharp attack of gout followed. He had to keep to his room through the weekend and to cancel most of his engagements for the following week.

By 25 June, however, he was sufficiently recovered to make his speech at the 1900 Club banquet. Herbert Maxwell, who presided, was astonished at his total disregard for all 'dietary precautions'.

... I was in the chair, and, of course, he, as principal guest, sat next me on my right. He had quite recently recovered from a prolonged and severe fit of gout and I could not but wonder at the freedom with which he ate, drank and smoked large cigars. 'My friend,' I thought to myself, 'It is hardly possible that you can escape paying smartly for this.'[1]

He was on the eve of his seventieth birthday.

The weekend of 30 June was spent at Sandon, where Lord Harrowby had gathered a house party of enthusiastic Tariff Reformers. Again, as at Taplow, Chamberlain complained of feeling tired and seemed rather bored by the conversation. Back in London, he developed a bad cold. Denison, however, who lunched with him on 4 July, thought him 'looking in perfect health'. Chamberlain, however, told him that

he was anxious to have a rest as the burden of leading a great movement was very heavy.[2]

X

Chamberlain had now completed 30 years as one of Birmingham's Members of Parliament. On 8 July, he would be seventy years old. The City fathers, accordingly, decided to celebrate this double anniversary in high pomp and style. The birthday itself fell on a Sunday; and it was, therefore, arranged that Birmingham, irrespective of party, should pay homage to its illustrious citizen on the Saturday. The Unionist supporters, for their part, were to stage a great demonstration on the Monday evening.

Chamberlain travelled to Birmingham on Thursday, 5 July.

[1] Unpublished papers of Sir Herbert Maxwell.
[2] Memo. by Col. Denison sent to Chamberlain for comment and correction, 28 December 1908.

Friday was spent quietly in the family circle. Meanwhile, Birmingham was throbbing with excitement. There was no organised scheme of street decoration, but, quite spontaneously, the people began decorating their streets with ribbons, lanterns and bunting.

Few things are harder to recapture than the relationship between a man and his city. Our modern cities have grown so rapidly and so lost their personalities that we may search in vain in Britain today for any counterpart of the great urban leaders of the turn of the century. The position enjoyed by M. Herriot in Lyon is perhaps the nearest parallel in recent years.

The speeches Chamberlain made during the celebrations were necessarily formal; but we can recapture something of the blend of intimacy and almost royal authority of his relationship with Birmingham from the following sentences. They are taken from his speech at a garden party during the Whitsun recess.

> I want to take the opportunity to say a word to all of you . . . who contributed so much to my triumph and above all to the triumph of the cause for which I stand. (*Cheers.*) You all worked well (*a voice —* '*You deserved it*') and the result was even more of a triumph than any of us could have anticipated. I am always proud of Birmingham, but I was never more proud than on that Wednesday night, because the result confirmed all that I ever said about you.[1]

The first event in the Saturday's celebration was a luncheon given in Chamberlain's honour by the Lord Mayor. The streets from Highbury to the Council House were filled with cheering crowds. Flags flew from all public buildings and business houses. Some two hundred Birmingham dignitaries were gathered at the Council House table, including the Aldermen and Councillors, the Bishops and Church leaders, the Members of Parliament, the Lord Lieutenant of Warwickshire, the chief men of the University, and a goodly contingent of the Chamberlain clan.

After luncheon, the Lord Mayor proposed Chamberlain's health. Chamberlain then rose to reply. Neville Chamberlain has described the scene :[2]

'However strenuously . . .' he began and then stopped. There was a long and most painful pause as he struggled to command himself. The audience was deeply moved, and I saw tears in the eyes of the man opposite me. At last, he began again :

> However strenuously I endeavour to express my thanks to the people of Birmingham for their constant kindness to me, I feel that my words

---

[1] *The Times*, 6 June 1906.   [2] Unpublished letter of Neville Chamberlain.

2 G 2

must always be inadequate to represent the depth and the sincerity of my feelings. I can never keep pace with your goodness. As soon as I have acknowledged one claim upon my gratitude, you immediately proceed to confer upon me another obligation.

Few leaders in English politics have found it harder to strike the personal note, but this time, his touch was sure. The honour done to him, he declared :

... fills my heart with pride and thankfulness that, with the greater part of my life behind me — an open book which all of you may read and criticise — I yet have been able to retain the distinction which I have most coveted and which I most prize — the affectionate regard of those amongst whom I live. Few men have been more fortunate than I — happy in the home that I have made amongst you ; happy in the wide circle of my public friends ; and, above all, happy also in having had behind me during the whole course of my career the confidence and support of this democratic community.

My Lord Mayor, I assure you that my wife joins me in this, as in everything else with which she has been associated with me during many years of my strenuous life. She feels, as I do, that from the moment she came among you, eighteen years ago, she has been the adopted daughter of Birmingham, and she feels a sympathy and interest which even I cannot surpass in all that concerns your public life and the welfare and the happiness of the people.

The rest of the speech remains one of the finest declamations in modern times on the value of public service in municipal life. He began with a backward glance at his own career in Birmingham local politics.

My Lord Mayor, in this building, and under these circumstances, you have naturally recalled the associations which are connected with my municipal life. Thirty years ago I resigned the position which you now occupy in order to become a representative of the city in Parliament. I did not accept the change without many misgivings and searchings of heart. I was not certain that I was not giving up a sphere in which I felt I might be of some service, and entering upon unknown waters, upon a future which neither I nor any one could foresee, and even now, after thirty years of considerable and wide experience, after full knowledge of the opportunities which a position in the House of Commons may give to a man, I still feel there is no more honourable position, and there are few in which any man can be more useful to his time and generation, than in the performance of civic duties. And I look back with unmixed pleasure to my association with the local life of the city in which I have passed more than half a century, and with admiration — constant admiration — for those who, whether in my time or since, have given unstinted and unselfish service to fulfil the duty which lies nearest to them, to endeavour to leave the world a little better than they found it.

Never can I have more loyal supporters than those that I found in my old municipal time. They were men who did their work with ability and power, and, above all, with absolute unselfishness. . . . I know there have been times, then as now, when people were inclined to under-estimate the dignity and importance of this local life, and yet it seems to me that there is no work which men of education and ability can do with greater satisfaction to themselves and greater advantage to others than this.

When I think of the changes which have been carried out in my time, the constant and successful struggle with disease, the provision which has been made for health, for recreation, and for everything which contributes to raise the standard of life and increase the happiness of the masses of the population, I admit I am inclined to doubt whether this silent, almost unhonoured, but unceasing display of local patriotism has not done more for our country than the sensational reforms which we owe to great statesmen and to the labours of the House of Commons. In any case, my Lord Mayor, it is not given to every man to play a distinguished part in national politics, but every man may take a hand in the work of local administration.

Then came a note of warning. In Chamberlain's youth, the chief men in every urban community had lived in the centre of the towns and cities. They had lived among the people at home as well as in their works. They were thus the natural leaders in every sphere of activity. But towards the end of the century, the drift to the suburbs and the country had begun. There was a growing tendency for the leaders of commerce and industry to take a smaller part in local affairs.

If complaint is made, and I think it is made justly sometimes, that our local administration occasionally falls off from the high ideal which it ought always to keep before it — if there is inefficiency, ignorance, extravagance — the fault does not lie with these great democratic institutions which express so well every form of public need and public opinion, which give such full opportunity to every class and every form of ability. It lies with those who, having advantages, denied, it may be, to others, advantages of influence, wealth, and education, yet refuse, or fail, from indifference, to place their talents at the disposal of the com-munity, leaving all this great work to be accomplished by others whose willingness is perhaps greater than their capacity to perform it.

After recalling old colleagues of his municipal days, he closed with a glowing tribute to Birmingham and its people :

My Lord Mayor, I thank you once more, I thank this great and representative company for the splendid reception which they have given to me and to mine, and I thank through you the people of Birming-ham for their generous recognition of what, at all events, has been an honest endeavour to serve them. Surely that is even more honourable to them than it is to us. Who can say in the presence of such circumstances as these which we witness to-day that the democracy is ungenerous or ungrateful? I feel that if I have been permitted to serve this community no man has ever had more generous masters. They have been my teachers also. What I am, for good or for ill, they have made me — this people and this city of my adoption and my affection. It has been the home of strong convictions, of great ideals, of frank expression, of earnest endeavour to carry out its ideals; and I, in my time, have tried to interpret what I believe to be the spirit of the town, and have found in the affection of my own people an overwhelming reward for a strenuous life of work and contest.

At half past three, Chamberlain and the guests emerged from the Council House into the brilliant sunshine of a July afternoon. There was a roar of cheering from the dense crowd assembled in Victoria Square and it was taken up by the crowds in New Street and away down the route along which he would pass.

Eighty cars had been assembled. Chamberlain and Mrs. Chamberlain entered the first. Austen and his fiancée the second. Other members of the family, guests at the luncheon and supporters made up the line. A few minutes later, the cavalcade started off on a 17-mile tour of the city. Dense crowds, often several deep, lined the whole route and it was estimated that there were 50,000 people in each of the six public parks. All Birmingham was there, for certain, and special excursion trains had brought in the curious and the ardent alike from all over the country.

The procession halted at each of the six public parks when addresses were presented from the different wards and political associations. Altogether 62 addresses were presented in the course of the afternoon. Fortunately for Chamberlain, a local by-law forbade speeches in the parks; and he firmly declined any suggestion that it should be waived in his favour. Tea was taken with the Mayor of Aston. Then came West Birmingham, his constituency, where the reception was the heartiest of all.

Towards seven o'clock, Chamberlain left Calthorpe Park, the last in the series, and a few minutes later, was back at Highbury. He took a very hot bath. Then, after dinner, he and his family returned to Calthorpe Park to watch fireworks. There were displays of these in each park and the centrepiece in every case was a 'fine portrait' of Chamberlain.

By the end of the day, Mrs. Chamberlain felt 'more than tired, just as if I had been beaten all over with little sticks'.[1] Next morning,

---

[1] Mrs. Chamberlain to her mother. Undated; probably 9 or 10 July 1906.

his birthday, Chamberlain too admitted to feeling 'very tired'.
It was a beautiful day, however, and he spent most of it in the
garden reading the telegrams — more than 2000 of them are in
his papers — which poured in from every part of the country and
the Empire, and from every section of society from the King to
an elementary schoolboy in New Zealand.

Monday's demonstrations were confined to a great meeting at
the Bingley Hall. More than 10,000 people were in the building,
including delegates from Liberal Unionist and Conservative
Associations and Tariff Reform Federations from all over the
country. A massed band played patriotic songs.

The first stage in the proceedings was the presentation of 125
addresses from the different Liberal Unionist, Conservative, and
Tariff Reform delegates. Each was announced by a herald and
shook hands with Chamberlain, who remained standing on the
platform. This proceeding occupied fully half an hour. The band
played 'Rule, Britannia!', the vast audience taking up the chorus.
Chamberlain then stepped forward to make his speech. He was

received with wild delight. Such a scene has never been witnessed in
Bingley Hall, the great Gladstone demonstrations not excepted. The
people rose and shouted and thousands of hands waved the programmes
of the morning's proceedings. . . . Scarcely had this unique demonstration of feeling ceased, when the audience began to sing, 'for he's
a jolly good fellow'.[1]

The Bingley Hall speech may stand as Chamberlain's political
testament. After returning the customary thanks to the Chairman,
he began with a reference to the many controversies through which
he had passed and a word on the temper of public life.

Mr. Chairman, you said just now something of the unnecessary bitterness of political controversy. Perhaps too much is made of that. I admit
very readily that all my life I have been a strenuous fighter for the causes
that I have thought to be righteous. I have received hard blows, and I
have endeavoured to return them. I bear no malice. I make no complaint, though, sometimes, I may have thought that my motives have been
unfairly represented. In that case I have always felt that any such
unfairness has merely acted as a rallying cry to the friends who hastened
to my side. And while the attacks have been forgotten, the friends remain.

I have been your representative for thirty years, which is a long time
in the life of a man. I think there are not many members of the House of
Commons who have sat in that House for a longer period, and certainly
there are very few, if there are any, who have sat there representing
continuously one constituency, and that a constituency with which all

[1] *The Times*, 10 July 1906.

the interests of their home and private life are most closely connected. And during all this time Birmingham has been behind me. Birmingham has cheered me when I might have been discouraged. Birmingham has strengthened my hands, and has given me an assurance of ultimate victory.

He turned next to the charge that he had been inconsistent and turned his coat.

Sometimes, it is strange, I find myself taunted with having changed my opinions and forgotten my ideals. Well, ladies and gentlemen, if indeed that be a fault, and if I have committed it, I have done so in good company. But have we changed? And if we have changed, is change a crime? During the space of a whole generation that I have been your political representative, what is there that has not changed? The conditions of the people, the needs of the people, they have altered. The state of parties has altered. Old names have no longer their old meaning; the position of the country has altered, especially in relation to other nations; and if, under these circumstances, we alone had remained unchanged we should have been false to our progressive principles.

I came across, the other day, a quotation from my old leader, for whom, though I differed from him in later years, I have always entertained a respect amounting almost to devotion. I found this quotation from Mr. Gladstone. He said, '*People talk of a change in opinion as if it were a disgrace. To me it is a sign of life. If you are alive you must change. It is only the dead who remain the same. And of all charges brought against a man or a party, that of inconsistency because of changed opinion is the most inept. As trumped up against a political opponent it is usually a mere party trick.*' So, ladies and gentlemen, on the authority of Mr. Gladstone, I say that change is not necessarily a crime.

But the people who accuse you and me of change are wanting in the intelligence which should enable them to distinguish between change in principles which can only be accepted under the stress of some great circumstance, and change in details and method of application which every wise man applies to everything in the course of his life.

He went on to claim that he had shown the truer consistency in defence of his principles and pursuit of his aims. Why had he changed sides in the House of Commons?

What has been the great event in our generation? Surely it was the event — I am referring to the introduction of Home Rule into the politics of the Liberal party — surely it was an event momentous in its issues which has altered the whole course of our political history, revolutionised our political relations, destroyed the Liberal party as we knew it, and as we in our time helped to cement and to strengthen it. But when Mr. Gladstone surrendered to Mr. Parnell, when he accepted Home Rule and allied himself with the men who a short time previously he had described as 'marching through rapine to the disintegration of the Empire' — when he did that who was it who changed? It was not

Birmingham. Birmingham remained true to the higher conception of patriotism which refused to weaken the heart of this great Empire in order to purchase the temporary political support of a few disloyal subjects.

But though Home Rule had made him change sides, it had never altered his purpose.

I maintain that at that time and since, Birmingham, and all who have joined with Birmingham, and sympathised with our views, have been consistently faithful to two great objects of policy. In the first place, they have been strenuous advocates of social reform. In the second place, they have been the most sturdy upholders of Imperial interests.

In domestic politics we, of every class and of every section of the Unionist party, have supported every constructive proposal for bettering the condition of the masses of the people, and for raising the standard of life amongst the great majority. We have had no sympathy with the negative policy which merely criticises and resists.

We have thought that an offensive policy, a definite concrete policy of reform, was the best weapon we could have to our hands in order to meet the purely destructive policy of our opponents. In a democratic State such as ours, with a Government which in our time has been made truly representative, we together have held the belief that advantage ought to be taken of the machinery which has thus been created to do for the people at large, for the whole community, what no individual can do for himself. What we have done at home in Birmingham with our City Council to help us — that we have done also in national affairs. We have been willing to trust the people, and the people's representatives. We have urged them to use their power in order to better the lot of the great majority of the people. Now, in this belief, you will remember that more than one unauthorised programme has been issued during the last thirty years with the Birmingham stamp. And let me say, looking back, I don't think we have any reason to be ashamed of our programmes, or to be discontented with the result of their adoption. The extension of local government, the provision of free education, the facilities given for the creation of allotments and small ownerships, the great development of factory legislation, the compensation provided for accidents in the course of employment — these constitute only a small part of the practical social reforms which have been carried by Conservative and by Unionist Governments during the generation to which I am referring.

He then reminded his audience that just as, in his Liberal days, his main opponents had been the Whigs, so they had remained his chief opponents to the end.

Now . . . these reforms were not carried without opposition. We had, of course, the opposition of our political opponents, 'Radicals', as many of them call themselves, that were false to Radical principles, not knowing what social reform meant, except as a cry at election time — to be dropped a few weeks later. But the bitterest opponents of all were those so-called Liberals, the descendants and representatives of the old Whig Party, the Duke of Devonshire, Lord Goschen, Lord James, with whom, although I am said to have changed, I still find myself in constant conflict. Both sides are consistent, both sides act after their kind, and these gentlemen, Free Traders as they are, were quite right in opposing the proposals of social reform, as they are right now in opposing proposals for fiscal reform. The same principles are involved. The Free Traders were against all State interference of any kind. They were against the Factory Acts; they were opposed to the laws to prevent fraud and adulteration, especially in the interests of the working classes; they were against trade unions, they were in favour of unlimited competition, they would buy everything in the cheapest market, and especially labour. Yes, but it is cheering to observe, in spite of their distinguished opposition, in spite of the efforts made twenty or thirty years ago by the same distinguished and superior persons, who are opposing me now as they opposed me then, that all these fine doctrines of Free Trade have gone to the wall. There are other equally absurd superstitions which are going to follow them, and the time is coming when, perhaps, even they will see that we cannot logically and consistently attempt to defend labour against unfair competition without defending at the same time and against the same unfair competition the products of that labour. We are moving, ladies and gentlemen, not so quick, perhaps, as the most impatient of us might desire, but we are moving on the right lines and entirely to my satisfaction.

Now, ladies and gentlemen, . . . the second object of the 'Birmingham school' was to maintain the strength and union of this Empire, and to hand down our great inheritance unimpaired to our descendants. But again, here, also, Birmingham is in conflict with Cobdenism. What were the views of the Free Traders? Mr. Cobden declared that he rejoiced chiefly in the federation of Canada because he thought it was a preliminary step to the entire separation of that great dominion from the British motherland. Mr. Cobden was opposed to our possession of India — I am not certain that he did not think that to be a crime. I am not questioning his perfect sincerity and honesty. I have no doubt his opinions were shared at that time by many of his followers. But let me impress upon you and upon the country that all these things go together, and that the men who imposed free imports upon this generation were the same men who, if they had had their way, would have had no Empire for us to be proud of, and no Colonies to which we might give a preference.

There followed what may stand as the noblest passage in all his speeches; a supreme justification of the cause and ideal of Empire.

I maintain that never in our history has Birmingham sympathised with the Little Englander. We have held to this Empire of ours as a trust received from our ancestors who were labouring for posterity as well as for themselves, and who, by great effort and self-sacrifice, built up the edifice of our dominion, whose privileges we are permitted to enjoy, and whose responsibilities, unless we are unworthy, we shall be proud to bear. Our glory! It will be the glory of this generation if we strengthen the foundations of this great and unparalleled dominion; it will be our eternal disgrace if we allow it to fall.

If Birmingham is a great city, what has made it a great city? No, not I. I could have done nothing without the unstinted and unselfish work of those who came so readily to my assistance. Birmingham is a great city to-day because a generation ago men were found — practically all its citizens — who were willing to work and, if necessary, to make sacrifices in order to maintain and support its reputation. If the Empire is to be great all its members must take in it a similar pride, and take upon themselves a similar obligation.

I have spoken of the 'Birmingham school'. I do not need to defend its tenets. There is another school, a very small school, that has always been with us — a school which seems to me to be utterly devoid of imagination, which can see nothing of the future, and nothing of the greater factors in our individual and national life. An individual, is he not the better for having some other interests than those which only concern his own pocket? Is he not the better for having a family to care for, for having a city for which he can do something, for having a country which he loves, for having an empire of which he is proud? The character of the individual depends upon the greatness of the ideals upon which he rests, and the character of a nation is the same. The moral grandeur of a nation depends upon its being sometimes able to forget itself, sometimes able to think of the future of the race for which it stands. England without an empire! Can you conceive it? England in that case would not be the England we love. If the ties of sympathy which have gradually been woven between ourselves and our children who are soon to become great nations across the seas, if these ties were weakened or destroyed, if we suffered their affection to die for want of food for it, if we allowed them to drift apart, then this England of ours would sink from the comparative position which it has enjoyed throughout the centuries. It would no longer be a power, if not supreme, at all events of the greatest influence, generally well exercised on the civilisation and the peace of the world. It would be a fifth-rate nation, existing on the sufferance of its more powerful neighbours. We will not have it.

He now pressed home the attack on the Little Englanders and then led up to his new policy.

The school to which I refer is blind to considerations of this kind. Its members appeal to what I consider are unworthy interests. They appeal entirely to the immediate material consequences of any act we may recommend to them. But they are short-sighted. They are not merely unpatriotic in the larger sense in which I like to use the word. It is not merely that they are selfish, but it is that they are foolish, and that these material interests for which alone they care would suffer under the system which they profess — would suffer as much as the national character and the national influence. What is it that we want? What is it that we desire for our country? National prosperity. Not indeed in the sense that we covet a greater aggregation of national wealth which, for aught we know, may never be properly distributed. It is not the amount of the income tax, not the number of cheques that pass through the clearing-house that marks the progress of a nation. It is our advance towards the great Radical aspiration, 'the greatest happiness of the greatest number'. That is what we desire. That is what we, you and I, have been seeking during this past thirty years, and I have told you more than once in the course of that time that there was a greater reform than any I had yet advocated publicly before you — there was a greater reform in the future which would do more for you than all these attempts at bettering your condition, and that was a reform which would secure for the masses of the industrial population in this country constant employment at fair wages. That is an end which, with all our labour, we have not yet attained. Even now, when trade is extraordinarily active, when our opponents are boasting of record exports and imports, as though, forsooth, they were the product of any activity of theirs — I say even now there is want of employment and something much worse. There is the fact that relatively, in proportion to our competitors, in the constant struggle for existence we are getting behindhand, and when the tide of prosperity recedes, as it always has done, as it must do again, and when a time of depression follows it, we shall be the sufferers. The working classes, especially, will be the sufferers, and we shall find then that it will be impossible, without a change, to find employment for the constantly increasing population of these islands. That is the danger. I am condemned for pointing it out after we have suffered from it? Let us provide against it. Let us find the remedy.

The remedy is at hand, and if we are not too careless, too apathetic as to the future, if we are not too timid to act, I say there is even now time to hold for ourselves and our people our own trade. And we can hold it against all fair competition. And we can do more. We can extend our trade in the best markets, with our best friends. We can benefit them in trading with them, while they give us reciprocal advantage in the preference which they give for our manufactures. We can do this. We can strengthen the union. We can draw closer the growing nations, the sister states, and by a commercial union we can pave the way for that federation which I see constantly before me as a practical object of aspiration — that federation of free nations which will enable us to prolong in ages yet to come all the glorious traditions of the British race.

He now moved to his climax. The economic argument was left behind.

Ladies and gentlemen, if we are to fulfil these aspirations, believe me, we must cultivate the affection and the sympathy of these children of ours in the Colonies. We must learn to understand them better, to appreciate more highly their mission and their work. They are our pioneers sent out from here, fighting against nature, fighting against dangers and difficulties of every kind. They have worthily maintained the honour of the flag and the interests of the Empire, and they deserve the sympathy which I claim you should give them.

But are we going the right way to produce this kindly feeling? You may be, who agree with the words I say, but what about those who profess to represent you? What are they doing at this time to draw closer together the British Empire? Only these last few weeks I have heard men in the House of Commons, ignorant — crassly ignorant — of all that concerns the British Empire, ignorant of the Greater Britain across the seas, careless of its future, careless indeed of everything but the petty interests which they claim particularly to represent — I have heard these men depreciating the motives of our colonists, treating their generous offers with neglect and scorn, and denying to them, whose shoes they are unworthy to unlatch, the common attributes of justice and humanity. There are men in the House of Commons who profess in a special sense to be the representatives of labour, who would not allow me, who represented a great working-class constituency, and for whom seven or eight thousand, most of them working men, voted at the last election — they would not allow me the claim to represent you. In order to do that, according to their theories, I should have to be a man who did some work thirty years ago, and never did any after. And it is these men who are at this time blackening the character of those who are upholding the British dominions and the British flag throughout the world. It is they who, with a fatuous conceit, dictate the policy of colonial statesmen and, forsooth, threaten the great Colonies to whom we have given self-government, threaten them with the veto of their petty standard of morality if they go contrary in any way to their views and party interests. They have no word of sympathy for the men who suffer for the Imperial cause. . . .

But one thing I will say, and I say it in your name : these men, at any rate, do not represent the working classes of England, and *never yet in our history of the British race, has the great democracy been unpatriotic.*

Then came the oft-remembered closing words.

The union of the Empire must be preceded and accompanied, as I have said, by a better understanding, by a closer sympathy. To secure that is the highest object of statesmanship now at the beginning of the twentieth century. And, if these were the last words that I were permitted to utter to you I would rejoice to utter them in your presence and with your approval. I know that the fruition of our hopes is certain. I hope I may be able to live to congratulate you upon our common triumph, but in any case I have faith in the people. I trust in the good sense, the intelligence, and the patriotism of the majority, the vast majority, of my countrymen. I look forward to the future with hope and confidence, and

> '*Others I doubt not, if not we,*
> *The issue of our toil shall see.*'[1]

[1] My italics.—J. A.

CHAPTER CXVIII

THE STRICKEN GIANT

(*July* 1906–*March* 1910)

Chamberlain's Stroke — A Well-Kept Secret — Balfour Inclines to Tariff Reform — Hopes of Recovery — Active Behind the Scenes — Views on South Africa — Asquith's Budget Disappoints — Trade Turns Traitor — High Hopes of the Tariff Reformers — The Lloyd George Budget — Socialism or Tariff Reform ? — Chamberlain Urges Rejection of the Budget — His View Accepted — The 1910 Election — Austen Seen as Unionist Leader.

I

ON the morning after his exertions at the Bingley Hall, Chamberlain insisted on returning to London. He was to be host at a men's dinner at the House that evening and did not like to disappoint his guests. At the end of the short journey from Birmingham, he admitted to feeling 'tired out' and was persuaded not to go to the House. His guests were invited to Prince's Gardens instead.

Next morning (11 July), Chamberlain went to the Hotel Metropole for a meeting of the Tariff Commission. As they went into the meeting, he confessed to Hewins, 'I am a wreck'.[1] He took the chair, however, and made a short business speech; the last he would ever deliver. At the close of the proceedings he was presented by the Commission with a George III silver salver.

He came back to Prince's Gardens after lunch, tired and, what for him was most unusual, rather flushed. Mrs. Chamberlain again persuaded him not to go to the House, and they had tea together. He then went to his library to read or work.

Chamberlain and his wife were due to dine that evening at Lady Cunard's house in Grosvenor Square. The dinner was to welcome Sir Arthur and Lady Lawley — she was Lady Cunard's sister-in-law — who had just returned from his tour of duty as Lieutenant-Governor of the Transvaal. Mrs. Chamberlain dressed for the dinner and came down to the drawing-room. Chamberlain was

[1] W. A. S. Hewins, *Apologia of an Imperialist*, vol. i, p. 172.

908

not yet down. The carriage came to the door. The minutes ticked by. There was still no sign of Chamberlain. Such unpunctuality was unusual in him, and Mrs. Chamberlain went to the bathroom which opened on to the library and also served as a dressing-room. The door was locked. She called to him and heard him answer faintly, 'I can't get out'. Guessing at once that he had suffered a stroke, she sent the footman for a crowbar to break down the door. But, while she waited, she saw the door handle turn, opened from the inside. She rushed in and found Chamberlain lying exhausted on the floor. He was paralysed on the right side and almost helpless. With the help of the servants he was got to bed upstairs, and an urgent message was sent to the doctor.

Meanwhile, at Grosvenor Square, the guests waited. It was Lady Cunard's first big party in London, and Chamberlain was the guest of honour. Dinner had been waiting nearly half an hour when an empty carriage drove up at the door. It brought a message to say that Mrs. Chamberlain had been taken suddenly ill and that Chamberlain had to stay with her. Mrs. Chamberlain's first thought had been to keep what had happened secret.[1]

The doctors could not tell at first the full extent of the injury Chamberlain had suffered. The right arm and leg seemed wholly paralysed and his speech had become slow and thick. For all that, they held out hopes of a full recovery. It was, accordingly, announced that he had had to cancel all engagements as the result of an unusually severe attack of gout. No one outside the inner circle of the family was told the truth. On 21 July, Austen was married. Chamberlain was far too ill to attend the service. But Austen and his bride paid him a visit before leaving for their honeymoon. His absence from the wedding naturally aroused comment, but the holiday season was approaching, and the political world dispersed for the summer with no idea of how ill he was.

For a whole month, Chamberlain lay in a darkened room in Prince's Gardens. Then, on 14 August, a month after his stroke, he was able to walk a few steps again. Three days later, he limped downstairs and, from this time, made steady progress. By mid-September, he was well enough to leave for Birmingham, and the fact that he had to be wheeled on and off the platform in a Bath chair only seemed to confirm the story of his severe gout. At Highbury, he lived as much as possible in the fresh air.

[1] This account of Chamberlain's stroke is based on conversations with Mrs. Chamberlain and Lady Cunard.—J. A.

MRS. CHAMBERLAIN TO HER MOTHER

21 *September* 1906.—He walks up and down the entire length of the terrace with a stick and only one person holding on to his right side and he has made a distinct advance in the ease and confidence with which he does it. He also walks up and down stairs : . . .

He felt stronger, and his brain remained as clear as ever. But no movement had returned to his right arm. His right foot dragged ; and his speech remained thick and not easily understood. He could not do without a nurse. Was this to be the limit of his recovery ? The doctors still held out hopes and, for the next few months, his whole will-power was bent to the single purpose of getting well.

No hint of Chamberlain's condition[1] was yet made public. As late as January 1907, even Balfour had no news of his health though he had a doctor examine a published photograph in an attempt to discover whether he could possibly get well again.[2] The doctor in fact diagnosed 'severe hemiplegia — and that having regard to the length of time which has elapsed since the stroke, recovery must be *very very* doubtful'. Nevertheless, great interests depended upon Chamberlain. Many Unionist members and candidates looked to him as their real leader. The Tariff Reform League had become accustomed to his almost daily direction. The writers of the Imperialist Press had come to expect his personal guidance. These forces had somehow to be held together, at least until it became clear whether Chamberlain could hope to lead again. This was far from easy to contrive. It was essential to Chamberlain's recovery that he should do no work. Austen was away on his honeymoon and when he came back, was busy setting up a home. He gave such help as he could.

AUSTEN TO GARVIN

25 *September* 1906 : *Private.*—You will probably have seen by the time this reaches you that my father has decided to cancel his Nottingham engagement & to undertake no public work this autumn. He is going on very well & is very much better than when I last saw him, but his doctor advises that he should take a real and complete rest & I am glad to say that he is willing to follow his doctor's advice. Mr. Wilson has just gone off on his holiday & I am therefore undertaking his work & so opened your letter. As he is to rest completely, my father prefers not to attempt to deal with his correspondence on public questions & I have not shown him your letter. You will understand therefore that

[1] See W. A. S. Hewins, *Apologia of an Imperialist*, vol. i, p. 189.
[2] Sandars to W. Short, 4 March 1907. B.M. Add. MSS. 49765.

in what I am going to say I speak for myself only tho' I have no doubt that on the main point at any rate my father would agree with me.

I think you are absolutely right that the success of the Tariff Reform policy depends on the strength of the Unionist party ; that that strength depends upon union in the party & above all on acceptance of the only possible leadership in that party. I am therefore entirely at one with you in thinking that constant attacks on Balfour are a great mistake tactically as well as on other grounds. From the moment that my Father decided for good or for evil — for good, I have always thought — not to allow himself to be put into competition with Balfour, Balfour became our only possible leader. Who is there besides who can hold a candle to him?

This being so the true policy of Tariff Reformers was to draw him as far as possible to one side & to make the division in the party, if division there must be, fall between Balfour and the Free Fooders & not between him and us. This was accomplished by the Valentine's day correspondence, & thereafter it was our business to back him through thick and thin on that basis.

I am sure that you are right in thinking that this is our proper line. All intrigue or even semblance of intrigue against Balfour only weakens us. It drives away the weaker brethren, the sitters on the fence & the man who is a party man *avant tout*. All these we can get on our side & must if we are to win. Let us keep Balfour to the Valentine letter — he is not unwilling — let us emphasise the fact that that is the official policy of the party and let us work for union on those lines.

Much of the time, however, Austen was away, and Mrs. Chamberlain had to do her best to represent Chamberlain's views to his correspondents. The following letter is typical of many written in these months.

MRS. CHAMBERLAIN TO RIDLEY

10 *October* 1906.—I am sure you will forgive me for sending you a dictated reply as my correspondence at the present moment is very large.

I read your letter to Mr. Chamberlain who was very much interested to hear what you had to say about the Tariff Reform League and asked me to tell you that he is perfectly satisfied with what has been done, and thinks that the condition of affairs is most promising for the future.

He regrets that his illness has been more protracted than he expected, and under these circumstances he thinks that you had better not delay any action in order to consult him. You may be quite sure that when he comes back again he will be quite ready to endorse everything that you have decided upon, and he has no doubt that he will find that much useful work has been accomplished in his absence.

I do not know whether Austen could give you any assistance, but he will be in London after 16 Oct. at the Hans Crescent Hotel and would at any time be most happy to do what he could to help you if you cared to consult him. He has for some time been meaning to join the Tariff Reform League, but owing to the press of other affairs has been unable to do so, but he now asks me to tell you that he would like to become a member and would be very glad if you could arrange it.

Mr. Chamberlain and I read your speech the other day and his comment on it was 'That is the right spirit'. I can assure you that it is a great satisfaction to him to know that those who are associated with him in the cause which he has so much at heart are throwing themselves heart and soul into the work and are doing all that in them lies to carry it forward during his temporary withdrawal from active work.

I am glad to be able to confirm the good reports which you have had of him, for he is steadily regaining his strength and, now that he has made up his mind to take no part until he is thoroughly rested, he is giving himself up to the cure of fresh air and idleness.

II

Chamberlain remained at Highbury till the end of February 1907. On New Year's Day of that year, Austen wrote of his health:

> My father goes on well but very slowly. He follows with keen interest all that is done and I have had some very useful talks with him about policy.[1]

The following letter to Northcote, written with an eye to the coming Colonial Conference, shows his continuing interest in affairs.

CHAMBERLAIN TO NORTHCOTE

6 *February* 1907: *Private.*—I fear that with the present Government nothing like a satisfactory lead will be given to our guests and it becomes of the greatest importance that they should themselves be prepared to state their wishes very clearly. The death of Seddon is a great loss as we could always rely upon him for an outspoken and Imperial policy. I hope that Deakin will take his place. I do not trust to Laurier, as I think that while prepared, if his hand is forced, to support a preferential policy, he is not anxious to take the whole matter on his own shoulders, and would perhaps rather make an agreement with the United States as his neighbours than with Great Britain, to which he has no sympathetic attraction.

I am not very happy at the policy or speeches of our present Government. I thought beforehand that they would not take a very different line in foreign or colonial affairs to what the previous Government had adopted, but I see that I was mistaken, and they are ready to upset all we did with very little consideration. Their policy in South Africa, the New Hebrides, and tariff reform, has been most unfortunate, as I think, for the future of the Empire. The majority is for the first time a Little Englander majority and the Government can rely upon the support of the Nonconformists, the Labour men, and the extreme

---

[1] Austen to Garvin, 1 January 1907.

Radicals for any proposal for reducing armaments or ignoring the wishes of the Colonies. I expect that their proposals for Irish Home Rule will be carried by an enormous majority and we shall again have to trust to the House of Lords to secure union. The same majority will be opposed to any attempt to meet the Colonies in the matter of reciprocity and they will be quite safe with their present majority.

I find that I shall not be able myself to attend Parliament at the commencement of the present session : although my doctors all declare that I am getting on well, I am not yet able to take up my usual work. My progress though slow is sure, and I hope that before long I shall be able to join my colleagues on the front Opposition bench.

There seems, at the time, to have been some justification for the optimism of the last paragraph. On 1 March, Chamberlain returned to London. Next day, he visited Austen's new house and insisted on exploring every room. On 3 March, he set out with Mrs. Chamberlain for the south of France and found the journey no particular effort. He had taken a villa at Valescure, near St-Raphael, and stayed there till the end of May.

These months in the south of France saw Chamberlain gradually preparing to reassert some influence on affairs. Austen kept him posted on political developments in almost daily letters;[1] and he now began to resume his own correspondence. He was still too weak to work for any length of time and could not hold a pen even to sign his name. Mrs. Chamberlain became adept at turning his general instructions and comments into clear and carefully argued letters. Usually, she wrote in her own name, diffidently at first but with increasing authority in later years. The more important letters, however, were drafts for Chamberlain to correct and sign.

Would the movement for Fiscal Reform break up in Chamberlain's absence? This was the immediate political issue confronting the Unionist party. In the first phase, as it happened, the exact opposite took place. While Chamberlain had held the centre of the stage, the younger Tariff Reformers had felt inhibited from pressing their views too far. They had left the conduct of the struggle in the Party to their leader. But now their inhibitions were cast aside and they tried by their ardour to make up for Chamberlain's absence. Meanwhile, Balfour began to move cautiously towards the Tariff Reformers. Sandars too had reported to Balfour the view of Acland-Hood, his Chief Whip, that what the Party wanted was :

---

[1] Most of these letters were published by Sir Austen Chamberlain in a volume entitled *Politics from the Inside*. They belong to his life rather than to Chamberlain's, but form an essential companion to any student of the issues raised in this chapter.

A statement on broad lines touching Fiscal Reform in its relation to finance, both Imperial and local : they would like a sympathetic reference to closer commercial union with the Colonies ; they would like a point made of the fact that schemes for social reform depending on public money cannot be accomplished without that elasticity of revenue which alone can be obtained from a wider basis of taxation ; and finally that until the fiscal question is tackled the British manufacturer will never get better treatment for his wares abroad.   A speech on these lines . . . would in Hood's opinion pull the Party together.

Sandars favoured this course himself and Balfour took his advice. He saw much of Hewins and took a new and unexpected interest in the work of the Tariff Commission.   Hewins' account of their talks certainly suggests that Balfour's earlier differences with the Tariff Reformers had sprung more from fear of Chamberlain's personality and methods than from any issue of policy.[1]   With Chamberlain withdrawn from the scene, Balfour's fears were quietened and he now moved to attach the Tariff Reformers more securely to himself.

Balfour's new tendency was presently stimulated by the attitude of the Liberal Government representatives at the Colonial Conference.   Austen was, of course, in regular touch with the Colonial Premiers and reported regularly to Chamberlain.   He also addressed a great demonstration at the Albert Hall (26 April) and made a strong plea for Preference.

AUSTEN TO MRS. CHAMBERLAIN

27 *April* 1907.—How I should like to have half-an-hour's talk with Father about the précis of the Conference's proceedings published today. I think that what they have done is all to the good, but I wish Deakin had had his way and got its own Secretariat for the Conference.   It is curious to see how this question, and the question of the Prime Minister of Great Britain presiding, have come to the front the moment Father's commanding personality is no longer there to make everyone feel that the Colonial Secretary is the biggest President the Conference could have.   As long as father was C.S. no one thought of these matters ; and having in mind father's tenure of office I was at first prejudiced against the change.   But apart from his personality, I think the change is right.

11.30 p.m.   Well, I delivered myself of an hour's further criticism of Asquith to my own satisfaction and then we dined at Stafford House, a non-party dinner to the Premiers.   I sat next Ward, who regretted they had not done more but was pleased with what they had done. They had found Laurier very difficult and it had needed much pressure in private conversations to carry him as far as they had done.   Ward hoped they would do something as to defence, and talked in the right spirit about Preference.   He was sure it would come, hoped they would

---

[1] See, in particular, W. A. S. Hewins, *Apologia of an Imperialist*, vol. ii, pp. 185–189.

arrange a 33 1/3 per cent Preference among all Colonies while over here and believed they would so help the question along, even in this country. Anyway they would put forward their views and they were not discouraged by our election, which was no affair of theirs.

London is laughing over a story of Lady Derby at the Prince's dinner to the Premiers.

'Who', she asked of Sir Wilfred Laurier, 'who is the pleasant-looking gentleman next Lady Laurier, who is enjoying his dinner so much?'

'That', replied Sir Wilfred, 'is *your* Prime Minister!'

I spoke to both the Lauriers tonight. They send their greetings.

I hear the Liberals did not at all like Deakin's speech at the Pilgrims. 'One didn't know what was coming next', they say. I fancy they are nearly as much afraid of him as they used to be of Seddon.

Chamberlain replied at length a few days later.

CHAMBERLAIN TO AUSTEN

29 *April* 1907.—I congratulate you on the success of the Albert Hall meeting and still more on your speech. The latter was read to me from the Morning Post and I heartily admire and approve of it. It is evident that you have during the last twelve months made great advances in platform speaking, both in the matter, which is free from platitude and clear and definite, and in the manner which is free from monotony, and, as I am told by Hilda and others who have been present at recent speeches, is excellent in style. There is no-one as far as I can see that can hold a candle to you now, in the front rank, although Bonar Law is probably gaining ground as a speaker of the second class.

I do not believe that such a meeting as that of the Albert Hall could have been held two years ago. It shows that the cause is making great way, and in answer to your letter of the 25th inst, I attribute this in great measure to the interest now taken in the Imperial Conference. Although we cannot expect great immediate results as long as we have a Government pledged against all reform, the present Conference will make the ground still more certain for the Unionist Party whenever it returns to power. It gives us what we have always wanted — a positive as well as a negative creed, and I believe that when the inevitable depression comes to take the place of the present boom in trade a change such as we have been advocating is certain, and those who have been in the forefront of the new crusade must reap the benefit.

All that the Conference had done is, I think, good, as far as it goes. I doubt whether a secretariat selected by the Conference would have been possible. It means one representative at least from each of the Colonies. They would have small salaries and would not have great influence here. It is better for us that nothing should be done to detract from the importance of the four-yearly conferences in which the Colonies are represented by their leading men.

I agree with you that the nominal presidency of the Prime Minister is, on the whole, a good thing although I should not have liked it if I had remained in office, but then, if the Colonial Secretary is a man of influence, it is to him and not to the Prime Minister of the day that people will look for most important utterances.

I wish the Conference had agreed to a full report of their proceedings, but I expect that both Laurier and Botha would have opposed this. Sooner or later it will come, and their own constituents will demand to know what they are doing. Meanwhile they seem to me to be growing under the influence of the other representatives of the Colonies and certainly the Conference as a whole has aroused more interest than ever before.

We have still to see what they will do about preference, which I suppose they will discuss without coming to any definite decision. If we could possibly hope to influence them, we should desire I suppose unanimously that they should pass a strong resolution in favour of preference as being mutually beneficial and tending to promote the union of the Empire. Such a resolution would be a text for the future for all discussion between now and the next meeting of the Conference. If this is impossible at least I hope that *our* friends will bear in mind our difficulties and will not agree to anything which will in any way hamper our future agitation.

I wonder what effect all this is having on Arthur Balfour. I am afraid it will not move him beyond his present standpoint. If I am mistaken it would be desirable that when the Conference is over he should take some opportunity of commenting upon it. You might I think see him about this, and if he is inclined to take advantage of the opportunity you might get a meeting of the Compatriots or some other comparatively small Club in order to find him a pulpit for a new sermon on the subject.

In the event, Balfour proved readier to take a positive line than Chamberlain had expected. On 2 May, Asquith rejected the Colonial proposals on Imperial Preference out of hand. Four days later, Balfour spoke at the Albert Hall and uttered a withering denunciation of the Liberal Government's refusal to co-operate with the Colonies. His speech aroused widespread response, and this encouraged Balfour to persist in his new line. He became for a time the leader of the Tariff Reform Movement. Chamberlain was naturally delighted by the new turn of events, though he recognised at once that Tariff Reform had become more acceptable to Balfour and others by his own absence from the scene.

CHAMBERLAIN TO DEAKIN

16 *May* 1907: *Private.*—It is very kind of you to say what you do about my value to the party, and yet I am inclined by my observation from a distance to recognise that the policy has moved more quickly than it would have done had I been a protagonist in its support. My enforced absence and the cause of it, has at once diverted the personal feeling and abuse which prevented much of what I had to say from receiving im-

partial consideration. In my absence others have been found to take up my work, who do not bear the burden of my unpopularity with the opposite political party and undoubtedly the presence of the Imperial Conference and the attention which has been called to its proceedings has also greatly influenced many of those who would not yield to representations which they thought to be tainted by political feeling.

Has your attention been called to an extract from one of Rosebery's speeches in which he says that if I had been able to assure the country that the Colonies were in favour of Preference any proposal from them would have been entitled to serious consideration. In fact, I believe he said it would have been criminal not to accept them. I doubt whether he will now be consistent with this utterance but it shows what they wanted and what only the Conference could achieve. In my speeches I referred again and again to the language used by the Statesmen of the Sister States, but without effect. Now, the proceedings of the Conference have carried conviction with them, and everyone agrees that it is we, the English people, who stand in the way of an agreement with the Colonies, and that the proposals for preference come from them in the first instance, although they are careful to declare that they do not wish to press them upon unwilling hearers.

Although the actual results achieved by the Conference have not been great the effect produced has been much greater than I anticipated, and I agree with you that quite continuous argument addressed to the people of the United Kingdom must do the rest. I also agree with you that our positive programme should not be confined to preference alone and that we have to add to it other questions which have the greatest possible interest to the bulk of our people. A little more experience will show how completely the other side is without constructive ability, and I hope that we may devise another 'unauthorised programme' which will once more show that in the matter of social reform our party is ahead of that curious and heterogeneous association which still calls itself the Liberal Party, and which, since the great Reform Bill of 1832 and the Reform of the Poor Law which shortly followed it, has shown itself barren of practical suggestion.

The Conservative wing of our Party has become almost entirely democratic. There are very few remaining who belong to the old reactionary Tories. On the other hand, there are still a great many who are indifferent to progress and think they have done enough if they can maintain the existing system of things in what they consider the best of all possible worlds. They will be driven forward by the force of events. You cannot have a Franchise as wide as ours without the representatives being compelled to adopt change as the order of political being.

Insensibly the Colonies are doing us good service in this respect. They are making experiments, many of which prove to be perfectly safe and satisfactory, and much more attention is now given to what they are attempting than formerly.

If the next Conference is held four years hence as it ought to be, it will be just before the normal period for the dissolution of the present

Parliament, and you may be certain that the vital question with us will then be whether the Government to be returned shall be in sympathy with the Colonies or not.

I hope that you may be again the representative of the Commonwealth at that time and that I may be more fortunate than now in that I may have the opportunity of seeing you and working with you.

Chamberlain was heartened by Balfour's change of attitude and by the response of public opinion. He wrote to Austen and to Halsbury urging them to follow up their advantage and table votes of censure in both Houses.

CHAMBERLAIN TO HALSBURY

12 *May* 1907.—I have duly received your letter of 9 May as also the earlier one of 2 April, which was stupidly delayed by the carelessness of a servant. I am obliged to dictate my reply, as I am still unable to use my right hand, although I am certainly getting better, yet progress is very slow, and I require all the patience I can show.

I read the papers daily, and of course give special attention to all that is going on in the political world. Like you, I have been struck by the progress made in the last six months on our question. Undoubtedly there is a great movement in our direction, and many of those who were hostile are coming over. I agree entirely with what you say about the Free Fooders. Before I was taken ill I do not believe that I ever made any attack against them personally, or, without the strongest necessity, ever used their names. I think we should adopt the same policy now, though I regard the principal men amongst them as almost hopeless. They are determined not to be converted, and their opposition will only end with themselves. Fortunately for us they have no popular following. I believe the six hundred of whom Elliot boasts would about exhaust their strength in votes, although the position they have held in the past gives them a certain amount of influence out of proportion to their real popular strength. On the other hand we cannot allow them, who are only a small minority, to settle what shall be the programme and policy of the Party. I am convinced the time has come when we ought to declare ourselves clearly.

I have written to Austen, urging that having regard to the Imperial Conference and to other circumstances, there ought to be a vote of censure in both Houses of Parliament.

It should run somewhat as follows :—'That this House regrets that in view of the declarations made in the Imperial Conference by the Prime Ministers of the King's Dominions beyond the Seas, His Majesty's Government and the United Kingdom should have thought it necessary to meet this proposal with a flat refusal.'

I do not suggest these words as unalterable, but they give the substance of what I should be disposed to raise in both Houses.

I should think that we ought to carry this Resolution in the House of Lords, although of course it would be defeated in the House of Commons, but it would have very considerable effect out of doors. I suppose that the Duke of Devonshire and others of his way of thinking, might support the Government in the House of Lords, but I do not see that this would be any objection. They need not be replied to by name, although, as you say, their arguments might be answered.

I see that notice is to be given of a reasoned amendment to the Finance Bill, which will necessarily cover some of the same ground. I do not think, however, that this ought to be any objection to raising the same matter directly, by a separate Vote of Censure which would necessarily come on after the Whitsuntide holiday, while the Second Reading of the Budget would be disposed of beforehand.

As at present advised we shall leave here at the end of the month. I suppose I shall then go down to Highbury, where I shall complete my cure if it is to be completed according to the doctor's assurance.

This is very much the letter of a man who still expects to lead. Before leaving for England at the end of May, Chamberlain wrote to Chaplin. This letter summarises his view of the position of the Tariff Reform movement and gives an outline of his own intentions. He still hoped to be back in the House in 1908, and looked forward to a General Election that year.

CHAMBERLAIN TO CHAPLIN

25 *May* 1907: *Private.*—I have followed with the greatest interest the proceedings at the Conference, which have told, I think, very much in our favour although of course there is nothing new in what Deakin and others have been saying.

It is amusing, however, to find that at last even the most cantankerous of Free Traders admit that the Colonies have made an offer which the present Government has declined, and the speech of Balfour at the Albert Hall shows that he is prepared to accept their offer and meet it fairly. I agree with you that we are not likely to have difficulties in our own party on this question and we may hope that the next Government will be a Tariff Reform Government as well as a Unionist one. The fact is that circumstances have been too strong for the small knot of men who at first stood aside and boasted that they would smash Tariff Reform if it was not already dead. It has made on the contrary great and important progress, and it is now so firmly rooted in the public mind that it cannot be put aside.

You speak of my return. I am coming back to England at the end of this month. We have not had first rate weather here but there has been a great deal of sunshine, and I have been able to get out much more than I could have done at home. Complete recovery will however be slow and I am still very lame and have not yet recovered the use of my right hand although in both respects I am better than when I left England. I shall keep quiet at Highbury for this summer, and *then I hope that I may be again in my place at the beginning of next year.*[1] In any case

[1] My italics.—J. A.

it is a great pleasure to me to see that my policy has made such great progress in my absence, and that others have been found to take up the work which I was obliged to lay down. Our opponents were confident that it was a one-man fight, in which case of course there was ground for their feeling that when I was out of the way they would make quick work of my policy. That has not turned out to be the case and Tariff Reform has come to stay. This has been a great satisfaction to me during the long period in which I have had to be patient and stand aside.

I hope that next Session we may get an oppor tunity of appealing once more to the people, and I am pretty sure that the verdict will be very different from that of last time.

III

Chamberlain returned to London on 1 June and, a few days later, after consultations with his doctors, went on to Birmingham. As yet, his seclusion had been so complete that not even Collings had seen him. But this régime could be continued no longer. There were already rumours that his mind was weakened and, if he continued to refuse visitors, people might well think him worse than he was. Besides, the strain of isolation was beginning to tell. He was essentially a man of action, almost wholly devoid of those inner resources which alone make retirement bearable. He needed contact with human beings and that kind of political discussion among comrades in action which had been his staple intellectual diet for so long. Though still very much an invalid, he now decided to return to the fringes at least, of active life.

MRS. CHAMBERLAIN TO GARVIN

20 *June* 1907: *Private*.—It is not easy to re-assure one's friends when every day sensational rumours are published which gain credence or not according to the views of their readers, & I feel it is better to ignore them & let the hand of Time dispel them. One has to take them as one of the trials inseparable from the life of a public man.

You know, I think, how much Mr. Chamberlain values the services you have rendered to the great cause to which he has devoted himself & that he looks for your further co-operation in helping to develop & guide its future. The progress which the movement has made during the last six months has been the greatest source of encouragement to him, as I trust it has been to you & he feels now that it has reached a point from which there can be no retreat, & that it will go forward to its triumphant fulfilment.

You can imagine the disappointment it has been to him to have to stand aside, but he feels that, much as he would like to have taken his share of the work, the very fact that he has not been there has eliminated

Stanley Baldwin

*Neville and
Austen Chamberlain*

*David Lloyd George
and Leo Amery*

Winston Churchill

some difficulties, & has made it in many ways easier for others to come forward. In any case it has been a great comfort to him to feel that his absence has not retarded the onward march of Tariff Reform.

You will, I know, be glad to be assured that he is making uninterrupted progress. His convalescence has been slow, but after such a long strain of overwork that was to be expected, & his doctors are entirely satisfied with his condition. He is much stronger than when we went abroad & now begins to do more than before.

He follows all that goes on with unflagging interest & is glad to hear about all the questions of the day. If therefore at any time you have a spare half-hour, & have any gossip which would entertain him it would be very kind if you would write to him. I say gossip for want of a better word — only meaning to exclude anything which might worry him & thus make him feel his chains more heavy. When a man has been so active as he has life is rather dull when he is compelled to be an onlooker.

This, however, I hope & believe is only for a time.

On 2 July, Chamberlain had Balfour to lunch at Prince's Gardens and, thereafter, began to receive occasional visitors.

The Party Conference, that year, was held in Birmingham. 'Balfour's pilgrimage to Canossa', the Free Trade Press called it. Chamberlain, could not, of course, attend; but Balfour and several of the other leaders came to Highbury to see him. At the mass meeting at the end of the Conference, Balfour spoke at some length on Fiscal Reform. Austen had been pressing for a new pronouncement on Preference and for a programme to include Old Age Pensions.[1] Chamberlain may have had a hand in this. Certainly he was pleased with the speech.

CHAMBERLAIN TO MAXSE

22 *November* 1907: *Private*.—I rather hoped that I should see you when you were in Birmingham, but I suppose you were fully occupied with the work of the Conference. It was to me, as an outsider, thoroughly satisfactory, and I think that Arthur Balfour's speech shows great advance in our direction. I do not see how the Unionist Party can again come into office without putting tariff reform in the forefront, and you will see that Balfour no longer shies at the prospect of a moderate duty on corn & meat which I think essential for our negotiations with the Colonies.

I saw him and also Chaplin and others who attended the Conference. The reports they gave me, as well as Austen's separate one, were all the same, and pointed to great progress in our policy both on the part of the leaders and of the rank and file. Apparently the delegates were unanimously in favour of change and the free importers or free fooders were nowhere.

I think that our tactics should be to make the most of this unanimity,

[1] See *Arthur James Balfour*, by Kenneth Young, p. 264.

2 H

and we ought not in any case to play into the hands of our opponents whose interest it is to magnify differences and to declare that we are a divided party. I do not think this is true. As far as men can speak alike upon a subject on which they are agreed we are all saying the same thing. Some slight difference there may be, but it is verbal and certainly not practical. The 'Westminster', with its usual cleverness, is trying to point to some difference still existing between Balfour and his followers. I do not think there is ground for this allegation, and it would be small encouragement to him, if, after having made definite advances towards us, he found our strongest men unwilling to recognise this change and still harping upon the differences which may yet remain. My conversation with him was very satisfactory and I have come to the conclusion that there is no practical difference between us except, perhaps, as to the treatment of free fooders like Hugh Cecil. The best thing in my opinion is to leave these people strictly alone. They will find themselves in a small minority and I think we may safely and truly claim Balfour as one of ourselves.

The cause of Tariff Reform was making good progress. But what of Chamberlain, himself? Would he ever come back? In the spring, hope of a full recovery had been strong, but now doubt began to appear. We can trace a growing depression about his prospects from his letters in these months.

J.C. TO NORTHCOTE

14 *September* 1907.—. . . about myself. I have not much to tell that is new — in fact nothing. My recovery is slow, but the doctors hold the same language and assure me that only time and patience are required. Meanwhile,' I am resting and taking things quietly, postponing all matters of public interest.

Austen is taking my place, and I am glad to agree with Deakin that he is doing extremely well and is making great advances in the public confidence.

J.C. TO DENISON

6 *November* 1907.—I am very much better than I was but complete recovery is slow and I do not look for *immediate* return to public life.

J.C. TO DOWSON

9 *November* 1907.—I am much better than I was, but I am still rather lame and unable to make much use of my right hand. Whether I shall be able to take my place again in the full activity of public life I do not know, but I continue to base my hopes upon the reports of the doctors, which are still favourable.

In any case I do not regret anything, and I have some comfort in feeling that I have given my best to my public work, while I continued to have the power to do public service.

J.C. TO MAXSE

22 *November* 1907.—I fear it may be some time yet, if ever, before I again take an active part in subjects which have had so much interest for me. Although the doctors continue to preach patience, I am myself getting somewhat discouraged. I am thankful to believe that my personal presence is less necessary than some of us supposed and that our policy has made without me even more progress than it did before. That this will go on in my absence is my earnest hope and belief.

J.C. TO NORTHCOTE

24 *December* 1907.—. . . I keep very well except for the results of my illness which I do not get rid of as soon as I should like. Until there is a great improvement I cannot hope to take my part in public life.

J.C. TO KNOLLYS

10 *January* 1908.—I am making progress but it is necessarily slow, and I do not feel it probable that I shall be able to take my seat in Parliament during the forthcoming Session.

Despite this growing anxiety, he was certainly more active than in previous months. In December, he attended the christening of Austen's son Joseph in Birmingham. Towards the end of January, he returned to London, where he stayed till the end of February. His time now was as much occupied as his strength would allow. His diary shows that there were frequent visitors, and guests to lunch or dinner almost every day. Balfour, Gerald Balfour, Ridley, Buckle, Hewins, Chaplin and Collings were among his callers. Austen conferred with him almost daily. He might no longer appear in public, yet he was still a powerful influence. His name counted for much. Messages from him were anxiously sought by candidates at by-elections and for great demonstrations. Besides, he still had control of the Liberal Unionist Organisation, the Tariff Reform League and the Birmingham machine. Hewins has left a description of him at this time.[1]

12 *February* 1908.—I had lunch with C. yesterday at 40 Prince's Gardens. Before going down Mrs. C. explained that it was one of his bad days, as he had a cold and a slight attack of gout which prevented him from walking. So he was in his place at table when we went down. No one was at lunch, except Mr. and Mrs. C., Ida and myself. I was pleased with his appearance. He *looks* better than before his illness. He is fatter in the face and body, and his left hand with which he gave me a good grip has grown quite plump. He looks as young and well groomed

[1] W. A. S. Hewins, *Apologia of an Imperialist*, vol. ii, pp. 220–222.

as ever. There is just the slightest drawn look in part of his face, scarcely more noticeable than before his present illness. His right hand is still practically useless, though he has recovered power in some of his fingers. We discussed a wide range of subjects. His mental faculties seemed to me as alert as ever, and his knowledge of the fiscal question wider and juster. His memory is good, his judgment sound and his sentences finely formed, with the old distinction.

The one great, patent drawback to all this is his physical powerlessness of speech. His voice has lost all its old ring and is not exactly thick but dull. He speaks very slowly and articulates with evident difficulty. It is as though the old ringing human voice had quite gone and he had been fitted with some clumsy mechanical contrivance as a substitute. But I had no difficulty in understanding him. He laughed several times and shrugged his shoulders in the old manner.

The first question he asked me when I went into the dining-room was what constituency it was which I had decided to contest. I told him Wolverhampton (West), and he then said he remembered. He went on to talk of Wolverhampton, that it was within the sphere of Birmingham influence, and ought to be a safe seat for a Tariff Reformer. He thought I should win. As to the general course of events he seemed very pleased. He thought there was no doubt now that we should win the victory, but the difficulty would be to make full use of it. In that he said he looked to the Tariff Commission. I congratulated him on Austen's speeches. C. thought that Austen had come along very much lately. I said he had improved greatly since the baby had arrived, and told him some stories to show that unless men had children they had no right to an opinion on economic questions !

I gave him some account of my discussions with Balfour. He said Balfour had certainly advanced. In reply to remarks of mine on Balfour's type of mind, C. said he had so far only been a leader of the educated University classes and could scarcely understand men like himself who tried to represent the English people. We went on to discuss the methods of economic study in connection with which I said that no one could sit down in cold blood to get up economics; that the subject was best approached in connection with some subject of practical importance in which one was interested. C. said he entirely agreed with that. I mentioned my own early experiences in the great trade depression when I was a boy and Thorold Rogers' suggestion that I should write a history of the National Debt. This led C. to give his reminiscences of Thorold Rogers, who, he said, was a strange mixture. He referred to his extravagant views on landowners and said he had no doubt that many free traders now sincerely held the same view that anything done to aid agriculture could only increase the wealth of the landlords.

He thought the Liberals had been foolish to pledge themselves so unreservedly against particular measures, because some duties might be put on which would be no real violation of free trade. He remarked on the manner in which the Liberal Imperialists had 'gone under' and said he had never thought much of them. He thought finance might wreck the Government and referred to the division of opinion on the

Naval Estimates. He wanted to know the course of procedure in getting the tariff started when we were in power, and I told him about Balfour's questions. He approved of my suggestion of a Ministerial Tariff Commission to bring together the departments concerned and wanted to know about the attitude of the officials. I told him of Balfour's fears of official obstruction, but C. did not agree with him. He said the officials had no responsibility and could be trusted to work loyally.

Chamberlain's view of the political situation at the end of 1907 is perhaps best illustrated by the following letter.

CHAMBERLAIN TO NORTHCOTE

24 *December* 1907 : *Private.*—I think the present Government is weakening, and if the Opposition were prepared with a programme, we might hope to turn them out at the next trial of strength ; as it is, and judging by the bye-elections, there is not a great deal of change but much indifference.

Meanwhile Tariff Reform is certainly making progress and if, as seems likely, we have a bad time for trade in front of us, we may confidently anticipate a great movement in our favour.

Balfour has made great progress, and his last speech at Birmingham shows him to be a declared tariff reformer. The free fooders are now a very small minority indeed, and they have no popular influence or weight whatever.

Much depends upon the next session. I understand that the policy of the Government is to force as much as possible through the House of Commons with the hope that it will be rejected by the House of Lords, and in that case they will require a dissolution either in the autumn of 1908 or the spring of 1909. In this case they will try to make the issue the existence of the House of Lords. I do not, however, believe that this policy will be successful. They have such a great majority already that they may still have enough to work the Commons with after a dissolution, but it will be much less than the present one. I do not think, therefore, that it will be accepted as conclusive either by the House of Lords or by popular opinion generally, and they will come back very much weakened.

As the New Year advanced the Unionist stock began to rise. The by-elections, hitherto rather favourable to the Government, inclined towards the Opposition. Chamberlain became more sanguine.

CHAMBERLAIN TO DENISON

21 *February* 1908.—I do not suppose that with their enormous majority we shall get rid of the present Government during the present Session, and under these circumstances I do not feel inclined to attend Parliament ; but next year I hope we may see the back of them and certainly the by-elections show how weak they are in the country.

Since you wrote we have had Worcester and South Leeds, and . . . both confirm your idea that the policy of Tariff Reform is making progress, and the bad trade which naturally follows that of the United States and Germany will certainly have its effect. In fact I regard it as likely to have a cumulative effect and I expect will be evident in the bye-elections before long.

CHAMBERLAIN TO NORTHCOTE

27 *February* 1908 : *Private.*—The Government has received a good deal of set-back in the recent bye-elections, which have gone heavily against them. As I assumed when they came in they will not keep their popularity and a general election may come sooner than it is expected. At all events the Tariff Reformers are much encouraged and we find everywhere that the policy is progressing. I think it will be victorious at the next general election.

Though essentially partisan in his outlook, Chamberlain gave public support to Haldane's efforts to strengthen the Territorial Army.[1] The following letter shows him for a moment, at least, in the rôle of the elder statesman above Party strife.

CHAMBERLAIN TO HALDANE

16 *January* 1908 : *Private.*—I am in many respects as well as ever I was, but my recovery from the blow which I received nearly eighteen months ago is very slow, and my return to active politics must still be postponed.

I take great interest in all that goes on and especially in what is non-partisan in its character. I certainly include your gigantic work under this head, and I think your proposals ought to have fair and generous treatment. I hope they may turn out as successfully as you desire and I am very glad to have been able to do anything, however small it may be, to bring about this result.

From what I see from my quiet watch-tower there is great anxiety lest the present Government should place, what Adam Smith warns us not to do, opulence before defence. I am certain that the influence of the party which places first efficient defence cannot be over-rated, and although the party of economy at any price — especially in your own ranks — is perhaps more numerous at the present time, I am confident that those who sacrifice to it will make a mistake.

This applies to the Army and the Navy as well. I do not trust Fisher, and I feel that you, and those who think with you, have a difficult task in resisting him. He thinks only of immediate popularity and popularity which is noisy of its kind. Believe me that there is a better popularity to work for, and that is the kind which looks ahead and is non-party in its character.

[1] Chamberlain to Colonel Ludlow, 7 January 1908, published in *The Times* and other papers.

IV

Chamberlain left for the south of France at the end of February 1908, staying at a villa in Cannes. This time, he joined, to some extent, in the social life of the large English community, receiving visitors, entertaining at meals, and going for drives. Spring-Rice, among others, went to see him and they spoke of Campbell-Bannerman, who had retired from the arena and was known to be dying. Spring-Rice made the following note of their talk.[1]

I saw J.C. He looks all right but you know his situation. It was most touching to see the care taken of him by his wife and the family affection which surrounds him. He spoke a good deal of C.B. whom he described as a clever man and a brave man, and deprecated the attacks made on him by Balfour. He was most kindly in all he said of his past associates. I almost wish I hadn't seen him ; it is so sad to see that sort of power nearing its end.

The same day, by a strange coincidence, Devonshire died in a hotel in Cannes only a few hundred yards from Chamberlain's villa. 'Well, the game is over, and I'm not sorry', were said to have been the Duke's last words ; but his old ally and antagonist was by no means ready to leave the table. He followed affairs carefully, reading the newspapers and learning the inside story from Austen, Winterton, his Parliamentary private secretary, and other correspondents.

Among the latter was Selborne, who sent a long and detailed memorandum on South African policy. Chamberlain's reply to him deserves to be quoted at some length. It is his political testament on South Africa, and is striking in its criticism of Milner's policies and work.

CHAMBERLAIN TO SELBORNE

26 *March* 1908: *Private.*—I think we should have agreed very nearly indeed in all that you have done, & the opinions that you have formed. I feel that you have been very brave in undertaking this work, especially as the defeat of the Government was probable when you undertook it. I entirely disapproved of Chinese Labour & told Milner and Lyttelton of my settled opinion. However they were not persuaded — although I could not help them, I felt that I ought not to do anything to stand in their way. Accordingly they had to go on with their policy & take the consequences which, however, were foreseen by me as well as by you. Also I disapproved of Lyttelton's constitution. It went too far or not far

[1] See *Letters and Friendships of Sir Cecil Spring-Rice*, 24 March 1908.

enough & I am not surprised that the present Government when they came into office determined to make a clean sweep of it. I share your view that in spite of these mistakes & all that has since followed the result of the war was satisfactory.

I do not believe that the Transvaal can ever be placed in the same position that it was before Kruger's time & this is something to look back upon with satisfaction. At the same time I feel that the fear of a Transvaal which shall be like the Irish at home or the French in Canada is very real, & I do not feel certain that some such result may not be the ultimate consequence of the presence of the two races on one continent. The fact that racialism remains in Cape Colony after a hundred years of good government & a long period of constitutional government confirms my fear, & the war shows what power a small population have where a large territory is concerned. If the Dutch are in a majority over South Africa, & they appear to be in the Transvaal, the O.R.C. & Cape Colony, are we sure that they will not make any effort to be supreme? Anyway, we can do nothing or rather the only thing we can do is in the nature of good government & patience, & not in the shape of force. Force alone will not keep the majority with us & the war shows that they are numerous enough & strong enough to hold their own if they have got the larger part of South Africa to operate in.

I am glad that you like Botha. I thought when I saw him both in London & in South Africa that he was rather 'slim' & could not be relied upon. I formed a good opinion of Smuts who undoubtedly is clever if he is also straight.

Even Milner, if he had remained, could not have kept the Dutch with him, but he must have relied entirely upon the English. This I think would be bad & would not be a final settlement. I am glad that you have taken up your residence in Pretoria. I always thought that Milner made a mistake in going entirely to Johannesburg, where he necessarily saw too much of the mine owners and capitalists. However I do not suppose that this would have been a bad decision but for the split to which you refer, which was consequent upon the introduction of Chinese Labour.

I am struck with what you say about the influence of other nations, especially Germany, on South Africa. Of course I agree with you & think that the German presence in South West Africa will have to be reckoned with hereafter & no doubt meanwhile will have considerable influence over our Boer fellow-subjects in the Transvaal. If we had not conquered the French at Quebec we should never have lost the United States. We must remember that in South Africa. But I should like to hear further from you about Unification. Is the country to be unified? It is very large but the population is small. What is the Parliament to be? Are the natives to be represented or only those of European descent? If the latter will Cape Colony give up their native franchise which I gather the natives prize very highly & will not surrender without a struggle. In fact they hope to gain it in the Transvaal & the O.R.C. & when I was there I gathered that they attributed great importance to the vote.

Do not be anxious about the line taken by the present Parliament. It must be very provoking no doubt to be judged or to think you are judged at home with insufficient information, & nothing can be worse than the readiness to condemn which the Little Englanders and those who support them show upon information derived from a most partial study of the situation; but the present Parliament will not be long lived. Putting aside bye-elections, just now confirmed by the result of Peckham where the turnover is extraordinary, I think there is reason for supposing that the present action of the majority is only a temporary phase. They mistook this mandate & accepted the extraordinary majority which the last general election gave them, as representing a permanent agreement with Little England feeling & policy. I never believed this myself. I thought that it would pass away quickly & that speaking generally the people of this country are Imperialist at heart although the late Government became unpopular by staying too long, & by devoting itself to certain unpopular policies as for instance the Education Amendment Bill & the introduction of Chinese Labour in the Transvaal. Now it is seen that I was right & the present Government has been tried & found wanting. I do not think it will last long, & you will then be ready to deal with the African subject as you think fit.

Your second letter has just come to hand. I have read it & its enclosure with great care. It undoubtedly confirms your feeling that Krugerism is dead & that whatever the events may have still in store for us it is incompatible with Krugerism as it was before. May I venture to repeat to you what I said to Milner but which I think he forgot, or at all events did not accept, & that is that you should take a lesson from Cromer's experience, & having accepted a most disagreeable post you should stick it out as long as you can. I believe Milner felt the job beyond his health & he therefore resigned his position before any pressure was put upon him, but I hope that you are not likely to be influenced by the same reason. If so, & if your health stands the work, you must recollect that every day gives you greater authority, & you can accordingly do for South Africa what no one else is likely to accomplish. You also, thanks partly to Milner's experience, have been able to keep well with the Boers & not to confine yourself entirely to the support of the mine-owning British clan. Personally I think there has been great danger in the past that the mine-owning section of the community would demand too much & would think that their British citizenship justified them in ignoring the Boers which I certainly do not think was the case. Many of the mine-owners were foreigners, in fact the majority, & we were working for aliens and not for ourselves. Your position is a much better one than Milner's, & I feel that this is largely due to your wise action. You ought to have the full advantage of it, & you can only reap that by staying out at all events your full time.

Owing to my illness I have been for some time deprived of the use of my right hand. The doctors are hopeful of entire recovery, but meanwhile my daughter Ida is acting as my amanuensis and shorthand writer.

2 H 2

V

In April, Asquith introduced his Budget; and, at last, a sum of £1,200,000 was allocated for a scheme of Old Age Pensions. Here was the fulfilment of another reform in which Chamberlain had been the pioneer.

Meanwhile the by-elections continued to favour the Unionists; and Churchill, who had to face a contest on receiving promotion in the Government, was defeated.

CHAMBERLAIN TO COLLINGS

26 *April* 1908.—I think I am better since I came here but recovery is very slow and I have been rather discouraged of late. I suppose we shall go on to Aix when the weather permits, and thence we are likely to come home, but I think very little to London — just enough, I hope, to see you and hear what you are doing.

I have received the telegram announcing Churchill's defeat. I am almost sorry, and should be quite so if he deserved more sympathy, but he would have been intolerable if he had won.[1]

Chamberlain seems to have benefited from his stay in Cannes. In April, indeed, he had managed to walk a full mile. At the end of June, in a supreme effort to get well, he undertook a month's cure at Aix. But a further trial was now added to his weakness and paralysis. His eyesight began to fail; not that he became blind, but that he lost the power of focusing and found it almost impossible to read or to distinguish any object clearly. He visited Ouchy, after Aix, for eye treatment, but it did little good.

Chamberlain returned to England at the end of July. For the rest of the summer and autumn he was busy at Highbury or Prince's Gardens, with visitors or correspondence. Balfour, Gerald Balfour, Milner and Bonar Law were among those who came to consult him. Hewins was also among his visitors and made the following notes in his diary.[2]

5 *December*.—I had an interview with Chamberlain on Dec. 3rd He appeared to me to be better than when I saw him last. He talked more easily, sometimes speaking for five or ten minutes without stopping and quite clearly. He walked downstairs to the dining-room and up again to the drawing-room, with the aid of Mrs. C. and a stick. I found him rather fierce and very anxious about the Imperial situation, especially

---

[1] Chamberlain had a genuine liking for Churchill and later that year, when Churchill was married, sent him a wedding present. Churchill wrote, 'I value your gift very highly and it will always be preserved in my family with honour'. (24 August 1908.)

[2] See *Apologia of an Imperialist*, vol. i, pp. 225 *et seq.*

the gravity of the questions raised by the foreign negotiations with the Dominions.

On the action the Unionist Government should take on coming into office he said they should at once give the corn preference whether they came in before or after the Budget. He would, if possible, add the meat preference and selected duties on manufactured products. He would then have a Conference and introduce a complete tariff scheme in the next Budget. He was afraid a Unionist Government would not have the courage to take this course.

On the constitution of the next Cabinet he said he presumed Balfour would be Premier; Austen, Chancellor; and Bonar Law, President of the Board of Trade. I asked him whether he thought this team would have the necessary driving power and he said it all depended on Balfour. He said he knew what the Government ought to do. In his judgment they should go to the country on licensing and the House of Lords. He looks forward to their Budget with apprehension and thinks they may do irreparable harm.

15 *December.*—I went to see Chamberlain on the 10th and talked to him about my recent discussions (*with Balfour*). I think he was reassured, but not quite satisfied. It was not likely he would be. He is pre-eminently a man of action. He decides first and finds reasons and methods afterwards. 'Statesmen,' he said, 'are all ignorant, they rely on others for information.' The subjects that interest Balfour and which in fact he wishes to know before making up his mind, have no charm for Chamberlain. He said that business men and the mass of the people did not know and never would know anything about them. I said 'you believe that the great things of the world are not done by the intellect; you decide first and then find reasons.' Chamberlain agreed with that and I said I thought I could find reasons for and against any course of action, but that a balancing of reasons would never lead one anywhere.

To something else he said, I replied, 'There is a great Providence in things,' and Chamberlain said: 'yes, there is' — a fine acquiescence from the dying statesman, for vigorous as his mind now is, his career is over and he is in fact dying. We went on to talk of more general subjects. He does not like these constant appeals to the interests of particular trades. I told him how I had laboured against it, how difficult it was to prevent and what impossible questions they wanted answered. He told me his experiences, particularly how difficult he had found it to answer a letter from a costermonger who inquired about the interest of that class. He said he had always thought it hard to deal with agriculture, because if one made out a case for it one went too far and made difficulties with the urban population. I told him of the neglect of the Empire in Tariff Reform speeches. He had noticed it. But this is the only question he cares for. He said that with the exception of Fielding he doubted whether Canada really cared about these treaties, and that when we granted Preference they would think no more about them.

Chamberlain viewed the prospects for Tariff Reform with some confidence.

CHAMBERLAIN TO DENISON

9 *November* 1908.—'Here our policy is making rapid way,' he wrote, 'and it is almost certain that we shall have a complete victory the next time an appeal is made to the country.' [1]

But beneath the mask, he chafed at his enforced retirement.

CHAMBERLAIN TO COLLINGS

4 *January* 1908.—Thanks for your kind wishes which I heartily reciprocate to you and yours. I wish I could be with you in your usual work. Meanwhile I am getting better and I keep my patience as well as I can.

VI

The struggle for Fiscal Reform now moved towards its climax. By 1909, the Liberal Government had bored the public and disappointed its supporters. No great reforms stood on the Statute Book to justify the vast ministerial majority. There was no Home Rule for the Irish; no startling measures of social progress for the Labour party. The hard core of Nonconformity were furious that Ministers had tamely accepted the rejection of their Education Bill. The brilliant group of Liberal Imperialists were dismayed by the failure of the Colonial Conference. And now trade turned traitor. The good years which had so far belied Chamberlain's prophecies declined into depression. Works were closed down. Unemployment rose. Everywhere, men began to ask, 'Was Joe right, after all?'

The weakness of the Government, the deteriorating economic situation, and the shock which Asquith's handling of the Colonial Conference had administered to Imperialist sentiment brought the Unionists to the point of decision. With Balfour, Austen, Bonar Law and Wyndham in the van, they declared for what was virtually the full Chamberlain programme. Balfour even began to encourage Jesse Collings' League for the establishment of a peasant proprietary.

Wyndham and Austen moved a strong Tariff Reform Amendment to the Address from the Opposition front bench.

GEORGE WYNDHAM TO HIS MOTHER

20 *February* 1909.—It is sixty and odd years since Disraeli, bidding farewell to Protection, said 'But the dark and inevitable hour will arrive'.

Yesterday, for the first time since then, an effective party made an effective fight, for that cause.

I am glad that I led the attack yesterday.

I led the attack yesterday. But Austen Chamberlain led it on Thursday and made a *very good* speech.

Arthur was very good in his philosophic way. To win in the country it is necessary to attack more directly the position of the Free Traders and to state facts and figures, which other speakers can use. It is that which puts up a fight all along the line.

The Government, of course, crushed the Opposition Amendment under the weight of their vast Parliamentary majority. But the fact that the Unionists were now united behind a constructive alternative to Liberalism and Socialism was soon felt in the constituencies. The tide at the by-elections now began to run strongly in favour of the Opposition.

Chamberlain viewed the situation with confidence, as we have seen. In a New Year's message to the Tariff Reform League he wrote:

It seems likely that the year 1909 will not pass away without a dissolution of Parliament, and it behoves tariff reformers everywhere to take stock of the present situation and to decide on their action in any circumstances. The progress made has been very satisfactory, and it is possible that a general election may lead to a change of Government. The present Administration of the country has been found out after a fair trial has been given to its policy. The recent by-elections have proved that a great change has come over the opinion of the country and show how little foundation there was for the exorbitant pretensions with which the Government assumed office. Their minatory legislation has proved to be ineffective, while they have nothing to meet an exceptional time of bad trade except the old policy which suited their forefathers, but which no longer meets the requirements of the present situation. Yet, while they obstinately cling to a retrograde policy of 60 years ago, they have no remedy to suggest for the evils which it has brought in its train. This has come home to the people of this country, as we may claim, largely owing to the efforts of the Tariff Reform League, and we have only to continue these efforts to ensure ultimate and speedy success.

Meanwhile, the Government must choose between the adoption of our policy, which they scorned when we offered it to them, and the humiliation which attends their continued clinging to office without power. We must pursue without ceasing our efforts to educate the people and be prepared to table our practical proposals the moment the opportunity arises.

By the middle of March, he could write to Denison:

I have real hope that now the greatest part of our labours are completed and that the future will only be the fulfilment of what we understood in the past.[1]

[1] J. C. to Denison, 19 March 1909.

In the Liberal camp, meanwhile, hesitation and anxiety reigned. The Government's Labour allies and their own left wing pressed for more social reform. But where were they to find the money? The Unionists had a plan for raising revenue. They had none.

The Gladstonian policy of retrenchment could be carried no further. It was at this point that the genius of Lloyd George came to the Government's rescue.

Hewins, as we saw, had noted that Chamberlain looked forward to Lloyd George's first 'Budget with apprehension and thinks they may do irreparable harm'.

He had some grounds for this. For some months the Press had made much of Lloyd George's: 'Next year I shall have to rob somebody's hen roost and I must consider where I can get most eggs and where I can get them easiest and where I shall be least punished.' The young tribune from Wales had found the answer to Chamberlain's great initiative. He could raise more revenue by soaking the rich than the Unionists ever could from import duties; and the appeal to class hatred could prove as strong, in peace time, as the appeal to national unity and Imperial sentiment. For the Liberals, as the traditional party of the middle classes, Lloyd George's policy was the first step towards political suicide. Nor did it offer any defence against the dangers threatening the National economy from abroad. It might appease the growing hunger for social reform, but it was powerless to defend the workers from cheap foreign competition and the resulting unemployment. But the Liberal leaders were in no position to weigh such long-term considerations. They were faced with a Unionist policy which, left to itself, would surely overwhelm them. They could not make the policy their own and go one better. They were too deeply committed to the doctrine of Free Trade. Lloyd George showed them the one means by which they might spike the Unionist guns and hold on to power. It was contrary to the interests which they represented but at least it involved no breach of Free Trade. Thus it happened that rather than touch the heresy of Protection, the Liberal leaders chose the alternative of Socialism.

Asquith opened the campaign on 11 December 1908. In a speech linking the forthcoming Budget with the prospect of a veto by the House of Lords which he forecast as 'the dominating issue in politics', Lloyd George took up the theme at Liverpool on 21 December. Churchill reiterated it at Birmingham on 13 January.

On 29 April, Lloyd George introduced the People's Budget

in a five-hour speech. It provided for a super tax, a land values tax, and a tax on unearned increment. In the event these measures raised surprisingly little revenue; but, whatever their financial worth, they were a political master stroke. Every landowner in the country from the magnate to the landlord of slum tenements, felt his property in danger. The whole middle class shrieked 'revolution'. So loud, indeed, were the cries and groans of the privileged that every tenant and working man could only draw the conclusion that the Government was the people's friend.

Chamberlain heard the news of Lloyd George's Budget with rueful admiration. He was in the south of France at the time, but at once decided to return to London, foregoing any idea of a further cure at Aix. He was stronger then than he had been. Just before leaving Cannes, he managed to walk 390 steps alone; and a few days after returning to London he climbed three flights of steps to visit Collings, ill in bed. For all that, he had begun to abandon hope of full recovery, and, in a telegram to the King, we find him using the phrase, 'whether or not I am permitted to take part again in public life'.[1]

King Edward, who had just inaugurated the new Birmingham University buildings, visited Chamberlain at Prince's Gardens on 19 July. He afterwards

told J.M. (Morley) that it was painful because of C.'s inability to *speak* plain, although his brain works easily. J.M. says that his ardent spirit should have gone to heaven in a chariot of fire and not in a bath chair.[2]

Chamberlain was no longer fit enough to play a public part in this critical year. But, behind the scenes, he would wield a powerful influence. Balfour and Lansdowne's first reaction to the budget was to oppose a rejection unless a popular movement arose for so doing. Chamberlain was the first to declare for uncompromising resistance to the budget. His ideas were taken up by Maxse in the *National Review* and by Garvin in the *Observer*. Garvin described Chamberlain's position in the following note

GARVIN TO NORTHCLIFFE

27 *May* 1909.—. . . more tragic than ever to see him and listen to his smothered words but more inspiring than ever to be in contact with his cool and resolute will. 'This budget tries to knock the House of Lords out of the constitution' — 'hope the Lords will knock it out!' — 'fear

[1] J. C. to King Edward VII, 8 July 1909.
[2] *Journals and Letters of Viscount Esher*, p. 396.

they won't; fear they will prove rather a cowardly lot' — 'dangerous?
yes but quite safe. If I were them I would do it. I wouldn't be afraid' —
. . . 'it is on the whole a bad budget; besides that *we don't like* these
people!' This last with a touch of the old sardonic emphasis which made
us shout with laughter. After all Joe was very much a man.

VII

Chamberlain spent the summer in England, dividing his time
between Prince's Gardens and Highbury. He was, as always, in
daily touch with Austen and his diary records frequent meetings
with Balfour, Bonar Law, Lansdowne, Milner and other Unionist
leaders. Balfour in particular called several times. These were no
mere courtesy visits but serious consultations on the tactics the
Unionists should adopt.

The main problem facing the Unionist leaders was how to meet
the challenge of Lloyd George's Budget. There were obvious
dangers in pressing the defence of vested interests too hard. On the
other hand, the big subscribers to Party funds, the landowners and
the local stalwarts, were up in arms against Lloyd George. The
Party managers were convinced that the leaders must act while
tempers were up.

AUSTEN TO MRS. CHAMBERLAIN

4 *September* 1909.—Alec Hood asked, 'Your father is in favour of a
fight, is he not? I thought of writing to him and then I thought I should
see you and I would not bother him.'

'Of course he is,' said I, 'strongly in favour of a fight and has been
so from the beginning.'

'Well,' said Alec, 'I'll tell you what I hear. All our people are spoiling
for a fight and will be disappointed if they don't get it. If there is no
fight we can't keep them at boiling point. All my reports say that there
have been no defections on account of this Budget but that if we allow
them time to bring in a *bribing* Budget next year, my agents won't answer
for the result.'

Chamberlain was all for a fight. He was anxious, however,
that it should be a fight for Tariff Reform rather than against the
Budget. His plan was that the Unionist leaders in the Commons
should publicly appeal to the House of Lords to throw out the Budget
and so force a General Election. The Peers would then be acting
not on their own initiative but in response to the appeal of democratic forces. With the Budget defeated, the Unionists would then
concentrate on their positive policy of Tariff Reform and seek a

mandate for it. They would fight the campaign on the issue of Tariff Reform against Socialism.

Chamberlain saw much of Garvin during the summer; and Garvin pressed Chamberlain's views in his article in the *Observer*. These continually stressed the contrast between Tariff Reform on the one hand and Socialist finance coupled with Naval decay on the other. Garvin argued for a positive alternative to the straight-forward opposition to Land Taxes which seemed both selfish and negative and played into the hands of the Liberals.

A Budget Protest league was formed under Long. To secure the widest possible support from Free Traders as well as Tariff Reform-ers, they made no mention of Tariff Reform in their programme. But their defence of vested interests led directly to Lloyd George's Limehouse speech and to a resurgence of Liberal confidence.

Garvin was alarmed by the demagogic appeal of the Limehouse speech and took up Chamberlain's position of rejecting the budget entirely on constitutional grounds. He pressed the argument upon Balfour who accepted it.[1]

Balfour, indeed, proposed to speak in Birmingham the week after Asquith if the Bingley Hall could be secured. [2]

Three days later he confirmed to Garvin that his policy was to be 'Tariff Reform — full steam ahead!'

The Bingley Hall was secured for 22 September. Chamberlain could not come to the meeting, but he drafted a resolution to be put to it embodying his plan. Balfour, however, still demurred at the idea of an appeal to the House of Lords.

AUSTEN TO MRS. CHAMBERLAIN

20 September 1909.—Please let father and Neville see the following: I did not submit the draft resolution to Balfour but Councillor Brooks sent it to Alec Hood for his approval.

Hood was afraid that the reference to the House of Lords would be interpreted as Balfour signalling to Lansdowne and the Lords, would be bad for Lansdowne and the Lords and perhaps not good for the Party.

Balfour also took this view though he holds that there is 'only one policy for us', and thinks that if the Lords did not reject the Bill, he could not continue to lead the Party.

Balfour's idea of his speech is to say nothing directly of the Lords, but to say that those who think we can go on in the old financial ways are in a fool's paradise, there must be a great departure either towards Socialism or to Tariff Reform. This Budget is Socialism, the alternative

---

[1] *The Observer and J. L. Garvin* by Alfred Gollin, pp. 113–116.
[2] Balfour to Garvin, 10 August 1909.

is Tariff Reform. The people must choose between them. Is this as claimed the poor man's Budget or is Tariff Reform the real poor man's Budget? and so forth — always contrasting the Budget and Tariff Reform.

I felt I could not insist on the resolution as originally drafted in face of Hood and Balfour and the Conservatives on the Joint Committee and accordingly have agreed to one running somewhat as follows :

'This meeting — recognising that the Budget is intended to postpone indefinitely the policy of Tariff Reform — expresses its determined adherence to that policy as the necessary means for increasing employment at home and strengthening the Empire at large and condemns the Budget as not merely unjust to individuals but injurious to national trade and policy.'

Father will, I know, regret the appeal to the House of Lords, but I think we shall get in exchange a good T.R. speech and resolution.

I was afraid that A.J.B. would object to the 'Lords' if he heard of it. He is very anxious not to appear to dictate.

Balfour might not be prepared to appeal publicly to the Lords; but Chamberlain was determined to make his view known. He accordingly sent a message which was read out by the chairman and set the keynote for the whole Unionist party.

Your meeting to-night is our first answer to the latest of the attacks on the Unionist citadel. The final answer will be given when the Government is at last obliged to appeal to the country — (hear, hear) — and you again return seven members pledged to the Birmingham policy of union, Tariff Reform — (applause) — and social progress. (Hear, hear.)

The citizens of Birmingham have always been democratic, and in the present case I think they are likely to support any attempt to get the present controversy referred to the people, who in the last resort ought to decide between us and the Government. (Hear, hear.) I hope the House of Lords will see their way to force a general election. (Applause.) I do not doubt in this case what the answer will be.

The Prime Minister seeks to represent the Budget as an advantage to working men. But I have looked at it carefully and I cannot take this view. It is the last effort of Free Trade finance to find a substitute for Tariff Reform and imperial preference, and it is avowedly intended to destroy the Tariff Reform movement.

Personally, I am of opinion that Tariff Reform is necessary to remedy our present want of employment — (hear, hear) — and I do not believe that without it we can do any good. The Budget will supply us with money, but at the same time will deprive us of work, and I think it is work, even more than money, of which we stand in need. (Cheers.)

Mr. Asquith admits that Tariff Reform is the only alternative. It is, therefore, between the Budget and Tariff Reform that you have to choose — Tariff Reform which assists trade, increases employment, and secures a fair contribution to our revenue from foreigners using our markets — (hear, hear) — and the Budget which exempts the foreigner from all contribution — (*shame*) — whilst casting fresh burdens on our trade, hampering our industries, and taxing the commonest comforts of our people.

Balfour's speech was a powerful plea for Tariff Reform, the strongest he had yet delivered on that theme. He did not appeal to the House of Lords, but he made it clear that he wanted a General Election at the earliest opportunity. Chamberlain heard the speech at Highbury over 'electrophonic receivers' installed for the occasion by the *Daily Mail*.

Balfour stayed the night at Highbury so that he could have 'a good chat' with Chamberlain. He was most anxious for Chamberlain's approval and on sitting down after his speech turned to Mrs. Chamberlain and asked 'do you think Joe will be satisfied?' 'Joe was', Mrs. Chamberlain later wrote to her mother and reported Chamberlain as saying 'on thinking it over I have come to the conclusion that Balfour played up very well'.[1] Afterwards, Chamberlain received a correspondent from the *Daily Mail* and, in the course of commenting on Balfour's speech, took the opportunity to rub in his views on the action the House of Lords should take.

Mr. Balfour placed clearly the separate merits of Tariff Reform, such as we conceive it, and Free Trade finance — that is to say, Socialist finance such as the Government propose.

There will be no more *talk* about the House of Lords after this speech. I think they are sure to *act*.

As the House of Lords is the only body now that can refer the matter to the people, I think the House of Lords will do it.

It has been a truly great event. I regard this speech as making history. It is the most important utterance we have yet had.

Chamberlain and Balfour might differ on the way in which the House of Lords should be drawn into the situation. But they were in full agreement on fundamentals. Both wanted to fight the campaign on the positive policy of Tariff Reform rather than on a mere opposition to the Budget. Chamberlain's view on this point emerges clearly from the following letter, written a few days after Balfour's speech.

CHAMBERLAIN TO HENNIKER HEATON

27 *September* 1909: *Private.*—. . . I hold with you that too much stress has been laid upon the Finance Bill and we ought not as prudent men to confuse the agitation about it with that about Tariff Reform. I do not think we can notice any difference in the latter agitation, and I am

[1] Mrs. Chamberlain to her mother, 25 September 1909.

inclined to go back to it. I hold with you that that is our best course and that we ought not to lay stresss upon the Finance Bill at all events at the present time.

I am advised to keep free from all political & public affairs at the present time and I do not therefore wish to take an active part in them, but I send you word for your own information of my private view. I do not think we can avoid a contest now even if we wished to which I do not, and I think if our people stick to Tariff Reform & drop altogether the Finance Bill we shall find that the public is with us in the course of the general election.

Garvin approached Chamberlain with a proposal to encourage Liberal defection by attracting Rosebery's support in opposition to the budget and in defence of the House of Lords. He drew a pungent reply.

CHAMBERLAIN TO GARVIN

8 *October* 1909.—. . . I do not feel that we shall get any help from Rosebery or Lord St. Aldwyn or any of the other weak-kneed politicians. They do not like to fight but I think they cannot avoid it . . . on the subject of Rosebery, I may be wrong but his past career does not lead me to expect much of him.

Parliament met again in October for an autumn session and the time approached when the Finance Bill would go before the Lords. To reject and force an election was the obvious move if only there was a certainty that a Unionist Government would be returned. But what if the gamble failed? What if the people stood by the Government? None could doubt that the Liberals would then proceed to curb the powers and perhaps change the composition of the Upper House. As the critical time approached, doubts began to grow in some sections of the Unionist party. Even Balfour seems to have had a moment of hesitation. Was it right to use the House of Lords as a pawn in Chamberlain's game? To risk the whole structure of the British Constitution just to advance Tariff Reform?

In these critical autumn days, Chamberlain exercised effective leadership over the Unionist party for the last time. For about six weeks, Highbury was again the Unionist centre of gravity. Balfour went there for consultations on 20 October.

MRS. CHAMBERLAIN TO HER MOTHER

22 *October* 1909.—Mr. Balfour is perturbed in his mind for he cannot make out their game (*i.e.* the Liberals) whether they want an election at once or in January.

Balfour was followed in the next few weeks by the leaders of the House of Lords, Lansdowne, Milner, Curzon and Roberts.

As the crunch drew near Chamberlain moved to London to play his part.

17 *November* 1909.—We have had frequent guests and Joe has talked extremely well most of the time. Joe was more optimistic of the result than most people . . . 'we should be in a very different position in the House'.

All Chamberlain's influence over the leaders of the Unionist party and over the Unionist Press was thrown into the scales to force the election. His view prevailed. On 30 November, the Lords rejected the Budget.

A General Election was now inevitable and a few days later, Mrs. Sidney Webb wrote in her diary:

20 *December* 1909.—We are all awaiting breathlessly the issue of the great battle. The progressives of all shades are in mind united, however Labour and Liberal party exigencies may make them fight among themselves in particular cases. To the outside observer, it is amazing that the Lords should have dared democratic feeling at one and the same time on the political and economic side ! Those who have led them, men of the type of Hewins, Milner, Garvin, Curzon (encouraged by the old politician of Highbury), have apparently relied on the ignorance and snobbish prejudice of the non-political elector — the man *without social purpose* of any kind — the reader of the *Daily Mail* and *Express* intent only on keeping all he has, and leading his life undisturbed by social obligations.

Chamberlain seems, by this time, to have abandoned hope of fully recovering his health. 'I suppose we shall [have] a strenuous fight during the next few months,' he wrote to Dowson

but I am very sanguine, and although I can no longer look forward to taking a prominent part in the battle and holding my own in the forefront of the contest I am still as hopeful as ever.[1]

He maintained his candidature for West Birmingham, however, and by a pleasant courtesy on the part of the Government leaders, was not opposed.

There could be no speeches now, but he opened his campaign with a manifesto issued to the National Press and widely distributed as a pamphlet.

When His Majesty's Ministers and their supporters came to the belated conclusion that the House of Lords meant business, they changed their

[1] J. C. to Dowson. 2 December 1909.

tune. They have since endeavoured to convince themselves and others that the action of the Lords was unconstitutional and unwise. They have shown it to be their object to fight the coming contest upon a false issue, and not upon the policy of tariff reform, which has made its evident impression upon the country, and which they desire to put aside.

It is our duty and interest to prevent this very obvious attempt to shift the ground. We know that for us it is intended to mean no advantage. Tariff reform is the only alternative to the Budget. It is the only policy dreaded by the authors of the Budget. This is now generally recognized. Nothing would be more satisfactory to our opponents than to put this issue altogether aside by raising new disputes to distract the mind of the electorate.

Consider what is the alternative. The supporters of the Government would sweep away all the constitutional usefulness of a Second Chamber. Apparently they intend to attempt the practical destruction of the House of Lords, and not its genuine amendment. I need not say that any proposal of this kind is not likely to find favour with any sensible man. There is, on the contrary, a feeling that the Lords, in demanding that the whole question shall be submitted to the electorate, are acting within their powers, and much to the advantage of the constituencies themselves.

If the vote at the coming elections were given in favour of the Budget, not only would the new system of finance be accepted and extended in the future, but the House of Lords would be relegated to a position of impotence in face of the House of Commons. Once for all, the people of this country would find out that a chance majority of the House of Commons might at any time impose upon them its own ideas against the national will.

In that sense this election may fairly be described as a national crisis. Two things, then, have clearly to be decided.

In the first place, we have to determine once for all whether, in disregard of the experience of our own flesh and blood elsewhere throughout the English-speaking world, we, above all nations, can do without a Second Chamber. I do not think that our people are prepared for such a change as this, and I believe that a House of Commons entirely uncontrolled would be a great public danger. It would be much worse than the House of Lords, which, just because it is a hereditary Chamber, must depend for its whole strength and influence upon its success in interpreting the true mind of the people.

The second point is whether tariff reform is now to become the basis of our fiscal system, or whether Cobdenism — especially as regards the freedom of foreign imports from all taxation, while heavier burdens are laid upon our own trade — is to be considered the final principle. The new demands made by the Budget are having their natural effect. Our people must find means of providing for the fresh requirements that every day are pressing more hardly upon them. The time has surely come for the tariff policy, which would promote British trade and welfare, instead of the Budget policy, which in every respect would surrender our interests and our security to foreign rivals. It is better to abolish Cobdenism and not the Constitution; to pull down free imports and foreign privilege in our market and not the Second Chamber, whose only offence is in giving the nation a chance to speak for itself. Let the workers defend their work and stand by the Peers, who in this case are standing by them. If the issue of tariff reform were submitted by itself there would be no doubt whatever of the reply.

He followed this up with an election address and a number of letters of support sent to Tariff Reform candidates up and down the country. Beyond these, he made only one major intervention in the campaign. It arose in this way.

At the height of the struggle, Sandars received the following telegram from Balfour, then in Scotland.

BALFOUR TO SANDARS

13 *January* 1910 (telegram).—I think you must be prepared for Radical placards tomorrow or Saturday alleging that I mean to tax food of people perversion of yesterday's speech.

Sandars consulted with one of the Party managers and wrote as follows to Chamberlain.

SANDARS TO CHAMBERLAIN

13 *January* 1910.—Mr. Balfour, whom I only left this afternoon, spoke, as you know, at York last night and dealt with Food Taxation.

He sends me the enclosed telegram this evening. Mr. Percival Hughes and I have been considering the more effective method of dealing with this 11th hour perversion of our case, and we submit the following suggestion for your consideration, viz.—

That a *very brief* statement should be issued tomorrow (Friday) afternoon on the subject of Food taxation — something to the effect that the cost of living of the working classes will not be increased under Tariff Reform ; and that to this statement *your name and Mr. Balfour's should be appended.*

If this idea meets with your approval would you dictate a telegram (my messenger will dispatch it) with the suggestion and the form of words to Mr. Balfour at Escrick Park, York — and I will arrange for the communication by him to me in London : and this in time for all the London papers in anticipation of the Saturday Pollings.

Pray forgive me for troubling you but we are advised that the Government are making a desperate effort at *the last moment* to recover their lost ground.

Chamberlain at once telegraphed the necessary message to Balfour.

Tariff reform will not increase the cost of living of the working classes nor the proportion of taxation paid by them ; but it will enable us to reduce the present food taxes and will lessen unemployment and develop our trade with the British Dominions beyond the seas.

Balfour substituted the phrase 'articles of working class consumption' for 'present food taxes', and, with this alteration, the
message was issued in his and Chamberlain's name.

Chamberlain was declared re-elected on 15 January, being thus
the first member of the New Parliament. The Unionists held all
the Birmingham seats with increased majorities, though Austen
only scraped in with a majority of five.

We catch something of Chamberlain's mood as the results were
coming in, from the following letters:

MRS. CHAMBERLAIN TO ERNEST MARTINEAU[1]

15 January 1910.—We are anxiously waiting tonight's returns. I shall
be glad when they come and the first stage is over for the strain is great
for your uncle. He has been working more than at any time since his
illness and is rather tired, but he is full of hope and confidence.

If only he were not so inundated with applications for messages to
candidates and endless correspondence it would be a comfort.

MRS. CHAMBERLAIN TO LORD ROBERTS

20 January 1910.—It is an anxious moment still and he is unfortunately
less sanguine as to the final result of this Election now than when you
lunched with us but while he is disappointed that the big towns have
not declared more emphatically in favour of Tariff Reform he is losing
no faith in its ultimate victory — only it will not come quite so soon as
he hoped.

Birmingham was splendid, and we have done very well in the Midlands, and have won some good victories elsewhere, so there is no need
to be discouraged. One wishes the people were better informed as to
the real state of affairs and their danger instead of being so easily led
away by the campaign of misrepresentation, not to use a stronger word,
which is led by responsible Ministers of the Crown, who ought to have
greater respect for their high offices.

Mr. Chamberlain appreciates very much your co-operation in making
Tariff Reform the main issue — and feels sure that was right. As you
know he is in sympathy with you on the question of National Defence
and has admired the way in which you have brought it forward and
advocated it. He is convinced that it is absolutely right, but he feels
that it must be of gradual growth, for constituted as we are the Navy
has to come first. One wishes that on that subject the people could see
the peril we are in danger of.

When all this turmoil is over I hope all who love their country and
realise the risks it is running will set to work to open the eyes of the
ignorant and rouse the apathetic. Both the policy of Tariff Reform and
Imperial Unity, and National Defence are really bound together — and
I pray for England that she may understand it before it is too late.

[1] Chamberlain's nephew and Election Agent.

In the country as a whole, the Unionists made steady progress;
but in Scotland and Lancashire there was no swing in their favour.
The final results were:

Liberals	275
Labour	40
Irish Nationalists	82

Unionists	273

The only analysis of the result made by Chamberlain which has
survived, is in the following letter. It is rather surprising for its
complacency.

CHAMBERLAIN TO DENISON

18 *February* 1910.—You must remember that we are a slow going people
and do not make up our minds to change as quickly as our critics. I
think on the whole the last election was all that we could expect, and
that the time is certainly coming when Tariff Reform will be the policy
of the masses. I have been told that in Scotland the cause of the failure
is what you say. The people of Scotland are opposed to the Lords,
and whenever there is a question about them they give their vote against
them. In Lancashire of course the feeling is one of self interest and the
welfare of the Cotton Trade is assumed to be bound up with Free Trade,
but this I think will not last long and I shall be very surprised if there is
not a considerable change before very long.

Meanwhile we must wait patiently. The tendency of our people is
in favour of a change though they may be content to wait longer than I
like, but the incidents connected with this election are favourable to
greater progress in the future, and I am well satisfied although I wish
we had more to tell.

In public Chamberlain continued to strike an optimistic note. In
a press interview given just after the election results had come in
(January 1910) he declared:

I should think that Mr. Asquith must have gone away very cross with
his people . . . they told him they were going to sweep the country with
the budget, but now he is dependent on the Irish. He will find them hard
taskmasters but he won't give them Home Rule. He will get out of it
somehow.[1]

Looking back this sounds like whistling in the dark. And yet
many Liberals were in the mood of something like despair at the
thought of selling out to the Irish or the Labour group. It seemed
for a time as if both Asquith and Grey would refuse to accept such
a choice.

[1] *Joseph Chamberlain* by Peter Fraser, p. 296.

On 10 February, Redmond laid down the terms on which the Irish would continue to give the government their support. He insisted that the Lords be deprived of their power of veto. Asquith's speech on the address was a compromise. He explained that he had not sought any guarantees from the King. The Irish reacted violently and the Labour ranks showed hesitation. It seems likely that the uneasy alliance between Liberal, Labour and Irish was only held together by the activities of the Whip's office.

For a few days power still seemed within the grasp of the Unionists. But once the debate on the address was past a grimmer situation was revealed. The Liberal strength it is true was now no greater than the Unionist. But the Trade Union vote had been firmly riveted to the Liberal cause by the People's Budget. The Irish Nationalists, too, could only hope for Home Rule from a Liberal Government. Asquith could thus count on a majority of more than a hundred provided he pursued the paths of Socialism and Irish Home Rule.

Chamberlain's gamble on the House of Lords had failed. There was a new issue now — 'the Peers against the People' — and it would overshadow Tariff Reform, and much else for a time.

Looking back, Sandars would write:

> The great unpopularity of many of them (*i.e.* the measures of the Radical Government), driven home by Balfour and his followers, might have ultimately destroyed the Government, but the Budget of 1909 had a specious attraction for the ignorant, and Balfour must share with Chamberlain (whose age and illness made him impatient) the responsibility for the unwise decision to have it rejected by the Lords.

But this was hindsight. At the time, the Unionist leaders thought that power was still within their grasp.

VIII

Chamberlain returned to London on 4 February. The election had tired him and he knew now that his health would not return. Mrs. Asquith, who went to see him a week later, recorded their meeting in her diary.[1]

> 10 *February* 1910.—I was welcomed on my arrival by the lovely Mrs. Chamberlain and found her husband sitting erect in his arm-chair near the tea-table; his hair was black and brushed, and he had an orchid in his tightly-buttoned frock coat.

---

[1] *Autobiography of Margot Asquith*, part ii, p. 133.

The room we were shown into was furnished in early Pullman-car or late North-German–Lloyd style, and struck me as singularly undistinguished.

My host's speech was indistinct but his mind was alert. After greeting him with a deep inside pity and much affection, I asked him if he had been pleased with the results of the General Election. I added that I myself had been disappointed with the South, but that the North had gone well for us; to which he answered that he had expected to beat us, and wondered why Scotland was always so Liberal. I amused him by saying that we were an uninfluenceable race with an advanced middle class, superior to the aristocracy and too clever to be taken in by Tariff Reform, and added:

'You know, Mr. Chamberlain, I would not much care to be a Unionist today!'

Mistaking my tone for one of triumph, he said:

'But you also have great difficulties ahead of you.'

I explained that I meant that the Protectionist party could not feel any satisfaction at being led by Arthur Balfour, as he had never been one of them. To which he replied:

'He is coming on a little, but the truth is he never understood anything at all about the question.'

Continuing upon our Cabinet, he said of one of them, pointing to his heart:

'He is a vulgar man in the worst sense of the word and will disappear; give him enough rope and he will hang himself; I admire nothing in a man like that. Winston is the cleverest of all the young men, and the mistake Arthur made was letting him go.'

I indicated that, however true this might be, he was hated by his old Party; to which he replied:

'They would welcome him today with open arms if he were to return to them.'

We ended our talk by his telling me that he had always been a Home Ruler, and that nothing could be done till the difficulties in Ireland were settled.

Wanting to show some of the compassion I felt for him, I told him before leaving that I also had had a nervous break-down, and added:

'You know, Mr. Chamberlain, I was *so* ill that I thought I was *done*', to which he answered:

'Better to *think* it, Mrs. Asquith, than to *know* it as I do.'

I never saw him again.

Balfour, who lunched with Chamberlain a few days later, seems to have found him 'very unintelligible'. He told Esher of their conversation and left the impression on him that Chamberlain was absolutely paralytic and it is inconceivable that his brain power should not correspond in a great degree to the physical condition in which he finds himself.[1]

---

[1] *Journals and Letters of Viscount Esher*, p. 451.

This impression of Chamberlain's health is much at variance with other contemporary accounts. It may be that Chamberlain was off colour that day. Alternatively, Balfour may have been irritated at the election results and inclined to blame Chamberlain's programme of food taxes for the Unionist defeat. There was, however, general surprise, when, on 16 February, Chamberlain appeared at the House of Commons to take the oath. He came into the Chamber from behind the Speaker's chair supported on either side by Austen and Morpeth and took his seat on the front Opposition bench. He took the oath seated and, after Austen had signed the roll on his behalf, touched the pen to indicate his assent. He then shook hands with the Speaker, and went out as he had come in. Three days later he left for the south of France.

The Unionists met Parliament in high spirits. Their members now filled the whole of the Opposition side of the House. Gone were the days when the Liberals could rely on their crushing majority to steam-roller any opposition. On the contrary, the growing demands of their Irish and Labour allies opened a prospect of the Government's early defeat.

The Unionist front bench, with the enthusiastic support of the Whip's office and the whole party, took the initiative and tabled a Tariff Reform amendment to the King's Speech. Most of the Irish abstained; and the Government's majority slumped dramatically. Austen reported next day:[1]

AUSTEN TO MRS. CHAMBERLAIN

25 *February* 1910.—*Tempora mutantur!*

13 *March* 1906.—The Free Trade Resolution was carried in the new House of Commons by 474 to 98.

24 *February* 1910.—The Tariff Reform Resolution is beaten in another new House by only 31 votes — 285 to 254.

Congratulations to father!

In a newspaper interview just after the election (7 February 1910), Chamberlain had been asked:

'Would you have the Government out within six months if you were in the House of Commons?' He had replied with a broad smile, 'Well, I'd try.'

The threatening attitude of the Irish towards the Government now suggested that the chance might come in the first few weeks of the Parliament. Churchill seems to have felt that the Liberals would have to resign in 'a few weeks'.[2]

---

[1] Austen Chamberlain, *Politics from the Inside*, p. 204.

[2] Austen Chamberlain, *Politics from the Inside*, p. 208.

Chamberlain's view was that the Unionists should seize any opportunity to bring down the Government. They should then form a minority administration, bring in a full-blooded Tariff Reform Budget and go to the country to seek a popular mandate for it. He pressed this course insistently on Austen. His messages have not survived, but we catch the drift of his advice plainly enough from the following extracts from Austen's replies:

AUSTEN TO MRS. CHAMBERLAIN

25 *February* 1910.—We were in a majority in the House today for a long time during the discussion on hops and it was quite uncertain, even when we divided, who had a majority, so that many of us were kept back in the lobby till it was clear that the Government forces had come up, and only voted when it was clear that we should not put them out.

We might perhaps beat them on Monday by the aid of Irish or Radical malcontents on the question of taking the time of the House; but in spite of your advice that we should get them out at the first moment and on any question, we all feel that this would not do now and that you yourself if here would not advise it at this moment. The situation changes from day to day and from moment to moment. It is extraordinarily difficult and complicated and I quite believe that from your post of observation at Cannes, and with your mind filled with the pictures of things as they were a fortnight or a week ago, you will think us wrong. But all this brings discredit on the Government and discouragement to the Radical Party, and if we do beat them on the Budget that may be the *coup de grâce*. At any rate it would be a tremendous triumph for us and make their attack on the Lords a glaring absurdity. A General Election in June or July would suit us best. August we must strive our hardest to avoid, as so many of our supporters are away from home and cannot be brought back.

27 *February* 1910.—I have ever before me the thought that 'he who will not while he may, when he will, he shall have nay'. But to defeat the Government on a by-issue and to take office in such a situation would be suicidal. From the moment of the change the fortunes of the Radicals, which are now on the down-grade, would begin to mend, and we should be discredited before we had any real power. It would be April before we could dissolve and late May or June before we could set to work at our offices even if victorious (which under such circumstances I do not think we should be) and a Tariff Reform Budget cannot, in spite of all Hewins may say, be produced at a moment's notice.

It will not do therefore to defeat the Government on a side-issue. We must take the risks of delay — the risk, that is, of their coming together again, finding some *modus vivendi* between the warring sections of the majority and carrying both Budget and Veto Bill through the House of Commons.

5 *March* 1910.—Many thanks for your letter of the 3rd received today. I was very glad to get Father's comments, and find myself very much in agreement with them. If we could have turned the Government out on hops (which I do not think that we could) we ought to have done so, and it was a mistake even to hesitate about it, though on that Friday no one would have been more pleased at defeat than the Government itself. It was then more probable than not that there would be either resignation of the whole Government or of a section of it before Monday. It was only on Saturday that the different sections of the Government came to terms and resolved all to hang together.

Except on Friday we never came near to defeating them — never had a chance of it, I mean — and if there was ever a chance on Friday it would only have been by a snap division, i.e. by passing round word to our men to stop the debate while the discussion was still in full flow.

And what a mess we should have been in after all ! We could not have dissolved ; we could not even have adjourned whilst the new ministers were being re-elected, for there is not a day to spare between now and Easter if the necessary financial business is to be done, and we should have had to leave the House sitting in charge of Under-Secretaries.

No, I don't see how it could have been done. There has never been quite such a complicated situation before.

Chamberlain continued to press his views on Austen, and, in three long talks, on Balfour who had also been ordered to Cannes by his doctors. His arguments seem to have had some effect and on 9 March, Austen wrote that the chief Tariff Reformers were now unanimous in wishing to get the Government out on any 'fair issue'. But the psychological moment had passed. Asquith had reached a *modus vivendi* with his allies. Chamberlain always felt the Unionists had missed a chance. Looking back more than a year later, he would say :

After the election which followed the defeat of the Budget, we had an improvement in our position to the tune of a hundred seats. They (the Government) were a good deal discouraged by this and were in difficulties with the Irish. We ought to have got them on the run and kept them on the run. Instead of that we left them alone and treated them with too much consideration ; and, by degrees, they recovered their tone and established themselves in a strong position.[1]

One other aspect of this difference between Chamberlain and the Unionist leadership deserves our attention. The rank and file of the party, in the House and in the constituencies, were dispirited by what they looked on as a lost opportunity. This feeling that they had been badly led produced a revival of criticism against Balfour. Balfour's health that spring provided the smoking-room

[1] H. F. Wilson. Note of a conversation with Chamberlain, 16 July 1911.

with a good excuse for discussing the succession to the leadership. Chamberlain had some echo of all this from Collings.

COLLINGS TO MRS. CHAMBERLAIN

20 *March* 1910.—. . . There have been rumours about Balfour's health . . . and questions are often asked who is there to take his place if unfortunately he found himself unable to go on. In cases when such a question is put to me I have by a process of exhaustion led my questioners to the conclusion that there is no one so fit as Austen for the reversion. They . . . seem to take to the idea which I hope will quietly spread.

THE BITTER END

(*March* 1910–*July* 1914)

Chamberlain's Advice to King George V — The Constitutional Conference —
Food Taxes and the Referendum — The General Election — Laurier Signs the
Reciprocity Treaty — His Defeat — The Reform of the House of Lords —
Chamberlain Backs Halsbury — 'Balfour Must Go' — Austen Stands Down —
Amalgamation of Liberal Unionists and Conservatives — Bonar Law Abandons
Tariff Reform — Chamberlain Decides not to Stand Again — 'This Means
War' — Death of Chamberlain.

I

ON 7 May, while Chamberlain was still at Cannes, King Edward
died. Austen wrote to Mrs. Chamberlain suggesting that his
father should send a letter of condolence to the new King:

and Father in writing such a letter would naturally be led to speak of the
King and Queen's special knowledge of the Empire, and of what that
means both to them and to the nation.[1]

This sentence led Chamberlain to make a remarkable proposal.
Seen in the light of King George's subsequent services to the Empire,
it may well have been of decisive influence.

CHAMBERLAIN TO KING GEORGE V

22 *May* 1910.—With my humble duty I beg to acknowledge with
thanks Your Majesty's gracious enquiries to my son, when he had the
honour of seeing Your Majesty.

We are shortly coming home as the spring is nearly over here, &
there are now very few English at Cannes. The weather has been fine,
although it seems to have been a short season.

I have had Your Majesty & The Queen much in my thoughts
during the last two weeks, & the new responsibilities which have come
to you since your Father's lamented death.

The world is much occupied with our new Monarch, & I have made
up my mind that Your Majesty will carry on the family tradition, &
although I may not live to see it you will be like your Father, & your
Grandmother, a great King.

To be this you must take a different line from that which gained the

[1] Austen to Mrs. Chamberlain, 17 May 1910.

late King his reputation, & which worthily obtained for him the title of the great Pacificator. No one has yet made himself the Symbol of the Empire as a whole, & Your Majesty has travelled more than any Monarch that has preceded you, & in the distant Dominions across the Seas I think that this is appreciated & I am sure that you are felt to be in a special sense their King.

I do not doubt that in this capacity you will represent the Empire, & not the Kingdom only. In such a representation you will be further developing the influence of the Crown, & you will be the first King of England who has had the opportunity of showing special interest in your Dominions across the Seas. Every day they are becoming more influential, & such a position has never had the importance that it has to-day. Whoever occupies it will be at least the equal of the Kings who have gone before.

I humbly wish Your Majesty success in the great future which is now before you.

KING GEORGE V TO CHAMBERLAIN

26 *May* 1910.—I am deeply grateful to you for your kind & sympathetic letter on the irreparable loss which I have experienced, for you know how devoted I was to my dear Father. I am much touched at your saying that the Queen & I had been in your thoughts during these last sad weeks. It will be my earnest endeavour to justify what you so kindly forecast that I will carry on the Family traditions & try to follow in the footsteps of my dear Father & of Queen Victoria. I entirely agree with what you say that I must take a different line to that which gained the King his great reputation as 'Peacemaker'. Indeed it has always been my dream to identify myself with the great idea of Empire & having visited practically every part of the Dominions beyond the Seas & had personal proofs of their loyalty to the Throne & love for the Mother Country, I shall ever strive to consolidate & bind together these vast & rapidly developing Nations under the Crown. We *must* all realize that our interests are not merely confined to these small islands in the North Sea. I hope your health has improved during your stay in the South & that on your return home I may have an opportunity of paying you a visit in London. With many kind messages to Mrs. Chamberlain & Austen & with renewed thanks for your letter. . . .

The King would be true to this conception and purpose to his last words and dying breath.

Chamberlain returned to London on 28 May in the best of spirits. On 3 June, he received a visit from ex-President Roosevelt. Spring-Rice, who saw him the same evening, wrote down his comments on the new King and the American leader :[1]

3 *June* 1910.—I also saw old Chamberlain. The old lion said, 'He will be a Great King and I know it. Roosevelt has turned us all topside

[1] *Letters and Friendships of Sir Cecil Spring-Rice.*

2 I

down; he has enjoyed himself hugely and I must say, by the side of our statesmen, looks a little bit taller, bigger and stronger. I am not sure he doesn't look the right thing. Our statesmen looked the wrong one — some of them.'

The Liberal Government, smarting from the rejection of the People's Budget by the House of Lords, were determined to cut down the powers of the peerage and substitute a delaying power for the power of veto then enjoyed. If necessary, they would ask the King to create enough new peers to give them an assured majority in the Upper House. What should the King do if confronted with such a request? There was no precedent to guide the new and still inexperienced Sovereign. His father had reached no decision. His private secretaries — Knollys and Bigge — took different views. The King explained his embarrassment frankly to the Prime Minister. Asquith now recurred to an earlier proposal that the Liberal and Unionist leaders should call a truce and try to settle their differences at a private conference. The Liberal Cabinet were inclined to accept and Balfour was not unfavourable.

King George himself called the next afternoon and spent more than an hour at Prince's Gardens. The Chamberlain papers merely record that the 'talk was intimate and ranged over many subjects, especially the Empire'. The following letter, however, suggests that this visit — and that of Knollys next day — were also concerned with gathering Chamberlain's views on the King's position in the growing Constitutional crisis.

GARVIN TO NORTHCLIFFE

13 *June* 1910.—But there is something else that as yet I don't know, the King must have moved almost at the last hour. How and why? I don't yet know. I lunched with Chamberlain upon his return from Cannes on Wednesday June 1st he was flatly against the conference policy. I explained it fully to him and showed that I have carefully thought out all the possibilities and had two strings to my bow. He was at length largely converted. On the following Saturday afternoon there was an interview between the King and Chamberlain. Hawkin thinks that at that interview something happened. The King already knew the sentiments of the majority of the Cabinet. Our leaders were dispersed in all directions and had made no sign for Thursday evening June 2. Sandars met Esher and told him rather to Esher's surprise that if the Crown moved, Mr. Balfour would feel it his duty to respond. If Chamberlain said the same speaking in his own person that may very well have settled the business.[1]

[1] Garvin's letter reproduced on p. 195 of Alfred Gollin's *The Observer and J. L. Garvin*, dates the Garvin/Chamberlain lunch as 14 June. The Chamberlain Diaries suggest that this is a faulty transcription for 1 June.

The Constitutional Conference, as it came to be called, met for the first time on 16 June. Its members were Asquith, Lloyd George, Birrell and Crewe for the Liberals; Balfour, Austen Chamberlain, Lansdowne and Cawdor for the Unionists. Chamberlain was kept informed by Austen of what was passing; and his diary shows that he continued in close touch with other Unionist leaders throughout the summer and autumn.

The starting-point of the Conference was the conflict between the two Houses of Parliament which had arisen over the 1909 Budget. The Unionists were prepared to accept most of the Liberal demands for cutting down the powers of the peers. But on one point they would not yield. They insisted that the House of Lords should retain enough powers to defeat another Home Rule Bill. This was a limitation the Liberals could never accept. Had they done so, they would have lost their Irish allies and with them their Parliamentary majority.

One bold, imaginative attempt was made to break the deadlock. It was made by Lloyd George. With the knowledge and at any rate partial approval of his principal colleagues he proposed the formation of a Coalition to carry out an agreed policy involving major concessions by both sides. The Liberals would be asked to agree to a strong Navy, a measure of compulsory military service, the immediate grant of Preference on existing duties and the appointment of a Commission to advise within six months on what further Duties it might be in the interest of the Empire to impose. In return, the Unionists were to accept a reduction in the powers of the House of Lords, a system of devolution or Home Rule All Round — 'something on your father's lines' Lloyd George described it to Austen [1] —, the disestablishment of the Welsh Church and certain changes in the Education Act.

Lloyd George did not bring this great transaction before the Constitutional Conference. He and Churchill explained it privately first to F. E. Smith, and then to Balfour and Garvin. It was not a firm proposal and Balfour only passed on the broadest summary of it to his colleagues and it was some time before Austen discovered the exact terms. His natural inclination — and we may guess his father's — was to favour a deal which would bring about the two major policies of the Chamberlain family, Imperial Preference and Home Rule All Round. But the proposal bristled with difficulties. How far was Lloyd George speaking for his colleagues? How

[1] *Politics from the Inside*, p. 292.

would the new proposals affect the Reform of the House of Lords? What would be the division of spoils in the new Coalition Government? Above all, would the Unionist party agree to the new design?

F. S. Oliver broached the idea of Home Rule All Round at both Highbury and Whittingham early in October. According to his report to Garvin, (17 November 1910) he made only a slight impression. Garvin backed up his efforts but received in reply a series of questions suggesting hostility to the scheme.

Garvin had also written to Austen on the same subject (20 October 1910). Here the seeds fell on more fertile ground. Austen expressed his agreement while urging caution lest the Irish be encouraged to raise their demands. On 25 October Austen gave Garvin further encouragement but asked that the policy should be submitted to Chamberlain; though by this time it was already clear that Balfour was not attracted to it. By 31 October Garvin reported to Northcliffe, 'no new sign from Whittingham or Highbury'. Balfour was soon in full retreat and on 6 November Sandars made it clear to Garvin that 'federalism' was dead.

By 14 November Bonar Law seems to have been convinced in principle that food taxes should be dropped, but he did not see how this was politically possible unless Chamberlain agreed; and Chamberlain would not.

In exploring Lloyd George's proposals the Unionist leaders showed great, perhaps excessive, caution. Akers-Douglas in particular believed that their Party would be split by a deal of this kind. Balfour, as at so many turning-points in his career, declared that he would not follow in Peel's footsteps and break up his Party. The offer was accordingly spurned, to Austen's regret but with his full consent.

What Chamberlain thought, we do not know in any detail. We can only speculate that had he been well enough to take part in the Conference, he would have struck the hardest bargain he could with the Liberals and then used all his energy and skill to carry the bulk of the Unionist party for this great transaction. As it was, the Unionists lost their last chance of introducing Tariff Reform, of solving the Irish problem in the framework of the United Kingdom and — most crucial of all — of gearing Britain's defence preparations by land and sea to the growing danger of war.

The rejection of the Lloyd George offer doomed the Constitutional Conference to failure. On 10 November, Asquith announced that the Conference would not sit again. An immediate election was now certain, and within a few days Parliament was dissolved.

Already before the dissolution, a number of Unionists — some of them staunch Tariff Reformers like Garvin — began to get cold feet over food taxes. They judged that to win the election, Balfour must concentrate on Home Rule and promise not to impose any new food taxes without a further appeal to the country.

Balfour demurred and was stiffened by Austen in his determination to stand by the full Tariff Reform programme. On 17 November, he made a speech at Nottingham, which Chamberlain took the unusual step of blessing in a public letter.

I need not assure you that I am in the most cordial agreement with you on all points. You have placed before the country in definite terms and with great lucidity the policy of the Unionist party.

A few days later, he issued his own election address in the following terms :

I still maintain that the country must be fully prepared in the matter of defence. Our prosperity depends upon it, and weakness is likely to lead to attack. I should, therefore, support those who claim that our Naval standard should be at least equal to what it has been before, and I believe that our people will not be willing to adopt any different policy to that which in the past has secured the safety of this country. Without this protection against outside forces any attempt to increase the internal prosperity of the country may be rendered futile, and I am therefore of opinion that the maintenance of a strong Navy is an essential feature of the Unionist programme.

Further, I am in favour of land reform, which, I believe, will secure a greater production of food supply in this country by multiplying the number of farmers and by improving the position of the agricultural classes. This reform has long been advocated by one of our members (Mr. Jesse Collings), and I am sure we should all regret if he did not take part in what now appears the speedy fruition of his hopes.

But while we shall do our utmost for the agricultural interest we are not likely to forget the interests of the large towns. By Tariff Reform and by Preferential rates with our Colonies we may greatly extend the demand for our products, and thereby secure to our working class fuller and more regular employment. To this reform I attach the greatest importance. Next year has been fixed for the Colonial Conference, and it would be a misfortune if it were to pass without our being able to come to an agreement which would establish reciprocal trade arrangements with our Dominions Across the Seas. A slight Preference given to our Colonies on the articles which they produce will secure at least equal concessions from them as regards our manufactures, and these mutual benefits ought to be settled at the coming Conference.

Turning to the Constitutional question which the Government are seeking to make the prime issue of this election, I think that the readiness showed by the Lords to reform their own Constitution as exemplified in Lord Lansdowne's resolutions is a proof that the Second Chamber will tend to become more and more democratic. On the other hand, the disposition shown by this Government to create new officials, and to resort to what is practically Single Chamber Government, indicates a danger which threatens our democratic system and must be resisted with all our strength. These are the issues which have to be settled in the present election, and I am confident that Birmingham will once more be in the front in declaring its adherence to the cause of patriotism, progress and reform.

But other forces were at work to bring Balfour to drop the proposed duty on imported wheat. Bonar Law had been persuaded to abandon his own safe seat at Dulwich and to fight the marginal constituency of North-west Manchester instead. The idea was that he should lead a Unionist revival in Lancashire. Bonar Law was a convinced Tariff Reformer, but he was soon convinced by Derby and the local Party managers that Lancashire would not swallow food taxes. In the last week of November, he suggested to Balfour that, without departing from the policy of Preference, Balfour should give a pledge that no tax on food would be imposed until the issue had been submitted to the nation in a referendum.

Balfour could hardly disregard such advice coming from so strong a Tariff Reformer as Bonar Law. Lansdowne, too, favoured the proposal. He considered that, in promising a referendum over food taxes, the Unionists would be offering a *quid pro quo* for their own demand that major constitutional changes such as Home Rule should also be submitted to a referendum. What was more, the *Daily Mail* took up the idea and urged the electors to exact a pledge from individual candidates.

Before reaching a final decision, Balfour felt bound to consult Austen, who was campaigning in Scotland. On 28 November, therefore, he despatched a special messenger to Edinburgh with a letter explaining his own views and enclosing Bonar Law's proposal. Austen telegraphed his disapproval in the strongest terms. But Balfour held to the majority view and the pledge was duly given.

The blow to Chamberlain was made the harder by the apparent lack of candour with which Balfour had treated him. Lunching together the same week, the two men had seemed to be in full agreement.

MRS. CHAMBERLAIN TO HER MOTHER

2 *December* 1910.—A bolt from the blue fell upon us on Tuesday night and I could not believe my eyes when I saw what Mr. Balfour had committed himself to at the Albert Hall. He took up the Radical challenge and agreed to submit Tariff Reform to a referendum ! ! ! I could have

cried. Poor Joe! Poor Austen! Just when their efforts seemed ready to be crowned with success and the whole Party brought into line, Mr. Balfour strong for the policy and all going well. . . . Joe is his usual controlled self over it. But I felt it was the irony of fate that at lunch on Tuesday he should speak to Sir Savile Crossley more enthusiastically than I have ever heard him of Mr. Balfour's attitude and leadership. He thought every mood had been excellent — and then to have this sprung upon him.

Balfour's decision meant that even if the Unionists won the election they would be unable to introduce a Preference on the very commodities for which the Colonies most desired it — wheat, meat and dairy produce. There would first have to be a referendum and a minority in the Party might well prevent one from being held. Beatrice Webb's judgment on the referendum device is interesting : [1]

1 *December* 1910.—Balfour's sudden advocacy of the referendum, whatever effect it may have, at the eleventh hour of the election, completely alters our constitutional system.

. . . from the point of view of the leader of a party, it has one inestimable quality. It delivers him from the domination of a political sect that has got hold of the caucus. That advantage must appeal to A.J.B. who has been suffering from having had tariff reform foisted on him. It is the last move in his duel with Chamberlain ; it is a final checkmate to tariff reform. And it is a superlatively fine stroke in his duel with Asquith — though it may be it has been delivered too late for this time.

It was too late. Austen always held that the manœuvre cost the Unionists more votes than it gained them. The Unionists gained ground in Lancashire as Derby had predicted but not enough to secure Bonar Law's return. At the same time they lost seats in London which was generally regarded as pro Tariff Reform. Sandars thought the result 'a fair measure of success' despite the 'peevish moaning of Highbury'.[2] The final results were :

Liberals	272	Unionists	272
Labour	42		
Irish	84		

For all practical purposes the state of the Parties remained unchanged.

It is hard in this momentous year to determine how far Austen reflected his father's views. In the spring, while Chamberlain was at Cannes, they had been in disagreement over the expediency of turning out the Government on a snap vote. Later, when Chamberlain was back in England, correspondence ceases. Throughout the summer and autumn, however, father and son were in close

---

[1] *Our Partnership*, ch. viii.   [2] Sandars to Garvin, 11 December 1910.

contact, and, at week-ends, often under the same roof. There is no
doubt that both were deeply depressed by the election results and
still more by Balfour's last-minute defection. Austen has recorded
his own mood as follows : [1]

I was exhausted by the long fight over the Budget and by two General
Elections (then a more lengthy affair than now as the polls themselves
were not yet all held on one day) in which I had spoken nightly.

But worse than the physical fatigue and in part its cause was the intense
depression which settled down on me as a result of the Albert Hall
Pledge. To have fought so long and so hard to keep Tariff Reform in
the forefront of our programme and to prevent its being whittled away or
postponed, to have come so near, as it seemed to me, to success and then
to see this new obstacle suddenly interposed in haste and at the last
moment, though we had deliberately rejected it earlier and after full
consideration, left me miserable and exhausted. Only once before in
my political life had I felt so beaten and *humiliated*, and that was when
Balfour's Cabinet decided in its last year not to meet the challenge of a
Private Member's motion on Food Taxes, but to abstain from speech
and vote, and I had come to the conclusion that nevertheless it was my
duty not to resign and that I could best serve the cause of Tariff Reform
by remaining in the Government.

Chamberlain must have felt the position even more keenly. He
had staked his political life on Tariff Reform and ruined his health
for it. After endless toil, the Unionist leaders had been brought to
support the new policy only to run away from it in the crunch.
Two General Elections now pointed to the bitter truth. The
Liberal–Labour pact had stood firm. The People's Budget and the
cry of 'the Peers against the People' had outflanked the appeal of
Tariff Reform and Imperialism. Could more dynamic leadership
in the Unionist camp have led to different results? To have beaten
the Government in the spring or to have formed a Coalition with
Lloyd George in the autumn are 'might have been's' which could
have turned on personality. Both chances had been lost; the great
policy had been put aside; and there was little prospect of an early
change. All Chamberlain now had left to hope for was that Austen
would succeed Balfour as the Unionist leader. He, one day, might
yet turn defeat into victory.

II

Neville was married in London immediately after the election
(5 January), to Miss Annie Vera Cole. Chamberlain was not well
enough to attend. He came to London, however, at the end of the

[1] Austen Chamberlain, *Politics from the Inside*, pp. 316–317.

month and took the oath at the House on 2 February. As in the previous year, he had to be supported — this time by Austen and Arthur Lee — and could only touch the pen while Austen signed the roll on his behalf. The Lobby Correspondent of the *Standard* described him as looking 'decidedly better than a year ago'. After sitting for a few moments on the front bench and shaking hands with the Speaker, he went to the room behind the Speaker's chair, where he stayed for half an hour or so talking with friends. It was his last appearance in the House.

The early part of the year was depressing for Chamberlain. Deakin, the Australian Premier, who would have been the leading advocate for Preference at the Colonial Conference, had broken down in health. Meanwhile, Botha was publicly threatening to withdraw the offer of increased South African Preferences. Gloomiest of all was the news from Canada. To understand this, we must look back a little.

In the course of 1910, there had been renewed interest in Canada in the idea of a Treaty of Reciprocity with the United States. This would have amounted, in practice, to the creation of a Canadian–American preferential union. Denison took a leading part in attacking this proposal and sought Chamberlain's advice. The following exchange took place.

CHAMBERLAIN AND DENISON

Chamberlain to Denison: 16 August 1910: Private.—You have done service to your country in watching very carefully the present movement which is going on, and, although I think that people here are a little uneasy about the tendency of leading men in Canada to agree prematurely with the policy of reciprocity with the United States, I do not believe that it will in the long run be found as advantageous as will be a preference from this country which is now, I think, assured in a short time, and which alone can secure the real union of the Empire and nullify all efforts, from whomsoever they may proceed, to separate it into its several constituents.

I am convinced that on this side of the water the movement of Tariff Reform and Preference is making way and I hope before long an offer may be made to Canada as well as to other Colonies, and that the matter will not be settled by any offers made in advance by other nations.

Your speeches and general action in support of this policy show that you have it at heart now as always and I do not think that the Americans are making any progress. In the meanwhile I hope you will continue and when you see an opportunity do your best to help those who are endeavouring to unite the Empire not only in matters of defence but also in matters of trade.

2 I 2

Denison to Chamberlain: 8 *October* 1910: *Private.*—I went to see Sir Wilfrid Laurier last week and had a long talk with him. He spoke about reciprocity in coal, fish, lumber and agricultural implements, none of which would have much effect on our policy of preferential tariffs. I did not raise much objection to these articles but warningly told him to be careful as we might be tricked. He then spoke favourably of reciprocity in farm products. Then I broke out and protested vehemently against doing anything in that line — to my amazement he seemed to have never thought out the effect of it — did not seem to know that we could not accept a preference from Great Britain if we were tied up with a treaty allowing U.S. products into Canada free — talked about earmarking the imported products etc. I argued it out with him until he had to admit that such a treaty would kill the whole thing, and then I suggested that we might have a proviso in the Treaty that would enable us to cancel anything that affected Imperial Preferential Tariffs. He seemed taken with the idea and said he would discuss it with Mr. Fielding.

Chamberlain to Denison: 18 *October* 1910.—I thank you for your letter and have read it ... with much interest. I think the proposal has all the objections you state and I think you are right in supposing that its promoters have something else in view and ought not to be encouraged to proceed with it. In fact we have difficulty enough to secure Imperial Preference and I should clear the situation of everything else. Although there may not be much harm in the different items proposed by Sir Wilfrid Laurier in his conversation with you, I should be afraid that they would lead to others more dangerous and more invidious. I hope that nothing will come of it at present.

Laurier weighed the alternatives carefully. On balance he inclined to Imperial Preference. It was, after all, his policy. But when he learned the results of the General Election in England, he concluded that Preference was no longer practical politics. He turned, accordingly, to the United States. At the end of January, the Taft–Fielding Trade Agreement was signed. Under it Canadian wheat and fish were to be admitted free into the United States. American agricultural implements and other machinery were to be admitted to the Canadian market.

The news that Laurier had decided for reciprocity with the United States was a severe shock to the Tariff Reformers in England. *The Times* and the *Daily Mail* both pronounced Preference dead. The *Daily Mail* was particularly virulent:

28 *January* 1911.—The agreement makes a breach in the wall and puts an end to the hope of commercial union between Great Britain and Canada based on preferential Tariffs. . . .

30 *January* 1911.—Exit imperial preference.

Garvin, however, continued to support Chamberlain's
argued that 'the United States have no real wheat surplu:
preference was not dead. For a time he was a lone voi(
Law and even Max Aitken agreed to work with Nor\
destroy 'the food tax incubus'; and Garvin was driven
that imperial preference could be combined with Anglo-/
reciprocity to improve the commercial and political links between
all three countries.[1]

Austen Chamberlain denounced the agreement in a speech at the
Birmingham Jewellers dinner (4 February 1910). Chamberlain
also entered the lists. On 8 February, he sent the following letter to
the Tariff Commission. It was duly printed in *The Times* next day.

CHAMBERLAIN TO THE CHAIRMAN AND MEMBERS OF THE TARIFF COMMISSION

8 February 1911.—I am more than ever convinced that without Preference we cannot hope to maintain and develop the unity of the Empire.
Since the Tariff Commission first undertook the work, however, we have
had to take account of new arrangements with foreign countries; and
now have to consider the proposed Reciprocity Agreement with the
United States of America. Without presuming to offer advice to the
people of Canada about their own affairs, I cannot help feeling that they
are rather premature. I wish they might at least have waited till the
meeting of the Imperial Conference, which is now fixed for May in this
year, when an opportunity of discussing a principle of such Imperial
importance with the representatives of the other self-governing Dominions
would have presented itself, and when the question of Preference might be
fully considered.

There is, moreover, another aspect to be taken into consideration.
It should not be lost sight of that the ratification of this Agreement
would mean a radical change in the policy of Canada, and its results
may be far-reaching; but whatever be the outcome of the present situation
the cause of Imperial Preference must not be abandoned.

There must be no whittling away of a policy which we believe essential
to Imperial union, and those of us who have devoted ourselves to the
furtherance of this great ideal in this country are bound to see to it that
nothing which has happened shall weaken our aspirations and render
our work vain. The fight must be carried on with unabated vigour and
confidence.

Chamberlain's letter caused as much stir in Canada as in England
and helped to work up a strong reaction there to the Reciprocity
Treaty. Grey, the Governor-General, described it in startling
terms:

[1] *Observer*, 5 February 1910.

GREY TO CHAMBERLAIN

5 *March* 1911.—The Taft–Fielding agreement has raised a storm here which is now at its height. In Montreal & Toronto the feeling is as strong as if the United States Troops had invaded our territory. — It requires a brave man to stand up in either place & proclaim himself in favour of the agreement — & yet to the agreement as it stands there is not much serious opposition. — To secure a free entry to the market of 90,000,000 of People for the natural Products of Canada, without reducing materially the duties against the external manufacturer would appear to be a great stroke. — Increased Prosperity for the farmers & the fishermen, & a careful maintenance of Protected manufacturing industries is the policy of Sir Wilfrid Laurier. The storm it has raised has been a surprise to him. — The honest fear that the agreement will start Canada on a slide which will one day land her in the lap of the United States is partly responsible for this storm. From this point of view the evidence of the existence of a passionately sensitive National Spirit is most satisfactory. — Stronger however than the National Sentiment is the fear of the Protected Industries that this agreement will create an increasing, & eventually an irresistible, demand for free trade. — Laurier's supporters are pressing him to raise the British Preference to 40 % — with the object of increasing the imports of British Manufactures, & thus giving the lie to those who argue that the Taft–Fielding agreement will kill the E & W Trade. If he were to yield to this pressure he wd. certainly score a point off his Political opponents — but it wd. be at the cost of his own policy, which is to increase the market of the Farmers & Fishermen, & to keep the home market for Canadian Manufacturers. He speaks tomorrow — & will I fancy give expression to his desire to approximate as near to Inter Imperial Free Trade as the Revenue Requirements & the National Necessities of Canada will permit. Those national necessities being at the present time the maintenance of a prosperous & varied manufacturing Industry.

It is denied here by Ministers that the free entry of American wheat into Canada will kill the Preference by the U.K. to Canadian wheat. German goods are imported into Canada through British Ports without obtaining the advantage of the British Preference. It is contended here that it will be just as easy to refuse to American wheat reaching U.K. through Canadian Ports the advantage of the Canadian Preference. — If most favoured Nation Treaty obligations do not interfere I would submit for your consideration the suggestion that the U.K. shd. give a Preference to food Products coming from Canadian Ports, no matter what the place of origin may be. — Such a Preference would help to secure for the St. Lawrence Route the Wheat & Cattle Trade which after the adoption of the Taft–Fielding agreement will go from American Ports.—

I cannot offer an opinion at present whether the Preference, which in effect would be a Preference on Canadian over American railways, is a Preference which could be put forward by the Unionist party. I have not heard it discussed — but the advantages resulting from it, if it could be adopted are so obvious that I think it is worth considering.—

The Opposition here are full of fight, for there is no closure here. They may obstruct in the Hs. of Cs. as long as they please.—

Chamberlain must have been encouraged by Grey's news. He had little use, however, for the proposal to give a Preference to American wheat shipped from Canadian ports.

CHAMBERLAIN TO SELBORNE

7 April 1911.—Personally I still think that we ought to maintain as far as we can our original policy, amd make no alteration whatever in our principles. In reference to your suggestion I think we ought to offer the same terms as we did before, that is to say, to give a preference to all Canadian wheat, but I should not extend this to American exportations, whatever the temptation may be. I think it is perfectly possible to differentiate between the Canadian and American wheat, but be that as it may, I do not suppose that it will be very much longer that American wheat will continue to come to Great Britain.

I agree with your suggestion that the details should be examined by the Tariff Commission if they have not already done so. *I think our preference may be given on other articles as well as wheat. I should for instance include maize,* and also *wine and tobacco,* both of which are made by some of the Dominions across the Seas by whom our preference will be considered important.

Chamberlain reaffirmed his anxiety over the Reciprocity Treaty in an open letter of support for Amery, who had just been adopted as candidate for North Birmingham.

CHAMBERLAIN TO AMERY

26 April 1911.—I am sure that all who think with me about Tariff Reform and Imperial Preference will rejoice to have your support in the House of Commons, where we have long desired your presence.

The policy, in my opinion, is more urgent than ever, and the recent action of Canada in connection with the Reciprocity measure proposed by the United States makes it even more imperative than before that we should show an alternative, which hitherto has been neglected by the supporters of the Government, and which I think is more than ever necessary now if the Empire is to be kept together.

We have, I consider, neglected our plain duty in so long refusing the request of Canada and the other Dominions Beyond the Seas to unite more closely our interests with those put forward by the representatives at the last Imperial Conference.

These public pronouncements were necessary, for Unionist opinion had been very shaken by the Canadian decision. Even Bonar Law had told Hewins that the time had come to abandon Preference.[1] Balfour, however, still held to the official policy. Then,

---

[1] W. A. S. Hewins, *Apologia of an Imperialist,* vol. i, pp. 268–269.

in September, came the Canadian General Election, resulting in the rout of Laurier and his Party. The Reciprocity Treaty was stone dead.

Chamberlain was relieved and heartened by the news. He telegraphed to the *Pall Mall Gazette*:

I congratulate Canadians on repudiation of Reciprocity agreement.

A further exchange with Denison may conclude our account of this incident.

CHAMBERLAIN AND DENISON

Denison to Chamberlain: 23 September 1911.—We have had a great fight, and once more Canada has stood by you and your policy. The plot in the United States, sympathised with by many of your Little Englanders has utterly failed and has brought Laurier's Government tumbling to the ground in ruins. Eight members of his government defeated and his majority of 43 turned into a hostile majority of 45, which I think, will be more when the full corrected returns come in.

I am proud of my country. In spite of the slamming, banging and barring of the doors in our faces, in spite of insolent treatment of that kind, which inspired Taft to think we would yield to his apparent friendship, the Canadian people have risen in their anger, and smashed the whole thing. You made great sacrifices for us, and I am very proud that my fellow-countrymen have stood so firmly by you. I am proud of my province 73 seats to 12 — of my city in which six out of seven Liberals lost their deposits and where every seat was carried by majorities of thousands, and particularly of the constituency in which I have lived all my life, where the majority against reciprocity was 8006.

Toronto is the Birmingham of Canada and stands as staunchly behind you.

I think this election will settle reciprocity for 20 years, and if England does not come to her senses before then, why of course she is done, and our Empire will collapse but the blame will not be either on you or on Canada.

Chamberlain to Denison: 3 October 1911.—Naturally I followed with the greatest interest your recent fight in Canada and I congratulate you heartily upon the result. I think it is the most important incident in our long campaign for Tariff Reform and Imperial Preference. You have shown the way out and I really do not doubt that your example will be followed by our people. At any rate you have done your part, and I share your feeling that it is the fault of England if we do not know how to reciprocate the many offers that have been made to us by you.

I am a little disappointed that I do not hear of a counter movement on our part, but I think that this must come, and meanwhile most of our people are away taking their holidays at the close of the last Session of Parliament. I cannot see how the present administration are to hold their own at the next general election which will, I believe, bring about a much needed change. In any case I repeat that you have shown us the way and you may be sure that your fight will have a great influence on the future of our movement.

The results of the Canadian election did more than anything to keep the Tariff Reform movement alive in the dark years ahead. It had been fought and won on Preference and Imperialism.

III

The main object of domestic interest, meanwhile, was the Parliament Bill. For a time, it changed the whole political alignment, even reuniting Cecils and Chamberlains. The issue for Unionists was clear enough. Should the House of Lords throw out the Bill and so force the Government to create some hundreds of new Peers? Or should they surrender their powers but avoid the wholesale dilution of their order?

Chamberlain was for the former course. He thought the creation of new Peers would have the immediate party advantage of bringing the Liberal Government into contempt. In the longer run, it might also be of lasting benefit to the Constitution. The new Liberal Peers would naturally want to safeguard the influence of the House of Lords once they were in it. Chamberlain reckoned, moreover, that after a few months they

would very likely turn against the Government as other 'political' Peers had done in many cases.[1]

One other consideration weighed with him. He had done more than any other man to persuade the Peers to throw out the People's Budget. He was thus partly responsible for their present plight. Accordingly, when a section of Unionist Peers started a 'no surrender' movement, honour as well as policy decided Chamberlain to come out in their support. Thus it happened that his last major intervention in politics was in support of the privileges of the House of Lords, of whose members he had once said, 'They toil not, neither do they spin'.

The 'Ditchers', as the diehard Peers were known, in contrast to the more moderate 'Hedgers', were led by Halsbury. Salisbury, Selborne, Milner, Northumberland and Willoughby de Broke were among their chief men in the Lords. Austen, Wyndham, Carson,

---

[1] Chamberlain in conversation with H. F. Wilson, 16 July 1911 (from a contemporary note by Wilson).

F. E. Smith, Hugh Cecil, Amery and Garvin encouraged them from without.

Garvin throws a curious sidelight on Chamberlain's attitude at this stage. In the *Observer* on 9 July he had praised Chamberlain as an opponent of any compromise over the House of Lords and had referred to a speech of Austen's as evidence for this claim.

AUSTEN TO GARVIN

14 July 1911.—In your last Sunday's notes you assumed that in my speech to the Women's Association, I spoke my father's mind. As a matter of fact I had no opportunity of consulting with him beforehand. But I dined with him on the night before last and you were right, for he warmly approved of what I said, 'You can't do wrong if you fight to the end' were his parting words.

As July lengthened, the hour of decision for the Unionist leaders drew on. Lansdowne called a meeting of Unionist Peers and advised them to abstain on the third reading of the Parliament Bill. To support his view, he read out a letter from Balfour. It included the following passage:

Let the Unionists in the Upper House follow their trusted leader. But if this is impossible, if differ we must, if there be peers who (on this occasion) are resolved to abandon Lord Lansdowne, if there be politicians outside who feel constrained to applaud them, let us all at least remember that the campaign for constitutional freedom is but just begun. . . . It would, in my opinion, be a misfortune if the present crisis left the House of Lords weaker than the Parliament Bill by itself will make it; but it would be an irreparable tragedy if it left us a divided Party.

The suggestion that to vote against the Bill would be an act of disloyalty to the Party leadership touched Austen on his most sensitive nerve. He was to speak at a great demonstration of the 'Ditchers' who were giving a banquet to Halsbury. Before going to it, he addressed a sharp remonstrance to Balfour.

AUSTEN TO BALFOUR

26 July 1911.—As soon as I was able to leave the debate yesterday afternoon I went to your room to see you. You were absent, and no one could tell me where I could find you.

It now appears that you had retired to the Travellers, where you were at that moment composing the letter to Lord Newton in which you accuse us of 'abandoning our leader', whilst encouraged by your language *The Times* this morning roundly brands some of your most earnest and, I will add, most loyal colleagues as 'rebels'.

I have read your letter with pain and more than pain. I think we have deserved better treatment at your hands. You cannot say that those whom you thus pillory have ever been wanting in loyalty to yourself. Might they not have asked in return at least for such ordinary consideration and frankness as a leader customarily extends to his followers? I have discussed this matter with you in Council of your colleagues and in conversation. Nothing that you have said on any of these occasions has prepared me for the line you have now taken up or given me a hint of your intention to treat this as a question of confidence in the leadership of either yourself or of Lansdowne.

On the contrary, you have repeatedly stated that this was a question which must be decided by each individual for himself. The crisis at which we have now arrived has been visible for a year past. We have frequently discussed it. Yet till this morning you had given no lead and had never suggested to those whose views you knew to differ from those which you now express that you desired that they should alter or abandon a course of action to which they were publicly committed.

It would be worse than useless to recapitulate at this stage the arguments which have convinced us that acquiescence by the whole House of Lords in the passage without amendment of the Parliament Bill would be disastrous to that House, to our Party, and to the country. You have confronted us not with a reply to our arguments, but with a denunciation of our conduct, and to make the pill more bitter you have addressed that denunciation not to us but to the public Press.

Under these circumstances I only desire to recall to your recollection that you have repeatedly stated that you had no objection to enforcing the creation of some peers if that did not of necessity carry with it the creation of such a number as would make a majority for the Government on all questions in the Lords; that you even stated more than once that you believed that that would be the best solution; and that as late as Friday last after our council you corrected a list which included your name among those in favour of unconditional acquiescence, saying that it was not correct to interpret what you have said in that sense. We now know from the King's declaration to Salisbury that his promise only extends to the creation of such a number as will carry the Parliament Bill, and that he will not consent to make more, and therefore the only danger which you feared from our action does not now exist.

Is it fair under such circumstances to talk of 'standing or falling' by a policy which is not your own and which, till this moment, you have never asked us to adopt, or to accuse of 'abandoning their leader' men who are carrying out a policy with which you have repeatedly expressed sympathy and even agreement?

It was the determination of us all that there should be no criticism of yourself or of Lansdowne at the Halsbury dinner. It is still our determination, and not even your letter will shake it. But our relations would be less frank and confidential than they have always been if I did not tell you privately that you have given deep and I think undeserved pain to men who have served you with affectionate loyalty both by the manner and the matter of your communication.

That night, the great assembly of 'Ditchers' gathered at the Hotel Cecil for the banquet to Halsbury. Selborne was in the chair. 'My Lords and gentlemen', he said in opening the proceedings,

'I have received letters and telegrams regretting inability to be present here tonight from a score or so of Peers and members of Parliament. . . . But the only communication I will read is this one :
' "I hear that you will preside at a dinner to Lord Halsbury : I wish I could be present and I heartily support the object. The country owes a great debt to Lord Halsbury since in the crisis of its fate he has refused to surrender his principles. — Joseph Chamberlain".'

According to the *Standard* correspondent, Chamberlain's message raised the enthusiasm of the gathering to 'fever heat'. It also stirred Balfour. He replied next day to Austen's letter which we have already quoted.

BALFOUR TO AUSTEN

(*Undated, probably* 27 *July* 1911).—Your letter — which I have read with feelings of pain which you will readily understand — seems written under a misapprehension.
There is nothing in my letter which was intended to suggest — or which on a fair interpretation ought to suggest — that I accused any friends of mine of disloyalty to myself. I certainly advised the Unionist Peers to follow their leader, Lord Lansdowne ; I certainly hinted — nay, more than hinted — that if Lord Lansdowne felt that, through his lead not being followed, he must resign his leadership, I should follow his example. But I never for an instant thought, I never for an instant allowed anyone to say in my presence, that old and tried friends like yourself, like Selborne, like Salisbury, like George Wyndham either, were, or could conceivably become, guilty of disloyalty.
I think you underrate the difficulties of a situation which I at least did nothing to create. The shadow Cabinet showed irreconcilable differences of opinion. Had it been a real Cabinet one of two things would have followed. Either the dissentient minority would have resigned, or they would have silently acquiesced in the decision of the majority. There could be no question, in the case of a shadow Cabinet, of resignation. There certainly has been no silent acquiescence. Members belonging to the two sides at once set actively to work. They used all the means which printed correspondence or the public Press placed at their disposal, and in the face of all men the Party fabric was, for the moment, violently rent from top to bottom.
In these circumstances I could not remain a mere spectator. I had to speak, and if I spoke I could only say in public what I had already said at the shadow Cabinet. You state that I 'have confronted you not with a reply to your arguments but with a denunciation of your conduct'. How differently the same document strikes different readers ! I certainly endeavoured to indicate why I think the so-called fighting in the last

ditch is not fighting at all; and as for 'denunciation', I had thought that my letter — especially the final paragraph — made it perfectly clear :

(1) that the importance of the issue had to my thinking been exaggerated;
(2) that the division of opinion it has occasioned, even if inevitable, could and should be temporary.

Denunciation was never intended and was never used. It may be difficult to express differences of opinion when feeling runs high without giving unintentional pain. Your father, for example, observes that '*the country owes a debt of gratitude to Lord Halsbury because in this crisis of his country's fate he has refused to surrender his principles*'. Many people will read this as meaning that in Mr. Chamberlain's opinion those who follow a different course from Lord Halsbury *had* surrendered theirs. I do not so read it. *That* would be 'denunciation' indeed. But without going into these or other collateral questions I beg you to believe that while I did most assuredly advise the peers to follow Lansdowne, I never for a moment intended to express, or did express, anything at which my friends in or out of the House of Commons have reason to take umbrage.

Balfour's remonstrance, however, went no further. He 'steadily declined to administer any public rebuke to Austen Chamberlain, saying he might have to form a Government later on, and he did not want to be left with Mr. Chaplin and Mr. Long as his principal ministers!'[1]

Halsbury's movement failed to stop the Parliament Bill, which passed the House of Lords on 10 August. But it bore unexpected fruit in another direction.

IV

Balfour's concessions, first over food taxes, and then over the Parliament Bill, alienated some of the ablest of his supporters. During the summer, Selborne, Wyndham, Milner, Carson, F. E. Smith, Willoughby de Broke, Amery and one or two others met to form a 'Halsbury Club'.[2] Their declared objects were : full support for Tariff Reform and Imperial Preference, including the withdrawal of Balfour's pledge for a referendum; compulsory National Service; an elected Second Chamber; and all-out opposition to Home Rule. For such men to come forward with such an unauthorised programme was a direct challenge to Balfour's leadership.

[1] See *The Times* obituary notice on Balfour. The Sandars papers confirm this anecdote.
[2] They convened their first meeting for 12 October 1911.

Neville learned what was afoot, and on 4 October, telegraphed to Austen, who was on holiday at Lugano.

Expect telegram this afternoon urge you to return as soon as possible join movement feeling in country real and widespread.

There is no evidence as to the source from which Neville secured his information. But it is most unlikely that he would have sent such a message to Austen without first consulting Chamberlain. Both men were in Birmingham at the time, and Neville hardly had sufficient political experience to act entirely on his own initiative. It looks, therefore — and subsequent evidence rather bears this out — as if Chamberlain judged that the time had come for Austen to take over the leadership of the Party.

Austen came home to find the 'Balfour must go' movement in full swing. He was at once approached by Selborne and Wyndham who told him of the programme of the Halsbury Club and discussed the likelihood of Balfour's retiring from the leadership. There is some evidence that Austen at first inclined to Chamberlain's view that the time might have come for him to take the leadership.

MRS. CHAMBERLAIN TO HER MOTHER

18 *October* 1911.—. . . Joe has had some good talks with him (Austen) and has become very much interested in discussing with him all the difficulties and complexities of the present situation and of the immediate plan of campaign during the Autumn session. 'I am very pleased with Austen and approve his ideas' was his verdict one night (13 October).

But at an early stage Austen took the line that it would be a great mistake for Balfour to resign. He went out of his way to stress this view to Balcarres, the Chief Whip, and held fast to it even when Balcarres told him that Balfour was seriously contemplating resignation. It is clear from the following extract that Chamberlain would have had him take a very different line.

AUSTEN TO MRS. CHAMBERLAIN

23 *October* 1911.—Father . . . will not altogether approve what I said to Balcarres about the leadership but I am convinced it is right and in my case I must work in my own way among these very difficult problems. I am quite clear in my own mind that I don't want a vacancy in the leadership.

Balfour, however, was sick and tired of the Party factions he had sought so long to reconcile. Despite Austen's assertions of loyal support, he determined to resign before his position became impossible. The decision was taken on 4 November. Austen wrote at once to inform his father.[1] One passage from this letter must be quoted. It explains, like nothing else, why Austen so often deferred to Balfour against his own and his father's views.

AUSTEN TO CHAMBERLAIN

4 November 1911: Secret.—The blow has fallen and I am as sick as a man can be. Balfour has definitely decided to resign the leadership. . . . There is the great news, sad news to me whatever happens for I love the man, and though as you know he has once or twice nearly broken my heart politically, I now can think of nothing but the pleasure of intimate association with him, the constant personal kindness he has shown to me and the great qualities of mind and character he has brought to the discharge of the tremendous duties of his post. Well, it is another milestone in my life. The last of the elder generation resigns his post, and to no other man can I feel again what I have felt towards him.

Austen had already discussed the whole question of the succession to the leadership with Chamberlain. Next day (5 November), he made an objective assessment of his chances and gave a rather maudlin account of his feelings.

AUSTEN TO MRS. CHAMBERLAIN

5 November 1911.—Now as to my self and what Father said the other day.

There has been so much talk of late about the possibility of B.'s resigning that I think I know fairly well how the ground lies. As far as I can tell, all the Front Bench with the exception of Long and possibly of Law think, with more or less misgiving, that I am the best man to succeed to the leadership of the Party in the Commons. Lansdowne, it is hoped and believed, will go on in the Lords. Who will be leader of the Party time will show. It may be either or neither of us according to our deserts, but till we are called upon to form a Government that question does not arise.

Against me, however, there is Long's strong objection to my selection, his special group of friends, swelled for the moment by some others who are angry about the Halsbury Club, and the fact that I am both a Liberal Unionist and a Nonconformist. I cannot find that there is anyone in our councils who thinks that Long himself would do, but he will throw all his weight into the scale against me and might get Bonar Law chosen. Sandars says that he and Balcarres had never supposed that Law would allow his name to be put forward. I think they are mistaken and that Law would allow it and like it if he thought there was a chance of his being chosen.

[1] Austen actually learned of Balfour's decision two days earlier (2 November) and wrote at once to protest. (Balfour Papers, B.M. Add. MS. 49767).

As to my own feelings I think you pretty well know them. I wish there were another Balfour, clearly superior to us and obviously marked out for the post. How gladly would I play second fiddle to him! But there is no such man at present, and having given my life to this work and got to the position I now hold, I cannot shirk fresh responsibilities or heavier labours if they fall to my lot.

As early as the second week of October Goulding had joined with Aitken in urging Bonar Law as leader, having learned that Law was prepared to accept the post if offered. Austen too recognized the threat.

AUSTEN TO CHAMBERLAIN

27 *October* 1911.—I think that Bonar Law does feel that if Balfour retired and I were too unpopular with a section of the party to be chosen to succeed, the leadership must fall to himself . . .

When Balfour announced his retirement, Austen and Long agreed (8 November) that if the party should be divided equally 'the tertium quid will probably be the right solution and the tertium quid could only be Bonar Law'. Law announced his candidature on 9 November. Garvin tried to persuade him to withdraw it and Law actually drafted a letter (10 November) tantamount to withdrawal but was persuaded by Aitken not to send it. The same day Austen and Long agreed to stand down in Law's favour.

'Now' Austen told Garvin 'comes the hard part. I am just going to write to my father who has always been more ambitious for me than he ever was for himself'.

Chamberlain had already learned the news by telegram. It was followed by this letter.

AUSTEN TO MRS. CHAMBERLAIN

10 *November* 1911.—My telegram will have told you what by the time you receive this will, I expect, be public news; that I and Long have withdrawn our names and that we shall propose Bonar Law as leader.

I did not take this decision without a pang, but I am clear that it was the right thing to do, and this morning I told Balcarres to make the proposal in my name to Long.

I discussed it with Ivy and she agreed.

I fear it will be a great disappointment to my Father. But for that thought, the decision would be an unmixed relief to me now that it is once taken.

Give him my dearest love, tell him that I am sorry to have grieved him, but that I am sure that he would have done the same in my position, and that I have at least brought no discredit to the name.

I will write full particulars when I can for him. At this moment Bonar Law is coming to see me.

The news was a fearful blow to Chamberlain. Garvin wrote : 'I seemed to hear great heart strings snapping at last in Joe and I would have given my life to save him from going down uncomforted to the grave.'

Mrs. Chamberlain wrote to Austen : 'He received your news as he always does, in his strong firm way.' His first instinct was to take Austen's part.

'I do not see,' he said, 'that under the circumstances he could do otherwise.'[1]

MRS. CHAMBERLAIN TO HER MOTHER

18 *November* 1911.—Joe has been so strong about it. Of course he regrets it and perhaps wonders whether the course of things could have been altered — but he is reconciled by the thought that on these terms Austen could not have done justice either to the cause or himself.

Later, as he looked more closely into the transaction, he seems to have doubted whether Austen had been right.

MRS. CHAMBERLAIN TO AUSTEN

12 *November* 1911.—Perhaps today, as your father thinks of it more and more, the sense of disappointment is uppermost in his mind, and he can even conceive that possibly the *dénouement* might have been different, but he says to tell you that in a matter such as this your decision must be your own, and he approves whatever it is. 'In his place I do not think I could have done differently.' But he recognises the extent of the sacrifice and he wishes you had not been called upon to make it.

The truth is that Austen had no will to power. He would have accepted the leadership if it had been offered to him on a plate, but he would not fight for it. As it happened, the balance of forces within the Unionist party was such that his only chance of winning the prize lay in fighting for it. Whether he would have gained it, even then, must be a matter of conjecture. Austen, himself, believed that

if I had held on, I should have won at the second ballot by a small majority. This is Sandars' belief . . . and he tells me it was Bal.'s [Balcarres] also. I would have faced all the risks . . . if I could have been assured of one thing — really loyal cooperation and support from all my colleagues. . . . You know that Long wouldn't have given me a dog's chance. While I stood up to fight the enemy, he would have stabbed me in the back, and knowing what I do . . . of the feelings in his entourage I do not think that anyone can say that I shirked a duty when I decided to withdraw my name.'[2]

[1] Mrs. Chamberlain to Austen, 11 November 1911.
[2] Austen to Mrs. Chamberlain, 11 November 1911.

It is not for us to pass judgment, but Chamberlain always thought that Austen had been 'over-punctilious' and would have done better to take his father's advice to 'stick to his guns'.[1]

V

Austen found consolation in the general view that he had shown himself 'a great gentleman'. But this was little consolation to Chamberlain. His Party had been defeated at two General Elections. His policy had been thrust aside. And now his son's claims to the leadership had been passed over. This was bitter fruit for the old man; the more bitter because he felt the outcome might have been different if only they had taken his advice.

It was in this mood that Chamberlain now accepted Austen's view that the time had come to amalgamate the Liberal Unionist party with the Conservatives. A definite proposal was made by Steel-Maitland on behalf of the Conservatives. Chamberlain would have rejected it, had he still been in active politics, but since Austen thought otherwise, what was the use of resisting the change? He was, however, inclined to make conditions. He wanted, in particular, to safeguard the independence of the Birmingham organisation.

CHAMBERLAIN TO BORASTON

18 *December* 1911.—Personally if I were still able to take an active part in the organisation I should think Mr. Steel-Maitland's suggestion premature, but having regard to all the circumstances, I feel that the time has probably come to unite the two organisations of the Unionist party. Everything, however, will depend on what the details are and how far the Committee of the Conservative Association can meet the conditions of our Committee. I should attach much importance to two things:

(1) the name of the joint association ought in future to be the Unionist Association; and,

(2) I think that the local Committees should be allowed a large discretion in this matter. I can well understand, for instance, that the Midlands Liberal Unionist Association and the Conservative one may not care to join forces and may prefer to keep their separate Committees as at present. Although in general I am inclined to respond to Mr. Steel-Maitland's proposal everything depends upon the name and the necessary arrangements for the two bodies and their officials.

The negotiations dragged on for some months and ended with the virtual absorption of the Liberal Unionists by the Conservatives.

[1] From a talk with Mrs. Chamberlain.—J. A.

In the circumstances, Austen could hardly have got better terms; and Chamberlain was consulted at each stage. But, though he agreed to what was done, the following letter shows how reluctant he was to lose control of the instrument which had served him so well.

AUSTEN TO MRS. CHAMBERLAIN

29 April 1912.—Now it comes to the point of winding up, I share all Father's regrets at bringing the L.U. Council to an end. It has been an excellent body and done excellent work, but we really had no choice for we cannot recruit enough young men. The sons of L.U.s have not their fathers' memories of the pre-'86 times and naturally join the largest section of Unionists. Often indeed no other choice is open to them and in any case it gives them the best chances and the widest field. And as to the moment, though I would sooner have done it after the close of this final fight over Home Rule, we had now an opportunity, owing to the re-organisation in progress in the Conservative Central Office and staff, which would never have recurred. Indeed when you come to think about it, it is an amazing thing that their two chief officers will now be Boraston and Jenkins! What jealousies this would have awakened a little time ago.

For all the disappointments, there were still flashes of the old fire. In March, while Chamberlain was in the south of France, there was a serious wave of strikes. More than 2,000,000 men were out. The Government, afraid of their own left wing, hoped that the Unionists might support a Liberal proposal for compulsory arbitration and so help pull their chestnuts out of the fire. Chamberlain telegraphed to Austen from Cannes:

They are in a hole. — Don't do anything to help them out.

For a moment, he seems to have thought that the Government's majority might break. 'I believe I could smash them,'[1] he said.

At the suggestion of Wyndham and Amery, two funds were started in Chamberlain's honour that summer. Their purpose was to raise money for Tariff Reform propaganda. The first — the Chamberlain Birthday fund — was a popular movement with subscriptions limited to one shilling. Begun on 8 July 1912, this closed on 16 February 1913 with a total of 113,597 shillings. The other, known as the Imperial Fund, got off to a good start with a dinner given by the Duke of Westminster, at which £21,250 were raised from a company of 21.

[1] Austen Chamberlain, *Politics from the Inside*, p. 454.

VI

Chamberlain's remaining hopes now centred on Bonar Law. The new Unionist leader was dour and uninspiring. He was, nonetheless, reputed staunch for Tariff Reform and an inveterate opponent of Home Rule. Law lunched with Chamberlain soon after taking over the leadership, and a few weeks later volunteered an important pledge to Austen.

AUSTEN TO MRS. CHAMBERLAIN

17 *January* 1912.—I lunched with Bonar Law yesterday and had a pleasant talk. He is beset by letters asking him to abandon Food Taxes altogether but admits that he doesn't see how it can be done and volunteered the promise :

'Well, Austen, if ever I do think that any change ought to be made in our policy on this question, I promise you that I won't propose it till I have your assent. You and I stand too much together on this question for us to have any difference about it.'

The pressure on the Unionist leaders to abandon food taxes continued throughout the spring. The Government were bringing forward the third Home Rule Bill, and there was a strong feeling that Unionists should concentrate on saving the unity of the Kingdom and leave to the future an issue on which they were still divided. Hugh Cecil was the leading spirit behind this movement and even sought to persuade Chamberlain to postpone Tariff Reform for the sake of preventing Home Rule.

HUGH CECIL TO CHAMBERLAIN

7 *March* 1912.—I venture with many apologies for my presumption to send you a copy of a memorandum which my brother and I are submitting to the leaders of the party. And I write this letter with it to make an appeal to you to give it your friendly consideration.

You will see that we have striven to consider the matter from the point of view of Tariff Reform ; & I am sincerely convinced that what we suggest is wisest from that standpoint. But it is for the sake of the fight against Home Rule that I solicit your approval. That Home Rule was defeated in 1886 & 1895 was more due to your most brilliant advocacy than to that of any other living man. Could you not again take the bold course that is needed to make the Union safe?

If the recommendation that the Tax on corn & meat should be postponed over the next Parliament was made by yourself, no one would impute it to weakness or halfheartedness. The whole Party would respond to your lead, & you would have saved the Union in a third great contest. Tariff Reform with other things would reap the benefit of the victory: but the greatest result would be the final extinction of Home Rule.

Trusting that you will forgive me for my boldness in addressing you . . .

Chamberlain's reply was friendly but inflexible.

CHAMBERLAIN TO HUGH CECIL

14 *March* 1912.—As to Home Rule I hold the same opinion as I did when it was last before the H of C — but I do not think that any alteration in the policy of Tariff Reform would make it more easy to defeat Home Rule.

I still think that the inclusion of food taxes which is part of the original policy was the right one, & under these circumstances I should not feel justified in supporting your present proposal. I do not think it would be wise to postpone the tax now, & I do not think it would have any influence upon the public mind.

We have endeavoured, especially in the last bye-elections, to put forward our whole programme, & I am strongly of opinion that we have made such progress that it would be a grave mistake to confuse the mind of the electorate by an action which would certainly be misrepresented and which would jeopardize the success of the scheme from an Imperial standpoint.

The saying of President Lincoln is still true & in my judgment it would be fatal 'to swop horses when crossing the stream'. I am sure that any change now would give rise to as much difficulty in the future as you see in the present proposal. I quite believe that some M.P.'s would be glad if we were to declare once for all that for the present at any rate we would not propose to tax food but it is quite certain that they would raise other objections if this one were removed.

I also feel that the Canadians would have just cause for complaint if we were now for the first time to announce that we were not going to tax corn.

For this and other reasons I feel I cannot take any part in your proposal which I not only think would be bad tactics, but I should be at a loss to defend it in principle.

The Unionist leaders decided against the Cecil proposal at a meeting of the shadow Cabinet in April. They agreed that opposition to Home Rule was a negative policy with no social or economic appeal. Tariff Reform, on the other hand, was their positive alternative to Socialism. To put it aside would be to rob their movement of its main dynamic element.

It was accordingly decided in principle to go back to the full Tariff Reform policy. There remained the question of Balfour's pledge, at the 1910 election, to submit any proposal to tax food, to a referendum. Borden, the Conservative Premier of Canada, urged the Unionist leaders to abandon it. Accordingly, at a meeting of the Conservative National Union in the Albert Hall on 14 November, Lansdowne specifically repudiated Balfour's referendum pledge. Despite the wave of protest Law endorsed what Lansdowne had said; and on 12 December, Austen followed suit.

But now, a sudden gust of anxiety swept through the Unionist ranks. The *Daily Mail* denounced the action of the leaders. The Unionist Associations in Lancashire and Yorkshire expressed grave concern. Bonar Law decided to rally Unionist opinion and arranged to speak at Ashton-under-Lyne in the heart of the Free Trade country. In the course of his speech, he stressed that no food taxes would be introduced until the Colonial Governments, at a Colonial Conference, had made specific proposals. There was nothing in this qualification to which any Tariff Reformer could take exception. But the stress which Law laid on it suggested that he was on the defensive and so encouraged his opponents. The anxiety in the Unionist ranks turned almost into panic; and the cry was raised that Ireland would be lost because of the food tax policy.

F. E. Smith believed that a major revolt threatened from the Lancashire Conservative Association. According to him Derby and Salvidge were preparing what amounted to a public denunciation of the leadership. They would have staged their demonstration at the Party Conference. The signs were that the Lancashire revolt might well carry the day.

Austen urged Bonar Law to stand firm and suggested that they undertake a six weeks campaign together to educate the Party to their point of view. But Bonar felt he could not go against so strong an opposition in the Party. He proposed accordingly, to summon a Party meeting and to resign. This meant capitulation to the opponents of Tariff Reform. Bonar Law's position is best explained in a letter he wrote to Chaplin. This also shows that he left himself a line of retreat.

BONAR LAW TO CHAPLIN

31 *December* 1912.—Politicians are not the most stable of people but the change which has taken place is remarkable even for politicians. The strongest Tariff Reformers are all coming to me saying it is impossible to fight with food taxes. The position therefore is a very difficult one, and I really have no idea how it will end; but so far as the present is concerned I am not going to depart in the least from the policy we have laid down, though (between ourselves) I am convinced that it must in the end be modified. I doubt whether this modification will be possible under my leadership but that is a bridge which I need not cross till we come to it.

Austen explained the position to his father in the following terms.

AUSTEN TO MRS. CHAMBERLAIN

7 January 1913.—I have prepared you and Father for what this letter has to tell, yet I find it a very difficult one to write. I have done my best, but the game is up. We are beaten and the cause for which Father sacrificed more than life itself is abandoned! It is a bitter confession to make and it is difficult for me to speak calmly about it.

I found a note from Lansdowne on my return to town yesterday asking me to see him. We could not meet till nearly seven o'clock and then he had been closeted with Law, Carson and Balcarres for two hours.

Law's decision is to call a Party meeting on Thursday and to resign on the ground that his policy is impossible. I presume that he will be re-elected, though he says he means to make this impossible.

I will try to write more fully another time, but I have not the heart now. The Whips' report was that though fifty or sixty Members would gladly support Law if he determined to stick to his guns, not more than twenty-five wished him to do so. Law says that so good a Tariff Reformer as Page Croft confirms this estimate. Three weeks of hesitation have destroyed the chance of a successful fight!

As soon as Law's intentions became known, a movement began on the back benches, headed by Carson and F. E. Smith, to persuade him to abandon food taxes but to keep the leadership. They drew up a memorial to this effect, and began to canvass signatures for it from the back benches. They sounded Austen. He refused to give his support but said he 'would do nothing to dissuade men from signing'.

Bonar Law had hardly expected even this much co-operation from Austen, and wrote at once to express his gratitude.

BONAR LAW TO AUSTEN

8 January 1913.—Carson has told me something of his conversation with you yesterday, and I wish to say to you how well I understand what all this means to you. You cannot fail to look upon it as if it were going back upon your father's life-work, and though I believe that the tendency towards closer union on the part of the Colonies is the direct result of what he did, yet that cannot at the moment soften the blow much.

It is to me a great misfortune that I should be in such a position that it is I who seem to deal the blow at his policy. I have told you, and I am sure you believe me, that if you or your father wished it I should gladly resign my position but I have not the courage to go on and be responsible for a policy which, with the feeling in the Party such as it is, I am sure is bound to fail. If I had been your father, I might have carried it through successfully, but I cannot.

In this crisis as in the earlier one, you have acted as what I know you are, a great gentleman.

Austen's reply is typical of the man. As so often with Balfour, he repeats his disapproval of Bonar Law's policy and yet urges him to retain the leadership.

AUSTEN TO BONAR LAW

8 January 1913.—Many thanks for your letter. I reciprocate the spirit in which it is written, for in the midst of my own deep disappointment I can appreciate and sympathise with your feelings and difficulties.

As you know I wish that you could have felt differently and I still believe that the advice which I tendered you was the best for your reputation and for the Party, and that if it had commended itself to you and been acted on at once the position of the Party would have been stronger in three months' time than it will be now and your own reputation immeasurably enhanced.

But I recognise that, if you couldn't believe what I believed, you could not advocate it with success, and I saw that I could not make you share the confidence that I felt.

If you and I now consulted our own wishes, we should leave politics to others; but neither of us *can* do that and you least of all.

You must make your sacrifice as well as others. I think you had the right to invite the Party to fight on your lines or get another leader. But, forgive me, if I pain you, I don't think you have a right to say to the Party, 'I see that my line is impossible and I cannot pursue it further, but I will not lead you on any other'.

The whole Party desires you to continue your leadership and I do not think you have the right, as things now stand, to withdraw.

I have said more than I meant to. Indeed I only wished to tell you that if I have not sought you out yesterday or today it is only because I could not help you by anything I could say and I felt that things had now passed altogether beyond my control and that it was now for others to find a solution since the cause which I supported was definitely rejected.

I am deeply sensible of the difficulties of your position. I will try not to make them greater, and if you do not altogether like what I have to say when I come to speak, you must make allowance for a man whose dearest political hopes and personal affections have received from fate a cruel blow.

Austen's refusal to encourage resistance to the Memorial ensured its success. Only half a dozen members — including Aitken,[1] Amery, Chaplin, George Lloyd and Page Croft — refused to sign up though Austen pressed Amery at least to do so. The Memorial was

---

[1] There is considerable evidence that although Aitken personally believed in food taxes and refused to sign the memorial, he had been prepared at several stages during the crisis to help Bonar Law overcome opposition to the change of policy.

See *The Observer and J. L. Garvin* by A. M. Gollin, pp. 366–385.

This is a classic example of a clash between loyalty to principle and loyalty to a leader that so often arises in politics.

duly presented and on 13 January, Bonar Law wrote to Balcarres to say that he and Lansdowne were prepared to accept its terms. They kept the leadership; but the flag of Preference was hauled down.

The same night, Austen spoke at Acocks Green:

I have to recognise that the decision, for the time at any rate, is against me. I have to acknowledge that the great majority of the Party took and take a different view. But for the first time in my long connection with it, for the first time in the eleven years that I have been permitted to sit in the councils of that Party, I am unable to take any share of responsibility for the decision to which they have come. I cannot turn my back upon myself. I cannot unsay what I have said. I cannot pretend to like the change of attitude. I cannot pretend to view without misgivings its possible effect.

I am afraid that this change may be a calamity for the Party with which all my public life has been associated. I am afraid it may prove a misfortune for the Empire which it has been my earnest desire to serve. But I have been too long engaged in politics to suppose that I can always have my own way, too long to sulk because I cannot now persuade the Party to take a course in this one matter which I believe to be alike the right course and the wise course; and though I have to admit my disappointment and acknowledge my fears, I will do my best in the future as I have done my best in the past to support my leaders and to co-operate with my political friends. I care too much for the other great causes whose success is bound up with that of the Unionist Party to sit idly by and not render what help I can in their defence or their promotion.

Chamberlain's own feelings in this crisis emerge clearly from the following letter, written on his instructions.

MRS. CHAMBERLAIN TO AMERY

9 *January* 1913.—It has indeed been a depressing time, & we have thought of the small but loyal band who have wished to keep the flag flying with grateful hearts.

Mr. Chamberlain has met the disappointment with his usual strength of mind — but of course he feels it deeply — the more that he still believes that a strong attitude & determination to overcome difficulties which only conviction & confidence could overcome, would have won the day — but that was not to be. But in spite of everything he does not lose heart. 'Tell him they have got a bad time to go through, but I know they are all doing their best, & I rely on 'the handful' to go on preaching the doctrine'—

His fear is that that may be thrust aside, & his hope is that if our friends still go on trying to break down the prejudice that something may yet be saved from the wreck.

He appreciates your reference to Austen — who has had a hard time indeed, but he is proud of the way in which he has fought & believes he will do good work yet. Poor Austen — to him it is a bitter blow—

However, all that can now be done is to fight for what remains, & not let the present control the future more than is inevitable — for it is a sorry spectacle that the Unionist Party presents to the world just now.

Again thanking you, & those like you who have shown courage and resolution.

On 26 January, a loyal handful — Selborne, Wyndham, Ridley, Hewins, Amery, and George Lloyd — dined with Austen to consider the future of the Tariff Reform League. It would be their task to keep the movement alive and wait for the tide to turn.

VII

Chamberlain's cup was full. His Party had been defeated ; his son passed over for the leadership ; his policy repudiated. The spectre of Home Rule loomed close ahead. The war clouds were gathering on the European horizon. Chamberlain's life work seemed in ruins ; and it was far too late to build it again. He had little left to live for now.

As usual, he spent the winter and early spring of 1913 in Cannes. It was there that he took the decision not to stand for Parliament again.

MRS. CHAMBERLAIN TO COLLINGS

23 *April* 1913: *Confidential.*—. . . Joe . . . is not satisfied with our political affairs at all — as indeed are no real Tariff Reformers in their hearts, but his optimism does not desert him in spite of his deep regret at the turn affairs have taken. . . .

Since we have been here he has been thinking a great deal about the political situation in Birmingham. He feels that his continued absence from active work and the changes which have taken place in the last seven years, are having a bad effect upon our people there, and he thinks there is a great danger of our losing the splendid hold which the Liberal Unionist party has maintained there so long. And if the fort is to be held he thinks more work must be given, which alas ! he cannot do. He therefore has come to a decision which as yet is *absolutely private*, known only to his children & myself, but as you have always shared his most private concerns he wants you too to be in the secret, which he begs you will not speak of to anyone but his sons if you happen to see them — until he takes steps to make it known, which for obvious reasons he does not intend to do at present. He has decided quite definitely not to offer himself for re-election at the next General Election.

It is, of course, a decision which has cost him (& me) a great deal, but he feels it is right, and much as I deplore the necessity I agree. It has been wonderful, the way in which the loyalty of Birmingham has stood by him, and if he were to continue I am sure we could rely on its further endurance — but Joe feels the time has come to recognize it by his retirement, and to use such influence as he possesses in helping his successor by his sympathy & support to make for himself a position which will help to keep up the reputation & usefulness of the town in the troublous times before the country.

In May, Mrs. Chamberlain had to be operated on for a sudden attack of appendicitis. She made a good recovery, however, and they returned to England together in June.

Nineteen-thirteen made deep inroads into the circle of Chamberlain's colleagues and family. Wyndham died in Paris in June ; and Lyttelton in July. In October, Chamberlain lost his brother Arthur, after a long and painful illness.

MRS. CHAMBERLAIN TO DOWSON

27 *October* 1913.—This loss is a deep sorrow to him — for though he could not wish that Arthur's life should be prolonged with its ever increasing suffering, still the parting is full of pain and he feels it keenly. They were very near to one another, and though their opinions sometimes differed, their affection remained the same.

On 21 November, a week after Chamberlain's silver wedding, the Unionist leaders held a great demonstration in Birmingham. Austen took the chair. Bonar Law and Carson were the chief speakers. Chamberlain sent a message, 'Hold fast and fight hard'.

This message was intended to apply to Tariff Reform as well as to Home Rule. Austen, however, went out of his way to reaffirm his loyalty to Bonar Law's line :

We are Tariff Reformers — whole hearted Tariff Reformers because we believe that in Tariff Reform we can lay the foundation for the improvement of the social condition of the masses of our people and for the closest union of the great Empire of which we are the centre. We have made in this matter great sacrifices in order to preserve concord, but we accept the conditions, Sir, which you have laid down. We are content to move on the lines which you have indicated. We are ready to postpone the full fruition of our hopes so that there be no going back, and so that our progress if slow be steady.

Hewins lunched at Highbury next day, and has left an account of how Chamberlain received Austen's speech : [1]

On Saturday I went to Highbury, lunched with Chamberlain and had a long talk wth him. . . . Apart from his disability, I thought him very well and his mind as vigorous as ever. . . .

[1] W. A. S. Hewins, *Apologia of an Imperialist*, vol. i, pp. 304–305.

It was refreshing to talk to him and find oneself in such complete agreement. He is full of the Labour question and Tariff and allied questions. I told him that I should not change and that so far as lay in my power I should see the business through whatever the consequences. When he came in to lunch Austen asked him whether he had read the account of the meeting. He curled his lips in the old scornful way and said slowly, 'Yes, I've read it'. He made no comment.

As to Chamberlain's own view there is no room for the slightest doubt. He has never been wedded to details, but on the broad issues of his policy he would not give way an inch. He said that if I held to it unflinchingly I should come out top. I don't think that, but as to holding to it there can be no doubt. He said he should ignore Bonar Law and his pledges and go straight on. He parted from me with great affection, holding my hand for a long time. He said there was one thing he desired to say to me, before I left. He hoped that I would in no circumstances whatever abandon the cause to which I had devoted my life, until it was carried. I said, 'Of course not, Mr. Chamberlain. I promise you I will never abandon it.' I then left.

His health was failing now and slowly his constitution began to give way. Neville left a pathetic description of his father in these last months of his life.

'I thought the work might kill me, but I never expected this,' he said to me pathetically one evening and many times he must have wished to be dead. He who had been so self reliant was now dependent on a woman for every common act of life. Yet he submitted with amazing patience and allowed himself to be dragged out to walk his daily round panting and sweating with the exertion, to be thrust into his coat and piled up with rugs on the hottest day, to have his gloves pulled on and off, to have his cigars cut down and to be sent to bed early, in short to endure humiliations and discomforts without end every day of his life. His only real pleasure was in watching his grandchildren. He could not even talk to them. He could only make uncouth noises which often frightened them, and it was touching to watch his efforts to attract them. He was delighted with Dorothy, especially when she stayed for 10 days at Highbury as a baby. Frank he only saw twice or thrice, but he held him in his arms and gazed at him with the utmost satisfaction. We were all glad that he had the pleasure of knowing that there was another boy in the family to carry on the name.

Looking back over the 8 years of his infirmity it must be admitted that they were sad and weary ones for your grandfather. One of his sorest trials was the gradual failure of his eyesight. Not that he became blind but that he lost the power of focussing so that he could not read nor distinguish any object clearly. Many times he expressed to your grandmother his wish that he were dead. Yet there were consolations. His physical condition brought out his innate goodness, his care and thoughtfulness for others, his great tenderness to his own family. At the same time the bitter hatred he had once aroused among his political opponents died away and they too came to see his great qualities. On his birthdays messages of sympathy and affection came to him from many quarters causing him to say 'They think too much of me'.

His decision not to stand again for Parliament was made public early in the New Year.

CHAMBERLAIN TO TITTERTON

5 *January* 1914.—Before leaving home for the South of France I think I ought to communicate to you the decision at which I have arrived to retire from Parliament at the next General Election. I have not come to this decision without many regrets at the severance of a connection which has already lasted for over thirty seven years and has been marked on the part of my constituents by an ever growing confidence and support; but I cannot hope again to do my work in Parliament, and I feel that our City and the constituency need the services of a younger man who will take an active part in the parliamentary struggle and help you to maintain the supremacy of the Unionist Cause in Birmingham.

In announcing to my old friends and constituents that I shall not offer myself again for re-election when a general election comes, I would ask you to thank them all for their long continued kindness to me & for the loyal and undeviating support which has been my mainstay throughout my public life. Assure them of my abiding interest in all that concerns their welfare and of my lasting gratitude for their friendship and goodwill.

Austen was adopted as his successor. Faithful old Collings announced that he, too, would not seek re-election.

Chamberlain's words, 'I cannot hope again to do my work in Parliament' marked the end of his active political life. They gave rise to a series of leading articles and biographical notices such as are seldom published while any man is alive. With almost no exceptions the tributes were generous and whole-hearted. The bitter hatreds he had once aroused were stilled by the bitterness of his own calvary.

VIII

Chamberlain left for Cannes at the beginning of January 1914, and resumed his accustomed routine. This included occasional promenades in his bath chair along the Boulevard du Midi. One day that winter, two English ladies, walking down the Boulevard, stopped by his chair and stood for some moments staring at him. 'It's Mr. Chamberlain,' one said to the other. To their utter astonishment and alarm, the figure in the bath chair swept off his hat and exclaimed, 'Yes, I'm Joe', at which the two old things beat a hasty retreat.[1]

[1] From a note supplied by Mr. W. J. Kage.

Henniker Heaton, who visited Chamberlain in February, found him 'looking remarkably well'.[1] Hicks Beach, however, who saw him a few weeks later, came away greatly saddened.[2]

Another visitor that spring was Lord Charles Beresford. Beresford talked much about a book by the German author, Bernhardi, which in his view pointed to a certain and early war with Germany. Mrs. Chamberlain ordered the book and read it to Chamberlain. He concurred with Beresford's judgment and said : 'This means war'. Mrs. Chamberlain then asked him, 'What about my countrymen, the Americans? What part will they take?'

'They'll try to keep out,' Chamberlain answered, 'but in the end they'll have to come in.'[3]

Chamberlain returned to England in May. On 6 June he appeared in a bath chair at a farewell garden party given at Highbury to his constituents.

Despite this farewell to public life his interest in affairs continued unabated. The Liberal Home Rule Bill had passed the House of Commons for the third time and under the provisions of the Parliament Bill would become law that year, whatever the attitude of the House of Lords. Ireland, meanwhile, moved to the edge of civil war. On 23 June, the Unionists introduced an Amending Bill in the House of Lords ; and a few days later (29 June), Halsbury came to consult Chamberlain as to the line the peers should take. His advice was to resist to the end. Two younger men, Ware and Amery, also called that day.

'I have never seen the good of giving in', he said to Ware, 'If you don't give in, something always happens.' [4]

As Amery was leaving the room, he called him back and said, 'Amery, if I were the House of Lords, I would fight.' [5]

Next day, 30 June, Chamberlain had a slight heart attack. He stayed in bed that day and the next. On the night of 1 July, Mrs. Chamberlain, who slept next door, heard noises from his bedroom. She went in, and standing over him, heard him making a speech in his sleep. He was replying to Asquith on some aspect of the Fiscal issue. Curiously, his speech, which had been blurred and thickened since his stroke, seemed to her, that night, to have recovered all its former clearness.

---

[1] Henniker Heaton to Kage, 23 February 1914.
[2] Lady Victoria Hicks Beach, *Life of Sir M. Hicks Beach*, p. 160.
[3] From a conversation with Mrs. Chamberlain.—J. A.
[4] Sir F. Ware, *The Post Victorians*, p. 115.
[5] L. S. Amery, 'Joseph Chamberlain', a broadcast, 1 August 1952.

Next morning, 2 July, he seemed a little better. Mrs. Chamberlain read *The Times* to him as usual. The leading article that day was on the murder of the Archduke Franz Ferdinand at Sarajevo. Mrs. Chamberlain began to read it to him, but he stopped her as if it were more than he could bear. He saw clearly that the world was on the brink of war.[1]

Austen came in a little later, and Chamberlain questioned him about a recent debate. Austen told him of Asquith's speech and of his own reply to it.

'Quite right,' said Chamberlain, 'somebody has got to give way, but I don't see why it should always be us.'

In the afternoon came a second and more serious heart attack. The family were called in. 'I got up to Prince's Gardens about 7 o'clock' wrote Neville,

and was told he was better and sleeping. After dinner, Austen and I went up to his room and it was then clear that he could not live much longer. He was unconscious and breathing loudly, and oxygen was being administered. In about half an hour, there was a change for the worse, Mrs. Chamberlain and Beatrice, Ida, Hilda and Ivy (Austen's wife), came in with Mrs. Endicott and for a quarter of an hour we waited while his breathing became slowly fainter and fainter. He never regained consciousness and passed away peacefully in Mrs. Chamberlain's arms. ... That afternoon, his brother Arthur's name and that of Ethel were also on his lips. I think he was partly conscious that his end was approaching. I am sure that he was ready for it.[2]

So the long years of frustration and illness ended; years only endured at all, thanks to the devotion of his wife and to the care of Ida and Hilda. 'What life will be without him I do not dare to think' wrote Mrs. Chamberlain

but I can truly say that I would not have him back. He had so much to bear that the thought that he was spared any further suffering gives peace to us all.'[3]

The Dean of Westminster offered burial in the Abbey, but the offer was declined. It had been Chamberlain's express wish to be buried in Birmingham and his wish was respected On 6 July, after. a short service at the Unitarian Church of the Messiah, his body was borne through the crowded streets of Birmingham and laid to rest in Key Hill Cemetery, alongside of the other members of his family. He was true to himself in this last gesture, as throughout his life.

[1] From a letter of Mrs. Chamberlain's, 8 July 1948.—J. A.
[2] From an account of Chamberlain's life written by Neville in the course of July 1914.
[3] Mrs. Chamberlain to Dowson, 16 July 1914.

BOOK XXVIII

EPILOGUE
(1914–1968)

CHAPTER CXX

TARIFF REFORM AND THE
FIRST WORLD WAR

The man and his achievements — The fate of his causes — The leadership of
Tariff Reform — The war revives Imperialism — Intervention or *laissez-faire*?
— 'so the old fiscal system goes' — The Balfour of Burleigh Committee and the
Paris Economic Conference — Lloyd George in power — Triumph of the Interventionists — The Imperial War Cabinet decides for Preference — Lloyd
George accepts Tariff Reform — Another 'Khaki' election — Austen introduces
the first Preferences.

I

CHAMBERLAIN's life was symbolic of his times. The man's life-
span alone is revealing. He was born in the year when Lord Melbourne called Queen Victoria to the throne. He died a few days
before the First World War shattered for ever the political, economic
and social structure evolved over the century since Waterloo.
Sprung from Unitarian stock in an age when Unitarians were still
banned from the University, he lived to found a university himself
and to establish an Anglican diocese. He entered public life an
extreme radical, contemptuous of an aristocracy 'that toil not,
neither do they spin'. He died the acknowledged leader of British
Imperialism and a die-hard opponent of House of Lords reform.

Yet even bitter enemies — and he had many — seldom attributed
his changes of political position to careerism or ambition. Men knew
that, had he swallowed his principles and stuck to his party, he would
have become the leader of the Liberals and almost certainly Prime
Minister as well. Instead, by siding with the Tories, he virtually
excluded himself from the highest office in the state.

His progress across the political spectrum was accepted because it
was gradual and natural. It did not spring from any sudden change
of heart or Pauline conversion. Rather it reflected the changing
circumstances of the industrial middle classes to which he belonged.
While they still fought against a predominantly landowning and
High Church establishment, he was in the forefront of the social
struggle. As they conquered the commanding heights of power and

2 K 2   993

grew to feel that the country belonged to them, so the radical agitator became the constructive reformer, first at home and then in foreign and imperial policy. The end found him at bay, grimly defending the national heritage against a new challenge from the new radicalism of Lloyd George.

No British statesman has been more representative than Chamberlain. But he was no mere mirror of the opinions or prejudices of his age. On the contrary, he did much to mould them and left an indelible stamp upon them. The man's mind was essentially practical and constructive, little given to speculation or theorising, but original in its grasp of the right moment for bringing new ideas into the arena of affairs. He was a man of principle, rather than principles; more concerned with ends than with means; dedicated to serving the nation and seeing political parties, not as causes in themselves but rather as instruments to get things done.

This desire to get things done was the key to Chamberlain's character. It brought him inevitably and from the beginning into conflict with the prevailing philosophy of *laissez-faire*. All his life Chamberlain was an interventionist, holding that political power should be used to shape the pattern of society. As Lord Mayor of Birmingham, he used the municipal office to clear the slums and make his city a better place. As a radical back bencher, he used the House of Commons to give the country better schools. As President of the Board of Trade, he brought in laws to provide better working conditions. In all these measures, as in his 'unauthorized programme', he was demanding that vested interests should pay for social reform. This was a direct challenge to the accepted Liberal doctrine of *laissez-faire* and led on inevitably to the clash with Gladstone.

Laissez-faire leads logically to self-determination. Gladstone was not prepared to tax the British public either to bribe or to coerce the Irish into maintaining the Union. He came, thus, to Home Rule. Chamberlain had long advocated regional self-government for Scotland, Wales and parts of England as well as for Ireland. But he had done so on grounds of business efficiency and to head off Irish separatism. He had never contemplated the break up of the kingdom. When he realised that Gladstone was prepared to concede even this, he judged that the nation was in danger. He accordingly joined hands with the Tories to fight Home Rule, sacrificing power, personal friendships and, so it seemed at the time, all prospects of future influence.

The Conservative party was the heir to a long tradition of Government intervention in economic and social policies stretching back to the seventeenth century. Peel and even Disraeli had bowed before the Liberal wind of change. But the tradition still lingered. Salisbury and his colleagues were scarcely zealous for social reform. But, unlike Gladstone, they did not object in principle to state intervention in social affairs. Thus it happened that Chamberlain's greatest social reforms — free and compulsory education, the extension of small holdings, and workmen's compensation — were achieved in alliance with the Tories and thanks to their support.

The fulfilment of this social programme led to a gradual change in Chamberlain's political priorities. From his arrival at the Colonial Office, in 1895, he became increasingly absorbed with the opportunities of Empire and the dangers from abroad. These came to replace social progress as the main objects of his reforming zeal.

In foreign affairs Chamberlain soon came to the conclusion that Splendid Isolation was no longer a tenable policy. Britain must have allies. Thus he sought first a German alliance and, when rebuffed by Bülow, turned to France and prepared the way for the Entente Cordiale.

In Imperial affairs his achievements were even more spectacular. It was under his aegis that British power was consolidated in East Africa, in Ashanti, and in Nigeria. He waged war and made peace in South Africa greatly to Britain's advantage. He saved the West Indies from ruin. He encouraged the constitutional union of Australia.

Even more important than these individual acts of policy were his efforts to build an effective political, military and economic union of the self-governing Colonies. He developed the Colonial Conference into an accepted institution of regular Imperial consultation. He brought the Colonies to send their troops to fight alongside the British Army in the South African War. He discerned in the system of mutual preference a practical way to strengthen the economic union of the Colonies with Britain. In all these things he was working for the union and strength of the Empire as the deliberate and foremost aim of British policy. And he was the first man to do so since the loss of the American Colonies.

Chamberlain's advocacy of Imperial Preference led him on to challenge the Free Trade system which had prevailed in Britain for two generations. He was first drawn to Tariff Reform as a means of consolidating the Empire. But as he studied the question he became increasingly an advocate of Protection for its own sake. He came to see in tariffs a way of safeguarding British industry from foreign competition, of maintaining a high level of employment, and of raising revenue to finance social reform. Fiscal Reform thus appeared as a policy combining Imperialism, economic expansion, full employment, and social progress. As such it had a wide appeal to all classes.

In Chamberlain's lifetime Tariff Reform was defeated by the Old Guard of Free Traders and the New Guard of distributive Radicals led by Lloyd George. Lloyd George accepted the traditional *laissez-faire* view that the state should not interfere in the processes of production and trade. But he proposed to milk the rich on an unprecedented scale and so to finance a more ambitious programme of social reform than the Tariff Reformers could hope to pay for from the proceeds of import duties. From 1909 onwards public opinion in Britain swung uneasily between these two views. In practice, the Parliamentary majority remained with the Liberals, though, ironically enough, this was mainly due to the continuing presence of the Irish members; and Chamberlain had done more than anyone to keep them at Westminster.

Chamberlain's exertions in his crusade for Empire Preference and Tariff Reform led to the breakdown of his health. Then came the long years of paralysed frustration while his colleagues hesitated and finally denied his policies. Could his story have had a different ending? What would have happened if his health had held out a few more years? Between 1906 and 1910 pressures inside the Conservative party might well have brought him to the leadership. The result of the 1910 election was very finely balanced. Is it possible that his personal appeal to the constituencies might just have turned the scales? Had he then come to power at the head of a Unionist Government, could he have laid his Imperial and fiscal policies on secure foundations? With a firmer grasp of defence and foreign policies than Asquith and his colleagues showed, might he even have averted the drift to the First World War? All this is one of the 'might have beens' of history. The fact remains that he died a defeated and a disappointed man.

II

One test of statesmanship is the fate of the stateman's work. What became of Chamberlain's causes?

Social reform received a powerful impetus from the First World War and the sense of national unity engendered by it. After the war,

Chamberlain's son, Neville, took up the task, and, building on foundations layed by his father and Lloyd George, is recognised today as a principal architect of the modern Welfare State. We may question nevertheless whether Chamberlain or Neville would have approved the extent to which our present social services have departed from any genuine system of individual insurance. Both men, in their time, certainly held the view that state aid should supplement self-reliance and not be a substitute for it.

Irish Home Rule and presently Independence was one of the results of the war. The outbreak of the World War, it is true, banished the threat of civil war in England. But the strain of the war on Britain, the Sinn Fein rebellion and American pressures led to the victory of the separatists; though Ulster was saved for the Union. It is one of the ironies of the final settlement that Austen played a leading part in bringing about the Home Rule his father had so passionately opposed.

Were Chamberlain's warnings against Home Rule justified ? Was he right over Ireland, or was he wrong ? Certainly things did not stop at Home Rule, but went on to total separation, as he had predicted. In the Second World War Ireland was neutral and her ports were denied to us. We paid dearly for this in lives and tonnage. At the same time, individual Irishmen flocked in their thousands to the British flag, just as they still come in their thousands to earn their living and make their homes in Britain.

In material terms, independence has impoverished Ireland and weakened Britain. The ending of bitterness has no doubt been some compensation; but the Irish example has proved contagious. Scotland and Wales continue to muster substantial forces for Home Rule. Whitehall and Westminster are turning again to modern variants of Chamberlain's formula of ' Home Rule All Round '.

In foreign affairs, Chamberlain's main achievement was the Alliance with France. It did not prevent the First World War, but it secured our victory and for a time made Britain and France the arbiters of the world. Austen tried, at Locarno, to combine the Entente Cordiale with his father's earlier concept of an alliance with Germany. But Locarno foundered in the aftermath of the Great Depression. Neville, too, returned to the idea of an understanding with Germany, swallowing Hitler's camels where Joe had strained at Bülow's gnat. Neville fell between two stools. He weakened France. He did not win Germany. Chamberlain, in his day, had known how to choose between them.

Despite Churchill's efforts to raise France from the depths of de-feat and occupation, the Entente Cordiale has been sadly strained in recent years. Yet logic as well as experience suggests that its revival is the key to the establishment of a lasting European system.

The United States, when Chamberlain entered public life, scarcely ranked as a major power. But Chamberlain was one of the first British statesmen to sense the importance of Anglo-American friend-ship. The radical businessman felt a natural sympathy for the American democracy. The leader of Tariff Reform acknowledged the success of American Protectionism. Yet Chamberlain always advocated ' standing up ' to American pressures in trade policy and over Canada. He understood the Americans better than most English leaders of his day and held that they would value our friend-ship the more if they saw us stand up for our own interests.

In Imperial affairs Chamberlain enlarged the bounds of Empire by two great provinces: the hinterland of Nigeria and the Boer Republics.

Nigeria rose on Lugard's foundations to become the most popu-lated and prosperous of Britain's African Colonies. But sixty years of British guidance proved too short a preparation for independence; and the high hopes that were set on Nigeria's political stability have been disappointed by the event. Yet very strong links have been established between Britain and this greatest of the tropical African states; and these may well develop to our mutual advantage in the years to come.[1]

The South African War, for all its clumsiness of execution, must be reckoned a master-stroke of policy. Few victories in British history have done more to increase Britain's economic or military power. After the Peace of Vereeniging British settlers and British capital poured into the country. Today it has become Britain's second most important market in the world and the ground where well over £1,000m. of British capital are profitably invested.

Thanks to a generous peace settlement — Chamberlain's as much as Campbell-Bannerman's — the wounds of the Boer War were healed; and, in both World Wars, South Africans of Dutch as well as of Anglo-Saxon origin, fought with distinction on the British side. Outstanding among them were Chamberlain's old adversaries, Botha and Smuts.

---

[1] Miss Margery Perham's *Lugard*, vol. i (1956), contains valuable information about Chamberlain's interest in Nigeria which was not available to J. L. Garvin when he wrote Volume III of the present work.

The racial issue between European and African was largely ignored in Chamberlain's time by pro-Boers even more than by Imperialists. Chamberlain, Milner and Selbourne had some regard to it, as we have seen, though they never considered it as decisive. Since their time this issue has assumed quite different proportions, clouding Britain's relations with South Africa and leading to the latter's formal separation from the Commonwealth. But the real connection between the two countries remains very strong. British investment in gold, diamonds, uranium and a growing industry combine to make South Africa one of the main pillars of the British economic system. The strategic and commercial importance of the Cape route to Britain has been underlined by the recent closing of the Suez Canal. Nor can British opinion ever be indifferent to the fate of more than two million South Africans of British descent.

Chamberlain's social reforms, his stand against Home Rule, his launching of the Entente Cordiale and his conquest of South Africa were solid and, by ordinary political standards, enduring achievements. At the time each aroused fierce controversy. Later they became part of the accepted scheme of things until the tides of history buried or eroded them. Of a quite different order was Chamberlain's crusade for Imperial Union and Tariff Reform. Here was a vision, a political philosophy and a party programme, combining the main themes of his life — the industrial and the social, the National and the Imperial.

He prepared the crusade for eight years from high office in Government. For three years he preached it to the people. He continued to inspire it for another eight years after his health was broken.

Imperialism and Tariff Reform were more than a policy. They were a faith. And Chamberlain was its prophet, gathering around him a host of disciples who received his inspiration and developed his ideas. His supporters were more than a party. They were a popular movement with deep roots in industry and agriculture, in the professions and the universities, in the working classes and among the youth. A generation passed before the Imperial Idea prevailed. Another generation again before it was denied. All this time, Chamberlain's teaching was a dominant, perhaps the dominant, influence in British political life and thought.

We have sought in these pages to tell the story of Chamberlain's Tariff Reform Campaign. But that story did not end with his death, and no biography of the man could be complete without at least a sketch of what became of the movement he had called into being.

III

After Chamberlain's stroke, in 1906, the leadership of the Tariff Reform Movement devolved naturally upon Austen. Austen believed in the policy but he never had the faith that moves mountains. Later on, indeed, he would tell Beaverbrook that ' food taxes had been a millstone around his neck throughout his political career '.[1]

Bonar Law too had been an enthusiast for Tariff Reform, but, from electoral considerations, grew shy of food taxes. Curiously enough his natural caution was sometimes reinforced by Beaverbrook's advice. Beaverbrook himself was always a convinced Tariff Reformer. But in his advice to Bonar Law he often distinguished between his own principles and his judgement of what was most expedient for his leader.

The biggest man in the Imperialist movement after Chamberlain was Milner. But he had no gift for Parliament or for the platform. His temperament made him operate from behind the scenes. He inspired the movement. He could not lead it. In these circumstances, Hewins and Amery increasingly came forward as the spokesmen of the movement in Parliament.

Hewins, the energetic head of the Tariff Commission, was a highly qualified economist; and his speeches on the economic case for Tariff Reform were heard with respect. But he lacked authority or experience when it came to the great issues of Imperial Policy. He was said, besides, to look like Tenniel's drawings of the Mad Hatter in *Alice in Wonderland*, and, perhaps because of this, was never taken quite seriously. Amery had already made a name for himself as a journalist on *The Times*. But he was still new to the House and not yet in a position to lead. He was, however, very close to Milner; and this was known.

Bonar Law's renunciation of food taxes in 1913 had been a shattering blow to the Imperialist cause and to the Tariff Reformers. The movement towards Imperial Union had, so it seemed, reached a dead end. The Liberal Government's efforts to encourage closer political or military co-operation within the Empire had already failed. On top of this, the Unionist party had gone back on Imperial Preference. At the time of Chamberlain's death, indeed, the mounting Irish crisis put in question, not just the unity of the Empire, but the unity of the kingdom itself. Then the Kaiser came to the rescue.

[1] Lord Beaverbrook, *The Decline and Fall of Lloyd George*, p. 68.

IV

The outbreak of the First World War sparked off a revival of Imperialist sentiment at home and in the Empire just as the Boer War had done fifteen years before. But this time it was on the grand scale. Its first and most striking manifestation was military. Britain's war was the Empire's war; and the Dominions answered the call to arms without a moment's hesitation. South Africa, with Botha and Smuts in the lead, proved no exception. Strong Imperial armies were raised and fought with distinction on the battlefields of the Western front and the Middle East.

Co-operation in defence led on naturally to political co-operation, though this took longer to develop. The first move was the visit of 'Billy' Hughes, the Australian Prime Minister, to London in 1916. His speeches aroused great enthusiasm; and there was talk of offering him a permanent seat in the British Cabinet.

A year later Lloyd George summoned a War Conference of the Empire. This led to the constitution of the Imperial War Cabinet, made up in the first instance of the Prime Ministers of the Dominions. It was resolved that the Imperial War Cabinet should meet at least once a year and if necessary more frequently.

Borden, the Canadian Prime Minister, described the Imperial Cabinet as a 'Cabinet of Governments rather than of ministers' and added: 'For many years the thoughts of statesman and student in every part of the Empire have centred around the question of future constitutional arrangements. It may be now as in the past that the necessity imposed by great events has given the answer.'

The formation of the Imperial War Cabinet was a great step forward in the political union of the Empire. It involved, in essence, converting the Imperial Conference into a policy-making body. But, as Borden's words show, it also marked the end of any thought of Imperial Federation. The union of British nations was to be achieved, not by the delegation of powers to some supra national authority, but by continuous consultation between sovereign Governments.

V

War is a matter of money as well as men at arms. From the beginning the Dominion Governments had contributed to the common war chest. But it was a little time before the question of Imperial economic co-operation was placed on the agenda.

The Asquith Government's conception of waging war seems astonishing to our generation. So, indeed, it would have seemed to our forebears in the Napoleonic Wars. The Government did not expect more than a year of fighting. It was, thus, a deliberate aim of policy to disrupt ordinary life as little as possible. The war was to be waged by the Regular Army, the Territorials, and presently Kitchener's volunteers. Some increase in taxation was accepted as necessary to pay the new recruits and buy their equipment. Otherwise, it was to be business as usual.

Trading with the enemy, it is true, was stopped and a blockade instituted. But there was no question of interference with prices, wages or contracts. No organised search was made for alternative sources of those essential materials, previously supplied from enemy or enemy occupied territory. No thought was given to the pre-emption of raw materials in neutral countries so as to deny them to the enemy. There was, in short, no plan to mobilise the resources of Britain, let alone of the Empire, to wage war on the economic as well as the military front.

The Liberal Government's approach to these matters was perhaps less unnatural than it seems today. It was a fundamental tenet of Liberal philosophy that Government intervention in the business of production, distribution and exchange could only have negative consequences. Ministers believed in the absolute virtue of the free-market economy subject to only one qualification. They accepted that direct or indirect taxes could be raised, in time of peace, to pay for social reform or, in time of war, to pay for military operations.

The Unionists took a rather different view. The Tariff Reform Campaign had stirred memories of an earlier Tory tradition of Government management of the economy. It had also educated the Party to the idea of Imperial self-sufficiency. Unionists were familiar with the thought that Government regulation of exports and imports would make it possible to expand British production, to develop alternative supplies of raw materials, and to influence the level of employment. Up to the war the pros and cons of Chamberlain's proposals had necessarily been debated in the abstract. In peacetime, indeed, it must have taken years to demonstrate whether they were false or true. The war, by contrast, offered an immediate criterion by which to test their validity: would Government intervention help to beat the enemy?

Men like Milner, Hewins and Amery saw this at once. Before 1914 was out, Hewins was advising British industry, through the

Tariff Commission, where to buy alternative supplies of scarce raw materials. Next, from the beginning of 1915, he and Amery went to work on the Unionist Business Committee set up under the chairmanship of Walter Long. They argued the need to mobilise the resources of the nation and the Empire, both for victory in the war, and for the extension of British influence after the victory. Their audience was well conditioned by a dozen years discussion of the merits of Tariff Reform; and the response was immediate.

The First World War is mainly remembered in Britain for the bloody stalemate in the trenches of the Western Front and for the virulent intrigues between the politicians and the generals. But the main struggle on the political front during the first two years of the war was not about these things. It was between *laissez-faire* and intervention. On the one side were arrayed Asquith and the leaders of the Liberal party. On the other, the Unionist leaders with increasing support, as time went by, from the business community and from Lloyd George.

The first Unionist campaign for increased Government control of the economy was waged over munitions. This led to the creation of the Ministry of Munitions and, indirectly, to the formation of the First Coalition Government in May 1915.

The next battleground was conscription. On 16 June 1915 Milner proclaimed the need for universal service. This, he said, required ' organized effort and that means regulation '. He was urged by Amery ' to proclaim the outlines of a complete policy in which National Service fits in as an essential element, but which also deals with all the other problems; munitions, finance, food and so on '.[1]

The battle over conscription raged throughout the autumn and was not finally won until May 1916. But already in the previous summer the Tariff Reformers had scored a marked success in their efforts to regulate trade. Towards the end of August, the Cabinet had considered the introduction of tariffs as a means of limiting the import of luxury goods. McKenna, the Free Trade Chancellor of the Exchequer had at first rejected the proposal. Yet a fortnight later Ministers changed their minds. On 15 September the Cabinet decided that duties must be introduced on certain selected and unessential articles. Lloyd George threw a note across the table to Walter Long: ' So the old fiscal system goes, destroyed by its own advocates.'

The autumn Budget, introduced on 24 September, imposed duties

[1] Amery to Milner, 2 August 1915.

of $33\frac{1}{3}$ per cent on motor cars, cameras, clocks, watches and other luxury goods. Hewins recorded his pleasure 'at having smashed the Free Trade system at last '.[1]

VI

Hewins turned next from the national to the Imperial economic front. In January 1916 he tabled a motion:

> that with a view to increasing the power of the Allies during the war, H.M.G. should enter into immediate consultation with the Governments of the Dominions in order with their aid to bring the whole economic strength of the Empire into co-operation with our Allies in a policy directed against the enemy.

Hewins spoke of co-operation for wartime purposes. But he was even more concerned with post-war economic co-operation. Rather surprisingly, the Government met his motion by appointing a Committee on post-war trade relations with the following terms of reference:

> To consider the commercial and industrial policy to be adopted after the war with special reference to the following points:
>
> (a) What industries are essential to the future safety of the nation and what steps should be taken to maintain or establish them.
> (b) What steps should be taken to recover home and foreign trade lost during the War and to secure new markets.
> (c) To what Extent and by what means the resources of the Empire can and should be developed *so as to render it independent of foreign supplies.*[2]

By a curious irony, Chamberlain's old opponent, Balfour of Burleigh, was made Chairman of the Committee. But his views had undergone a sea change since the resignations of 1903.

The Tariff Reformers received a further shot in the arm that year from the speeches made by Hughes, the Australian Prime Minister, during his visit to Britain. Hughes devoted much of his time to attacking Free Trade and spoke out strongly in favour of Tariff Reform and Imperial Preference. At Birmingham, he paid tribute to Chamberlain, who had 'first sounded in these Islands the clarion call of Empire. . . . Joseph Chamberlain, who pointed the way along which our feet should tread to achieve our destiny'.

Asquith made Hughes a member of the British Delegation to the

---

[1] W. A. S. Hewins, *The Apologia of an Imperialist* (1929), vol. ii, p 53.
[2] The words in italics were deleted from the published text for fear of alarming our allies.

Paris Economic Conference. This Conference marked a further departure from the Free Trade system. Its resolutions fell into three groups. There were proposals to improve the blockade and enforce the sequestration of enemy-owned business. There were measures providing for reparations, protection against unfair competition and the denial to the enemy of most-favoured-nation treatment for a term of years after the war. Finally, there were proposals to encourage post-war trade between the allies and to make them independent of ex-enemy countries in raw materials and essential manufactures. Several of these Resolutions were inspired by Bonar Law and by Hughes. Had the post-war measures then agreed — and they were subsequently elaborated in detail — been carried out, they would have led to an organic combination of the British, French and Belgian Empires.

As it happened the Resolutions of the Paris Conference led indirectly to Asquith's fall. Carson had tabled an amendment that enemy business confiscated in Nigeria should be sold only to natural-born British subjects, or to wholly British companies. The Government opposed this as an excessively protectionist interpretation of the Paris Resolutions. In the division seventy-three Unionists supported the Government, while sixty-five voted with Carson. Bonar Law chose to take this as evidence that the Government had lost the confidence of the Unionist Party. He demanded its reconstruction. Long and devious negotiations followed. At the end of them Asquith resigned and made way for Lloyd George.

VII

Lloyd George's advent to power meant the victory of intervention over *laissez-faire* in the economic management of the war. Asquith had made concessions to the interventionists, but he had retreated reluctantly and step by step.

The idea that industry would have to be deliberately organized for war production encountered subconscious resistance in a Government committed to the doctrines of Free Trade and individualism. It is not surprising that the necessity for state intervention was only gradually admitted by ministers who had spent the greater part of their political careers in exposing the fallacies of Protectionism on the one hand and Socialism on the other.[1]

With Lloyd George all this was changed. The first few months of his administration produced a comprehensive system of economic

[1] Sidney Pollard, *History of the British Economy*, p. 43.

and financial controls. In the spring of 1917 came the Corn Production Bill, marking a complete break with the Victorian system of
free imports. It was virtually a return to the Corn Laws. There
followed the direct or indirect control of industry and trade by a
system of licences, the restriction of capital expenditure, the fixing of
prices, the regulation of transport, and the direction of labour. At
the heart of the system was Milner, reconciling the rival claims of
the armed forces, industry, and the Government; allocating tonnage
and manpower; determining import priorities and the level of food
stocks. By the end of the war, the Government had direct charge of
shipping, railway and canal transport. It bought about 90 per cent
of all imports and marketed 80 per cent of all food consumed at home.
Price control was almost universal.

It is interesting to reflect that this revolution from a free to a
managed economy was mainly brought about by the Unionist leaders
and the capitalist businessmen made Ministers by Lloyd George.
Opposition to it came principally from the Asquith Liberals and
from MacDonald's supporters in the Labour party.

VIII

The economic revolution was not confined to the home front. At
the end of 1916, Milner had persuaded the Government to summon
the Imperial War Conference. Wartime and post-war economic
co-operation between the Empire countries was on the agenda. This
was bound to raise the question of Preference. What was the
Government's policy to be ?

The Cabinet hesitated to put a definite proposal to the Conference.
Hewins, however, was determined that the Balfour of Burleigh Committee at least should agree a definite set of Resolutions for submission
to the Imperial leaders. There was much lobbying and discussion
in which Bonar Law showed himself characteristically cautious. But
in the end, Hewins had his way; and on 1 February the Committee
agreed the following Resolutions unanimously :

1. In the light of experience gained during the war we consider that
   special steps must be taken to stimulate the production of foodstuffs,
   raw materials and manufactured articles within the Empire wherever
   the expansion of production is possible and economically desirable
   for the safety and welfare of the Empire as a whole.
2. We therefore recommend that H.M. Government should now declare their adherence to the principle that preference should be
   accorded to the produce and manufactures of the British overseas

dominions in respect of any customs duties now or hereafter to be imposed on imports into the United Kingdom.

3. Further, it will be necessary to take into earliest consideration as one of the methods of achieving these objects, the desirability of establishing a wider range of customs duties which would be remitted or reduced on the produce and manufactures of the Empire and which would form the basis of commercial treaties with allied and neutral powers.[1]

The Report of the Balfour of Burleigh Committee came before the Cabinet on 11 April. Bonar Law turned to a neighbour and murmured nervously : 'This means Tariff Reform.'[2] Nevertheless, the Cabinet decided to publish the Report and to circulate it to the Imperial Conference, though for information rather than as a British Government proposal.

On 24 April Preference was discussed by the Imperial War Cabinet. Amery noted in his diary:

Lloyd George . . . frankly declared that the war had revealed fundamental facts which it was necessary to recognize and entirely accepted a summary of the case laid down by Milner to the effect that Preference on customs duty was certainly included within his purview wherever customs duties either existed or were imposed in future. All he stipulated was that when the Resolution was published it should be made clear that we were not actually committed to taxes on food.[3]

The drafting of the Resolution gave some trouble. But in the end, the Imperial War Cabinet, including the British representatives, unanimously accepted the principle of Mutual Preference within the Empire. The decision was so categoric that Amery, then a Secretary to the War Cabinet and present throughout the discussion, wrote in his diary:

Thus ended the twelve years fight on Imperial Preference.[4]

IX

Imperial Preference was now the official policy of the British as well as the Dominion Governments; and, after some prodding from the Tariff Reformers, a Committee was appointed under Walter Long to study how to give effect to this and other decisions of the Imperial War Cabinet. Hewins was made a member of the Committee and also appointed Under-Secretary at the Colonial Office. His hands and Long's were further strengthened by the final Report

[1] W. A. S. Hewins, *Apologia of an Imperialist*, vol. ii, p. 115.   [2] Ibid.
[3] L. S. Amery's Diaries, 24 April 1917.   [4] Ibid., 26 April 1917.

of the Balfour of Burleigh Committee. This was frankly protectionist. It proposed Government action to promote and safeguard the development of 'pivotal' industries. These 'should be maintained in this country at all hazards and at any expense'. It also recommended tariff protection for other selected industries, whenever these were unable to maintain themselves 'by reason of undue foreign competition, inadequate supplies of raw materials or any other causes'.

Meanwhile, the failure of Ludendorff's last great offensive had opened the way to victory. Lloyd George now turned his eyes from the battlefield to the constituencies. He determined to continue the Coalition and planned, like Chamberlain after the Boer War, to exploit his military triumph at an immediate 'Khaki' election. Bonar Law supported him. He believed that Lloyd George could bring a new accession of strength to the Conservative party, much as Chamberlain had done a generation earlier.

Lloyd George and Bonar Law were agreed that it would be bad election tactics to propose food taxes to a public which had so long endured the rigours of a siege economy. At the same time, if Lloyd George was to carry the Unionist party with him in peacetime, he would have to make concessions to the Tariff Reformers. On this Lloyd George sought Milner's advice. Milner replied that Britain should be guided by her own interests as to whether or not to impose tariffs, but that it was 'essential that on existing duties and such as we may from time to time see fit to impose, there should be some reduction for goods of British [Colonial] origin'. He went on to argue that, once tariffs had been imposed, Preferences could not raise prices. If the Government continued to 'tax certain imported articles of food, like sugar, tea, cocoa, then it is not an increase, but if anything an alleviation of the burdens of the consumer to admit these imports from our Dominions at a somewhat lower rate'.[1]

Several days before the Armistice, Lloyd George ratified his conversion to Tariff Reform in a letter drafted for his signature by Bonar Law. This opened with a statement that the promotion of the unity and development of the British Empire was a fundamental object of policy. It included acceptance of

the policy of Imperial Preference as defined in the Resolutions of the Imperial Conference to the effect that Preference would be given on existing duties and on any duties which may subsequently be imposed.

[1] A. M. Gollin, *Proconsul in Politics: a Study of Lord Milner* (1964), p. 582.

It also accepted the need for a policy designed to give British industries security against unfair competition. ' We must face all these questions', Lloyd George went on:

With new eyes without regard to pre-war views or to pre-war speeches. ... In order to secure better production and better distribution I shall look at every problem simply from the point of view of what is the best method of securing the objects at which we are aiming without any regard to theoretical opinions about Free Trade or Tariff Reform.[1]

The letter was duly published and, on 22 November, Lloyd George and Bonar Law followed it up with a joint election manifesto. They proposed to safeguard key industries and to take measures against the dumping of foreign goods. They would not impose new taxes on food or on raw materials, but they would give Preference to the Dominions and Colonies on existing duties.

Lloyd George won the election by a handsome majority. Austen became Chancellor of the Exchequer. It thus fell to Chamberlain's son in the Budget of 1919, to introduce Preference on all those customs duties then in force. $16\frac{2}{3}$ per cent Preference was given on imports of Empire sugar, tea and tobacco and $33\frac{1}{3}$ per cent on motor cars, cameras and clocks.

This first instalment of Preference was chiefly of interest to the Crown Colonies and to India. But it was taken in the Dominions as a promise of greater things to come and evoked an immediate response. Canada introduced mutual preferential arrangements with the West Indies and opened negotiations with Australia. New Zealand extended Preferences to all Empire countries. Canada, Australia and New Zealand all increased their Preferences to Britain.

The Asquith Liberals ridiculed the idea that Canada could have any interest in a Preference on motor cars. Yet very soon the Preference led the American motor-car companies to set up factories in Canada, sometimes almost within sight of the parent works across the border. They understood the advantages Preference would bring to the Empire producer. Here was the beginning of the Canadian motor-car industry.

[1] Lloyd George to Bonar Law, 2 November 1918.

THE ROAD TO VICTORY

Migration and Preference — Break up of the Coalition — Baldwin takes the plunge — 'dishing the Goat' — The 1923 election — Reactions of the Conservative leadership — Churchill v. Amery: the struggle over 'safeguarding' — The 'Safety First' election — Conservative tactics in Opposition — the Amery–Beaverbrook campaign — Baldwin accepts the full programme — The 1931 crisis — the Gold Standard abandoned — Britain goes protectionist — The Import Duties Act opens the way to Preference — The Ottawa Agreements — Triumph and Justification of Chamberlain's policy.

I

MILNER became Colonial Secretary in the new Coalition with Amery as his deputy.[1] The Government's election pledges left them little scope to press for any immediate extension of Preference beyond the limits of the 1919 Budget. They accordingly concentrated on the encouragement of overseas settlement. Amery introduced a scheme of free passages for ex-servicemen and, at the Imperial Conference of June 1921, persuaded both the Home and the Dominion Governments to put up what, in those days, were regarded as substantial funds. Under the Empire Settlement Act of 1922, the British Government agreed to contribute up to £3 m. a year for fifteen years towards migration schemes. In consequence, nearly half a million people migrated from Britain to the Empire in the next decade.

This was, in fact, much less than the Government had hoped for.

The reason for the shortfall was the collapse of the post-war boom. It was widely believed at the time that unemployment at home would stimulate migration to the Empire. In fact it worked the other way. If British industry was depressed, the British market for Empire food and commodity producers slumped correspondingly. There might be unemployment at home, but there were no new jobs in the Empire either. The Dominion Governments were quick to draw the lesson. Men and money were essential to development.

[1] Hewins had lost his seat at the election and never returned to the House of Commons.

But markets were even more crucial. It was no use stimulating migration and opening up new resources unless the additional food and raw material produced could be sold. To develop the Empire meant to reserve a substantial share of the British market for the Empire producers. And this meant Tariffs against the foreigner and thus taxes on food and raw materials.

Meanwhile, the trend at home was all the other way. With the end of the war there was a natural move to cut back Government expenditure and set the country free from wartime controls and restrictions. Liberals and Unionists were at one in this; though there was an important difference of emphasis between them. The Liberals wanted to go back to the unqualified *laissez-faire* system of pre-war years. Most Unionists wanted to convert some at least of the wartime restrictions on foreign imports into Tariffs with Preferences for the Empire. The Unionists were the dominant partners in the Coalition; and there was much talk from the front bench about the need to safeguard particular industries.

After some delay Horne drafted the Safeguarding of Industries Bill and this was accepted by the Cabinet in the spring of 1921. It was piloted through the House of Commons by Baldwin, the President of the Board of Trade, and, like his father, an early supporter of Tariff Reform. The Bill contained no provision for Preference to Empire countries.

On paper the Safeguarding of Industries Act seemed a major step towards Protection. But it was in the nature of an enabling Act and everything depended on how far the Government were prepared to follow it up and apply its provisions to particular industries. In practice each attempt to apply it encountered obstinate obstruction; and Baldwin even had to threaten resignation to secure the safeguarding of such a relatively unimportant industry as fabric gloves. This particular episode made him popular with the Tariff Reformers. But, from their point of view, the overall balance-sheet was disappointing. The wartime controls were dismantled. Very few safeguarding measures were introduced in practice. There were no additional Preferences.

There were many reasons for this. As the depression deepened and unemployment rose so Ministers became increasingly sensitive to the short-term dangers of any policies likely to raise food or raw material prices. Their fears on this count were underlined by the emergence of the Labour party as the main opposition to the Coalition Government. The Labour party of those days still advocated extremist policies and threatened to resort to direct action to achieve its ends rather than work through the framework of the constitution. This persuaded Lloyd George that his best course was to mobilise public opinion to resist a Socialist revolution. He would unite behind him the traditional forces in the country, Liberal as well as Conservative, to confront the 'Red menace'. But this meant abandoning or at least going slow on the one issue — the fiscal issue — which still divided the ' bourgeois ' parties. Churchill and Birkenhead were the real authors of this policy. But Balfour also backed it. So did Austen who, with Bonar Law's retirement, had at last become leader of the Unionist party.

This negative anti-Socialism no doubt suited ' the hard-faced businessmen who had done well out of the war '. It might even have won a General Election; but it could have no appeal to Imperialists like Amery.

With Milner's resignation in 1921 Amery had become the effective leader of the Tariff Reformers. But he was still only an Under-Secretary and his influence on Lloyd George was limited. As he saw matters, the Coalition leaders were turning their backs on the Empire. Their failure to consult the Dominion Governments over the Chanak crisis had alienated important sections of opinion in the Empire and especially Mackenzie King in Canada. Their conception of an anti-Socialist front made it virtually certain that the next election manifesto would be cautious over safeguarding and would repeat the pledges not to tax food or raw materials. And yet, without Tariffs and Preferences, the Unionists had no positive solution to the mounting economic crisis that could hope to compete with Socialism. Accordingly Amery and those who thought like him came increasingly to join forces with Baldwin and the growing number of Conservatives who disapproved of Lloyd George for many reasons, personal as much as political.

At the beginning of October 1922 Lloyd George and the Conservative leaders in the Cabinet decided on an early General Election. Baldwin threatened to resign in protest; and Amery organised what became known as 'the revolt of the Under-Secretaries'. This was a demand that the Unionists should go to the country as a separate party free to form a Government of their own without Lloyd George if they won a sufficient majority; and free, in that event, to introduce a full Tariff Reform programme.

At the critical Party Meeting at the Carlton Club, Austen, Balfour and the other Unionist Ministers declared their loyalty to Lloyd

George. But Bonar Law, moved by successive appeals from Beaverbrook, Baldwin, George Younger and — not least perhaps — his own sister, weighed in on the side of the rebels. His intervention decided the issue. The Coalition broke up, and a Conservative Government was formed. Bonar Law took office but he was already a dying man and in less than six months Baldwin became Prime Minister.

II

Amery had believed that a return to Conservative government offered the best chance of putting Tariff Reform into practice. And events seemed for a time to confirm his view. He had great influence over Baldwin and his views were shared by many of his Cabinet colleagues.

In the course of walks and talks with the Prime Minister at Aix-les-Bains, during the summer recess, Amery convinced him of the need to introduce a full-blooded programme of safeguarding of industry. The question of extending Preference was still undecided; but, here the Imperial Conference, in October 1923, brought Amery further support. The economic situation in Britain and in the Dominions was increasingly threatening. Bruce of Australia took the lead at the Conference and with strong backing from Smuts, for South Africa, and Massey, for New Zealand pressedthe British Government to break out of the slump by adopting a wide-ranging scheme of tariffs and preferences. They succeeded, indeed, in agreeing anumber of new preferential arrangements affecting in particular Government contracts and such industries as dried fruit and wines.

In the course of October Baldwin told his closest colleagues and later the whole Cabinet that he favoured an early election on a programme of Tariff Reform and Empire Preference. Amery proposed holding the election in the following June. This would give time to educate the constituencies and to prepare a budget with a complete scheme of tariffs in addition to the preferential arrangements already agreed with the Dominions. Most members of the Cabinet pleaded for time before going to the country. But Baldwin was in a hurry.

Lloyd George was away on a tour of the United States and Canada. Beaverbrook, Hamar Greenwood and others were urging him to return from the Great Dominion as the champion of a bold

Imperial policy, including Preference. Such a policy, they argued, would strengthen his influence over Austen, Balfour, Birkenhead and other Coalition Unionists who were also Tariff Reformers. It might even enable him to win back the whole Tory party. Lloyd George saw the opportunity to pinch his opponents' clothes. He began, while still overseas, to frame an Imperial programme. Baldwin heard of it from Younger, the Chairman of the Conservative party. As he told Tom Jones years later: ' I had information that he [Lloyd George] was going protectionist and I had to get in quick.'[1]

On 23 October in a speech at Plymouth, Baldwin declared his faith in the policy of safeguarding but his speech still seemed to look forward to an autumn session. On 2 November at Manchester he came out strongly in favour of Preference. The Liberal leaders, knowing something of Lloyd George's plans, hesitated to answer. On 3 November Lloyd George sailed from New York.

The knowledge that the formidable Welshman was on his way home decided Baldwin that he must strike at once and it was in the next few days that the decision to appeal to the country was taken.

Greenwood saw Lloyd George immediately on his return and urged Lloyd George to stick to his plans for an Imperial programme and smother Baldwin with his support. But the thought of backing Baldwin was too much for Lloyd George. He would fight on a Free Trade platform instead. 'Baldwin knifed me', he said 'and I shall knife him.'[2] In this he partly succeeded.

Baldwin asked for a dissolution on 13 November. For the first time the issue of Tariff Reform and Preference was put squarely to the electorate. But there had been too little preparation. Lancashire voted for Free Trade. The Farmers voted against the government because they had not been promised adequate protection. The result was disastrous for the Conservatives. They lost eighty-eight seats and were forced into Opposition.

Amery always believed that Baldwin had rushed into the election without giving himself time to educate his party or the public. But then he did not share Baldwin's overriding anxiety to 'dish the Goat', as Baldwin called Lloyd George. In later years he sometimes wondered whether Lloyd George might not have proved a far more determined and effective Imperial leader than Baldwin if the

[1] Baldwin in a statement to Tom Jones, September 1935.
[2] L. S. Amery, *My Political Life*, 3 vols. (1953–5), vol. ii, p. 281.

Coalition had been resumed in 1923 on an Imperial programme.[1]

III

The minority Labour Government which followed lasted only a few months. But with Liberal support, Snowden, the Chancellor of the Exchequer, swept away the duties and Preferences introduced by McKenna and Austen. He also repudiated the preferential arrangements agreed with the Dominions at the Imperial Conference of 1923. Britain was once again a Free Trade country.

The Conservative leaders, meanwhile, had suffered a traumatic shock and none more than Baldwin. In the course of the General Election of 1924, Baldwin pledged himself against a general tariff and against food taxes. He did, indeed, leave himself free to safeguard particular industries. But this was to be done on an industry by industry basis and with special legislation in each case.

The Conservatives won the election with a large majority; and the new Cabinet was broadened by the inclusion of the leading Coalition Unionists, Balfour, Austen and Birkenhead. Churchill also returned to the Conservative fold and became Chancellor of the Exchequer. These four were united by personal friendship and because they had remained loyal to Lloyd George in 1923. They formed a group within the Cabinet. Churchill was the strongest character among them and, though he remained a Free Trader while they were Tariff Reformers, they tended to take their lead from him.

Amery became Dominions and Colonial Secretary. But his influence in the Cabinet was weakened by the defeat of 1923. He might not have been responsible for the timing of the election, but the policy on which the Conservatives had been beaten was his policy. He continued to advocate it, undismayed, and, in this, Bridgeman supported him. But such staunch Tariff Reformers as Neville Chamberlain, Cunliffe-Lister and Steel-Maitland all joined in counselling caution on Baldwin. Baldwin's own views seem to have remained unchanged. But after his victory in 1924 his overriding preoccupation was to hold his party and his Cabinet together. As a result his approach to the fiscal issue became increasingly Balfourian. In principle he was a Tariff Reformer; in practice he acted as a brake on the policy.

[1] For a detailed account of the events leading up to the 1923 election see the forthcoming biography of Stanley Baldwin by John Barnes and Keith Middlemas.

How were Baldwin's election pledges on Preferences and the safeguarding of industry to be interpreted ? Churchill was determined to restrict them to a minimum; Amery to stretch them to the maximum.

Amery succeeded, easily enough, in securing the restoration of the McKenna duties and the 1919 Preferences. Next he proposed the introduction of those Preferences, agreed by the Imperial Conference of 1923 and subsequently repudiated by Snowden. Churchill argued that the Cabinet was precluded from this course by one of Baldwin's speeches at the election. By way of compromise, it was agreed that the approximate cash value of Preferences, about £1 m. a year, should be set aside to encourage the marketing of Empire produce in Britain through an Empire Marketing Board. This proved an outstanding success.

In February 1925, after considerable argument, the Cabinet accepted a new procedure for safeguarding which gave tariff protection to a few industries, in particular lace. But the central issue for Tariff Reformers was the safeguarding of the iron and steel industry.

In June 1925 the iron and steel industry applied for Protection. A Cabinet enquiry followed and, after the recess, Amery pressed for immediate action. Churchill replied that to safeguard iron and steel was tantamount to imposing a general tariff. Baldwin let it be known that he was personally in favour of safeguarding. But, as a former ironmaster, he was concerned not to champion the cause of his industry too directly and in view of Churchill's objections decided to do nothing. He accordingly told Parliament that the industry had proved its case but that he was precluded by election pledges from taking action to help it in the lifetime of the Parliament.

The main Imperial business of 1926 was the Conference of Dominion Prime Ministers. This agreed the definition of Dominion status later enshrined in the Statute of Westminster. Balfour and Amery were its chief architects. Its importance was that it put into words the new constitutional concept that had been developing since Chamberlain's time — the concept of a union of wholly sovereign states.

No further progress was made that year over safeguarding though the economic situation worsened and was further aggravated by the consequences of the coal dispute and the General Strike.

In 1925 Churchill had returned to the Gold Standard under the inspiration of Montagu Norman. This was part of a grand if anachronistic design aimed at stabilising prices and encouraging freer international trade. Opposition to safeguarding policies was a natural accompaniment to it. Amery regarded Churchill's policy as dangerously deflationary and one of the main causes of the industrial unrest of 1926. He accordingly sought to bring the difference between them on economic policy to a head.

In April 1927 Amery wrote to Baldwin proposing that he should take Churchill's place at the Treasury. He even suggested that, failing action over safeguarding, he might have to follow Joseph Chamberlain's example and 'try what I can do outside. I might well fail where Chamberlain failed. Still, I am many years younger than he was and the situation is many years riper. Anyhow, if I must, I can but try. Like Martin Luther, I cannot do other.'[1]

Baldwin temporised, and in July Amery left England on a tour of all the self-governing Dominions, thus fulfilling an earlier ambition of Chamberlain's. His original purpose had been to counteract the centrifugal forces then at work in the Empire and to explain the conception of Dominion status agreed at the 1926 Conference. But he also hoped to return with a moral mandate from the Dominion Governments to press for action over Preference. The tour was in itself a triumph, and the Dominion Governments encouraged him in his advocacy of Preference. But, like Chamberlain after his visit to South Africa, he came home to find his position in the Cabinet weakened. He had been away six months and had lost touch with his colleagues. In particular, he found that Churchill had convinced the Cabinet that the best way to help industries in difficulty was by derating them. And the derating proposals had been explicitly advanced by the Chancellor as an alternative to safeguarding.

But the world was now drifting into the Great Depression and no scheme of derating could hope to stem the rising tide of unemployment. By the summer of 1928 a majority of Conservative members had come round to Amery's view that something must be done to safeguard industry. In July two hundred members called for a debate on the iron and steel situation, but the Government refused it.

There was, indeed, a general economic debate, but Baldwin and Churchill only managed to infuriate the back-benchers by their negative attitude towards safeguarding. The Whips feared an explosion and on 2 August Amery and Neville Chamberlain persuaded the Cabinet to make a concession to feeling in the party. A letter from Baldwin to the Chief Whip explained that while the Government were still opposed to new food taxes or to a general tariff they

[1] Amery to Baldwin, April 1927.

would be free, after an election, to safeguard iron and steel or, indeed, any other industry.

This compromise failed to satisfy Conservative opinion and at the Party Conference of 1928 a resolution deploring 'the slow progress made' over safeguarding was passed by an overwhelming majority. Baldwin in his reply acknowledged the force of the arguments advanced, but once again took refuge behind his election pledges.

The King's speech was silent on the subject. Yet Amery, at Brighouse a day or two later, went far beyond the official programme and called for a general tariff to redress the heavy burden of taxation.

But Churchill and the Free Traders had the last word. In the Budget of 1929 Churchill removed the tea duty, and consequently the Preference that went with it. He also refused a further preferential remission on Empire sugar, which Amery had proposed in the interests of the West Indies.

But now time was running out. The Cabinet failed altogether to agree on a policy to meet the mounting economic crisis. Baldwin accordingly drifted into the General Election of 1929 under the uninspiring slogan of 'Safety First'. The wonder is that the Conservative defeat was only marginal.

Unemployment by this time was over a million and a half; and the only party leader with a clear programme for dealing with it was Lloyd George. Armed with some brilliant pamphlets, prepared by Keynes and Hubert Henderson, he argued the case for spending our way out of the Depression by a major programme of loan-financed public works. It was a British forerunner of Franklin Roosevelt's New Deal. Yet there was a fundamental weakness in Lloyd George's scheme. Public works create employment, but they also lead to an increase in imports. The works themselves require raw materials and machinery. Those who work on them need food and consumer goods. Unless measures are taken at the same time, therefore, to restrict imports, a programme such as Lloyd George's is likely to lead to a balance-of-payments crisis.

The essence of Amery's policy was that to fight unemployment without risking a balance-of-payments crisis required two things: the protection of British industry against foreign competition by a Tariff, and the creation of new markets in the Empire by a system of Mutual Preference. Amery believed that a combination of Lloyd George's policy and his own might be the best solution. But he had to recognise that the Conservative party of those days would not accept the necessary increase in public expenditure. A year later

Mosley would propose a rather similar combination of public works at home, backed by import quotas and bulk-buying arrangements with the Empire. But the Free Trade influences on the Labour Government side were too strong for him and brought him to resignation.

IV

'Safety First' had been a bad enough slogan for a Government. For an Opposition it was meaningless. What course then were the Conservatives to follow ? Churchill and Austen were attracted by the idea of working for an anti-Socialist Coalition with Lloyd George. This would have meant abandoning Tariff Reform to close the ranks between Liberals and Conservatives. But it would have formed an alternative majority in the House of Commons and so brought down the MacDonald Government. Here was a quick way back to office but without any agreed plan to solve the economic crisis.

The other course, urged by Amery, was to proclaim Tariff Reform and Empire Preference as the only practical solution to the problem of unemployment. This meant to accept a spell in Opposition. But if the Labour Government failed to solve the nation's problems then the electors would almost certainly give the Conservatives a mandate to put the Empire policy into practice.

On 9 July, a few weeks only after the election, there was a debate on Empire trade. Amery, speaking from the front bench, made a strong plea for a return to Tariff Reform and Empire Preference. Two days later his speech was discussed in the Shadow Cabinet. The pros and cons of a Tariff Reform policy and of a Coalition with Lloyd George were vigorously debated. Baldwin and Neville Chamberlain demurred at the idea of a junction with Lloyd George. At the same time the weight of opinion inside the Shadow Cabinet was against a clear commitment to Tariff Reform and Preference.

But, meanwhile, a new Empire crusader had entered, or rather re-entered, the lists. On 30 June Beaverbrook published a flamboyant article entitled *Who is for the Empire ?* In this he took himself to task for lack of zeal in the Imperial cause and pledged himself henceforth to its service. He followed up the article by forming the Empire Free Trade Movement. A number of prominent businessmen and several Conservative candidates joined him, and after ten weeks, he could claim 200,000 members.

Amery and Beaverbrook met and found themselves in substantial

agreement on the main issues at stake, though there were shades of
difference between them. Beaverbrook's campaign slogan was
'Empire Free Trade'. This had the advantage of being simple. It
was also misleading. None of the Dominion Governments, as Amery
knew only too well, were prepared even to consider Free Trade with
Britain. Preference they would give, sometimes by lowering duties
in favour of Britain, more often by increasing them against the
foreigner. But nothing would persuade them to dismantle the tariffs
protecting their own industries then, any more than in Chamberlain's
time. Beaverbrook agreed that this was true but held that the
appeal of a slogan was more important than its accuracy.

Another point of difference was in their attitude towards the
Conservative leadership. Amery thought it necessary to win over
Baldwin and Neville Chamberlain for a Tariff Reform policy, much
as Chamberlain had thought it necessary to win over Balfour. He
was ready to put maximum pressure on the official leadership, but
was frankly sceptical of the chances of success of a breakaway movement. Beaverbrook disliked and despised Baldwin. He wanted to
oust him from the Conservative leadership and sometimes thought
in terms of starting a new party in competition with the Conservatives.

The two men, however, agreed to work closely together, though
in parallel, rather than as a team: Amery inside the Conservative
party, Beaverbrook from outside. Beaverbrook, with Rothermere's
support, began campaigning for the Empire Free Trade movement.
Amery, with the help of Melchett and Abe Bailey, formed the Empire
Economic Union as a successor to the Tariff Reform League.

These moves soon took effect. At the end of July Neville Chamberlain declared that the General Election had wiped the slate clean
of past pledges setting limits to Tariff Reform or Imperial Preference.
But this was not enough for Amery or Beaverbrook. On 22 October
Amery addressed a gathering of industrialists at Abe Bailey's house,
where Melchett drafted a manifesto calling for an Empire Economic
policy. Beaverbrook came out two days later with a more violently
worded proclamation of the United Empire Crusade.

Baldwin and Beaverbrook met, appropriately enough on Armistice
Day. Their talk was general but a few days later Beaverbrook spoke
in the House of Lords as a supporter of Baldwin's. Baldwin returned
the compliment in a speech to the National Union where he praised
Beaverbrook's work for the cause of Empire. A further meeting
followed and for a few days harmony reigned.

On 5 February 1930, however, Baldwin, speaking in the Coliseum Theatre, urged the need to safeguard industry but declared against any taxing of food. Two days later Amery spoke in Birmingham and said bluntly that he disagreed with Baldwin about food taxes. There were demands for Amery's expulsion from the Shadow Cabinet; but in an exchange of letters Baldwin agreed that, in view of the position he had always taken on the issue, Amery should be free to advocate food taxes.

On 13 February, however, Baldwin told Beaverbrook that the latitude accorded to Amery was personal and could not be extended to others of his colleagues. Beaverbrook took this as a rebuff and, on 18 February, converted the Empire Free Trade Movement into the United Empire Party with himself as its leader. Ten days later, however, in a speech at Gloucester, he declared that his purpose was to reach an agreement with Baldwin. He saw Baldwin on 3 March and proposed by way of compromise that the question of food taxes should be the subject of a referendum. Baldwin accepted this proposal and announced their agreement at a meeting in the Hotel Cecil next day. Amery also came out in favour of the referendum.

The different sections among the Conservatives thus seemed to be agreed; and Beaverbrook resigned the leadership of the United Empire party. His place was taken by Rothermere. But the honeymoon was short-lived. Baldwin's subsequent speeches and some of the literature put out by the Conservative Central Office suggested that he regarded food taxes as unrealistic, and this aroused Beaverbrook's and Amery's suspicions.

As it happened there was a by-election at West Fulham that spring. Sir Cyril Cobb ran as the United Empire party candidate, and was duly elected. Cobb's victory over the official Conservative candidate convinced Beaverbrook that the tide of opinion was running his way. Accordingly, on 19 May, he repudiated his own proposal for a referendum on food taxes, thus striking at the root of his compact with Baldwin. A month later (17 June) he called on Conservatives to subscribe to a special fund to finance opposition to any Conservative candidates who stood as Free Traders.

Baldwin took up the challenge. He appointed Neville Chamberlain as Chairman of the Party to placate the Tariff Reformers. He then called a special meeting of Conservative members and candidates at the Caxton Hall (24 June). He told them that he would not submit to dictation by the press lords and carried the meeting by a two-thirds majority.

But, as the summer wore on, opinion veered increasingly towards the Tariff Reformers. On 2 July a group of leading bankers and businessmen, all previously Free Traders, met at Hambros Bank and passed a resolution in favour of Safeguarding and Imperial Preference. Very similar views were expressed in the following weeks by the Associated Chambers of Commerce, the Economic Committee of the T.U.C. and the Federation of British Industries.

But Baldwin failed altogether to respond to the changing mood in the country; and, in September, Beaverbrook wrote to Amery offering to serve under him if he would take over the leadership of the Conservative party. Amery made no direct response but, in a speech at Birmingham on 29 September, joined Beaverbrook in repudiating the idea of a referendum on food taxes. Baldwin sensed that a challenge was developing to his leadership; and, though no public statement was made, Amery was no longer invited to the meetings of the Shadow Cabinet.

Meanwhile, the Imperial Conference had assembled; and Bennett, the Canadian Prime Minister, came forward with a proposal that all Empire countries including Britain should grant an increased preference of 10 per cent on all existing or future import duties. The Labour Government rejected Bennett's proposal out of hand. Amery, though out of the Shadow Cabinet, pressed Baldwin and Neville Chamberlain to respond to it. Baldwin wrote an open letter to Neville endorsing the Bennett proposal so and committing the Conservative party to Imperial Preference.

Baldwin's statement, foreshadowing, as it did, the introduction of food taxes, led Churchill to threaten resignation from the Shadow Cabinet. The Tariff Reformers would have welcomed his departure; but Austen persuaded him to hold his hand. Indeed when Amery asked what were his intentions, he replied: 'I propose to stick to you with all the loyalty of a leech.' In January 1931, however, he broke with Baldwin over Indian policy, and the main Free Trade influence in the Shadow Cabinet was thus withdrawn.

Despite Baldwin's favourable response to the Bennett proposal, the feud between him and Beaverbrook smouldered on. Beaverbrook had lost all confidence in Baldwin; and some of Baldwin's speeches in the autumn — aimed perhaps at placating Churchill — only darkened his suspicions. Feeling, too, was mounting against Baldwin in the party and even in the Shadow Cabinet.

Matters came to a head in March with the by-election in the St. George's (Westminster) division. Beaverbrook ran Sir Ernest Petter against the official candidate Duff Cooper; and Central Office were far from confident of victory. But in the event, Petter was defeated. Baldwin's face was saved and the scene was thus set for a reconciliation. Amery returned to the Shadow Cabinet. Neville Chamberlain and Beaverbrook exchanged letters (29 March). In these Beaverbrook undertook to support the Conservative Party and Baldwin as its leader. Neville on his side confirmed that the Conservative party's policy included the protection of British agriculture by duties, quotas or prohibitions; the protection of industry; and Empire Preference. Baldwin thus retained the leadership of the Conservative party but in return accepted the full Tariff Reform programme.

V

In the summer of 1931 the Free Trade system of fixed exchange rates combined with free imports finally collapsed. Unemployment rose to over two millions. At the height of the crisis the Labour Cabinet considered the introduction of a General Tariff but only to reject it. On 19 August, however, they decided — by fifteen votes to five — in favour of a tariff on manufactures. But this was too much for Snowden, who threatened resignation. To lose the Chancellor at the height of a crisis seemed unthinkable; and the decision was accordingly reversed. In the absence of some control of imports there was nothing for it but to resort to savage deflation. Even then the foreign bankers demanded assurances, in return for their support, which could not have been given without cutting back on unemployment benefits. Snowden and MacDonald prepared to yield to these demands. Several of their Cabinet colleagues — though a minority — refused. The Labour Government broke up and was replaced by a Coalition.

The first Coalition formed on 24 August was intended as a purely temporary steering committee designed to see the country through the immediate crisis. A General Election was held to produce a new House of Commons; but Ministers did not go to the country on an agreed programme. They asked instead for 'a doctor's mandate'.

They received, in the event, an overwhelming majority and decided to continue as a team. This second Coalition was predominantly Conservative. But it included MacDonald, Simon, Runciman, and Samuel from the Liberal side; all of them Free Traders. Churchill was excluded, mainly because of his rift with Baldwin over

India. At MacDonald's insistence, Amery was also excluded to reassure the Liberals and Snowden that Baldwin would not press for fiscal reform.

But the momentum of events proved stronger than any Coalition compact. Already before the election, the Government had abandoned the gold standard. This, like any devaluation, was in itself a form of protection: a temporary general tariff.

In the autumn, the Cabinet Committee concerned accepted proposals from the Melchett study group and the Conservative Research Department as the basis of a new Protectionist policy. Thereafter, the fiscal revolution made rapid progress. In November, the Government introduced the Abnormal Imports Bill. This gave the President of the Board of Trade power to impose duties up to 100 per cent on a wide range of consumer goods. In February 1932, Neville Chamberlain fulfilled the first part of his father's fiscal programme with the introduction of the Imports Duties Bill. This provided a 10 per cent Tariff against most imports. Certain basic necessities were specifically excluded; but, for the rest, the Chancellor was free to impose additional duties on the recommendation of an Imperial Advisory Committee. In addition, a 10 per cent Preference was given, across the board, to imports from the Empire. Later in the year, the Wheat Bill — also based on proposals prepared by Melchett's group — at last implemented Chamberlain's original proposal though by way of quota rather than duty.

All this was stiff medicine for the Free Traders in the Government. The Liberal Ministers, in particular, more than once threatened to resign. But they were persuaded to remain by the offer of an unusual exemption from the rule of collective responsibility. They were specifically authorised to criticise this part of the Government's policy in public as well as in private.

VI

The Imports Duties Bill meant, in effect, the introduction of a General Tariff. This opened the way for the fulfilment of the other branch of Chamberlain's fiscal policy — Imperial Preference. It created the conditions where the British Government could sit down with the Dominion Governments to hammer out a series of mutual trade agreements, based on preferential tariff concessions.

In July of 1932, Baldwin set out at the head of a strong delegation to meet the Dominion Prime Ministers at Ottawa. His team included Neville Chamberlain, Hailsham, Runciman, Thomas, and Cunliffe-Lister. The host to the Conference was R. B. Bennett, the Canadian Prime Minister, a strong protectionist and close friend to Amery and Beaverbrook. Bruce, the leader of the Australian delegation and the dominant figure in the Conference of 1923, was also to play a leading and constructive part. Amery also went, but in a private capacity.

Baldwin set out in a generous frame of mind. Before leaving, he told the lobby that Ottawa would be 'a bigger thing than Party or National Government. It was one more attempt to keep the sane forces of the world together.' To Tom Jones, then Secretary of the Cabinet, he said: 'No-one knows what Bennett will do. He will want the Conference to be a success. I shall try to keep to the big things on which Canada can help us. Iron and steel, coal, cotton and wool. If we could divert some of her trade with America in these four groups, it would help.' Above all he wanted 'to go for a few big things in the way of freer trade within the Empire'.

An Imperial Conference to agree the details of preferential arrangements had been a goal of Unionist policy since 1903. Chamberlain had always known that it would be an occasion for tough bargaining. But, in the intervening years, Tariff Reformers had talked so much about the eagerness of the Dominions for Mutual Preference that they had taken it for granted that once the Conference met these would have no difficulty in reaching agreement.

In the event the Conference engendered much heat and some bitterness.

Thirty years had gone by since Laurier and Fielding had made their first firm offer to Chamberlain of a Mutual Preference agreement. Since then, the Dominion Governments had granted successive and substantial Preferences to British goods but had received nothing in return. It was only now, after repeated rebuffs, from Conservative as well as Liberal and Labour administrations, that a British Government had at last agreed to meet them and discuss what had been the dominant economic issue in the Empire since the turn of the century. The Empire leaders welcomed Britain's change of heart. They could not conceal that they thought it overdue.

The British delegates for their part thought the Dominion leaders parochial and insufficiently appreciative of what Britain was already doing for them. Were they not receiving free entry for their raw materials and many of their foodstuffs? Had they not been given

a 10 per cent Preference under the Import Duties Act? Who
provided the bulk of their investment capital to say nothing of their
defence?

Such arguments would have been telling in Chamberlain's day.
But Baldwin and his colleagues were playing their hand from weakness. In 1903, Chamberlain had called for Tariff Reform not as an
immediate cure to present ills, but as a means of safeguarding Britain
and the Empire against perils looming ahead. Britain's economic
leadership in those days had been scarcely challenged; and Chamberlain had focused opinion not on the problems of the present but
on his vision of the future. Thirty years later, the position was very
different. The British leaders had not come to the Conference table
as missionaries of Empire. They had been driven to it by an
unprecedented economic and financial crisis which had shattered
Britain's established fiscal system and created nearly three million
unemployed.

The Dominions, for their part, faced a calamitous fall in commodity prices. Both sides were, thus, drawn together not by a great
ideal and positive purpose, but by 'the ties of common funk'. They
met in a climate of fear rather than of faith.

There were other difficulties. MacDonald was still Prime Minister of Britain, and had set his heart on an International Economic
Conference. The Liberal members of the Cabinet had only with
difficulty been persuaded to swallow their Free Trade principles and
accept the Import Duties Bill. Baldwin and Neville Chamberlain
were thus always looking over their shoulder to make sure that no
action of theirs should break up the Coalition.

Nor were matters much easier within the delegation. Runciman,
the President of the Board of Trade, was a Free Trader. So were
most of the Treasury and Board of Trade officials who accompanied
the British delegation. Proposals from the Dominions side were thus
scrutinised with suspicion and even hostility. Little allowance was
made for the lower quality of the Dominion Civil Services. The
British delegates tended to bargain with the Dominions as opponents,
rather than try to lead them as a team.

On the Dominions' side, too, things had greatly changed since
1903. Industry had grown, economies had become more diversified
and Governments were subject to stronger pressures from vested
interests. These things accentuated the old difference as to how
Preferences should be given. Most British Tariff Reformers had
begun life as Free Traders and always felt that Preferences should

take the form of a lowering of duties within the Empire. Baldwin felt this very strongly as his opening statement to the Conference shows. It was, moreover, only by a lowering of inter-Imperial trade barriers that the Empire policy could be reconciled with the internationalist aspirations which formed part of the official policy of the Coalition.

But at this stage the Dominion leaders were not greatly concerned with the reactions of third parties. Most of them were avowed protectionists, and preferred to give Preferences by increasing duties against the foreigner rather than by lowering them in favour of Britain. They did not want to increase the total of their import trade. They were prepared to turn that trade away from the foreigner and towards Britain.

As in most Conferences, there were moments of crisis and talk of breakdown. Yet in the end, common interests, the pressure of public opinion and the lobbying activities of Amery and his friends — though rather resented by their British colleagues — led to agreement. Yet a certain disillusion and bitterness remained, especially in the minds of Neville Chamberlain and of Bennett.

VII

The conclusions of the Conference were embodied in a set of general resolutions and specific trade agreements. The resolutions declared that:

by the lowering or removal of barriers among themselves provided for by these agreements, the flow of trade between the various countries of the Empire will be facilitated and that by the consequent increase of purchasing power of their peoples, the trade of the world will also be stimulated and increased.

They went on to proclaim that the principle of trade impartiality contained in the most-favoured-nation agreements did not apply to inter-Imperial trade and pledged the signatories to denounce any trade treaties inconsistent with the principle of Empire Preference.

Essentially the agreements provided that in return for increased Preferences over a wide range of commodities from the Dominions, Britain would continue to grant free entry to Dominion producers. And this right of free entry was increased in value by the promise to impose new restrictions on a wide variety of foreign imports. Britain also pledged herself not to reduce the existing 10 per cent *ad valorem* duty on specified foreign goods without the consent of the Dominions — a surrender of fiscal independence which came as near to federation as the Commonwealth would ever come.

Britain, however, retained the right to regulate the import of eggs, poultry and dairy products from the Dominions as well as from abroad by duties subject to Preference or by quotas. Meat imports, too, were later fixed by quota, but in quantities which, compared to foreign meat imports, were clearly preferential.

On the British side the agreements treated all the Dominions alike, but provision was made to review them after five years.

VIII

Baldwin and Neville Chamberlain had leant over backwards at Ottawa to avoid giving offence to their Free Trade colleagues at home. In vain. The package proved too much for Snowden and for most of the Liberal Ministers. They argued:

> that the bargaining method adopted will soon break the Empire: that the five and seven years fiscal commitments are thoroughly unconstitutional and improper; that the bargain from the point of view of business is all against us, and from the point of view of politics is irredeemably bad; that it destroys the chances of a successful International Economic Conference; that it continues the influences which have brought this distress upon the world; that it is so contrary, not only in its immediate contents but in its inevitable far reaching and more continuing results, to Free Trade and low Tariffs that they cannot support it.[1]

They accordingly resigned, though continuing for a few months to support the Government on other issues.

Despite their predictions of woe, the economic validity of Chamberlain's policies of Tariff Reform and Empire Preference was soon confirmed by the results of the Ottawa Agreements. The next few years saw the gradual recovery of world trade from the Great Depression largely as a result of the American decision to increase the price of gold. But the recovery of the Empire and the Sterling Area was much more marked than that of other countries. Britain's trade expanded in all directions, foreign as well as Imperial. But its most striking feature was the rise in the proportion of Empire trade to total trade. Between 1932 and 1937, British exports to foreign

[1] MacDonald to Baldwin, September 1932 — quoted by G. M. Young in *Stanley Baldwin* (1952), p. 170.

countries rose from £200 m. to £269 m.; an increase of 35 per cent. Exports to Empire countries, on the other hand, rose from £166 m. to £252 m.; an increase of 52 per cent. Exports to the Empire thus amounted to very nearly half (48·3 per cent) our total export trade. The change was even more marked in our imports; naturally enough, seeing that our exports had long enjoyed the benefit of Preferences in Dominion markets. Between 1932 and 1937 British imports from foreign countries rose from £454 m. to £624 m.; an increase of 27 per cent. Our imports from Empire countries rose from £248 m. to £405 m.; an increase of 64 per cent. Imports from the Empire thus rose from 35·3 per cent to 39·4 per cent of our total imports.

These figures are striking enough; but even more significant are those of our imports of raw materials. Between 1931 and 1937 British imports of food, drink and tobacco rose from £416 m. to £432 m.; i.e. by £15 m. Our imports of manufactures rose from £261 m. to £275 m., i.e. by £14 m. Meanwhile, our imports of raw materials rose from £173 m. to £315 m.; an increase of £142 m., or 82 per cent. And of this increase, over £65 m. came from Empire countries. This increase in raw-material consumption reflected a comparable growth in manufacturing production. This, in fact, went up over the years in question by 51 per cent including an increase in our steel production from five million to thirteen million tons a year. Much of the credit for this expansion of the British economy must go to the combined effects of the domestic tariff, and of the Imperial Preference.

Scarcely less important in its contribution to our recovery was the formation and development of the Sterling Area. The gold standard by its very nature had been rigid and restrictive, tending to depress prices and make credit scarce. Sterling, on the other hand, could be adjusted in volume — and with it the sterling price level — to meet the needs of production and trade. So long as there was confidence in British integrity and expertise and in the productive resources of the Sterling Area, it was a cushion against depression and a stimulus to expansion.

These three elements of the fiscal revolution — Tariffs, Preference and Sterling — had a direct influence upon the level of employment. At the time of Ottawa, unemployment had stood at nearly three millions. By 1935 it was well under two millions. By 1938 it was down to about one million; a figure which Lord Beveridge in his wartime Report on social security would regard as acceptable.

But the Ottawa Agreements were not confined to bilateral agreements between Britain, the Dominions and India. They included a considerable development of inter-Imperial Preference between the Dominions, India and the Colonies. Between 1932 and 1937 the total trade between Empire countries, other than the United Kingdom, increased from £70 m. to £157 m.; an increase of 124 per cent.

The British Fiscal Revolution of 1931/2 was as far-reaching in character as the Free Trade Revolution of 1846. It was even more dramatic in its results. It conquered the problem of unemployment in Britain and brought about a return to prosperity at home and in the Empire. But it did more than that. The Ottawa agreements and the creation of Sterling gave the Commonwealth and Empire the economic strength and financial flexibility to wage the Second World War. But for them the British peoples could scarcely have mobilised the resources to go on 'alone' when France fell and while the United States and Russia still sought safety, the one in an inglorious, the other in an unfriendly, neutrality.

DEFEAT IN VICTORY

The Centenary of Chamberlain's birth — The American challenge to Ottawa —
Cordell Hull and the Reciprocal Trade Agreement — Amery urges Preference
for Europe — The Second World War and the Commonwealth — Alone but in
good company — Britain's need, America's opportunity — Cash and Carry —
Lend-Lease — The strings — Exports to South America — Preference and the
Atlantic Charter — The struggle in the Coalition Cabinet — The Washington
Loan Agreements — Amery's opposition — The convertibility crisis — GATT
and the Conservative Party — Amery defeated at Blackpool — The Suez base
abandoned — The Suez expedition — The retreat from Empire.

I

The Import Duties Act, and the Ottawa Agreements mark the
high tide of our story. Tariff Reform and Empire Preference had
prevailed; and Chamberlain's faith was soon confirmed by
works.

Men like Amery and Beaverbrook at home, Bennett, Smuts and
Bruce in the Empire, believed that a new age had opened. They
looked on the Ottawa Agreements as the sure economic foundations
on which they and their successors could build a Commonwealth
of sovereign states co-operating freely in every aspect of policy. On
8 July 1936, at a mass meeting held to commemorate the centenary
of Chamberlain's birth, Amery declared:

Now at long last, and after the wasted and unforgiving years, we have
seen his predictions justified, his arguments proved true. In time, but only
just in time, to avert utter collapse, we have seen the first instalment of his
policy carried out. It is only an instalment. A tariff is, after all, only the
groundwork of a policy of national strength and stability. Imperial fiscal
preference, carried, as we hope it will be, steadily forward, is only a part of
a policy of economic co-operation. That policy has still to deal with finance;
it has still to deal with the urgent plight of our shipping, with our air
communications, with the vital problem of migration. Yet economic
co-operation itself was always for Chamberlain only a means towards effective co-operation in defence and foreign policy in a world of increasingly
formidable and menacing powers, a means towards the collective security
of Empire which is the only collective security on which, in the long run,
we can always rely.

Neville Chamberlain was the guest of honour at the Albert Hall that night. But he had little of his father's heart or vision. He consolidated the Fiscal Revolution of 1931/2. He did nothing to extend it. Tariffs and Preferences became an accepted feature of our economic defences. The Sterling Area grew to meet the needs of its members. But there was no follow through after the victory of Tariff Reform as there had been after the victory of Free Trade in 1846. Nor was there any attempt to establish the universal validity of the principles of the British Fiscal Revolution. Cobden, in his day, had not only practised Free Trade but preached it to others. Cordell Hull would preach it even more than he practised it. Not so Baldwin or Neville Chamberlain. There were many far-sighted statesmen in Europe, Van Zeeland among them, who wanted to follow Britain's lead. Yet when Belgium and Holland sought, at Ouchy, in the very year of the Ottawa Conference, to establish a system of Mutual Preferences, the British Government took the lead in denouncing their plans as a breach of the most-favoured-nation clause.

The same forces in London which frustrated the Ouchy Convention stimulated, in the years before the Second World War, a slight but perceptible retreat from the Ottawa policies.

Australia followed up Ottawa with more enthusiasm than any other Dominion and with great advantage to many of her industries. But barley suffered a serious blow from Belgian retaliation, as did wool at the hands of the Japanese. By 1938, when Australia came to negotiate a new trade agreement with Britain, the wool lobby had raised a considerable agitation against the Ottawa policy. In the event the revised agreements reaffirmed the importance of Preference to both parties; but they also laid stress on the need for Britain and Australia to take account of each other's interest in trading with third parties.

The Canadian Government, even in Bennett's time, had a dual interest in the Ottawa Agreements. They valued them for their own sake, but they also came to see them as a means of strengthening their bargaining position against the United States. The Americans understood this and, in 1934, made certain proposals to Mackenzie King. These involved some sacrifice of Preferences in return for reciprocal tariff reductions between Britain, Canada and the United States. In themselves, these proposals were not of very great significance. But they mark the beginning of the American challenge to the economic unity of the Commonwealth. In the circumstances of the war and its aftermath, this challenge would prove fatal to Chamberlain's policies.

II

Chamberlain's Tariff Reform campaign, as we have seen, had caused some concern in the United States at the beginning of the century; though American protectionists, like Theodore Roosevelt, had thought it only natural that Britain should seek to do for her Empire what the United States were doing for themselves. In the event Britain held fast to Free Trade, so no problem arose.

Woodrow Wilson, in his Fourteen Points, had attacked economic discrimination as a major cause of war. Yet despite Europe's post-war dependence on American economic support, there is little evidence that the President's views had much influence on the policies of the Lloyd George Government. In any case, the United States soon relapsed into isolationism and still higher Protection, while Britain, after 1923, reverted to Free Trade.

The Republican Administrations of the 1920s had been primarily concerned with protecting American industry against foreign competition. Their Trade barriers rose ever higher, culminating, as the Great Depression drew on, in the Hawley–Smoot tariff. But with the New Deal and the recovery from the Depression there came an important change in American economic policy. Powerful American interests, and particularly those backing the Democratic party, pressed the Administration to help them to secure new outlets for American exports. They found their spokesman in Roosevelt's Secretary of State, Cordell Hull.

Like Cobden and Bright for Britain a century before, Hull led the American attack on the world's markets in the name of morality and peace. In his own words, 'unhampered trade dovetailed with peace; high tariffs, trade barriers and unfair economic competition with war'. His declared aim was 'the reconstruction of a multilateral system of world trade'. This was to be based on full convertibility of currencies, the reduction of trade barriers and the complete elimination of all forms of discrimination.

Convertibility of currencies as yet presented no great problem, though sterling was already suspect to Americans because of the credit facilities which the system gave to its members. It is fair to add that currency restrictions were also a major American grievance against the Axis Powers and the Soviet Union. But the real objects of Hull's wrath were tariffs and discrimination or Preference.

As between these two, Hull made an important distinction. He regarded tariffs as regrettable, preferences as sinful. His zeal for tariff reductions, indeed, had necessarily to be limited. The United States was still a very high-tariff country; and the most he could persuade Congress to accept was the reciprocal reduction of tariffs. The Reciprocal Trade Agreements Act was, no doubt, a liberalising measure. But its main purpose was to help Americans sell more abroad rather than to help foreigners earn dollars by selling to the United States.

Hull defended American tariffs on the ground that tariffs were an expression of nationalism and that, within limits, nationalism was respectable. But he saw no similar excuse for Preference or other forms of trade discrimination. These were expressions of Imperialism. They were the fruit of past aggression and reflected combinations based on military power. As such it was the duty of liberal-minded men to work for their complete elimination. The Ottawa Agreements in particular aroused his wrath, and he described them as 'the greatest injury in a commercial way that has been inflicted on this country since I have been in public life'.[1]

Hull's campaign to reduce tariffs and eliminate preferences took the form of invitations to foreign Governments to conclude reciprocal trade agreements with the United States. This approach offered Mackenzie King a chance to convert part of the Ottawa Agreements into a tripartite agreement between the United States, Britain and Canada. It also conformed with a recommendation made by Van Zeeland to the British and French Governments. In a report, specially commissioned by them, Van Zeeland had concluded that since the United States and the British Empire controlled between them over 40 per cent of the world's commerce, an Anglo-American trade agreement was likely to stimulate world trade as a whole.

Accordingly in 1937 negotiations began for a reciprocal trade agreement between Britain, Canada and the United States. These were prolonged. At one stage, Hull asked for the complete abandonment of Commonwealth Preferences as his price for agreement. This was, of course, rejected. But Chamberlain, though resentful of such pressures, judged that the international situation demanded some concession to American views. 'The reason,' he wrote,

why I have been prepared (*pace* Amery and Page Croft) to go a long way to get this treaty is precisely because I reckoned it would help to educate

[1] House of Representatives: Committee on Ways and Means hearings on H. J. Resolution 407: 76th Congress, 1st Session.

American opinion to act more and more with us and because I felt sure it would frighten the totalitarians.[1]

In their final form, the agreements committed Canada and Britain to sacrifice significant preferential advantages in each other's markets. In return they secured some real compensation in the United States market. The wheat preference was dropped and certain other preferences modified. On their side, the Americans made specific cuts in their tariff affecting almost a third of Britain's exports to the United States.

The agreement was well received in London; and, indeed, it was difficult to argue that Britain had struck a bad bargain for her exports. Amery, however, attacked the agreement on the ground that it had regard only to trade and not to the need to expand British or Commonwealth production. Such agreements, he argued, would do nothing to remedy the excess of American exports over imports which had been at the root of the Great Depression. The only remedy, as he saw it, for the imbalance in world trade was to encourage other groups of countries, and notably the countries of Europe, to co-operate among themselves on a preferential basis, just as the countries of the British Commonwealth were doing and so make themselves less dependent on American supplies. In a speech in the House of Commons (2 November 1937) he developed these ideas in terms which gave a universal instead of a purely national and imperial significance to Chamberlain's ideas.

I believe that we, without any real sacrifice, could give substantial help to the economic and political regeneration of Europe if we announced boldly and definitely that we would no longer adopt a dog-in-the-manger policy in regard to the Most Favoured Nation Clause, but would encourage other nations to get together, even if we were partially excluded. In our history we have often given a lead not only in political freedom but also in economic matters. We once led the world in the development of scientific protection. In the last century we led it in the development of free international trade. Let us give a lead now in the development of such freer trade as world tendencies today allow, and encourage the formation of groups like our own in the world. If the Prime Minister were able to say to the world that we would not stand in the way of the formation of such an economic grouping of the European nations, including their Colonies, but would use our influence with the Dominions and the United States to encourage such a grouping, it would be the dawn of a better day in Europe.[2]

[1] Sir Keith Feiling, *The Life of Neville Chamberlain*, (1946), p. 308.
[2] M. Van Zeeland's report, mentioned above, also advocated relaxing the most-favoured-nation clause so as to encourage the formation of a European Preferential Union.

It is arguable that Amery overestimated the extent to which inter-Commonwealth trade could have been increased. But events rapidly confirmed his view that trade tends to expand much more rapidly between members of a group of politically associated countries than on a universal and multilateral basis. Dr. Schacht's economic empire over Eastern Europe and the Japanese co-prosperity sphere were crude pre-war examples of this thesis. But it has found striking confirmation in more recent times in the EEC, the EFTA, the Organization of American States and even in the COMECON. In all these there has been a rapid expansion of trade and investment within the group and a consequent though slower development of trade between the group and the rest of the world.

III

The ebb and flow of Imperial patriotism follows a fairly constant pattern through our story. Major crises like the Boer War, the First World War and the Great Depression drew the nations of the Empire together. In the intervals of peace and prosperity, national self-interest tended to take precedence over the common cause. After Ottawa, there was some return to parochialism. But it was short-lived. The outbreak of the Second World War found the Empire more united than ever in its history.

The sovereignty of the individual Dominions had been fully recognised in the Statute of Westminster. But, with the single exception of Ireland, they joined in the war from the beginning. All of them raised substantial forces by land, sea and air. India, despite neutralist and even hostile agitation by the Congress party, put forth all her power. So, on a far greater scale than in the First World War, did the Crown Colonies. It was not, indeed, until well into 1944 that the American manpower contribution to the war effort surpassed our own. And yet only forty years had passed since Chamberlain had brought the self-governing Colonies of his day to send what were little more than token contingents to join Britain in the South African War.

Political co-operation between the Governments of the Commonwealth and Empire was even more intimate than in the First World War. The Imperial War Cabinet, indeed, was not formally revived, mainly because of Mackenzie King's hesitations; but Australia, New Zealand and India had permanent representatives attached to the British Cabinet. More important, the development of air transport made it easy for Dominion statesmen to visit London. They attended meetings of the Cabinet and of the British Chiefs of Staff. Some, like Casey, took ministerial or pro-Consular office under the British Government. Others like Menzies or Smuts visited Washington and Allied Commands, not just as representatives of their own countries but as spokesmen of the Home Government and sometimes of the whole Commonwealth.

No less impressive was the co-operation on the economic front. The system of exchange control introduced with the outbreak of war completed the conversion of the Sterling Area into a formal financial block. The Sterling Area countries allowed Britain to run up almost unlimited debts. Canada, too, became virtually a part of the Sterling Area, accepting sterling as money after 1941 in unlimited quantities. There were vigorous and successful efforts to make good shortages of food and raw materials. There was also extensive joint planning to share out essential materials and machinery.

It was thanks to this co-operation among its members that the Commonwealth and Empire was able to fight on alone for a whole year from the fall of France to the German attack on Russia. In this time we had no ally save Greece and no financial support from abroad until April 1941, when the first shipments of Lend-Lease materials reached our ports.

War is a very expensive business. To wage war effectively, Britain had to cut back her living standards drastically and at the same time to spend far more than she could earn. The Commonwealth countries gave us virtually unlimited credit. The American approach to the problem was very different.

Two great themes dominated the policies of the Roosevelt Administration. They were determined to defeat Germany and Japan. They were scarcely less determined to break up the European Empires — British, French and Dutch — when the war came to an end. Roosevelt planned to build 'One World'; and it was to be a world safe for American exports. Here Britain's need was America's opportunity.

IV

At the outset of the war the American Neutrality Acts prevented us from either buying war material from the United States or from borrowing dollars. In November 1939 the 'Cash and Carry' legislation was introduced. We were still forbidden to borrow in the United States. We were allowed to buy from them on condition that we paid in hard cash. To do this we sold up the bulk of our American investments at what, under the circumstances, were knock-down prices. Later on we threw in our gold and dollar reserves. Significantly enough, the American authorities discouraged us from paying in gold. They wanted to see us liquidate our American investments and the annual outflow of dollars which they represented. We were fighting for our lives and had to pay heed to the only country which could help us stand the siege.

In his first personal message to Roosevelt, after becoming Prime Minister, Churchill wrote: 'I should like to feel reasonably sure that when we can pay no more, you will give us the stuff all the same.' By August 1940 the British position was becoming critical. We had cashed the bulk of our American securities and had begun to run down our reserves. We proposed that the United States and Canada should run up sterling balances. Canada presently agreed. The United States, on Cordell Hull's advice, refused.

In the autumn of 1940 Churchill set out 'a statement of the minimum action necessary to achieve our common purpose' and warned that Britain would soon be unable 'to pay cash for shipping and other supplies'.

In the winter, as bankruptcy stared us in the face, Roosevelt at last moved and, despite opposition from Congress and inside the State Department, introduced the Lend-Lease legislation. This became law in March of 1941; and the first shipments reached us a few weeks before the Nazi attack on Russia.

Churchill once described Lend-Lease as 'the most unsordid act in history'. It was generous, indeed, in the sense that vast quantities of materials were supplied to Britain and little or no payment was required for them. But a word of qualification is needed. These were supplies given to Britain to fight a war which the American Administration recognised as in their vital interest. The conditions of Lend-Lease, moreover, were far more restrictive than any Britain had ever attached to the subsidies paid to our continental allies in the wars of the eighteenth century and against Napoleon.

V

One specific condition attached to Lend-Lease was aimed at British exports, particularly to South America and Canada. The Americans wanted to support the British war effort. But they were reluctant to allow any part of their supplies to Britain to be converted

into British exports to South America or Canada where they com-
peted directly with comparable American exports. Britain's export
trade was, of course, already well below its peacetime level. But,
in order to acquire dollars for war purposes, a need not ended by
Lend-Lease, and with an eye on the post-war situation, Britain had
made special efforts to maintain some exports to the American
continent. The British Government thought it only reasonable that
part at least of the aid received from the United States under Lend-
Lease should be devoted to maintaining British exports, in the
interest both of the war effort and of Britain's post-war survival. The
Americans disagreed.

Some idea of the difference in perspective on opposite sides of the
Atlantic appears from an official American communication which
called on the United Kingdom:

> to concentrate her exports in the field of traditional articles, such as Scotch
> whisky, fine textiles, etc. and other similar articles and cut down the ex-
> portation of articles similar to those being provided through Lend-Lease
> funds to the irreducible minimum necessary to supply or obtain materials
> essential to the war effort.

On this Professor Robertson commented drily that the impression:

> of a picturesque little nation whose trading reputation depends on a few
> specialities, popular in fashionable circles in Boston and New York, but
> which had presumptuously under the temptation of Lend-Lease gone out-
> side its 'traditional' field to try its hand at real industry like metallurgy or
> the staple textile trade, and has now humbly promised to draw in its horns
> again, has to be corrected.[1]

The British Government accepted that they should not use
'materials similar to those supplied under Lend-Lease in such a way
as to enable their exporters to *enter new markets* or *to extend* their export
trade at the expense of the United States exporters '.[2] But this was
not enough for the United States. The Americans were not content
that we should abjure any extension of trade. They wanted us to
abandon existing markets in their favour.

By the beginning of 1942 the United States themselves had entered
the war. The British Government sought at once to introduce the
concept of joint planning of exports 'on a basis of equality and
maximum efficiency'. There was a good deal of sympathy in the
State Department for this view, but to no avail. The Lend-Lease

---

[1] Quoted by R. S. Sayers in *Financial Policy* (1956), 1939–45, p. 402.
[2] Cmd. 6311; E. L. Hargreaves and M. M. Gowing, *Civil Industry and Trade* (1952), pp.
145–51.

office proved obdurate. The Americans were determined to secure our South American markets for themselves. In this, they very largely succeeded.

VI

Far more serious was the condition contained in Section 3 (*b*) of the Lend-Lease Act. This provided that in return for the supplies sent to Britain the United States should receive 'some consideration which the President deems satisfactory'.

The consideration which the Administration had in mind was a commitment from Britain to support Cordell Hull's economic policies and in particular to reduce Britain's tariffs and eliminate Imperial Preference.

On 28 July 1941, Keynes was handed a first draft of Article 7 of the Mutual Aid Agreement. This contained a strict commitment to non-discrimination; and Keynes was frankly told that its acceptance would preclude Britain from maintaining the system of Imperial Preferences.[1]

When Churchill and Roosevelt met in Newfoundland, at the beginning of August, Sumner Welles tried to introduce a similar commitment to non-discrimination into the draft of the Atlantic Charter. His wording, indeed, was very close to the draft of Article 7, already submitted to Keynes.

Churchill, advised by Beaverbrook, realised that the American intention was to preclude Preferences. He accordingly told Roosevelt that he would have to submit the text, not only to the British Cabinet, but to the Dominion Governments as well. 'I should have little hope that it would be accepted.'[2] The Americans pressed him very hard; but, as he cabled to his colleagues, he insisted that the draft should

safeguard our obligations contracted in Ottawa and not prejudice the future of Imperial Preference. This might fall into its place after the war with decisive lowering of tariffs and trade barriers throughout the world, but we cannot settle it now.

Churchill had his way at the time, but the Americans soon returned to the charge and kept up their pressure on the British Government throughout the autumn. In its final form Article 7 of the Lend-Lease Agreement (Mutual Aid Agreement) pledged the British Government 'to the elimination of all forms of discriminatory

---

[1] See R. S. Sayers, *Financial Policy*, 1939–45 (1956), p. 408.
[2] Winston S. Churchill, *The Second World War* (1950), vol. iii, p. 387. See also Kenneth Young, *Churchill and Beaverbrook* (1966), pp. 201–2.

treatment in international commerce and to the reduction of tariffs and other trade barriers'.

This commitment, however, was subject to the conclusion of a general international agreement after the war. It also begged the question whether inter-Imperial trade was international or domestic. Churchill told the House of Commons that the agreement in no way conflicted with Ottawa and that he had assurances to this effect from the President. Cordell Hull maintained precisely the opposite.[1]

This is not the place to elaborate the details of the campaign mounted by the United States Administration, during the war, against the economic and administrative framework of the Commonwealth and Empire. Suffice it to say that at the Allied Conferences at Quebec, Yalta and Potsdam, and at more specialised meetings like those at Bretton Woods, Dumbarton Oaks and San Francisco, the Americans returned again and again to the charge. Their themes were always the same; the reduction of tariffs; the elimination of preferences; the convertibility of currencies, and the outlawing of sea or air cabotage between sovereign countries.

They also pressed relentlessly for the grant of self-determination to Colonial peoples. Their main targets here were Indo-China, the Dutch East Indies, Burma and India. Their main purpose was to break down those political and administrative ties which gave the business interests of Britain, France and Holland an advantage over their American competitors.

The British Cabinet were divided on how to deal with these American demands. Churchill, Attlee and a majority of the Cabinet inclined to compliance over the economic issues, partly on the merits of the case and partly because of the importance of keeping friends with the United States. Amery, Beaverbrook, Ernest Bevin and Rob Hudson were for standing up to the Americans. On India Churchill was unyielding.

In the daily stress of war men of action find it difficult to give their minds to peace aims and long-term plans 'sufficient to the day.' The Churchill Cabinet recognised the dangers to our system inherent in American policies and stopped short of selling the pass. But our dependence on American support and the stubborn survival of Free Trade thinking, particularly in the Board of Trade, inclined ministers to 'roll with the punch'. They did not capitulate to American pressure, but they retreated steadily before it.

[1] For a fuller account of this imbroglio see R. N. Gardner, *Sterling–Dollar Diplomacy* (1956), pp. 60–1 and 65, and Cordell Hull, *Memoirs* (1948), vol. ii, p. 1152.

VII

Roosevelt died. Churchill fell. The deep differences which existed between American and British economic policies were no longer mitigated, as they had been until then, by personal friendships.

A week after the ending of the Japanese war (15 August 1945) Lend-Lease was cut off. This had been foreshadowed at the Potsdam Conference in June. But the decision, when it came, was a body blow to the new British Labour Government, committed, as it was, to an ambitious programme of social reforms and nationalisation.

At the time of the 'cut off', Lend-Lease was enabling Britain to overspend her income by rather more than £2,000m. a year. The Labour Government judged that, assuming a strict regulation of imports and a lowering of living standards even below wartime levels, the balance of payments could be brought into equilibrium by 1949. But the deficit over the intervening three years would amount to at least £1,700m. Britain's gold and dollar reserves stood at about £500m. at the end of 1945 and half of these might be committed. A further £200m. might be borrowed from the Sterling Area. But, even on these optimistic assumptions, there would still be a gap of £1,250m. This, it was argued, could only be bridged by borrowing from the United States and Canada.

Honourable but rather pathetic attempts were made to persuade the United States to give Britain a grant in aid or, at least, an interest-free loan. But the talk of 'equality of sacrifices' fell on deaf ears in Washington. Leading men, like Churchill's friend, Baruch, questioned whether the United States could or should aid Britain at all. Winthrop Aldrich, the banker, urged that

The British Commonwealth should agree to do away with exchange controls on current account and give up the so called sterling area . . . relinquish the system of Imperial Preference . . . and eliminate quantitive trade controls.[1]

Congress was equally determined. The Houses Special Committee on Post-War Economic Policy and Planning urged the Administration to secure commitments to multilateral trade policies before even writing-off Lend-Lease. They proposed that aid should only be given to countries willing to abandon state trading and prepared to give 'a guaranty of non-discriminate treatment for all

[1] *New York Times*, 5 October 1945.

business of United States citizens'. For Britain they demanded specifically 'the removal of discriminatory treatment, of quotas, exchange controls, and Tariff Preferences'.[1]

The views of the Administration were similar but more cautious. They feared that in the absence of American aid, Britain would strengthen the preferential arrangements between herself and the other sterling countries and so make the Sterling Area permanently independent of imports from America. They accordingly favoured giving Britain a loan but on conditions which tied her Government irrevocably to American trade policies — a commitment which the Churchill Coalition had narrowly eluded.

The arguments employed by the Administration to secure Congressional agreement to the loan show their purpose only too clearly. Creighton, the Under-Secretary for Foreign Affairs, told the Senate Committee (7 March 1946) that:

> Britain will withdraw from Bretton Woods if she does not get the loan. She will then expand her agreements [preferential agreements] all round the world. If I were sitting in the position of power in Britain, that is exactly what I should do.

Similarly, Vincent, Secretary of the Treasury, foretold the consequences of a rejection of the loan as follows (14 May 1946):

> Egyptian and Indian cotton will replace American cotton. Rhodesian and near Eastern tobacco will replace American tobacco. British automobiles and machinery will replace American automobiles and machinery. In half the trading areas of the world, American products will be at a serious disadvantage in competing with the products of the sterling countries.

After painful and long-drawn-out negotiations, the Administration agreed to make Britain a loan of £937 m., repayable over fifty years at 2 per cent interest. This was accompanied by a generous final settlement of Lend-Lease.

The loan was smaller than the £1,250 m. sought by the British Government, but the difference was substantially bridged by a Canadian loan of £300 m. The financial terms of the American loan were very reasonable. But stout political strings were attached to it.

The Americans demanded that sterling should be made convertible by 15 July 1947. They also required that Britain should join the United States in setting up an International Trade Organisation.

---

[1] House of Representatives, No. 1205; 79th Congress, 1st Session, 12 November 1945.

Members of this organisation were pledged to work against all forms of discrimination, and in particular:

In the light of the principles set forth in Article 7 of the Mutual Aid Agreements, Members should enter into arrangements for the substantial reduction of tariffs and for the elimination of Tariff Preferences, action for the elimination of Tariff Preferences being taken in conjunction with adequate measures for the substantial reduction of barriers to world trade, as part of the mutually advantageous arrangements contemplated in this document.

As an initial step in the process of eliminating Tariff Preferences, it should be agreed that:

(a) existing international commitments will not be permitted to stand in the way of action agreed upon in respect of Tariff Preferences.

(b) All negotiated reductions in most-favoured-nation tariffs will operate automatically to reduce or eliminate margins of Preference.

(c) margins of Preference on any product will in no case be increased and no new Preferences will be introduced.[1]

To accept the loan on these terms meant that Britain was committed to dismantling the two main bulwarks of inter-Imperial trade: the temporary bulwark of an inconvertible sterling currency and the more permanent bulwark of Empire Preference.

The Labour Government, under pressure from the Treasury and the Board of Trade, took the loan and accepted the conditions attached to it. Churchill hesitated to come out openly against their decision. He did not want to be accused of seeking to prolong wartime austerity. He, accordingly, advised his followers to abstain. Amery, though no longer in the House of Commons, led the resistance to the loan from outside, using the Empire Industries Association, an offshot of the old Tariff Reform League, as his main instrument.

Amery believed that more of our requirements, especially of tobacco, sugar and foodstuffs, could be met from the Commonwealth than the Government allowed. He also maintained that in their own interest the Americans would have to lend us some money even without political strings, if only to dispose of their surpluses. Conservative opinion inclined to Amery's view. So did a small but significant section of the Labour party on the ground that the conditions of the loan deprived a Socialist Government of almost every means of regulating or planning Britain's foreign trade. Informed opinion outside Parliament was almost equally critical of

[1] *Proposals for Consideration by an International Conference on Trade and Employment*, ch. iii, section B.

the loan. *The Economist* deplored the agreement; and Hubert Henderson described its conditions as 'calculated to ensure default'. In the event the loan passed the House of Commons by 343 votes to 100 (70 Conservatives and 30 Socialists) with 169 abstentions. The opponents of the Washington Loan Agreements were soon proved right. In accordance with their commitment under the loan, the Labour Government made the pound fully convertible on 15 July 1947. By that time half the money borrowed had already been spent. With convertibility there was an immediate run on sterling, and, within six weeks, the bulk of the money remaining had been lost to Britain. By the end of August, indeed, all that remained to Britain of the £1237m. borrowed from the United States and Canada, was £125m. of the Canadian loan and £100m. of the American. The convertibility crisis led the Government to reverse engines. Strict exchange control was reintroduced and quotas were imposed on all imports from outside the Sterling Area. The Americans, too, had learned their lesson and attached very few conditions to the credits subsequently supplied under the Marshall Aid programme. Nevertheless, the Labour Government felt obliged to sign the General Agreement on Tariffs and Trade. The GATT virtually prohibited the unilateral raising of tariffs. It did not abolish existing Preferences but committed its signatories not to introduce any new Preferences. This meant that with the passage of time the existing Preferential agreements between the different Commonwealth countries were condemned to lose much of their significance.

VIII

The convertibility crisis convinced most Conservatives that Amery and his friends had been right in opposing the Washington Loan Agreements. As a private enterprise party, however, the Conservatives accepted that convertibility was a desirable objective. They were, likewise, opposed to quotas and bulk-buying arrangements. They concluded, therefore, that the right way for a Conservative Government to regulate foreign trade would be by recovering their freedom to increase tariffs and introduce new preferences. They planned with the help of these flexible and, by modern standards, liberal economic defences, to bring about an increase in Sterling Area trade which would make Britain much less dependent on imports from the United States.

The Conservative Party Conferences of 1948, 1949 and 1950 called on the Conservative leadership to denounce the 'no new Preference clauses' of the GATT and to recover Britain's freedom to raise Tariffs and extend Preferences. These resolutions were accepted by the Conservative leaders, and the policy underlying them was embodied in the election manifestos of 1950 and 1951.

The Conservative Government elected in 1951 determined to sweep away the bulk of wartime and post-war controls, much as the Lloyd George Coalition had done after the First World War. Import controls were dismantled. Sterling moved steadily towards convertibility. But what was to be the positive side of the programme? Were Ministers still determined, as they had been in Opposition, to denounce the relevant sections of the GATT and to erect a new network of Tariffs and Preferences?

At the Sydney Conference of Commonwealth Finance Ministers efforts were made to canvass Commonwealth support for an extension of the policies underlying the Ottawa agreements. But the initiative in this was half-hearted. So was the response. India and Pakistan were far more interested in American aid than in the marginal trade advantages of new Preferences. Canada, under Mackenzie King, was closely ranged with the United States. Australia, New Zealand and South Africa, though more favourably inclined, hesitated to quarrel with the Americans. The United States were at this time virtually the only supplier of new investment capital, and the American market was assuming an ever increasing importance for primary producers.

Amery, from his retirement, called for Britain to give a lead, if necessary without prior agreement with the Commonwealth. He urged that Britain should denounce the no new Preference clause of the GATT, raise the level of British tariffs unilaterally and so increase Preference margins to the Commonwealth. He believed that the Commonwealth countries would respond once they saw the benefits of such a policy to themselves. But Conservative opinion was deeply divided. The break-up of the Liberal party had brought large numbers of Liberal recruits into the Tory ranks; and they had been raised in the Free Trade tradition. The Soviet danger worked against pressing any difference with the Americans to the point of a quarrel. Despite some encouraging speeches by Menzies of Australia and Diefenbaker of Canada, the response from the Commonwealth was lukewarm.

Nevertheless, amendments calling for a withdrawal from the

GATT were moved and carried at the Conservative Party Conferences of 1952 and 1953. They were accepted, albeit, with reservations, by the leadership; and the impression was given that they would be seriously considered at Commonwealth Conferences. But in 1954, the Government decided upon a showdown with the Tariff Reformers. At the Party Conference in Blackpool, that year, they declared that they would stand by their obligations under the GATT.

The supporters of the Empire Industries Association had moved an amendment calling on the Government to recover their freedom to increase Preferences. Amery spoke in support of it. He was answered by Thorneycroft, the President of the Board of Trade. Amery had used the familiar Imperial and economic arguments to which Conservative Conferences had never failed to respond over two generations. Thorneycroft attacked Preference and Protection and made a classical defence of Free Trade. A vote was taken; and, for the first time since Chamberlain had raised his standard, the Tariff Reformers were beaten.

Amery's defeat that day, marked the end of the campaign for Tariff Reform and Empire Preference. There would still be efforts to save something from the wreck and to gain the same ends by other means. But this was the last stand of the crusade which Chamberlain had launched at Glasgow half a century before.

IX

In abandoning Chamberlain's fiscal policies, the Conservative Government had yielded to American pressures. In the same year they also yielded to American pressures in the Middle East. Against Churchill's better judgment[1] Eden persuaded the Cabinet to agree to the withdrawal of British forces from the great military base in the Suez Canal zone.

The earlier withdrawals from India and from Palestine had already worn away much of Britain's military muscle and striking-power. Yet, so long as we retained Gibraltar, Malta, Suez, Aden and Singapore, Britain could still provide an articulated bone structure for a concerted Commonwealth strategy. With the withdrawal from Egypt, the back of that strategy was broken; and the development of substitute bases in Cyprus and at Aden could not

[1] See Lord Moran, *Winston Churchill: the Struggle for Survival, 1940–65* (1966), pp. 478 and 482.

prevent the growth of an air and sea barrier between Britain and the Commonwealth East of Suez.

The Conservatives had returned to power in 1951, pledged to stay *in* Suez and get *out* of GATT. In the event they reversed the prepositions, and the Government stayed *in* GATT and got *out* of Suez. These two decisions were fatal alike to the military and the economic unity of the Commonwealth. Both owed much to the combination of American pressure and the Little Englander reaction which followed the exertions of the war. So it happened that the aged Churchill came, against every instinct and intention, to preside over the liquidation of the British Commonwealth and Empire.

X

There was still one more chance to avert disaster.

Within little more than a year of the signing of the Anglo-Egyptian treaty, Eden recognised the danger facing Britain in the Middle East. In alliance with France he sought, in 1956, to retrieve his mistake. Had the Suez expedition succeeded there are good reasons to believe that the dissolution of the Commonwealth, as of the French Union, would have been postponed; and what is postponed in history is often averted. As it was, the failure of the Anglo-French expedition marked the end of any effective political, military or even economic co-operation between the nations of the Commonwealth. Many Commonwealth countries ranged themselves against Britain at the United Nations. None offered military support. The weaknesses of the British war machine were glaringly exposed. So, even more, was our financial weakness. The threat of a Soviet nuclear strike on Britain and France was discounted in London and Paris as the bluff it was. But the Administration's request to the American banks to sell sterling proved decisive. The American threat to break the pound broke the will power of the British Government and led to a premature cease fire and an inglorious withdrawal.

The failure of the Suez expedition had far-reaching consequences for Britain and France. The French presence in North Africa was fatally undermined. De Gaulle soon recognised this and, to clear the decks for an Algerian settlement, gave independence to all the French Colonies in Black Africa. Belgium followed suit in the Congo.

British Government planning had envisaged another decade at least of Colonial rule in East Africa. But, in face of the French and

Belgian examples, the British Government threw in their hand. Tanganyika, Kenya, Uganda and Zanzibar were swiftly granted independence. So, after the break up of the Central African Federation, were Zambia and Malawi. None of these countries was fully prepared for independence. But once they had become sovereign members of the Commonwealth, it became important to British interests to try and retain their goodwill. One way of doing this was to support them in their controversies with South Africa over racial issues. This led to an increasing estrangement between Britain and South Africa and ultimately to South Africa's withdrawal from the Commonwealth. It led on too, in 1965, to Rhodesia's Unilateral Declaration of Independence. Since then Britain has imposed an arms embargo on South Africa and stringent sanctions against Rhodesia.

Meanwhile, Britain's armed forces have gone from Aden and — at the time of writing — the remaining British garrisons have begun their withdrawal from the Persian Gulf and from Malaysia and Singapore. These countries, as well as Australia and New Zealand, have pleaded against this decision; so far to no avail. The Legions are under orders to return. How long will Britain's investments overseas and her trade survive their withdrawal?

2 M

CHAPTER CXXIII

CONCLUSION

An essay in interpretation — Chamberlain and Europe — Churchill launches
the European Movement — Amery supports him — Empire and Europe — A
lost opportunity — Europe and Suez — Macmillan's Commonwealth tour —
The Free Trade Area proposal — Macmillan's bid to join the Common Market
— Its failure — Wilson follows suit — Europe and the world overseas —
Chamberlain's ideas and the future.

I

The withdrawal of the British presence overseas and the erosion
of the systems of Imperial Preference and of sterling mark the
dissolution of the Commonwealth as a military, economic or political
entity. The curtain is falling on the work of Chamberlain and
his successors. And yet there is a sense in which Chamberlain's
political ideas may outlive the causes which inspired him and even
lead to a revival of his vision. It may therefore be appropriate to
conclude these volumes of research into the past with a brief essay
in interpretation and conjecture.

Chamberlain was the first British statesman of the front rank to
realise that Britain's future no longer lay wholly in her own hands.
He designed an Imperial destiny for his country but he also recognised the need to buttress it with a European alliance.

Chamberlain himself was the architect of the Entente Cordiale
with France. His son, Austen, sought at Locarno to devise a more
ambitious scheme. France, Germany and Britain were to 'observe'
each other within the framework of an alliance, and this was to be
the cornerstone of international security.

After the fall of France in 1940, British opinion turned away from
European alliances and sought security in 'the open sea' and the
special relationship with the United States. But in 1946, Churchill,
alarmed by the advance of Soviet influence into Eastern Europe and
the hesitations of American policy, called at Zürich for a United
Europe. To the surprise of those who had not read his pre-war
speeches in detail, Amery, the veteran leader of the Imperial Movement, came out in full support of his appeal.

Both Churchill and Amery thought in terms, not of a federal Europe with supra-national institutions, but of a combination of the Commonwealth and the Continental powers. This was to be a grouping associated with the United States, but developing an independent power of its own. Their reasons for promoting European unity were simple. The first was as a means of containing the westward advance of the Soviets. The second was concerned with Britain's own relations with the world overseas.

Both men recognised that Britain alone could no longer offer the Commonwealth all the investment, markets or migrants which it needed. Britain's military power was much reduced. The future of Sterling was in question. In a world where the standards of power were set by the United States and by the Soviet Union, there seemed to be only one way to renew our strength and to match the needs of an expanding Commonwealth. This was to bring about a junction with the nations of the Continent. If the great industries of Britain and of continental Western Europe could be harnessed together, these would form an industrial base strong enough to provide the markets and the investment for which the Commonwealth and the French Union were looking.

The exact links which would bind the new Union together were never worked out in detail. But plainly, Sterling might have formed the basis of a European currency. Preferential agreements between the European countries and their overseas partners or dependencies could have led to an increase in inter-European trade and perhaps in the longer run to a complete customs union. Meanwhile, defence policies might have been co-ordinated and the British and French bases overseas could have ensured a European presence worldwide. At the summit, a Council of Ministers could have served as a forum for regular political consultation, somewhat after the model of the Commonwealth Conference or the Imperial War Cabinet of the First World War.

Had Churchill's Government given a positive lead along these lines, in 1951, they might well have welded the Commonwealth and the French Union into the foundations of a new Europe.

Inside the British Government, Macmillan, Maxwell Fyfe, Sandys and Eccles saw the opportunity. Macmillan fired a number of memoranda at his colleagues, but, as Minister of Housing, was scarcely in a position to press his views. Moreover, Eden at the Foreign Office was persuaded that Britain's best interest lay in building up her special relationship with the United States. The

American attitude towards Britain's role in Europe was ambivalent. The dominant opinion in Washington wanted Britain to abandon her Imperial role. At the same time there was a fear that British leadership of Europe might call into being a Third Force discriminating against American trade and seeking even to hold a balance between the United States and the Soviet Union.

Matters came to a head over the proposal to establish a European Defence Community. Maxwell Fyfe, speaking from a text agreed by the Cabinet, told the Council of Europe, in November 1951, that Britain was ready to join the Community. The same day Eden, moved by Eisenhower, told a meeting of the North Atlantic Treaty Organisation in Rome that Britain could not join. In the ensuing clash of wills, Eden prevailed.

As a result, the Churchill Government never gave the lead to Europe which so many of their friends on the Continent had confidently expected. The golden opportunity was lost. In 1955 and 1956, however, despite Britain's negative attitude to the Messina Conference, co-operation between Britain and France again grew closer. Had the Entente powers prevailed in their expedition against Egypt an Anglo-French leadership of Europe might well have been one of its consequences. But the failure at Suez shattered confidence between Paris and London. Britain hastened to repair her relations with the United States. France plunged into an anarchy from which she was only rescued by de Gaulle.

Macmillan came to power in 1957 in a dark hour for Britain and for the Conservative Party. But even before he had consolidated his position at home, he set out on a tour of Commonwealth countries — the first Prime Minister to do so when in office. He came back from it confirmed in his earlier view that a junction with Europe offered the only way forward for Britain and for the Commonwealth. To attempt it would put some strain on the Commonwealth relationship. But if the attempt was not made, the British economy was likely to decline to a point where the Commonwealth would break up.

His first initiative was the proposal for a European Free Trade Area. This would have led to Free Trade between Britain and Western Europe in industrial goods while still enabling Britain to maintain a managed market in agriculture and to continue to give free entry to Commonwealth food and raw materials. The Free Trade Area was rejected by the French Government. The nations of Western Europe had already gone a long way down the road to a Common Market and were not prepared to accept a compromise which gave Britain all the industrial advantages and none of the agricultural obligations of European unity.

Macmillan saw the danger of falling between two stools — of losing the Commonwealth and being left outside Europe. He could see no practical way of arresting the centrifugal trends in the Commonwealth or of reasserting British leadership of it. He accordingly took the decision to apply for full membership of the Common Market.

This decision involved a political and a fiscal revolution as far reaching as that attempted by Chamberlain. But Macmillan, unlike Chamberlain, was Prime Minister and, though he had to move cautiously in a divided Cabinet, he was in a position to decide when to launch his new policy. The General Election of 1959 gave him an overwhelming majority and he judged that the moment was ripe. The British Government accordingly applied for membership of the Common Market.

Macmillan's bid to take Britain into the Common Market was blocked by de Gaulle. Its failure proved fatal to his Government and yet his European policy took root. Experience of Government, indeed, presently convinced Harold Wilson, hitherto a sworn opponent of the European policy, that entry into the Common Market offered the best way forward for Britain. His bid, like Macmillan's, has so far broken on the rock of French resistance. But a junction with Europe remains, at the time of writing, the official policy of all the major political parties in Britain.

At long last, in fact, all the dominant currents of opinion in Britain have accepted one at least of the basic tenets of the Chamberlain policy. This is the belief that Britain can only hope to solve her economic problems within the framework of a wider trade and payments system — a system designed to foster freer trade between its members and at the same time to stimulate the Development of their resources and techniques by protecting them all against the full force of competition from outside.

Industrial Western Europe may well provide the basis for such a system and Britain's entry into the Common Market would be, perhaps, a natural extension of the policy of European alliances of which Chamberlain was, in modern times, the pioneer. But a Little Europe would scarcely be better placed to solve its problems than a Little England. Europe will always be far more dependent than the United States upon the world overseas for its raw materials and for its markets. It is no accident that the West European nations, Portugal, Spain, France, Holland and Britain, all built great colonial

empires. They did so because they could not find within their own
confines or in the rest of Europe the necessary resources to achieve
the power and prosperity they sought. If Europe should unite,
economic and demographic pressures will tend once again to make
it the heartland of a more widespread community of nations. This
may not be an Empire, in the old sense of the word, but it may well
reproduce many of the features of that Commonwealth of Nations
which Chamberlain, more than any other man, called into being.
If so, it will pose again the central problem which confronted
Chamberlain; the problem of how sovereign states can unite and
yet preserve their individual personalities.

II

Chamberlain's vision of a union of self-governing British countries
dominated the political thinking of two generations of his countrymen at home and in the Empire. It exercised a powerful influence
on their actions, and led to results which even he had never dreamed
of. In two World Wars, and in the world economic crisis of 1931,
the nations of the British Empire achieved a degree of political,
military and economic unity which raised them to the summit of the
world and led them to write the most glorious pages in all of Britain's
history.

In measuring Chamberlain's part in this story, we have to remember how far the Empire had fallen apart in the years before he
came to the Colonial Office — the years of Gordon's murder and of
the defeat at Majuba. When these humiliations are compared with
events in the generation that followed his death, we are left astonished
and perhaps encouraged at how fast the trends of history can be
reversed. It was not, of course, the work of one man. But the chain
of cause and effect is broken at the individual link. Chamberlain
was the prophet and leader of the Imperial Movement. He gave it
its form and content. His themes, his policies, even his slogans have
continued into our time. Without him the whole development
would have been different. It might have been stillborn.

Two World Wars and their aftermath wore down the British
Empire's strength and strained its unity to breaking-point. Its
peoples were left between the hammer of Soviet aggression and the
anvil of American economic imperialism. Once again the centrifugal forces have taken charge; the ebb tide has set in; and the
Imperial vision has faded.

This does not mean that Chamberlain failed, or that his work was in vain. For a man's vision to dominate the thinking of two generations is rare enough; and the history of the British Empire since his death is a sufficient monument to his achievement. Nor is that, of necessity, the end. The British Empire, as Chamberlain knew it, will not return, nor even the Commonwealth of Churchill's day. But Britain remains a great industrial power; and her ties of interest and affection with rising nations beyond the seas are abiding, and will long continue to influence the march of events.

Chamberlain, besides, was more than the leader of British Imperialism, and many of his ideas still retain a universal value. The experience of nineteenth-century individualism and of twentieth-century totalitarianism have led to a strong reaction against absolute concepts of the economic and the social order. Instead, there is a growing recognition of the truth of Chamberlain's philosophy that freedom and social justice can only be secured in combination by a balance between private enterprise and Government direction.

In the same way the experience of the world wars and their aftermath has led to a deep disillusion both with the concept of absolute National Independence and that of an absolute World Order such as the League of Nations and the United Nations were intended to provide. Interdependence between nations is increasingly regarded as the true goal of statesmanship. But this calls for a fine and flexible balance between the duties of co-operation and the rights of nationhood. Here again, Chamberlain's conception of a partnership of sovereign states, based on the principle of Mutual Preference — applied in all spheres, not only the fiscal — may still prove to be the most practical way of linking like-minded nations together.

BIBLIOGRAPHY

VOLUME ONE

Adams, Francis. *History of the Elementary School Contest in England*. Chapman & Hall, 1882.
Allen, Bernard M. *Gordon and the Sudan*. Macmillan, 1931.
Annual Register, 1882, 1883, 1884. Rivingtons, 1883, 1884, 1885.
Arch, Joseph. *The Story of his Life told by Himself*. Hutchinson, 1898.
Armstrong, R. A. *Henry William Crosskey: His Life and Work*. Simpkin, 1895.
Arnold, Matthew. *Letters (1884–88)*, ed. G. W. E. Russell. 2 vols. Macmillan, 1895; new ed. 1901.
Bagehot, Walter. *The English Constitution*. Chapman & Hall, 1867.
—— *Works and life*, ed. Hutton. Kegan Paul, 1910–13; Oxford U.P., 1925; Watts, 1962.
Balfour, Lady Frances. *Memoir of Lord Balfour of Burleigh*. Musson Book Co., 1925.
Baxter, Richard. *The Saint's Everlasting Rest*. Epworth Press, 1961.
Blachford, Frederic, Lord. *Letters*, ed. G. E. Marindin. Murray, 1896.
Bloomfield, Robert. *The Farmer's Boy*. Van Voorst, 1800.
Blunt, Wilfred Scawen. *Secret History of the English Occupation of Egypt*. T. Fisher Unwin, 1907.
Bright, John. *Diaries*. Cassell, 1930.
Bunce, John Thackray. *History of the Corporation of Birmingham*. Vol. 1. Cornish, Birmingham, 1878.
Calamy, Edmund. *The Nonconformists' Memorial*. 2 vols. 1802.
Chamberlain, (Sir) Austen. *Notes on the Families of Chamberlain and Harben*. Privately printed, 1915.
Chamberlain, Joseph. *Memorandum of Events, 1880–1892*.
—— and others. *The Radical Programme*. Chapman & Hall, 1885.
Churchill, (Sir) Winston Spencer. *Lord Randolph Churchill*. Macmillan, 1905; Odhams, 1952.
Corder, Percy. *Robert Spence Watson*. Headley Bros., 1914.
Cromer, Earl of. *Modern Egypt*. 2 vols. Macmillan, 1908.
Dale, A. W. W. *Life of R. W. Dale of Birmingham*. Hodder & Stoughton, 1898.
Dent, Robert Kirkup. *The Making of Birmingham*. J. Allday, Birmingham; Simpkin Marshall, 1894.
Die Grosse Politik der Europäischen Kabinette, 1871–1914, 1923.
Dilke, Sir Charles W. *Problems of Greater Britain*. 2 vols. Macmillan, 1868; reissues, 1869, 1907.
Fergusson, James. *History of Architecture, 1865–76*. 5 vols. Murray, 1865–76.
Fitzmaurice, Lord Edmond. *Life of Lord Granville*. 2 vols. Longmans, Green, 1905.

Foxe, John. *Actes and Monuments.* 4th ed. by J. Pratt and J. Stoughton. Religious Tract Society, 1877.

Gardiner, A. G. *Life of Sir William Harcourt.* 2 vols. Constable, 1923.

Gathorne Hardy, A. E. (ed.). *Gathorne Hardy, First Earl of Cranbrook.* 2 vols. Longmans, Green, 1910.

George, Henry. *Progress and Poverty.* Kegan Paul, Trench, Trübner & Co., 1881.

Grote, Mrs. G. *Personal Life of G. Grote.* 2nd ed. Murray, 1873.

Gwynn, Stephen, and Tuckwell, Gertrude M. *Life of Sir Charles W. Dilke.* 2 vols. Murray, 1917.

Harris, William. *History of the Radical Party in Parliament.* Kegan Paul, 1885.

Harrison, Henry. *Parnell Vindicated: The Lifting of the Veil.* Constable, 1931.

Healy, T. M. *Letters and Leaders of My Day.* 2 vols. Thornton Butterworth, 1928.

Hirst, F. W. *Early Life and Letters of John Morley.* 2 vols. Macmillan, 1927.

Holland, Bernard. *Life of Spencer Compton, 8th Duke of Devonshire.* 2 vols. Longmans, Green, 1911.

Hutton, Edward. *Highways and Byways in Wiltshire.* Macmillan, 1917.

Kruger, Paul. *Memoirs.* 2 vols. Unwin, 1902.

Leslie, (Sir) Shane. *Henry Edward Manning: His Life and Labours.* Burns, Oates, 1921.

Liddell, A. G. C. *Notes from the life of an Ordinary Mortal.* Murray, 1911.

Llewellyn Smith, Sir Hubert. *The Board of Trade.* Whitehall Series. Putnam, 1928.

Lorne, Marquis of. *Palmerston.* 'Prime Ministers of England' Series. 3rd ed., Dent, 1906.

Lucy, (Sir) H. W. *A Diary of Two Parliaments: The Gladstone Parliament, 1880–85.* 2nd ed. Cassell, 1886.

McCarthy, Justin Huntly. *Our Book of Memories: Letters to Mrs. Campbell Praed.* Chatto, 1912.

Mackenzie, John. *Austral Africa: Losing It or Ruling It.* 2 vols. Sampson Low, Marston, 1887.

Marris, N. Murrell. *Joseph Chamberlain, the Man and the Statesman.* Hutchinson, 1900.

Monypenny, W. F., and Buckle, G. E. *Life of Disraeli.* 6 vols. Murray, 1910–1920.

Morley, John (Viscount). *Life of Cobden.* 2 vols. Unwin, 1881 and 1896; Nelson, 1913; Macmillan, 1936.

—— *Life of Gladstone.* 3 vols. Macmillan, 1903.

—— *Struggle for National Education.* 3rd ed. Chapman & Hall, 1874.

—— *Recollections.* 2 vols. Macmillan, 1921.

O'Brien, Barry. *Life of Charles Stewart Parnell, 1846–1891.* 2 vols. Smith & Elder, 1898.

O'Connor, T. P. *Gladstone's House of Commons.* Ward, 1885.

O'Shea, Katharine. *Charles Stewart Parnell.* 2 vols. Cassell, 1914.

Ostrogorski, M. *Democracy and the Organisation of Political Parties,* trans. F. Clarke. 2 vols. Macmillan, 1902.

Paul, Herbert. *History of Modern England.* 5 vols. Macmillan, 1905.

Purcell, E. S. *Life of Manning.* 2 vols. Macmillan, 1896.

Reid, T. Wemyss. *Life of William Edward Forster.* 2 vols. Chapman & Hall, 1888.

Rumbold, (Sir) Horace. *Further Recollections of a Diplomatist.* E. Arnold, 1903.

Seeley, (Sir) John Robert. *The Expansion of England.* Macmillan, 1925.

Selborne, Roundell Palmer, Earl of. *Memorials.* Parts I–II. 4 vols. Macmillan, 1912.
Smith, Frank. *The Life and Work of Sir James Kay-Shuttleworth.* Murray, 1923.
Solly, Henry. *These Eighty Years.* 2 vols. Simpkin, 1893.
Stanford's Handy Atlas and Poll Book. Stanford, 1892.
Trevelyan, George Macaulay. *Sir George Otto Trevelyan, O.M.: A Memoir.* Longmans, Green, 1932.
Tuckwell, Rev. W. *Reminiscences of a Radical Parson.* Cassell, 1905; popular ed., Cassell, 1906.
Victoria, Queen. *Letters,* ed. G. E. Buckle. 2nd series. 3 vols. Murray, 1926.
Walker, John. *Sufferings of the Clergy.* Parker, 1862; epitomised, Parker, 1913.
Watson, Robert Spence. *The National Liberal Federation.* T. Fisher Unwin, 1907.
West, (Sir) Algernon. *Contemporary Portraits.* T. Fisher Unwin, 1920.
Wilson, Walter. *History and Antiquities of Dissenting Churches in London.* 4 vols. 1808–14.
Wingate, Major F. R. (Sir Reginald). *Mahdiism and the Egyptian Sudan.* Macmillan, 1891.
Wolf, Lucien. *Life of the First Marquess of Ripon.* 2 vols. Murray, 1921.

ARTICLES, REVIEWS, ETC.

Chamberlain, Joseph. 'The Liberal Party and its Leaders', *Fortnightly Review,* Sept. 1873.
—— 'The Next Page of the Liberal Programme', *Fortnightly Review,* Oct. 1874.
Fortnightly Review, Dec. 1876, Nov. 1878, Feb. 1886.
National Education League Monthly Paper, Aug. 1873.
Punch. 14 Nov. 1874; 30 June 1883.
Russell, G. W. E. 'Joseph Chamberlain: A Phase', *Cornhill Magazine,* Sept. 1914.
Searchlight, special number, Birmingham, 13 Nov. 1913.
Spectator, 12 July 1879.

VOLUME TWO

Armstrong, R. A. *Henry William Crosskey: His Life and Work.* Simpkin, 1895.
Askwith, Lord. *Lord James of Hereford.* Benn, 1930.
Balfour, Earl of. *Chapters of Autobiography,* ed. Blanche E. C. Dugdale. Cassell, 1930.
Chamberlain, Joseph. *Memorandum of Events, 1880–1892.*
—— and others. *The Radical Programme.* Chapman & Hall, 1885.
Childers, Spencer. *Life and Correspondence of Rt. Hon. Hugh C. E. Childers.* 2 vols. Murray, 1924.
Churchill, (Sir) Winston Spencer. *Lord Randolph Churchill.* Macmillan, 1905; Odhams, 1952.
Clayden, P. W. *England under the Coalition.* T. Fisher Unwin, 1908.
Crewe, Marquess of. *Rosebery.* 2 vols. Murray, 1931.
Dale, A. W. W. *Life of R. W. Dale.* Hodder & Stoughton, 1898.
Davitt, Michael. *The Fall of Feudalism in Ireland.* Harper & Bros., 1904.

Denison, Col. George T. *The Struggle for Imperial Unity.* Macmillan, 1909.

du Parcq, Herbert (Lord). *Life of David Lloyd George.* 4 vols. Caxton Publishing Co., vol. 1, 1912; vols. 2–4, 1913.

Edwards, J. Hugh, and Hughes, Spencer L. *From Village Green to Downing Street: Life of Rt. Hon. D. Lloyd George.* Newnes, 1908.

Fitzmaurice, Lord Edmond. *Life of Lord Granville.* 2 vols. Longmans, Green, 1905.

Gardiner, A. G. *Life of Sir William Harcourt.* 2 vols. Constable, 1923.

Gathorne Hardy, A. E. (ed.). *Gathorne Hardy, first Earl of Cranbrook.* 2 vols. Longmans, Green, 1910.

Gladstone, Lord. *After Thirty Years.* Macmillan, 1928.

Gwynn, Stephen, and Tuckwell, Gertrude M. *Life of Sir Charles W. Dilke.* 2 vols. Murray, 1917.

Hardinge, (Sir) Arthur. *Life of Henry Howard Molyneux Herbert, fourth Earl of Carnarvon, 1831–90.* 3 vols. Oxford U.P., 1925.

Healy, T. M. *Letters and Leaders of My Day.* 2 vols. Thornton Butterworth, 1928.

Holland, Bernard. *Life of Spencer Compton, 8th Duke of Devonshire.* 2 vols. Longmans, Green, 1911.

Leslie, (Sir) Shane. *Henry Edward Manning: His Life and Labours.* Burns, Oates, 1921.

Life of Joseph Chamberlain, by various writers. Associated Newspapers.

Lucy, (Sir) Henry W. *A Diary of the Home Rule Parliament, 1892–95.* Cassell, 1896.

—— *A Diary of the Salisbury Parliament, 1886–92.* Cassell, 1892.

McCormick, Charles. *Memoirs of the Rt. Hon. Edmund Burke.* London, 1798.

Macdonald, John. *The Parnell Commission.* Revised from *Daily News.* Unwin, 1889.

Mackintosh, Alexander. *Joseph Chamberlain; an Honest Biography.* Hodder & Stoughton, 1906.

Maycock, (Sir) Willoughby. *With Mr. Chamberlain in the United States and Canada, 1887–1888.* Chatto, 1914.

Morley, John (Viscount). *Life of Cobden.* 2 vols. Unwin, 1881 and 1896; Nelson, 1913; Macmillan, 1936.

—— *Life of Gladstone.* 3 vols. Macmillan, 1903.

—— *Recollections.* 2 vols. Macmillan, 1921.

Newton, John. *W. S. Caine, M.P.: a Biography.* Nisbet, 1907.

O'Brien, Barry. *Life of Charles Stewart Parnell, 1846–1891.* 2 vols. Smith & Elder, 1898.

O'Brien, William. *Evening Memories.* Maunsel, 1920.

O'Shea, Katharine. *Charles Stewart Parnell.* 2 vols. Cassell, 1914.

Paul, Herbert. *History of Modern England.* 5 vols. Macmillan, 1905.

Shaw, Bernard. *John Bull's Other Island.* Constable, 1904.

Stead, W. T. *Deliverance or Doom?* Review of Reviews Office, 1892.

Temple, (Sir) Richard. *Character Sketches from the House of Commons.* Long, 1899.

Thorold, Algar. *Life of Henry Labouchere.* Constable, 1913.

Trevelyan, G. M. *Life of John Bright.* New ed. Constable, 1925.

Tuckwell, Rev. W. *Reminiscences of a Radical Parson.* Cassell, 1905; popular ed., Cassell, 1906.

Victoria, Queen. *Letters,* ed. G. E. Buckle. 2nd series. 3 vols. Murray, 1926.

—— *Letters,* ed. G. E. Buckle. 3rd series. 3 vols. Murray, 1930.

Watson, Robert Spence. *The National Liberal Federation.* T. Fisher Unwin, 1907.
West, (Sir) Algernon. *Private Diaries,* ed. Horace G. Hutchinson. Murray, 1922.
—— *Recollections, 1832 to 1866.* Nelson, 1910.

ARTICLES, ETC.

Further Correspondence respecting the Termination of the Fishery Articles of the Treaty of Washington, Jan. to June 1886. Foreign Office Confidential Paper 5307.
Labouchere, Henry. 'The Secret History of the First Home Rule Bill', *Truth,* 14 Oct. 1908.
New Review, Apr. 1895.

VOLUME THREE

Amery, L. C. M. S. (ed.). *'The Times' History of the War in South Africa.* Vol. 6. Times, 1909.
Annual Register, 1897, 1900. Longmans, Green, 1898, 1901.
Askwith, Lord. *Lord James of Hereford.* Benn, 1930.
Boyd, Charles W. (ed.). *Mr. Chamberlain's Speeches.* 2 vols. Constable, 1914.
Brandenburg, Erich. *Von Bismarck zum Weltkriege (From Bismarck to the World War),* trans. Annie Elizabeth Adams. Oxford U.P., 1927.
Bryce, James (Viscount). *Impressions of South Africa.* Macmillan, 1897.
Buchan, John. *Lord Minto.* Nelson, 1924.
Bülow, Fürst von. *Denkwürdigkeiten* (Memoirs), ed. F. von Hammern. English translation by F. Voigt and G. Dunlop. Putnam, 1931.
Clarke, (Sir) Edward. *The Story of My Life.* Murray, 1918 ; new ed. 1923.
Colonial Office List, 1896.
Correspondence of Theodore Roosevelt and Henry Cabot Lodge, 1884–1918. 2 vols. Scribner's, 1925.
Colquhoun, A. R. *Dan to Beersheba.* Heinemann, 1908.
Colvin, Ian. *Life of Jameson.* 2 vols. E. Arnold, 1922.
Cook, (Sir) E. T. *Rights and Wrongs of the Transvaal War.* E. Arnold, 1901.
Crewe, Marquess of. *Rosebery.* 2 vols. Murray, 1931.
Dilke, (Sir) Charles W. *Problems of Greater Britain.* 2 vols. Macmillan, 1868 ; reissues 1869, 1907.
du Parcq, Herbert (Lord). *Life of David Lloyd George.* 4 vols. Caxton Publishing Co., vol. 1, 1912 ; vols. 2–4, 1913.
Durand, (Sir) M. *Life of Field-Marshal Sir George White.* 2 vols. Blackwood, 1915.
Edwards, J. Hugh. *From Village Green to Downing Street: Life of Rt. Hon. D. Lloyd George.* Newnes, 1908.
Fitzpatrick, Sir J. P. *The Transvaal from Within.* Heinemann, 1902.
Gardiner, A. G. *Life of Sir William Harcourt,* 2 vols. Constable, 1923.
Goetz, Walter (ed.). *Briefe Wilhelms II an den Zaren.* Berlin, 1920.
Gooch, G. P., and Temperley, H. W. V. (eds.). *British Documents on the Origins of the War, 1898–1914.* H.M.S.O., 1938.

Hensman, Howard. *Cecil Rhodes.* Blackwood, 1901.

Hertslet, Sir Edward. *The Map of Africa by Treaty.* 3rd ed. revised and completed to 1908 by R. W. Brent and H. L. Sherwood. 3 vols. H.M.S.O., 1909.

Hole, Hugh Marshall. *The Jameson Raid.* P. Alan, 1930.

Holland, Bernard. *Life of Spencer Compton, 8th Duke of Devonshire.* 2 vols. Longmans, Green, 1911.

Jebb, Richard. *The Imperial Conference.* 2 vols. Longmans, Green, 1911.

Johnston, Sir Harry. *The Nile Quest.* Alston Rivers, 1905.

Kaiserreden. Leipzig, 1902.

Keith, A. Berriedale (ed.). *Selected Speeches and Documents on British Colonial Policy, 1763–1917.* 2 vols. Oxford U.P., 1918.

Kingsley, Mary H. *West African Studies.* Macmillan, 1901.

Kruger, Paul. *Memoirs.* 2 vols. Unwin, 1902.

Laurence, (Sir) Percival. *Life of John Xavier Merriman.* Constable, 1930.

Lavisse, Ernest, and Rambaud, Alfred. *Histoire générale.* Paris, 1884.

Lucas, (Sir) Charles. *Historical Geography of the British Dominions:* vol. 4, pt. 2 : *History of the Union of South Africa.* New ed., Macmillan, 1915.

Lucy, (Sir) Henry W. *A Diary of the Unionist Parliament, 1895–1900.* Arrowsmith, 1901.

Mackintosh, Alexander. *Joseph Chamberlain: an Honest Biography.* Hodder & Stoughton, 1906.

Michell, (Sir) Lewis. *Life of the Rt. Hon. Cecil J. Rhodes, 1853–1902.* 2 vols. E. Arnold, 1910.

Mills, J. Saxon. *Sir Edward Cook.* Constable, 1921.

Milner, Alfred (Viscount). *England in Egypt.* E. Arnold, 1892.

—— *Milner Papers: S. Africa 1897–99; 1899–1905,* ed. Cecil Headlam. 2 vols. Cassell, 1931–3.

Mockler-Ferryman. *Imperial Africa,* vol. 1 : *British West Africa.* Imperial Press, 1898.

Morley, John (Viscount). *Life of Gladstone.* 3 vols. Macmillan, 1903.

—— *Recollections.* 2 vols. Macmillan, 1921.

Murdoch, Walter. *Alfred Deakin.* Constable, 1923.

Newton, Lord. *Lord Lansdowne.* Macmillan, 1929.

Pratt, Edwin A. *Leading Points in South African History (1486–1900).* Murray, 1900.

Quick, (Sir) J., and Garran, R. R. *Annotated Constitution of the Australian Commonwealth.* Angus (Sydney and Melbourne), 1901.

Reid, T. Wemyss (ed.). *Memoirs of Lyon Playfair.* Cassell, 1900.

Seeley, (Sir) John Robert. *The Expansion of England.* Macmillan, 1925.

Smalley, G. W. *Anglo-American Memories.* 2nd series. Duckworth, 1911.

Spender, J. A. *Life, Journalism and Politics.* 2 vols. Cassell, 1927.

—— *Life of Sir Henry Campbell-Bannerman.* 2 vols. Hodder & Stoughton, 1923.

Stevenson, Robert Louis. *A Footnote to History.* Cassell, 1893.

Thorold, Algar. *Life of Henry Labouchere.* Constable, 1913.

Victoria, Queen. *Letters,* ed. G. E. Buckle. 3rd series. 3 vols. Murray, 1930.

Walker, Eric A. *Lord de Villiers and his Times.* Constable, 1938.

Webb, Sidney (Lord Passfield), and Beatrice. *Industrial Democracy.* 2 vols. Longmans, Green, 1897, 1901.

Whates, H. *The Third Salisbury Administration, 1895–1900.* Vacher, 1900.

Williams, Basil. *Cecil Rhodes* (Makers of the Nineteenth Century). Constable, 1921.
Willison, Sir John. *Reminiscences Political and Personal.* McClelland, Toronto, 1920.
Wolf, Lucien. *Life of the 1st Marquess of Ripon.* 2 vols. Murray, 1921.
Worsfold, Basil. *Lord Milner's Work in South Africa.* Murray, 1906.

ARTICLES, ETC.

Bechuanaland Blue Book: C. 7962, 1896.
Cape Committee Report on Jameson Raid: C. 8380, 1897.
Correspondence relating to the Bloemfontein Conference: C. 9404, 1899.
Correspondence on . . . Recent Disturbances in the South African Republic: C. 7933, 1896.
Correspondence Relative to the Closing of the Vaal River Drifts: C. 8474, 1897.
Command Papers: C. 8063, 1896. C. 8721, 1897. C. 9317, 1899. C. 9345, 1899. C. 9507, 1899. C. 9518, 1899. C. 9521, 1899. C. 9530, 1899. Cd. 43, 1900. Cd. 261, 1900. Cd. 264, 1900. Cd. 369, 1900. Cd.420, 1900. Cd. 625, 1901.
Journal of the African Society, Apr. 1931.
Report of Conference at the Colonial Office: C. 8596, 1897.
Report of the Select Committee on British South Africa (Raid Inquiry): H.C. 311, 1897.
Wilson, Sir Harry. 'Joseph Chamberlain as I Knew Him', *United Empire*, Feb. 1917.

VOLUME FOUR

Allen, Bernard M. *Sir Robert Morant.* Macmillan, 1935.
Amery, L. C. M. S. (ed.). '*The Times' History of the War in South Africa.* Vol. 6. Times, 1909.
Annual Register, 1902, 1903. Longmans, Green, 1903, 1904.
Askwith, Lord. *Lord James of Hereford.* Benn, 1930.
Asquith, Margot (Countess of Oxford and Asquith). *Autobiography.* Thornton Butterworth, 1920–2.
Arthur, (Sir) George. *Life of Lord Kitchener.* 3 vols. Macmillan, 1920.
Balfour, Lady Frances. *Ne Obliviscaris.* 2 vols. Hodder & Stoughton, 1930.
Bell, E. H. C. Moberly. *Life and Letters of C. F. Moberly Bell.* Richards Press, 1927.
Boyce, Sir R. W. *Mosquito or Man?* Murray, 1909.
Bruce, Sir Charles. *The Broad Stone of Empire.* 2 vols. Macmillan, 1910.
Bülow, Fürst von. *Denkwürdigkeiten* (Memoirs), ed. F. von Hammern. English translation by F. Voigt and G. Dunlop. Putnam, 1931.
Churchill, (Sir) Winston S. *Great Contemporaries.* Putnam, 1937.
—— *Lord Randolph Churchill.* Macmillan, 1905 ; Odhams, 1952.
Colvin, Ian. *Life of Jameson.* 2 vols. E. Arnold, 1922.
De Wet, Gen. Christiaan. *Three Years' War.* Constable, 1902.

LIFE OF JOSEPH CHAMBERLAIN

Denison, Col. George T. *The Struggle for Imperial Unity.* Macmillan, 1909.
Die Grosse Politik der Europäischen Kabinette, 1871–1914, 1923.
Dugdale, Blanche E. C. *Arthur James Balfour.* 2 vols. Hutchinson, 1936.
Eliot, (Sir) Charles. *Turkey in Europe.* By Odysseus. E. Arnold, 1900; new ed. 1908.
Ensor, (Sir) R. C. K. *England, 1870–1914.* Oxford, 1933.
Esher, 2nd Viscount, *Journals and Letters.* 4 vols. (Vols. 1–2 ed. M. V. Brett; vols. 3–4 ed. Oliver, Viscount Esher.) Nicholson, 1934–8.
Fitzroy, (Sir) Almeric. *Memoirs.* 2 vols. 3rd ed. Hutchinson, 1925.
Gardiner, A. G. *Life of Sir William Harcourt.* 2 vols. Constable, 1923.
Gooch, George Peabody. *Life of Lord Courtney.* Macmillan, 1920.
Gooch, G. P., and Temperley, H. W. V. (eds.). *British Documents on the Origins of the War, 1898–1914.* H.M.S.O., 1938.
Gwynn, Stephen L. (ed.). *The Letters and Friendships of Sir Cecil Spring Rice.* 2 vols. Houghton; Constable, 1929.
Halévy, Élie. *A History of the English People. Epilogue (1895–1905).* 2 vols. Trans. E. I. Watkin. P. Smith, and Benn, 1929, 1934.
Hamilton, Lord George. *Parliamentary Reminiscences and Reflections, 1868–1885* (1916); *1886–1906* (1922). Murray.
Hayashi, Count. *Secret Memoirs of Count Tadasu Hayashi.* Eveleigh Nash, 1915.
Herzl, Theodor. *Tagebücher, 1895–1904.* Berlin, 1922.
Hicks Beach, Lady Victoria. *Life of Sir Michael Hicks Beach.* 2 vols. Macmillan, 1932.
Holland, Bernard. *Life of Spencer Compton, 8th Duke of Devonshire.* 2 vols. Longmans, Green, 1911.
Hope, James F. (Lord Rankeillour). *History of the 1900 Parliament.* 2 vols. Oxford U.P., 1904.
Jebb, Richard. *The Imperial Conference.* 2 vols. Longmans, Green, 1911.
Lee, Sir Sidney. *King Edward VII.* 2 vols. Macmillan, 1925–7.
Manson-Bahr, P., and Alcock, A. W. *Life and Work of Sir Patrick Manson.* Wood, n.d.
Milner, Alfred Milner (1st Viscount). *Milner Papers: S. Africa 1879–99; 1899–1905,* ed. Cecil Headlam. 2 vols. Cassell, 1931–3.
Newton, Lord. *Lord Lansdowne.* Macmillan, 1929.
Skelton, Oscar Douglas. *Life and Letters of Sir Wilfrid Laurier.* 2 vols. Century, 1922.
Steed, Wickham. *Through Thirty Years, 1892–1922.* 2 vols. in 1. Doubleday, 1924.
Ullswater, Viscount. *A Speaker's Commentaries.* 2 vols. Longmans, Green and E. Arnold, 1925.
Walker, Eric A. *Lord de Villiers and His Times.* Constable, 1938.

ARTICLES, ETC.

Brussels Sugar Bounty Conference: Cd. 1013, 1902.
Command Papers: C. 8359, 1897. C. 8655, 1897. Cd. 528, 1901. Cd. 633, 1901. Cd. 732, 1901. Cd. 893, 1901. Cd. 906, 1902. Cd. 1096, 1902. Cd. 1162, 1902. Cd. 1284, 1902. Report of West Indian Commission: C. 9412, 1899.
Establishment of Schools of Tropical Medicine: Cd. 1598.

'From Amurath to Amurath', *Fortnightly Review*, Aug. 1902.
National Review: Feb. 1902, Apr. 1902, May 1902, June 1902, Aug. 1902, Dec. 1902.
New Liberal Review, Mar. 1901.

VOLUME FIVE

Allen, Bernard M. *Sir Robert Morant*. Macmillan, 1935.
Amery, L. S. *My Political Life*. 3 vols. Hutchinson, 1953–5.
Annual Register, 1902. Longmans, Green, 1903.
Askwith, Lord. *Lord James of Hereford*. Benn, 1930.
Asquith, Herbert Henry (Earl of Oxford and Asquith). *Fifty Years of Parliament*. 2 vols. Cassell, 1923–6.
Asquith, Margot (Lady Oxford and Asquith). *Autobiography*. 2 vols. Thornton Butterworth, 1920–2.
Balfour, Lady Frances. *Memoir of Lord Balfour of Burleigh*. Musson Book Co., 1925.
Balfour, Lady Frances. *Ne Obliviscaris*. 2 vols. Hodder & Stoughton, 1930.
Bell, E. H. C. Moberly. *Life and Letters of C. F. Moberly Bell*. Richards Press, 1927.
Caillard, (Sir) Vincent. *Imperial Fiscal Reform*. E. Arnold, 1903.
Churchill, (Sir) Winston S. *Great Contemporaries*. Putnam, 1937.
Clapham, (Sir) John. *Economic History of Modern Britain*. 2 vols. Macmillan, 1931–2; Cambridge U.P., 1932.
Denison, Col. George T. *The Struggle for Imperial Unity*. Macmillan, 1909.
Die Grosse Politik der Europäischen Kabinette, 1871–1914.
Dilke, (Sir) Charles W. *Problems of Greater Britain*. 2 vols. Macmillan, 1868; reissues 1869, 1907.
Dugdale, Blanche E. C. *Arthur James Balfour*. 2 vols. Hutchinson, 1936.
Elliot, Hon. Arthur D. *Life of Lord Goschen*. Longmans, Green, 1911.
Ensor, Sir R. C. K. *England, 1870 to 1914*. Oxford U.P., 1936.
Esher, 2nd Viscount. *Journals and Letters*. 4 vols. (Vols. 1–2 ed. M. V. Brett; vols. 3–4 ed. Oliver, Viscount Esher.) Nicholson, 1934–8.
Fitzroy, (Sir) Almeric. *Memoirs*. 2 vols. 3rd ed. Hutchinson, 1925.
Forster, Mary A. *Rt. Honourable Hugh Oakeley Arnold Forster: a memoir*. E. Arnold, 1910.
Fraser, Peter. *Joseph Chamberlain*. Cassell, 1966.
Froude, J. A. *Oceana*. Longmans, Green, 1886.
Gardiner, A. G. *Life of Sir William Harcourt*. 2 vols. Constable, 1923.
Gollin, Alfred. *Balfour's Burden*. Blond, 1965.
Gooch, George Peabody. *Life of Lord Courtney*. Macmillan, 1920.
Halévy, Élie. *A History of the English People*, vol. VI: *The Age of Peel and Cobden*, trans. E. I. Watkin. P. Smith, Benn and Saunders, 1948.
—— *A History of the English People. Epilogue (1895–1905)*. 2 vols., trans. E. I. Watkin. P. Smith, and Benn, 1929, 1934.
Hamilton, Lord George. *Parliamentary Reminiscences and Reflections: 1868–1885* (1916); *1886–1906* (1922). Murray.

Hewins, W. A. S. *Apologia of an Imperialist.* 2 vols. Constable, 1929.
Hicks Beach, Lady Victoria. *Life of Sir Michael Hicks Beach.* 2 vols. Macmillan, 1932.
Holland, Bernard. *Life of Spencer Compton, 8th Duke of Devonshire.* 2 vols. Longmans, Green, 1911.
Hyde, H. Montgomery. *Carson.* New ed., Heinemann, 1956.
Jebb, Richard. *The Imperial Conference.* 2 vols. Longmans, Green, 1911.
Lyttelton, Edith. *Alfred Lyttelton.* Longmans, Green, 1923.
Marshall, Alfred. *Official Papers.* Macmillan, 1927.
Masterman, Lucy. *C. F. G. Masterman.* Nicholson & Watson, 1939.
Morley, John (Viscount). *Life of Cobden.* 2 vols. Unwin, 1881, 1896; Nelson, 1913; Macmillan, 1936.
—— *Recollections.* 2 vols. Macmillan, 1921.
Newton, Lord. *Lord Lansdowne.* Macmillan, 1929.
Pigou, A. C. *The Riddle of the Tariff.* R. Brimley Johnson, 1903.
Ronaldshay, Earl of. *Life of Lord Curzon.* 3 vols. Benn, 1928.
Salvidge, Stanley. *Salvidge of Liverpool.* Hodder & Stoughton, 1934.
Seely, J. E. B. (Lord Mottistone). *Adventure.* Heinemann, 1931.
Skelton, Oscar Douglas. *Life and Letters of Sir Wilfrid Laurier.* 2 vols. Century, 1922.
Spender, J. A. *Life of the Rt. Hon. Sir Henry Campbell-Bannerman, G.C.B.* 2 vols. Hodder & Stoughton, 1923.
Ullswater, Viscount. *A Speaker's Commentaries.* 2 vols. Longmans, Green and E. Arnold, 1925.
Webb, Beatrice. *Our Partnership,* ed. Barbara Drake and Margaret I. Cole. Longmans, Green, 1948.

ARTICLES, ETC.

'Memoirs of Joseph Chamberlain', J. Parker Smith. *National Review,* May 1932.
'Mr. Chamberlain's Balloon', Leonard Courtney. *Contemporary Review,* Aug. 1903.
National Review: Feb. 1902, Apr. 1902, May 1902, June 1902, Aug. 1902, Dec. 1902, Mar. 1903, May 1903.
Spectator: 20 May 1902, 12 July 1902.
African Review: 15 Mar. 1902.
Fortnightly Review: Aug. 1902.

VOLUME SIX

Amery, L. S. *My Political Life.* 3 vols. Hutchinson, 1953–5.
Ashley, (Sir) William James. *The Progress of the German Working Classes.* Longmans, Green, 1904.
—— *The Tariff Problem.* P. S. King, 1920.
Askwith, Lord. *Lord James of Hereford.* Benn, 1930.
Asquith, Herbert Henry (Earl of Oxford and Asquith). *Fifty Years of Parliament.* 2 vols. Cassell, 1923–6.

Asquith, Margot (Lady Oxford and Asquith). *Autobiography.* 2 vols. Thornton Butterworth, 1920–2.

Balfour, Lady Frances. *Ne Obliviscaris.* 2 vols. Hodder & Stoughton, 1930.

Beaverbrook, Lord. *The Decline and Fall of Lloyd George.* Collins, 1963.

Chamberlain, (Sir) Austen. *Down the Years.* Cassell, 1935.

—— *Politics from the Inside: 1906–1914.* Cassell, 1936.

Churchill, (Sir) Winston S. *The Second World War.* 6 vols. Cassell, 1948–54.

Clarke, (Sir) Edward. *Story of My Life.* Murray. New ed. 1923.

Croft, Lord. *My Life of Strife.* Hutchinson, 1948.

Die Grosse Politik der Europäischen Kabinette, 1871–1914, 1923.

Eckardstein, Baron Hermann von. *Ten Years at the Court of St. James, 1895–1905,* Trans. and ed. G. Young. Thornton Butterworth, 1921.

Esher, 2nd Viscount. *Journals and Letters.* 4 vols. (Vols. 1–2 ed. M. V. Brett; vols. 3–4 ed. Oliver, Viscount Esher.) Nicholson, 1934–8.

Feiling, Sir Keith. *Life of Neville Chamberlain.* Macmillan, 1946.

Fitzroy, Sir Almeric. *Memoirs.* 2 vols. 3rd ed. Hutchinson, 1925.

Fraser, Peter. *Joseph Chamberlain.* Cassell, 1966.

Gardiner, A. G. *Life of Sir William Harcourt.* 2 vols. Constable, 1923.

Gardner, R. N. *Sterling–Dollar Diplomacy.* Oxford U.P., 1956.

Gollin, Alfred. *Balfour's Burden.* Blond, 1965.

—— *The Observer and J. L. Garvin, 1908–1914.* Oxford U.P., 1960.

—— *Proconsul in Politics: Lord Milner.* Blond, 1964.

Gooch, George Peabody. *Life of Lord Courtney.* Macmillan, 1920.

Gwynn, Stephen Lucius, and Tuckwell, Gertrude M. *Life of Sir Charles W. Dilke.* 2 vols. Macmillan, 1917.

Hargreaves, E. L., and Gowing, M. M. *Civil Industry and Trade.* (History of Second World War. U.K. Civil Service.) H.M.S.O., 1952.

Hewins, W. A. S. *Apologia of an Imperialist.* 2 vols. Constable, 1929.

Hicks Beach, Lady Victoria. *Life of Sir Michael Hicks Beach.* 2 vols. Macmillan, 1932.

Holland, Bernard. *Life of Spencer Compton, 8th Duke of Devonshire.* 2 vols. Longmans, Green, 1911.

Hull, Cordell. *Memoirs.* 2 vols. Hodder & Stoughton, 1948.

Inge, W. R. (ed.). *The Post Victorians.* Essay by Sir Fabian Ware on Joseph Chamberlain. Nicholson & Watson, 1933.

Masterman, Lucy. *C. F. G. Masterman.* Nicholson & Watson, 1939.

Moran, Lord. *Winston Churchill: the Struggle for Survival, 1940–65.* Constable, 1966.

Nevill, Lady Dorothy. *Reminiscences,* ed. R. Nevill. E. Arnold, 1906.

Newton, Lord. *Lord Lansdowne.* Macmillan, 1929.

Perham, Margery. *Lugard: The Years of Adventure, 1858–98.* Collins, 1956.

Petrie, (Sir) Charles. *Life and Letters of Austen Chamberlain.* 2 vols. Cassell, 1939–1940.

Pollard, Sidney. *Development of the British Economy, 1914–50.* E. Arnold, 1962.

Ross, Sir Ronald. *Memoirs.* Murray, 1923.

Salvidge, Stanley. *Salvidge of Liverpool.* Hodder & Stoughton, 1934.

Sayers, R. S. *Financial Policy, 1939–45.* (History of Second World War. U.K. Civil Service.) H.M.S.O., 1956.

Seely, J. E. B. (Lord Mottistone). *Adventure.* Heinemann, 1931.

Spender, J. A. *Life, Journalism and Politics.* 2 vols. Cassell, 1927.
—— *Life of the Rt. Hon. Sir Henry Campbell-Bannerman, G.C.B.* 2 vols. Hodder & Stoughton, 1923.
Spring-Rice, (Sir) Cecil. *Letters and Friendships of Sir Cecil Spring-Rice.* 2 vols. Constable, 1929.
Webb, Beatrice. *Our Partnership,* ed. Barbara Drake and Margaret I. Cole. Longmans, Green, 1948.
Weizmann, Chaim. *Trial and Error.* Hamish Hamilton, 1949.
Young, G. M. *Stanley Baldwin.* Hart-Davis, 1952.
Young, Kenneth. *Arthur James Balfour.* Bell, 1963.
—— *Churchill and Beaverbrook.* Eyre & Spottiswoode, 1966.

ARTICLES, ETC.

'Memoirs of Joseph Chamberlain', J. Parker Smith. *National Review,* May 1932.

INDEX TO VOLUMES ONE TO SIX

Sub-headings are in chronological order wherever possible. Joseph
Chamberlain is shown as JC throughout the index.

(1930), vi 1022; at Ottawa Conference (1932), vi 1024–8
Balfour, Alice, vi 699, 784, 801–3
Balfour, Arthur James (1st Earl of Balfour) (1848–1930), ii 59, 144, 155, 265, 348, 355, 364, 415, 440, 555, 587, 600, 611, 632, 637–8, 642: iii 19, 169, 232, 283, 324, 333, 340, 365, 461, 505, 537, 547–8, 553, 565, 619: iv 272, 279, 287; v 3, 53, 69, 104, 138, 141–2, 145, 147, 157, 161, 176, 227, 253, 262, 274, 285, 296, 303–4, 310, 315, 410, 431–2: vi 453, 458–9, 468, 482, 486, 492, 495, 509–10, 512–513, 515, 534, 553, 564, 569, 573, 592–3, 639, 641, 667, 719, 728, 773, 787, 795, 888, 894, 927, 947–8, 982, 1014: and JC, ii 189–91; Chief Secretary for Ireland (1887), ii 300, 351–3, 420–2; and coercion, ii 300; Irish Land Bill, ii 303–5; Irish Land Purchase Bill, ii 420–1; JC's admiration and liking for, ii 424–6, 617; Leader of the House (1891), ii 529; on JC, ii 532; Irish Local Government Bill, ii 532–3; and Austen Chamberlain's election for E. Worcestershire, ii 537; on dissolution (1892), ii 538; and 1893 Home Rule Bill, ii 577; progressive tendencies, ii 617; and bimatellism, ii 623; and Warwick and Leamington by-election, ii 628, 630; condemns attacks on JC, ii 631; formation of Salisbury Ministry, iii 4–5; Leader of the House (1895), iii 5, 154; relations with Salisbury and with JC, iii 7–8; and reinforcements for South Africa, iii 140–1; disagrees with JC on educational policy, iii 154–5; and Suez Canal shares, iii 177; and negotiations with Germany, iii 257–9, 266, 268–9; and Cuban War, iii 299; and Portuguese colonies, iii 307, 317, 321; signs secret Anglo-German treaty, iii 318; and Uitlanders' petition, iii 393; on South African franchise question, iii 422, 438; war session (Oct. 1899), iii

486–7; weakness, iii 519; and appointment of Roberts and Kitchener to South Africa, iii 525; and Khaki Election, iii 595, 599; and reconstruction of Ministry, iii 610–611; and attacks on Chamberlain family interests, iii 616; and Old Age Pensions, iii 626; chosen successor to Salisbury, iv 4; at Blenheim meeting (1901), iv 16–17; and welcome to Milner, iv 33; and JC's proposal to visit South Africa, iv 76–7; and Milner's resignation, iv 130; and China, iv 138–9; and final attempts at German alliance, iv 157; enthusiastic motorist, iv 166; Mansion House tribute to JC (1902), iv 175; and Anglo-French rapprochement, iv 182; and Siam, iv 185; and Kaiser's visit to Sandringham (Nov. 1902), iv 198; Balfour Declaration, iv 256; and Zionism, iv 270; on JC's South African visit, iv 383; and Corn Duty, v 16, 43, 117, 121–5, 149, 154–156, 158–60, 162; Education Bill (1902), v 55, 77, 82, 85–8, 90–1, 95–99, 101–2, 106–7, 110, 112–13; vi 775, 794; becomes Prime Minister (1902), v 60–2, 64–7, 71–2; co-operation with JC, v 69–71; JC attends his first Cabinet, v 72; reconstruction of Government, v 72–8; on JC's Empire tour, v 80–1; and Brodrick's Army reforms, v 136; and Ritchie, v 151, 154–6, 179; on JC's state of depression (1903), v 175; and opposition to repeal of Corn Duty, v 181–3; receives Unionist back bench deputation, v 181, 183, 225, 228; on fiscal reform, v 218–19; and JC's Birmingham speech (1903), v 225; speech in fiscal debate (May 1903), v 228–31; emphasises solidarity with JC, v 228–229; and unwisdom of tax on raw materials, v 230; on food tax, v 230, 246–7, 266; favourably inclined to JC's policy, v 230; extent of agreement with JC, v 235–6; in weak

721–2; Tariff Reformers' deputation to him, vi 696; discusses JC's proposals with Wyndham, vi 696, 699–702; discussions with JC, vi 697–9, 702–6, 712; 'running with Free Trade hare and Tariff Reform hounds', vi 699; accused by Opposition of breach of pledges, vi 702–3; Albert Hall speech (June 1905), vi 706–9; JC's interpretation of speech, vi 709–11; JC attacks his indecision, vi 723–7; withdraws resolution on Redistribution, vi 729; against early dissolution, vi 730–1, 733; compromise proposals for election policy, vi 734–6; consultation with JC on election tactics, vi 734–40; JC's criticism of his leadership, vi 741; and recriminations between Londonderry and the Chamberlains, vi 743–4; and Gerald Balfour's proposals for establishing unity, vi 745–751; JC seeks to force choice on him, vi 748–50; at Newcastle Conference (Nov. 1905), vi 752–4; talks with JC and decision to resign, vi 755–6, 760–3; improved relations with the Chamberlains, vi 755; and JC's Bristol speech, vi 757–60; resigns, vi 763, 768–9; JC's tribute to him, vi 763–4; and Austen Chamberlain, vi 765–6; Campbell-Bannerman's judgment on his Government, vi 767; election speeches and address, vi 770, 778, 779; JC's irritation at his tactics, vi 770–1; JC rejects proposals for compromise with him, vi 771–2; loses his seat at Manchester, vi 782–5; 790–1, 796; JC reaffirms loyalty to him, vi 782–3; and rise of Labour party, vi 790; verdict on the election, vi 795; blamed for defeat, vi 797; and City of London seat, vi 797–8, 803, 808–9, 845; negotiations with JC, vi 800–5; suggests JC as temporary leader, vi 801–2; JC's terms, vi 803–5; dines with JC (2 Feb. 1906), vi 812–18; opposed to general tariff, vi 814–15; question of Party meet-

ing, vi 824–7, 832–43; meeting with Gilbert Parker, 838–9; Merchant Taylors Hall speech, vi 843–5; Valentine Compact, vi 845–51, 862–863, 891, 911; at Party meeting, vi 848–9; dinner to Opposition leaders, vi 855; elected for City and resumes leadership in Parliament, vi 860–1, 865, 868, 883–4; attack of influenza, vi 860, 862, 883; and Kitson's Resolution, vi 862, 864–6; ordered to rest, vi 876; and 1906 Education Bill, vi 879, 881; and party organisation, vi 883–5; and JC's health, vi 910; movements towards Tariff Reformers, vi 913–914; interest in Tariff Commission, vi 914; and Colonial Conference (1907), vi 916, 919; JC heartened by his change of attitude, vi 918, 924–5; visits to JC, vi 921, 923, 930, 936, 940; speech at Birmingham Conference (1907), vi 921–2, 925; discussions with Hewins, vi 931; in van of Tariff Reform programme, vi 932–3; and 1909 Budget, vi 935–940; Bingley Hall speech (Sept. 1909), vi 937–9; and taxation of food, vi 943–4; finds JC 'very unintelligible', vi 947; talks with JC at Cannes, vi 950; ill health, vi 950–1; and Constitutional Conference (1910), vi 954–5; and proposals for Coalition, vi 955–6; election campaign (Nov.–Dec. 1910), vi 957–959; JC approves his Nottingham speech, vi 957; promises referendum before food-taxes, vi 957–9, 979–80; treats JC with apparent lack of candour, vi 958; holds to official policy, vi 965; and Parliament Bill, vi 968–71; Halsbury Club and challenge to his leadership, vi 971–3; 'Balfour must go' movement, vi 972; announces retirement (1911), vi 974; and anti-Socialism, vi 1012; and Carlton Club meeting (1922), vi 1012; Baldwin's Cabinet (1924), vi 1015; and Statute of Westminster, vi 1016

2 N

974–6; and amalgamation of Liberal Unionists with Conservatives, vi 976–7; repudiation of his policy, vi 983–4; decides not to stand for Parliament again, vi 984, 987; death of Arthur Chamberlain, vi 985; failing health, vi 986; last illness and death, vi 988–9; and the new Radicalism, vi 994; opposition to *laissez-faire*, vi 994; change in his political priorities, vi 995; achievements in Imperial affairs, vi 995; advocate of Protection for its own sake, vi 995–6; outcome of his causes, vi 996–1000; centenary of his birth (1936), vi 1031–2
Chamberlain, Joseph, son of (Sir) Austen, vi 923
Chamberlain, (Sir) (Joseph) Austen (1863–1937), son of JC, ii 269, 356, 367, 372, 497, 547 and n., 558, 624, 626: iii 108, 486, 548, 612: iv 233, 272, 275–6: v 62, 74, 103, 133, 137, 144, 160–1, 168, 184, 285–6, 360, 385, 420, 423, 427, 435: vi 486, 502, 519, 554, 589, 610, 639–40, 645, 653, 673, 730, 732, 799, 803, 812, 821, 913, 922, 931, 961, 972, 985–6, 1000, 1014, 1015, 1019: birth, i 78; at Rugby, i 269; at Cambridge, i 494; candidate for Border Boroughs, ii 356 n., 536; returned unopposed for East Worcestershire (1892), ii 536–7; Gladstone's compliments on maiden speech, ii 563; Civil Lord of the Admiralty (1895), ii 639: iii 6; Financial Secretary to the Treasury (1900), iii 609; and attacks on family interests, iii 614–15; and Pacific Cable, iv 13; JC on him, iv 275; Postmaster-General (1902), v 75; and 1902 Education Bill, v 95; and Corn Duty, v 122–3; on Alaska boundary dispute, v 139; and Ritchie's intrigues over Corn Duty, v 152, 154–8; and Ritchie's 1903 Budget proposals, v 152; position on Tariff Reform, v 357; influence on him to remain in Cabinet, v 392–

395, 403, 405, 410; at Cabinet of 14 Sept. 1903, v 400–2; agrees to continue in Cabinet, v 411, 417: vi 547; appointed Chancellor of the Exchequer, v 421–2, 429, 439, 448; 'hostage to the Government', v 439; speaks in JC's defence, vi 481, 550; Wyndham on him, vi 482; in 11 Downing Street, vi 541–2; lacks authority with Balfour, vi 545; unsuccessful deputy for Balfour, vi 552–553; and Powell Williams's death, vi 556; first Budget, vi 561; and Albert Hall demonstration (July 1904), vi 591; speeches on Preference, vi 607, 641; interviews and correspondence with Balfour, vi 615–625, 628; and private members' resolutions (Mar. 1905), vi 677–90; difficulty of his position, vi 680–5, 765–6; JC declines to advise him, vi 681; reasons for not resigning, vi 682–4; at conference between Balfour and JC, vi 703; and assurance required from Balfour, vi 705–6; Balfour's Albert Hall speech (June 1905), vi 706–7; on time for dissolution, vi 737–8; asks Balfour to repudiate Londonderry, vi 743–4; and Gerald Balfour's proposals for promoting unity, vi 745–51; and resignation of Government, vi 761, 763–766; loses office and house, vi 764–765; and Balfour, vi 765–6; and 1906 election, vi 780–2, 785, 787–8, 790, 792, 800–2; at meeting between JC and Balfour (2 Feb. 1906), vi 812; with JC at Torquay, vi 817, 826, 837, 839; helps JC to form compromise Resolution, vi 837; and Valentine Compact, vi 843, 845–6, 848–9; on Balfour as Opposition leader, vi 860–1; and Kitson's Resolution, vi 864, 866–7; illness and recuperation in Algeria, vi 891, 894; engagement, vi 895; and JC's 70th birthday celebrations, vi 900; marriage and honeymoon, vi 910–11; on JC's health, vi 910–12;

Gibbs, Vicary, vi 797 : letter to JC,
v 437
Giffen, Sir Robert (1837–1910), i 410–
411 : ii 305 : v 44, 47, 284 : vi 604 ;
letter to *The Times* on Free Trade
and Imperial Unity, v 293–4 ; and
JC's statistics, vi 479–80
letters from JC, vi 479, 528–9
letter to JC, v 480
Gladstone, Herbert John (Visct. Gladstone) (1854–1930), ii 118–19, 132,
134–6, 141–2, 145, 152, 546 : iii 579 :
v 306 : speech on Home Rule at
Leeds (1885) ii 25–6, 88 ; and Home
Rule Bill, ii 227
letter from Campbell-Bannerman,
vi 549
Gladstone, Mrs., i 295 : ii 145, 593–4
Gladstone, William Ewart (1809–
1898), i 123, 129, 132–3, 145, 150,
157–9, 236, 241, 248–9, 263–5, 307,
337, 344, 386, 401, 409, 412, 417,
432, 436, 479, 496–7, 536–8, 541,
544, 566, 623–4 : ii 15–16, 26, 47,
55–6, 65, 71–2, 77–8, 81–4, 120, 129,
210–11, 214–18, 220, 269, 299, 321,
345–6, 362, 389, 391, 406, 408, 414–
415, 443, 452–3, 473, 476, 488–90,
494, 502–3, 512, 528–9, 583, 602,
631, 638, 643 : iii 4, 9, 152, 169, 194,
360, 379, 401, 484, 486, 565, 579,
592, 604, 606 : iv 16–17, 272, 277,
279, 288 : v 13, 61–3, 65, 67, 70, 74,
96, 107, 111, 141, 151, 172, 196, 209,
220, 247, 263, 311, 380, 399, 425,
442, 447 : vi 453, 583–4, 590, 666,
687, 723, 844, 891, 902–3, 934, 994,
995 ; Education Bill (1870), i 106,
107–9, 111–13, 115–18, 120 ; outlook on education, i 106 ; his
Churchmanship, i 106, 128 : ii 33 ;
first meeting with JC, i 111–13, 148 ;
last phase of 1868 Ministry, i 134–6,
162 ; Irish University Bill, i 136,
139 ; and Bright, i 138–41 ; electoral reform, i 154 ; proposes abolition of income tax, i 163–4 ; resignation of Liberal leadership, i 221–2 ;
on Bulgarian atrocities, i 238–40 ;

Resolutions on Eastern Question,
i 242–3 ; stays with JC, i 259–60 ;
addresses Bingley Hall Conference,
i 261 ; Midlothian campaigns, i 276,
281 : ii 58, 91 ; and the Queen,
i 280, 286–7, 293–6, 312, 379, 531 : ii
80, 111–12 ; and Premiership (1880),
i 285–96 ; becomes Prime Minister,
i 296 ; formation of Ministry, i 296–
304 ; takes JC into Cabinet, i 300–3 ;
psychological enigma, i 312–13 ;
Eastern policy, i 314–15 ; European
policy, i 315 ; and Forster's Irish
policy, i 320 ; JC's threat of resignation, i 328–30 ; Irish Land Bill,
i 335–6,345,347 ; denounces Parnell,
i 340 ; and negotiations with O'Shea,
i 350–5, 357 ; Forster's resignation
and successor, i 358, 360–2 ; opinion
of JC, i 362 : ii 115 ; JC's deference
to him, i 362 ; and Phoenix Park
murders, i 364–5, 367–8 ; Crimes
Bill, i 370–4 ; ii 24 ; strain on him,
i 378 ; fiftieth anniversary of public
life, i 379 ; reconstruction of Cabinet,
i 379–84 ; moves towards Home
Rule, i 387–8 ; Irish Local Government, i 387–90 ; franchise extension,
i 390, 399, 402–5 ; and Queen's dis-
pleasure at JC's speeches, i 395–8,
469–75 ; Merchant Shipping Bill,
i 427–8, 430 ; South African policy,
i 438–42, 493, 529 : iii 133, 352, 415 ;
Egypt and Sudan, i 445, 447–50,
452–3, 455–6, 499, 522–3, 567–8 : ii
455, 520, 531, 556 ; Franchise Bill
(1884), i 460, 462–4, 477, 481–6 ;
attempts to restrain JC, i 489–75 ;
and General Gordon, i 504, 510–11,
514–18, 524–8 ; ill health and question of retirement, i 531–6 ; and
'unauthorised programme', i 550,
552, 554, 558–65 : ii 58, 87, 95, 113–
114, 165–6 ; Penjdeh incident, i 571–
574, 598, 600 ; and Parnell, i 575–6 :
ii 13, 27, 29–30, 87–8, 107–10, 137,
166–8, 257–8, 346, 352, 382, 396,
400, 409, 426 ; JC's negotiations with
Parnell, i 582, 587, 595, 602–4 ; ii

University College School, i 33–4,
62 : Liberalism of, i 34, 41
Keynes, John Maynard (Lord
Keynes), vi 1018, 1040
Khaki Election (1900), iii 593–607 : v
3, 77
Khalifa, the, iii 169–70, 226
Khama, Bechuana chief, iii 37, 81 : iv
349 : visit to England (1895), iii
40–1, 49–50, 56
Khartoum : siege and fall of, i 510–16,
524–7, 566 ; recaptured (1898), iii
226–7
Kiao-Chau, German seizure of, iii
248, 310
Kidd, Benjamin, v 305
Kilmainham Treaty (1882), i 353,
356–7, 364, 368–9, 384, 463 : ii
378–9
Kimberley, 1st Earl of, i 439, 490, 607 :
on JC's 'long-spoon' speech, iii 284
letter to JC, i 495
King, Sir H. Seymour, vi 867 :
Unionist Free Trader, vi 863
King, William Lyon Mackenzie, Prime
Minister of Canada, vi 1012, 1032,
1034, 1036, 1046
Kingsley, Mary, iii 206
Kingston, Charles Cameron : and
Australian Federation, iii 559–61,
565 : and JC's tariff proposals, v 335
Kipling, Rudyard, iii 199, 202 : verses
on JC, vi 597–8 : letter to JC, iv 375
Kitchener, (Sir) Horatio Herbert (1st
Earl Kitchener of Khartoum) (1850–
1916), i 525 : ii 454 : iii 234 : iv 49,
79, 167–8 : vi 1002 : Sirdar, iii 169–
172 ; JC on him, iii 170 ; forward
move in Sudan (1898), iii 172, 175,
225 ; Battle of Omdurman, iii 226–
227 ; meets Marchand at Fashoda,
iii 228 ; appointed Chief of Staff to
Roberts in South Africa, iii 525 ; in
South Africa, iii 545–6 ; succeeds
Roberts, iii 618 ; and farm-burning,
iii 620 ; Rosebery on him, iv 20 ;
sets up block-houses, iv 27, 52 ; and
JC's peace proposals, iv 30–2 ; war
of attrition, iv 35 ; issues Banish-
2 0 2

ment Proclamation, iv 37–9 ; his
conduct of war criticised, iv 40–6 ;
and peace proposals, iv 54–9 ; discussions with Boer leaders in Pretoria,
iv 61–4 ; and Boer Generals' visit to
Europe, iv 81–3, 87–8 ; feud with
Curzon, vi 720–1
letter to JC, iv 83
Kitson, Sir James (1st Lord Airedale),
resolution on fiscal policy (Mar.
1906), vi 862–8
Knollys, 1st Visct. : dislike of JC, iv 9 ;
and proposed creation of peers, vi
954 ; visits JC, vi 954
letter from JC, vi 923
Knutsford, 1st Visct., Colonial
Secretary, ii 466 : iii 10–11
Kotze, (Sir) John, Chief Justice of
South African Republic : ruling on
Constitution (1897), iii 356–7 ; dismissed by Kruger, iii 359, 363, 367–8
Kruger, President Paul, i 438, 489–91,
493 : iii 60–1, 63, 65, 68, 74, 79, 81,
86, 91, 104, 107, 125, 163, 165, 333,
336, 366, 370, 372, 393, 411, 414,
418, 451, 468, 470, 481–2, 485–6,
580, 589–90 : iv 16, 32, 57, 64, 69,
79, 86, 131, 300, 304–5, 313, 320,
371 : vi 541, 928–9 : London
Convention, i 490–1 : iii 101 ;
closing of Vaal River drifts, iii 41–5,
54 ; Delagoa Bay railway, iii 41–2,
308 ; speech on Kaiser's birthday
(1895), iii 42 ; his character, iii 47 ;
Jameson Raid, iii 87, 90 ; Kaiser's
telegram to him, iii 92–7, 178, 353 ;
meetings with Sir Hercules Robin-
son, iii 97–101, 126–7 ; requires
unconditional surrender of arms in
Johannesburg, iii 98–9 ; and JC, iii
126–47 ; JC invites him to London,
iii 127–8, 130, 134, 137–8 ; grievance
at publication of JC's dispatch, iii
128–30 ; and suzerainty, iii 130, 135,
137, 352, 354 ; and Germany, iii
131 ; attempts to weaken restrictions,
iii 135–7 ; claims to indemnities for
Raid, iii 140 ; tactical retreat, iii
142 ; JC hopes for concessions from

Education Bill, v 89; and Alaska boundary dispute, v 139; Free Trade and Tariff Reform, v 243–4, 247–8, 357, 367, 427; Harmsworth's hostility to him, v 296–7; censured by Royal Commission on South African War, v 358; at Cabinet of 14 Sept. 1903, v 400, 403–4; Vice-President of Liberal Unionist Association, vi 590–3, 595; closeness to Balfour, vi 591; at Albert Hall demonstration (July 1904), vi 590–3, 595; Campbell-Bannerman's motion of censure on him, vi 660; and Dogger Bank incident, vi 643; at discussions between JC and Balfour (May 1905), vi 697, 699, 703; and JC's interpretation of Balfour's Albert Hall speech, vi 711–12; and resignation of Government, vi 761; opposed to JC as temporary leader, vi 808–9, 811–12; divided from Devonshire, vi 809; and Valentine Compact, vi 843, 845, 862; Party meeting at Lansdowne House, vi 848–9; and 1909 Budget, vi 935, 937; visits JC, vi 936, 941; at Constitutional Conference (1910), vi 955; and Balfour's referendum proposal, vi 958, 980; and Parliament Bill, vi 968–71; on Bonar Law's intention to resign, vi 981; accepts terms of Memorial to Bonar Law, vi 983
letters to Balfour, vi 808–9, 811–812
letters from JC, iv 163–5, 188–9: v 22, 327, 429–30: vi 590–3
letters to JC, iv 165, 184, 253, 430: vi 591–3
letter from Duke of Devonshire, vi 809

Lascelles, Sir Frank (1841–1920), iii 510: iv 139, 157, 188: v 325: vi 503: discussions with Bülow and with JC, iii 290; interview with Kaiser, iii 290–1; and British policy in South Africa, iii 426; and Boer Generals' visit to Berlin, iv 196–7; on German navy, iv 197

letter from JC, iii 512
Laurier, Sir Wilfrid, Prime Minister of Canada (1841–1919), iii 183–4: iv 11; v 115–16, 158, 165, 180, 188, 348: vi 477, 1025: at Colonial Conference (1897), iii 186–7, 190–2; and South African War, iii 529–34; and proposed Imperial Council, iii 630; statement on preferential trade (May 1902), v 15–16, 18, 43; at Colonial Conference (1902), v 26, 29, 44–5, 47–9; and Imperial defence, v 33; JC on him, v 44: vi 912; on JC, v 44; seeks exemption from Corn Duty for Canada, v 45; and reciprocal preference, v 47–9, 51–3, 114, 338; and JC's Birmingham speech and Preference proposals, v 194, 337–41, 345, 349–51; conversations with Minto, v 339–41, 350–1; response to JC's policy, vi 521–3, 526–7; supports Fielding on preferential trade, vi 608; and Colonial Conference (1907), vi 914–916; and Reciprocity Treaty, vi 962, 964; defeated at General Election (1911), vi 966
letter to JC, v 81
Law, Andrew Bonar (1858–1923), v 384: vi 457, 571, 931, 965, 978, 985–6, 1000, 1006–8: on Corn Duty, v 14, 76; junior Minister (1902), v 76; Chester speech on fiscal question (May 1903), v 228; Tariff Reformer, v 358; speeches defending JC's policy, vi 550; loses his seat, vi 795; JC on him, vi 915; visits to JC, vi 930, 936; in van of Tariff Reform programme, vi 932; and food taxes, vi 956, 963; suggests referendum to Balfour, vi 958; defeated in Manchester (Dec. 1910), vi 959; chosen as Party leader (1911), vi 973–4; repudiates Balfour's referendum pledge, vi 980; on defensive, vi 980; proposes to summon Party meeting and resign, vi 980–1; Memorial to him, vi 981–3; he accepts its terms, vi 983; renounces food taxes (1913),

Mason, Sir Josiah, and Mason College, iv 210, 212, 217
Massey, William Ferguson, vi 1013
Massingham, Henry William, iii 28; iv 15; v 254: on JC and Workmen's Compensation Bill, iii 157–8; on JC and reorganisation of armed forces, v 19; and Tariff Reform campaign, v 298–9
Masterman, C. F. G., vi 880
Matabele rebellion (1896), iii 116, 124, 132
Mathews, C. E., i 57, 85 n., 113 n.: friendship with JC, i 77: ii 371
Matthews, Henry (Visct. Llandaff), ii 121, 123: elected in Birmingham (1886), ii 254
Maxse, Capt. (Admiral) F. A., i 97, 156–7, 165, 178, 239: iii 235: v 286: and Clemenceau, ii 457–9, 462
Maxse, Leopold James (1864–1932), v 18, 137, 194, 218, 286: and the 'Coefficients', v 286; strong Preferentialist, v 286; at Sheffield Conference (1903), v 439, 443–4, and 1909 Budget, vi 935
letters from JC, vi 921–3
letters to JC, v 297, 443–4
Maxwell, Sir Herbert (1845–1937), ii 627: iii 537: v 210–11, 306, 384; vi 573, 722, 896: leading Protectionist, v 258, 261: vi 559; opposed to bringing down Government, vi 664–5; on deputation to Balfour (Apr. 1905), vi 696; and discussions between JC and Balfour, vi 697–9, 703–5; appeals to JC not to break with Balfour, vi 704–5; and Valentine Compact, vi 847
letters from JC, vi 457–8, 665–6, 705
letters to JC, vi 664–5, 704–5
letter from Winston Churchill, v 277
Maxwell, Sir John Stirling, v 434: vi 617
Maxwell Fyfe, Sir David (Earl of Kilmuir), vi 1051–2
Maycock, Sir Willoughby, ii 370

Meade, Sir Robert, iii 17, 22, 37, 73, 92, 109, 115: and imminent Transvaal rising, iii 76–2; breakdown, iii 143
letter from JC, iii 72
letters to JC, iii 69–71
Melchett, Lord, vi 1020, 1024
Méline, Jules, iii 207, 221, 225: v 322
Mellor, J. W., Chairman of Committee in Commons, ii 573–4; letter to JC, ii 574
Menelek, Emperor of Abyssinia, iii 230
Mennell, Philip, Australian editor, v 334
Mensdorff, Count Albert, iv 181
Menzies, Sir Robert, vi 1037, 1046
Mercantile system, the, v 199–201
Merchant seamen, JC and cause of, i 413–14, 420–30: 'coffin ships', i 420–1, 429; Plimsoll's agitation, i 421–2; Merchant Shipping Bill (1884), i 424–8; JC's threat of resignation, i 427–8; lack of support from colleagues, i 428; withdrawal of Bill, i 428–30; Royal Commission, i 430; JC supports Lloyd George's Bill (1906), vi 876
Mercier, General, iii 484
Merriman, John Xavier (1841–1926), iii 372: on JC, i 529–30; on Kruger's attitude, iii 362–3; and Bloemfontein Conference, iii 402; on Kruger and Milner, iii 405; and JC's visit to South Africa (1903), iv 373
Messiah, Church of the, Birmingham, i 65, 182: JC teaches in Sunday school, i 84
Methuen, Field-Marshal Lord: in South African War, iii 492, 519–20: attack at Magersfontein miscarries, iii 522–3; captured at Tweebosch, iv 50, 52, 54
Metternich, Count, iii 231: iv 136, 148, 150–1, 170: interview with JC (Mar. 1900), iii 514–16; and JC's Edinburgh speech (Oct. 1901), iv 168–70; and Anglo-French rapprochement, iv 179–81
Meyer, General Lukas, iv 83

Miall, Edward, i 116
Milk Street, Cheapside, Chamberlain home and business premises in, i 12, 36, 38 : ii 368 ; closure of business, i 77, 78
Mills, Saxon, v 305 : letter from JC, vi 733
Milner, (Sir) Alfred (Visct. Milner) (1854–1925), iii 199, 307, 343, 394, 411–12, 427, 439, 442, 450, 464, 470–471, 473, 483, 580, 587, 618, 627 : iv 9, 29, 49, 53, 87, 233, 257, 303, 336, 353 : v 176, 261, 286, 343 : vi 642, 999, 1007–8 : on JC, iii 18 ; chosen by JC as High Commissioner in South Africa, iii 142–5, 147, 347–349 ; *England in Egypt*, iii 143 ; on Delagoa Bay, iii 311 ; relations with JC, iii 347–9, 355 8, 361, 363–80, 394–9, 413–21, 423, 474–5, 572–8, 620–4 : iv 33–5, 98, 107–12, 115, 117–20, 124–32, 340–2 ; JC discusses suzerainty with him, iii 354 ; long tours of South Africa, iii 355–6 ; Graaf Reinet speech (Mar. 1898), iii 361–3, 378 ; sees issue as 'reform or war', iii 364–5, 370, 378, 413 ; JC counsels strict restraint, iii 366–8, 379 ; criticises Colonial Office, iii 369 ; wish for discussion with JC, iii 370–1 ; on Cape election, iii 371–373 ; goes on leave (Nov. 1898), iii 376, 384 ; discussions with JC, iii 377–80 ; and Edgar incident, iii 382 ; and Uitlanders' petition, iii 392–3, 396–7 ; 'helot' dispatch, iii 394–6, 412 ; JC authorises his meeting with Kruger, iii 397–401 ; Bloemfontein Conference, iii 401–9 ; contrasted with Kruger, iii 405 ; unbending attitude, iii 428–9 ; and Smuts's proposals, iii 434–6 ; and rupture of negotiations, iii 444–5 ; and Sir William Butler, iii 453 ; on military problem, iii 455–6, 462–3 ; on proposed British ultimatum, iii 467–468 ; South African War, iii 480, 520; criticises Buller, iii 538 ; and Roberts's campaign, iii 545 ; seeks

drastic measures, iii 573–4 ; JC declines to suspend Cape Constitution, iii 574 ; seeks enhancement of his office, iii 577 ; and situation in Cape Colony, iii 621–4 ; JC on, iii 623–4 ; Rosebery condemns him, iv 20 ; and JC's peace proposals, iv 30–1 ; on leave in England (1901), iv 32–5, 37–9 ; JC plans welcome for him, iv 33 ; raised to peerage, iv 33 ; JC gives lunch in his honour, iv 33–4 ; Privy Councillor, iv 35 ; receives freedom of City, iv 35 ; visits JC at Highbury, iv 35 ; plans for South African rehabilitation, iv 36 ; and concentration camps, iv 37 ; wishes to see Kitchener superseded, iv 44–6 ; and peace proposals, iv 55–9 ; in favour of 'unconditional surrender', iv 55–7 ; discussions with Boer leaders in Pretoria, iv 61–4 ; and reconstruction in South Africa, iv 67–8, 71 ; and British settlement, iv 74 ; and JC's proposal to visit South Africa, iv 75–6 ; and Boer Generals' visit to Europe, iv 79–81, 88–90 ; favours suspension of Cape Constitution, iv 100–8, 124 ; and South African Federation, iv 101, 324–9 ; and Sprigg, iv 101–2, 113 ; 'calculated indiscretion', iv 104, 106, 108 ; JC's warnings and rebukes, iv 107–9 ; JC defends him in Commons, iv 120 ; tenders his resignation (1902), iv 125–32 ; JC meets him in South Africa, iv 300 ; at Raadzaal meeting, iv 305 ; deliberations with JC, iv 312, 315–17, 322, 328, 355, 357–8, 382–3 ; JC stays with him, iv 313 ; agenda for 'Johannesburg Conference', iv 313–35 ; and preferential trade, iv 328–9 ; and Rand labour problem, iv 331–2, 334–5 ; and Chinese labour, iv 334–5 : vi 561, 569 ; and JC in Johannesburg, iv 337–9 ; withdraws resignation, iv 340–1 ; JC's tributes to him, iv 341 : v 147 ; and JC's outline of Tariff Reform scheme, v 126–9 ; and South

203